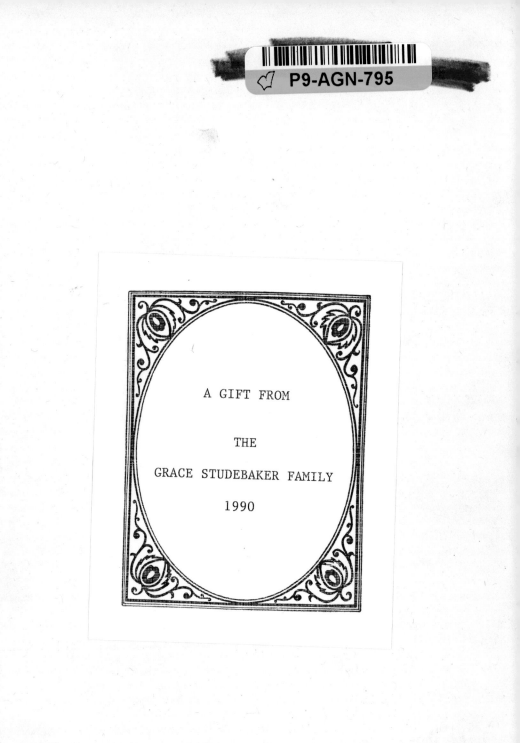

A GIFT FROM

THE

GRACE STUDEBAKER FAMILY

1990

AFRICA TO 1875

A Modern History

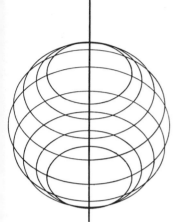

The University of Michigan History of the Modern World

Edited by Allan Nevins and Howard M. Ehrmann

AFRICA TO 1875

A Modern History

BY ROBIN HALLETT

Ann Arbor: The University of Michigan Press

Copyright © by The University of Michigan 1970
All rights reserved
SBN 472-07160-2
Library of Congress Catalog Card No. 72-83452
Published in the United States of America by
The University of Michigan Press and simultaneously
in Don Mills, Canada, by Longmans Canada Limited
Manufactured in the United States of America by
Vail-Ballou Press, Inc., Binghamton, New York

For D. F. M.

Preface

It has been my good fortune to write the greater part of this volume while holding the post of research officer in the Institute of Commonwealth Studies of the University of Oxford, and I would like most cordially to thank the members of the Committee for Commonwealth Studies for their support. With the superb range of its libraries and the distinguished company of its Africanists Oxford is a university peculiarly well equipped to assist the student of the African past. I am grateful to the staff of many libraries both in Oxford and in London for their unfailing courtesy and efficiency and particularly to Mr. R. J. Townsend, librarian at the Institute of Commonwealth Studies. Any one who has been engaged on a long historical study must be deeply conscious how much he owes to all those, the living and the dead, who have stimulated and enlightened him by their thoughts and words. Thinking of the books I have read, recalling the seminars I have attended, the conversations about the African past I have enjoyed during the last few years in Oxford, reflecting too on the truly humane internationalism of mid-twentieth-century African studies, I find that the best way to express my own sense of obligation is to follow the example of my friend and colleague, Thomas Hodgkin, in the Introduction to his anthology, *Nigerian Perspectives,* and repeat the formula of the Fulani scholar and statesman, Abdullah dan Fodio:

I cannot now number all the shaikhs from whom I acquired knowledge. Many a scholar and many a seeker after knowledge came to us from the East from whom I profited, so many that I cannot count them. Many a scholar and many a seeker after knowledge came to us from the West, so many that I cannot count them. May God reward them all with his approval.

As for the help I have received from my wife, all I would say here is that without her constant encouragement and her practical assistance this book might never have been finished.

Institute of Commonwealth Studies
Oxford

Contents

MAPS

Introduction

AFRICA—how many and how varied are the images that word has called up in the minds of men of different lands and different ages. "There is always," the ancient Greeks used to say, "something new coming out of Africa"; and Pliny, the Roman encyclopedist who recorded their saying, entranced the imagination of Europe for more than fifteen hundred years with his stories of strange African beasts—elephants and cameleopards and hippopotami—and of men even stranger—Strapfoots and Goat-pans and headless Blemmyes with eyes in their breasts.

For Europeans a sense of the extraordinary strangeness of Africa persisted, at least until very recent times, though the dominant images changed from age to age. Thus, to the Portuguese of the Age of Discovery Africa was the land of white Moors and black Moors, of fabulous gold mines and of a mysterious Christian monarch, the fabled Prester John of the Indies. Europeans of the Age of Romanticism, three hundred years later, found Africa no less mysterious, as their imagination called up parching deserts and lion-infested wildernesses and barbarous monarchs disporting themselves with savage magnificence. By the middle of the nineteenth century, however, the growth of humanitarian feeling and of Christian missionary activity presented Africa in a different guise, as a theater of the blackest ignorance and crime, where brutal slave dealers and tyrannical chiefs held sway over the suffering millions of heathendom.

The Age of Imperialism produced a new crop of images, the most prominent of which was that of the beneficent white man, shouldering his burden, as he brought the blessings of civilization to the "new caught, sullen peoples." But the sense of mystery remained. The Africa of *Sanders of the Rivers* and *Beau Geste* was also the Africa of *King Solomon's*

Mines and *The Heart of Darkness* and *Journey Without Maps*. In the last twenty years, however, the images have changed yet again. Africa has become less exotic: its rulers are seen now as exuberant black politicians in European suits or tight-lipped white men ruthlessly intent on preserving the supremacy of their "race." The talk is of revolution and development, of army coups and political refugees, of dams and universities, of oil deposits and the tourist trade.

Africa, the romantically minded outsider may find himself observing with regret, is becoming far less mysterious. But then—and this is really the truth of the matter—within the conventional images of the past there was always a large measure of absurdity. Africa was mysterious only in the eye of the ignorant beholder, only insofar as all human life is mysterious, since all of us, in the words of Sir Thomas Browne, "hold all Africa and her prodigies in us." So the first operation that many people coming new to Africa need to perform on themselves is to clear their minds of misleading preconceptions of the exotic. The sooner one grasps the ordinariness of Africa, the easier it becomes to appreciate that people in Africa, however primitive their culture, are concerned with the same basic tasks—earning a living and raising a family—as people anywhere else in the world.

Of course the contrasts are very striking. But these contrasts spring from the environment, not from something innate in the character of the people. To explore this environment in all its complexity is the task of those who give themselves up to the study of Africa. To perform this task effectively one needs to appreciate what a social anthropologist has called "the morality of amorality," the rightness, that is, of examining a society or a situation without constantly passing moral judgments upon it. There is much in the past to cause anger and revulsion. Such emotions only serve to fog the mind. Students of human society—whatever name they choose to give their discipline—are concerned not so much to pass judgment as to learn to understand. A wise compassion, a sympathetic grasp of other men's lives, whatever their "race" or culture, is the sovereign virtue of their profession.

⚓ THE TRADITION OF AFRICAN STUDIES

A generation ago the idea of constructing a history of Africa on the same lines as a history of Europe, Asia, or the Americas would have seemed to almost all Western scholars an undertaking at once eccentric and impracticable. Africa, in the cliché of the age, was the continent without a history—or rather a continent whose "history" only began when it was drawn into the orbit of "civilization" by the coming of the Europeans. Europeans produced historical records; Africans, it was argued, living in preliterate societies, had no documents to illuminate their past. The material remains of ancient African societies and the languages and customs of the present inhabitants might throw some light on earlier stages of Africa's development, but their study was the concern of archeologists, linguistic experts, or anthropologists, not of historians. Africa, "barbarous," "primitive," "uncreative" continent, though it might attract the attention of those who worked on the fringes of the world of scholarship, was really an area of little interest to the high priests of the academic tradition.

Views such as these were the product of a particular time and place. Those who expressed them lived in the superficially untroubled afternoon of the age of European imperialism, when most men of the Western world doubted whether Africans could ever govern themselves or handle with any competence the tools of modern technology. To those influenced by such preconceptions a derogatory view of the African past came easily enough. For the present generation, on the other hand, brought up in an age of triumphant African nationalism, it is not very difficult to perceive the limitations of their fathers' vision. Africa in all its aspects is now accepted as a subject for study in universities in every part of the world. Nevertheless, it is still a sufficiently novel subject in academic circles for Africanists to feel an almost revolutionary élan, the exhilaration of standing at one of the frontiers of knowledge, the iconoclastic pleasure that comes from knocking down the accepted images of an earlier generation. Yet, those who now engage in the study of Africa are not pursuing quite such a novel line as they sometimes suppose. The history, geography, and ethnology of Africa have engaged the attention of scholars within the continent and without for many centuries. Modern students of Africa are not academic revolutionaries, but the heirs of a long tradition of scholarship.

In tracing this tradition one cannot make a hard and fast distinction between different disciplines and especially between anthropologists, geographers, and historians, for their studies are complementary. Ideally, the anthropologist needs to acquire the time perspective of the historian, the historian to develop that awareness of the complexity of society possessed by the anthropologist, while both ought to possess that sense of the importance of the physical environment that comes naturally to the geographer. It is peculiarly appropriate that the earliest-known scholar in the tradition of African studies should be the Greek Herodotus. For Herodotus, who traveled in Egypt and Libya in the fifth century B.C., is not only the Father of History but also the first great geographer and anthropologist.

The tradition which Herodotus established was continued and enriched by later scholars of the Greek and Roman world. One might mention Sallust, a contemporary of Julius Caesar, whose vivid account of the war between Rome and the Numidian prince Jugurtha contains many incidents reminiscent of later campaigns in Algeria; or the elder Pliny with his encyclopedic mass of curious information about Africa, much of it obtained from the voluminous works, unfortunately no longer extant, of an erudite Berber king, Juba II, a puppet ruler in the time of Augustus; or Procopius, the official historian of the Byzantine reconquest of Africa from the Vandals in the sixth century A.D. and author toward the end of his life of a scathing indictment of Byzantine imperialism; or any one of a score of other historians or geographers from the Age of Antiquity.

Classical writing about Africa was confined almost exclusively to the lands bounded by the Mediterranean and the Red Sea. The works of medieval Arab scholars embraced all the lands that had been touched by the expansion of Islam, including the Sahara, the Sudan, the Horn, and the East African coast. The remoter provinces of the *dar al-Islam* (land of Islam) attracted the attention of geographers rather than historians. The earlier Arab geographers, of whom the most eminent was al-Idrisi, the compiler in the twelfth century of the most encyclopedic of Muslim geographies, derived most of their information at second hand from the reports given them by Muslim traders. But the later Middle Ages saw the appearance of two outstanding accounts of travel in Africa, both by Moroccan writers, ibn Battuta of the fourteenth century and Hassan ibn Muhammad al-Fasi, better known by his Christian names of Leo Africanus, in the early sixteenth century.[1]

A vigorous tradition of historical writing developed in the Muslim world, and a number of scholars writing in Arabic devoted themselves to the history of Egypt, Andalusia (Muslim Spain) and the Maghrib (North Africa). Their narrations are not unlike the works of medieval European chroniclers. But in the records of Muslim historiography one work stands supreme, the *Universal History* of ibn Khaldun, not for its narrative which followed conventional lines but for its massive introduction or *Prolegomena*. In this section ibn Khaldun, a Berber aristocrat of the fourteenth century with an adventurous political career behind him, "conceived and formulated a philosophy of history which is undoubtedly," in the opinion of the most eminent of modern historical philosophers, "the greatest work of its kind that has ever yet been created by any mind in any time or place."[2] The practice of historiography was transmitted to some of the communities on the periphery of the Muslim world. Among the places which became for a time important centers of scholarship must be counted Timbuktu in the sixteenth and seventeenth centuries and Sokoto, the capital of the Fulani empire that embraced most of Northern Nigeria, in the nineteenth century.

An interest in the past has never been confined exclusively to those societies in Africa—the Berbers, the Hausa, the Swahili, and others with a knowledge of Arabic, and the Ethiopians with a knowledge of Ge'ez—which possessed a written language. Oral traditions, "testimonies of the past deliberately transmitted from mouth to mouth," [3] preserved something of the history not only of major kingdoms, but also of much smaller units, of villages, clans, or families. In most African societies, moreover, these historical records are not to be regarded as dry-as-dust lists of kings, or battles, or migrations. "The recital of History," one European scholar with much experience in gathering oral traditions in Ghana has pointed out, "goes right to the roots of the African's emotions." And he illustrates the point by recording how an elder once told him "in a voice restrained into monotony" the story of "a gallant feat of arms performed by an ancestor of his seventy years ago." "When he had finished, he broke down, got up hastily, and left the circle and walked up and down for twenty minutes striving to recover his self-control." [4] It is easy for an outsider to think of the records of African historiography only in terms of the contributions of outsiders. In fact work of the utmost value to historical studies, involving the preservation and transmission of historical material, has been done by the members of many African communities. That many of these historical records should not yet have been preserved in print, that some of them should be known only to a small circle of initiates, should not lead anyone tracing the tradition of African studies to ignore their existence or depreciate their importance, even when confronted with the massive amount of work done by alien scholars in Africa.

The late fifteenth century saw the opening of a new age of European interest in Africa. Steadily from this time onward the works of European Africanists, the books, the maps, the articles, have piled up, their volume, at least in recent times, continuing to increase with every passing year. Among the Europeans who lived in Africa in the precolonial period were a number who composed vivid and detailed accounts of their surroundings. Many of these authors, particularly in West Africa, were traders, some were missionaries, a few adventurers. Among the explorers who provided Europeans in the eighteenth and nineteenth centuries with their first accounts of the interior of Africa were men who combined toughness and courage with a deep and scholarly interest in every aspect of the countries they visited. The writings of travelers such as the Scotsman James Bruce in Ethiopia, the Englishman Richard Burton in Somalia and

East and West Africa, the German Heinrich Barth in the Western and Central Sudan, the Frenchman Emile Grandidier in Madagascar, may well be regarded as laying the foundations of modern African studies.

The establishment of European rule over the greater part of Africa in the course of the nineteenth and early twentieth centuries naturally brought many more outsiders to the continent. Among two groups in particular, the colonial administrators and the missionaries, there were men who realized the importance of acquiring a better knowledge of African societies. Some stressed the importance of the study of African languages, others the need to acquire a deeper insight into the laws and customs of the people, a few devoted their leisure to collecting information of a historical nature. Official encouragement of research varied from territory to territory. The greatest contributions to historical scholarship were made in Egypt in a movement that can be traced back to the work of the scholars who accompanied Bonaparte's expedition of 1798. In North Africa, to a greater extent than in any other colonial territory, French scholars produced a remarkable range of works designed to render the historical development of the region fully comprehensible both to its own people and to outsiders. Over most of the rest of Africa the record of research of interest to historians was more patchy. But the works of a handful of professional anthropologists, of academic historians, and of scholarly missionaries or administrators stand out as the classics of this period. And behind them, continuing a tradition established in the early nineteenth century with the appearance of the first scholarly journals to publish articles on Africa, must be ranged the periodicals founded during the colonial era, most of them printed and published in Africa, whose articles contain a mass of material of interest to Africanists of a later generation.

The period after 1945, marked by the growing confidence of African nationalism, the massive expansion of African education, the creation of many new universities and the emergence of a worldwide interest in the continent, provided ideal conditions for the rapid development of African studies. Africans were anxious to learn about their continent and to explore or rediscover its past. University lecturers or secondary-school teachers coming new to Africa from overseas found themselves faced with the exciting possibility of engaging in original research. For the first time graduates from African universities had the opportunity to work for higher degrees and in so doing made substantial contributions to the field of knowledge. The building up of collections of national archives in some, though regrettably not all, of the countries of Africa at once facilitated and stimulated the work of historians. The establishment of research institutes and university departments specializing in African studies not only in Africa but in all the other continents, the foundation of new learned societies, many with their own journals, the proliferation of academic conferences, activities such as these provided meeting places of a kind that had hardly existed before, where scholars following different disciplines and drawn from a great variety of countries could come together to discuss problems of common interest.

The 1950's and 1960's may well be regarded, at least in comparison with earlier periods, as a golden age of African studies. Never have so many people been able to devote themselves to the study of Africa in all its aspects. Never has there been such a vigorous cross-fertilization of ideas, never such a spate of valuable works in so many fields of knowledge from archeology to political science. In hailing the achievements of the present one must not forget the foundations on which they are laid. Anyone now engaged in African studies should indeed think of himself as the fortunate heir of a long tradition and remember with gratitude and admiration the pioneer scholars of earlier generations.

THE SOURCES OF AFRICAN HISTORY

What are the sources of African history? What material can the historian make use of in his attempt to reconstruct the African past? These must be among the first questions that occur to anyone with some historical training when he turns to study the history of a continent so often described as "dark" and "mysterious." The brief account just given of the long tradition of African studies falls far short of providing a sufficient answer to these questions, even though some of the works mentioned, the writings of classical historians, Muslim geographers, or European travelers, obviously provide valuable historical evidence. The historian in Africa derives his material from a great many other sources, some of a kind familiar enough to historians of other continents, others at first sight of a more exotic or specialized nature.

Evidence for the African past comes from sources both written and unwritten. The unwritten sources are derived from the work of scholars in a variety of disciplines, including archeology, anthropology, linguistics, art history, botany, zoology, and epidemiology. Something needs to be said about the significance of each of these disciplines to the student of African history, but first it is important to stress the wealth of written sources at the historian's disposal.

Written sources can conveniently be divided into two groups, library material (books and printed reports) and archive material (manuscripts). If one leaves aside the secondary sources (historical reconstructions contained in the books and articles of modern scholars) and the works of scholars in other disciplines, the library material can be said to fall into a number of classes: early works of history and geography, travelers' accounts, autobiographies, novels, and other literary works and reports usually of an official nature. Much of this material makes easy and attractive reading. Indeed, anyone making his first acquaintance with African studies will be well advised to read as widely as possible among the narratives of the great nineteenth-century European travelers or the novels produced by recent African writers. Works such as these are fuel for the imagination, and without a vigorous imagination, without a willingness to attempt to picture past scenes and to relive past lives, the student of history will deprive himself of much of the enjoyment he should receive from his reading.

For the professional historian archive material often provides reading quite as exciting as any novel. Fortunately, there is an immense amount of archive material relating to Africa contained in record offices and other depositories in many different countries of the world. The greater part of this material was produced in the period from 1500 onward, but there are some earlier records. A major source of the history of Egypt in Ptolemaic and Roman times, for example, is to be found in documents written on papyrus miraculously preserved in that dry soil. Most of the available manuscript material was produced not by Africans but by aliens intimately connected with Africa—missionaries, traders, foreign consuls, explorers, colonial officials, and others. Naturally, this material is of particular importance in tracing the development of alien contacts with Africa, but some of it also throws a flood of light on the history of African societies. Thus, it has been possible to reconstruct the history of the sixteenth-century kingdom of Kongo from the reports of Portuguese agents and missionaries and from some of the surviving letters of Kongolese monarchs, to chart the involved politics of the mid-nineteenth-century Yoruba states from the letters of the first Protestant missionaries, both American and English, to obtain statistical data on the caravan trade of the Sahara from the information supplied by French army officers in Algeria or British consuls in Tripoli during the course of the nineteenth century.

In recent years a certain amount of manuscript material of a purely African nature has come to light. The national archives in Khartoum contain the correspondence of the Mahdist administration of the Sudan after 1885; many of the letters of the nineteenth-century Fulani sultans and their officials are preserved in Sokoto, and valuable collections of manuscript material have been reported from other major Muslim centers. No doubt it is true that hardly any part of Africa possesses even a tenth of the mass of archival material to be found in England, France, or Italy. No doubt in some parts of the continent there is little or no relevant manuscript material before the nineteenth century. But so far as professional historians are concerned, they may be confident that the proper study of the material now known to exist will never be completed in their own lifetime.

If much manuscript material still remains to be collected and properly preserved, the same is equally true of oral tradition, one of the major sources of African history. Here indeed the need is far more urgent. Most of those who carry in their minds the records of the past are elderly men and women, and the rapidly changing pattern of African societies makes it less certain that the chain of transmission will be preserved. Oral traditions may be divided into three different categories: myths concerned with supernatural beings or designed to explain natural phenomena, accounts of the ancestors, and fables and tales told for entertainment. The historian naturally tends to concentrate on the second of these categories, but a careful study of myths and fables is also likely to provide some evidence for the past. The recent work of a number of scholars, both African and European, has revealed the wealth of oral tradition in certain localities and demonstrated convincingly the degree of detail that can be achieved in the reconstruction of the more recent past.

For the remoter past archeology is naturally of paramount importance. Until about 1930 archeological research was confined almost entirely to North Africa and the Nile Valley. Recently, however, the number of archeologists working in sub-Saharan Africa has slowly begun to increase. At the same time cooperation with other scientists has led to the development of new techniques for dating sites, techniques which have given archeological research an exactness that would have seemed impossible to achieve a generation ago. In East Africa our knowledge of the earliest stages of human evolution has been transformed by the discoveries of Dr. Louis Leakey and others in the Olduvai Gorge and other sites. In West Africa an entirely new and unexpected culture, known as Nok after its type-site in Northern Nigeria, has been brought to light. In Central Africa the riddle of the famous ruins at Zimbabwe has been solved and a great deal learnt about the early history of the area. All this is only a beginning. There are numerous sites in every part of the continent still to be explored. Indeed, in the course of the next generation no field of African studies is likely to produce such exciting results as archeology.

Anthropologists have been primarily concerned with the study of contemporary African societies, examining the variations of physical types, gathering information on the range of a people's material culture, some aspects of which may be of especial concern to art historians, investigating thought processes and religious and philosophical ideas, tracing the complex structure of a society and describing its forms of law and government. Inevitably, however, many anthropologists have found it necessary, in the strenuous process of attempting to understand the present, to ask questions about the past. For the historian contact with anthropologists can be immensely stimulating. From their works he can gain not only a clearer concept of the complexity of African societies and cultures, but also a measure of vicarious experience, an opportunity to see the world as it looks through the eyes of a people brought up in an environment very different from his own.

Linguistics is an extremely arduous discipline, many branches of which the historian may find himself ill-equipped to understand. But he cannot ignore that every language represents an important historical document and that certain aspects of its study, notably the nature of its relationship with other languages and the derivation of its loanwords, may provide him with the material from which to construct valuable hypotheses about the past. Taken by itself the evidence from linguistics may never appear completely convincing, but it can prove an invaluable auxiliary in the reconstruction of the broad lines of development in distant periods of the past.

The study of the plants and animals used by man is primarily the concern of the botanist and the zoologist, but certain aspects of their research are of great interest to the historian. To know the exact area of the original domestication of a plant or animal, to be able to trace the routes by which it came to be more widely diffused, to possess some account of the flora and fauna of a particular region at a particular period in the past—information such as this, which the botanist and the zoologist may be able to supply, represents an extremely valuable contribution to the stock of historical knowledge.

In much the same way the historian in his concern to reconstruct the life of men in the past needs to know something about the nature and spread of disease and particularly of those diseases such as malaria or trypanosomiasis which have had such a profound influence on human movement and settlement in Africa.

In general, then, a wide range of sources lies at the disposal of the historian in his exploration of the African past. In practice, of course, it often happens that the student of the history of a particular area finds the amount of easily available material extremely limited—oral traditions uncollected, archive material uncatalogued, archeological sites unexplored, and so on. Such limitations are natural in a field of study still in its early stages. In compensation the student of African history can enjoy the exhilaration of feeling himself a pioneer. And if later he returns to more familiar fields, he may well find that the strenuous and exciting process of investigating the African past has helped to open his eyes to new aspects of the history of his own country and has led him to formulate questions which may never have occurred to historians whose work has lain in more conventional fields.

✻ THE SCOPE AND PURPOSE OF A HISTORY OF AFRICA

It remains to say something about the scope in space, time, and subject matter of the present work and to define its purpose.

This history embraces the entire continent with its adjoining islands. To some readers such a field of study may seem far too large. Yet it is hard to devise a satisfactory alternative. Some scholars in recent years have favored the bisection of the continent into two unequal parts—North Africa and sub-Saharan Africa, *Afrique blanche* and *Afrique noire*. But this division makes no allowance for that persistent interplay between the two parts which provides one of the major themes of the continent's development. If one is going to divide Africa, it is more satisfactory to distinguish not two large parts but seven or eight smaller but still very extensive regions. Each of these may well be studied in isolation, as indeed they have been in certain parts of this book, but it is also useful to draw all the regions together and to try to discern themes that are common to the entire continent.

Moreover, there can be no doubt that the term "Africa" is constantly on people's lips. Africa may well be thought to have suffered more from simplifying and distorting generalizations than any other continent. To show that "Africa" is a phenomenon of the utmost complexity, to convey some impression of the continent's immense variety, these are worthwhile objects for a general historian to try to achieve.

A history of Africa is, of course, concerned with all the people who have left their mark on the continent, whatever the color of their skin. This point is so tautologous that one would apologize for making it were it not that the habit of laying excessive stress on the contribution of the people of one skin color to the neglect or denigration of those of another persists in some quarters and is developing in others. A general historian is concerned both with the growth of indigenous societies and with the activities of outsiders. Even if his gaze is fixed most of the time on the continent, he must not lose sight of what is happening beyond its shores. He needs to try constantly to keep in mind the comings and goings of men on the seas that surround Africa and to develop a keen awareness of activities relevant to Africa in the lands beyond those seas, to look over the Atlantic to the United States and Cuba, Jamaica, and Brazil, over the Mediterranean to Spain and Portugal, France and Italy, England and Germany, Greece and Turkey, over the Red Sea to Arabia, over the Indian Ocean to India and Indonesia and China. To be fully understood the general history of Africa, as indeed of every continent, needs to be seen in the context of world history.

In time, this history goes back, albeit very briefly, as far as the record of human evolution permits. Again this may seem too vast a span to cover at all adequately. But the alternative is to adopt a purely arbitrary starting point, and this creates other problems of understanding and explanation. Moreover, to take as one's field the entire sweep of African history from *Homo habilis* two million years ago to the newly independent African states is to make oneself more vividly aware of the dynamic element in history, the sense of purposive movement, the nature of progress.

As for the subject matter of a general history one cannot do better than recall the definition of history given by ibn Khaldun six hundred years ago:

> History is the record of human society, or world civilization; of the changes that take place in the nature of that society . . . ; of revolutions and uprisings by one set of people against another with the resulting kingdoms and states, with their various ranks; of the different activities and occupations of men, whether for gaining their livelihood or in the various sciences and crafts; and, in general, of all the transformations that society undergoes by its very nature.[5]

With such a definition in mind it becomes impossible to impose on the past the limiting and conventional divisions implied in the terms "political," "social," and "economic." One needs to acquire a sense of the interrelatedness of all fields of human activity, the ruler in his council chamber, the general on the battlefield, the merchant in the marketplace, the farmer tending his crops, the priest in his temple, the scholar in his study. One needs to become deeply aware of what ibn Khaldun calls "the transformations that society undergoes by its very nature," to think of change as a continuous process, though with its rate varying from period to period and from society to society. Thus, the identification of the particular manifestations of change and of the forces behind them becomes a matter of particular importance. In attempting to grasp the sweep of the past the historian has to weave his own intellectual pattern. In the pattern presented here the process of change is thought of as the warp of history, regional and local variations as the woof.

Finally, it needs to be said that no historians can be so aware of the extent of their own ignorance as those who chose a vast and general theme. In part this ignorance comes from ordinary human limitations, for any historian, conscious of the almost infinite amplitude of his sources, must be haunted by the feeling that he has never read widely enough or thought deeply enough about his subject. In part it is a product of a particular moment in time, for clearly if research continues at its present rate the historians of twenty years hence will know much more about Africa than we do today. In part the sense of ignorance is inseparable from the nature of the historian's profession, in that there are many things about the past that will never be known. To brood too long on these limitations is simply to discourage action; to be keenly aware of all that one does not know is to provide oneself with a stimulus and a goad. No historical work is ever absolutely authoritative, ever completely definitive. Basically, it is no more than a temporary framework fated to be superseded sooner or later by the work of other scholars. But if for a time it can provide new insight to the past and contribute to a better understanding of the present, it will have served a worthwhile purpose.

CHAPTER I

Africa and Other Continents: Some Historical Comparisons

✻ DIFFERENT PERSPECTIVES

The most isolated, the least well-endowed in natural resources, the most backward in its technology—thus did Africa appear for many centuries when set against the other major continents of the world. As for the pattern of Africa's political geography, at least until the latter half of the nineteenth century, how different it was with its multiplicity of independent communities and its extraordinary variety of forms of political organization from the relatively simple political pattern of Europe, Asia, and the Americas.

Generalizations such as these are related, it must be realized, to particular periods in history. To move forward or backward in time is to acquire a different set of comparisons. Thus, today one might well regard not Africa but that part of Asia occupied by China as the most isolated portion of the world. Mindful of the previously unsuspected natural resources discovered within recent years in many parts of the continent, one might wish to revise earlier assumptions of Africa's basic poverty. And one would certainly consider that the political map of Africa in the 1960's with its patchwork of nation-states reproduced a pattern familiar enough from other continents.

Moving backward to the remote era of paleolithic man, the comparisons change dramatically, for then Africa was the center of human activity, technical invention, and development. Indeed, it was only with the evolution of neolithic civilization in western Asia, ten thousand years ago, that Africa ceased to occupy this central position.

One needs, then, to develop a sense of the long perspectives of the past in order to free oneself from the simple absolute judgments, the glib convictions of the "natural superiority" of one people over another, of the present day. Only by looking back far into the past can one begin to trace

the evolution of Africa and to understand why Africa should have come
to differ so greatly from other continents.

❧ THE IMPACT OF ASIA AND EUROPE

It was not unreasonable to regard Africa, especially from the sixteenth to
the late nineteenth century, as the most isolated of the major continents.
Over the span of five thousand years there had developed an immensely
subtle, an exceedingly fruitful relationship between Asia and Europe. In
the course of a mere three hundred years Europe had powerfully imposed
its stamp on what Europeans chose to call their "New World" of the
Americas. But the impact of Asia and of Europe on Africa—or at least
on the great mass of the continent that lay beyond the coastal fringes—
seemed tenuous and insignificant.

In the development of Africa the effect of external influences, the impact of men, ideas, and techniques emanating from other continents, had
been far more profound than outside observers, blinkered by their sheer
ignorance of most of African history, suspected. To trace these influences
one must go back at least ten thousand years, to the beginning of a movement that brought light-skinned Caucasoid people from Southwest Asia
into Africa. This movement continued until quite recent times; it populated most of the northern half of Africa with people of Caucasoid stock
and created a living bridge along which cultural innovations could easily
be transmitted from one continent to another.

The earliest invention to reach Africa from Asia was also the most
important. About 4500 B.C. small groups of immigrants brought both
domestic animals and the newly developed technique of cereal cultivation to Lower Egypt. From Egypt a knowledge of the pursuits of the pas-
toralist and of the farmer spread westward and southward to be diffused
in time throughout almost the entire continent. Four thousand years later
another revolutionary technique, the craft of ironworking, possibly introduced into Egypt by Assyrian invaders in the seventh century B.C.,
spread very much more rapidly. By 1500 A.D. there were few communities in Africa which did not possess some iron implements.

Asia made two other major contributions to the economy of Africa: the
camel and certain tropical food crops. The camel reached Egypt toward
the end of the first millennium B.C. and was gradually taken over by
peoples living on the northern fringes of the Sahara. Had the camel with
its remarkable powers of endurance in arid conditions not been available,
men could hardly have developed and maintained the caravan routes that'
spanned the desert in medieval times. The tropical crops, notably the
Asian yam and the banana, were brought from Southeast Asia, where
they had been domesticated, to the east coast of Africa by Indonesian sea-

farers of the first centuries of the Christian era. Hitherto, Africa had lacked a plant that could serve as a staple food crop in hot and humid conditions. The gradual dispersal of the yam and the banana across the Congo basin and into West Africa greatly accelerated the settlement and exploitation of the lands of heavier rainfall.

Agriculture, stock raising, and ironworking affected the lives of almost every community in Africa. Asia's other cultural contributions were of great but less than universal significance. In the first millennium B.C. Phoenician adventurers founded a string of trading posts along the coast of North Africa and introduced to the Berber people some of the concepts of urban civilization. At the same time other Semitic colonists from the rich states of South Arabia were establishing settlements in the northeastern highlands of Ethiopia. Later, in the fourth century A.D. Syrian missionaries grafted the new religion of Christianity onto the elaborate civilization that had evolved in the Ethiopian kingdom of Axum. Ethiopia represented one of Christendom's remotest provinces, but despite many tribulations the faith endured. In the Berber lands of North Africa, on the other hand, where the number of early Christian converts was far greater and their intellectual vitality more intense, the Church, weakened by internal dissensions, failed to survive the onslaughts of Islam.

The faith and culture of Islam formed Asia's last major contribution to the development of Africa. Islamic culture implied far more than a religion: a new language, new concepts of law and government, and new standards of dress and architecture accompanied the new faith. Islam was carried across North Africa by the armies that burst out of Arabia in the middle of the seventh century A.D. Later, Bedouin nomads began to cross into Africa, passing westward along the northern belt of the Sahara and southwestward into the less arid lands of the Sudan. Their slow pastoral migrations represent the last phase in that movement of people of Caucasoid stock out of Southwest Asia that had begun so many centuries earlier. Meanwhile, Islam was being carried not by the sword but by the peaceful penetration of merchants and of wandering scholars into many other parts of Africa—along the trans-Saharan caravan routes into the Western Sudan, across the Red Sea to the marches of Ethiopia and the Horn, along the coast of East Africa, and on to Madagascar and the archipelago of the Comoros. The extension of Islam, with the steady process of attraction and conversion, is a movement that continues to this day.

Compared with the massive contributions made by Asia to the development of Africa, the impact of Europe, at least until the twentieth century, appears very much less profound. Greek and Roman rule in North Africa, though it lasted in Egypt for close to a thousand years, brought with it no major innovation of more than ephemeral significance. The renewal of intensive European intercourse with Africa in the fifteenth century had more revolutionary consequences. The commercial activities of the maritime nations of Western Europe powerfully affected the pattern of African trade, weakening, even destroying old trading connections and calling new trade routes into existence. Moreover, Europeans introduced, almost incidentally, a number of new food crops of American origin, the most important of which—maize and manioc (cassava)—came to provide the basis of the diet of many African communities. But the activities of foreign traders, both Asian and European, Muslim and Christian, affected more than the economy of African communities. By their demand for gold, slaves, and ivory—the three staples of Africa's external trade—they called forth in previously self-sufficient societies new concepts of wealth. By their introduction of firearms they provided acquisitive local rulers with an instrument to help them satisfy their ambitions.

Of course, much of this external influence was indirect, and other factors of a purely local nature entered into every situation. But still it would be true to say that by the mid-nineteenth century the evolution of large parts of Africa was being affected by external forces, even though the major settlements of Asians or Europeans were confined to the coast. And even in those many remote, isolated communities, lost in the bush, the forest, or the swamp, the farmer tending his maize crop or his yams, the hunter with his iron-tipped arrows, the herdsman rounding up his cattle, all testified to the impact, however remote, however indirect, of a wider world. And yet the arrival of a stranger from another continent was an event to fill the minds of such people with astonishment, with wonder, even with awe.

By the nineteenth century, then, Africa was not, as most external observers imagined, a world utterly apart. For centuries it had absorbed techniques and ideas from other continents. And it had made its own contribution to the development of Asia, Europe, and the Americas. The radiant culture of ancient Egypt was one of the great civilizing forces of the Mediterranean and Near Eastern worlds. The intellectual life of early Christianity and of medieval Islam was enriched by contributions from men of Egyptian or Berber origin. Crops such as coffee or sorghum, domesticated in Africa, provided a valuable supplement to the agricultural economy of parts of Asia and of the Americas. Finally, the labor involved in the colonization of the tropical regions of the Americas was largely provided by Negro slaves, and these reluctant immigrants enriched by their contributions almost every aspect of the cultural life of their new homelands.

Yet it was not altogether unreasonable, at least for one group of humanity at a certain period of history, Western Europeans in the eighteenth and nineteenth centuries, to think of Africa as being more isolated than other continents. How much more vigorous, after all, was the intercourse of Europeans with Asia and the Americas than with Africa, how much more extensive their dominions in those continents, how much more lucrative their trade. One has only to compare the great cities called into existence by European enterprise in the Americas and in Asia— New York and Rio de Janeiro, Bombay and Singapore—with the handful of European settlements in contemporary Africa to realize the difference.

Some historians have sought the reasons for the relative paucity of Europe's contacts with Africa in the physical obstacles presented by the continent to outsiders who attempted to penetrate the interior. Others have stressed the power possessed by Africans to repel the intruders. But there was another more cogent and far more important reason to account for the modesty of European activities: the simple fact that in an age when resources of men and of money were strictly limited, Asia and the Americas presented much more attractive opportunities for trade and for settlement. Of all the great continents Africa clearly seemed during the formative centuries of the modern world the least well endowed in natural resources.

NATURAL RESOURCES

Africa's comparative poverty had different aspects. Its deserts were very extensive: indeed, the proportion of economically valueless land was far higher than in the other great continents. Over wide areas the rainfall was irregular and the soil poor. The range of destructive pests or disease-bearing parasites was far wider than in other temperate or tropical lands: it extended from the elephants, the baboons, and the locusts which trampled or devoured a man's crops to the tsetse fly which killed his cattle, the guinea worm which reduced his vitality, and the anopheles mosquito which caused the death of many of his children.

For a variety of reasons communications over long distances were extremely difficult. There was the sheer size of the continent and the fact that two-thirds of its coastal lands faced not easily navigable inland seas but vast stretches of ocean. There was the lack of navigable rivers in all but a few parts. There were the natural hazards of travel over waterless desert, trackless forest, or tsetse-infested bush. There was the shortage of natural harbors on a surf-beaten coast. All these factors served to isolate many of the major communities of Africa both from one another and from the outside world. And isolation restricts development.

Over most parts of the continent the density of population was very low. The thinness of the population was a reflection of the poverty of the environment, but it was also a contribution to that poverty. Modern development planners are familiar enough with the almost intractable problems presented by areas of very low population density. The vicious circle of poverty existed in most parts of precolonial Africa.

Nevertheless, the continent possessed some resources to attract outsiders. Gold was to be found in a number of areas, particularly in West and Central Africa. In medieval times West African gold, carried across the Sahara, made a vital contribution to the economy of Mediterranean lands. But by the mid-nineteenth century the production of African gold had declined greatly and far more lucrative sources of precious metals had been discovered in other continents.

From the sixteenth to the mid-nineteenth century slaves formed Africa's major export. The export of human livestock brought some material return to Africa in a wide range of manufactured goods. But with the exception of firearms these imports were of articles for immediate consumption or adornment. They could not compensate for the destruction caused by the slave trade in certain areas of the continent.

As for other traditional forms of African produce—ivory, gums of various kinds, animal skins, tortoise shell, ostrich feathers—their total value can never have been very great. Less exotic but potentially far more valuable were the products that various parts of Africa were beginning to export in the first half of the nineteenth century: cotton from Egypt, corn from Algeria and Morocco, palm oil from the West Coast, wool from South Africa, sugar from the Mascarenes, cloves from Zanzibar. But though a steady expansion in the continent's external trade could be traced from the beginning of the nineteenth century, its total volume was still very modest. Thus, in the 1860's less than 1 percent of the external commerce of the United States was carried on with Africa. Even the British, who possessed a wider range of contacts with the continent than did other nations, had no more than 6 percent of their trade with Africa. Indeed, for the British in the 1860's the white colonists of Australasia, numbering about a million, presented a more valuable market than the entire continent of Africa from Egypt to the Cape.

It would be a mistake to derive an impression of African poverty from the statistics of international trade. Most African communities were self-sufficient, a few participated vigorously in the continent's internal trade. The accounts of many nineteenth-century travelers suggest that given the right conditions, especially political stability and a regular rainfall, African communities could enjoy a level of material comfort and social well-being that might be regarded as hardly inferior to that of peasant communities in other parts of the world. Nor can one assert that the life of a factory hand in one of the new industrial towns of the technologically most advanced countries of the world offered many benefits not possessed by independent African farmers or pastoralists.

But there was one advantage which the proletariat of the Western world possessed over their African contemporaries. They were living in societies which had been able to create the conditions for rapid economic growth, and they could look with hope to a more prosperous future. African societies, by contrast, were involved in a cycle of change that moved so slowly that it was inevitably mistaken for complete stagnation.

TECHNOLOGY

The technological backwardness of Africa was an obvious fact to mid-nineteenth-century travelers from Europe. One can trace a certain sense of superiority in the writings of Europeans about Africa from classical times onward. But this conviction of greater natural ability was immensely strengthened by an intense pride in the mechanical marvels of the Industrial Revolution. Even in lands such as Egypt or Morocco whose material culture had been equal, indeed superior, to that of most European countries a few centuries earlier, the contrast between European progress and African backwardness was vivid enough. It became positively glaring as one moved deeper into the continent.

In many African communities men went naked or covered themselves with the skins of beasts. Their dwellings were simple structures made from mud or grass or the branches of trees. Their tools for agriculture were of the crudest. They had no knowledge of the wheel. They had not acquired the art of writing. Their notions of the world were vitiated by the grossest forms of superstition.

Generalizations such as these, the clichés of so much European small talk about Africa, made no allowance for the variety to be found in the continent, the marked differences in the technology of African societies. Some African peoples had acquired remarkable skill as wood-carvers, others as metalworkers, others as weavers or makers of bark cloth. Nakedness was far from universal, and in societies in which differences of status could be detected, the wealthy and the noble often exhibited great elegance or lavishness in their dress and personal adornments. Those societies which lay within the pale of Islam had taken over the Arabic script and in some cases adapted it to enable them to write in their own language. In Arabic, in Hausa, in Amharic, and in Swahili there existed a considerable body of literature. And even in preliterate societies a pleasure in words, expressed in songs and stories and historical recitations, was often to be found. As for men's notions of the world in its widest sense, some African societies had evolved highly complex theologies and philosophies; and the knowledge of their environment, of the ways of animals and the qualities of plants, to be found among such people as the Bushmen, whom European ethnographers placed on the lowest rung of the "ladder" of human evolution, revealed exceptional powers of observation.

And yet the contrast remains. African achievements in art and literature are far from negligible, but they seem very modest when set beside the art and literature of Europe and of Asia. The great historical monuments, the palaces and the temples, the castles and the cathedrals that are to be found in almost every country of Asia and of Europe bear witness to the existence of a remarkable technology in ancient or medieval times. Why should Africa's monuments be confined to so few countries, limited indeed almost entirely to the Mediterranean coast, the valley of the Nile, and the highlands of Ethiopia? Above all, why should Europe have achieved a rate of technological progress that made Africa seem utterly backward?

Questions such as these could best be answered, so it seemed to many nineteenth-century Europeans, by the assumption that Africans were afflicted by a certain congenital inferiority. The reasons for this inferiority were diagnosed by a process of pseudoscientific reasoning as being somehow connected with the physical characteristics that distinguished the majority of Africans from the peoples of other continents. The real answer lay elsewhere—in the simple facts of the African environment.

The down drag of poor soils, irregular rainfall, and an abundance of pests made it impossible for many African communities to achieve that regular surplus of foodstuffs needed to support those whose labor was not immediately productive—especially the full-time craftsman and the highly skilled technician. At the same time the remoteness of most parts of Africa from the major centers of invention deprived local communities of the shock and stimulus of new ideas.

Whenever a substantial surplus could be accumulated, development almost invariably began to take place. And this would be carried still further once contact had been established with other societies possessing different patterns of technical knowledge, religious belief, social structure, or political institutions. This is what had happened in ancient Egypt. It happened in Ethiopia and Morocco and all the great kingdoms of sub-Saharan Africa.

But there was another element needed to ensure the gains of technical progress—political stability. And in this field Africa once again found itself at a disadvantage when set beside other continents.

✤ POLITICAL ORGANIZATION

In its social and political evolution Africa appeared at least until the nineteenth century to present a pattern quite different from that of Asia and of Europe. In those two continents certain dominant cultures had emerged and wide areas of cultural homogeneity—marked most obviously by the fact that the people in such areas spoke the same language—had been established. In Africa linguistic groups were far smaller, and much of the continent had not been affected by the international civilizations associated with Christianity and with Islam, civilizations capable of lessening the force of local differences.

In Europe and in Asia a relatively simple political pattern had evolved by the mid-nineteenth century with the nation-state and the supranational empire as the dominant forms of political organization. Some of the nation-states of Asia and of Europe—Japan, Korea, England, and France, for example—could trace their growth back more than a thousand years and present their history as a steady process of unification and consolidation. Some of the supranational empires—the Russian, the Turkish, and the Chinese—had what might be regarded as a nation-state as their nucleus, a state which had gradually spread its power over minor nationalities in adjoining areas. The history of imperial states reached back to the end of the first millennium B.C. in Europe, to an even more remote period in parts of Asia.

Africa, by contrast, presented a political pattern of great complexity that endured until the European conquest at the end of the nineteenth century. The continent contained a few states—Morocco, Tunis, Egypt, Ethiopia—of considerable, even great antiquity. There were in sub-Saharan Africa a number of substantial kingdoms, such as the states created by the Ashanti, the Fulani, the Ganda, or the Zulu, of more recent origin. But these major states were rarely contiguous, and the greater part of the continent was occupied by a very large number of small independent communities ranging from the hunting bands of the Bushmen and the Pygmies to the tribal chieftaincies and the minor kingdoms to be found in almost every region.

In a nineteenth-century context such variety, such a multiplicity of miniscule polities seemed unusual. But if one compares nineteenth-century Africa with Europe or Asia in the middle of the first millennium B.C., one is struck by the similarities, by the existence at one time in Europe and in Asia of forms of political organization more readily associated with precolonial Africa. Thus, it may be inferred that the differences between Africa and other continents of the Old World have their origin not in basic dissimilarities but rather in varying rates of political development.

But why was this so? Why did the nascent nation-states of Africa— for one may not unreasonably apply this term to states such as Morocco or Buganda or the Zulu kingdom—appear so much later than comparable polities in Europe and in Asia? And why did Africa's few supranational states, notably the medieval empires of the Western Sudan, fail to establish themselves as really powerful and enduring political communities?

The factors already suggested to explain Africa's technological backwardness provide part of the answer. Powerful states can only be built on the solid foundations of surplus wealth. Kings must be able to raise tribute from their subjects, whether in the form of taxes on agricultural products or tolls on trade, in order to maintain the servants about their court, the officials who assert their authority in the provinces, the soldiers who protect their dominions. Moreover, in order to produce such a surplus, a certain density of population is essential. Now it is clear that over the greater part of Africa, as indeed in certain parts of Europe and Asia, the natural resources were too meager, the population too small to support a large political superstructure. Conversely, one can almost make the generalization that a major state was to be found wherever the natural resources were sufficient to support a fairly dense population. This is true of many parts of the continent, although in a few areas, notably among the Kikuyu of Kenya and the Ibo of Eastern Nigeria, a dense population coincided in the mid-nineteenth century with an absence of the major forms of political organization.

The process of creating major forms of political organization always appears to involve an element of conflict. Local groups fight one another until one has achieved the hegemony; the threat of a hostile neighbor induces a number of groups to combine and eventually perhaps to merge; foreign invaders conquer previously disparate groups and establish themselves as a dominant state-building aristocracy in their midst. Conflict breeds on constriction; men fly most eagerly to arms when there is competition between them for valuable resources, for land or cattle or other forms of wealth. Conversely, conflict's best antidote is space for expansion. The sheer size of Africa tended to minimize conflict. In many regions disputes could be resolved by the simple expedient of the defeated party moving away. When such safety valves are removed, when the defeated have no place to which they can retreat, then local societies have to evolve new forms of political organization. The history of the Bantu of South Africa in the first half of the nineteenth century shows this process very clearly: rising population leading to increasing conflict, conflict leading local groups to evolve new forms of political organization.

There was another aspect of the spaciousness of Africa that affected the emergence of major states—the lack in most parts of the continent of obvious natural frontiers. The situation of Egypt was exceptional: the long narrow oasis of the Nile Valley provided an ideal forcing ground for the process of state-building. Elsewhere, and especially in the great savanna plains that occupy so much of the continent, major states were faced with a situation in which it was easy to expand, but difficult to build up a really strong nucleus at the center. Most African kingdoms were inland states; they could not enjoy the partial protection afforded by a boundary that is also a seacoast. If they could expand in all directions, they were also vulnerable to attack from all directions.

The vulnerability of some African states was increased by the fragility of their economic foundations. The decline of the two ancient states, Ghana and Meroe, that lay on the edge of the desert is associated with a process of gradual desiccation caused by overgrazing and soil erosion. The Songhai empire was completely shattered by a small Moroccan force and the resulting anarchy appears to have caused a decline so disastrous that no major state emerged again in the heartland of the empire. In much the same way some of those parts of Africa which suffered most gravely from slave-raiding in the nineteenth century bear a scar clearly visible to this day in the ruins of deserted villages. The richer a country is the greater its powers of recuperation. Conversely, for peoples living just above the level of subsistence disasters such as war or plague or famine can inflict irreparable harm.

The sheer size of the continent, the low density of the population, the meager resources of many environments, the lack of natural frontiers— it is to a combination of factors such as these that one must look if one is to explain the reasons for Africa's political development proceeding at a rate so much slower than that of Asia or of Europe. But the difference between Africa and other continents has never been immutable, never really fundamental. And the history of Africa is clearly concerned with the same themes as the history of Asia or Europe or the Americas.

CHAPTER II

Land and People

𝕏 GEOGRAPHY

Africa is the second largest of the continents. With a total area of eleven million square miles, it is two-thirds the size of Asia, three times the size of Europe and about one and a half times the size of either North or South America.

Africa stands out, set against other continents, by virtue of the regularity of its outline. The simple lines of its coasts are complicated by no elongated peninsulas, no deep inlets of the sea. And this regularity of physical features is carried on into the interior, for though the continent contains individual mountains of great size and certain massive highland plateaus, there are no ranges to serve as natural barriers, comparable to the Alps, the Himalayas, or the Andes.

Indeed, Africa is not a continent that divides up easily into natural regions, and the divisions that are used in this book are purely arbitrary. Some—West, East, and South Africa—represent territorial groupings with half a century of convention behind them. Others—Northeast, Equatorial, and Central—are designations convenient only for the purposes of study.

The historian needs to acquire a deep familiarity with the geography of the continent, for in Africa, more obviously perhaps than in any other continent, the lives of men have been molded by their environment: the character of the landscape, the nature of the soil and of the vegetation, the distribution of the rainfall. One needs to bear in mind, too, that in many parts of the continent sharp local contrasts exist. Thus, to take a particularly striking example, standing on the slopes of Kilimanjaro, Africa's highest mountain, surrounded by a landscape of fir trees, mountain torrents, and mossy banks reminiscent of the European Alps, one can look down on parched, brown plains, covered with a vegetation of thorn scrub and wiry grasses, the home still of elephant, lion, and giraffe.

Inevitably, maps which depict the main features of Africa on a continental basis can only represent broad generalizations. One needs to be aware that tropical rain forests have many extensive clearings, that highland plateaus are often dissected by deep valleys, that all the great rivers of Africa have their courses interrupted by impassable rapids. Nevertheless, it is essential to hold constantly in mind the main features of African geography.

⚒ PEOPLES AND TRIBES

In its broad outline the physical geography of Africa is not difficult to grasp. The human geography by contrast presents a much more confusing picture, and this confusion may become quite overpowering when one is faced for the first time with a really detailed map giving the location of the hundreds of identifiably distinct ethnic groups to be found on the continent.[1]

At this point it is essential to define the terms used in any description of the inhabitants of Africa. In Europe cultural homogeneity and political unity tend to coincide. The majority of those whose culture is Italian, for example, live in a single sovereign political community, the republic of Italy. In precolonial Africa, on the other hand, as indeed in Italy before its unification, people who possessed the same culture were often to be found living in a number of independent political communities. Alternatively, a single polity—a term used here as a synonym for independent political community—might contain a number of people of differing culture.

The term "tribe" has often been used by Africanists in a very confusing manner. Sometimes the sense is cultural: thus the Yoruba who number several million and who founded a large number of polities are called a tribe. Sometimes "tribe" is given a political connotation: among the southern Bantu a particular chief sometimes gave his name to his followers whose numbers might vary from a few hundred to several thousand but who were henceforward known as a tribe. Social anthropologists favor the use of the term "tribe" in the first sense, to imply cultural homogeneity. But there are other terms that can be used with the same meaning: one can refer to a "people" or to an "ethnic group" or simply insert the definite article. In these circumstances it seems less confusing to restrict the term "tribe" to the second meaning, the followers of a chief in certain societies in which political groups are constantly changing their shapes. Almost all African societies have experienced this peculiarly fissiparous form of political organization at some periods of their history. "Tribe" will be used, then, in this limited sense, to describe a certain form of polity. When the inhabitants of a definite area all speak the same language or show other signs of cultural homogeneity, they will be termed a "people" or an "ethnic group."

Between adjoining ethnic groups the differences may be comparatively modest. But taken over a wider area, as large as the territory of some of the present states of Africa, the contrast between ethnic groups—in physical features, language, social structure, political organization, religion and so on—may be very great indeed. Certainly, no European country, apart from the Soviet Union, possesses a population made up of so many diverse elements as are to be found in Kenya or Nigeria, Ethiopia or the Sudan, South Africa or the Republic of Chad. How, one may wonder, can one possibly trace a connection between the ebullient Ibo communities of Eastern Nigeria and the conservative Hausa cities of the North, between the sophisticated Amhara aristocracy of Addis Ababa and the simple Negroid villagers of Ethiopia's western borderlands, between the wandering pastoral Herero of Southwest Africa and the black urban proletariat of the Rand?

Yet as one's knowledge of Africa becomes more extensive, a more coherent picture begins to emerge. One learns of underlying similarities beneath surface differences; one sees how different peoples have been influenced by the same broad historical movements; one begins to understand how the people of Africa have come to evolve so many different cultures. Diversification is to be regarded as one aspect of the complex process of change, a theme to be discussed in Chapter IV. At this stage, however, it is convenient to consider two of the most obvious ways— physical features and language—in which the peoples of Africa differ one from another.

PHYSICAL FEATURES: "RACE"

In the physical features of its inhabitants Africa presents sharper contrasts than does any other continent. The first outsiders to comment on this were the ancient Greeks. They coined the word *Ethiopian,* "burnt-faced," and applied it to all those darker-skinned peoples who lived beyond the southern fringe of the Mediterranean lands. In much the same way the Arabs designated all that part of the continent that lay to the south of the Sahara *Bilad as-Sudan,* "land of the blacks."

In the nineteenth century European scholars developed the concept of "race," and physical anthropologists came to identify five distinct "races" in Africa—Caucasoid (sometimes referred to as the Brown or Mediterranean race or as Hamites), Negroid, Bushmanoid, Pygmoid, and Mongoloid.

The European concept of race had two serious flaws. In the first place it became the practice to think of "races" in terms of "ideal types." Thus, some peoples were regarded as being physically "pure" or true representatives of their race, while others were classified as hybrids. In fact it is now clear that "races" cannot be defined in such hard and fast terms, for every "race" contains many different strands. The concept of a "pure race" is a myth, since all "races" are hybrids.

The second flaw in the concept of race was the tendency of those who used it to equate race with culture. Thus, because light-skinned people, such as the ancient Egyptians or the Arabs, had created elaborate civilizations in Africa, it was assumed that there must be some connection between light skins and the ability to create highly evolved societies. This deduction represented a gross and distorted simplification. The evolution of any culture is a highly complex progress; but there is no evidence to suggest that the characteristic physical features of a people are a factor of major importance in the development of their culture.

But though the concept of "race," as it is generally understood, is now outmoded, it is clear that great physical differences do exist in Africa and the old racial divisions are of some use in the initial process of classifying the peoples of the continent. Moreover, for the historian a study of the physical features of any one people may provide some clues as to the nature of the different elements that have come together to form the present population.

Of Africa's five racial types three are today of comparatively minor importance—the Bushmanoid, Pygmoid, and Mongoloid. People of Bushmanoid stock are distinguished by short stature, light yellowish brown skin, thin lips, flat noses, and high cheek bones. Two thousand years ago they were probably the dominant element in the population of most of South, Central, and East Africa. Today they are confined for the most part to the remote fastnesses of the Kalahari Desert.

People of Pygmoid stock are most obviously distinguished by their very short stature. A yellowish-brown skin and downy body hair are physical characteristics found in some Pygmy groups. The ancestry of the Pygmies is a matter of controversy. Some scholars regard them as being of Negroid origin, others relate them more closely to the Bushmanoids. It is probable that they have undergone a process of dwarfing in the last ten thousand years during which the dense tropical rain forest has been their habitat.

Mongoloid groups—people with yellowish brown skin and straight hair—are confined to Madagascar. They are the descendants of the Indonesian immigrants of the first millennium A.D.

With Bushmanoid and Pygmoid groups numbering far less than 1 per cent of the total population of twentieth-century Africa, the mainland of the continent is left divided between two broad racial groups, Caucasoids and Negroids. The original homeland of the Caucasoids was probably western Asia. From there they moved in a steady series of migrations extending over a period of at least ten millennia into much of the northern half of Africa from the Horn to the Western Sahara. The most prominent peoples of Caucasoid stock are the descendants of the ancient Egyptians, the Berbers, the Arabs, the Amhara, the Galla, and the Somali. Their most characteristic physical features are light or medium brown skin, narrow nose, thin or medium lips, and straight or wavy hair.

People of Negroid stock dominate the rest of Africa. There has been much controversy about the original homeland of the Negroes. The most likely location for the evolution of Negroid features is the savanna country to the north and west of the equatorial forest. From this homeland one group of Negroid peoples—the speakers of Bantu languages—moved southward to populate most of Central, Eastern, and Southern Africa. Other groups spread over the savanna lands of the Sudan and penetrated the forests of West Africa. Dark brown skin, broad noses, thick lips, and kinky hair represent their most characteristic features.

Among both Caucasoids and Negroids considerable variations in physical features are found. Sometimes this can be ascribed to intermarriage between people of different racial stocks. Some of the Southern Bantu, for example, clearly possess physical features of Bushmanoid origin. Again, the basically Caucasoid characteristics of many of the Fulani of West Africa or of the "Hamites" of East Africa—the Hima of Ankole or the Tutsi of Rwanda—have been modified by intermarriage with other people of Negroid stock.

But there are some ethnic groups whose racial history is more obscure. These groups occupy an area between the Central Sahara and the Ethiopian highlands. They include such people as the Teda or Tebu of Tibesti, the Dinka of the White Nile, and the Masai of modern Kenya. The physical features of these peoples fit uneasily into either the Caucasoid or the Negroid pattern. Though their skin may be very dark, some of their other physical characteristics—the shape of nose or lips or legs—are often quite unlike those of most Negroids. Most physical anthropologists have seen these groups as representing a mingling of Negroid and Caucasoid stocks. But most of these people speak languages belonging to a family that is quite distinct from the language families of the Caucasoids and the Negroids. It may well be that the original ancestry of these people is to be found neither in the Caucasoids nor in the Negroids, but in a third racial stock, at present unidentified and unnamed.[2] Such a stock, if indeed it existed, must clearly have received a considerable admixture of Caucasoid and Negroid blood.

❧ LANGUAGE

Africa contains a greater number and a wider variety of languages than does any other continent. For a century scholars have been engaged in the complex task of determining the exact nature of the relationship between African languages. Linguistic classification is still a subject for controversy, but a considerable measure of agreement has been reached in defining the main linguistic stocks, even though no universally accepted terminology for the description of several of these stocks has yet been evolved.

Most of the Caucasoid peoples of the northern half of Africa speak languages which belong to a stock variously described as "Afro-Asiatic" (Greenberg), "Hamitic" (Murdock), or "Hamito-Semitic." Afro-Asiatic —the terms used by Greenberg seem the least confusing—has five main branches: ancient Egyptian, Semitic (Arabic and Amharic), Berber, Cushitic (Beja, Somali, and many Ethiopian languages), and Chadic (Hausa and many languages spoken south and west of Lake Chad).

Not all the people of Caucasoid type in Africa speak Afro-Asiatic languages. There are some isolated Caucasoid groups, such as the cattle Fulani in West Africa and the Hima and Tutsi in the interlacustrine area of East Africa, who have adopted the languages of their Negroid neighbors. Conversely, all the speakers of the Chadic branch of Afro-Asiatics are basically Negroid in physical appearance.

The languages spoken by Bushmanoid groups belong to a stock now usually termed Khoisan, a term compounded from *Khoi,* the Hottentots' name for themselves, and *san,* their name for the Bushmen. The most conspicuous feature of Khoisan languages is the presence of click sounds.

The classification of languages spoken by Negroids presents much greater difficulties than those of the Caucasoids or Bushmanoids. Greenberg, the only scholar in recent times to work out an overall system of classification, has divided Negroid languages into two great stocks which he terms Congo-Kordofanian and Nilo-Saharan. But his classification has been criticized by other scholars who point out that it is based on insufficient evidence and who consider that it does not pay enough attention to alternative conclusions.

There is, however, a considerable measure of agreement that the languages of West Africa (with the exception of Songhai and Kanuri and the Chadic branch of Afro-Asiatic) belong to a single linguistic stock which has been termed "Western Sudanic." Western Sudanic has six main branches.

Greenberg considers that Bantu is no more than one subsection of a branch of Western Sudanic. He therefore coined the term "Niger-Congo" to replace the term Western Sudanic. But other scholars prefer to see Bantu as a separate stock, though related to Western Sudanic. For the historian it is certainly an advantage to think of Bantu separately and so to acquire a clearer impression both of the essential unity and the wide spread of Bantu languages.

It has long been recognized that the languages spoken by some of the people living in the Nuba Hills of Kordofan in the Republic of the Sudan are quite unlike other languages spoken in the same area. Greenberg has recently asserted that these Kordofanian languages are related to the languages of West and Central Africa. This conclusion led him to change the term "Niger-Congo" to "Congo-Kordofanian." [3]

Linguistically, the most confusing part of Africa is that which lies between the Central Sahara and the Ethiopian highlands. Some of these languages appeared to represent distinct stocks spoken by very small groups: Maban, for example, spoken by a few thousand people in Central Chad, or Koman, spoken on the Ethiopia-Sudan border. Other languages were seen as belonging to large groupings. Greenberg has now suggested that most of the languages of this area should be regarded as forming part of a basic stock he terms "Nilo-Saharan." Nilo-Saharan includes Songhai (languages spoken by a people living far to the west on the Niger bend), Saharan (Teda and Kanuri), and the branch which Greenberg terms "Chari-Nile." Chari-Nile is subdivided into two main branches: Eastern Sudanic, which includes Nubian and the languages spoken by the people usually termed Nilotes (Luo, Nuer, and others) and Nilo-Hamites (Masai, Turkana, etc.), and Central Sudanic, which is made up of various groups living in the Bahr-al-Ghazal province of the Sudan and adjoining area in Uganda, Congo, and Chad.

The languages spoken by the Malagasy peoples of Madagascar are closely related not to any African language, but to the languages of Indonesia, which form one of the branches of Malayo-Polynesian.

Given the paucity of written records, the historian in Africa has to press every possible type of evidence into his service. The language of any people represents a massive historical document, a document that contains many clues to help elucidate the relationship of a people with their neighbors. A study of the Arabic loanwords in Hausa, for example, would throw a great deal of light on the nature of the influences that reached the Hausa people from across the Sahara. And a study of loanwords from the languages of other neighboring peoples—Kanuri, Tuareg, Songhai, Yoruba—would serve to increase still further an understanding of the different strands in Hausa culture.

As one pushes further into the past, the evidence of linguistic relationships provides, as Murdock has pointed out, "the most dependable evidence of historical connections." [4] If two peoples speak related languages, then, however much they may now differ in race or culture, however geographically remote one from another their present locations may be, it is reasonable to assume that important elements in both peoples are either derived from some common stock or alternatively that they had such intimate contact with peoples speaking the basic language that they adopted it in favor over their own original tongue. (The spread of English from England to North America and the adoption of English by many non-English immigrants provides a convenient illustration of these two processes.)

The evidence from linguistics is often extremely difficult to interpret. At best it can provide not much more than broad indications or material for intelligent hypotheses. These hypotheses need to be set alongside the deductions derived from other sources of evidence, particularly archeology and oral tradition. But without the evidence provided by linguistics our knowledge of Africa's remoter past would at the present stage be very hazy indeed.

CHAPTER III

Periods of African History

To grasp the history of the African continent is a formidable under-taking. Not only is Africa very large and very varied, but the record of man can be traced to a past more distant than that in any other continent. In the Americas human history begins a mere thirty thousand years ago; in Africa the remains of the earliest known tool making hominids are now reckoned to be close to two million years old.

The story of man in Africa as in other continents is concerned, at least until quite modern times, with a process of ever-increasing diversifica-tion. Nevertheless, for all but the last six or seven thousand years of Afri-can history so great a measure of uniformity appears to have existed in the economy and social structure of African people that it is legitimate during this long introductory phase to consider the continent as a whole. After 5000 B.C., however, for parts of Northeast Africa, after 1000 B.C. for Northwest Africa, after the beginning of the Christian era for the rest of the continent, the differences among regions become so clearly marked that one cannot trace the history of any region adequately unless one studies it in isolation. On the other hand, since there has always been a considerable measure of interaction between regions, it is necessary to present some account of the state of the entire continent at different peri-ods in the past. This chapter is, therefore, concerned first to trace the main features of African history up to 5000 B.C. (this early period is not touched on in the regional chapters), then to describe very briefly the main stages of African history from 5000 B.C. to 1850 A.D.

A chronological framework provides a form of scaffolding into which one can insert the histories of individual regions and so construct a more complex whole. Yet this is not the end of the matter. Historians cannot dispense with dates and facts, but they need to be on their guard against too mechanical a view of the past. And so it is particularly important for them to acquire an imaginative awareness of the processes of change that are continually transforming human societies. These processes are discussed in the next chapter; the forces and manifestations of change, as there defined, form the perennial themes of the history of every society in Africa.

Finally, something should be said here of the nomenclature applied by historians to periods of the past. "The Stone Age," "the Dark Ages," "the Era of Firearms and the Slave Trade"—all such labels are basically impressionistic in that they seize on a single aspect of a particular period that appears to be of especial significance to individual historians. There is a good deal to be said, especially in a continent so varied in its development as Africa, for adopting a more austere approach and giving to periods of continental history no more than the designations of formal chronological divisions.

FROM 1,750,000 TO 50,000 YEARS AGO

Africa appears almost certainly to have been the birthplace of mankind. This hypothesis was first put forward a century ago by Charles Darwin, who based his argument on what was then known of the distribution of the higher apes. The fossil remains of early hominids discovered in East and South Africa go far to confirm Darwin's hypothesis, but the latest evidence undermines the generally accepted view that man, passing in the space of a few million years through the stages of ape (pongoid) and near-man (Australopithecine), evolved far more rapidly than other species of animal. The fossil remains found in Kenya in 1963, of a creature known provisionally as *Kenyapithecus wickeri* and regarded as being a member of the family Hominidae, date back at least twelve million years. Clearly, the common ancestor of both men and apes must be sought in a past even more remote. As new species of the superfamily Hominoidea to which both apes and men belong are brought to light the process of human evolution assumes an ever-increasing complexity.

Of all the African sites that have produced evidence of early hominids Olduvai Gorge is at once the most spectacular and the most informative. Olduvai lies in one of the wildest and most arid parts of East Africa, not far from the famous game reserves of Ngorongoro and Serengeti in northern Tanzania. The gorge, a great gash in the floor of the Rift Valley, looks like a smaller Grand Canyon, cutting down through three hundred feet of ancient lake sediments and thus exposing, neatly stratified, layer upon layer of deposits rich with the remains of the lake-side camps of generations of early man. Here in 1959 Dr. L. S. B. Leakey discovered the skull of a hominid nicknamed "Nutcracker man" on account of its huge molars but known as *Zinjanthropus boisei,* a creature that lived, according to the potassium-argon method of dating, at least 1,750,000 years ago. Bed I in which *Zinjanthropus* was discovered also contained a large heap of animal bones together with a mass of crude stone implements, many of them being pebbles flaked to give them a chopping or cutting edge. Naturally, it was assumed that *Zinjanthropus* was responsible for producing these earliest of human tools. In this tool making capacity there lay, so it seemed, the vital difference between *Zinjanthropus* and the physically similar australopithecines whose fossil remains had been discovered in a number of sites in South Africa but never in clear conjunction with stone implements. Defining man as a "creature capable of making tools to a set and regular pattern," Leakey suggested that *Zinjanthropus* in possessing this capacity could be regarded as a man, while the australopithecines who lacked it must be regarded as "near-men."

These views Leakey has now modified as a result of recent discoveries.[1] In the first place research on chimpanzees in their wild state has shown that they too make tools to a set and regular pattern, shaping pieces of wood to be used in fishing termites from their nests. In defining man one can still lay stress on his capacity to make *cutting* tools, but one must also look for a wide range of physical characteristics—the size of the brain, the structure of the hand, and so on—to distinguish him from "near-man." In 1960 further hominid remains were brought to light in a lower deposit of Bed I at Olduvai. Though older than *Zinjanthropus,* these remains proved to be those of a different species of hominid, which has been named *Homo habilis. H. habilis* possessed a larger brain than *Zinjanthropus.* Moreover, his teeth indicate that his diet contained a considerable amount of meat, whereas *Zinjanthropus* was a vegetarian. It seems more likely that *Homo habilis* not *Zinjanthropus* was the maker of the earliest stone tools which were used for cutting up dead animals and smashing their bones to extract the marrow.

Some change in the ecology must have forced these hominids to extend their diet from vegetable foods and small animals to the carcasses of antelopes and pigs. Faced with skin too tough to be pierced by blunt teeth and weak nails, *Homo habilis* must have hit on the device of using sharp stones to cut through to the meat. At first he was a scavenger rather than a hunter, but the additional supplies of food his simple tools enabled him to obtain greatly increased his chances of survival. Gradually, as the numbers of these earliest toolmakers increased, they must have spread to new areas. Stone tools of the Oldowan type have now been found as far afield as the Maghrib.

Oldowan culture probably lasted for about a million years. One can hardly talk of progress or change in the face of such an almost unimaginable span of time. And yet imperceptibly changes were taking place. Man himself was evolving toward the dominant strain of *Homo sapiens*. The human population was slowly increasing. Slightly more efficient stone tools of the type known as Chellean were being manufactured in the post-Oldowan period. From scavenging men moved on to develop the techniques of the hunter, steadily improving their methods to enable them to deal with the larger animals. By Chellean times elephants were being successfully hunted; an advance which implies the development of more evolved social institutions, for a considerable number of individuals must have cooperated in the battue. Chellian artifacts are rare, but hand axes of the type known as Acheulian, a development from the Chellean, are fairly common. Though Acheulian artifacts have been found from England to Ceylon, no continent is so rich in them as Africa, where they occur in every region except the tropical forest areas. Clearly, Acheulian times, which lasted from about three hundred thousand to fifty thousand years ago, must have seen a great increase in population in Africa and a movement of men into many parts that had previously held little to attract them.

Of all the forces making for change in the earliest period of human history the one of which archeologists are most aware is that exerted by alterations in the natural environment as a result of changes in the climate. Africa experienced climatic changes in paleolithic times no less profound than those that transformed the face of Europe, Asia, and North America, the glacials or Ice Ages and interglacials of northern latitudes corresponding roughly to pluvials and interpluvials in tropical regions. Four pluvials have been identified in the geological record of East Africa in the period of the Pleistocene that covers most of the Old Stone Age, followed in more recent times by two "wet phases." During pluvials the rainfall of Africa was increased, if only by a few inches. Lakes spread out to cover areas that are now dry land, and desert regions, such as the Sahara or the Kalahari, acquired a modest vegetation. Interpluvials, by contrast, were marked by a lower rainfall which caused rivers to run dry, lakes to diminish, and the vegetation of the desert regions to disappear. Much of Acheulian times had coincided with a long pluvial. With most of northern Europe, Asia, and America lying under a covering of ice, the savannas and even the present deserts of Africa, their plains teeming with game, presented an ideal environment for the hunters of the Old Stone Age.

FROM 50,000 TO 5000 B.C.

Acheulian culture was distinguished by its widespread uniformity: men living in Kenya or Morocco, England or India all manufactured almost

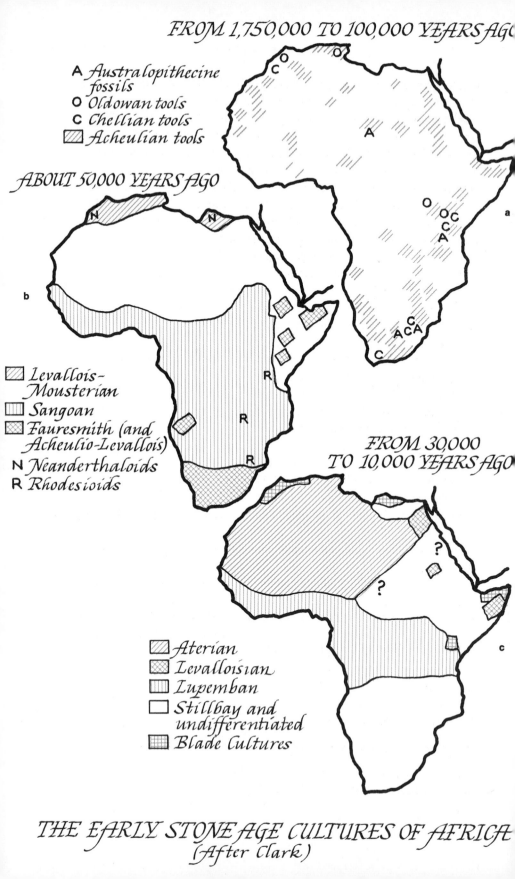

FROM 1,750,000 TO 100,000 YEARS AGO

A *Australopithecine fossils*
O *Oldowan tools*
C *Chellian tools*
▨ *Acheulian tools*

ABOUT 50,000 YEARS AGO

▨ *Levallois-Mousterian*
▨ *Sangoan*
▨ *Fauresmith (and Acheulio-Levallois)*
N *Neanderthaloids*
R *Rhodesioids*

FROM 30,000 TO 10,000 YEARS AGO

▨ *Aterian*
▨ *Levalloisian*
▨ *Lupemban*
☐ *Stillbay and undifferentiated*
▨ *Blade Cultures*

THE EARLY STONE AGE CULTURES OF AFRICA
(After Clark)

identical types of implements. Gradually, however, differences began to emerge, making it possible for the archeologist to trace a slowly increasing number of distinct cultures.

The most obvious characteristic of these post-Acheulian cultures is the presence of a much greater variety of stone tools. The all-purpose hand axe disappeared to be replaced by many different implements usually much smaller in size and involving new techniques of stoneworking. Thus, the Aterian culture of North Africa is marked by a proliferation of delicate tanged arrowheads, the Sangoan of equatorial regions by picks used for grubbing up roots and knives and "planes" for woodworking, the Stillbay of Southern Africa by triangular or leaf-shaped "points" for arrows and spears. Many of these stone artifacts imply the use of other materials, such as wood for the hafts of spears and gut or rope for bow strings. A few bone and ivory implements have been found for this period, and it is likely that men were also using skins and an increasing variety of vegetable products. To these material innovations must be added a new process—the regular use of fire—of which there is evidence in Africa only from late Acheulian times.

Many of the new techniques acquired in the Middle Stone Age arose in response to the need for men to adapt themselves to different environments. A period of intense aridity that occurred about fifty thousand years ago led to the desiccation of many areas previously favorable to human settlement and forced men to move into regions which in wetter periods had been impenetrable swamp and forest. Thus, it was at this time that the first settlements, identified from Sangoan artifacts, were made in the forest regions of West and Equatorial Africa. At the same time steadily accumulated experience taught men to make ever more productive use of their environment. Improved hunting techniques and increased knowledge of edible roots and plants made it possible to obtain a regular food supply from a more limited area and to substitute more permanent homes in caves and rock shelters for the open-air camps of earlier peoples. These changes must have been accompanied by the development of more complex forms of social organization and the gradual improvement of another technique hardly less important than toolmaking, that of language. The origin of languages is a highly obscure subject, but the latest methods of linguistic research suggest that the divergences of present-day languages must be traced back to a very remote past. Thus, it has been estimated that Yoruba and Idoma, two Nigerian languages both members of the Kwa division of the Western Sudanic family, have been growing apart from one another for at least six thousand years.[2] If this is so, then the basic forms of the main language families of Africa may well have emerged as early as the Middle Stone Age.

Technological changes were at once stimulated and accompanied by the evolution of man himself. Fossil skulls from a period between fifty thousand and one hundred thousand years ago reveal the existence of a number of different types of man in Africa: Neanderthal in North Africa, "Rhodesian," marked by extremely prominent brow ridges, in Southern Africa, and the earliest traces of *Homo sapiens* from sites in Kenya and Morocco. Gradually, the Neanderthalers and the "Rhodesians" were replaced by men of the sapient type, even as the australopithecines of the earliest Stone Age had given way to men of more advanced type. Ten thousand years ago it must have been possible to distinguish men to whom one could apply the racial terms in use today. Southern Africa and Eastern Africa were the domain of a stock ancestral to the modern Bushman. In the savannas of the southern Sahara and the Sudan an ancestral Negroid stock had probably emerged, though the earliest Negroid skull so far discovered dates back only to the fourth millennium B.C. In Northwest and Northeast Africa earlier stocks had begun to be modified by Caucasoid immigrants from western Asia.

In the earliest stage of human history one may postulate a gradual dispersion of toolmakers from an African center. By the Middle Stone Age the currents of migration had become increasingly complex. In the present state of knowledge it is impossible to chart these population movements with complete assurance. Thus, it is not known for certain whether the Neanderthalers of North Africa are the descendants of an ancient African stock or immigrants from Europe or Asia. But it is clear that at this remote period, fifty thousand years ago, North Africa had begun to be differentiated from the rest of the continent.

𝕫𝕡 FROM 5000 B.C. TO THE BEGINNING OF THE CHRISTIAN ERA

About ten thousand years ago communities in western Asia began to domesticate cattle, sheep, and goats and also to practice the regular cultivation of certain wild grasses, thus taking the first steps toward an economy based not on the collecting but on the producing of food. There is no evidence of these revolutionary new techniques occurring in Africa before the fifth millennium B.C. In 5000 B.C. all the people in the continent could be termed hunters and gatherers. But this generalized description fails to convey an impression of the varied types of economy which archeological research has shown to have existed at the beginning of what is termed the Late Stone Age in sub-Saharan Africa and the Mesolithic period in the northern part of the continent.

Some communities—in Tunisia, in the southern Sahara, in the neighborhood of Khartoum and in the Kenya Rift Valley, for example—

lived beside well-stocked lakes and rivers and obtained a food supply rich in protein from fishing and hunting water animals. In areas of heavier rainfall, where the savanna merged with the forest, other communities gained most of their food from the great variety of edible plants and fruits at their disposal. The regular collection of foodstuffs from a limited area has been termed "vegeculture" and is regarded as an "incipient form of cultivation." Finally, there were those who roamed the great plains of the drier savannas of Southern and Eastern Africa and even, during the Makalian Wet Phase, which lasted from about 5500 to 2500 B.C., made their homes in the Central Sahara, preying on the larger game animals as their ancestors had done for tens of thousands of years.

Most of these people had at their disposal far better equipment than their predecessors of the Middle Stone Age. They benefited from what has been termed the "microlithic revolution." Microliths are narrow flakes of stone used in the making of composite tools. Crescent-shaped microliths, for example, inserted in the haft of a wooden spear served as barbs and made the weapon very much more effective for hunting purposes than the simple pointed spear. The earliest microlithic cultures in Africa are represented by the Upper Capsian of Kenya and Tunisia, which appeared about ten thousand years ago. It has been suggested that both cultures had their origin in Palestine. They appeared during the period of increasing aridity that occurred between the end of the last pluvial about 10,000 B.C. and the beginning of the Makalian Wet Phase. Hunting communities in the drier savannas of East Africa must have found themselves forced to move over wider areas in search of game. Population movements such as these may well account for the diffusion of microlithic techniques to people of other cultures. The Capsians themselves, living by the lakes of the Kenya Rift Valley or the Schotts (saltwater lakes) of southern Tunisia, were able to lead a more sedentary life: indeed the Tunisian sites are marked by artificial mounds made up of a debris of snail shells, which indicate permanent settlement in the same spot for generations. Such favorable conditions facilitated invention. The Kenyan Capsians produced what is possibly the earliest pottery in the world, the Tunisian Capsians some of the earliest examples of sculpture and engraving on stone.

About 4500 B.C. immigrants from the Levant brought the new food-producing techniques to Lower Egypt. Their arrival coincided with the height of the Makalian Wet Phase, when much of the Sahara was covered with a vegetation of bush and grass that made it ideal grazing country. In these circumstances the people of the Sahara must have taken readily to the newly introduced domestic animals. Agricultural techniques made a less immediate appeal. Indeed, for two thousand years they were confined almost exclusively to the valley of the Lower Nile. Here, however, an amazing transformation took place. Within the space of fifteen hundred years, an extremely short span of time when set beside the millennia required for earlier developments, changes of a truly revolutionary nature took place in the population structure, the technology, and the social institutions of a people who began as groups of primitive hunters and cultivators and ended as the subjects of a large, highly organized state. Slowly, the agricultural techniques on which Egyptian prosperity was founded spread up the Nile Valley and across the Sahara. The desiccation at the end of the Makalian Wet Phase must have encouraged their diffusion by forcing people of the Sahara to move toward the savannas of the Sudan. Here they found it necessary to develop a new range of cereals, for the wheat and barley of Egypt would not grow in more humid regions. Local crops, millets and sorghum, provided the substitutes needed for food producing in the tropics.

By the middle of the first millennium B.C. Egypt had ceased to be the only "civilized" community in Africa, for three polities—Kush, Carthage, and Cyrene—had emerged as centers of urban culture. All of them were the product of colonization, Kush by the Egyptians, Carthage by the Phoenicians, Cyrene by the Greeks. Farther south in the northeastern highlands of Ethiopia another group of colonists from the rich city-states of South Arabia was laying the foundations of Axum. In 525 B.C. Egypt became a province of the Persian Empire; two centuries later it was conquered by the Macedonian Greeks.

Most of the communities of sub-Saharan Africa were far too remote to be influenced by these advanced and sophisticated polities. Only in parts of the Sudanic belt and on the East Coast is there evidence that commercial links had begun to be established before the beginning of the Christian era. But one technique—that of ironworking—which only reached Egypt about 700 B.C., was diffused with remarkable rapidity from the main centers of civilization, though it was not until after the beginning of the Christian era that most sub-Saharan communities acquired the new metal. At the end of the first millennium B.C. most African peoples could accurately be described as still living in the Stone Age.

THE FIRST MILLENNIUM A.D.

Five major themes can be traced in the history of Africa in the first millennium A.D.:

The consolidation and decline of Roman and Byzantine rule in North Africa and the expansion of Christianity.

The impact of the Arabs and of their religion of Islam on the northern half of
Africa.
The emergence of organized states in the Western and Central Sudan.
The influence of Indonesian seafarers on Eastern Africa.
The expansion of Bantu-speaking Negroids in the southern half of Africa.

The Romans took the first step toward establishing an African empire
when in 146 B.C., after more than a century of violent but intermittent
warfare, they occupied the homeland of Carthage. From this point they
extended their rule over the entire North African littoral, thus preventing
the rise of any substantial Berber state and absorbing the Macedonian-
ruled kingdom of Egypt. To Egypt the Romans contributed little; in Barbary they continued the steady process of development begun by the
Phoenicians. From the fourth century A.D. Egypt was controlled by the
"new Rome" of Byzantium, and the eastern part of Barbary, after a century of Vandal occupation, was also brought under Byzantine rule. For
the people of North Africa acceptance of the new religion of Christianity
probably represented the most profound transformation experienced in
the centuries of Roman and Byzantine rule. From North Africa the
Christian faith was carried to Axum and to the Nubian kingdoms that
succeeded Kush. Only in Egypt and in Ethiopia did Christian communities find a way of surviving the onslaught of Islam.

Between 639 and 700 Arab invaders, powerfully influenced by the new
religion preached by the Prophet Muhammad, conquered Egypt and
most of Barbary. By 1000 A.D. the North African territories that had once
been provinces in a unified Arab empire had broken away to form independent states. The Arab invasions brought Muslims from other parts of
western Asia to settle in North Africa, and their contributions enriched
existing cultures and greatly stimulated commercial activities. By 800
regular trade was established across the Sahara, a development facilitated by the introduction of the camel some centuries earlier. At the same
time Muslim traders from Arabia and the Persian Gulf brought about the
expansion of trade on the African coasts of the Red Sea and the Indian
Ocean and laid the foundation of a number of city-states in the Horn and
along the East Coast.

The second half of the first millennium A.D. saw the emergence of the
first organized states, such as Ghana and Kanem, among the Negroid
peoples living at the southern edge of the Sahara. The origins of these
states are still extremely obscure, but local traditions suggest that outsiders, possibly mainly of Berber origin, played an important part in the
process of state-building. Expanding trade with North Africa, based on
the export of gold and slaves, provided these Sudanese kingdoms with the
economic foundations essential for their development.

Indonesian seafarers appear to have made their first contact with East Africa about the beginning of the Christian era. During the course of the first millennium they played a major part in the colonization of the large, uninhabited island of Madagascar. No trace of any Indonesian colonies on the African mainland has yet been found, but they are known to have introduced a number of important food crops, including the Asian yam and the banana to the people of East Africa.

The expansion of Bantu-speaking Negroids is thought to have begun about the beginning of the Christian era and to have been associated with the introduction of iron. The Bantu homeland has been placed on linguistic evidence in the central area of the northern savannas. From here it seems likely that small groups followed the rivers that traverse the rain forest till they reached the central part of the southern savannas. From this point the steady pressure of population probably caused the migration of Bantu groups in all directions, thus bringing them into contact with peoples of different racial stocks, the Bushmanoids of Southern Africa, the Caucasoids (ancient Azanians) of East Africa, the Indonesians, and the Arabs of the coast, with whom they merged to form the Swahili. The new food crops obtained from the Indonesians were widely diffused throughout the area of high rainfall and made it possible for the Bantu to colonize parts of the continent that could previously have supported only a small population dependent on vegeculture. In time the new crops were transmitted to Western Sudanic Negroids and so facilitated the colonization of the Guinea forests.

By 1000 A.D. one can no longer assert that the majority of Africans were living in the Stone Age. Iron implements and food-producing techniques had come to be widely diffused. Important innovations—notably the yam and the camel—were profoundly influencing the lives of people in large areas. More regular lines of commercial contact had been established with peoples of other continents. Some communities had developed more elaborate forms of social organization and acquired in Christianity and Islam an ideology that facilitated contact with a wider world. Finally, in many areas, especially in the tropical regions, a substantial increase in population must have taken place.

FROM 1000 TO 1500

Of the five themes listed for the first millennium A.D., two cease to be of much significance for the greater part of the next five hundred years. The influence of European peoples and of the Christian religion cannot be considered a really important factor in the development of Africa during the period that lies between the Arab conquests of the seventh century

LINGUISTIC GROUPS

- Berber (Caucasoid)
- Chadic (Negroid)
- Nilo-Saharan (Negroid)
- Western Sudanic (Negroid)
- Cushitic (Caucasoid)
- Khoisan (Bushmanoid)

- Roman/Byzantine/Arab colonies
- A⟩ Arab trading contacts
- ⋯→ Bantu migrations
- → Indonesian colonists
- Ax Axum
- G Ghana
- K/N Kush/Nubia

AFRICA IN THE FIRST MILLENNIUM A.D.

and the renewed European involvement in Africa in the fifteenth, though Europeans played a substantial part in the commerce of North Africa in medieval times and the Christian faith helped shape the destiny of Axum's successor-state, Ethiopia. The impact of Indonesian sea voyagers is also a theme whose importance declines as the contacts between Indonesia and Africa gradually lapse, but Indonesian colonists and Bantu immigrants continued their pioneering work in Madagascar throughout this period. The continuation of the three remaining themes—the influence of the Arabs and of Islam, the process of state-building in the Western Sudan, and the migrations of the Bantu—account for much of the history of Africa in the five centuries after 1000 A.D.

In North Africa the eleventh century saw the emergence of the first major Muslim Berber dynasties and the arrival of the first Bedouin Arabs. The Bedouin migrants transformed the face of the Maghrib more profoundly than did the Berber conquerors, at once destroying the fertility of areas that the toil of centuries had rendered prosperous and furthering the process of arabization among the Berber people. At the same time other groups of Bedouin Arabs moved southward from Egypt into the Eastern Sudan, undermining as they did so the Christian kingdoms of Nubia. Arab expansion was from the start accompanied by the extension of Islamic culture, a culture of an international character to which people of many different countries from Andalusia to Indonesia made contributions. Traders, wandering scholars, and political refugees rather than soldiers carried Islam beyond the territories conquered in the seventh century; they played a leading part in creating the first urban centers that certain regions had ever known. Some Muslim foundations—notably Kairwan (Tunisia) and Cordoba (Andalusia)—had grown into large and wealthy cities well before 1000 A.D. Others, including Cairo (Egypt), Fez (Morocco), Zeila and Mogadishu (Somalia), and Kilwa (Tanzania), whose history begins toward the end of the first millennium A.D., achieved their greatest prosperity in the period between 1000 and 1500. Marrakesh (Morocco) and Timbuktu (Mali), founded after 1000, grew rapidly into important political and commercial centers. A vigorous trade with other continents or with other regions of Africa gave some of these Muslim cities a position among the most prosperous centers of urban culture to be found in the contemporary world.

In the Western Sudan the process of state-building was further stimulated in part by the profitable trade with North Africa and by the new concepts introduced by Muslim immigrants or by others with some knowledge of the more evolved polities of the Mediterranean and the Nile Valley. States emerged among the Hausa, the Songhai, the Mossi, the Yoruba, the Malinke, and others. The Soninke kingdom of Ghana collapsed, but first the Malinke state of Mali and then the state created by the Songhai developed into substantial empires.

Among the Bantu the steady work of pioneering continued. By 1500 Bantu groups were firmly established in the interlacustrine area of East Africa, on the Kenya highlands, and in parts of the Transvaal and Natal, and a number of substantial Bantu states appeared, notably on the lower Congo (Kongo) and in the Zambezi (Monomotapa), while Bantu Negroids formed the main element in the population of the Swahili city-states of the East African coast and of Kitara, a kingdom north of Lake Victoria founded by "Hamitic" pastoralists, possibly of Sidama origin. The Sidama themselves, benefiting from contact with the powerful Christian kingdom of Ethiopia and with Muslim traders from the Red Sea coast, created a cluster of kingdoms along the southern borders of Ethiopia.

In 1500 the majority of African peoples were still living in small-scale polities based on self-sufficient economies of a kind that had changed little in the course of a thousand years. Yet these modest societies made their own contribution to the development of Africa, as their slowly increasing population of farmers or herdsmen spread into areas that had previously only supported scattered bands of hunters. At the same time an increasing number of Africans, though still only a very modest percentage of the continent's total population, found themselves subject to more elaborate forms of political organization, affected by the consequences of more intense commercial activity, and brought into contact, in a few favored parts, with urban cultures and ideologies of an international character.

FROM 1500 TO 1850

Two general themes dominate African history in the three and a half centuries after 1500: the renewed impact of outsiders and the extension of the process of state-building to areas which had previously only contained small-scale polities. These two themes are only partly interconnected.

Seven alien peoples—five Europeans: the Portuguese, the Spanish, the English, the French, and the Dutch; and two Asians: the Ottoman Turks and the Omani Arabs—exercised a powerful influence on the development of particular areas of Africa after 1500. This new movement by outsiders into Africa began in the fifteenth century, when the Christian peoples of Spain and Portugal finally succeeded in expelling the Muslims of Arab or Berber origin who had dominated the Iberian Peninsula since the eighth century. In 1415 the Portuguese carried the war into Africa when they captured the Moroccan port of Ceuta. In 1492 the

Spanish overran Granada, the last Muslim state in Andalusia. In the next half century Portuguese and Spaniards captured most of the ports of the Maghrib. This Christian onslaught provoked a fierce Muslim reaction, in which the Ottoman Turks played a leading part. In the fifteenth century the Ottomans had built up the most powerful Muslim state in the Mediterranean. In 1517 Egypt was added to the Ottoman empire and Turkish influence spread down the Red Sea. At the same time Turkish naval power was used to expel the Spaniards from the Eastern and Central Maghrib, and Turkish colonies were established in Algiers, Tunis, and Tripoli. Meanwhile, in Morocco a nationalist movement drove the Portuguese from most of their coastal bases.

By the end of the fifteenth century a revolutionary development had taken place along the western coast of Africa. Western European mariners, with the Portuguese taking the leading part, audaciously felt their way around the western bulge of Africa. The Atlantic islands—Madeira, the Canaries, and the Cape Verde Archipelago—were settled by Europeans of varied nationalities, while the Portuguese, eager to tap the gold trade of the Western Sudan and to discover a sea route to the Indies, went on to establish trading posts on the Guinea coast, then to make contact with the states of Benin and Kongo, and finally, in the last decade of the century, to complete the circumnavigation of the continent, sailing past the prosperous Swahili city-states of the eastern seaboard to reach the rich markets of the East Indies.

In the second half of the sixteenth century the English, the French, and the Dutch began to break into the Portuguese preserve. The long stretch of coast from the Senegal to the Congo became the sphere of the most intensive European commercial activity. Nowhere along this coast, with the exception of a few small French posts up the Senegal, were there any European trading establishments in the interior. But farther south in Kongo, Angola, and on the Zambezi the Portuguese succeeded in penetrating far inland. They also dominated the Swahili cities of the East African coast until their garrisons were driven out at the end of the seventeenth century by the Arabs of Oman, a state possessing considerable maritime power and lying at the mouth of the Persian Gulf. Sofala and Mozambique, the East Coast ports that remained firmly in Portuguese hands, provided them with staging posts on the route to the Indies. By the beginning of the eighteenth century the other maritime powers with a stake in the East had founded similar bases in southern latitudes, the English on the island of St. Helena, the Dutch at the Cape, and the French, after an abortive attempt to colonize Madagascar, at Mauritius and Réunion.

By 1800 the most substantial polities created by outsiders in Africa were not those of European origin but the territories dominated by the Turks in North Africa and nominally subject to the Ottoman sultans. Nevertheless, though the European presence was at this stage far less imposing than it had been when Roman power was at its height, European influence was felt over a much wider area than in classical times and exerted an increasingly profound effect on indigenous polities. Some communities, such as the Bushmen of the Cape, were destroyed by the European impact. Others, notably some of the Swahili city-states of the East Coast, found their prosperity shattered. Yet others, the kingdoms of Kongo and Monomotapa, were gravely weakened by European interference. On the other hand some African polities, kingdoms such as Ashanti or Benin in West Africa or the Ovimbundu states in Angola, gained an immense access in wealth from the new commercial opportunities, particularly the trade in slaves, opened by Europeans. And there were other polities, such as the trading communities of the Niger Delta, which would never have been created had it not been for the profits the Atlantic trade offered to African middlemen who passed on the products of the interior to European traders.

The involuntary movement of peoples as the result of the trade in slaves can be traced back, at least on a modest scale, to the emergence of the first organized states with military power at their disposal in the Nile Valley in the fourth millennium B.C. By the end of the first millennium A.D. the trade in slaves, mostly of Negroid origin, was put on a regular basis by the Muslim merchants who did business in the Sudan and on the Indian Ocean and Red Sea coasts. But it was the demand of Europeans for Negro labor to work the plantations established first in the Atlantic islands and later in the tropical colonies of the Americas that led to a really massive increase in the trade and so set in motion the greatest and longest drawn-out involuntary migration in the course of human history.

The most important material innovations introduced by outsiders in this period were two food plants of South American origin—maize and manioc (cassava)—and one manufactured object, the firearm. The slave trade was conducted in a way that inevitably led to some increase in violence; firearms, which from the seventeenth century on were frequently given in exchange for slaves, made it easier for the wealthier and better-organized polities to dominate their neighbors; and the tide of violence rose steadily as the number of firearms increased and their efficiency improved. There was some compensation for the lives lost as a result of the slave trade in the lives saved from death by famine by the introduction of the two new crops, both of which spread rapidly throughout the tropical regions of the continent. Certainly, there is no evidence to suggest that the period of the slave trade coincided with any substantial fall in the population of Africa, except in a few limited areas after 1850.

The end of the eighteenth century saw the beginning of a massive increase of alien interest in Africa. The French made a spectacular but abortive attempt to conquer Egypt (1798–1801), embarked a generation later on the immensely costly task of occupying Algeria, and extended their interests in Senegal and Madagascar. Humanitarian sentiment impelled the British to decree the abolition of their slave trade and to set up a colony for freed slaves in Sierra Leone; strategic interest led them during the Revolutionary and Napoleonic wars to annex the Dutch colony at the Cape and the French colony of Mauritius. Some of the Dutch settlers of the Cape (the Boers), influenced by expansive concepts of *lebensraum,* pushed deep into the heart of South Africa and founded the first European polities in the interior of the continent. Egypt was modernized by an exceptional Turkish governor, Muhammad Ali, and a large part of the Eastern Sudan conquered and transformed into a colony of this province of the Ottoman Empire. On the East African coast the Omani sultan, Sayyid Said, transferred his capital from Muscat to Zanzibar and gave vigorous support to the penetration of the interior by Arab and Swahili traders.

To these local developments must be added three movements of continental significance: a deliberate attempt, supported by many different bodies, to lessen the outside world's ignorance of Africa by the dispatch of missions of exploration into the interior of the continent, an increasingly vigorous effort to spread the Christian gospel to African peoples, a slowly mounting interest in the commercial possibilities of Africa, and an encouragement of the production of the raw materials needed by the rapidly expanding industrial economies of Western Europe and North America.

And yet, despite the steadily mounting rate of alien activities, there were many parts of the continent which, at least until the middle of the nineteenth century, were hardly affected by the impact of outsiders. In these parts the major events of the period between 1500 and 1850 relate to the emergence of more elaborate forms of political organization.

In West Africa, Bornu, Oyo, Ashanti, Dahomey, and the Fulani empire of Sokoto were the most substantial kingdoms to be created or to be consolidated during this period. The Fulani empire, based on the conquest of the Hausa states in the early nineteenth century, was the product of a movement of Muslim reforming zeal that affected many other communities in the Western Sudan between 1720 and 1880. Farther east the kingdoms of Baguirmi, Wadai, Darfur, and Sennar came to control wide areas of the Central and Eastern Sudan. To the south of the Central Sudan smaller kingdoms such as Bamun and the chieftaincies of the Zande and other peoples were created in this period.

In the highlands of Ethiopia the Christian kingdom and its neighboring Muslim principalities were disastrously weakened by their constant wars and by the invasion of the pagan Galla, but the concept of a unified monarchy survived in the Ethiopian successor-states such as Shoa and Tigre, while the stateless Galla began to merge with the conquered Sidama and created, at the beginning of the nineteenth century, a group of Galla-Sidama kingdoms.

In East Africa the process of state-building was concentrated in the interlacustrine area, though concepts of chieftainship spread slowly southward. Among the lakes invaders from the north and northeast, "Nilotes" and "Hamites," played a major part in the creation of a large number of states, of which Bunyoro, Buganda, and Rwanda were the most substantial. In the heart of Central Africa the closely related Luba, Lunda, and Bemba peoples were the main agents in the building of states among the scattered Bantu communities.

In South Africa no large polities emerged until the beginning of the nineteenth century, when a period of revolutionary violence, known as the *Mfecane,* produced the conditions that led to the emergence of the kingdoms of the Zulu, the Swazi, and the Sotho (Basuto) and sent powerful groups—the Ndebele, the Ngoni, and the Kololo—northward to found conquest states along the southern belt of Central Africa.

In Madagascar the process of state-building produced a mass of petty chiefdoms in the sixteenth and seventeenth centuries and culminated in the early nineteenth century in the emergence of one kingdom, Merina, powerful enough to undertake the conquest of the entire island.

Many factors contributed to the development of states in this period. Particularly favorable economic conditions, the product of a rich soil (Buganda), control over mineral wealth (Ashanti), or an advantageous position on an important trade route (the Ovimbundu states), enabled some communities to acquire a surplus wealth that could be used either for peaceful or for violent purposes. Some states, born in violence, developed a superiority in military techniques that made it easier for them to dominate their neighbors: the Sokoto Fulani with their cavalry, the Zulu with their well-disciplined impi illustrate this point. Other states— Merina is a notable example—showed themselves particularly adept at taking over the military techniques of other peoples. But in whatever manner they came to be formed, one point is clear: alien influence was a matter of comparatively minor importance in most cases in this period.

After 1850, however, the situation was radically transformed, as aliens thrust their power deep into the interior, breaking down as they did so the relative isolation of many African communities and forcing their peoples to become aware of ideas and techniques that had developed in other continents. One may trace a steady increase in the rate of change from paleolithic times onward, but after 1850 the tempo of change was immensely accelerated. History's fabric is seamless, and there is something highly artificial about picking on a single year to mark the beginning or the end of a period. But if one has to choose a date to mark the opening of modern times in the history of Africa, then 1850, the middle of the nineteenth century, is perhaps the most suitable. For it is only after 1850 that one can begin to see the two themes that have formed the subject of this section—the impact of alien influences and the process of indigenous statebuilding—coming together to produce through their fusion the face of Africa as we know it today.

CHAPTER IV

Change in Africa

THE ILLUSION OF CHANGELESSNESS

To many outsiders Africa has presented the illusion of uncreative stagnation. "Generations of men in Africa have lived in vain," wrote a late-nineteenth-century Africanist, "if life be measured by the invention of an Art, or the propagation of an Idea. In imagination we can depict them, migrating through their grand forests, huddled together in their straw huts, fighting their cruel fights, dancing their wild dances, and giving way to their abominable customs of Cannibalism, Human Sacrifice and bloody ordeals." [1] Within the last few years one of the most widely read writers on African themes has spoken of the people of Central Africa in the nineteenth century as appearing to be fated "to remain in a state of arrested development." "In a mysterious way the light of human ambition was extinguished, the village stayed chained to the Stone Age, and from century to century life revolved in an endless ant-like cycle of crude customs and traditions." [2]

It is hardly surprising that over the last century Europeans and Americans, brought up in an environment where rapid change is accepted as normal and constant stress is laid on the value of individual initiative, should have been struck by the apparently intense conservatism of many African societies. Some African societies were indeed deeply wedded to the past. "Have not the Hereros been cattle-breeders since God created them?" an old man of the Herero (a pastoral people from Southwest Africa) remarked rhetorically, when asked about his people's history. "As a cattle-breeder does not one always live in the self-same way? That is the life of the Herero," he went on, after describing the migrations in search of water and of grazing and the occasional conflicts with neighboring groups. "That is the life my great-grandfather lived, and my father lived it too. When we all live in exactly the same way, there is not much to be told." [3]

It is not difficult to account for the factors which produce an apparent immunity to change in certain societies. There is the simple fact of isolation: the villages lost in the bush, where no stranger ever comes to settle, bringing with him the disturbing shock of novel experiences, of new modes of doing things. There is the down-drag of a harsh environment, where men have neither the proper sort of leisure nor the incentive to develop their inventive faculties. There is the conformist pressure of societies in which, for entirely practical reasons, far greater stress is laid on cooperative effort than on individual initiative.

It was not unreasonable for Europeans to think of many African societies of the nineteenth century and even of the twentieth century as reproducing features comparable to those of European societies in medieval or even in late prehistoric times. But it was misleading to imply that these African societies were somehow immune to change, that their history could only be presented in terms of the "unrewarding gyrations of barbarous tribes," [4] that they were somehow stuck on one of the lower rungs of the ladder of human evolution. In reality the picture that Africa presents at any period in its history is at once more confusing and more dynamic. Its confusion results from the sheer variety of forms of social organization within the continent, its dynamism from the fact that in a continent of such size the process of change has always been taking place. To chart this process and to identify its forms is a task particularly conducive to a proper understanding of historical development.

FORCES OF CHANGE

In analysing the nature of change in history one needs to draw a distinction between the forces through which change occurs and the actual manifestations of change in a particular society. Often such distinctions are not easy to ascertain. The construction of a new road, for example, may be taken as a clear manifestation of change. Yet it is also a force making for change, encouraging intercourse, breaking down isolation, and so on. But the force exerted by the road can be defined in more general terms. One can see in this strip of laterite or tarmac laid across the landscape an example of the profound effect of any alteration in the natural environment; one can also see the road as a product of human action inspired by a desire for a greater measure of well-being.

By adopting this more generalized approach, at least six forces productive of change may be identified:

alterations in the natural environment;
population growth and pressure;
the peaceful pursuit of well-being (various forms of political, social, and economic development);

the violent pursuit of well-being (war and conflict);
the impact of ideas;
the stimulus of intercourse with peoples of different cultures.

Each of these forces must be examined in more detail.

Alterations in the Natural Environment

Men tend to think of the landscapes they see before them as being un-changing. In fact the natural environment in many parts of the world is almost as much subject to the forces of change as human society. Altera-tions in the natural environment may be produced by forces over which men have no control (climatic change, volcanic action, floods, and storm), or they may be the consequence of human activities (desiccation or soil erosion as the result of overgrazing or careless methods of cultiva-tion, the irrigation and reclamation of swamps and marshes, the cutting down of forests, the destruction of wild life, the introduction and diffu-sion of new plants, animals, and diseases). The changing face of the Sahara in prehistoric times and the transformation of the Lower Nile Val-ley from a jungle-choked swamp to one of the most productive areas in the world provide particularly striking examples of this theme, but the process of landscape change can be traced in almost every part of Africa.

Population Growth and Pressure

There is no aspect of the past on which historians stand so much in need of accurate information—and are so little likely ever to obtain it —as the field of population statistics. In all but the most unfavorable environments population tends to increase. The actual rate of growth must vary from period to period and society to society, being dependent on so many other factors, food supply, current diseases, medical facil-ities, social customs, political security, and so on. Population pressure must not be thought of as being limited to areas with a high density of population. Men become conscious of the pressure of their neighbors whenever there appears to be a shortage of the basic means of livelihood. Hunters or pastoralists probably tend to be more conscious of population pressure than do agriculturists in that the commodities they require, game animals, grazing grounds, and water holes, are likely to fall into short supply quicker than the land which is the agriculturalist's basic resource.

Population pressure may well be regarded as the major force, though not of course the only one, behind most *large-scale* migrations in African history: the movement of prehistoric hunters, the expansion of the Bantu, the spread of Arab and Somali nomads, the "Great Trek" in South Africa, the settlement of many foreigners in nineteenth-century Egypt and Algeria, the movement of Ibos into Northern Nigeria during colonial times, and so on.

The Peaceful Pursuit of Well-being

The natural desire of men to achieve for themselves or for their families what they regard as a sufficiency clearly supplies part, at least, of the motive force behind many human activities. The hunter devises or adopts a more efficient weapon with which to ensure his game supply; the farmer takes over an unfamiliar plant because he believes it may provide him with a better return for his labors; the trader undertakes arduous journeys to increase his stock of wealth; the peasant leaves the countryside to seek a better living in the town; the student devotes himself to acquiring a better education than his father received in the hope of obtaining more remunerative employment. Security is an essential concomitant of well-being; men may seek it by evolving new institutions or, if they conceive the supernatural to possess certain powers, by devising new forms of ritual. Well-being also involves an active enjoyment of life, and men may choose to create certain arts, sports, or ceremonies to this end. Thus, the peaceful pursuit of well-being involves a whole range of human activities, political, social, economic, religious, and aesthetic.

The Violent Pursuit of Well-being

The peaceful pursuit of well-being may turn to violence when men, whether as individuals or in groups, find themselves in vigorous competition for the same object. Often this object can be defined in simple material terms, as when men fight over land or cattle or trading rights. Sometimes the object takes a more abstract form, freedom to be preserved from those who threaten it, honor to be defended against those who smirch it, an ideology to be imposed on those who scorn it. Freedom, honor, or a particular ideology may provide as great a part of the content of well-being as the more obvious material forms of satisfaction.

In African history four types of conflict may be identified: feud, raid, war of conquest with its converse war of resistance, and revolt. The feud is characteristic of small-scale, stateless societies, where it may serve as an institutionalized form for settling disputes, particularly those associated with homicide. The raid (*razzia*) has as its object the removal of easily portable forms of wealth. Among pastoralists animal livestock, particularly camels and cattle, provided the main booty; among agriculturists human livestock to be turned into slaves represented the most attractive form of easily obtainable wealth.

Both feuds and raids were endemic in many African societies at least until the establishment of the temporary colonial peace in the early twentieth century. But the intensity of these conflicts varied from society to society. In the more elaborately organized polities feuding was replaced by peaceful methods of settling disputes. On the other hand, with greater numbers of men and better supplies of the instruments of destruction at their disposal, such states were more efficiently equipped for raiding the small-scale polities of their neighbors.

Wars may be distinguished from raids in one or more ways, the greater number of men involved, the longer duration of the campaign, or the more enduring and decisive consequences of the conflict. Wars of conquest can only be waged by a polity with an organization elaborate enough to maintain an army in the field and to possess some means of controlling for its own benefit the conquered territory. Thus, over a large part of Africa, especially in the southern half of the continent, wars, as distinct from feuds and raids, represented a type of conflict that could not occur before more elaborate polities had been created, a development that did not take place until quite recent times. Wherever such polities were to be found occupying contiguous territory, a record of belligerency can be traced no less sanguinary than that which stains the history of the states of Europe and of Asia. In the Maghrib, in the area around Lake Chad, in the interlacustrine area of East Africa, and in other parts of the continent war between states was of frequent occurrence.

On the other hand it should be noted that the most elaborate and possibly the most destructive campaigns fought on African soil—certain phases of the Punic Wars, for example, the Anglo-Boer War, or the North African battles of World War II—were those in which the dominant groups on either side were aliens. In view of the technological backwardness of Africa such a fact, though curious, is in no way surprising.

Wars of resistance may be regarded as the instantaneous reaction of certain societies to the threat of conquest, revolts as a later reaction to foreign domination. Resistance and revolt provide the reverse side of the coin of imperialism, the same situation viewed from a different angle. Few, if any, acts of conquest are completely bloodless, but the amount of fighting is likely to vary greatly from situation to situation. Thus, in their conquest of Algeria in the nineteenth century the French occupied the major Turkish-controlled towns fairly easily, only to find themselves drawn into a long and savage conflict with the Arab and Berber tribes of the interior. Clearly, the nature of resistance is likely to depend on a variety of factors: the suitability of the terrain for guerilla warfare, the military tradition of the people under attack, the behavior of the invaders, and so on. Most of the same variables bear on the likelihood of revolt against a dominant power.

Both wars of conquest and revolts may be inspired by motives that can be expressed in ideological terms. Such varied manifestations of violence as a Muslim jihad, a Christian crusade, the "civilizing mission" of an imperialist power, the revolt of an unorthodox Muslim sect, or a nationalist insurrection, all have one element in common, the dynamic of a strong ideological content. In civil wars, too, which can almost be defined as large-scale feuds within a society, ideology may have some influence on the actions of the combatants. But many conflicts of a kind frequently mentioned in the history of every major African polity have been almost completely devoid of ideology: the wars between rival states escalating out of a series of trivial incidents, the civil war provoked by a disappointed contender to the throne, the revolt of an ambitious provincial governor or of a group of people tired of paying tribute to a distant overlord. In conflicts such as these, inspired by the anger, ambition, and frustration of a small number of men, it would be absurd to involve so grandiose a concept as ideology. And even in conflicts in which the ideological element is clearly of importance, other forces must be taken into account. Thus, the Arab invasion of North Africa cannot be understood only in terms of the dynamic power of a new religion. Islam may be seen as the binding force which provided the unruly inhabitants of Arabia with that measure of unity essential for the success of their assault on the great empires surrounding them. But without the goad provided by the frustrations of life in a desert land, without the lure of plentiful booty, and without the impetus built up by a run of easy successes, the Arab invasions would never have developed into so cataclysmic a movement. Indeed, it is significant that the second Arab invasion of the Maghrib in the eleventh century, a movement no less profound in its consequences than the first, was almost completely unaffected by ideology.

Ideology is not the only external influence bearing on the nature of conflict. Changes in the instruments of destruction, brought about as the result of material innovations or the acquisition of new techniques, produce an effect even more profound. The substitution of iron for stone weapons, the advent of cavalry, and the introduction of firearms of ever-increasing efficiency must be regarded as major events in the history of any region in which they occur.

It is customary to think of the changes wrought by conflict in simple political terms, such as the domination of one people by another. Conflict can have more profound consequences. It may lead to the emergence of new institutions: the history of the Zulu kingdom provides a striking illustration of this process. It may bring new patterns of settlement into existence, with the construction of military bases and fortified posts in a recently conquered territory. Any conquest of long duration, such as the Arab conquest of the Maghrib, is likely to lead to the introduction of many new material goods, techniques, institutions, and ideas. And the revolt against the conquerors is no less likely to bring about the development of novel forms of political organization and the emergence of new ideologies.

The Impact of Ideas

One cannot interpret human actions only in terms of practical responses to particular situations. Men are also influenced to some extent by the codes of manners and conduct developed within specific social groups, by the intellectual traditions associated with particular professions and, in some societies, at certain periods of history, by well-defined ideologies.

Well-defined ideologies, though they may represent complex bodies of ideas influencing a wide range of human activities, are the easiest of thought systems for the historian to examine. Christianity and Islam, the two major ideologies in the history of Africa, at least until very recent times, have possessed basic texts and a massive exegetical literature. Both are universalistic, both subject to considerable local variations, both capable of influencing many different aspects of life. Thus, when the adherent of a traditional African religion becomes a convert to Islam, he may experience changes in his dress, his diet, his education, his system of family relationships, his social status, his attitude toward authority and toward people of other countries, and his concepts of the supernatural.

Universalistic ideologies clearly have a profound influence on codes of conduct. In the past, however, many African societies were untouched by such elaborate systems, and even today their influence is very slight in many parts of the continent. Irrespective of the impact of ideologies, every society or social group naturally evolves a code of manners or conduct that lays particular stress on certain virtues. The virtues stressed vary from society to society, and even within the same society institutional changes may lead to the adoption of entirely new codes of conduct. Thus, among the Zulu the reorganization of society on military lines accomplished by the despot Shaka in the early nineteenth century was accompanied by the acceptance of a different set of social virtues. "Informality, hospitality and naive curiosity . . . [were] replaced by a more reserved attitude. A pride almost amounting to arrogance and an indifference to human life were accompanied by a sense of discipline, order and cleanliness." [5] This new ethos of Zulu society was the result of a highly successful process of social engineering, but it was also a force in itself, helping to produce further changes in the lives of neighboring peoples.

Every specialized form of human activity possesses what has been termed here an "intellectual tradition," a refined body of accumulated knowledge handed down from generation to generation. The lore of a Bushman hunter, the agricultural skills of a Hausa farmer, the techniques of a Bambara wood-carver, the knowledge of the ways of cattle of a Masai herdsman, the style and verse form of a Somali poet—all these may be regarded as different examples of intellectual traditions. Such traditions are never static, for every tradition may gain accretions, suffer diminution, or even disappear completely. Certain intellectual traditions, those associated with modern sciences and technologies, have become universalistic. None of these sciences can claim an African origin, but African intellectual traditions may well contribute to universalistic systems of thought. This may easily be seen in the field of music and art, but it can also happen in other fields—certain traditional African medicines, for example, may be found to possess therapeutic powers of value to modern medicine.

In comparison to the dynamism and the assured rationality of modern science, the intellectual traditions of most African societies may seem to lack both force and rightness. Yet every intellectual tradition does possess its own vigor, its power to influence the minds of men within the society in which it is accepted. The lore of witchcraft may serve to illustrate this. In many African societies people still accept the notion that disease or ill-fortune is caused by the action of witches, of malevolent human or superhuman agents, and this belief may have a powerful influence on their actions. Similar beliefs were common enough in Europe and America three hundred years ago. They have almost completely disappeared as a result of the changes within European and American society: the development of modern medicine, the spread of education, the breaking down of the isolation of rural communities, and so on. Should the same changes take place on a comparable scale in Africa, belief in the existence of witches is likely to disappear. Nevertheless, there may well be certain elements in the lore of traditional African witch doctors that can be incorporated into the modern science of psychotherapy.

The Stimulus of Intercourse

Societies and peoples are often spoken of as being isolated. Yet isolation is a relative term and complete isolation over a very long span of time an impossibility. Certainly, there must have been many people in the African past who lived their lives without ever meeting anyone possessing a culture markedly different from their own. But it is equally true that in many parts of Africa contact between peoples of different culture was a commonplace occurrence. The meeting of Arab and Berber in the Maghrib, of Axumites and Agau in Ethiopia, of Masai and Kikuyu in East Africa, of Hausa, Tuareg, and Kanuri in the Western and Central

Sudan, of Bushman and Bantu in South Africa may be cited as examples.

Encounters such as these serve as a force making for change, for the transmission of material innovations, new techniques, institutions, or ideas from one people to another. One might almost state it as a law of historical development that the more cosmopolitan a society, the greater the intellectual vitality it is likely to display. Alexandria in Greco-Roman times provides an apt illustration. Another less familiar, but no less apposite example is to be found in the European society of Port Louis, the capital of Mauritius, in the early nineteenth century. A perceptive French visitor noted that quite ordinary Mauritian traders possessed much less limited minds than most Parisian businessmen. This he ascribed to the fact that their everyday activities brought them into contact with a very wide range of places—from Philadelphia to Canton. Such cosmopolitan experience left no room, he concluded, for conventional prejudices.[6]

The stimulus of intercourse may also operate within a single society, if that society is itself sufficiently diverse and sufficiently open to allow people of different classes and occupations the opportunity of meeting one another. Clearly, many African societies have been affected not only by the limited extent of their intercourse with outsiders but also by their social homogeneity, a homogeneity that was in the main a product of their material poverty.

MANIFESTATIONS OF CHANGE

Change may manifest itself in at least five different ways:

the appearance of material innovations (plants, animals, and manufactured objects);
the acquisition of new techniques;
the development of new patterns of settlement and new lines of communication;
the transformation of existing institutions and the establishment of new ones;
the emergence of new modes of thought.

Material Innovations

Material innovations provide the most obvious manifestations of change. The Coca-Cola sign on the wall of a mud hut, the petrol pump in the medieval alley, the occasional European dress in the throng of a native market: sights such as these, commonplace enough in contemporary Africa, are not to be regarded as distasteful incongruities, but rather as outward symptoms of a process of cultural transformation.

One can classify material innovations in two groups, living things (plants and animals) and manufactured objects. Something has already been said of the introduction of certain plants and animals to Africa. Their diffusion and diversification today may be regarded as a fairly rapid process, with research institutes developing new breeds and species and extension workers bringing them to the attention of farmers. In the past diffusion must have taken place very much more slowly, new plants or animals passing from community to community, partly through inter-marriage and other forms of local migration, partly also no doubt as the result of intervillage trading.

The range of manufactured objects relevant to the study of African development—tools, weapons, domestic utensils, clothing, furniture, vehicles, articles for adornment, objets d'art, forms of currency, musical instruments, and so on—is vast, and many of these objects have a history reaching far back into the past. Prehistorians, forced by the nature of the evidence at their disposal to concentrate on material goods, tend to have a greater appreciation of their significance than do those concerned with more recent periods of the past. Yet every material innovation affects in some way the society into which it is introduced. The importance of the development and diffusion of improved stone tools in the earliest African societies has already been stressed. For a more recent example of a manufactured object of major importance the firearm may be considered.

Firearms were first used with any frequency in Africa in the early sixteenth century, when they were introduced by the Turks and the Portuguese. Those states that acquired firearms gained a certain military advantage over their neighbors, but by no means a decisive one, for the early muskets were cumbersome and unreliable weapons. Until the middle of the nineteenth century firearms were comparatively rare in most of the states of tropical Africa, and the victories gained by certain peoples, notably the Fulani under Usuman dan Fodio and the Zulu under Shaka, owed nothing to their use. But the rapid expansion of European armament industries and the production of ever more efficient types of weapon led to the dumping of large quantities of obsolete firearms on the African market. Those who acquired them—the Arab traders of the Congo or the Southern Sudan, for example, or such states as Buganda, Ethiopia, or Wadai—were able to dominate neighboring peoples far more effectively than ever before. At the same time rulers who could afford to import large numbers of firearms found it necessary to establish permanent bodyguards or small standing armies, a development that had a profound influence on the social structure of the polities in which it took place.

Sometimes the study of a particular type of object may lead the historian to ask questions which other sources at his disposal would never have suggested to him. Thus, an eminent musicologist, A. M. Jones, has drawn attention to the remarkable similarities between the xylophone as found in Southeast Asia and in West Africa.[7] He discounts the possibility of separate invention in the regions and suggests that the xylophone was brought directly to West Africa by Indonesian seafarers. This is a hypothesis that other historians, pointing to the practical difficulties that would have faced the Indonesians in rounding the Cape and sailing up the west coast and above all to the apparent lack of motive for such a voyage, are unwilling to accept. But by drawing attention to the xylophone and by asking awkward questions about it, Jones has helped in a highly original way to stimulate thought about the African past.

New Techniques

The acquisition of material innovations does not necessarily imply the emergence of new techniques. Many of the consumer goods imported into Africa for centuries—beads, alcohol, and clothing, to give three disparate examples—did not lead those who obtained them to develop new skills. But some innovations—domestic animals, firearms, or motor vehicles, for example—require special maintenance, and others may be associated with techniques of manufacture that are easy to copy. The introduction of cotton plants, for example, may well be accompanied by the acquisition of the techniques of spinning and weaving. The appearance of iron implements probably preceded the arrival of blacksmiths in most societies. But the development of a caste of professional metalworkers, some of whom earned their living by moving from community to community, soon led to the wide diffusion of the techniques of metallurgy.

The amount of specialization to be found within a society provides perhaps the most accurate gauge of the extent of its technological development. In many African societies today no less than in the past, the number of specialists able to devote all their time to their profession has been very small. Indeed, a striking characteristic of many African societies is the variety of skills ordinary men and women need to acquire. Thus, among the Tuareg of the Central Sahara most men and women have some proficiency in the working of leather, wood, grass stalks, and goat hair, the extremely meager range of raw materials that the environment puts at their disposal. The leather is used for making tents, camel harnesses, water bottles, and some articles of clothing, the wood for bowls and tent pegs, the grass for mats, and the hair for ropes. Metalworking, on the other hand, is left to a special caste of smiths, who are regarded as being of alien origin. For Tuareg men the manufacture of useful objects occupies only a minor part of their time; primarily they have been, at least until recently, pastoralists and warriors, possessing all the skills that these arduous professions demand.

The Nupe of Northern Nigeria may be taken as an example of a people who have developed a wide range of specialization. A survey made in the

1930's [8] listed the following industrial specialists: blacksmiths, iron miners, brass and silver smiths, glass makers, bead workers, builders, carpenters, weavers, tailors, embroiderers, leatherworkers, indigo dyers, straw-hat makers and mat makers. To these should be added a considerable number of other professions from administrators, teachers, and traders to drummers and barber doctors. Nupe barber doctors, it may be noted, were remarkable for their "far-reaching competency"; their activities included not only cutting hair and dispensing medicines for every known disease, but also tattooing, the performance of minor surgical operations, and sometimes the treatment of lunacy.[9] In other words, they combined in one person a range of skills that in a more highly developed society would be performed by many different specialists.

One technique of universal significance requires special mention — language. The evolution of any language, the refinement of its grammar, the enlargement of its vocabulary, the whole process by which it develops into a more effective tool for expressing thought, is a historical process of the utmost importance to any society. Equally significant to the historian are the processes of change to which all languages are exposed in their relationship one with another, processes which may lead to the rapid expansion of one language, the complete disappearance of another, and the stubborn preservation of a third.

The emergence of new techniques and professional skills may occur in a number of different ways. Sometimes it may result from the arrival of small groups of alien specialists. Thus, some of the smiths among the Ahaggar Tuareg are said to be the descendants of Jews who sought refuge with the Tuareg after their community in the oasis of Tuat had been dispersed by Muslim persecution in the late fifteenth century. Alternatively, the arrival of a substantial number of foreigners displaying attractive material innovations of their own manufacture and creating a steady demand for such products may lead local people to acquire the new techniques. The emergence of a cotton industry in the Western Sudan toward the end of the first millennium A.D. provides an example of this process. Although a species of cotton is native to the Western Sudan, no use appears to have been made of it, and people either went naked or dressed themselves in leather, leaves, or bark cloth until Muslim traders from North Africa introduced both cotton cloth and a better species of cotton plant of Indian origin. The stress which the new religion laid on decency of dress forced its converts to acquire cotton robes for themselves and thus created a demand that could support a local industry.

Sometimes new forms of specialization in a society may owe nothing to the influence of outsiders but arise in response to largely self-generated changes. The society of ancient Egypt, for example, in its period of revolutionary change during the fourth millennium B.C. appears to have been little influenced by outsiders; but the rapid growth in the population, itself a product of the increased food supply, made it possible for many individuals to devote themselves full-time to occupations of a nonproductive nature such as the carving of statues or the painting of pictures on the walls of tombs, activities which less prosperous societies lacked the means to support.

The more rapid the pace of change, the more frequently particular techniques become obsolete. Conversely, when a society changes very slowly, old techniques linger on. In Europe and America one may occasionally come across nineteenth-century techniques still being practiced; in Africa on the other hand it is not difficult to find people using methods —the grinding of corn in stone querns, for example—that have not changed since neolithic times. Most contemporary African societies use techniques derived from many different periods of the past, and the incongruities that result present perhaps the most striking characteristic of African material culture in modern times.

New Settlement Patterns and Lines of Communication

Settlements in Africa may take many different forms: the movable camps of hunters or pastoralists, the isolated homesteads or compact villages of sedentary agriculturists, the towns and cities created by more diversified communities varying greatly in function, size, and pattern. Lines of communication are also of various kinds, ranging from bush paths, bridle tracks, and navigable waterways to constructed roads, air routes, and telecommunication systems. For the modern visitor to Africa the great cities and the roads, railways, or air routes that link them together present the most spectacular manifestation of change. But the historian cannot afford to ignore the humbler settlements, the more obscure lines of communication, for every village, even though outwardly no more than a collection of crumbling mud huts, every winding path through the bush represents, it must be realized, the end product of some local process of development.

Patterns of settlement develop in response to the nature of the environment, the size of the population, the character of its political and social institutions, and the dynamics of its economy. In some parts contrasts in settlement pattern may be ascribed to the pressure of different environments. Thus, in South Africa shortage of water forced the Tswana, living on the edge of the Kalahari, to create considerable towns around the few permanent water holes. The Zulu, on the other hand, whose land receives adequate rainfall, lived for the most part in isolated homesteads scattered fairly regularly over the countryside. In Southern

Nigeria the contrast between the existence of many substantial towns in Yoruba country and their relative absence in the equally well-populated Ibo territory would seem to be due not to any major variation in the environment but to differing institutions. Among the Yoruba there arose a large number of states with hierarchical forms of government, while the Ibo lived in innumerable independent village communities, most of which lacked a state organization.

Different settlement patterns account for some of the most striking contrasts between the regions of Africa. Egypt, the Maghrib, the East Coast and parts of the Sahara, the Sudan, and the Guinea forest saw the emergence of major urban centers: Memphis and Thebes, Carthage, Cyrene, and Alexandria, Cairo, Tunis, Fez, and Marrakesh, Kilwa and Mombasa, Sijilmasa and Ghadames, Timbuktu, Gao, Kano and Sennar, Oyo, Kumasi and Benin, and many others. Over most of the rest of Africa permanent urban centers were almost lacking until the major European settlements, Luanda and Cape Town, St. Louis and Freetown, began to take on the character of cities.

This contrast was a reflection of the differences in economic development, of the greater accumulations of wealth that occurred in parts of northern and western Africa and along the East Coast. Many of the old cities of Africa—Carthage, Kano, and Kilwa, for example—grew slowly into important commercial and consequently political centers. The story of the origin of such commercial cities is usually lost in obscurity or in legend, but in the case of Timbuktu a seventeenth-century Sudanese historian, Abd ar-Rahman as-Sadi, has described its origin in a passage that has the ring of authenticity about it.[10] Timbuktu owed its importance, as-Sadi pointed out, to its position, for its site provided a natural meeting point for traders coming across the Sahara and canoemen carrying agricultural produce along the highway of the Niger. At first, in the twelfth century, Timbuktu was no more than the encampment of a local Tuareg tribe, its dwellings huts of straw surrounded by thorn zeribas. But gradually more and more traders, some from countries as distant as Egypt, came to settle in the town and to build substantial houses there. In the fourteenth century Timbuktu passed under the sway of Mali and began to acquire some political importance; two centuries later it became the second capital of the Songhai empire. The city's wealth and importance attracted many learned men of religion, and it became in the sixteenth century the major center of Muslim scholarship in the Western Sudan. At the height of its prosperity in the sixteenth century its population was about twenty-five thousand.

Not all the great cities of Africa grew up in this way. Some of them owed their foundation to the political decision of a powerful ruler. Alexandria was laid out by Alexander the Great in 330 B.C.; Cairo was founded by the Fatimids after their conquest of Egypt in 969 A.D., Marrakesh by the Almoravids when they occupied Morocco in 1060; Khartoum was transformed from a small village into a great provincial capital by the Turco-Egyptians in the 1820's.

All human settlements face the possibility of decline or destruction. Sometimes destruction can be ascribed to a single political act: the ruined villages in many parts of Africa destroyed by nineteenth-century slave raiders or the cities of the East African coast shattered by the Portuguese in the early sixteenth century. Sometimes settlements are the victims of a longer period of political change: the grandiose urban centers of Roman Africa pillaged and dismantled by Berber and Arab nomads in the long centuries after the collapse of imperial rule. Sometimes a change in the natural environment appears as the main cause of decay: the neolithic settlements of the southern Sahara abandoned in the face of growing desiccation, a process that was also a major factor in the ruin of Nepata, capital of ancient Kush, and of Kumbi Saleh, capital of ancient Ghana.

Lines of communication are the product of human action no less than the various forms of settlement, but usually their history is far more obscure. Archeological research may throw some light on the identity and the date of the earliest inhabitants of a particular settlement, but who can tell what men first trod one of those paths through the bush that still serve as the main line of communication for many African communities? With the growth of interregional trade, however, it becomes possible to throw some light on the development of certain major highways. Thus, one can see how many African trade routes gradually came into prominence as the demand for African products—slaves or ivory, gold or copper, salt or kola nuts—or for that enticing variety of goods of Asian or European manufacture led enterprising men, African, European, or Asian, to venture far from their homes. Berber traders set out for the Western Sudan, Hausa for Ashanti, Nyamwezi for Zanzibar, Arabs for the Great Lakes, Ovimbundu for the Lunda country, Boers for the "Far Interior."

The record of traffic on the lakes, rivers, and coastal waters or lagoons of Africa is very obscure in its early stages, except in Egypt where archeological evidence throws some light on the type of ships used on the Nile or the Red Sea. But there can be no doubt that wherever an easily navigable waterway existed, men made use of it. The Songhai fishermen of the Middle Niger, the people of the Niger delta with their massive war and trading canoes, the Buduma pirates of Lake Chad, the Ganda with their navy on Lake Victoria, the Sakalava sea raiders of Madagascar—these are a few of the African peoples who skillfully adapted themselves for peaceful or for violent purposes to the waterways of their homeland.

The development of the great maritime highways that led to Africa can be traced in the records of the sailors and merchants who pioneered and regularly sailed them. They range from the Phoenicians in their great "ships of Tarshish," the Arabs in their dhows, and the Indonesians in their outriggers to the Portuguese in their caravels, the British in their men o'war, and the men of diverse nationality in ships flying Liberian or Panamanian colors and doing business in ports of modern Africa.

As for those lines of communication—constructed roads, railways, air routes, and telecommunication systems—that play so important a part in the life of modern Africa, they may be more appropriately considered later.

The Development of Institutions

The term "institution" is understood here to cover all forms of social organization designed to promote orderly intercourse or the well-regulated conduct of affairs. In size institutions range from the family to the supranational body of modern times; in function they may be concerned with any aspect of human activity. Broad headings such as political, economic, social, religious, and cultural afford a rough and ready means of classifying institutions. But many institutions, especially in less evolved societies, have a dual purpose. Thus, age grades as found among many African peoples may serve both political and social purposes.

The development of a society implies increasing elaboration in the number and variety of its institutions. In the simplest form of African society known today, the hunting bands of the Bushmen, the extended family is the only institution, at once social, political, and economic in its functions. On the other hand the substantial African kingdom of the nineteenth century contained a considerable number of institutions: the monarch and his court, the royal councils, the great officials, the military organizations, the legal establishment, the priests of the traditional religion, the market administration, territorial officials, village councils, and so on. In a modern African nation-state the range of institutions becomes still greater: presidents and political parties, parliaments and ministries, schools and churches, trades unions and development corporations, shops and social clubs. To the historian concerned with tracing the process of change every human institution is of some relevance. At the same time the historian in Africa must also direct his attention to all those alien institutions that have had some influence on the development of the continent: trading companies and missionary societies, colonial ministries and imperial parliaments, and international organizations of many different kinds.

Within any society institutions may develop in two different ways. There may be a process of internal evolution in response to other changes affecting a society. Alternatively, novel institutions, introduced from the outside, may either be grafted onto existing institutions or established on entirely new foundations.

In the early history of Africa the introduction of alien institutions is easier to trace with some assurance than is the development of indigenous institutions. In certain states, such as Carthage, Kush, or Axum, the machinery of political administration appears to have been introduced by alien invaders or immigrants, whether Phoenicians, Egyptians, or Semites. Again it is possible to trace the profound influence of Islam in many parts of the northern half of Africa, either calling entirely new institutions, such as Koranic schools or Muslim fraternities, into existence or transforming the character of others by grafting onto the structure of existing states Muslim principles of law and administration. Even so basic an institution as the family may experience a radical change when exposed to the pressure of alien cultures. Thus, the Beja of the Eastern Sudan are known from the accounts of Arab geographers to have followed the practice of matrilineal descent, at least until the fifteenth century when the influx of Arab settlers and the consolidation of Islam led the Beja to accept patrilineal descent, though they retain to this day certain practices characteristic of a matrilineal society.

The evolution of institutions in response to the internal pressures of a society is obviously a process more likely to occur when that society is large and complex. The history of such states as Ashanti and Buganda from the seventeenth to the nineteenth centuries provides examples of such internal changes, leading to the concentration of power in the hands of the monarch. It seems likely the extraordinary development that took place in Egypt in the fourth millennium B.C., the creation of a single unified kingdom in a country that once consisted of a chain of independent villages, was largely the result of processes confined to the valley of the Lower Nile.

To trace the development of institutions is one of the historian's most obvious tasks. In dealing with Africa he is particularly fortunate in being able to draw on the work of so many social anthropologists and political scientists, work which at its best adds a new dimension to the historian's vision by giving him greater awareness of the complexity of the social structure of most African peoples.

New Modes of Thought

The emergence of new modes of thought—new concepts of the world in its widest sense, of the natural and supernatural order of things or new ideas about the positioning of man in society—is clearly a theme of major importance to the historian. But it is one that is extremely difficult to trace in the past of many African societies, where the most satisfactory form of evidence, that derived from written records, is completely lacking. The contrast between the history of Christianity and Islam in Africa and of traditional African religions provides an effective illustration of this point.

The extensive literature associated with Christianity and with Islam makes it possible to trace the intellectual development of the two religions and to gain some understanding of the violent disputes that occasionally rent their adherents. The writings of Donatus, for example, the leader of a schismatic movement in fourth-century North Africa, or of Usuman dan Fodio, the prophet of Muslim reformism in the early nineteenth-century Western Sudan, together with those of the two men's followers and opponents, throw a flood of light on the intellectual climate of their ages. Traditional African religions, on the other hand, appear almost completely ahistorical. A straightforward description of the pantheon of a particular people and of their forms of ritual tells one nothing of the way in which that ritual was evolved or those deities conceived. Yet, every religion, not only the so-called historical religions, has a history behind it insofar as it must have been shaped by the thoughts and actions of individual men and women.

In certain circumstances particular aspects of the material culture may throw some light on a people's thoughts. Forms of burial, for example, often provide some indication of the way in which an afterlife is regarded. In some societies with elaborate aesthetic traditions the art forms—paintings, sculpture, or styles of architecture—may give some insight into the people's beliefs. Nowhere is this better illustrated in Africa than in ancient Egypt. But in Egypt the historian has written records at his disposal to help elucidate the subjects depicted. Where such records do not exist and where the practitioners of an art form who might be able to explain the significance of their images or designs have died out, the task of deriving from artistic material historical information of a kind that will illuminate the intellectual development of a people is one of exceptional difficulty.

Occasionally, the oral traditions of a people may throw some light on important stages in their intellectual history. The Hausa legend of Bayajidda provides an example of evidence of this kind. Bayajidda or Abu Yazid, as the name is sometimes given, is one of the folk heroes of the Hausa of Northern Nigeria. According to the legend, he was the son of a king of Baghdad, who arrived in Bornu with a great company and later passed on to the Hausa state of Daura. There he slew a sacred snake and married the queen. His descendants became the founders of the main

Hausa states. It is probable that Bayajidda was, if not a single historical figure, at least the personification of a definite historical group. A modern historian, Mr. W. K. R. Hallam, has produced much circumstantial evidence to show that this group is probably to be identified with a large band of Berber political refugees from North Africa, the supporters of the Kharijite rebel, Abu Yazid, whose insurrection against the Fatimids of Tunisia was crushed in 946.[11] Snake worship has been a phenomenon in many parts of the world, and other instances of its practice in West Africa have been recorded. But if one is right in interpreting the snake incident in the Bayajidda legend as the destruction of a local cult by a group of alien Muslim invaders, the episode can be regarded as no more than a single event in the intellectual history of an area almost all of whose other features are completely unknown to us. One would like to be able to trace the history of snake worship among the Hausa and other West African people, to discover its origins, to assess its significance in the life of the people, to chart the stages of its disappearance. Regrettably, historians may never have sufficient evidence at their disposal to undertake such a task.

Examples of this sort of ignorance could be multiplied. Indeed, there is no aspect of change so difficult to trace as the development of the complex intellectual traditions of most African peoples. It is only in very recent times that the researches of anthropologists and the autobiographies and novels of African writers provide the material needed to illuminate the way in which a people respond to new experiences.

⚜ THE EXERTIONS OF MEN AND WOMEN

To analyse the processes of change one must employ fairly abstract terms; to visualize such processes one needs to re-create imaginatively the exertions of individual people. For all change is associated with human action, with the movement, conversation, or purposeful thought of men and women.

Movement may be a matter for isolated individuals or for small groups or for large, well-disciplined bodies. One thinks of adventurous men setting out on lonely journeys: blacksmiths taking their mysterious craft from settlement to settlement, itinerant traders spending a lifetime on the roads of Africa, wandering Muslim scholars undertaking the arduous pilgrimage to Mecca, soldiers of fortune moving from court to court, European explorers braving the unknown, Christian missionaries carrying the gospel to the heathen, colonial officials working in lonely stations in the bush, young men caught up in the "revolution of rising expectations" leaving their sleepy villages for the brash, alluring cities. One holds in the mind's eye the migrations of small groups of men and women: bands of hunters, from paleolithic times onward, roaming the savannas or the forests in their constant search for food; pastoralists following the slow perambulations of their livestock from grazing ground to grazing ground; farmers and their families leaving their ancestral settlements to clear new land in the swamps of the Nile Valley, the bush of the Sudan, or the forests of the Congo. Hunters, pastoralists, and farmers — the accumulation of their modest movements forms one of the major themes in the history of Africa. As for the movement of larger bodies of men, the first image that comes to mind is of the march of armies: the foot soldiers and the chariots of Egypt advancing to the conquest of Kush, the squadrons of Arab horsemen sweeping across North Africa, the hordes of the Jaga or the Ngoni leaving a wake of desolation across the plains of Central Africa. But the movements of other large bodies may be recalled: gangs of slaves limping wearily to the barracoons of the coast, the ox wagons of the Boer trekkers lumbering across the veld, the lorry loads of refugees fleeing from the threat of tribal massacre.

Conversation, the interchange of experience between man and man, may best be imagined by thinking of the places where people congregate. Thus, one may catch the hubbub and clamor of markets, the low tones of men talking at nightfall in the camping sites of some well-frequented trade route, the hush of the throng in a royal court when the ruler or some great official rises to make his address, the arguments of men in council, whether elders sitting under a tree or delegates to an international conference, the voice of teachers stimulating, chiding, or questioning, Muslim scholars surrounded by their disciples, or westernized schoolmasters in modern classrooms.

One must try too to re-create those moments of creative thought that occur in the lives of many men and women. The wife of the paleolithic hunter racking her brains to discover some new foodstuff for her half-starved children, the Egyptian craftsman working out means to construct some new form or object, the Maghribi merchant weighing the risks of sending a load of trade goods across the Sahara, the ruler of some kingdom of the savannas brooding on means of holding his domains more effectively together, the missionary struggling to present his gospel to an alien people, even the modern schoolboy working to master a European language: all such people in their different ways may be regarded as contributing to the process of change, as helping to shape the evolution of Africa.

To think of the past in terms of the actions, words, and thoughts of individual men and women is to gain a clearer impression of the variety and complexity of history and of the dynamism innate in all human affairs, in Africa no less than in any other continent.

CHAPTER V

Northeast Africa

✱ GEOGRAPHY

Northeast Africa is taken here as a region that embraces modern Egypt, the Sudan Republic, Ethiopia, and Somalia. Thus defined, this area of about two million square miles may be thought of as little more than a convenient academic division, lacking the closer unity or simple geographical pattern of other regions of the continent. But various parts possess certain common features that distinguish them sharply from adjoining regions. Thus, the Red Sea, one of the least formidable maritime barriers in the world, washes all the main territories of the region, laying them open, throughout historical times, to movements of peoples coming out of western Asia. And the Nile, one of whose streams has its source in Ethiopia, links the Sudan with Egypt and dominates much of the life of both countries.

In its relief Northeast Africa possesses considerable variety. To the west lie the Nuba hills of Kordofan, the Jebel Marra of Darfur, the Tibesti massif of the Central Sahara. To the east rise the jagged chain of hills along the Red Sea coast, the mountains of northern Somalia, and, most prominent of all, the highlands of Ethiopia, the loftiest and most extensive plateaus in the continent. Where there are no mountains the land is usually harsh: the deserts on either side of the Nile, the burning flats of the Red Sea coasts, the swamps and cracking-clay plains of the Bahr-al-Ghazal, the thorn scrub of the Somali country. Yet the region also contains in the well-watered Ethiopian highlands and above all in the valley of the Lower Nile some of the most fertile districts in the entire continent.

✱ CAUCASOIDS, NEGROIDS, AND OTHERS

The present population of Northeast Africa displays a considerable variety of physical types, languages, and cultures. The history of the peoples of the region is very unevenly known. In Egypt written records go back to

NORTHEAST AFRICA

Names of countries – (in capitals)

Mainly Caucasoid peoples speaking Cushitic
  languages – (in capitals underlined)

Mainly Caucasoid peoples speaking Semitic
  languages – (in capitals, doubly underlined)

Mainly Negroid peoples speaking Eastern Sudanic
  languages – (in upper & lower case, wavy underlining)

Mainly Caucasoid peoples speaking Eastern Sudanic
  languages – (in capitals, wavy underlining)

Mainly Negroid peoples speaking other
  languages – (in upper & lower case)

Names of towns & countries mentioned in
  antiquity – (in parentheses)

Lines of Semitic migration – (←——)

Highlands are shaded

Alexandria
Cairo
←(Memphis)
Siwa
(Ammonium)
EGYPT
(Thebes)
(Berenice)
ARAB
Medina
BEJA
Jidda
Mecca
RED SEA
NUBIA
(KUSH)
Dongola
(Napata)
Suakin
(Meroe)
YEMEN (SABA)
Massawa
(Adulis)
HABABISH
Khartoum
TIGRE
Mocha
Fur
Sennar
Axum
Aden
Nuba
AMHARA
Gondar
Zeila
BHQQARA
AGAU
Berbera
Shilluk
Nuer
GALLA
Harar
Dinka
SIDAMA
SOMALI
Central Sudanic Speakers
Nilotes
NILO-HAMITES
Mogadishu
Merca
Brava
DANAKIL

3000 B.C., and archeological research has made it possible to trace the development of the country from an even more remote period. The history of Nubia—the name applied to the country south of Egypt—is known in broad outline for the last four thousand years. Surviving monuments and references in the works of classical writers make it possible to describe the development of a part of Ethiopia from the second half of the first millennium B.C. But these three areas comprise only a small part of the total extent of the region. In Somalia, southern Ethiopia, and Darfur local chronicles throw some light on developments in the last seven or eight hundred years. But the earlier history of these areas is almost completely dark. And the darkness comes still closer to modern times in the southern Sudan where historical records date back no further than a century.

In time archeological research should be able to throw a flood of light on the early history of many more parts of Northeast Africa. But for the time being the historian must make do with the hypotheses put forward by physical anthropologists and linguistic scholars. To many physical anthropologists Northeast Africa appears as a region where people of Caucasoid and Negroid stock meet and sometimes merge. But many of the Negroids of the region are markedly different in appearance from the Negroids of West and Central Africa, and, as has already been noted, some scholars would prefer to see in them traces of a third, distinct racial stock.

One group, however, the Nuba of southern Kordofan, does possess physical characteristics remarkably similar to those of West African Negroids. Moreover, the languages of the Nuba appear to be more closely related to Western Sudanic than to any other linguistic stock. But the history of the Nuba is completely obscure. Do they represent the last remnants, protected by the hills in which they live, of a once much wider spread of western Sudanic Negroids? Or are they no more than an isolated group long separated from the main body? For the moment one can only speculate.

The evidence provided by physical types is vague and confusing. The evidence provided by language is somewhat more precise. Broadly speaking, the region is divided between two great linguistic families, Afro-Asiatic and Nilo-Saharan. Three branches of Afro-Asiatic have existed in the area: ancient Egyptian, Cushitic, and Semitic. Of these the first is now extinct. The Cushitic branch of Afro-Asiatic has been divided into five sections: Northern, Central, Western, Eastern, and Southern. The most prominent of the Northern Cushites are the Beja, a pastoral people living between the Sudanic Nile and the Red Sea. Central Cushites today form a small group—the Agau and kindred peoples—in northern

Ethiopia; but Central Cushitic languages were probably spoken over a much larger area until they were replaced by the Semitic languages introduced by colonists from South Arabia in the first millennium B.C. Western Cushitic languages are spoken by some of the Sidama peoples of southwestern Ethiopia, Eastern Cushitic by other Sidama groups and by the Danakil (Afar), Galla, and Somali of the Horn of Africa. Finally, there is a small isolated group of Southern Cushitic speakers represented by the Iraqw of northern Tanzania.

All the other languages of the region, with the exception of those spoken by the Nuba, fall into the family Greenberg has termed Nilo-Saharan. Most of the Nilo-Saharan languages of the region come into the Chari-Nile branch—Eastern Sudanic and Central Sudanic being the two main sections of Chari-Nile. Eastern Sudanic embraces many of the languages spoken in the Nile Valley (before the introduction of Arabic) from Nubia to Lake Victoria, while Central Sudanic languages are spoken south of Darfur. There are also some isolated Nilo-Saharan languages, such as Koman, spoken in Ethiopia.

Archeological evidence suggests that the movement of peoples of Caucasoid stock from western Asia into Northeast Africa began at a very remote date, at least ten thousand years ago. The first Caucasoids were hunter-gatherers, who must have kept to the drier lands and avoided the cool Ethiopian highlands and the swamps of the southern Sudan. Some of these early Caucasoid groups probably remained on the Red Sea coast, others moved westward along the North African littoral, yet others followed the line of the Rift Valley that divides the Ethiopian highlands on to the highlands of East Africa. The Caucasoids introduced the different Cushitic languages of Africa. But of the relations between the speakers of the different branches of Cushitic nothing definite is known. Did the divisions between them take place after their arrival in Africa, or do these divisions represent different movements of migration? Only archeological research can throw light on these questions.

The early history of the Nilo-Saharan speakers is even more obscure. One important fact about their environment must be borne in mind. The country between Tibesti and the Red Sea, now almost waterless desert, received a modest rainfall during the Makalian Wet Phase that lasted from the sixth to the third millennium B.C. And even as late as the beginning of the Christian era much of the country north of Khartoum had a cover of grass and trees. In these circumstances the movement of men with horses or cattle over the eastern Sahara must have presented no great difficulty.

Two archeological discoveries throw some light on the composition of the early population of the present Sudan. At Singa on the Blue Nile a skull of Bushmanoid type has been found on a site which also produced paleolithic artifacts. Did Bushmen once represent an important element in the population of the Sudan? Until further discoveries have been made it is impossible to answer this question.

On a site near Khartoum the remains of a Stone Age community, dated to about 4000 B.C., have been found. Skeletal remains indicate that these people were of Negroid stock. But there is no evidence to suggest that Negroids were to be found north of the Sixth Cataract of the Nile. Toward the end of the third millennium a Caucasoid people known to archeologists as the C-group settled in Nubia. But the present Nubian language, classified as Eastern Sudanic, appears to have been introduced by another group of migrants possibly coming from Kordofan or Darfur in the first half of the first millennium A.D.[1]

The first attempt to classify the peoples of Northeast Africa was made by a Greek scholar, Agatharchides, of the second century B.C. He divided the peoples living south of Egypt into four types: riverain agriculturalists, "marsh-dwellers," nomadic pastoralists, and fishers on the seashore. The first three groups accord well with the present divisions (represented by such groups as the Nile Nubians, the Nuer, and the Beja) in that large part of the population of the modern Sudan that is not of Arab origin. It seems reasonable, then, to assume that by the beginning of the Christian era Northeast Africa already contained all the basic elements in its modern population—with one important exception, the Arabs whose movements beginning in the seventh century were to have such a profound impact on the culture of many parts of the region.

THE GROWTH OF EGYPTIAN CIVILIZATION

Seven thousand years ago the valley of the Lower Nile and its broad delta were jungle-choked swamps. The paleolithic hunters kept well away from the valley bottom and sited their camps on the terraces overlooking the river or by the shores of the lakes that filled the broad depressions to the west of the Nile. Culturally, these early Egyptians were no more advanced than other hunting communities elsewhere in Africa. But their location gave them one immense advantage: no African people lived closer to those parts of western Asia where two revolutionary developments—the cultivation of cereals and the domestication of animals—were taking place. Indeed, Jericho, where food-producing communities are known to have existed since the eighth millennium B.C., lay no more than five hundred miles from the Nile Delta.

It was not, however, until the middle of the fifth millennium B.C. that immigrants from the east brought the new food-producing techniques to Egypt. Their earliest-known settlement was in the Fayum Depression. By the beginning of the fourth millennium food-producing communities had come into existence in Middle Egypt. A slow but significant improvement could be traced in their material culture. Thus, the people of Badari (c. 3800 B.C.) used finely carved ivory spoons in notable contrast to the crude pottery ladles of the earliest cultivators of Fayum. But the Badari people still lived well above the valley, and as with the people of Fayum, hunting still played an important part in their economy. Gradually, in the course of the first half of the fourth millennium, the cultivators of the Nile ter-races found themselves forced—partly, it would seem, because of the steady encroachment of the desert, partly, no doubt, as a result of the pressure of a growing population—to undertake the arduous task of clearing the jungle and draining the swamps of the valley.

The consequences of this slight change in habitat were truly astound-ing. The soils of the narrow valley of the Lower Nile, annually rejuve-nated by the silt spread by the flooding river, are among the richest in the world. A farmer was able to produce more than he and his family could consume. One consequence of this new development was a phenomenal increase in population. In the fifth millennium B.C. the population of Egypt has been estimated at less than twenty thousand; the lowest esti-mate for Egypt's population in the mid-third millennium is three million. With a growing population went increasing specialization and a vast im-provement in the material culture of the people. New settlement patterns emerged: farming communities grew into villages, villages into towns, and each advance called for a more elaborate system of political organi-zation.

Already then in this predynastic period of the late fourth millennium B.C. Egypt, in its great leap forward, had achieved a level of development that was to lie beyond the reach of most other African peoples until quite modern times. Moreover, once the entire land had been united under a single ruler (the First Dynasty arose about 3100 B.C.), still greater achievements became possible. More land was brought under cultivation, higher standards of craftsmanship were reached (one historian has spoken of the craftsmen of this period "playing with the hard stone as though it were clay" [2]), traders roamed farther afield in search of precious materials: all these were manifestations of the advances of early dynastic times, advances which culminated in the construction of the great pyra-mids of Giza, the largest and most spectacular of Egyptian monuments.

By 2500 B.C. Egyptian civilization had established a pattern whose basic features were to endure with astonishing consistency for the next two thousand years. An ideal of political stability and economic well-being was achieved. The later history of ancient Egypt was far from being uniformly peaceful: there were periods of anarchy, civil war, and foreign invasion. But the great period of the Old Kingdom (2700–2200 B.C.) provided the model of a golden age that was re-created under the Middle Kingdom (2100–1800 B.C.) and under the New Kingdom (1600–1100 B.C.).

Harmony, not progress, became the Egyptian ideal. The Egyptian state was regarded as the gift of the gods. "What is the King of Upper and Lower Egypt?" one vizier inscribed on his tomb. "He is a god by whose dealings one lives, the father and mother of all men, alone by himself without an equal." ³ The pharaoh appeared as a totally impersonal ruler, standing at the apex of a centralized bureaucracy. In theory he possessed totalitarian powers: by him officials were appointed, transferred, removed, rewarded; the ownership of land was a royal grant, the import trade a royal monopoly. In practice every pharaoh was dependent on the men around him, his own kinsmen, officials, priests, army officers. Ideally, the system was a beneficent one: "the distinction of a prince," one vizier was instructed, "is that he does justice." ⁴ The society of ancient Egypt during its greatest periods, so rich in its artistic achievements, so well endowed with the skills of administration, was in many ways the most remarkable Africa has ever known.

🜂 THE IMPACT OF EGYPT: THE SPREAD OF PASTORALISM AND AGRICULTURE

Superficially, ancient Egypt seems isolated and distinct from the rest of Africa, isolated by the deserts that hem in the narrow valley of the Nile, distinct by virtue of the unrivalled achievements of its people. Yet the Egyptians were in constant contact with their immediate neighbors, the Libyan Berbers to the west, the Beja to the east, the peoples of Nubia to the south, and they maintained occasional intercourse with the peoples of the Horn of Africa.

War and trade brought strangers together. When Egypt was weak, the desert tribes raided the fat lands of the Nile; when Egypt was strong, punitive expeditions held the nomads in check. Moreover, the Nile Valley was not completely self-sufficient. If the Egyptians wanted gold, ivory, and incense—essentials for the adornment and the service of their temples—they had to go far beyond their borders. Gold came from the Nuba hills, ivory from still farther south, incense from the land of Punt, probably to be identified with northern Somalia. Libyan tribesmen who had visited the Nile Valley passed on some notion of what they had seen to their neighbors. (Clear signs of Egyptian influence have been detected in some of the rock paintings of the central Sahara.) Caravans of merchants or garrisons of soldiers introduced Egyptian products and techniques to the inhabitants of Nubia. From Nubia local traders or migrating tribes must have carried these innovations westward along the savanna toward Lake Chad, southward to the highlands of Ethiopia.

Through this obscure movement of unrecorded individuals the techniques of agriculture and of pastoralism spread out from the valley of the Lower Nile across the northern half of Africa. For the hunting peoples of the Sahara domestic animals, goats, sheep, and cattle, must have provided a particularly welcome supplement to their economy. Until the end of the Makalian Wet Phase in the third millennium B.C. much of the Sahara provided ideal cattle country. And the wide distribution of Saharan rock paintings depicting cattle provides particularly vivid testimony to the presence of pastoralists in areas now completely desert.

It is not yet known when cattle were first introduced to the Sahara, but the movement must have begun well before 3000 B.C. The herds of domestic animals increased at a time when the rainfall was declining. Overgrazing accelerated the process of desiccation. Faced with the gradual disappearance of their traditional pastures, the pastoralists were forced to move into new areas. Some began to penetrate the savanna country south of Tibesti, others, such as the C-group Caucasoids, began to settle in the Nile Valley south of Egypt. Later some of these C-group people appear to have moved, possibly after the Egyptian occupation of Lower Nubia in 2000 B.C., into highland Ethiopia. By the end of the first millennium B.C. some pastoralists, whose ancestors may have come not from Nubia but from South Arabia, had moved up the Rift Valley to the Kenya highlands.

The transmission of agricultural techniques was a slow process. Barley and wheat, the two main crops of Egyptian farmers, are not well adapted to the climatic conditions of the tropical savanna. The development of agriculture in this region was dependent on the domestication of different plants. Sorghum (guinea corn) and various types of millet provided the necessary substitutes. There is no archeological evidence at present available to indicate when or where these new cereals were first domesticated. An ethnographer, G. P. Murdock, has argued that agriculture was developed by the Negroids of the Upper Niger before 4500 B.C. and that this development owed nothing to external influences.[5] The evidence on which Murdock's theory is based has been severely criticized by botanists and archeologists, and a far more persuasive explanation has been put forward to account for the initial development of agriculture in sub-Saharan Africa. It is reasonable to assume that even if the actual crops grown in Egypt and North Africa could not be used south of the Sahara, a knowledge of the techniques of cereal cultivation must have become familiar to many different peoples living in the savanna. Having grasped the basic techniques, they could begin experimenting with local plants.

These experiments must have been carried on in many different parts of the savanna, but it seems likely that the most significant area for the development of the new food plants was that part of the Central and Eastern Sudan stretching from Nigeria to western Ethiopia.[6]

Certain parts of highland Ethiopia were almost the only area south of Egypt where barley and wheat could be grown. These crops may have reached the Central Cushitic people of the plateau in the course of the second millennium B.C. But the Ethiopians went on to domesticate other plants, including coffee, castor oil plant, and ensete (the Abyssinian banana). "Central highland Ethiopia ranks with China and India," Murdock has claimed, "as one of the world's important minor centres of origination of cultivated plants." [7]

KUSH

None of the territories bordering Egypt came so markedly under Egyptian influence as the lands lying immediately to the south. At the time of the Old Kingdom (c. 2500 B.C.) the Egyptian frontier was established in the area of the First Cataract, but soldiers raided the country to the south and traders with their donkey caravans penetrated deep into the interior, possibly even reaching the country of Darfur. During the period of the Middle Kingdom (c. 2000 B.C.) the frontier was pushed more than two hundred miles farther south to the Second Cataract, where a chain of massive fortresses was built to protect it. Finally, at the beginning of the New Kingdom (c. 1500 B.C.) the Egyptians conquered and annexed all the country as far as the Fourth Cataract and thus made themselves masters of the land which they called Kush.

The Egyptians had two powerful motives for extending their frontiers to the south: the search for security against a potentially hostile neighbor and the lure of gold. The Nuba hills east of the Nile formed one of the richest gold-bearing areas known to the ancient world. The Egyptians began to exploit these deposits at the time of the Middle Kingdom. Five hundred years later gold from Nubia served to finance the New Kingdom's policy of imperial expansion in the Eastern Mediterranean.

The pharaohs of the New Kingdom did not attempt to colonize their new province of Kush by settling farmers on the land, but substantial numbers of Egyptians, officials and priests, soldiers and traders, made their homes in the country. Under the influence of this powerful minority the people of Kush, many of them probably the descendants of the C-group Caucasoids, became increasingly Egyptianized.

After 1100 B.C. the Egyptian New Kingdom collapsed and in the ensuing anarchy Kush broke away and became an independent state. By 725 B.C. the rulers of Kush were powerful enough to invade and conquer

Egypt, where they were recognized as pharaohs of the XXVth Dynasty. For sixty years, for the first and indeed the only time in history, a state based on the interior of Africa played an active part in the politics of the Mediterranean. In an attempt to stem the expanding power of Assyria the Kushitic pharaohs established close relations with the states of Palestine and Syria. Their policy ended in failure. In 663 B.C. an Assyrian army advanced into Upper Egypt and sacked Thebes, the ancient capital. A new dynasty, based on the Delta, arose in Egypt. The princes of Kush fell back on their homeland.

The conquest and the retreat from Egypt were only the first act in the history of Kush as an independent state. The kingdom lasted for a thousand years, a record of longevity as an organized state unrivaled by any other polity in the interior of Africa. The ruins of pyramids and of temples at Napata and at Meroe, the successive capitals of the country, and at other sites provide striking evidence of the wealth of the ancient kingdom. Yet they lie in country that today is almost completely desert. In 500 B.C., however, the land of Kush was rich enough to support great herds of cattle, and the rainfall was probably sufficient to allow a flourishing agriculture. Kush had many other resources of which gold and iron were the most important.

The use of iron was a novelty in Africa. The technique of producing iron had been discovered by people living in the mountains of Armenia in the second millennium B.C. Gradually, the closely guarded secret of the new craft leaked out, first to the Hittites, then to the Assyrians. It may have been introduced to Egypt by the Assyrian invaders of the seventh century. Egypt had no supply of iron ore. In Kush, however, in the country around Meroe there was an abundance both of ore and of the wood needed to provide fuel for smelting. But technical innovations spread slowly, and the iron industry of Meroe does not appear to have developed before the fourth century B.C.

The rulers of Kush faced the constant problem of holding in check the nomadic pastoralists, akin to the modern Beja and Tebu, living to the east and west of the Nile. A regular supply of iron weapons and the possession of a considerable number of horses must have contributed in no small measure to their military superiority. Military power served not only to defend the kingdom but also to control the trade routes that led to Egypt and to the Red Sea coast.

These trade routes kept Kush in touch with a wider world. Throughout the kingdom's history pharaonic Egypt provided the dominant cultural influence. Temples were dedicated to Egyptian deities and bore inscriptions in Egyptian hieroglyphs. The ceremonial of the court followed Egyptian practice, and indeed the rulers of Kush continued for centuries to style themselves kings of Upper and Lower Egypt. Some historians have seen in the culture of Kush nothing but a degenerate replica of an Egyptian ideal. Yet the monuments of Meroe in the first century A.D. suggest a civilization vigorous enough to absorb new ideas and new techniques from other sources, from Greco-Roman Egypt, from Axum, even possibly from India.

The basic cause of Kush's decline would seem to lie in the increasing desiccation of the country around Meroe. The pastures were overgrazed, the woodland destroyed, the soil eroded, and the actual rainfall may have decreased. Meroe had been the great commercial metropolis of the Eastern Sudan. By the third century A.D. it was faced with a declining market in Egypt, impoverished by Roman exploitation, and a powerful competitor in its eastern neighbor, Axum. Moreover, the decline in Kush's military power, consequent no doubt on the acquisition of horses and iron weapons by neighboring peoples, must have rendered the trade routes, Kush's lifelines to the outside world, increasingly insecure. The invasion of Kush by an Axumite army in 350 A.D. marks the kingdom's final collapse.

For close on two thousand years Kush was a land through which new ideas and new techniques of Egyptian or Mediterranean origin could percolate into the heart of Africa. There is no doubt that it was through Meroe that a knowledge of ironworking, carried by itinerant blacksmiths, reached many neighboring peoples.

The diffusion of religious and political ideas presents a much more complex problem. Forms of ritual and ceremonial which undoubtedly had their origin in ancient Egypt can be found among certain societies in Negro Africa. And it has been argued that after the collapse of Meroe members of the royal house fled westward and by introducing new political concepts—in particular the idea of divine kingship—became the founders of new states in the Central Sudan. It is reasonable to assume that political refugees, traders, and adventurers, familiar with Kush's elaborate system of government, must occasionally have come to settle among the peoples living to the south and west. But until something is known of the political organization of these peoples in the first millennium A.D. (at the moment our knowledge of this period is almost completely blank), bold hypotheses about the diffusion of Egyptian or Meroetic institutions should be treated with extreme skepticism.

⚡ GREEK AND ROMAN RULE IN EGYPT

In 525 B.C. Egypt lost its independence and became a province of the Persian Empire. Two centuries later that great empire was shattered and its provinces absorbed into the still vaster empire created by Alexander of Macedon. Egypt, occupied by him in 332, was entrusted to Ptolemy, one of the generals of the victorious army. When the empire of Alexander broke up after its founder's death, Ptolemy made himself ruler of an independent kingdom and founded a dynasty that lasted for nearly three hundred years.

The Greek occupation of Egypt can be seen as the culmination of a long process of intercourse between the Aegean and the Nile. During the second millennium B.C. there were periods of brisk trade between Minoan Crete, Mycenean Greece, and Egypt. About 1200 B.C., however, the Eastern Mediterranean was ravaged by bands of predatory northern barbarians, "the Peoples of the Sea" of Egyptian records. "The islands were restless," runs a contemporary inscription, "disturbed among themselves, they poured out their people all together. . . . They advanced on Egypt, their hearts relying on their arms." [8]

Five centuries elapsed before Greek contacts with Egypt were resumed. A combination of circumstances drove Greeks overseas. Their homeland, whether on the islands of the Aegean or on the mainlands of Greece and Asia Minor, was a poor contracted region in which the pressure of population soon made itself felt. Some sought their livelihood overseas as individual adventurers, as pirates, or mercenaries. Others were sent out by their own cities to found daughter colonies in other lands. Yet others sought a living as merchants, for trade was becoming increasingly important when farmers began to specialize in the production of wine and olive oil, and it became necessary to import corn from overseas.

In the mid-seventh century B.C. the three types of Greek immigrants —mercenaries, colonists, and traders—were to be found in Egypt and in neighboring parts of North Africa. On the coast and fertile plateau of Cyrenaica, Greek settlers laid the foundations of a group of city-states. Greek mercenaries were welcomed by the pharaohs of the XXVIth Dynasty and employed both in internal struggles and in foreign wars. Greek traders were allowed as an unprecedented privilege to found their own trading center, Naucratis, in the Nile Delta. Naucratis of the seventh century B.C. might well be compared to early twentieth-century Shanghai. And indeed the relations between Greeks and Egyptians— brashness and vigor on the one side, arrogance and conservatism on the other—are reminiscent of the attitudes of Europeans and Chinese to one another before World War II.

The Greek conquest of Egypt established the first substantial European colony—using the word in its modern sense—in Africa, and the parallels with later episodes in the history of European imperialism are remarkably close. The Ptolemies set about developing their "estate" of

Egypt with energy and efficiency. The peasantry were strictly supervised: legally they were regarded as the king's tenants and were required to bring half their produce as rent to the royal storehouses. New crops and animals were introduced—fig trees from Asia Minor, vines from the Aegean, sheep from Arabia, pigs from Sicily. Agricultural implements made from the new metal, iron, replaced the old wooden ones.

The state vigorously encouraged the development of trade and industry. Currency replaced barter. Mines and quarries in the eastern desert were worked by slave labor. Caravan routes were developed and the camel became more common as a beast of burden. New harbors were created on the Red Sea coast and trading posts established farther south. Gradually, the Red Sea became a regular highway of maritime commerce. By the end of the first century B.C. Greek merchants from Egypt had developed a regular trade with India and were beginning to feel their way down the East African coast.

The produce of the Nile Valley and the commerce of eastern seas made possible the rapid growth of the new city whose ground plan had been laid out by Alexander himself. The young conquerer had been inspired by a vision of the unity of mankind. It was appropriate then that his foundation, Alexandria, which contemporaries described as being *by* Egypt rather than *in* Egypt, with its Greek, Jewish, and Egyptian quarters, should provide an ideal meeting place for men of different cultures. In its first two centuries Alexandria proved itself one of the most remarkable centers of intellectual activity that the world has ever known, a center not like Athens of the creative arts but of scholarship and science, where the stock of accurate human knowledge was marvelously increased by research into many fields from anatomy to geography and mathematics.

The remarkable achievements of the Ptolemies could not, however, disguise the contradiction inherent in every form of imperial rule. "The Greeks in Egypt," as Rostovtzeff has pointed out, "felt themselves masters and rulers, and they would never think of sharing with the despised natives the right acquired by conquest and maintained by force." [9] Intermarriage and the mutual attraction of remarkable cultures—the Greeks accepting Egyptian deities, the Egyptian upper classes taking up the Greek language—did something to blur racial antipathies. But for the mass of Egyptians the Ptolemaic state was a bureaucratic machine functioning in the interests of an alien governing class. By the first century B.C. Egypt presented the spectacle of a dynasty grown increasingly effete and corrupt, a Greek middle class of officials and partially Egyptianized landowners, and a peasantry restive and oppressed.

The Roman occupation of Egypt, beginning in 30 B.C., brought with it some initial improvement, but produced in the long run still greater afflictions. The rulers of Rome needed corn to feed the swollen population of the capital; Egypt was one of the granaries of the Mediterranean; by levying tribute in corn and money the emperors developed and maintained for centuries a ruthless system of exploitation. The Greek middle classes were impoverished and the Egyptian peasantry, driven to despair by oppressive tax-gatherers, began to leave their lands uncultivated and turned to banditry or to begging for their livelihood.

The growing discontents of the third century A.D. made the Greek intellectuals of Alexandria and the rural proletariat of the Nile Valley listen more attentively to the teachings of a new religion that had been cherished by a small band of devotees for two hundred years. The old gods had failed. Christianity, at once radical and international in its teaching, spoke of the joys that awaited true believers in another life. No religion could have been so well adapted to the needs of ordinary men and women in Roman Egypt. By 330 A.D., when Christianity was accepted as the religion of the empire, Egypt had become an almost entirely Christian country.

Egypt made notable contributions to the development of the early church. Here monasticism was practiced as one of the patterns of the Christian life by a multitude of holy men who retreated to the deserts on either side of the Nile and devoted themselves to the struggle against the invisible powers of the Devil. Here the intellectual foundations of the faith were laid by Clement and Origen and other Alexandrine scholars. In the fourth century, after the capital of the Empire had been transferred from Rome to Constantinople, Alexandria emerged as the foremost stronghold of Eastern Christendom, its patriarchs triumphant defenders of the faith against the deviations of Arianism and Nestorianism. But the power of the patriarchs, "spiritual Pharaohs" in their own land,[10] aroused the resentment of the emperors and of other members of the Church. At the Council of Chalcedon in 451 the tables were turned and the patriarch of Alexandria found himself condemned as a heretic for embracing a doctrine—Monophysitism—which by stressing Christ's divinity disregarded his humanity.

Thereafter, the Church in Egypt was divided. The Orthodox "Melkite" congregations had the support of the Imperial authorities. The Monophysite, "Coptic" Church expressed the nationalist aspirations of the masses. For nearly a thousand years Egypt had been intimately involved in the life of the Mediterranean. Now it began to turn its back on the outside world: Coptic began to replace Greek as a language, decaying Alexandria became an intellectual backwater, the economic decline continued. But a revolutionary change was at hand.

𝕏𝕗 AXUM

Arabia may well be the original homeland of some of the Cushitic-speaking peoples of Northeast Africa. In time archeologists should be able to throw some light on the historical development of the lands on either side of the Red Sea before the first millennium B.C., but for the present this period is completely obscure. It is clear, however, that about 1000 B.C. the Semitic-speaking people of the Yemen in the southwestern corner of Arabia had created a number of small but highly prosperous states, one of which, Saba, is possibly to be identified with the biblical Sheba.

The Yemen enjoyed three advantages. It was almost the only part of Arabia that received enough rain to support a flourishing agriculture. It produced an abundance of some of the most sought-after commodities — spices, myrrh and frankincense—of the ancient world. And it occupied the lucrative position of an entrepôt linking two of the most important trade routes of western Asia; its ports were well placed for voyages to India and the Horn of Africa, and its cities were the starting points for caravan routes through the Hejaz to the lands of the Fertile Crescent.

By the seventh century B.C. the pressure of overpopulation must have been felt in the Yemen, for bands of Yemenites began to cross the narrow straits and settle on the northeastern edge of the Ethiopian plateau. Here, in a country not unlike their homeland, they found themselves among a Cushitic-speaking population with a political organization and a technology far less evolved than their own. The immigrants were indeed highly efficient farmers who used plows and constructed terraces, dams, and irrigation canals. By the third century B.C. one group of colonists, the Habashat, had established a substantial kingdom, later known after its capital, Axum. Within its steadily extending borders the local Cushites began to accept the social customs, the language (Ge'ez), and the technology of the dominant Semites.

Axum was founded at a time when the Ptolemies of Egypt had begun to encourage the development of Red Sea trade. The kingdom was particularly well placed to take advantage of the new commercial opportunities. Its hinterland produced probably the most extensive supply of ivory known to the ancient world, along with other exotic commodities, such as tortoise shell, rhinoceros horn, and at a later date gold. Its main port, Adulis (near modern Massawa), attracted Greek, Persian, and Indian merchants. By the fifth century A.D., if not earlier, Axum was the main commercial center between the Mediterranean and the Indian Ocean.

With a flourishing commerce and a prosperous agriculture went military power. The inscriptions of fourth-century Axumite kings tell of their campaigns northward as far as the Nile and crumbling Meroe, southward into the mountains of Ethiopia, eastward across the straits to the old homeland of the Yemen. Enriched by commerce and by war the rulers of Axum were able to adorn their capital with splendid monuments, some of which, notably a group of massive stone obelisks, survive to this day. The architecture of ancient Axum bears witness to the dominant influence of South Arabia. But already by the first century A.D. other cultures were beginning to contribute to the development of Axumite civilization.

The growth of international trade had brought small groups of Greek and Jewish merchants to settle in the country. At a later date there may have been an immigration from the Hejaz and the Yemen. Many of the Jewish settlers must have penetrated deep into the interior, for some of the Cushitic Agau were converted to Judaism. One group, the Falasha, retain the faith to this day. Other Judaized Agau were later converted to Christianity and became the main source of Jewish customs in the Ethiopian church.

Greek influence was felt in the most exalted circles. Already in the first century a king of Axum was noted for his Greek education. In the third century inscriptions on monuments and coins appeared in the Greek language. And Greek bureaucratic practices may have well been followed in the administration of the kingdom. In the fourth century the presence of Greek Christians in the capital prepared the way for the new religion. Before the end of the century Christianity had been accepted as the official religion of the country. This revolutionary change appears to have been brought about largely through the initiative of a Syrian Christian, named Frumentius. As a boy Frumentius was shipwrecked on the Red Sea coast. Taken into the royal household, he rose to a position of great influence and did all in his power to promote the firm establishment of the faith.

Frumentius was ordained first bishop of Axum by the great patriarch, Athanasius, thus establishing with the church of Alexandria a link that was to have a profound influence on the development of Ethiopian Christianity. In the fifth century nine Syrian monks, Monophysites to a man, arrived as missionaries, founded monasteries, introduced the Alexandrine liturgy and translated the Gospels into Ge'ez. Christianity took firm root. Nowhere in all Africa was the faith to be defended with such tenacity or to exert so profound an influence on the culture of the people.

The sixth century saw Axum at the height of its power. A Greek visitor, an ambassador from Byzantium, described the splendor of the royal court: the king, wearing many ornaments of gold, standing in a gold-plated chariot drawn by four elephants. For a time the Axumites made themselves masters of South Arabia, but they were expelled by a Persian expeditionary force and their defeat marked the beginning of their decline. The temporary Persian occupation of the Yemen and later the Arab conquest of Egypt disrupted commerce in the Red Sea. Even more serious than the economic crisis caused by these events was the threat presented by the growing power of the pagan Beja. About 700 A.D. the Beja began to move into Axumite territory, ravaging the farmlands and settling on the plains that lay between Axum and the sea. The city itself was not destroyed and its rulers continued to issue coins for another two centuries. But the foundation of the kingdom's prosperity had been shattered and the trade links with India and the eastern Mediterranean broken.

Gradually, groups of Axumites began to move deeper into the highlands of Ethiopia, merging in time with the pagan or Judaized Agau and so continuing a process of Semitization begun by the first settlers from South Arabia a thousand years earlier. From this blending of different stocks came the people of Amhara, Tigre, Gojam, and Shoa, the "Abyssinians proper," the nucleus of the great kingdom of Ethiopia.

THE RISE OF ISLAM

The spread of Christianity in the first two centuries after its Founder's death was slow and secretive. Islam, by contrast, burst upon the world with astonishing force and suddenness. In 622, the year of the Hijra, which marks the beginning of the Muslim era, the Prophet Muhammad and his followers were a handful of men and women who had been expelled from their native Mecca and forced to take refuge in Yathrib (later renamed Medina), an obscure oasis settlement in central Arabia. A generation later the Muslims had vanquished the armies of the two greatest military powers of their day, Persia and Byzantium, and made themselves masters of the entire Fertile Crescent from the Nile to the Euphrates. By 732, the centenary of the Prophet's death, the caliph of the Faithful could claim to rule an empire that stretched from the Pyrenees to the Himalayas.

It was equally astonishing that a movement of such dimensions should have had its origin in one of the most backward areas of the seventh-century world, among a people whom their neighbors could only regard as a race of turbulent savages. And yet there are some pointers in the early history of the Arabs that help to explain the explosion of Islam. The dwellers in Arabia were for the most part pastoralists in a barren land, where population easily exceeded resources and where men were exposed to the attraction of an easier life in the richer lands to the north and west. For centuries, then, there had been a steady movement of people out of the desert. But Arabia was not entirely isolated from the richest societies on its periphery. Important trade routes traversed the peninsula, and there were communities of foreign merchants in the main centers. The Jews were particularly prominent: they dominated the economic life of the Hejaz and provided the agricultural population of many oases. Traditional Arab religion involved the worship of many deities, but by the sixth century A.D. the Arabs were becoming increasingly familiar through the conversation and the ritual of their Jewish and Christian neighbors with the concept of monotheism.

The majority of the Arabs of northern and central Arabia were Bedouin nomads, famed as horsemen and warriors, fiercely independent and scornful of the restrictions of an organized state. Politically, they were divided among a multitude of independent tribes, each tribe being made up of a number of family groups, bound together by ties of kinship. Within the tribes government was rudimentary, with the tribal chief, the sheikh, acting not as a ruler but rather as an arbitrator. Between tribes relations were dominated by interminable feuds and constant raids. But although there was not a vestige of political unity within Arabia, the tribes had achieved a remarkable degree of cultural homogeneity through the development of a common language. And this language had been shaped into an instrument of great power and beauty, to be prized by orators and loved by poets.

Muhammad, the founder of Islam, possessed a remarkable combination of qualities; he was endowed with the visionary power of a seer, the mastery of language of a great poet, and the astuteness of a consummate politician. His political achievement was extraordinary; in the space of ten years this obscure Meccan trader succeeded, by a blend of force and diplomacy, in inducing most of the tribes and communities of Arabia to accept his overlordship. His career provides an outstanding example of the power of ideology, of the way in which the vision of a prophet, profound thoughts expressed in passionate words, moves the hearts and minds of men. Muhammad saw himself as the last of the prophets, the successor of Moses and Jesus, the spokesman of the Almighty. The Koran, in which his utterances were collected, represented in the minds of his followers the infallible word of God.

> *Praise be to Allah, Lord of the Creation,*
> *The Compassionate, the Merciful, King of the*
> *Last Judgment!*
> *You alone we worship and to You alone we pray*
> *for help.*
> *Guide us in the right path, the path of those*
> *whom You have favored.*

The opening verses of the Koran express the core of the new faith—complete resignation to a single all-powerful God (the word "Islam" means in fact "resignation"). This resignation was to be expressed by the performance of the ritual duties of prayer, fasting, almsgiving, and pilgrimage to the sanctuary at Mecca, said to have been established by Abraham.

The new faith introduced to the Arabs a new concept of brotherhood. In the past men were brothers only through the ties of blood; now they could regard one another as brothers in the faith. The Romans had evolved within the Mediterranean world the idea of a single great society. The followers of Muhammad came in time to establish an even larger international community. And the annual pilgrimages to Mecca provided—and still provide—the opportunity for peoples of many different cultures, from Asia, Africa, and Europe, to come together under the aegis of a common faith.

But the cement of Muslim unity has always been cracked by the force of sectional divisions. From the start these divisions were apparent. The death of the Prophet was followed by the rebellion of many of the Bedouin tribes. Unity was only restored by diverting the energies of these predatory nomads into a series of raids on the Fertile Crescent. Soon these raids developed into wars of conquest as the weakness of the two great empires of Byzantium and Persia became apparent. Purely mundane motives—the need to satisfy a restless soldiery's desire for booty or the imperatives of strategic necessity—serve to explain the stages of Muslim expansion. But without the binding force of the new ideology the Arabs would never have maintained the unity that was essential for their success, and the profession of the new faith gave to these comrades in arms a sense of overwhelming moral superiority that led them to perform extraordinary feats of audacity and valor.

THE ARABS IN EGYPT

Muhammad died in 632. Within five years of his death the Arabs were masters of Syria and Iraq. In 639 an army under Amr ibn al-As invaded Egypt. By 641 Alexandria, the last Byzantine stronghold, was in Arab hands. An attempt to advance up the Nile was halted by the Christian kingdom of Nubia, and for six hundred years the First Cataract marked the southern boundary of Muslim Egypt. To the west, however, there was no force strong enough to halt the Arab onslaught, and in the second half of the seventh century all North Africa from Cyrenaica to Morocco was brought under Arab domination.

For the next two hundred years Egypt remained a province in the great Islamic empire whose capital was first at Medina, then under the

Umayyads (661–750) at Damascus, and finally under the Abbasids at Baghdad. To begin with the Arabs in Egypt were organized as an army of occupation, based on the newly created garrison town of Fustat (Old Cairo) and numbering under the first Umayyad caliph, forty thousand men. Soon, however, they came to assume the position and the privileges of a dominant aristocracy, their numbers swollen by a steady stream of new arrivals from Arabia.

For the mass of Egyptians the Arabs may well have seemed slightly less alien masters than their Byzantine overlords. Certainly, for the Coptic Church the change in regime was an advantage, for it put an end to the persecution suffered at the hands of the Orthodox authorities. The first Muslims showed themselves remarkably tolerant of other religions, and there was no movement of mass conversion to Islam. But non-Muslims were subject to taxes from which Muslims were exempt. Inevitably, the social prestige and the economic advantages enjoyed by the Arabs induced many Egyptians to adopt the new religion and with it the language of the conquerors. But the movement of conversion from Greek or Coptic and Christianity to Arabic and Islam was a very slow one, and it was not until the fourteenth century that the majority of Egyptians were Arabic-speaking Muslims. In the intensely conservative villages of the Nile Valley it seems likely that a change so profound as the adoption of a new language could only have been made possible by the absorption through intermarriage of a substantial number of Arab immigrants, many of them probably of Bedouin origin.

Under the Abbasids a change took place in the social structure of the empire. The Arabs gradually lost the privileged position they had enjoyed under the Umayyads, as Muslims of different nationalities, previously regarded as second-class citizens, were appointed to important posts in the great bureaucratic machine constructed by the rulers at Baghdad for the administration of their vast empire. One new group, the Mamluks, came to occupy a position of especial importance in Egypt. The word "mamluk" means "a possession" and hence "a slave" in Arabic, but the term came to be applied to a special category of slaves, boys purchased in the markets established by the Turkish-speaking peoples to the north and east of the Black Sea. Brought to the capital these youths were converted to Islam and given a vigorous education in which military training played a large part. They were then appointed to the army or to the administration and by the ninth century some had attained the posts of provincial governors.

The court of the caliphs of Baghdad became a byword for oriental magnificence, but for all their power and wealth the Abbasids were never able to establish a really firm grasp of the remoter provinces of their empire. By 800 Spain and North Africa had broken away, and in 868 a Mamluk governor of Egypt, Ahmad ibn Tulun, proclaimed his independence of Baghdad and established his own dynasty. From 868 to 1517, when the Ottoman Turks conquered the country, Egypt succeeded, except for a brief period of Abbasid rule in the tenth century, in maintaining its position as an independent state.

🜲 MEDIEVAL EGYPT

During Egypt's six and a half centuries of independence the country was ruled by five different dynasties: Tulunids (868–905), Ikshidids (935–969), Fatimids (969–1171), Ayyubids (1171–1250), and Mamluks (1250–1517). These dynasties possessed one outstanding feature in common: all five were founded by foreigners, not by native Egyptians. In other respects they differed greatly. The Ikshidid dynasty, like the Tulunid, was founded by a Mamluk governor in Abbasid service. The Fatimids were the leaders of a revolutionary Muslim sect, the adherents of the Ismaili branch of Shi'ism. They claimed descent from the Prophet through his daughter Fatima, regarded themselves as divinely ordained rulers, and damned the Abbasid caliphs as usurpers. The Fatimids invaded Egypt from the west, having first secured a base for themselves in Tunisia. Their army was largely made up of Berber tribesmen. Salah al-Din, the famous Saladin of medieval European chroniclers, supplanted the Fatimids, restored the orthodox faith, and founded the Ayyubid dynasty. By birth he was a Kurd who had risen to prominence as a general in the service of one of the independent rulers of Syria. The Mamluk rulers were first of Turkish and later of Circassian origin. Their assumption of power coincided with the destruction of the Caliphate by the Mongols. By maintaining a puppet Abbasid caliph at their court these "slave" sultans gave to their regime a semblance of Muslim orthodoxy and legitimacy.

The ablest rulers of these dynasties rendered great services to the country of their adoption. No longer was the surplus wealth of Egypt dispatched as revenue for imperial potentates in distant capitals. Instead, it was in every ruler's interest to concentrate on developing the country's resources. Under the Fatimids Egypt recovered its position as a great commercial entrepôt between the Mediterranean and the Indian Ocean. Trade contacts were established both with India and with the city-states of Italy. Later events increased still further the importance of Egypt as a commercial center. Political disturbances dislocated the rival trade route from the Persian Gulf to the Syrian coast. At the same time the Crusades brought more merchants from Western Europe to settle in the Levant. By 1215 no less than three thousand "Frankish" merchants were established in Alexandria. In exchange for the timber, cloth, iron, and other goods brought by Europeans Egypt offered some products of local manufacture such as sugar and cotton, but above all spices imported from the East. The profits from this transit trade were very great. In the fifteenth century pepper, the most sought-after of spices, bought at Cairo for 50 dinars, was being sold to European merchants in Alexandria for no less than 130 dinars.

With a flourishing economy to support them Egypt's rulers were able to make the country the greatest military power in the Muslim world. Syria, Palestine, and the Hejaz were brought under Egyptian suzerainty, and under the Fatimids, who possessed a highly efficient underground organization for spreading propaganda and encouraging subversion, Egyptian influence was felt even further afield. At the same time Egypt was defended against foreign invasion. In the 1090's that motley group of European adventurers, the warriors and pilgrims of the First Crusade, established a chain of petty Frankish kingdoms based on the main cities of Syria and Palestine. But the Crusaders never secured a permanent foothold on Egyptian soil and Egyptian-based rulers such as Saladin played a major part in expelling the invaders from their Levantine strongholds. No less formidable, though of shorter duration, was the threat presented by the Mongols. In 1260 the Mongol horde that had sacked Baghdad invaded Palestine. It suffered a decisive defeat at the hands of Baybars, the first and one of the greatest of the Mamluk sultans.

During these centuries Cairo, which the Fatimids had founded as their capital in 970, developed into a magnificent city which all of its great rulers sought to adorn with splendid buildings. Christian visitors marveled at the city's size and opulence, while Muslims revered it as a center of learning whose great collegiate mosque, al-Azhar, attracted students from every part of the world of Islam.

✳ CHRISTIAN NUBIA AND THE ARABS IN THE EASTERN SUDAN

After the destruction of Meroe the name Kush disappeared from the annals of the Eastern Sudan, to be replaced by Nubia. The new term was applied to the country south of the First Cataract and was associated with the arrival of the Nobatae, whose earlier home was probably in Kordofan. The Nobatae, together with the Blemmyes (Beja) who invaded the Nile Valley from the east, merged with the old inhabitants of Kush to form the population of medieval Nubia. By the sixth century there were three substantial kingdoms in the valley of the middle Nile. Their rulers accepted Christianity as the state religion less than a hundred years before the Arab invasion. In the eighth century the two northern states merged to form the kingdom of Nubia, with its capital at Dongola. Farther south lay the kingdom of Alwa, whose capital, Soba, lay near the confluence of the two Niles.

In the Eastern Sudan the Christian kingdom of Nubia occupied a position comparable to that of the far better-known empire of Ghana in the Western Sudan. At the height of its power its domains stretched from the First to the Fourth Cataract, and its influence may have reached as far west as Darfur, where the ruins of a Christian monastery have recently been discovered. Little is known of the foundations of Nubian economy, though there are references to a flourishing trade in slaves with Egypt in Fatimid times. But it has long been clear from the abundance of ruined churches and fortresses that the kingdom must once have been rich and powerful, and archeological research is now beginning to throw some light on its culture. The decorated pottery of Nubia is particularly striking, and the recently discovered frescoes in the cathedral at Faras are proof of an elaborate artistic tradition.

With its military strength based largely on its well-trained bowmen, Christian Nubia was strong enough to hold its own against Muslim Egypt for six centuries. But it was not possible for the Nubians to check Arab infiltration into the country lying between the Nile and the Red Sea coast. In the eighth century Muslim traders began to settle in the Red Sea ports, in the Beja country, and even in Nubia itself. But a much more substantial immigration occurred in the ninth century when groups of Bedouin Arabs, deprived of many of their privileges by the new Mamluk administration, began to move south in search of new grazing grounds. Other Arabs were attracted by the gold mines of Nubia and by the growing importance of the Red Sea ports. The settlement of Arabs in northern Nubia and in the Beja country to the east appears to have taken place gradually and peacefully. Intermarriage was not infrequent, and since the Beja observed the custom of matrilineal succession, when a prominent Arab married the daughter of a Beja chief, the children of the union succeeded to the chieftaincy.

Few border areas in the Muslim world were, indeed, as peaceful as that between Egypt and Nubia, but relations deteriorated in the thirteenth century. In 1275 the Mamluk Sultan Baybars invaded Nubia and installed a puppet ruler who agreed to pay regular tribute to Egypt. Forty years later a Nubian prince who had been converted to Islam ascended the throne. The old religion lingered on, and as late as 1520 there were said to be 150 churches in the country. But as more and more Arabs moved into the riverain lands, Islam became established as the dominant and eventually as the only faith.

The southern kingdom of Alwa survived for another century. But with its frontiers lying open to Muslim penetration it was clearly doomed to disappear. The Arabs, however, were not the only contenders for the rich lands at the Nile confluence. Just after 1500 another military group, the Funj, suddenly appeared, forced the Arabs to accept their overlordship, and established a kingdom—known after its capital as Sennar—that developed into the most powerful state in the Eastern Sudan. In Sudanese traditions the rulers of Sennar are known as the "Black Sultans." It is clear they were neither Arabs nor Muslims, though the rulers soon adopted Islam, but no one can yet say with certainty where they came from.

Meanwhile, a steady stream of Bedouin nomads were moving westward away from the Nile. Some stayed in the steppe country of Kordofan. Others moved still farther west. Indeed, as early as 1391 the ruler of Kanem, a kingdom northeast of Lake Chad, wrote to Cairo to complain that Bedouin tribes were raiding his subjects and selling them to Egyptian merchants. In Darfur there appears to have been an Arab strain in the first Muslim dynasty, which emerged in the seventeenth century. Gradually, some of the Arab nomads, the ancestors of the Baqqara of Kordofan and the Shuwa of Chad and Bornu, found themselves pushed farther south into parts of the savanna where their camels could not survive. Cattle provided a substitute that enabled them to retain their nomadic way of life.

The Bedouin Arabs introduced a superficial notion of Islam to the people of the Eastern Sudan. The consolidation of the faith was the work of individual teachers and missionaries. Some of these teachers came from far afield, from the Yemen, from Baghdad, even from Fez in Morocco. Others were Sudanese who had studied in Cairo or Mecca. Their activities were concentrated in the valley of the Nile, but their schools attracted students from more remote districts. Thus, gradually, between the fourteenth and the eighteenth centuries. Arab blood, the Arabic language, and the Muslim religion were diffused throughout the area that now forms the northern half of the Sudan Republic, distinguishing it sharply from the lands immediately to the south whose peoples were almost completely untouched by external influences.

✥ CHRISTIANS AND MUSLIMS IN ETHIOPIA AND THE HORN

Ethiopia and the Horn were almost the only parts of Northeast Africa not to be affected by the incursions of Bedouin Arabs. But both areas possessed close ties with Arabia, and the gradual spread of Muslim influence represented the continuation in another guise of that movement of men, ideas, and institutions that had been going on across the southern end of the Red Sea for centuries. As early as 702 Muslim Arabs occupied some islands off the Eritrean coast in order to root out a gang of pirates. But it was not until the early tenth century that Muslims began to settle in substantial numbers and to develop a string of coastal trading posts of which Zeila and Mogadishu became the most important.

These settlements thrived on the export of Abyssinian slaves to many parts of the Muslim world. The traders, mostly of Arab but some of Persian origin, came to form local aristocracies, intermarrying with the neighboring Danakil and Somali and converting them to Islam. From Zeila Muslim traders pushed up the line of the Ethiopian Rift Valley into the interior. By the thirteenth century the highlands had been brought under the control of a number of recently created Muslim sultanates of which Ifat in eastern Shoa was the most substantial.

Except on its eastern fringes highland Ethiopia was little affected before 1200 by Muslim expansion. On the plateau the dominant groups were the Christian Semitized Agau and the pagan Cushitic Sidama. Ethiopia, as the old Axumite kingdom should now be called (Abyssinia is derived from the Arabic equivalent, Habash), still survived as a Christian monarchy. After being ravaged by the Beja in the eighth century it recovered sufficiently to be described by Muslim geographers of the tenth century as a populous and extensive kingdom, whose rulers exacted tribute from the Muslim communities of the coast. But the closing years of that century brought a terrible disaster, an invasion by a pagan people—probably the Sidama of Damot—that brought the kingdom to the verge of complete ruin. The invasion must have been accompanied by the revolt of many of the recently subjugated Agau, for the kingdom reemerged, after an exceedingly obscure period, greatly shrunken in size.

Steadily, from the twelfth century on, first under the Zagwe, a dynasty of Agau origin, then under a line of rulers who claimed descent from the Axumite kings, and ultimately, by a cleverly fabricated legend, from no less a person than Solomon, the kingdom grew in strength and size. Church and state worked hand in hand. Battalions of monks, based on hundreds of monasteries scattered throughout the country, dedicated themselves with passionate zeal to the conversion of the pagan Agau. Those who accepted Christianity accepted also the divinely ordained Solomonid dynasty. But as it spread, Ethiopian Christianity, already impregnated by "archaic Semitic elements," began to absorb from its Agau converts many pagan or Judaic practices. Thus, the once-alien faith developed its distinctive indigenous character and became with its innumerable ceremonies and its splendid and elaborate ritual, "the storehouse of the cultural, political and social life of the people." [11]

Regular links were established with the outside world. The *abuna,* the head of the Ethiopian church, was always an Egyptian Copt appointed by the patriarch of Alexandria. Hundreds of Ethiopian monks undertook the arduous pilgrimage to Jerusalem. Coptic masons are reputed to have built the amazing churches, sculptured out of solid rock, at Roha, the capital of the Zagwe kings. Works from Coptic and Arabic were translated into Ge'ez. Muslim merchants from countries as remote as Morocco visited Ethiopia, Turkish Mamluks were employed as armorers, and by the fifteenth century Ethiopia contained a small colony of European adventurers, among them a painter from Venice.

From the central core of provinces, Tigre, Shoa, and Amhara, the kingdom expanded southward to dominate the pagan polities of the Sidama and the Agau, eastward to establish its suzerainty over the Muslim sultanates. Fittingly, the ruler of Ethiopia called himself *negus nagasti,* "king of kings." Only as a warrior could the negus hold his wide-flung dominions together, only by remaining constantly on the move, surrounded by a massive retinue accommodated in a great tented camp, could he overawe his vassal kings and ensure the steady flow of tribute needed to reward his followers and to provide for the enrichment of his staunchest supporter, the Church. In the fifteenth century the system worked splendidly. Contemporary chronicles tell of churches adorned with gold and silver and precious stones from India, and in Europe men heard extraordinary tales of the fabulous wealth of that mysteriously remote Christian monarch the Prester John. But the sixteenth century brought two long-drawn-out crises that shook the kingdom to the foundations.

The first shock came from the Muslims of Adal. Adal, with its capital at Harar, escaped by virtue of its remoteness the fate of the other Muslim states lying on the edge of the plateau. But though not absorbed, it was constantly under attack from Ethiopia. Some Muslims with a practical interest in trade were in favor of accepting Ethiopian domination as the price of peace; others, inflamed by religious zeal, clamored for a jihad. The war party had the support of the nomadic Danakil and Somali, who looked enviously to the rich pasture lands of the Ethiopian highlands. In the 1520's a leader of genius appeared, the Imam Ahmad, nicknamed Gran, "the left-handed." Uniting the nomads behind him Ahmad Gran invaded the plateau. Everywhere the Ethiopians were defeated, everywhere churches were destroyed, everywhere all but a small minority of resolute Christians accepted forced conversion to Islam. Despairingly, the Ethiopians appealed to the Portuguese whose naval power had already been felt in the Red Sea. In 1540 four hundred musketeers, sent from Portuguese India, provided Ethiopian resistance with the stiffening it needed. After many dramatic incidents Ahmad Gran was killed and his Somali followers retreated in disarray.

In the 1560's Ethiopia and Adal, exhausted by their long wars, were faced with an invasion from an entirely unexpected quarter. The Galla were Cushitic-speaking pastoralists forming a loose confederacy of tribes. Their homeland was probably to the south of Lake Abaye in the Ethiopian Rift Valley. In the 1560's, for reasons that have not been satisfactorily determined, they suddenly began to expand. Some Galla bands went eastward to the Juba River, others ravaged the highlands around Harar, yet others struck deep into the heart of the Ethiopian kingdom or moved among the independent Sidama states. The Galla were not a passing predatory horde. They settled in the countries they had occupied, but kept themselves distinct from the local inhabitants. Had they been able to unite their tribes, they could have overwhelmed Ethiopia, for they were formidable warriors. Instead, they were a major cause of the anarchy which came to engulf the Christian kingdom.

Nevertheless, at the end of the seventeenth century Ethiopia seemed to have made a considerable recovery. The Muslim threat had been eliminated. Adal, torn apart by internal dissensions, had ceased to exist. Meanwhile, Ethiopia had cut all its links with Christian Europe and indeed come to regard all Europeans with intense distrust. Jesuit missionaries were to blame for this dramatic reversal. First invited to the country in the 1550's they had succeeded seventy years later in converting the ruler of the day to their form of Christianity. The tactless zeal with which they followed up this advantage provoked a national rising which drove the king from his throne and the missionaries from the country. With Muslim powers, on the other hand, relations were not unfriendly. Indeed, the number of Muslims within Ethiopia steadily increased. Though subject to many restrictions they were allowed to engage in trade and so dominated the commercial life of the country. As traders, the Muslims traveled in areas not yet brought within the bounds of the kingdom and among people for whom Christianity was associated with the dominion of the arrogant Amhara. And as the weakness of the Christian monarchy and the decadence of the established church became increasingly apparent, Islam began not only to make converts among the pagan Galla and Sidama but also to win over some of the Christian nomadic tribes of Tigre.

The anarchy which afflicted Ethiopia throughout most of the eighteenth and much of the nineteenth century had many causes. In the seventeenth century the kings made the mistake of substituting a fixed capital at Gondar for the moving camp that had enabled their predecessors to keep a check on the great provincial magnates. The new division caused by the Galla migrations increased the isolation of individual provinces and so made it easier for local warlords to assert their independence. By the mid-eighteenth century the rulers at Gondar were puppets in the hands of their Galla mercenaries or of their great provincial feudatories. The country had fallen apart, and the annals of the time grow tedious with the record of revolt, intrigue, and massacre. And yet, as in earlier dark ages of Ethiopian history, the inspiring ideal of a great Christian monarchy ruled by kings of the House of Solomon never entirely faded from men's minds.

𝕏 THE OTTOMAN TURKS IN EGYPT

The two and a half centuries of Mamluk rule in Egypt coincided with the rise of an entirely new and extremely formidable military power on the northern side of the Eastern Mediterranean, that of the Ottoman Turks. By the middle of the sixteenth century the Ottoman sultans, who took their name from Osman, the founder of their dynasty, were masters of an empire that stretched from the eastern Alps to the Yemen and from the Atlas to the Persian Gulf. No empire of comparable extent—the Ottomans controlled almost as much territory as the Caesars and the Abbasids—has ever developed from so modest a nucleus. At the beginning of the fourteenth century the Ottoman Turks were no more than a band of freeborn soldiers of fortune gathered under the banner of a certain Osman, a successful war leader in the unending Muslim jihad against the Christian Byzantines on the marches of Anatolia. But Osman was more than a warrior; as an administrator he was able to provide the modest emirate that he founded in 1307 with institutions effectively designed to hold together his heterogeneous collection of followers. For more than two centuries the House of Osman continued to produce leaders of the same stamp as its founder. With one of the most efficient fighting machines the world had yet seen at their disposal, the Ottomans conquered Asia Minor and most of southeastern Europe. In 1516 Mamluk hostility provoked the Ottoman invasion of Syria. The next year a brief and bloody battle decided the fate of Egypt.

As masters of Egypt, the Ottomans found themselves occupying a country in decline. The last century of Mamluk rule had been marked by increasing inefficiency and corruption in government, by devastating famines due to a natural failure of the Nile waters, and by a galloping inflation. A final blow came in 1498 when the Portuguese discovered the sea route to the Indies and so acquired direct access to the producers of spices. By 1520 these newcomers in their stout caravels were masters of the Arabian Sea. For the Egyptians and their Italian trading partners this was a disastrous blow. The transit trade in oriental commodities, from which they had reaped such fat profits, was almost completely ruined. Even the Ottomans could not rescue the situation. But by establishing posts in the Yemen, at Aden, Massawa, and Suakin they prevented the Portuguese from dominating the southern end of the Red Sea.

For the Egyptian people the Turkish conquest brought little change in the composition of the governing class. Nominally, as a province of the Ottoman Empire, Egypt was under the control of a pasha (viceroy) appointed by the sultan in Istanbul. In fact, by the end of the seventeenth century power had passed to a small class of local military grandees, the beys, most of whom were of Mamluk origin. But the beys were too divided among themselves to provide the country with a vigorous system of administration or to make a concerted bid to secure the country's independence.

From its state of stupor and virtual isolation during these centuries of Ottoman rule Egypt was roused by a shock from quite an unexpected direction. In 1798 a French army under the command of the young General Bonaparte invaded the country. For the French the Egyptian expedition was both a colonial venture, designed to secure a territory capable of producing tropical crops to replace the islands lost in the West Indies, and a move in the grand strategy of the war against England. This first major episode in the history of nineteenth-century European imperialism in Africa ended in failure, for the French were defeated and forced to withdraw. Nevertheless, the expedition remains a seminal event in the history of Egypt and indeed of all Africa. It provided the first opportunity for an African country to gain some awareness of the remarkable technological advances that had been taking place in Western Europe in the past three centuries. ("We must take from Europe all the sciences which do not exist here," one of the sheikhs from al-Azhar exclaimed, after visiting the Institute which the French scholars and scientists who accompanied the army had set up in Cairo.[12]) For France the expedition, despite its failure, established an enduring link with Egypt and served to strengthen in the minds of many influential Frenchmen that concept of a "civilizing mission" that served as one of the principles of later French imperialism. For the British, engaged in expanding their great new empire in India, the expedition was no less significant. Hitherto, Egypt had been a country of no interest to them; now its strategic importance as halfway house to India was clear. Finally, for the Egyptians it opened the door for Muhammad Ali.

𝕏 MUHAMMAD ALI

A Turk of Albanian origin, Muhammad Ali came to Egypt in 1801 with a contingent of Albanian soldiers. In the confusion that followed the French withdrawal this force became one of the major power groups in the country. Muhammad Ali took over command of the Albanians in

1803; two years later the sultan appointed him pasha (viceroy) of Egypt. By a series of astute maneuvers which culminated in the peculiarly atrocious massacre of his most dangerous opponents, the Mamluk beys, the new pasha made himself undisputed master of Egypt, then turned to consolidate his impoverished province into a powerful and, if possible, independent state.

For such a purpose a large, well-disciplined army was imperative. The Albanian soldiery with whose aid the pasha had risen to power were dangerously restless. Muhammad Ali sent them off to fight and die in Arabia where the fanatical Wahhabi of Najd had recently seized the holy cities. By 1818 Wahhabi power was broken, Mecca and Medina returned to their protector, the sultan, and the Egyptians gained control of the Red Sea's eastern coast. In 1820 Muhammad Ali dispatched a motley army, four thousand strong, up the Nile. Within a year the petty riverain polities, the decaying kingdom of Sennar, and the plains of Kordofan were in Egyptian hands to form the nucleus of a colony more extensive even than that established by the pharaohs of the New Kingdom.

Muhammad Ali's prime purpose in occupying the Sudan, as the territory came to be known, was to secure a steady supply of black slaves for the army of his dreams. (The Caucasus, from which so many white Mamluks had been dispatched to Egypt, was now coming under Russian control.) But as the Sudanese slave recruits did not live up to the pasha's expectations he decided on a step unprecedented in the annals of foreign rule in Egypt, the conscription of the despised fellahin (peasantry). To train these new soldiers and to educate their Turkish or Mamluk officers a well-qualified cadre of European army officers was engaged, mostly Frenchmen and Italians who had served in the Napoleonic wars and were now eagerly seeking employment.

To meet the costs of training and equipping such an army it was necessary to reorganize the administration and the economy of the country. The pasha's basic aim was to concentrate as much power in his own hands as possible. He made himself the apex of a system of centralized administration, became by far the largest landowner in the country, and asserted a monopoly over the export trade. Yet this despotic policy involved a number of measures of permanent benefit to the country. To train administrators special schools were set up and students sent on courses in Europe. The discovery of long-fibered cotton and the spectacular increase in its production—from less than a thousand hundredweight in 1821 to more than three hundred thousand hundredweight in 1837—provided the basis for a flourishing export trade. New land was brought under cultivation, communications were improved, and the endemic banditry of past centuries was repressed. And Europeans traveling to the East were encouraged to make use of the route up the Red Sea, which earlier rulers had kept strictly closed to all non-Muslim shipping.

Muhammad Ali made Egypt the most prosperous and powerful province in the Ottoman Empire, but he was not able to achieve complete independence. His new model army proved its worth against Greek rebels in 1824–27 and against the forces of his own suzerain in Syria and Anatolia in 1831–32 and again in 1839. Half a century earlier the pasha would undoubtedly have been free to assert his independence and to retain a hold on Syria. But since the 1780's all the four major powers of Europe had developed an interest, unprecedented since the time of the Crusades, in the affairs of the eastern Mediterranean. The Russians were advancing around the Black Sea; the Austrians, after liberating Hungary from the Turks in the early eighteenth century, were deeply concerned about the state of the Balkans; the British, now firmly established as masters of India, appreciated the strategic importance of the countries astride the overland route to the East; and the French could not afford to disregard a region of such concern to their international rivals. The European powers were not prepared to see the Greek rebellion crushed or the Ottoman Empire shattered. Three times, therefore, Muhammad Ali found himself compelled by the irresistible pressure of European sea power to withdraw—from Greece in 1828, from Anatolia in 1833, and from Syria in 1841.

All great men arouse controversy. To some historians Muhammad Ali has seemed no more than a successful military adventurer or a ruthless despot concerned only with his own interests; others have regarded him as an outstanding administrator and "the founder of modern Egypt." "When I came to this country," the pasha himself remarked toward the end of his life, "it was barbarous, utterly barbarous. Barbarous it remains to this day. Still I hope that my labours have rendered it somewhat better than it was." [13] This modest self-appraisal does not lay sufficient stress on the originality of the pasha's work. In the history of the Afro-Asian world Muhammad Ali stands out as the first ruler to make a successful attempt to bridge the gap between traditional society and the new civilization created by the technology of Western Europe.

THE SOMALI EXPANSION

For many centuries the Somali have been the dominant people of the Horn of Africa, and their expansion provides the main theme of the area's history. But documentary material is so meager, traditions are so confusing, and so little archeological work has yet been done in Somalia that it is impossible to speak with assurance about the early stages of this great movement.

Linguistic evidence suggests that the homeland of the speakers of Eastern Cushitic languages, the Somali, the Galla, the Danakil, the Sidama, and others, lies in the Rift Valley area of southern Ethiopia.[14] The Galla are known to have expanded from the area in the sixteenth century. The dates of the Danakil and Somali migrations are quite uncertain, but since all the Somali clans, though now dispersed over more than a thousand miles of territory, speak the same language with minor variations of dialect, it is reasonable to assume that the Somali expansion must have taken place within comparatively recent times, probably in the course of the last thousand years.

The majority of the Somali were and still are nomadic pastoralists, herding camels, sheep, and cattle. Among the pastoralists the basic political unit was a group of a few hundred men, claiming descent from a common ancestor and bound together by an obligation to assist one another in pursuing blood feuds. A number of such groups, again linked by ties of descent but from a still remoter ancestor, formed a clan whose head, sometimes termed sultan, possessed very limited powers. The Somali lived in a harsh land, with water scarce and grazing restricted. Such an environment inevitably produced among the pastoralists an intensely competitive society. They were and are a warlike and fiercely independent people. "Small incidents, such as the seizure of a few camels, or a quarrel over precedence at a well, readily lead," as a modern anthropologist has noted, "to bitter feuds, involving an ever-widening circle of clansmen on each side as incident follows incident." [15] Thus, the Somali clans, though they may have possessed a certain sense of common nationality, never formed a political nation, and their migrations are not to be seen as "a concerted operation under a single direction" but rather as "a disjointed series of clan and lineage movements in which there were many cross currents of migration as group jostled group in the search for new pastures." [16]

There is no documentary evidence of the Somali presence in the Horn of Africa before the fourteenth century, when the Hawiye, one of the branches of the Somali, are described by an Arab geographer as living in the neighborhood of Merca on the Indian Ocean coast. Obviously, the Somali must have been established in the northern part of the Horn long before this date. But there is no evidence to indicate whether or not the Somali are to be regarded as the descendants of the "Berberi," the name applied by Greek traders of the first century A.D. to the inhabitants of the coast of northern Somalia.

As the Somali expanded over the Horn, they came into contact with other peoples. In some parts they encountered small groups of hunters and gatherers in whose modern descendants, such as the Boni, some anthropologists have seen traces of a Bushmanoid ancestry. Farther south, the comparatively fertile valleys of the Juba and Shibeli were already occupied by Bantu-speaking Negroid agriculturalists, who are known to have been settled in the area by the tenth century. The Somali clans who moved into this area became sharply distinguished from the northern Somali, merging with the Negroids, adopting agriculture, and accepting a hierarchical social structure in sharp contrast to the egalitarian society of the pastoralists. In the sixteenth and seventeenth centuries Galla groups began to move into the same area. Indeed, Galla expansion brought them into contact with the Somali on a very wide front from the Juba to Harar.

In the early nineteenth century one group of clans, from the Darod branch of the northern Somali, crossed the Juba River, lived peacefully for a time with the Galla of the area, then in the 1860's fought and defeated them and advanced still farther south.

If Somali expansion forms the main theme of the history of the Horn in the past thousand years, the spread of Islam from the settlements founded by Arab traders on the coast provides an important secondary motif. Many Somali clans today trace their ancestry back to Muslim sheikhs who came from Arabia and married into Somali lineages, and it is not unreasonable to see in these traditions the recollection of a broad historical process. Certainly, the Somali acquired a passionate devotion to Islam that contrasts sharply with the laxness of belief of many other African converts.

LONG-DISTANCE TRADE ROUTES

The spread of Islam is one of the themes that binds together the history of Northeast Africa. Another interconnecting theme is provided by the development and maintenance of long-distance trade routes. The trade routes of this region are the oldest in Africa. Many of them were in existence at the beginning of the Christian era, and some can be traced back to the third millennium B.C.

Egypt was connected with the lands to the south by three main routes: the "Forty Days' Road" that struck southwestward across the desert to Darfur, the route directly to the south which at some periods followed the Nile and at others cut across the Nubian Desert to the riverain area north of Khartoum, and the caravan trail from Upper Egypt to the ports of the Red Sea coast. From these ports passages could be obtained to Suakin, Massawa, and Zeila.

In the Sudan the main transversal route, running from east to west, started from Suakin, passed through Beja country to Sennar, Shendi, or Khartoum and continued across Kordofan to Darfur and on to the countries around Lake Chad. From Darfur a route which may not have come into existence before the eighteenth century led southward to the copper mines of Hofrat en Nahas. The White Nile presented an obvious highway to the south, but the warlike disposition of the riverain Shilluk deterred traders until the area was pacified in the mid-nineteenth century and beyond the Shilluk country stretched apparently impenetrable swamps whose local name, Sudd, was derived from an Arabic word meaning "barrier." Not until 1840 was the barrier surmounted when an expedition of exploration launched by Muhamad Ali and led by a Turkish officer succeeded in making its way through the Sudd and sailed up the river as far as Gondokoro.

There were three main approaches to the highlands of Ethiopia. The shortest and easiest route started from Massawa and climbed the steep escarpment to Tigre. Another route from the Red Sea coast passed through the arid country of the turbulent Danakil and reached Shoa. A third route ran from Sennar through the wild Ethiopian borderlands to Gondar. Zeila and Berbera, the main ports of the northern Somali coast, served as the termini for caravans from Harar and the Ogaden. From Harar, Gondar, and Shoa routes ran to the rich Sidama kingdoms of southern Ethiopia. Before the Galla expansion there are reports of a route between Mogadishu and Ethiopia, but in the nineteenth century Mogadishu's trading connections were with its own hinterland. There is no evidence of any route connecting the Sidama states with the country to their west.

To appreciate their full significance these overland trade routes need to be fitted into the pattern of maritime trade. The ports of the Red Sea coast and the Horn attracted merchants from Arabia, the Persian Gulf, and western India—and on two occasions in the fifteenth century from as far afield as China. In the seventeenth century merchants of the European East India companies settled in Mocha and Jiddah on the Arabian coast of the Red Sea. But the region's main port for contact with Europe was Alexandria, which attracted merchants from every country in the Mediterranean.

Every port, trade route, and market center in the region experienced many vicissitudes in the course of its history. Alexandria, for example, which in the late Middle Ages could, indeed, be described as a "Queen of Cities and Metropolis of Africa," [17] shrunk by the eighteenth century into a wretched provincial town with rubble-filled streets and a population of a mere ten thousand, until the development of the Egyptian cotton trade restored its prosperity. As a trade route the Red Sea was affected by the rise and fall of empires: at some periods it was a great international artery, at others a maritime backwater. Political changes of a purely local nature influenced the flow of traffic on the overland routes. A feud between two Somali clans, for example, could prevent caravans from reaching Zeila and Berbera for one or two seasons. Sometimes these disturbances were of longer duration. Trade between the Sidama kingdoms and the coast was impoverished for more than two centuries by the anarchy caused by the Galla invasions.

With the exception of cotton, which became Egypt's major export in the first half of the nineteenth century, the products of Northeast Africa varied remarkably little in the course of two thousand years. Slaves, gold, ivory, hides, and skins, and a variety of exotic produce such as civet, myrrh, ostrich feathers, and rhinoceros horn were the commodities exported by the countries south of Egypt in the early nineteenth century, even as they had been in pharaonic or Greco-Roman times. Slaves, drawn mainly from the pagan peoples living in the Ethiopian borderlands, the Nuba Mountains, and the country south of Darfur, formed probably the most lucrative item of commerce, but the trade was on a much smaller scale than in West Africa. Even after the Egyptian conquest of the Sudan not more than twenty thousand slaves a year were sent to Egypt and to Arabia. Gold was no longer as important as it had been in the days of the Ptolemies, for the deposits in the Nuba hills were exhausted, but a certain amount of the precious metal continued to come from southern Ethiopia. The trade in ivory, on the other hand, stood in the 1840's at the beginning of a boom period, for the growing prosperity of the middle classes of Europe and of America created a widening market for fine combs and knife handles and other articles, such as billiard balls and piano keys, which in that age could be manufactured only from ivory. This new demand—both the price and the quantity of elephants' teeth sold on the London market more than doubled between the 1840's and the 1870's—provided one of the major incentives for the commercial exploitation of the southern Sudan.

𝕫𝕝𝕖 NORTHEAST AFRICA IN THE 1850'S

Ever since its unification at the end of the fourth millennium B.C. Egypt had almost always been the major polity in Northeast Africa. This was clearly the case in the middle of the nineteenth century. Indeed, never in the country's long history had its power reached so deep into the interior of Africa, even though it was still nominally only a province of the Ottoman Empire. And when Muhammad Ali died in 1849 he bequeathed to his successors not only a hereditary throne—the sultan had agreed in 1841 to maintain the viceroyalty of Egypt in the pasha's family—but also the strongest government, the most efficient army, and the most prosperous economy to be found anywhere in contemporary Africa.

The "Turks," as the local people called the invaders, were firmly in control of a large part of the Sudan. Kordofan and the riverain provinces of Dongola, Berber, Khartoum, and Sennar had been occupied in the first year of the conquest. In the 1840's the southern Beja country was pacified and a trading port established at Gondokoro far up the White Nile. On the coast Suakin and Massawa were still under the sultan's nominal control. To the west of Kordofan lay the independent sultanate of Darfur. The wild border country between Sennar and Ethiopia was occupied by a heterogeneous collection of polities, ranging from the independent villages of the Negroid Kunama to the strongholds of outlaws and political refugees from the Sudan. Farther south, in country at the time almost completely unknown to the outside world, were to be found innumerable petty Negroid polities. Strung out along the banks of the White Nile lay the settled communities of the Shilluk, loosely bound together by their recognition of a single divinely ordained ruler. The swamps and plains of the Bahr-al-Ghazal were the domain of the Dinka and Nuer, tough pastoralists moving from wet-season villages to dry-season cattle camps, their tribes regularly raiding each other's cattle, their tribal subsections constantly feuding with one another. Beyond the swamps in the wooded parklands to the east of the Nile or on the ironstone plateau to the west, lay a multitude of independent village communities founded by settled agriculturists such as the Bari or the Bongo. Nowhere in this great semicircle of territory stretching from Darfur to the Ethiopian highlands was there to be found a political community substantial enough to be described as a state.

In 1850 the ancient kingdom of Ethiopia still presented a spectacle of complete disorder, with power lying in the hands of the great warlords of Tigre, Gojam, Shoa, and other provinces. But an outsider, a young war leader named Kassa, from the western frontier province of Kwara was attracting more and more followers to his banner and was dreaming of restoring the glory of the Solomonid dynasty. In 1855, after defeating all the great provincial rases, he achieved his ambition and was crowned as the Emperor Theodore.

Most of the old Sidama kingdoms had disintegrated under the assault of the Galla in the seventeenth century. At the beginning of the nineteenth century some of the Sidama kingdoms were reestablished under Galla dynasties. Galla-Sidama polities such as Limu-Enarea or Jimma-Kaffa were states as prosperous and extensive as many of the far better-known kingdoms of East or West Africa. The Galla living among the Sidama and among the Amhara had become settled agriculturists; their kinsmen in the Hawash Valley and the eastern highlands still retained their ancestral pastoralism. These pastoral Galla knew no overlord, nor did their neighbors, the Danakil to the north and the Somali to the east. Harar, once the capital of the kingdom of Adal, was now no more than a city-state of some significance as a center for Islam but of little political importance. Mogadishu, too, and the other towns of the southern Somali coast had also declined in importance since the sixteenth century. In the 1820's they were forced to accept the suzerainty of the sultan of Oman and Zanzibar.

In one important respect Northeast Africa differed in 1850 from almost every other region in the continent: no part of it, not even a small enclave, was under European sovereignty. And yet, ever since the French expedition to Egypt, no region of Africa had been of such interest to the statesmen of the major powers of Europe. Within the region European interest was confined almost exclusively to Egypt. For that province of the Ottoman sultan was powerful enough, as Muhamad Ali had demonstrated, to threaten the stability of the entire empire. And if the empire collapsed, with it would fall that elaborate structure of international relations, the European balance of power.

The British had an additional reason for being concerned about Egypt. The extent of British dominions in the East increased dramatically in the first half of the nineteenth century, and with expanding dominion went an ever-more lucrative trade. British exports of cloth to India, for example, rose in value from £200,000 in 1814 to over £3,000,000 in 1832. As the demands of commerce and of empire called more and more Englishmen to serve in the East, the speed of communications became a matter of major importance. The long passage to India by the Cape took five to eight months. But in the 1820's Egyptian cooperation made it possible for passengers to travel overland across the Suez isthmus and on down the Red Sea, thus cutting the time for the journey by more than half. In 1830 the first steamship reached Suez from Bombay; in 1835 officers of the Indian navy completed their survey of the Red Sea coasts; in 1839 the derelict port of Aden, already in use as a coaling station, was annexed by the British. By 1850, then, well before the construction of the Canal, the Suez–Red Sea route had become established as one of the lifelines of the nineteenth-century world.

"The English," an Arab sheikh on the Euphrates remarked in the 1830's, "are like ants; if one finds a bit of meat, a hundred follow." The Arab's observation might with equal justice have been applied to most European peoples at this time. The European population of Alexandria was a particularly striking example of this sudden burst of expansion. In 1798 Alexandria had less than a hundred European residents; in 1864 the city contained more than fifty thousand, more than half of them Greeks or Italians, with ten thousand Frenchmen and six thousand British, mostly of Maltese extraction. Among this motley populace were to be found "the best and worst elements of the European and Mediterranean world . . . staid English brokers and mercurial Levantine peddlers, proper clerks for the offices of the Peninsular and Oriental, painted harlots for the Square of the Consuls in Alexandria, dedicated scholars for the temples of Abydos and Karnak, cutthroats and confidence men for the alleys of Cairo." [18] A few of the Europeans in Egypt followed Muhammad Ali's armies into the Sudan. In the 1850's Khartoum had about two dozen European residents, and among the pioneers of the ivory trade in the southern Sudan were a Welshman and a Savoyard, both of whom had come to Egypt as technical experts in Muhammad Ali's service.

Ethiopia was of little commercial and no strategic interest to mid-nineteenth century Europe. But that fascinating, if anarchic, country attracted a number of adventurous European travelers, first and foremost among them, James Bruce, a Scottish gentleman of eccentric character whose *Travels to Discover the Source of the Nile* published in 1790 is one of the most splendid narratives in the literature of African exploration. In the 1830's European missionaries returned to Ethiopia after an interval of two hundred years, but both the Germans of the Anglican Church Missionary Society and the Italian Lazarists found the country a grueling and unrewarding field for their labors.

The writings of scholarly minded travelers and missionaries made Ethiopia one of the best-known countries in the continent for European Africanists. The interior of Somalia was completely unknown ground until 1855, when Richard Burton, an Indian Army officer and traveler of genius, made a daring journey to Harar. The Harari had a legend that their ruler would lose his independence once a European had entered the city. In that age of incipient European imperialism such a legend might well be regarded as evidence of shrewd political foresight.

CHAPTER VI

Northwest Africa

✻ GEOGRAPHY

Bounded on the north by the Mediterranean, on the south by the savanna of the "geographical Sudan," [1] on the west by the Atlantic, and on the east by the western frontier of Egypt and the Sudan Republic, Northwest Africa stretches over an area no less than three million square miles in extent. The region falls into two unequal parts: the Sahara and the area termed North Africa or Barbary by Europeans and *al-Maghrib*, "the West," by Arabic speakers. Today North Africa comprises Morocco, Algeria, Tunisia, and Libya, while the Sahara, which should really be thought of as stretching across the continent to the Red Sea coast, is divided between ten independent states and one colonial territory under Spanish control.

Two geographical factors—relief and rainfall—have had an immense influence on the historical development of North Africa. About half the land of the western Maghrib (Morocco, Algeria, and Tunisia) lies three thousand feet above sea level, but the pattern of the area's relief is extremely complex with the highlands taking many different forms. Morocco is dominated by the range of the High Atlas, whose peaks rise to over thirteen thousand feet. Subordinate ranges run to the southwest (the Anti-Atlas) and to the east (the Tellian Atlas and the Saharan Atlas of Algeria). Isolated mountain chains or massifs are represented by the Rif of northern Morocco and the Aurès and the Greater and Lesser Kabyles of eastern Algeria, while across Algeria, between the Tellian and the Saharan Atlas, stretches a broad belt of high plains.

The Mediterranean coast of the western Maghrib receives an adequate rainfall, but in most parts of the interior and in the coastal plains of southern Tunisia and southern Morocco the average rainfall is less than sixteen inches and annual variations are so great that drought is an ever-present danger. Such a meager rainfall means that the Maghrib possesses

MUSLIM DYNASTIES OF THE MAGHRIB AND ANDALUSIA

A—dynasty of Arab origin; B—dynasty of Berber origin; T—Turks

		Area	Capital	Date
				(in centuries)
A	Umayyad and Abbasid governors	Maghrib/Andalusia	Kairwan	7/8
A	Umayyads	Andalusia	Cordoba	8/11
A	Aghlabids	Tunisia/E. Algeria/Sicily	Kairwan	9
A	Idrisids	N. Morocco	Fez	8/10
A	Rustamids	C. Algeria	Tahert	8/9
A	Fatimids	Tunisia/E. Algeria/Egypt	Cairo (after 969)	10/12
B	Zirids	Tunisia	Achir/Kairwan	11/12
B	Hammadids	E. Algeria	Qala/Bougie	11/12
B	Almoravids	Morocco/W. Algeria/Andalusia	Marrakesh	11/12
B	Almohads	Maghrib/Andalusia	Marrakesh	12/13
B	Hafsids	Tunisia/E. Algeria	Tunis	13/16
B	Merinids	Morocco	Fez	13/15
B	Abd al-Wadids	W. and C. Algeria	Tlemcen	13/16
B	Wattasids	Morocco	Fez	15/16
A	Saadians	Morocco	Fez	16/17
A	Alawites	Morocco	Fez	17/20
T	Ottoman beys	Algeria	Algiers	16/19
T	Ottoman beys	Tunisia	Tunis	16/17
T	Hussainids	Tunisia	Tunis	18/20
T	Karamanlis	Tripolitania	Tripoli	18/19
T	Ottoman governors	Libya	Tripoli	19/20

few perennial streams and none adequate enough to serve for navigation. To the formidable disadvantage imposed by the Maghrib's pattern of rainfall must be added other geographical limitations: a coast ill-provided with good natural harbors; a lack of easily accessible mineral resources; and large areas of poor soil, some of which, around the stagnant lakes of the Algerian steppe, is so impregnated with salt as to be quite uncultivatable.

Thus, of all the lands around the Mediterranean the Maghrib appears in many ways the least well-endowed to support a flourishing civilization. The area as a whole lacks the natural unity of Egypt and of the peninsular lands of the northern seaboard, and its major parts—Morocco and Algeria—are deeply segmented by their mountains. Few communities have resisted external domination so fiercely and so effectively as the mountain villages of the Atlas, the Rif, or the Aurès; by contrast, the coastal plains have constantly been exposed to the assaults of foreign adventurers. Every substantial polity in the history of the Maghrib has based its power on control of the plains, yet suffered from the fundamen-

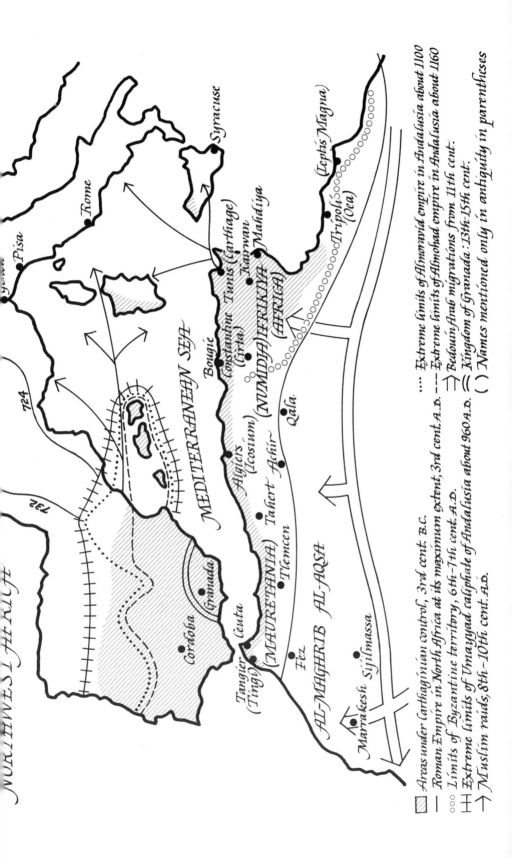

NORTHWEST AFRICA

Pisa
Rome
Syracuse

MEDITERRANEAN SEA

724
732

Granada
Cordoba
Tangier (Tingi)
Ceuta
(MAURETANIA)
Tlemcen
Fez
AL-MAGHRIB AL-AQSA
Marrakesh   Sijilmassa

Algiers (Icosium)
Tahert Achir
Qala

Bougie
Constantine (Cirta)
Tunis (Carthage)
Kairwan
Mahdiya
(NUMIDIA) IFRIKIYA (AFRICA)

Tripoli (Oea)
(Lepis Magna)

.... Extreme limits of Almoravid empire in Andalusia about 1100
━ ─ ─ Extreme limits of Almohad empire in Andalusia about 1160

▭ Areas under Carthaginian control, 3rd cent. B.C.
── Roman Empire in North Africa at its maximum extent, 3rd cent. A.D.
ooo Limits of Byzantine territory, 6th-7th cent. A.D.
╫ Extreme limits of Umayyad caliphate of Andalusia about 960 A.D.
→ Muslim raids, 8th-10th cent. A.D.

⇒ Bedouin Arab migrations from 11th cent.
⊂ Kingdom of Granada: 13th-15th cent.
( ) Names mentioned only in antiquity in parentheses

tal weakness of never being able to dominate effectively the mountainous interior.

The aridity of the North African steppe turns to desolation in the Sahara, the most extensive desert in the world. In popular imagination the Sahara is seen as a wilderness of sand dunes; yet it is a region of most varied landscapes, ranging from the great massifs of Ahaggar and Tibesti with their extraordinary rock formations and their lofty volcanic peaks to vast stretches of gravelly plains or broad belts of constantly shifting dunes. The desert is not completely waterless—in certain parts, particularly on the northern fringes, excellent supplies of subterranean water support the rich culture of the oases—nor is it completely bereft of vegetation. Men have thus found it possible to gain a livelihood in the Sahara whether as cultivators in the oases or pastoralists in other areas.

There is one other point that needs to be recalled in considering the historical geography of North Africa. The region has been profoundly affected by the climatic change which accompanied the ending of the Makalian Wet Phase in the third millennium B.C. As the rainfall declined the vegetation of the desert grew more sparse and the marshy lakes of the southern Sahara gradually disappeared. From being one of the most favorable environments known to men in paleolithic times, the Sahara became one of the harshest.

⚜ "LIBYAN" BERBERS AND "ETHIOPIANS"

In no region of the continent has the basic stock, the population that occupied the territory three thousand years ago, been so little diluted by external migrations as Northwest Africa, in spite of the fact that the northern part of the region, the land of Barbary, has been subjected to waves of foreign settlers from the Phoenicians and the Romans to the French, Spanish, and Italian *colons* of the age of modern European imperialism. But the immigrants have never come in overwhelming numbers—even the Arabs of the seventh and eighth centuries who exerted so profound an influence on the culture of the region are reckoned not to have exceeded two hundred thousand—and so by far the greater part of the present population may be regarded as descendants of a people that has occupied the Maghrib and part of the Sahara for many millennia.

The ancient Greeks called these people Libyans, a term derived from a single tribe, the Lebou, who lived on the western borders of Egypt. Later, the Romans lumped together all the native inhabitants of North Africa who had not been affected by Roman culture and dubbed them *barbari,* "barbarians," a term which has passed into modern usage in the Arabized form Berber. Thus, the ancient Libyans are the direct ancestors of the modern Berbers. Basically, the Berbers of Northwest Africa are a people of Caucasoid stock, but many varieties of physical type are found among them, including even some groups with blond hair and blue eyes, and archeological research has revealed the existence in Paleolithic times of a number of distinct cultures. It is clear then that the Berber represent a blending of many different peoples. Some of these peoples probably came from Europe, but the fact that the Berber language forms one of the main branches of the Afro-Asiatic family suggests that the dominant groups came from the east, spreading along the southern littoral of the Mediterranean.

The movements of peoples which led to the emergence of the Berber population of Northwest Africa must have taken place well before the fourth millennium B.C. Egyptian records make it clear that the Libyans living to the west of the Nile delta were a substantial and formidable people from the beginning of Dynastic times. Herodotus, writing in the fifth century B.C., provides a description of Libya, some of whose tribes were already living deep in the Sahara. Hunting, food-gathering, and pastoralism formed the basis of the economy of the vast majority of the inhabitants of the Maghrib and the northern Sahara until as late as the end of the first millennium B.C.

Classical writers clearly distinguished the light-skinned Libyans from the Negroid "Ethiopians," the people with "burnt faces," of the central Sahara. Even today, when people of Caucasoid stock, the Berber Tuareg and Arabo-Berber Moors, have spread to the borders of the Sudan, a substantial proportion of the population of the Sahara is still of Negroid stock. Many of these Negroid Saharans are the descendants of slaves brought from the Sudan to serve as cultivators in the oases in the course of the past thousand years, but some—notably the black-skinned Tebu of Tibesti—are undoubtedly the descendants of a very ancient race of desert dwellers. How far north these Negroids of the Sahara once lived cannot at present be ascertained, but both archeological evidence and the oral traditions of such areas as Air make it clear that the southern Sahara was occupied by peoples of Negroid stock until increasing desiccation and the pressure of the nomadic pastoralists forced most of them to move farther south.

🜨 THE PHOENICIANS: CARTHAGE

Pharaonic Egypt of the third millennium B.C. was completely ignorant of the lands lying far to the west along the North African coast. But in the course of the second millennium some of the maritime peoples of the eastern Mediterranean began to probe the unknown waters of the western half of the great inland sea. In essence this movement was not unlike the "reconnaissance" carried out by Western European navigators of the fifteenth and sixteenth centuries on a much vaster scale. The basic motive of these Cretan and Aegean explorers would seem to have been a desire to discover new sources of precious metals, particularly tin, which was needed for the production of bronze and which could be obtained from Tarshish in southern Spain. Some recollection of this period of exploration is probably to be found in a number of the episodes woven into the *Odyssey*.

Toward the end of the second millennium B.C. a new people, the Phoenicians of Tyre, profiting no doubt from the collapse of the Aegean states under the attacks of northern barbarians, began to participate in the western trade and eventually to assert a monopoly over it. To protect their monopoly and to meet the needs of their seamen, who rarely sailed out of sight of land and preferred to beach their ships every night, the Phoenicians built a chain of trading stations and other posts, carefully sited on the mainland coasts and islands of the southern half of the western Mediterranean. The most important of these settlements was *Qart Habasht* or Carthage, the "new city," founded according to tradition in 814 B.C. by Dido, queen of Tyre.

Although the circumstances of its foundation obviously invested it with a special significance, Carthage developed slowly and it was not until the sixth century B.C. that the city emerged first as the protector, then as the overlord of the other Phoenician settlements which found themselves faced with powerful competition from newly established Greek colonies in Sicily and southern Italy. Much of Carthaginian history in the fifth and fourth centuries B.C. is taken up with wars against the Greek city-states of Sicily, wars whose causes were too complex and too local to be explained in terms simply of a clash of rival economic imperialisms. Nor can one provide any easy explanation to account for the first Punic war (264–241 B.C.) with Rome, which escalated from comparatively trivial incidents into the most terrible and the most long drawn-out conflict in the annals of the classical world. The defeat of Carthage in the first Punic war led to a deliberately planned war of revenge. Deprived of their settlements in Sicily and in Sardinia, the Carthaginians built up a new empire in southern Spain and produced in the young commander, Hannibal, one of the greatest military leaders of all time.

Never have Europeans been made more conscious of an African power as when Hannibal, advancing from Spain with an army whose largest contingent was made up of Berber mercenaries, crossed the Alps, struck deep into the heart of Italy, and inflicted on the Romans three massive defeats. But numbers were on the Roman side, and this was ultimately decisive. In 201 Carthage was forced to accept a peace that stripped the city of all its overseas possessions and left it virtually a vassal of Rome.

The Romans now found themselves faced with a new threat. In the third century a number of kingdoms had been created among the independent Berbers of North Africa. When the second Punic war ended, the most powerful of these kingdoms covered most of eastern Algeria (Numidia). Its king, Masinissa, was a man of exceptional ability; indeed the French historian, Gsell, the foremost authority on North Africa in antiquity, considered him the greatest ruler the region has ever produced.[2] Masinissa talked like a latter-day nationalist: Livy recorded him as saying to all foreigners, whether Romans or Phoenicians, that Africa belonged to the Africans. Clearly, his dream was to build up a great Numidian empire, and he took advantage of the weakness of Carthage to extend his own dominions eastward, hoping in time to seize the great metropolis itself.

Rather than see Carthage fall into Numidian hands, the Romans decided that the city should be destroyed. They carried out this policy in a peculiarly odious and brutal manner in the third Punic war (149–146 B.C.). In annihilating Carthage they also put themselves in a position to stifle an effective Berber nationalism. A Roman colony was established in the Carthaginian homeland in northern Tunisia, Roman intrigues brought about the division of Masinissa's kingdom after his death, and Roman dominions spread in the course of the next hundred and fifty years over all the coastal districts of North Africa. The murder of Ptolemy, ruler of Mauretania (northern Morocco and western Algeria), by the loathsome Caligula in 40 A.D. gave the Romans control of the last substantial Berber kingdom of antiquity, but nothing could extinguish the indomitable Berber spirit of independence.

The Romans destroyed Carthage; they could not erase the effects of Phoenician influence felt over the course of close on a thousand years. At the beginning of the first millennium B.C. the Berbers were the most isolated of Mediterranean peoples; the Phoenicians introduced them to the concepts and techniques of a more elaborate civilization. The ablest Berber princes gladly followed their example. Masinissa, for example, forced many of his subjects to turn from nomadic pastoralism to agriculture and to live in compact villages where they could, of course, be more easily governed. But the plan of urbanization and economic development which Masinissa carried out in Numidia with the aid of foreign technicians was one that the Carthaginians had already successfully implemented in their own home territory in Tunisia.

"The Carthaginians," wrote Plutarch, "are a hard and gloomy people, submissive to their rulers and harsh to their subjects . . . they are austere and care little for amusements and the graces of life."[3] Modern scholarship tends to confirm this characterization. The Carthaginians were, par excellence, a nation of shopkeepers, most of whose wealth came from their control of the carrying trade of the southern Mediterranean. Their own products were of a quality far inferior to those of Greek manufacture; they contributed nothing to literature or pure science and little to applied technology; and their traditional religion involved the repulsive practice of sacrificing newborn children to their high god, Baal Hammon. But the Carthaginians were never completely immune to outside influences, and in the last century of their existence as an independent people they showed themselves, so archeological evidence suggests, particularly responsive to the attractions of Hellenic culture.

The solemn curse which the Roman conquerors pronounced on the ruined site of Carthage was peculiarly ineffective. The city recovered under the emperors to become once again the metropolis of North Africa and also one of the great cosmopolitan intellectual centers of the Mediterranean world. The Punic language continued to be spoken in the first centuries of the Christian era, and religious concepts of Punic origin were taken over by the neighboring Berbers. Indeed, it is possible, as some scholars have surmised, that these early contacts with a Semitic language and a Semitic religion eased the way for the eventual triumph of Arabic and Islam.

ROMAN RULE IN NORTH AFRICA

The coastal tract of North Africa is filled—in Gibbon's orotund phrase —"with frequent monuments of Roman art and magnificence." [4] Nowhere, indeed, in Africa were there to be found, at least until the second half of the nineteenth century, such imposing memorials to European colonialism as in the lands of Barbary. Yet these spectacular and time-resisting structures—amphitheater, triumphal arch, or pillared forum —were not for the most part built by Latin hands but by Romanized Africans of Berber or Punic origin. Italy itself suffered in imperial times from a serious shortage of population, and most of the men of Roman stock who went to North Africa were not settlers but officials, businessmen, or absentee landlords visiting their estates.

That this infusion of new blood should have been so modest makes all the more remarkable the changes that took place. Urbanization was vigorously promoted, with the result that about half the population of the Roman provinces of North Africa is reckoned to have lived in towns, no less than five hundred of which have been counted. A massive advance occurred in the economic development of the territory with the construction of roads and irrigation works, the draining of marshes, the clearing of bush, and the establishment of plantations. North Africa, once in Horace's phrase "the arid nurse of lions," became one of the granaries of the Empire, an exporter of corn and of olive oil, a noted exporter too of wild animals to figure in the ghastly holocausts of the Colosseum, staged by the emperors to appease the brutalized populace of the imperial city. Flourishing trade and agriculture made the North African provinces among the most prosperous in the Roman Empire and supported a rich urban culture. Africa produced some of the most remarkable men of the later Roman Empire: Septimius Severus, one of the most able and energetic of emperors; Apuleius, a writer of encyclopedic genius, now chiefly renowned for his entertaining satire, *The Golden Ass;* Tertullian, a fiery apologist of the early Church, who "retained beneath the Christian veneer the passions, the intransigence and the indiscipline so typical of the Berber people"; [5] greatest of all perhaps, Augustine of Hippo, saint, theologian, autobiographer, administrator, and resolute defender of the established Church.

Looking at the monuments and thinking of the great men, it is easy to overestimate the extent of the Roman achievement. It suffered from two fatal limitations. The Romans never attempted to conquer the whole of the Maghrib. Most of modern Morocco, western Algeria, and Libya lay beyond their grasp. Indeed, from the fourth century onward the area under Roman and later Vandal and Byzantine rule was largely confined to the northern half of modern Tunisia. The Berbers living beyond the *limes* (the frontier zone of Roman territory) constantly threatened the colony with their raids, and the meager chronicles of Roman Africa—most of our information about the territory comes from the rich horde of inscriptions and archeological sites—present an almost unbroken series of native "revolts."

These disturbances beyond the *limes*—comparable perhaps to the Northwest Frontier of India in the days of the British Raj—had their counterpart in acute tensions within imperial territories. There was a sharp contrast between the opulence of the landed aristocracy of mixed Roman, Punic, or Berber descent and the miserable living conditions of the exclusively Berber rural proletariat, and this contrast was accentuated by differences of language and culture. In the fourth century A.D. after the Christian faith had come to be widely accepted in North Africa, these social tensions took the form of a violent religious controversy between the leaders of the established Church and the followers of Donatus. The immediate cause of the dispute was a matter of church discipline: the ecclesiastical Establishment seemed in the eyes of the Donatists too easygoing in accepting back into the fold those Christians who had renounced their religion in periods of persecution, when other Christians had suffered martyrdom for their faith. In 411 half of the nine hundred bishops were reckoned to be Donatists, and the schismatics were strengthened by their close association with a movement of agrarian revolt whose adherents were known as Circumcellions, those who prowl "around farms." The conflict between the Donatists and the Circumcellions on the one hand and the imperial authorities of the established Church and the landed aristocracy on the other was savage and long drawn-out. The forces of the Establishment could gain no more than ephemeral victories, and the harshness of their methods only made the grandiose imperial structure appear the more oppressive to the mass of the people.

VANDALS, BYZANTINES, AND ARABS

In 429 the Vandal horde, eighty thousand strong, whose movements can be traced back to the Baltic in the first century A.D., crossed from Spain into Barbary and established itself in Africa Proconsularis (northern Tunisia), the richest of the Roman provinces, as a conquering minority. Genseric (d. 474), the leader of the migration, transformed his African dominion into one of the most powerful states of the Mediterranean, occupied the Balearics, Corsica, Sardinia, and Sicily and raided with his fleets the coasts of Greece and southern Italy. But Genseric's successors were less able men, their supporters were corrupted by a life of ease on the confiscated estates of the Romanized aristocracy, and the regime collapsed completely before a sea-borne invasion launched by the Byzantine Emperor Justinian in 535.

The Vandals could be overcome with relative ease; the Berbers presented the Byzantines with a far more formidable enemy. In the past two centuries a development of revolutionary significance had taken place among the Berber tribes of Tripolitania and southern Tunisia: they had acquired camels in large numbers. The introduction of the camel into North Africa is a subject as obscure as it is important. The animal was probably known in Egypt in the sixth century B.C.; it is first mentioned in North Africa in an account of Caesar's campaign in 46 B.C., but there is no evidence of camels being used in any numbers until the fourth century A.D. No really satisfactory explanation has yet been put forward to account for the slow spread and tardy adoption of so useful an animal. Those Berber tribes which eventually acquired large numbers of camels presented the foreign masters of the Maghrib with some of their most formidable opponents. Meanwhile, other Berber tribes living on the border of the Romanized territory had taken advantage of the disorders which accompanied the Vandal invasion to assert their independence. Consequently, the Byzantines were only able to impose their authority on the reconquered territory by subjecting it to a stringent military occupation.

In 647 the Arabs launched their first plundering expedition against

North Africa. They had conquered the richest lands of the Middle East in less than a decade; North Africa, the Far West of the Muslim world, was only occupied—and even then not fully subdued—after seventy years of hard fighting, not against the Byzantines, who were swept aside with relative ease, but against the Berbers, some of whose tribes resisted the invaders with ferocious determination.

In the early centuries of Islam the Maghrib represented, as Bernard Lewis has pointed out, "a colonial frontier," to which men looked as Europeans from the sixteenth century onward looked to the Americas. "At first it was the still unconquered West of Islam, offering the alternatives, equally seductive to different minds, of booty or martyrdom. Then, as the West was conquered and colonized, it became the land of hope and opportunity, where fortunes could be made, and where, in the freer spirit of the frontier, the persecuted and the unfortunate might hope to find a home and a refuge." [6]

The Muslim invaders made a far more profound impact on the Berber population than Rome and Christianity had ever done; they transformed the cultural orientation of Barbary by turning its face from the Latin West to the Arab East. Not that the process of de-Romanization was completed within a generation or two. Christian bishoprics and the Latin language survived in parts of the Maghrib until as late as the twelfth century. But already by the eighth century a majority of the Berbers appear to have adopted Islam. Two major episodes from this period of North African history reveal the extent of the transformation that had already taken place.

In 711 a Muslim army invaded Spain, overthrew the Visigoth kingdom, and within twenty years conquered the greater part of the Peninsula; it was an army composed largely of Berber troops, commanded in the initial stages not by an Arab but by a Berber general in the service of the Umayyad caliph of Damascus. The Berber soldiers who fought in Spain and raided France till checked at the battle of Poitiers (732) recall the armies of Hannibal. The second indication of the leavening power of Islam presents an analogy with a more recent period of Berber history. When in the eighth century the Berbers continued their struggle against Arab despotism, they took as their ideology a schismatic form of Islam, a Muslim Donatism, one might say, known as Kharijism.

The original Kharijites had been followers of the fourth caliph, Ali (656–61), who resented their leader's decision to negotiate with his political opponents rather than submitting the dispute to the will of God and the chance of battle. Developing into a revolutionary sect with their stronghold in Iraq, the Kharijites stressed certain political and social ideals, notably egalitarianism, puritanism, and nonconformity, that were peculiarly congenial to the Berber temperament. Little wonder then that Kharijite agents should receive a ready welcome in many parts of the Maghrib.

By the ninth century the political transformation of Barbary since Byzantine times was symbolized by three new cities, Kairwan, Fez, and Tahert, which had been founded since the collapse of Byzantine rule. Kairwan was planted in the plains of central Tunisia by the Arab invaders in 670; it was intended, in the words of its founder, the general Uqba ibn Nafi, "to serve as an armed stronghold for Islam until the end of time." In the eighth century Kairwan was the administrative center of the Arab empire in the Maghrib, in the ninth the principal city of the Aghlabids, an Arab dynasty founded by an Abbasid governor of Ifrikiya (the medieval Arab name for Tunisia, the Roman Africa). Fez, which occupied a highly favorable position in the plains of northern Morocco, was founded by Idris I, an Arab refugee of distinguished ancestry, at the end of the eighth century. Almost from the start Fez appeared as the principal city of the western Maghrib, and the Idrisid state, though it covered only a modest extent of territory, served as a model for later Muslim dynasties in Morocco. In the ninth century Tahert was the principal city of the central Maghrib, the capital of a state founded in 761 by ibn Rustan, a Kharijite of noble Persian ancestry. Lying amid the high steppes, it enjoyed the support of many Berber groups, from the peasantry of the Aurès and the Djebel Nefousa (south of Tripoli) to the nomadic Zenata of the steppe and served as a highly congenial haven for the radicals of Kharijite persuasion of the Middle East.

With their palaces and their fortresses, their mosques and their bazaars the major Muslim urban foundations were designed to serve a fourfold purpose as administrative capital, garrison headquarters, religious center, and commercial entrepôt. Since the population was largely of alien origin, it was naturally somewhat divorced from the life of the Berber countryside, but it maintained close connections with the outside world. Fez and Kairwan in particular developed into centers of major importance in the intellectual life of the world of Islam. ("What are the citizens talking about these days?" a ninth-century traveler asked on arriving in Kairwan. "Of the names and attributes of God" was the reply.) From the cities a knowledge of Islam spread out among the Berber masses, and with the new religion went inevitably the language of its holy book. But in these early centuries of Islam a knowledge of Arabic must have been as rare among the Berber as it is today among the Muslim Hausa of Northern Nigeria. The first Arab invasion of the seventh and eighth centuries brought about the Arabization of the towns of Barbary;

the Arabization of the countryside was the consequence of a second invasion that did not occur until nearly four centuries after the first.

❋ THE SAHARA IN CLASSICAL AND EARLY MUSLIM TIMES

The influx of so many foreigners into the remotest parts of the Maghrib in the first two centuries of the Muslim era had a profound effect on the economic development not only of the lands of Barbary but also of the Sahara. Not that the great desert had ever been completely isolated in Punic or Roman times from the Mediterranean world, for there is documentary evidence that two areas at least of the Sahara maintained contact with the people of the coast.

The more important of these areas was the Fezzan, inhabited by the Garamantes, a people of basically Berber stock. The Garamantes are first mentioned by Herodotus in the fifth century B.C. Even at this early date they must have maintained a vigorous intercourse with the coast and the Nile Valley, for they possessed chariots drawn by horses, vehicles that could only have reached them from Egypt or the great cities of Cyrenaica. After a period of initial hostility, the Romans established friendly relations with the Garamantes; a community of Roman traders settled in the Fezzan in the third century A.D., and a flourishing commerce was maintained with the coastal cities of Tripolitania. The exact nature of Garamantian exports remains something of a mystery: classical authors refer only to a precious stone, the "carbuncle," but it has been surmised that the Garamantes also sent slaves and ivory to the coast. Of the contacts established by the Garamantes with the countries to their south three curious pieces of information are available. Herodotus states that the Garamantes used their chariots to chase "the cave-dwelling Ethiopians," usually identified as the Tebu of Tibesti. Ptolemy, the geographer writing in the second century A.D., records a Garamantian expedition to the unidentified country of Agisymba, "where rhinoceroses abound," four months' journey from the Fezzan. Finally, the French archeologist Henri Lhote has found rock engravings of chariots along a route leading from the Fezzan through the Ahaggar massif to the Niger bend. From information such as this one can hardly deduce the existence of a flourishing trans-Saharan trade in classical times.

The second area of commercial importance was the northwestern corner of the desert. According to Herodotus the Carthaginians traded for gold on the coast of southern Morocco, while a famous Carthaginian document, the *Periplus* of Hanno, describes an elaborate expedition down the African coast. (Many scholars have interpreted this controversial document as proving that the Carthaginians reached Sierra Leone and even Cameroun, but the difficulties of a maritime expedition in boats propelled by oars down the barren Saharan coast makes it extremely unlikely that the Carthaginians ever got beyond southern Morocco.) The gold obtained by the Carthaginians probably came from the Senegal area; and another series of rock engravings of chariots provides some evidence of an early route across the western Sahara. But this early gold trade must have been extremely spasmodic, for it does not appear to have been of much importance in Roman times.

If the Sahara is thought of as a sea—an analogy which makes the history of the desert a little less strange—then the oases are its island bases, camels its ships, the nomadic tribes its mariners, pilots, and pirates, and the merchants of the Maghrib the supercargoes and capitalists of the desert trade. As no work has yet been done on the archeology of the oases outside the Fezzan, it is impossible to say when they first became human settlements. But some are clearly of great antiquity. Augila in southern Cyrenaica is mentioned by Herodotus as being famous for its dates. Ghadames possessed for a time a Roman garrison. In the second century A.D. Jews, fleeing persecution in Cyrenaica, are said to have settled in Tuat and to have introduced the *foggara,* an ingenious system of oasis irrigation. Sijilmassa, the main terminus for the trans-Saharan trade in southern Morocco, was founded in the eighth century. Awdaghast in southeastern Mauritania may have been founded even earlier; by the eleventh century it had grown into a flourishing town with a large and wealthy population which included Berbers from every part of the Maghrib and a few merchants from the other major cities of Islam.

The camel would seem to have been introduced into the central and western Sahara in the first five hundred years of the Christian era. It will probably never be possible to trace the stages of its diffusion, but there is no doubt that its arrival represented a development as revolutionary in its way as the replacement of the stagecoach by the railroad. In the precameline era men had used both horses and pack oxen in the Sahara. Neither of these animals fell completely out of use, but the camel with its extraordinary capacity for traveling long distances with little or no water, was far better adapted for the strenuous conditions of the desert. The camel made possible the establishment of regular trading caravans across the Sahara. It also increased the insecurity of desert life by enabling the strong to prey more effectively on the weak and thus gradually transforming the political patterns of the Sahara.

By the beginning of the Muslim era there were three great groups of Berber nomads established in the desert. The Zenata dominated the northern Sahara, the Sanhaja, whose name survives in a slightly different form in Senegal, were masters of most of modern Mauritania, while the ancestors of the Tuareg lived in the massifs, Ahaggar and Air, of the central Sahara. Both Tuareg and Sanhaja were distinguished by the wearing of a face veil, the *litham*. The nomadic tribes profited from the development of the trans-Saharan trade, finding employment as guides or escorts, levying tolls on passing caravans, or holding them to ransom by threats of violence.

The Arabs showed an early interest in the Sahara. In 666 Uqba ibn Nafi raided the Fezzan; in 734 an expedition was sent against Ghana from Sus in the western Maghrib and returned with great booty in slaves and gold. These commodities and other products of the Sudan, such as ivory or gum (used in Andalusia to give a luster to silk), were well adapted for transport across the desert and provided Maghribi merchants with a handsome profit. The trade appears to have developed rapidly. By the ninth century three major trade routes were in operation: from Fezzan to Kanem north of Lake Chad, from the central Maghrib to Gao on the Niger bend, and from the western Maghrib to Ghana. The complete absence of statistics makes it impossible to estimate the exact importance of the trans-Saharan trade in the economy of the medieval Maghrib, but it was clearly one of the foundations of the region's prosperity.

✿ THE MEDIEVAL MAGHRIB

For more than two hundred years after the Arab invasion, the major dynasties of the Maghrib were created by aliens and derived a large measure of their support from immigrants of eastern origin, but the end of the ninth century saw the opening of a period of more than half a millennium, when for the first time in their history the Berbers were able to create and maintain really substantial states of their own.

The period began with the overthrow of the Aghlabids of Ifrikiya by the Kotama, a Berber tribe from Kabylia, who were incited to invade the rich country to their east by a certain Abu Abdallah, the agent of yet another Muslim sect, the Ismaili or Fatimid Shia. Once in control of Ifrikyia Abu Abdallah invited his master, Ubaid Allah, who was regarded as the Mahdi, the "Rightly Guided One," to come from Syria and enter into his kingdom. For Ubaid Allah and his successors in the Fatimid dynasty the Maghrib was only a base for the conquest of the central lands of the Abbasid caliphate. In 969 the Fatimids succeeded with the aid of a Berber army in conquering Egypt and transferred their capital from Mahdiya, the capital they had founded on the coast of central Tunisia, to Cairo.

During the half century between their occupation of Ifrikiya and their conquest of Egypt, the Fatimids made their influence felt far to the west, destroying Tahert and dominating Fez. Only one power was strong enough to resist them, the Umayyads of Cordoba in southern Spain. The Umayyad dynasty had been founded in 756 by Abd ar-Rahman, a refugee prince who managed to escape from the clutches of the Abbasids; he made his way to Spain and ousted the Abbasid governor of Andalusia. To weld into a unified state the diverse groups, Arabs, Berbers, Jews, Spanish Muslims, and Arabic-speaking Christians (Mozarabs), was a formidable test of statesmanship, and revolts against the dynasty were frequent. But by the tenth century the Umayyad caliphs—Abd ar-Rahman III assumed the supreme title in 929—appeared to have established a firm grip on the country. Andalusia, which in Roman times had provided the empire with some of its greatest men, developed under Muslim rule into one of the richest and most cultured countries of the Mediterranean.

Never, indeed, were the Christian states of Western Europe made so conscious of Muslim power as in the last two centuries of the first millennium A.D. Sicily was occupied by the Aghlabids in the ninth century and most of southern Italy was for many years exposed to sudden devastating raids by Muslim freebooters. Meanwhile, almost the entire Iberian peninsula was either in Muslim hands or ravaged by plundering expeditions. So great was Muslim mastery of the western half of the Mediterranean that in ibn Khaldun's words "the Christians could not so much as float a plank on it."

The eleventh century brought a series of dramatic changes that completely transformed the situation in Andalusia, in Ifrikiya, and in the western Maghrib. In Andalusia the Umayyad caliphate fell from its state of greatest splendor into complete collapse in the space of thirty years. Twenty-six new-sprung Muslim principalities divided among themselves the territory of the caliphate; but their weakness and disunity presented the rulers of the petty Christian kingdoms to the north with an ideal opportunity to begin the long struggle of the *reconquista*. The anarchy that afflicted Andalusia led "thousands of Muslims of all classes and professions" to seek refuge in the western Maghrib with the result, as a contemporary historian noted, that "agriculture was developed by newly arrived farmers, springs were discovered and used for irrigation; trees were planted; watermills and other useful machinery constructed." [7]

Ifrikiya, too, was on the verge of disaster. After the removal of the center of Fatimid power to Egypt, the control of Ifrikiya had been vested in a dynasty of hereditary governors, the Zirids, a family of Sanhaja Berber origin. Under the Zirids Ifrikiya enjoyed a state of prosperity such as it had not known since the most fruitful period of Roman rule in the third century A.D. Inevitably, the Zirid governors thought of independence, but in 1042 when the break with Cairo became final the Fatimid caliph, al-Mustansir, had it in his power to exert a terrible vengeance—he directed toward the Maghrib two large tribes of Bedouin Arabs, the Banu Hilal and the Banu Sulaim, whose depredations were already causing him trouble in Upper Egypt.

For the Berbers of the Maghrib the Bedouin invasion brought consequences no less momentous than the original Arab conquest. The prosperity of Ifrikiya was destroyed. The Bedouins, according to ibn Khaldun, pulled down houses when they wanted stones on which to prop their cooking pots and cut up roof timbers for tent pegs. Large areas of the eastern and central Maghrib, rendered fertile and prosperous by a thousand years of careful farming, were transformed within a few generations into desolate steppe. Many towns and villages disappeared completely. The Zirids were forced back to the coast. Another rival Sanhaja dynasty, the Hammadids, abandoned their capital, Qalaa, in the plains of the central Maghrib and retreated to Bougie, which they made into a center of vigorous maritime activity. The Bedouin influence affected the culture of Barbary as profoundly as its politics and its economy. Many Berbers, especially the nomadic tribes, adopted the Arabic language, until in time Berber became the language of a minority, being spoken today for the most part only in the remoter mountain districts and by the Tuareg of the central Sahara.

While the Arab nomads were pouring over Ifrikiya, another group of nomads, the Sanhaja Berber of the western Sahara, were establishing a massive empire in the western Maghrib. This movement from an unusual direction—never before had the Saharan nomads exerted a decisive influence on the Maghrib—had its origin in the preaching of a single Muslim divine, a certain ibn Yasin, who came from the western Maghrib. He had been invited by a Sanhaja chief returning from the Meccan pilgrimage, to settle in the camps of the nomads and teach them the proper observance of the faith. Finding his teaching little regarded by the impious men of the desert, ibn Yasin withdrew to an island probably off the Mauritanian coast, where he established a *ribat,* a fortified "fraternity center" to which he attracted a small band of devotees. As their number increased, he was able to launch his strictly disciplined *murabitun,* "men of the ribat" or Almoravids in a jihad, first against the recalcitrant Sanhaja tribes, then, with thousands of camel men avid for booty placing themselves under his banner, against the Sanhaja confederation's most powerful neighbors, the Zenata to the north and Ghana to the south.

The Almoravids were astonishingly successful. Within the space of thirty years (1050–80) they overran all the petty principalities of the western Maghrib and occupied for a time much of the territory of Ghana.

Reluctantly, the effete and sophisticated Muslim rulers of Andalusia decided to invite the rough puritanical warriors of the desert to deliver them from their Christian assailants. The Almoravids under their great amir, ibn Tashfin, won a decisive victory over the Christians at Zallaqa in 1086, and went on to bring all the petty Muslim states under their control. When ibn Tashfin died in 1107 the Almoravid dominion embraced southern Spain, Morocco, and western Algeria. But as ibn Khaldun observed, "conquest tends to be followed by luxury and softening," and the wide-flung empire collapsed as rapidly as it had grown.

But the Almoravids' achievement was not entirely ephemeral. For the first time in history the tribes of the western Maghrib had been forced to obey a single ruler. Thus, the concept of Moroccan unity was born. It was appropriate that the country should derive its very name Morocco from the great new city Marrakesh, founded by the Almoravids as their capital in 1062.

The Almoravids were overthrown by a remarkable movement not altogether dissimilar from their own. Ibn Tumart, a divine from one of the Berber tribes of the Atlas, who preached a more spiritual religion than the formal orthodoxy encouraged by the Almoravids, gathered a small band of disciples around him—known as *al-Muwahiddun* (Almohads), "Unitarians"—and gained widespread notoriety for his attacks on the "immorality" of the governing classes. Persecuted by the Almoravids but regarded by his followers as the Mahdi, ibn Tumart fell back on his kinsmen in the Atlas and succeeded before his death in 1130 in creating a political structure strong enough to hold together many of the mountain tribes who felt a natural hostility to the dominant Sanhaja.

Abd al-Mumin, the Mahdi's favorite disciple and successor (*khalifa*), proved an outstanding leader. Bringing his followers down into the plains, he overthrew the power of the Almoravids and extended his own northward into Andalusia and eastward over Ifrikiya. Under Abd al-Mumin and his two immediate successors the Almohads maintained their sway over the entire Maghrib. The latter half of the twelfth century was, indeed, Barbary's finest hour. The great Almohad sovereigns were not only able soldiers and administrators but men of great intellectual stature, who entertained philosophers and encouraged architects. Andalusian culture reached its apogee in their reigns, when the great philosopher ibn Rushd (Averroës) served as court physician and the Kutubia mosque in Marrakesh and the Giralda tower in Seville were the work of the same Andalusian architect.

The collapse of the Almohads in the first half of the thirteenth century was accompanied by the loss to the Christians of most of Andalusia except for Granada and by the emergence of three new dynasties in the

Maghrib. The Hafsids of Tunis, originally governors of Ifrikiya under the Almohads, maintained an uneasy hold on the eastern Maghrib for three centuries. The Abd al-Wadids, a dynasty drawn from the nomadic Zenata, were based on Tlemcen, but found it difficult to control more than a small part of the central Maghrib. The Merinids, also of Zenata origin, with their capital at Fez, ruled most of Morocco. These three dynasties regarded themselves as successors of the Almohads, yet lacked a military base large enough to serve as the foundation for a great empire. In comparison with the great age of the Berber empire, the later Middle Ages in the Maghrib may seem to present "a long stagnation and a slow decadence," [8] but the three Berber kingdoms provided for the areas they controlled substantial periods of stability and prosperity.

Meanwhile, the Bedouin Arabs strengthened their hold on the plains of the Maghrib. Some of their tribes had been forced by the Almohad Abd al-Mumin to settle in the vicinity of Marrakesh; thus, the Bedouin were brought to the Atlantic coast. In the central Maghrib the Berber Zenata were gradually transformed into tribes which spoke Arabic and claimed an Arabic ancestry. A similar development took place among the Sanhaja of the western Sahara, as a result of contact with the Maaqil, a branch of the Banu Hilal. As the Bedouin tribes spread over the Atlantic plains, the western Maghrib found itself suffering the same fate as its neighbors. Indeed, throughout the entire Maghrib the fifteenth century was a time of mounting anarchy, for which the nomads were largely responsible.

In the later Middle Ages Islam in the Maghrib came to acquire certain marked local characteristics. The heresies of the earlier period disappeared before a strict observance of the orthodox faith. At the same time a vigorous cult of saints, which had some connection with the ancient cult of nature spirits, developed. Religious fraternities whose rites had a strong mystical appeal attracted many of the unsophisticated Berber of the countryside. And holy men who distinguished themselves by their learning (marabouts) or who could claim descent from the Prophet (*sharif,* Maghribi plural *shorfa*) were regarded as possessing *baraka,* "the charismatic power of emitting blessing and producing well-being" [9] and attracted many followers.

✻ CHRISTIANS, TURKS, AND MOORS

In 1415 the Portuguese occupied the port of Ceuta on the Moroccan side of the Straits of Gibraltar. It was by no means the first time since the collapse of Byzantine rule that the Christians had established themselves on the coast of the Maghrib. In the middle of the twelfth century the Normans, who had wrested Sicily from the Arabs in the previous century, captured most of the ports between Tripoli and Tunis but held them little more than a decade. The Portuguese, on the other hand, never let go of their grip on Ceuta; the first of their overseas possessions, its capture and retention marked not only an important stage in the shift of the balance of power between Muslims and Christians in the western Mediterranean but also the beginning of Western European expansion into a wider world.

Between 1460 and 1520 the Portuguese occupied almost the entire coast of Morocco as far south as Agadir and their raiding parties reached to the walls of Marrakesh. At the same time the Spaniards, who had over-run Granada in 1492, carried the war across the sea and took most of the ports of the central Maghrib.

The Christian assault on Muslim territory provided the circumstances that enabled a new dynasty to come to the fore in Morocco and allowed the Ottoman Turks to intervene in the central and eastern Maghrib. The Merinids and their successors, the Wattasids, were quite unable to deal with the Portuguese menace in Morocco, but an Arab family of sharifian origin, the Saadians, coming from the extreme south of the country, took the lead in opposing the Portuguese, drove them from most of their strongholds, and established themselves as rulers of Morocco. Ahmad al-Mansur, the greatest of Saadian sultans, took his honorific title, "the Victorious," from the battle of Alcazar at which in 1578 a Portuguese expeditionary force was decisively defeated, with Sebastian, the young king of Portugal, among the slain. The twenty-five years of al-Mansur's reign (1578–1603) brought a remarkable revival of Moroccan prosperity and prestige. The sultan acted on a larger stage than most Moroccan rulers; he established close commercial and diplomatic ties with Elizabeth of England, who saw in him a valuable ally against Spain; he also sent an army across the desert which utterly overwhelmed the Negroid Songhai Empire, founded a Moroccan protectorate on the banks of the Niger, and sent back so much gold that the sultan was able to assume a new title, al-Dhabi, "the Golden."

Meanwhile, the coastal cities of the central Maghrib had found an unexpected champion against the Spaniards in two Muslim corsairs from the Aegean, Aruj and Khair ad-Din, nicknamed Barbarossa, "Redbeard." In 1516 the people of Algiers, a port of secondary importance, asked Aruj and his followers to assist them against the Spaniards. Their liberators made themselves masters of the town and later strengthened their position by accepting the overlordship of the Ottoman sultan. From Algiers the rule of the *beylerbeys,* the Turkish governors, spread westward to Tlemcen, southward to the edges of the Sahara, and eastward to Tunis and Tripoli. Throughout the sixteenth century with Turks and

Spaniards fighting for naval supremacy in the central Mediterranean, Algiers occupied a position of immense strategic importance.

In the seventeenth century the three "regencies" of Algiers, Tunis, and Tripoli became virtually independent states. Their internal politics were monotonously violent; the political history of Algiers, where the turbulent Turkish soldiery acquired the power to elect their own leaders, has been described as "one long tale of plots, riots, and massacre," and much the same could be said of Tunis and of Tripoli until these two regencies saw the emergence of hereditary dynasties of their own, the Husainid beys and the Karamanli pashas, in the early eighteenth century. The governing minority derived most of its wealth from the sea, for this was the great age of the "Barbary pirates." Piracy was nothing new, of course, in the Mediterranean, and every maritime people had engaged in it. But in the seventeenth century it provided the basis of the economy not of small independent communities but of substantial states. Most of the corsair captains were neither Turks nor Berbers but renegade Europeans from Calabria or Sicily, where in other circumstances their talents might have led them to find employment as bandit chiefs. So successful were their depredations that Algiers grew into an opulent city with a population of one hundred thirty thousand people, of whom thirty thousand were Christian slaves.

After the death of al-Mansur in 1603 Morocco fell into a state of complete anarchy which lasted until order was restored in the 1660's by a new dynasty, founded by the Alawites, a sharifian family from the Tafilet, a remote district south of the Atlas. The second Alawite sultan, Mulay Ismail, who ruled from 1672 to 1727, became, at least in European eyes, the most notorious of Morocco's rulers. The builder of a palace at Meknes intended to equal Versailles, the sire according to legend of more than a thousand children, a monster of cruelty in his treatment of his slaves and subjects, he was also an extremely able ruler who kept a tight hold on the country and based his power on a standing army of Negro slaves, many of whom were obtained in military expeditions that took the Moroccans as far south as Senegal. But Mulay Ismail was no more successful than al-Mansur in guaranteeing order after his death. And though after a generation of anarchy the later Alawite rulers achieved a measure of stability, Morocco entered the nineteenth century as a deeply divided country—the sultans lacking the power to dominate the Berber communities of the Atlas—with a stagnant economy and an intense distrust of the outside world.

Algiers too presented irrefutable evidence of decline. The population of the city had shrunk to thirty thousand and the number of European captives to less than a thousand by the end of the eighteenth century. The improved efficiency of European navies produced so sharp a reduction in the profits of privateering that the Turks turned to squeezing what they could out of their own hinterland. Yet there were many areas that escaped their control completely, and their garrisons in the main towns were faced with constant revolts. In the regency of Algiers the Turks always remained an alien class. In Tunis, on the other hand, they were absorbed as so many other foreign invaders had been, and the Husainid beys were gradually able to assume the character of national rulers.

In the eighteenth century the European powers had not yet acquired sufficient strength to impose their will on the states of the Maghrib. Indeed, the rulers of these states had far more to fear from internal dissension or from the activities of their own Muslim neighbors—the Algerians, for example, occupied Tunis in 1756 and executed the ruling bey, while the Algerian-Moroccan frontier was an area of constant tension— than from the ambitions of England, France, or Spain. By the middle of the nineteenth century the situation was to acquire quite a different complexion.

✺ TRADE IN NORTHWEST AFRICA

Berber culture, the Muslim religion, and Arab nomadism combined to give Northwest Africa a certain unity. Another unifying theme was provided by the development of trade. It was a theme with a long and complex history, for commercial relations in the region fall into three distinct but interconnected compartments: maritime, internal, and trans-Saharan.

Trade with foreigners coming across the sea to the coasts of Barbary can be traced back to the Phoenician settlements of the first millennium B.C. From Carthaginian times Barbary's exports of local origin (as distinct from reexported goods brought from the Sudan) consisted mainly of agricultural or pastoral produce—corn, dates, cattle, wool—or simply processed commodities such as olive oil or leather. Corn, a major export, was particularly subject to the vagaries of the climate, a poor harvest following a failure of the rains naturally leading to a drastic fall in exports. Even more disruptive, however, was the impact of political changes. The Arab conquest of the Maghrib shattered the economic unity of the Mediterranean. Two hundred years elapsed before Italian traders began to do substantial business in North African ports, first Amalfi, then Pisa, and finally Genoa playing the most active commercial role in the early Middle Ages.

By the thirteenth century European merchants were to be found in most of the ports of the Maghrib. In the main ports they possessed their own trading establishments (*funduq*), and their position was guaranteed by commercial treaties. Many of the goods they obtained in exchange for manufactured products—cloth, arms, beads, and so on—were of Sudanese origin. Gold, carried across the Sahara, was a particularly important item of exchange; passing from Muslim into Christian hands it provided a major stimulant for the economy of the increasingly prosperous trading republics of northern Italy. In the fourteenth century traders from Florence, Venice, Marseilles, Aragon, and Castile joined in the North African trade. Two hundred years later the English and the Dutch began to establish commercial relations with the Maghrib, particularly with Morocco.

By 1600, however, the vast expansion that had taken place in the commerce of Western Europe made North Africa an area of less interest to European traders than it had been in the Middle Ages. Gold in particular could now be obtained far more easily by trade on the coast of West Africa. The obstruction which European merchants had to face in the Maghrib also discouraged commerce. And so, though the Maghrib could still offer some commodities of value, its contribution to the international economy was very modest. In the middle of the nineteenth century Great Britain, then the greatest trading nation in the world, was obtaining no more than 1 percent of its imports from the Maghrib.

The internal trade of the Maghrib was based on the large towns, with Jewish traders playing a particularly important part in the commerce. The main towns of the interior—Fez, Marrakesh, Tlemcen, Constantine, and Kairwan—were linked by well-trodden paths both to the coast and to one another. The major towns had their own craft industries and acted as distribution centers for goods brought from Europe and the Sudan. One factor of some importance in the internal commerce of the Maghrib was the annual pilgrimage to Mecca, for the pilgrims in their large caravans traveled across the length of North Africa, doing business as they went.

The trans-Saharan trade was intimately linked with the internal trade of the Maghrib. By the later Middle Ages the desert was covered by an elaborate network of routes. (One important route, however, linking Wadai with Cyrenaica by way of the lonely oasis of Kufra did not come into use until the nineteenth century.) Traffic on these routes was subject to the vicissitudes of local politics in the Sahara and the Sudan. The absence of any commercial statistics makes it quite impossible to chart the fluctuations of Saharan trade up to 1850. After 1850 the information obtained by European travelers and consuls provides a much more precise picture. It is clear that by the middle of the nineteenth century the trade in gold was no longer of much importance. But the trade in slaves was still flourishing: about ten thousand slaves reached North Africa every year from the Sudan. And Sudanese ostrich feathers began in the late 1850's to find such a good market in Europe, where they satisfied the needs of contemporary haute couture, that the entire trans-Saharan trade experienced a period of marked prosperity in the decades that preceded its final collapse.

In exchange for these and other products the caravans brought to the Sudan a great variety of goods, mostly of North African or European manufacture, cottons and silks, mirrors and glassware, needles, sword blades, and paper. Such items might be regarded as luxuries, but some of the caravans also carried a commodity that was a necessity for the people of the Sudan. Salt is essential for physical well-being in tropical climates. But the Western Sudan suffered from a marked shortage of salt deposits. The Sahara, on the other hand, produced excellent salt, with major deposits at Idjil, Taghaza, Taodeni, and Kawar. Since these deposits lay in mid-desert, the Saharan nomads were well placed to control them. They exchanged the salt for the agricultural produce of the Sudan. In much the same way the nomads of the northern Sahara bartered dates, the main produce of the oases, for corn with the settled population of the Maghrib.

🌾 NORTHWEST AFRICA IN THE 1850'S

In the middle of the nineteenth century many of the inhabitants of Northwest Africa—the citizens of Fez or Kairwan, the Berbers in their mountain villages, the nomads of the Sahara—followed a pattern of living that seemed not to have changed for hundreds of years. But already by 1850 it was apparent that the region was once again coming under severe external pressure of a kind as revolutionary in its impact as the Roman conquest or the Arab invasions had been.

The decisive date was 1830, when the French launched an expedition against Algiers. The pretext for the attack was trivial; the basic consideration was the desire of the Bourbon monarchy to restore its waning prestige through a successful military expedition. Algiers fell easily—so too did the Bourbon monarchy in the revolution of July 1830. But the new regime of Louis Philippe found it impossible to extricate itself from the adventure and was drawn on by Berber and Arab resistance into a war of total conquest, the largest and most destructive military campaign in the annals of modern European imperialism in Africa.

In 1835 the Ottoman Turks took advantage of the virtual collapse of the Karamanli dynasty to make themselves masters of Tripoli, Cyrenaica, and the Fezzan. Thenceforward, the former regency was kept strictly under the control of the government at Constantinople. Tunis, too, was still nominally a province of the Ottomans, and its rulers took the precaution of sending tribute to the Porte. It was undoubtedly the most prosperous of the Barbary States, at least until 1837, when a new bey, Ahmad, inspired by the example of Muhammad Ali of Egypt, embarked on the extravagant policy of trying to build up a modern army and navy, and so started his country down the slope that led to the disasters of bankruptcy.

Up to 1850 Morocco had proved the most successful of the states of North Africa in keeping the West at bay. In 1850 there were fewer than five hundred Europeans in Morocco, compared with twelve thousand Europeans in Tunis and more than a hundred thousand, excluding the army, in Algeria. The policy of the sultan of Morocco was similar to that of contemporary rulers of China and Japan: to keep Europeans confined to certain ports and impose stringent restrictions on all commercial relations with the outside world. But Morocco was even less well placed than the Far Eastern powers to ward off external pressures. Foreign businessmen, especially in such places as Manchester and Marseilles, were beginning to show an interest in the potential Moroccan market, and the Moroccans themselves were acquiring a taste for foreign products; imports of tea, for example, rose from thirty-five hundred kilograms in 1830 to twenty thousand in 1840. At the same time the French conquest of Algeria gave Morocco a powerful and dangerous European neighbor. In 1844 in a brief Franco-Moroccan war the Moroccans, who had provoked the French by the assistance they were giving to the Algerians, suffered their first major defeat at European hands.

Even in the remote Sahara there was some evidence of European penetration. In the years after 1815 a handful of British explorers sent out by their own government and one remarkable Frenchman, René Caillié, had brought back a mass of information on a part of the world until then completely unknown to Europeans. In the 1840's the British government established consulates at Ghadames and Murzuk, partly to keep a check on the slave trade, partly to investigate the possibilities of engaging in trans-Saharan trade. The consulates in themselves were of no great importance and they were only maintained for a few years, but their establishment was symptomatic of the rising tide of European activities. Well-informed Muslims were far from indifferent to what was happening, for news passes rapidly along the arteries of the world of Islam. So there were men in Timbuktu or Tuat or the Tafilet (not remote, outlandish places, as Europeans thought them, but centers of vigorous, commercial activity), who heard with foreboding the stories of European arms and European victories in Egypt (the French expedition of 1798), in Algeria, and even on the distant plains of Hindustan.

CHAPTER VII

West Africa

✿ GEOGRAPHY

West Africa is a region about two million square miles in extent. Clearly bounded to the west and south by the Atlantic Ocean, to the north its savanna plains merge gradually into the waterless wastes of the Sahara, while to the east the mountains of Cameroun and the shallow depression of Lake Chad serve as a conventional boundary, though these natural features are not formidable enough to act as a barrier to human movement. In West Africa, with greater reason than in some other regions, the historian must accustom himself to looking beyond conventional divisions, northward to the Sahara and the Maghrib, eastward to the lands of plain and forest that have been included in this study under the heading of "Equatorial Africa," still farther east to the valley of the Nile and the countries bordering the Red Sea.

In broad outline the geography of West Africa is remarkably simple, for the region may be divided into two belts of territory stretching from east to west, the savannas of the "geographical Sudan" and the forests of the Guinea coast.[1] The differences between the two belts are very striking, but they derive not so much from contrasts in relief as from variations in rainfall and in climate and vegetation. Compared with other parts of the continent most West African landscapes—dusty bush or claustrophobic forest—suffer from a certain monotony. There are some highland areas—the Jos Plateau of Northern Nigeria, for example, or the Futa Jallon of Guinea— but they cover comparatively small parts of the region and their mountains rarely exceed five thousand feet. Far more spectacular as natural features are the great rivers—Senegal, Gambia, Volta, and, above all, Niger with its extraordinary course, rising little more than two hundred miles from the sea, flowing northeastward to brush the fringes of the desert before completing its great bend by a southeasterly course across the savanna and the forest to the labyrinthine creeks and mangrove swamps of its long-mysterious delta.

The mountains have served as places of refuge, the rivers, though frequently barred by shallows or rapids, have assisted communications; but of far greater importance in its impact on historical development has been the nature of the region's rainfall. There are some coastal districts of West Africa that receive more than a hundred inches of rain a year. In general, in the forest areas rainfall is considerable, humidity intense, and the vegetation exuberant. Over most of the savanna belt rainfall is higher than is often imagined. The famous Nigerian city of Kano, for example, which lies in the northern savanna, receives on average more rain than does London. Thus, in spite of long rainless periods every year—four to five months in duration in the southern savanna and increasing steadily as one moves northward—most parts of the savanna receive sufficient rain to support a flourishing agriculture.

The savanna has another advantage. In the dry season, when many of its rivers lose all their water, it provides ideal conditions for traveling. Moreover, there is one part in the area of modern Togo and Dahomey where savanna country reaches to the sea. As for the forests of the Guinea coast, nowhere do they present a really formidable barrier, and there are no high mountains or deserts to restrict movement within the region. Thus, internal communications have been easier to maintain in West Africa than in any other region of the continent. In the development of its economy and in the evolution of the cultures of its peoples this has been of fundamental importance.

﷽ THE PEOPLES OF WEST AFRICA

At present very little is known of the history of West Africa before 1000 A.D. Accurate information about the remote past can only come from documentary material or from archeological research. Arab geographers of the eighth and ninth centuries provide—if one excludes certain debatable passages in classical authors—the earliest written records of West African history. As for archeology, there are no sites as spectacular as Luxor or Leptis, Olduvai or Zimbabwe; consequently, no outside attention has been paid to the region, and only within the past decade have two West African countries, Ghana and Nigeria, been able to afford to employ professional archeologists. The results of the first scientific excavations undertaken in West Africa are extremely promising and suggest that in time archeology should completely transform our picture of the dark centuries of the West African past. At present, however, archeology can do no more than throw a few brilliant flashes of light on certain areas of the past; it cannot provide an adequate framework for the region as a whole. In these circumstances the historian must turn to the less precise evidence provided by physical anthropology and linguistics to gain some

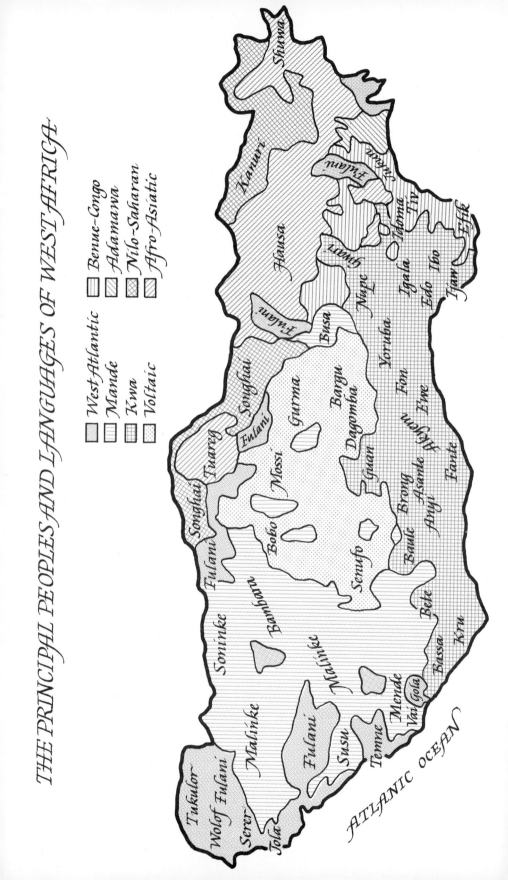

THE PRINCIPAL PEOPLES AND LANGUAGES OF WEST AFRICA

West Atlantic
Mande
Kwa
Voltaic
Benue-Congo
Adamawa
Nilo-Saharan
Afro-Asiatic

Shuwa
Kanuri
Fulani
Jukun
Tiv
Hausa
Gwari
Idoma
Igala
Edo
Ibo
Nupe
Ijaw
Efik
Busa
Yoruba
Songhai
Fulani
Bargu
Fon
Ewe
Tuareg
Songhai
Gurma
Dagomba
Anyi
Ashanti
Akwapin
Fante
Fulani
Mossi
Bobo
Guan
Brong
Baule
Soninke
Bambara
Senufo
Bete
Kru
Malinke
Bassa
Tukulor
Wolof
Fulani
Serer
Malinke
Fulani
Susu
Mende
Vai Gola
Jola
Temne

ATLANTIC OCEAN

insight into the history of West Africa before the beginning of the second millennium A.D.

Most West Africans are of Negroid stock, but the northern part of the region has received a considerable infusion of peoples of Caucasoid origin. For many centuries groups of desert pastoralists have been forced by increasing desiccation or by the pressure of more formidable neighbors to move farther south. Certain Tuareg tribes crossed the Niger in the region of its great bend in the eighteenth century and still retain their language and customs. Farther east some of the traditions of the Hausa of Northern Nigeria suggest that groups of Berber origin formed at one time a dominant minority in some areas. But the most remarkable example of the dispersal of people of Caucasoid stock in West Africa is afforded by the pastoral Fulani. Today, cattle Fulani are found in almost every part of the savanna from Senegal to Darfur. Their distinct physical features, particularly their olive skin and straight hair, and their pastoral way of life distinguish them sharply from their Negroid neighbors, yet their language, Fufulde, is closely related to the languages spoken by other people of Negroid stock in the Senegal area. It seems likely that the Fulani were once a group of desert nomads, possibly originally of Berber speech, who crossed the Senegal to pasture their cattle on the Ferlo plateau. Finding themselves cut off from their kinsmen by the Negroid communities occupying the fertile Senegal Valley, they gradually adopted the language of their new neighbors. As their herds increased, small groups of Fulani found themselves forced to move eastward and so initiated a series of largely peaceful migrations that continue to this day. Sometimes they were accompanied by their Negroid neighbors, also known as Fulani, for they spoke the same language as the pastoralists. These Negroid Fulani, agriculturists and town-dwellers for the most part, were to play a major role in the expansion of Islam in West Africa.

Linguistically, the pattern presented by West Africa is one of considerable complexity. Most West Africans speak languages of the Western Sudanic stock. But the northeastern part of the region is largely occupied by speakers of Chadic languages that form a branch of the Afro-Asiatic stock, and there are two important languages, Songhai and Kanuri, which have been classified as branches of Nilo-Saharan.

Western Sudanic is made up of six branches: West Atlantic, Mande, Voltaic, Kwa, Benue-Congo, and Adamawa. The differences between languages of the same branch are considerable, and in most cases it is reasonable to assume that people who speak distinct languages of the same branch, though they may originally be derived from a common ancestor, must have been living apart from one another for many hundreds, possibly some thousands of years. If one is to infer a common origin for all the speakers of Western Sudanic languages, then the original stock must have been in existence at a very remote period. Archeological research makes it clear that the West African savannas were inhabited from at least as early as Acheulian times. When men first began to move into the forests of the Guinea coast is not yet known, but the recent excavation of an important site at Akure in the forest area of Western Nigeria, from which more than half a million stone artifacts have been recovered, suggests considerable penetration fairly early, for the lower level of this site has been given a radio-carbon date of about 9000 B.C.[2]

The existence of a broad wedge formed by the speakers of the Chadic branch of Afro-Asiatic languages in the northeastern corner of the region suggests that this part must have received a stream of migration coming from the north or east. It is not unreasonable to associate this movement with the pressures exerted by the increasing desiccation of the Sahara from the third millennium B.C. onward. Possibly—but this is no more than a guess—the original speakers of Chadic languages are to be identified with the early pastoralists who gradually spread across the Sahara from the fifth millennium B.C. The area around Lake Chad has long been recognized as one of particular importance in the early history of the Sudanic belt. Very little satisfactory archeological research has yet been carried out in the area, but recently the excavation of a site at Daima thirty miles south of Lake Chad indicates that it was probably under continuous occupation from about 500 B.C. and that the earliest inhabitants were a cattle-rearing people using implements of stone and bone.[3]

Several hundred miles to the southwest of Lake Chad a belt of territory bordering the southern half of the Jos Plateau of Northern Nigeria has provided archeologists with the remarkable artifacts of the Nok culture, most of which were brought to light as a result of open-cast mining operations. The culture, which takes its name from the village where the first discoveries were made, is distinguished for its remarkable terra-cotta figures, the realistically modeled heads of men and animals. The Nok people were agriculturalists who possessed some knowledge of ironworking, but appear to have still made use of a variety of stone implements. Radio-carbon dates suggest that their culture developed toward the end of the first millennium B.C. Of its origin nothing definite is known, but it will be recalled that a knowledge of agricultural techniques is thought to have spread from the Nile Valley after the fifth millennium B.C., while itinerant smiths whose skills were ultimately derived from Kush and Carthage must have introduced the revolutionary new metal iron to the peoples of the Western Sudan in the last centuries of the first millennium B.C.

Already, by the beginning of the Christian era, the pattern of population in West Africa must have been one of considerable complexity, with a great variety of groups differing from one another in language, in culture, and in economy. Fishing no doubt provided much of the livelihood of the peoples living in the valleys of the great rivers; cattle were probably the major asset of those living in the drier parts of the savanna; a knowledge of agriculture must have been spreading among many of the Sudanic communities, while the dwellers in the forest, not yet possessed of the crops that were to form the staples of their agriculture (certain kinds of yam, manioc, plantains or bananas, all introduced at a much later date from Asia or America), must have combined vegeculture with hunting. Nothing definite is known of the political organization of these early communities, but it is reasonable to assume that they lived in small groups, held together partly by ties of kinship, partly by the prestige possessed by certain ritual experts, "earth priests" who served as spiritual mediators in contact with the forces of nature. Small-scale societies of this type may be found in some parts of West Africa to this day, but throughout most of the region the character of these miniscule polities was to be completely transformed as the more sophisticated structure of the state was laid over them. In time, West Africa was to acquire a greater number and diversity of states than any other region of the continent.

✣ THE WEST AFRICAN STATES OF THE FIRST MILLENNIUM A.D.

By the end of the first millennium A.D. regular trade routes had been established across the Sahara, hundreds of Maghribi or Levantine merchants had visited and even settled in the commercial centers of the Sudan, and Muslim scholars from Cordoba to Baghdad were able to obtain first-hand descriptions of the lands beyond the desert. The accounts composed by these early geographers, such as al-Masudi (d. 956) or al-Bakri (d. 1094), make it clear that by 1000 A.D. a number of states, varying considerably in size and importance, had come into existence in those parts of West Africa that are most conveniently described as the Western and Central Sudan.[4]

The most westerly kingdom known to the Arabs was Takrur in the Senegal Valley, whose people, the ancestors of the modern Tukulor, enjoyed the distinction of being the first Negroes to accept Islam. Farther east, covering much of the southeastern part of modern Mauritania, spread the extensive domains of Ghana, the best known and to many Muslims the most powerful of Sudanese states. South of Ghana lay the kingdom al-Bakri knew as "Malel," possibly the nucleus of the future empire of Mali. Still farther east, at the bend of the Niger, was the town usually known as Kawkaw, the modern Gao, the capital of a state of the same name described by a ninth-century geographer as the greatest of all

Sudanese kingdoms. The Hausa country was not described by any Muslim geographer until the sixteenth century, but at least two Hausa states, Daura and Kano, are known from traditional sources to have been in existence by this time. Beyond Hausa the country north of Lake Chad, known as Kanem, was regularly visited by Muslim traders and contained at least one considerable kingdom. Naturally, Maghribi merchants were most familiar with those parts of the Sudan that provided the southern termini of the trans-Saharan routes, and it is of these areas, such as Ghana and Kanem, that the most detailed descriptions have been preserved.

Ghana—the kingdom took its name from the title of its ruler—was mainly populated by Negroid Soninke (Sarakole), a branch of the great family of Mande-speakers and a people who still form one of the major ethnic groups of the Western Sudan. At its height in the early eleventh century Ghana appears to have dominated a territory well over a hundred thousand square miles in extent, stretching from the Senegal to the Niger and reaching northward to include the steppes of the Sahil that formed the borderland of the desert. It is clear from the account given by al-Bakri in 1067 that the ruling dynasty had at its disposal an administrative machinery of considerable efficiency. The king could call upon two hundred thousand warriors of whom one-fifth were bowmen. He was supported by a revenue based in part on carefully graded taxes on the major imports and exports. He maintained a magnificent court: al-Bakri mentions the horses with gold trappings and the guard dogs with collars of gold that stood outside the audience chamber. And though a conscientious upholder of the traditional religion, whose priests practiced their rites in strictly guarded groves near the royal palace, he welcomed Muslim strangers to his country, employed them as officials and interpreters, and allowed them to establish a town of their own, adorned with mosques and houses of stone, only a short distance from his capital. (The remains of a substantial Muslim settlement dating from this period have been found at the site of Kumbi Saleh in southern Mauritania.)

Kanem shared with Ghana the commercial advantage of lying at the end of one of the main trans-Saharan routes; but while Ghana was exceptionally well placed to control the trade in gold brought from districts beyond its southern borders, the main export of Kanem appears to have been slaves, a less lucrative commodity but one which, by the ninth century if not earlier, was providing a flourishing business for traders coming down from the Fezzan. At this time the dominant people of the area were the Zaghawa. Today the Zaghawa are a small group of black nomads in northwest Darfur, speaking a language closely related to Tebu. A thousand years ago they were much more widely dispersed or at least the name Zaghawa was applied to the dominant groups of nomads, of non-Berber origin, between Chad and Darfur. In the tenth century there appear to have been a number of Zaghawa principalities, one of which developed into the powerful kingdom of Kanem. In 1085 the ruler of Kanem was converted to Islam—in a contemporary document he describes the Muslim traders in his country as the "pillar" of his kingdom. Only a generation earlier, however, al-Bakri had referred to the people of Kanem as "idolatrous blacks." An earlier geographer, al-Muhallabi, defined their religion as "king-worship," noting that the Zaghawa regarded their kings as the cause of life and death, sickness and health, and describing the elaborate precautions taken to give the king his food in secret. The Zaghawa kings were nomads with no fixed capitals, but their subjects appear to have been mainly sedentary cultivators. Nevertheless, the royal authority cannot have been great for al-Muhallabi noted in his account that "whoever wishes to do so, tries to steal the king's goods." [5]

The Arab geographers of the tenth century appear to be describing states that had already been in existence for a considerable time, but their accounts throw no light on the initial process of state-building. However, most of the peoples of the Western and Central Sudan have preserved traditions of origin and these, though often confused or distorted, throw some light on one of the most intriguing and important developments in African history, the emergence of the earliest organized states in sub-Saharan Africa. In Ghana twenty-two kings "of white race" were said to have reigned before the hijra (622 A.D.). As-Sadi, the seventeenth-century Timbuktu historian who preserved this tradition, also recorded the Songhai legend which told how a stranger known as Za al-ayaman, "the man from Yemen," came to the ancient town of Kukia on the Niger, found the people being terrorized by a fish (possibly intended, so a later commentator has suggested, to symbolize river pirates), killed the monster, was gratefully accepted by the people as their ruler, and thus became the founder of the first Songhai dynasty.[6] The dynasty of the rulers of Kanem, known as the Saifuwa, also traced their ancestry back to Yemen, while the earliest rulers of Daura claimed descent from a family that had originated in Palestine and migrated across the Sahara. All these states lay within the northern belt of the savanna, but traditions of migration from countries far to the east have been recorded among some peoples living much farther to the south. The Yoruba claim to be sprung from Lamudu, "one of the kings of Mecca," whose son, Oduduwa, was driven out of the holy city on account of his idolatrous practices and finally settled at Ife within the forest area of Western Nigeria. Among the Jukun of the Benue and in Bussa and other petty states on the middle Niger there are stories of a migration from the Nile Valley of a powerful group known as "the people of Kisra." Farther west, many of the dynasties of the Mossi-Dagomba states of Upper Volta and northern Ghana claim to have been founded by "red men," coming on horseback from farther east. All these legends are connected with the impact of outsiders, of red men or white men from the east or from the north. But legends of this type are by no means universal. The establishment of the kingdom of Mali is not ascribed to strangers; and the founder of the major Hausa city of Kano is described as a black man of uncertain origin.

The process of state-building must undoubtedly have been a highly complex one, varying considerably from area to area within the region. But certain broad lines of development may be distinguished. There can be no doubt that for most of the first millennium A.D. many of the Negroid cultivators living in the northern savanna country were subjected to the pressure of nomadic pastoralists from the Sahara, some of Berber origin, others—notably the Zaghawa—akin to the modern Tebu. The nomads possessed certain obvious tactical advantages over the cultivators: they were mobile, more experienced in the craft of war, and their social groups were probably larger than the scattered communities of the black farmers. Without much difficulty they could levy tribute in agricultural produce and slaves and so assume the position of a dominant aristocracy. But only through intermarriage could the conquerors become fully integrated with their subjects. As Saharan chieftains turned into Sudanese kings, their followers began to abandon the traditional nomadism, and their descendants gradually lost the physical characteristics that distinguished the original conquerors so sharply from their subjects, but in the process the social framework of a more enduring polity was constructed.

The fact of conquest must not be taken to imply that the nomads possessed any great cultural superiority over their Negroid neighbors. Even if the Saharans were slightly more aware than the Sudanese of the great civilizations of the Mediterranean and the Nile, their contact with these regions can hardly have been other than tenuous and peripheral, and certainly not of a kind to make them effective carriers of more sophisticated political techniques or more complex religious notions. But it is reasonable to assume that there were also to be found in the Saharan borderlands some men who had lived in Kush or Axum or Roman and Arab North Africa—political refugees, adventurers, soldiers of fortune, who really had acquired some knowledge of the workings of a centralized state. Such men would not necessarily require force to impose their ideas; sometimes—the Songhai legend of Za al-ayaman suggests such an incident—they might be invited to assume the leadership of a community on account of their special talents.

Not every West African state was formed through the agency of outsiders. On some occasions, no doubt, a number of small local groups may have acquired the means to dominate their neighbors. The gradual expansion of long-distance trade must have played an important part in fostering this type of political development. The Sudanese ruler who found himself in a position to control the sale of gold or ivory or slaves to the merchants from North Africa enjoyed all the benefits of increasing wealth. Enterprising men, attracted by his bounty, flocked to his town to swell the number of his warriors and enlarge his retinue. Local chiefs found it prudent to court his friendship, confirming the relationship by the payment of tribute or the arrangement of a diplomatic marriage. The Muslim traders with their experience of a wider world and of a more evolved technology were ideally suited to act as political and technical advisers, men who could put forward practical suggestions about the most effective means of holding together a new state. In ways such as these, through the evolution of heterogeneous communities and the concurrent absorption of new techniques and new ideas, the earliest West African states would seem to have emerged.

Two other points need to be made about this early period. It has sometimes been suggested that this was a time of *Völkerwanderungen,* of the massive movements of people, of great "tribes" on the march. If one discounts such obscure traditions as the Kisra legend, there is really no evidence to indicate large-scale migrations. Instead, it is more realistic to imagine a constant process of small-scale movements, not only of nomads or adventurers, but also of hunters or farmers forced by the pressure of their neighbors to seek new lands for themselves. But the proportion of such movements in relation to the population as a whole should not be exaggerated. The early traditions of West African peoples are full of stories of migration, but these stories must usually be taken as referring only to a small section of the community. The linguistic map of West Africa, with its remarkable number of languages sharply differentiated one from another, suggests a state of cultural stability maintained over a very long period.

The second point concerns the origin of the political and religious ideas that helped to shape the emergent states. Some scholars,[7] struck by what they regard as the apparent similarity of political organization throughout sub-Saharan Africa, argue that it is only possible to account for such a similarity by assuming the existence of a common fund of politico-religious ideas. These ideas, they suggest, must have originated in the Nile Valley. To other scholars this seems a hypothesis based on a highly questionable premise. No doubt some ideas ultimately derived from Kush or ancient Egypt reached West Africa, but they must have suffered considerable modification in the process of transmission, and they can have represented only one element in the complex pattern of the cultures that developed in the region. One must hope that this pattern will come increasingly to be illuminated by historical research.

✵ THE EMPIRE OF MALI AND THE MANDE EXPANSION

For the greater part of the last thousand years speakers of Mande languages have dominated the savanna country and its forest fringes lying between the Atlantic Ocean and the Niger, thus including in their sphere of influence most of modern Mali, extensive stretches of Senegal, Guinea, Sierra Leone, Liberia, and the Ivory Coast, and parts of modern Ghana and Upper Volta. The medieval empire of Mali, one of the greatest states Africa has ever known, was created by the Malinke, the most numerous group of Mande speakers, while Mande warriors, traders, and clerics have for centuries played a leading role in the political, economic, and cultural life of surrounding countries.

Local traditions and the writings of a number of medieval Muslim travelers and historians make it possible to trace with a fair measure of assurance the growth of imperial Mali from the twelfth century and the expansion of Mande-speakers from the fifteenth. But the earlier period of Mande history is still completely obscure. It seems likely that the area of the upper Niger, the heartland of the great empire, was also the homeland of the Mande, that a certain measure of expansion occurred at an early date, and that this expansion was associated with the development of a more efficient system of food production. But only when effective archeological research has been carried out in this area will it be possible to know the time and understand the manner in which this early expansion took place.

By the end of the first millennium A.D. a number of petty Mande chiefdoms had been founded in the Upper Niger area. Politically, they were overshadowed by their northern neighbors, Ghana and Takrur. Indeed, Arab geographers report that in the twelfth century their country was being raided for slaves to sell to Maghribi merchants. By this time, however, Ghana itself was in decline. The kingdom had been temporarily overwhelmed by the Berber Almoravids in the 1070's, Berber nomads from the north were continually harrying Soninke cultivators, subject provinces were in revolt, and vassal rulers were able to assert their independence. In the early thirteenth century one breakaway Soninke group, the Susu, was strong enough to dominate the entire kingdom and to conquer much of the Mande country to the south. In the 1230's the Malinke revolted against Susu oppression, and their leader, Sundiata, a warrior of heroic stature whose exploits form the subject of legends still recited among the Malinke, succeeded not only in overthrowing the Susu but also in taking over all their dominions, including the old kingdom of Ghana, thus laying the foundations of a great new empire.

Medieval Mali differed from ancient Ghana in a number of ways. Ghana's homeland lay in the semiarid steppe country of the Sahil; the central provinces of Mali, by contrast, were made up of fertile agricultural land in mid-savanna. Moreover, Mali was much better placed to control the rich gold-bearing lands of Bure and Bambuk, the main source of Sudanic gold at this time. Occupying such a favorable situation the *mansas* (rulers) of Mali were able to extend their hegemony over an area about twice as large as that formerly controlled by Ghana. At the empire's apogee in the mid-fourteenth century Berber nomads in the southern Sahara, Songhai princes at Gao, the rulers of the kingdoms of the Senegal, and a multitude of petty Mande chiefs in the southern savanna all accepted the overlordship of the rulers of Mali.

The Mansas were also able to establish a harmonious relationship with the rulers of Morocco and Egypt. Sundiata was a pagan, but his successors accepted Islam with enthusiasm, encouraged the building of mosques and the establishment of Koranic schools, and even undertook the long and arduous pilgrimage to Mecca. The most famous of these royal pilgrimages, that undertaken by the Mansa Kankan Musa in 1324, afforded the Mediterranean world an opportunity of gauging the wealth of this remote Negro kingdom, for the Mansa and his numerous entourage stayed for some time in Cairo, whose inhabitants were amazed by the gold brought by these black pilgrims and entranced by their monarch's courtesy and generosity.

Fortunately, we possess a number of accounts of Mali written by contemporary North African scholars, the most vivid of which is a first-hand description by the most famous of all Muslim travelers, the Moroccan ibn Battuta. The impression formed by this sophisticated and critical observer was a remarkable one. Three features of the country roused his admiration: "the small number of acts of injustice one finds there," "the complete and general safety one enjoys throughout the land," and the punctilious devotion shown by Sudanese Muslims.[8]

Ibn Battuta visited Mali in 1352 when the empire was at the height of its power. A century later the great state, weakened by internal dissension resulting from disputes over the succession and harassed by the attacks of aggressive neighbors, began to break up. The process of dissolution continued unchecked until by the seventeenth century even the heartland of Mali was divided among innumerable petty chieftaincies. The completeness of Mali's decline makes the achievement of its rulers during the age of imperial greatness all the more remarkable, for they had found a way of holding together for a period of close to two hundred

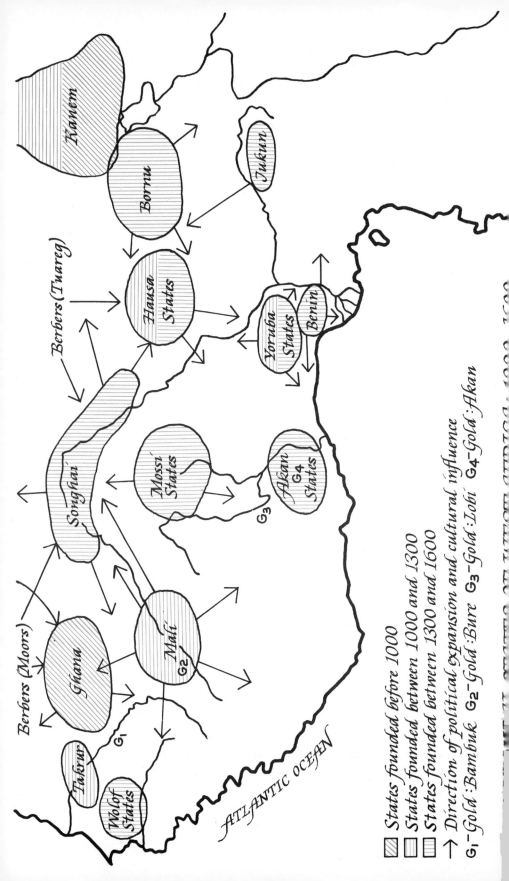

THE RISE AND FALL OF STATES OF WEST AFRICA 1000–1600

Kanem

Bornu

Tukun

Hausa
States

Berbers (Tuareg)

Songhai

Yoruba
States

Benin

Mossi
States

Akan
G4
States

G3

Berbers (Moors)

Ghana

Mali
G2

G1

Takrur

Wolof
States

ATLANTIC OCEAN

▨ States founded before 1000
▥ States founded between 1000 and 1300
▤ States founded between 1300 and 1600
→ Direction of political expansion and cultural influence
G1–Gold : Bambuk   G2–Gold : Bure   G3–Gold : Lobi   G4–Gold : Akan

years peoples of diverse ethnic groups spread over a vast stretch of territory. Clearly, one reason for their success was the wealth at their disposal. The Mansas could make use of the services of a large number of domestic serfs, and they profited from their control of a trade whose volume must have increased as a result of the security established throughout their domains. Moreover, this trade enabled them to import horses from across the desert and so build up a substantial force of cavalry, which gave them an obvious military advantage over most of their opponents.

It was impossible, of course, to establish a system of direct administration over the entire empire. The metropolitan provinces and some important towns were governed by royal officials, but for most of the incorporated states a system of indirect rule was developed which left local rulers a large measure of independence once they had been invested with authority by the Mansa and had agreed to render regular tribute. The fissiparous tendencies of an empire made up of so many different ethnic groups was partly counterbalanced by the growth of a common culture through the expansion of Islam. Only a very small proportion of the people of the empire accepted the new religion, but those who did, officials and merchants for the most part, formed an elite most of whose members must have possessed a clear appreciation of the advantages of the imperial organization. An empire of such a kind threw up many enterprising men who found it to their advantage to pursue their careers in the countries beyond their suzerain's immediate sphere of influence. Some went eastward, some to the south, some to the west. In the fourteenth century a group of Malinke, known to the Hausa as Wangarawa, arrived in Kano and persuaded the ruler to become a Muslim. In the fifteenth century Mande traders, usually termed Dyula, pioneered a major trade route designed to tap the gold of the Lobi and of the Akan in the northern part of modern Ghana. By the early sixteenth century Mande traders were even doing business with the Portuguese on the seacoast. At the same time another pioneering movement carried some Mande groups into the valley of the Gambia where they established a number of petty chiefdoms.

Mande expansion continued while the empire was falling apart and may indeed well have been accelerated by the anarchy that afflicted the Malinke homeland. The Mande migrants possessed a spirit of enterprise which made their influence felt in many different ways. The Dyula, many of whom were Muslims, naturally preferred to settle on the main trade routes. To the rulers of rising states they rendered invaluable service as commercial agents and diplomatic and legal advisers. Elsewhere, the Mande proved themselves vigorous state-builders. In the seventeenth century the scattered communities living in the bend of the Black Volta were forced to recognize the overlordship of a group of Mande invaders, the creators of the new kingdom of Gonja. Farther west Mande adventurers penetrated the forested hinterland of Sierra Leone. Known as the Mende, they set up a series of petty chiefdoms organized on a military basis, the raids of whose warriors occasionally reached as far as the coast. But the most substantial of the Mande successor states were found not on the periphery but close to the heartland of the old empire among the Bambara, a people closely akin to the Malinke, whose center of population lay downstream from Bomako in the valley of the upper Niger. In the eighteenth century warrior groups among the Bambara established the two substantial kingdoms of Segu and Kaarta and dominated much of the country between the Niger and the Senegal. The Bambara kings tolerated Islam but gave their personal devotion to the traditional religion of the country, thus incurring in the eyes of Muslim and pro-Muslim historians the odium of "paganism."

🌿 THE SONGHAI EMPIRE

At the height of their prosperity the Mansas of Mali could number among their vassals the Songhai, a people living along the northeastern bend of the Niger, who were later to prove their most formidable opponents and to become the creators of an imperial state that rivaled and possibly even surpassed fourteenth-century Mali in size, wealth, and power.

At least three different elements had merged to form the Songhai people. Originally, their homeland—a stretch of the Niger Valley upstream from the present Nigeria-Dahomey frontier—appears to have been occupied by cultivators and fishermen of the same stock as the Voltaic peoples to their west. Then at an uncertain date—possibly early in the first millennium A.D.—groups of fishermen known as the Sorko began to move up the river, coming originally perhaps from the Lake Chad area. Finally, in the latter half of the first millennium A.D. another alien group, whose arrival is commemorated in the legend of Za al-ayaman, founded a dynasty known from the title of its rulers as the Za. The Za may have been of Zaghawa origin. At any rate the linguistic evidence which separates Songhai from the surrounding Western Sudanic and Afro-Asiatic languages and links it with languages of Nilo-Saharan stock suggests that the area must have been strongly influenced by people akin to the Zaghawa.

By the eleventh century the Za were the rulers of a substantial state. Gao, their capital, was one of the major terminals of the trans-Saharan trade, amicable relations had been established with some of the kingdoms of the Maghrib, and the Zas had become at least nominally converted to Islam. For much of the thirteenth and fourteenth centuries the Zas accepted the hegemony of Mali, but by 1400 their independence was complete, and in the 1460's they produced a ruler, Sonni Ali, whose career marks him out as one of the great conquerors of African history.

Sorko fishermen extending their activities up the Niger as far as Lake Debo prepared the ground for the expansion of the Songhai state. But the occupation of the great commercial centers of Timbuktu and Jenne and the defeat of the Tuareg and the Mossi, Songhai's most formidable rivals as successors to the declining power of Mali, were the work of Sonni Ali and his armies. Though a nominal Muslim, Sonni Ali had little respect for the ulama, the intellectual elite of the great cities, and preferred to base his prestige on the awe in which he was held by the mass of his subjects as a master of the traditional religion, a magician credited with the ability to turn himself into a vulture and to render his soldiers invisible.

Sonni Ali transformed his kingdom into a multinational empire, but within a year of his death in 1492 the ancient native dynasty was overthrown in a military coup led by one of Sonni Ali's generals, Muhammad Ture, who assumed supreme power under the dynastic title of Askia. To the Songhai their new ruler was a foreigner, for he was of Soninke origin. Inevitably, therefore, Askia Muhammad turned to the cosmopolitan group of ulama for support. To increase his standing in Muslim eyes he made an imposing pilgrimage to Mecca and returned invested with the prestigious title of caliph, and he regularly sought the advice and assistance of the Muslim elite. Under his patronage Timbuktu, the second city of the empire, developed into a considerable center of learning. "Here," wrote the Moroccan traveler Leo Africanus, who visited the city in 1513 and whose account became the main source of Timbuktu's glamorous reputation for the outside world, "are great store of doctors, judges, priests, and other learned men, that are bountifully maintained at the king's cost." [9]

Askia Muhammad had come to power as a soldier and much of his reign was taken up with military expeditions. As a result Songhai overlordship was accepted in places as remote as Agades and Kano to the east and to the north the salt-mining center of Taghaza in mid-Sahara. To hold his far-flung dominions together Askia Muhammad built up a system of administration which has been described as "more despotic" than the normal state structure of the Sudan, for power was carefully centralized and the ruler had at his disposal a large number of officials whom he could remove at will. [10]

Superficially, the Songhai empire might be compared to pharaonic Egypt in that both states based their power on the control of a river. Indeed, their massive fleet of canoes was probably the most effective instrument of power in the hands of the Songhai rulers. But the empire suffered from many serious weaknesses. Its population—Songhai, Tuareg, Moor, Malinke, Fulani—contained many mutually hostile groups. It possessed no nuclear area comparable in agricultural prosperity to the Mali homeland. The acceptance of Islam as the religion of the state widened the gulf between the governing elite and the mass of the population. Finally, the Askia dynasty never succeeded in working out an effective system of succession. The great Askia Muhammad was himself deposed toward the end of his life by his ambitious sons, and the reigns of his successors present an almost continuous tale of palace revolutions and fratricidal strife.

And so it was that the great empire collapsed with astonishing speed when confronted with a threat from an unexpected direction. In 1590 al-Mansur, the sultan of Morocco, inspired solely by a desire to acquire for himself the fabulous gold deposits of the Sudan, sent an army of four thousand men across the Sahara. At first this conquistadorial gamble scored a spectacular success. The small Moroccan force, many of whose fighting men were European renegades, highly disciplined and equipped with firearms, overwhelmed the bowmen and the horsemen of Songhai in a pitched battle fought near the banks of the Niger and went on to occupy Gao, Timbuktu, and Jenne, the principal cities of the empire. But the Moroccans, starved of reinforcements, could never hope to reconstruct the administrative framework of the empire. And so the whole region found itself given up to anarchy.

For a century Moroccan pashas, increasingly independent of their distant suzerain, held sway at Timbuktu, while the survivors of the Songhai ruling class established themselves in Dendi, once the southernmost province of the empire. There was no revival of Songhai power: the descendants of Sonni Ali and Askia Muhammad, quarreling constantly among themselves, became the sovereigns of a score of miniscule chiefdoms. As for the Moroccans they gradually merged with their Negroid subjects to become one more caste, known locally as the *arma,* in the cosmopolitan population of the cities of the Niger. Effective power passed into the hands of the enemies of the old empire, the Bambara, the Tuareg, and the Fulani. Few military campaigns can have produced such dire consequences as the Moroccan invasion of the Sudan. "The Sudan was one of God's most favored countries in prosperity and fertility at the time the expeditionary force entered the country. Now," wrote the Timbuktu historian, as-Sadi, about 1650, "all that has changed. . . . Security has given place to danger, prosperity to misery and calamity. . . . Disorder spreading and intensifying has become universal." [11]

✺ THE STATES OF THE UPPER VOLTA

Until the thirteenth and fourteenth centuries the peoples living to the south of the Niger bend in the basin of the Upper Volta (a territory now contained within the boundaries of the Republic of Upper Volta and of the northern provinces of modern Ghana) appear to have been quite unaffected by the political developments that had taken place in other parts of the Western Sudan in the course of the past five hundred years. Culturally, these peoples had many features in common. Most of them spoke languages of the Voltaic (or Gur) branch and possessed similar religious and social institutions. But they had not found cause to create over their innumerable independent kinship groups the political superstructure of a state organization.

At some uncertain date, however, probably about the fourteenth century, bands of "red men," as the legends call them, began to move across the Niger from the east. They came on horseback, and their cavalry clearly gave them a measure of military superiority over the peasant farmers with their bows and arrows; they must also have brought with them some knowledge of the workings of a state system of government. These immigrants were the founders of the Mossi-Dagomba group of states.

At first the immigrants may have been organized in war bands comparable to those of the Jaga and the Ngoni in other parts of Africa in more recent times. Certainly, they possessed considerable force, for the Timbuktu chroniclers tell of a number of Mossi raids on the settled lands of the middle Niger, one of which in 1480 reached as far north as Walata on the edge of the Sahara. But the growing power of Songhai checked their depredations and possibly forced them to turn south. So it would seem that the groups of states—Wagadugu, Yatenga, Dagomba, Mamprussi, and others—which trace their ancestry back to a common origin came into existence in their present locations about the end of the fifteenth century. A hundred years later another powerful immigrant group of Mande origin and coming from the west created the kingdom of Gonja on Dagomba's western borders.

The political pattern that came into existence in the Volta basin about 1600 endured with little change until the European conquest nearly three hundred years later. Between themselves these kingdoms achieved a convenient balance of power. The cluster of stateless peoples living on their borders presented no threat to their existence. Only to the south were they faced with a really formidable threat in the growing power of Ashanti. In the mid-eighteenth century Ashanti armies invaded Gonja and Dagomba and secured the payment of regular tribute, but though these states were in part incorporated within the Ashanti empire little attempt was made to transform their existing institutions.

The vigorous conservatism of their political institutions is the most remarkable feature of these Voltaic states. The Mossi, it has been said— and the same judgment could be passed on the rulers of Gonja and Dagomba—were "past masters of the art of incorporating diverse groups into their politico-religious system." [12] This political sagacity was most clearly shown in the relations between the immigrants and the leaders of the autochthonous peoples, the priests of the Earth-cult. Political power rested clearly in the hands of the king and his nobility, the descendants of the immigrant state-builders, but the Earth-priests continued to perform their religious duties on which, it was universally agreed, the prosperity of the kingdom depended.

The stability which these kingdoms enjoyed was not the product of isolation. Important trade routes connecting commercial centers such as Jenne, Timbuktu, and Kano with the rich gold and kola-nut-producing areas of the forest passed through their territory, and most of their towns attracted communities of foreign merchants, mainly of Hausa or Mande-Dyula origin. Many of these merchants were Muslims who brought with them to the fringes of the forest that compendium of stimulating new ideas and attractive new techniques that Berber Muslims had carried across the Sahara a thousand years earlier. And the consequences were much the same as they had been in the northern belt of the western Sudan. Among the Mossi, whose country produced little to export to Kano or Timbuktu, commerce was slack and the Muslim community correspondingly small and uninfluential. But in Gonja and Dagomba, whose towns such as Salaga and Yendi were major centers of the gold and kola-nut trade, Muslims were numerous and their importance considerable. So it was that while the Mossi rulers of Wagadugu and Yatenga remained devoted adherents of the old religion, the governing elite of the southern kingdoms had come by the beginning of the nineteenth century to accept Islam.

🐾 KANEM-BORNU AND THE HAUSA STATES

During the first half of the second millennium A.D. the Central Sudan— that thousand-mile stretch of savanna reaching from the middle Niger to Darfur—saw the emergence and the consolidation of a number of substantial states. None of these polities could be said to rival the great Western Sudanic empires of Mali and Songhai in size or power, for at this period the Central Sudan did not possess the kind of base on which an imperial state could be constructed. Culturally, with its many different linguistic groups, it lacked the benefits of that measure of homogeneity that the spread of Mande speakers afforded the rulers of Mali. Geographically, it had no axis comparable to that long stretch of the middle Niger, control of which enabled the rulers of Songhai to knit together for a century many different ethnic groups. Economically, it had no mineral resources comparable to the gold of Bure and Bambuku to stimulate the development of trade and create that surplus of wealth so vital in forcing the pace of political evolution. Confronted with the task of fusing highly disparate groups made up of Saharan nomads and Sudanic cultivators and of discovering other sources of wealth, the major polities of the Central Sudan took shape more slowly, but in compensation they eventually achieved a measure of stability which protected them against the fragmentation that accompanied the downfall of Mali and Songhai.

Kanem-Bornu and the Hausa states—the kingdoms east of Lake Chad, none of which emerged as major polities until after 1500, are considered in the setting of Equatorial Africa—differed greatly in character and in the pace of their development. The kingdom of Kanem was in existence, it will be recalled, as early as the ninth century. Its rulers dominated the steppe country north of Lake Chad. South and west of the lake there lived a conglomeration of peoples known collectively as So. The So, whose closest modern descendants may be found in a group such as the Kotoko living south of Lake Chad, spoke languages of the Chadic branch of Afro-Asiatic. Their neighbors, the Hausa and numerous other groups living to the west, also spoke languages of the same branch. Traditions associated with the So speak of migrations from the north and east about the middle of the first millennium A.D., but one must assume a very much longer period of population movements. The area around Lake Chad was one of the first parts of sub-Saharan Africa to be affected by the new techniques of food production, and to the pressures produced by a growth in population must be added the disturbances caused by the increasing desiccation of the Saharan borderlands. Both So and Hausa developed elaborate cultures long before they came under the influence of Islam. (Archeological research has shown that the So were highly skillful potters, who at one period made massive urns to bury their dead.) Both peoples lived in compact settlements, the most important of which were destined to become substantial walled towns.

Some indication of the character of these early Hausa polities, at a time when each major settlement was an independent unit, is afforded by the *Kano Chronicle,* one of the most extraordinary documents in the history of sub-Saharan Africa. The opening section of the chronicle tells how a certain Barbushe "by his wonders and sorceries and the power he gained over his brethren, became chief and lord over them." [13] Some years after the death of this "priest-king" the country was invaded and conquered by a great host, led by one of the descendants of the great folk-hero Bayajidda, who may have been of Maghribi Berber origin. These invaders established the dynasty of the *sarkis* (kings) of Kano, but for at least three hundred years according to the chronicle, the Kano *sarkis* found their power opposed by the priests of the traditional religion. The pattern of events in Kano may not have been typical; elsewhere foreign invasion may not necessarily have occurred. But at least it would seem clear that among the Hausa and So there was in the first centuries of the second millennium A.D. no state of more consequence than a petty chiefdom. In this Hausa and So polities presented a sharp contrast to the situation in Kanem.

Before 1000 A.D. Kanem had possessed the character of a loose hegemony established by the Saifuwa, a dynasty of Zaghawa origin, over the peoples living mostly to the north of Lake Chad. By 1200 the state had acquired much more secure foundations. Its *mais* (sultans) had accepted Islam, but they still retained much of the mystic ritual of pre-Islamic rulers, rarely appearing in public and giving audiences from behind a screen. Unlike the great Western Sudanic rulers, however, the *mais* of Kanem appear to have attached little importance to a fixed capital. But it may well have been the need to provide for a large retinue and to supervise an extensive kingdom rather than instincts inherited from nomadic ancestors that kept them continually on the move.

Though the character of their rule was changing and though the Saifuwa themselves were becoming increasingly Negroid in appearance —a thirteenth-century Mai was described in the king list as being the first ruler with a black skin, all his predecessors being regarded as red— their sphere of influence was still largely Saharan. The towns of the Fezzan acknowledged their hegemony, thus insuring their control of one of the main trans-Saharan trade routes. At the same time good relations were maintained with the rulers of North Africa. In 1257 presents sent from Kanem to the Hafsid sultan of Tunis included a giraffe, "an animal whose external characteristics," ibn Khaldun noted in his history, "are most diverse." [14]

In the fourteenth century the kingdom of Kanem began to break up as the *mais* came under attack from the Bulala, a powerful nomadic group also of Zaghawa origin, who lived between Lake Chad and Darfur. The Bulala, assisted by various Arab tribes who had recently entered the area from the Eastern Sudan, pushed the Saifuwa westward. But though forced to abandon Kanem, the old dynasty reestablished its power in Bornu, the country west of Lake Chad. To do so they had not only to guard themselves against Bulala attacks but to conquer one by one the wellstockaded settlements of the So. After a long time of troubles the six-teenth century brought an age of military glory for the Saifuwa. Most of the *mais* of this period are commemorated as great warriors, one of whom, Idris Alooma, gained a considerable tactical advantage over his opponents by recruiting a corps of Turkish musketeers from Tripoli. Conquest was followed by assimilation as the So mixed with the immigrants from Kanem to become the modern Kanuri. By 1600 the kingdom of Bornu was clearly the most powerful state the Central Sudan had ever known.

One consequence of the shift of the Saifuwa from Kanem to Bornu was to bring the Hausa states closely in touch with a major power. Until the fourteenth century the Hausa were insulated by their remoteness from the main currents of activity in the Sudan, the work of empire-builders, traders, and Muslim clerics on the middle Niger or in the neighborhood of Lake Chad. During these centuries of freedom from external pressures a process of internal crystallization took place which reduced the multiplicity of Hausa polities to seven substantial states, the Hausa *bakwai* (seven), of which Kano, Katsina, Gobir, and Zazzau (Zaria) were the most important. At the same time another group of states known to the Hausa as the "bastard seven" and including Zamfara, Kebbi, Nupe, and Yoruba, began to be formed to the west and south. These "bastard" states may well have been founded by immigrants from Hausa country who imposed themselves on peoples of different culture.

The appearance of Mande traders and clerics in Kano and Katsina in the mid-fourteenth century marked the end of Hausa isolation and established a connection with the intellectual and commercial centers of the middle Niger. Under Mande influence some of the *sarkis* accepted Islam. At the same time they learned of the values of slaves as an export commodity—the *Kano Chronicle* records a significant increase in slave raiding at this period. There is no evidence that Mali ever exerted any political power over the Hausa states, and Songhai appears to have done no more than establish a brief hegemony in the reign of Askia Muhammad. But the influence of Bornu was more profound and more lasting. Until the Fulani wars of the early nineteenth century the rulers of Bornu regarded the Hausa states as lying within their sphere of influence and obtained from the Hausa rulers periodic payments of tribute. The Saifuwa *mais* had much to teach the petty Hausa princes about methods of administration and court ceremonial. And it seems likely that most of the innovations attributed to the late fifteenth-century *sarki* of Kano, Muhammad Rimfa—they range from the introduction of long trumpets and ostrich-feather fans to the appointment of eunuchs to major offices of state—were almost certainly derived from Bornu.[15]

As the power of the Hausa monarchs increased conflicts between states became more violent. The chronicles of the seventeenth and eighteenth centuries tell of many wars, with the military advantage going now to one state, now to another, but with no kingdom powerful enough to establish an unchallenged hegemony over its neighbors. South of the Hausa states and Bornu were to be found a great variety of polities. Some, statelets formed on the Kanuri or Hausa model, could be regarded as satellites of their more powerful neighbors; others, particularly in inaccessible mountainous areas such as parts of the Jos plateau, were tiny autonomous units ferociously resisting any form of external domination; yet others were substantial independent states. Of those in the last category the most spectacular history attaches to the Kwararafa or Jukun. In the seventeenth century these people built up a formidable military power in the valley of the middle Benue and raided as far afield as Kano and Katsina, only to collapse into complete obscurity a few generations later.

At the end of the eighteenth century the Central Sudan presented a pattern that had changed little in the course of three hundred years. This pattern was soon to be shattered by the most dramatic revolution the Sudan had ever known—a revolution of which Islam was to be the ideology and the Fulani, a people whose role in the history of the Central Sudan had hitherto been a modest one, the agents.

☆ THE PEOPLES OF GUINEA UP TO 1450

Until as late as 1400 the development of Guinea, the second of West Africa's lateral divisions, proceeded at a much slower pace than that of the Sudan with its substantial kingdoms, its thriving cities, and its stimulating contacts with the Mediterranean world. Guinea was held back primarily by its remoteness. In contrast to the northern and eastern coasts of Africa, visited continuously by alien traders from the first millennium B.C. onward, the western littoral was shut off against outside intercourse by a combination of geographical factors, the width of the Atlantic, and the nature of the prevailing winds and currents on the Saharan coast. These winds blow throughout the year from north to south, while the current follows the same direction. Thus, for a sailing ship or an oared galley the passage down the Saharan coast was not excessively difficult, but for such vessels to return the way they had come was practically impossible. Only by heading straight from the coast of Guinea for the middle of the Atlantic where trade winds blow from the south or west could a sailing ship make its way back to northern latitudes. Seamen of the Mediterranean had little incentive to explore these dangerous waters, and it needed a peculiar combination of factors before the people living on the

Atlantic seaboard of Europe felt the urge to venture into the unknown reaches of the great ocean.

Unconscious then of the enlivening experience of maritime trade, the communities living on the Guinea coast before the arrival of European seafarers in the mid-fifteenth century presented a striking contrast to those of the East African littoral. In Guinea there were no opulent city-states such as Kilwa or Sofala, only the modest villages of farmers and fishermen, maintaining some intercourse with their hinterland through a local trade in salt and dried fish, but living well beyond the range of the great centers of the Sudan. These coastal communities represented, however, only one element in the population of Guinea. Other groups, living on the southern edge of the savanna or in the northern fringes of the forest, lay well within the orbit of the traders and adventurers fanning out from the states of the Sudan in the first half of the second millennium A.D.

But these contacts between Guinea and Sudan reach back to an infinitely remote period. Sharp though the contrast may be between the humid, luxuriant forests of the one and the dusty plains of the other, the two subregions are so closely interlocked that their historical development possesses a certain unity. Indeed, geographically Guinea reproduces many of the features of the Sudan, with Sudanic landscapes reaching the sea in Senegambia and again in a broad corridor cleft between the forest areas of modern Ghana and Nigeria. As for the rain forest, the most characteristic geographical feature of Guinea, in few places is it more than two hundred miles across and in most places its width is very much less than that. In few parts does the forest present a really formidable obstacle to movement, and in one major area of population the forest is traversed by a magnificent waterway, the Niger, the creeks and estuaries of whose delta with the lagoons that adjoin them provide a network of routes for inland navigation. The same favorable conditions for water transport exist in other parts of Guinea, in the estuary of the Gambia, for example, or among the islands and inlets of the Windward Coast (a convenient designation applied in the days of sail to the westward-facing stretch of Guinea between the Gambia and Liberia). Within this environment—dense forest and intrusive savanna, lonely seacoasts and populous inland waterways—the peoples shaped their culture before being drawn into the wider community of the Atlantic.

Obscure though the early history of Guinea may be in our present state of knowledge, two broad themes stand out clearly—the diversification of peoples and the pioneering of the forest. Linguistically, the population of this part of West Africa is divided between two branches of the Western Sudanic family—West Atlantic and Kwa. The West Atlantic branch comprises a fairly compact assemblage of peoples living in the neighbor-hood of the lower and middle Senegal (Wolof, Serer, Tukulor, together with the now widely dispersed pastoral Fulani) and a variety of minor ethnic groups spread along the Atlantic seaboard as far south as Sierra Leone. The Kwa branch is very much more extensive. It ranges from the Kru of Liberia to the Ibo of Eastern Nigeria and includes the Akan of modern Ghana and the Yoruba. Although the Kwa people are often thought of primarily as forest-dwellers, many of them—the Guan of Ghana, for example, or the Gwari, Nupe, and Northern Yoruba of Ni-geria—live well outside the forest belt. It is reasonable to assume that the original home of the Kwa peoples lay in the savanna, but it is clear from the profound differences that exist among many Kwa languages, even between some of those spoken by peoples living in adjoining areas, that the major ethnic groups must have been separated one from another for a period to be measured not in centuries but in millennia.

Archeological evidence already cited reveals that parts of the forest were peopled at least as much as ten thousand years ago. It is possible that these early forest-dwellers developed a system of cultivation, based on the African yam and other indigenous crops, that can almost be called agriculture. But two major innovations—the introduction of iron im-plements and of Asian food crops—must have taken place before the forest could become the home of a substantial population. A knowledge of ironworking probably reached the people living in the southern sa-vanna about the beginning of the Christian era. Asian food crops, of which the Asian yam was by far the most important, cannot have reached Guinea until several centuries later. How they were passed from the East African coast to which they had been carried by Indonesian seafarers is one of the mysteries of African history. The most reasonable hypothesis is that the use of these crops spread across the continent carried by the natural processes of local trade and intermarriage on a number of differ-ent routes. One such route may have lain through the Bantu-speaking peoples of Equatorial Africa, another through the Eastern Sudanic groups living farther north.

About 1000 A.D. polities more substantial than the independent kin groups began to emerge among some of the peoples of Guinea. In the West Atlantic area the first kingdoms were founded on the middle Senegal, Takrur, the most substantial, occupying the country later known as Futa Toro, the home of the Tukulor. According to oral traditions, Takrur's history was a turbulent one with frequent changes of dynasty associated in part with the arrival from the north and northeast of dominant groups of Berber or Soninke origin. To the south of Futa Toro there emerged during the fourteenth century the first important Wolof state, Jolof. For several generations Jolof maintained its hegemony over the other Wolof polities in the area.

The Wolof of the lower Senegal came under pressure from Berber nomads, and the substantial Negroid population living north of the river was forced to abandon its homes or accept servile status in Berber society. Farther south a more peaceful process of infiltration brought Malinke settlers into the valley of the upper Gambia, where they created a number of chiefdoms under the suzerainty of distant Mali. Yet another current of migration was to be seen in the movements of pastoral Fulani from the overgrazed Ferlo plateau between the Gambia and the Senegal, some going eastward to the Niger and beyond, others southward to the lush pastures of the Futa Jallon massif. As for the Windward coast its peoples were largely insulated from the movements taking place in the far interior by a hinterland of forest and mountain, or they found in the swampy margins of the coast a sanctuary where they could preserve their miniscule village-states remote from alien intruders.

Many small, independent communities lost in the forest, swamp, or bush were also to be found among the Kwa peoples in this time. But by 1400 certain Kwa groups had already laid the foundations of major polities. Of all the Kwa peoples the Yoruba possess the longest traditions, reaching back perhaps as far as eight hundred years. The earliest legends stress the fact that Ife, a town on the northern edge of the forest, was a great religious center, whose influence spread over a wide area. Archeology confirms the legends, for here in this Yoruba Rome have been discovered the famous "Ife heads," naturalistic sculptures in bronze and terra-cotta, today placed among the supreme artistic achievements of mankind. Art historians have pointed to the similarities of style between the artistic traditions of Ife and of Nok, but no light has yet been thrown on the millennium that separates the two cultures. Indeed, the prehistory of Ife presents one of the most intriguing gaps in our knowledge of Africa's past.

On the creation of Yoruba states the traditions indicate that some of them, though not necessarily the earliest, came to be ruled by dynasties that had their origin in a movement of conquering groups from farther north. The legend, already mentioned, that speaks of Oduduwa, the first great Yoruba leader known by name, as coming from Mecca would seem to have been originally a theory put forward by some Muslim interpreter; far more realistic are the traditions that associate Oduduwa with the Hausa-Bornu area. Oduduwa, it may be suggested—though this is only a hypothesis—represents a group of political adventurers thrown up in the turmoil that accompanied the development of the Hausa states and establishing their domination by virtue of their greater political sophistication over some of the Yoruba. Of the states said to have been founded by Oduduwa's offspring, Oyo, lying in full savanna country, was to become preeminent. But in 1400 Oyo was no more than one among a number of Yoruba chiefdoms.

It is often assumed that the tropical forest presents the least propitious environment for state-building activities; yet it is one of the most remarkable facts of West African history that a state which was certainly among the most substantial of all the early kingdoms of Guinea grew up in the midst of the forest belt. This was Benin whose people, the Edo, are the Yorubas' eastern neighbors. At an early date, though at a time when an Edo state was already in existence, Benin was drawn into the orbit of Ife: local traditions speak of a son of Oduduwa being invited to come from Ife to rule the Edo, finding the country uncongenial, but impregnating before he left a local princess whose son became the first ruler in a new dynasty. It is clear that Benin derived much in ideas and techniques from the cultural metropolis of Ife; it is equally clear that the Edo were never politically subordinate to the Yoruba.

East of Benin among the Ibo of the lower Niger and the Ijaw of the river's delta historical traditions are very much thinner than those of the Yoruba and the Edo. Their thinness seems to reflect a situation in which there existed no polity larger than a village state at this time.

Much the same may be said for the period before 1400 of the Kwa peoples living to the west of the Yoruba. Here in the area of modern Ghana the major group was made up of the Akan, a term applied to a cluster of peoples, of whom the Ashanti and the Fante were to become the most prominent, speaking the same language, Twi, and possessing many institutions in common. The Akan came to dominate a forest area of exceptional importance in the economy of West Africa, for it produced both gold and kola nuts, two of the major staples of West African trade. By the middle of the fifteenth century if not earlier Mande and Hausa traders had begun to do business in the northern Akan territory. The stimulus of new sources of wealth must have begun to have had some effect on the political development of local communities. This stimulus was soon to be felt even more powerfully when African communities living on the coast of Guinea found themselves faced with an extraordinary phenomenon— white men in strange ships appearing from out of the sea and offering a tempting range of merchandise in exchange for slaves and ivory and gold.

🎴 THE IMPACT OF EUROPE: THE ERA OF THE SLAVE TRADE

To men of the Mediterranean world, in the Middle Ages no less than in antiquity, the Atlantic was the Ocean of Darkness, a boundless sea whose fogs and storms would surely engulf the too audacious voyager. The Moroccan coast was reasonably familiar ground to Iberian sailors, but beyond it stretched the desolate shores of the Sahara, *terra ignota* to Muslims and Christians alike. For men to think of undertaking the exploration of these dangerous waters a rare combination of factors was necessary. It so happened that all the required factors—incentive, technical skill, capital, and efficient direction—came together in fifteenth-century Portugal.

As early as the thirteenth century a few European seamen and merchants had begun to speculate on the riches that might reward a voyage of discovery down the mysterious western coast of Africa. It was known that the Moors carried on a lucrative trade in gold with the Negro lands beyond the desert; there were rumors of delectable islands off the coast of Africa; and some daring minds believed it might prove possible to circumnavigate the continent and so find a sea route to the fabulous spice markets of the Orient. As early as 1291 two galleys were sent from Genoa on a voyage of exploration; after passing the Moroccan coast both vessels disappeared without a trace. Then, in the fourteenth and early fifteenth centuries seamen from many European ports took a hand in the discovery and exploitation of the Canaries and other western Atlantic islands. But only in Portugal was there to be found that peculiar combination of motives needed to forge a resolution steely enough to survive the dangers and the frustrations of more extensive exploration.

The Portuguese had been involved in African affairs for many generations. Their nation had been born of the struggle against the Andalusian Moors, a struggle that was carried into Africa with the capture of Ceuta in 1415. The minds of certain Portuguese, though still obsessed with the crusade against the Infidel, now began to be haunted by three alluring images—gold, spices, and Prester John. Gold was to be found beyond the Sahara, spice markets reached by a new route to the East, while Prester John represented a fabulous Christian monarch reported as possessing vast resources and as living somewhere in the unknown parts of Africa. To control such wealth, to acquire such an ally—what a victory that would represent in the struggle of rival faiths.

Unique in its dreams, Portugal was unique, too, in possessing men who could translate them into reality: sailors trained in the hard school of the Atlantic fishing fleet and willing to adopt the new navigational techniques developed by Italian seamen; wealthy merchants willing to risk capital on hazardous enterprises; above all, royal princes prepared to take a lead in the practical tasks of organizing exploration.

The most famous name in this early period of Portuguese expansion is that of Prince Henry, misleadingly called "The Navigator," for he was not a seaman himself, but a man with a genius for organizing, coordinating, and encouraging the maritime skills of others. In 1419 the prince began to send ships down the Moroccan coast, but it was not until 1434 that he achieved a notable success when one of his captains sailed beyond Cape Bojador, till then the southern limit of European knowledge. Shortly afterward the Portuguese must have hit on the trick of using the Atlantic trade winds for the return journey (a discovery that was kept a closely guarded secret and not mentioned in contemporary chronicles), for the pace of exploration quickened marvelously, and in the next twenty years the Portuguese made themselves familiar with fifteen hundred miles of coast as far south as Sierra Leone. Henry died in 1460, his ambition still unachieved, for his captains had not yet discovered the source of "the golden trade" of the Moors, nor had they been able to make contact with any major African ruler. But he had established a vigorous tradition, and his initiative had shown that profitable trade in slaves and other commodities could be carried on along the coast of Guinea. When the work of exploration was resumed, first through the initiative of a private merchant, then again under royal patronage, the Portuguese scored a long run of spectacular successes. In the 1470's they reached the Gold Coast, in the 1480's the mouth of the Congo and the Cape of Good Hope, and before the century ended Portuguese ships under Vasco da Gama's command had succeeded in charting the last stage of the revolutionary new sea route to the Indies.

Until the 1530's the Portuguese were able to keep the greater part of the trade of Guinea in their own hands. Their expectations had in the end been entirely fulfilled. Along one stretch of coast they had found the people wearing a profusion of gold ornaments. Believing that the precious metal must come from a single source, they called this part Costa da Mina, "coast of the mine," and immediately built there a great fortress, later known as Elmina, to deter foreign interlopers. Gold from the Costa da Mina was of crucial importance in financing the later feats of Portuguese explorers. But inevitably as profitable commitments were taken up in other parts of the world, in Angola and Mozambique, the Indies and Brazil, Portuguese resources of men and ships were strained to the utmost. Inevitably, too, Guinea, the nearest part of the newly discovered world to Europe, attracted an ever-increasing swarm of foreign ships and traders. But it was not until the 1630's when the Dutch captured Elmina, that the title assumed by Portuguese kings, "Lord of Guinea," took on a hollow ring.

By the end of the seventeenth century European traders had established a pattern of commercial activity that changed little in the course of the next hundred and fifty years. Some parts of the coast—particularly

the Gold Coast and the Niger delta—presented a scene of regular commercial intercourse, steadily mounting in volume; on other stretches the
arrival of a foreign ship was a comparatively rare occurrence. The
French controlled the trade of the Senegal area and maintained trading
posts up the river. The Portuguese were particularly active in that deeply
indented coast that forms the seaboard of the territory later to be known
as Portuguese Guinea. Along the Gold Coast stood some thirty trading
stations occupied by Englishmen, Dutchmen, and Danes, and for a time
by German Brandenbergers. Elsewhere in Guinea, on the Gambia, in
Sierra Leone, on the Ivory Coast, and in the Niger delta there were no
substantial European posts and trade was open to all comers.

European traders of the eighteenth century followed commercial practices worked out by the Portuguese three hundred years earlier. At first
the Portuguese had made a vigorous attempt to penetrate the interior: in
the 1480's King John II had despatched diplomatic missions to Mali and
other inland kingdoms. Nothing came of these efforts and it was soon
evident that it was vastly more convenient to attract African merchants to
the entrepôts on the coast or to the posts established on the lower Senegal.
The more important of these entrepôts gradually developed into small
towns. Those which grew up around European establishments, such as
the French St. Louis on the Senegal or the English Cape Coast Castle on
the Gold Coast, acquired a distinctly cosmopolitan character, comparable to the trading settlements established by Phoenicians in North Africa or by Arabs along the East African coast; their population included a
substantial number of half-castes, many of whom found employment in
European service. Other coastal towns, such as Bonny or Old Calabar
(now in Eastern Nigeria), where Europeans never resided permanently,
retained their African character.

Even in the mid-eighteenth century there can never have been more
than two or three thousand Europeans, exclusive of the crews of trading
vessels, residing and doing business on the coast of Guinea at any one
time. But their influence was out of all proportion to their numbers. In the
first place Europeans were responsible for the introduction of a considerable range of new material objects. Textiles, either of European or of Indian manufacture, headed the list of European exports to West Africa, a
list that also included metalware, ornaments, alcohol, tobacco, and, in
increasing quantities from the late seventeenth century, firearms. Economic historians have pointed out that with the exception of firearms all
these commodities fall into the category of consumer goods, that they
merely supplemented existing African manufactures, and that their import probably had a deleterious effect on local industries. On the other
hand it can be argued that the provision of cheap articles of clothing and

of more efficient domestic utensils did something to improve the local standard of living. Europeans were responsible for another type of material innovation which represented an unquestioned blessing for the peoples of Africa. They brought with them, though only as a by-product of the process of trade, a wide range of new food crops with most of which they themselves had only recently become familiar through their contacts with America. Of the American plants maize and later manioc (cassava) were by far the most important, for they could be used over a wide area as a basic food crop, an invaluable supplement to millet or yams. New fruits and vegetables brought over from America—including pineapple, pawpaw, and tomato—made possible a substantial improvement in the quality of African diet. By reducing the risks of famine and by providing an added resistance to disease these new crops served to accelerate the growth of the population and so to render a major service to the development of the region.

In the way of new techniques the European contribution was less substantial. Many Africans on the coast picked up a smattering of European languages, a few learned how to read and write, a handful were taken to Europe for their education. Some of the more prosperous African merchants adopted European dress and had houses built and furnished in the European style. Far more important than these outward signs of the adoption of European culture was the commercial education that Africans acquired through the practical experience of trade and the development of new methods—the gradual replacement of simple barter, for example, by various forms of currency—to expedite the processes of commerce.

Something has already been said of the new settlements called into existence by European commerce, settlements connected with the interior by new or greatly improved trade routes. But it would be wrong to assume that the coming of Europeans completely revolutionized the pattern of West African trade. Except in so far as they were interrupted by political disturbances the trade routes of the Sudan and the Sahara were used no less vigorously than before. The real significance of the arrival of Europeans on the coast was that it opened a new "frontier of opportunity" for West Africans.

In the field of ideas about man's place in society and in the universe Europeans imparted little to West Africa. At this stage a number of attempts were made, particularly by the Portuguese, to establish Christian missionaries in some of the principal kingdoms of Guinea. In contrast to the kingdom of Kongo, where the Portuguese achieved for a time a remarkable success, nothing came of these efforts. Until as late as 1800 Christianity was of negligible significance in West Africa.

But though Europeans had little direct influence on African ideas, their presence and the nature of the trade in which they were principally engaged had a very substantial indirect influence on the development of the polities which provided them with their main export from West Africa —slaves.

The Atlantic slave trade with its consequences is by far the most controversial subject for this period of African history. Many of those who have thought about it—particularly European humanitarians or African nationalists—see it in a dark but simple light as "a monstrous aberration," "the greatest crime in the annals of humanity," or, in the phrase of the Senegalese poet and statesman Leopold Senghor, as "a bush fire, ravaging Black Africa, wiping out images and values in one vast carnage." The historian, true to the discipline of his profession, must examine the subject more coolly. In so doing he will find himself faced with a highly complex situation in which it is not easy to make sweeping moral judgments.

The outline history of the trade can be told briefly enough. In the first years of exploration Portuguese sea captains made a point of kidnapping unwary Africans whose sale for use as domestic servants helped to defray the expenses of the voyage. This was a practice familiar enough to both Muslim and Christian pirates in the Mediterranean. But the trade soon began to assume a larger scale when African labor was found essential for the sugar plantations of the recently colonized Atlantic islands. And the demand for African slaves became more and more insistent when the same process of development was applied to the virgin lands of the Caribbean and tropical America. Thus, the number of Africans sent overseas steadily increased: in the sixteenth century the annual export of slaves rose to about thirteen thousand, in the seventeenth century to twenty-seven thousand, in the eighteenth to seventy thousand, and in the first decades of the nineteenth century before the final abolition of the trade, numbers of slaves exported sometimes exceeded a hundred thousand. These figures indicate that at least fifteen million Africans were forcibly transported across the Atlantic. But the actual loss of life and manpower to Africa was far greater, since many slaves died as a result of the hardships incurred on the journey to the coast or during the notorious "Middle Passage," and many more individuals lost their lives in the wars that accompanied the trade. For every slave landed in America, another African may have died as a result of the processes of the trade. Thus, it would seem that perhaps as many as thirty million people were lost to Africa as a result of the Atlantic slave trade.

In considering these figures—appalling as they must seem to a later generation—a number of points should be borne in mind. The total figure relates to a very long period of time, while the annual figures refer to slaves drawn from an area which at its widest extended from the Senegal to the Zambezi. There are no means of estimating the population of tropical Africa in these centuries, but a figure of two hundred thousand—a rough maximum for the greatest loss in any one year—cannot represent more than a small percentage of the total population. Clearly, one cannot speak of tropical Africa as a whole being depopulated by the slave trade. Nor can one assume that such a loss produced a drastic weakening of Africa's vitality. Europe in the nineteenth century suffered an even greater loss of population as a result of emigration.

But it is misleading to discuss the trade in such general terms when the nature of its impact varied so greatly from area to area. Some limited parts, notably in Angola, were undoubtedly ravaged very severely by the trade. This represented one extreme; the other was to be found in those areas remote from major kingdoms and thriving trade routes whose communities were completely unaffected by the demands of the traders. Some villages, particularly those of small-scale stateless societies, might find themselves lying in a belt of territory regularly raided by more powerful neighbors; for these peoples the hazards of life were greatly increased. In other communities the trade came to provide a convenient and profitable means for removing criminals, "witches," and other individuals regarded as socially undesirable. Finally, for a few dominant polities the trade brought with it an opportunity to acquire wealth and power on a scale previously unknown.

In Guinea the coast lying between the western borders of modern Ghana and the eastern borders of Nigeria was the scene of the most vigorous commerce. Inevitably, the rich profits to be gained from the trade stimulated intense rivalry not only among Europeans but also among the local African polities. And after the introduction in the mid-seventeenth century of substantial numbers of firearms, local conflicts became still sharper. From competition of this kind no ruler could afford to stand aside. To defend himself he needed firearms; to procure firearms he had to engage in the slave trade, either by taking over the slave markets of his neighbors or by raiding communities less well equipped to defend themselves. In stimulating the development of larger forms of political organization firearms and slaves, together with a certain amount of gold, may be said to have played the same part in Guinea as did cavalry, gold, and slaves in the Sudan.

Although the trade may have increased the wealth of some communities, its ultimate economic effects, recent commentators have pointed out, were harmful to African development. In exchanging men and women whose labor could theoretically be used for productive purposes at home for a shoddy range of consumer goods, Africans made an extremely bad bargain. And yet this is not the way it seemed to contemporaries. Africans engaged in the trade because they wanted the goods Europeans offered, and they soon proved themselves extremely shrewd customers. No doubt it would have been far better for the people of Guinea if they could have developed a plantation economy of their own to provide Europeans with the tropical crops they needed. But the social and political conditions necessary for the establishment of such an economy did not exist before the nineteenth century. The choice with which the greater part of Guinea was faced before 1800 was not between the slave trade or a legitimate commerce of equal value but the slave trade or little or no trade at all. But to speak of a choice is to deal in unrealities. The compulsions of the time were such that neither Europeans nor Africans had any alternative but to engage in the trade.

On the social consequences of the slave trade most modern commentators feel that it is possible to speak in terms of confident generalization; the trade, they assert, stunted African development, brutalized human relationships, increased the oppressive power of chiefs, and in general had a demoralizing effect on those involved in it. Once again, however, a word of caution seems necessary. Many different societies were affected by the trade, and its impact varied from society to society. Moreover, the slave trade represented only one element in the evolution of these societies. Thus, while it is tempting to think of the ghastly human sacrifices practiced in Ashanti, Benin, and Dahomey in the eighteenth and nineteenth centuries as a direct product of the slave trade, it seems more likely that the emergence of these hideous rituals was the consequence of a complex process in which local political tensions and religious beliefs merged with the peculiar assumptions associated with a slave trade economy. Fully to comprehend the nature of the slave trade the historian must have at his disposal a large number of detailed local studies. Until such studies become available, sweeping generalizations about demoralization and degeneration need to be regarded with a good deal of skepticism.

There are three aftereffects of the slave trade that can be described with more assurance. The first is concerned with the development of racial attitudes. The trading partnership between Africans and Europeans on the coast of Guinea was marked by remarkably harmonious race relations. In general, the two sides dealt with one another on a basis of equality. But there were often occasions when Europeans found themselves in a position of some inferiority. "The British interest" on the Gold Coast in the mid-eighteenth century was, in the opinion of a contemporary official, "chiefly, if not entirely, dependent on the good will and friendship of the natives." [16] Half a century earlier a French trader commented that the "great wealth" of the Fantes "makes them so proud and haughty that a European trading there must stand bare to them." [17] But for most Europeans without first-hand experience of Africa the terms "African" or "Negro" and "slave" became almost synonymous. And this impression of African inferiority became all the more intense as the technological gap between Europe and Africa widened. The slave trade thus played an important part in the formation of European notions of racial superiority—notions that later served to bolster European assurance in the rightness of their "civilizing mission" in Africa.

When thinking of the victims of the slave trade a sense of bereavement and suffering predominates. And yet the lives of the men and women forced to toil in the dreary plantations of the New World were not entirely wasted. The labor of African slaves represented a great pioneering effort, a major contribution to the development of the tropical regions of the Americas. However little significance it may seem to possess for the internal evolution of Africa, this work undoubtedly represents one of Africa's major contributions to the shaping of the modern world.

Finally, the slave trade brought about its own demise when greater public awareness of its brutality provoked in Britain, the country that had come in the eighteenth century to take the largest share in the trade, a movement that lead not only to its formal abolition but also to the emergence of dedicated groups of individual men and women determined to compensate Africans for their suffering by bringing to them the "blessings of civilization" as conceived by nineteenth-century Europeans. This urge to "do good" to Africa soon served to justify an increasing interference in African affairs and so proved one of the main forces behind European imperialism.

✻ THE STATES OF GUINEA: 1450 TO 1750

The dominant theme in the history of Guinea in the period 1450 to 1750 is provided not by the impact of Europe but by the emergence and consolidation of a considerable number of substantial states. Certainly, this process of state building owed a good deal to the stimulus of European trade, but it had begun before Europeans arrived and it would undoubtedly have continued, although perhaps at a slower pace, if the coastal trade had been maintained on a much more moderate scale.

The largest polities of Senegambia were those established by the Wolof. At first subordinate to the inland state of Jolof, the three states of the Atlantic littoral, Walo, Cayor, and Baol, asserted their independence in the sixteenth century and maintained it for the next three hundred years. Their political organization was characterized by an elected monarchy—the king acting as leader in war and supreme magician in the rites to ensure his people's prosperity—and by the degree of power possessed by the class of nobles. Though their political history appears to be one long tale of wars and revolutions, the Wolof states obviously possessed a certain basic stability. And it is notable that despite the proximity of powerful Muslim neighbors the political structure of the Wolof states was not seriously affected by Islam until late in the nineteenth century.

In the valley of the Gambia the political pattern differed considerably from that in Wolof territory. Few parts of West Africa contained such a heterogeneous population, made up of Jola, Wolof, Serer, Malinke, Fulani, and Soninke elements; and the activities of dominant groups led to the creation of a score of petty kingdoms along the lower reaches of the river. Beyond the Gambia the pattern changed again, for the peoples of the Windward coast in their self-sufficient village communities remained remarkably little affected by the activities of European traders or—with the exception of the Mende in Sierra Leone—of immigrant groups from the interior. Not until the eighteenth century when the Futa Jallon plateau became the scene of a revolutionary Muslim war was there a major change in the political life of these peoples.

Along the Gold Coast and in its hinterland the process of political evolution followed somewhat different lines. Here at the beginning of the seventeenth century were to be found more than thirty independent kingdoms, some of which had been in existence for more than a hundred years. As these small states began to participate in the growing trade with the outside world, whether with Mande and Hausa traders from the north or with Europeans on the coast, they found themselves increasingly exposed to accelerated processes of political change. An efficient ruler could control trade to his own great advantage by requiring alien traders to pay tolls and customs duties or by asserting a monopoly on certain commodities; if he were an ambitious man he could think of increasing his wealth by using force to extend these measures of control over his neighbors. In this fiercely competitive situation the coastal states found themselves handicapped by the presence of European posts in their midst, for they were drawn into the frequent conflicts between the rival European trading companies, and their internal politics were rendered all the more complicated by the intrigues of European traders. The states lying farther inland were spared these difficulties, and so it was among them that the first major hegemonies arose—Denkyra in the west and Akwamu in the east. Significantly, both kingdoms began their campaigns of expansion in the middle of the seventeenth century at a time when the Dutch, abandoning the cautious policy of the Portuguese who had refused to sell firearms to Africans, began to export "incredible quantities" [18] of guns and gunpowder to the Gold Coast. But mere force was not enough to hold a loose-knit collection of vassal states together, and both Akwamu and Denkyra failed to devise an enduring form of political organization. Akwamu lasted till the 1730's, when it fell apart as a result of its own internal tensions. Denkyra, a kingdom "so arrogant," a contemporary observer noted, "that it looked at all negroes with a contemptible eye," [19] suffered a catastrophic defeat a generation earlier. Appropriately enough, its conquerors were a group of peoples who had recently formed themselves into a new kingdom known as Ashanti, solely in order to defend themselves against Denkyra's aggression.

In the middle of the seventeenth century the forest area that was to become the core of Ashanti contained a number of small Akan states whose rulers, all members of the Oyoko clan, regarded one another as brothers. These dynastic ties made it natural for them to cooperate when faced with the threat from Denkyra. They were fortunate, too, in occupying a country rich in gold and kola nuts and traversed by trade routes that led northward to the Mali and Hausa areas, southward to the European posts on the coast. These political and economic advantages created favorable conditions for rapid development, but could not automatically ensure that a temporary military alliance would crystallize into a permanent political union. For this task high qualities of leadership were required; they were supplied by the chiefs of one of the Oyoko states, Kumasi. Osei Tutu, the late seventeenth-century chief of Kumasi, had spent some time as a young man in the court of Akwamu and had seen at first hand the constitutional and administrative problems involved in holding together previously independent political units. From Akwamu, too, he had learned of new and effective forms of military organization. And he possessed as his closest adviser a man of genius, a priest-magician named Anokye, who provided the political union of the Oyoko states with a legend, regalia, and ritual. In what must have been one of the most extraordinary scenes in the whole course of African history Anokye astounded a vast concourse of chiefs and their followers by making a golden stool appear to descend from heaven and come to rest beside Osei Tutu. This stool Anokye declared embodied the soul of the Ashanti people; henceforward the ruler of Kumasi was to be recognized as the Asantehene, the divinely ordained ruler of the entire people, while the other Oyoko chiefs were to swear allegiance to him in newly devised festivals to be held at yearly intervals.

The new kingdom proved astonishingly successful. Under Osei Tutu and his able successor, Opoku Ware, Ashanti armies achieved an almost unbroken run of victories that extended the kingdom southward to include most of the old hegemonies of Denkyra and Akwamu and northward to conquer parts of Gonja and Dagomba. But even more remarkable than these military successes was the skill with which the eighteenth-century Asantehenes managed, despite occasional reverses, to devise a political structure which could hold their growing empire together.

Despite the fact that by 1720 they were by far the strongest kingdom in the area the Ashanti were not masters of the coast. Just as the Oyoko states had come together to defend themselves against Denkyra, so a group of coastal states, formed by the Fante in the central part of the Gold Coast, founded a confederacy to meet Ashanti aggression. The Fante never achieved so close a measure of unity as the Ashanti, but their position was bolstered by increasing support from European traders on the coast.

Thus, by the latter half of the eighteenth century the political map of the Gold Coast had come to assume a pattern very much simpler than that of a hundred years earlier, with two great hegemonies—the Ashanti union and empire and the Fante confederation—imposing new superstructures over the mass of previously independent polities.

East of the Volta River, in territory that now forms the southern part of Togo and Dahomey, there lived a cluster of peoples who can most conveniently be described as Adja-speakers. By the eighteenth century a striking contrast in political organization was beginning to emerge between the western and the eastern Adja. The western Adja, later known as the Ewe, never established a kingdom of any size; as late as the end of the nineteenth century their country was divided up between more than a hundred miniscule chieftaincies. Among the eastern Adja, there came to be founded in the late sixteenth and seventeenth centuries three states of some importance: Allada (Ardra), Ouidah (Whydah or Hueda), and Abomey, the last of which developed into the powerful kingdom of Dahomey.

The reason for this sharp disparity in the political evolution of different sections of a culturally similar people must lie in the varying intensity of the external stimuli to which the two halves of the Adja were exposed. All the Adja appear to have been affected by the culture of their eastern neighbors, the Yoruba, but this influence, implying as it must have the transmission from the old established Yoruba kingdoms of more sophisticated notions of political organization, was obviously more strongly felt among the eastern Adja. Indeed, in the 1690's many of these people came under Yoruba domination, when Oyo sent an army against Allada and forced the ruler to pay tribute. By this time the two kingdoms of Allada and Ouidah had begun to carry on a vigorous trade in slaves, and European merchants had found it worth their while to establish trading posts in the territory of the latter kingdom. The western Adja, by contrast, remained among the most isolated peoples of the Guinea coast; there were no trading posts in their territory, which seems indeed to have been little visited by alien traders, either African or European.

In the 1720's Abomey, which lay some sixty miles from the coast, conquered Ouidah and Allada. But though Agaja, the victorious king of Abomey, owed much of his success to his skill in building up an efficient army, he could not match the military might of Oyo. In 1730, after his country had been ravaged by the cavalry of Oyo, Agaja was forced to acknowledge himself a vassal of the *alafin* (the title of the ruler of Oyo). And for the remainder of the century Dahomey, though developing internally into one of the most tightly governed states in Guinea, was forced to accept this humiliatingly subordinate status.

In the middle of the eighteenth century Oyo was at the height of its power. Very little is known of the kingdom's early history, but it would seem that much of its success was due to its position. It lay in a stretch of the savanna that brought its peoples into touch with traders coming from the Hausa states to the north and the Akan states to the west. From the Hausa the rulers of Oyo obtained horses, which enabled them to build up a force of cavalry that became the scourge and terror of their neighbors. But horses are of no use in forest country and so Oyo, whose territory was said at one time to have contained no less than six thousand towns and villages, remained an empire of the savanna, including under its suzerainty a considerable number of people of non-Yoruba stock but leaving outside its borders probably more than half of all Yoruba-speakers.

Those Yoruba who were not subject to Oyo lived in a multitude of states, numbering in time as many as fifty and varying greatly in size, political structure, and history. Ife retained its mystical primacy in the Yoruba community, but the physical force at its rulers' disposal was far less than that possessed by other Yoruba *obas* (chiefs). Some kingdoms such as Ijebu could trace their history back to a remote past; many others were recent creations established in certain cases by political adventurers breaking away from the older kingdoms.

To the east Yoruba-speakers merged with Edo-speakers among whom the kingdom of Benin occupied a position of unchallenged paramountcy. Benin was a powerful state in the fifteenth century, and it reached its apogee in the course of the next hundred years at a time when there was no other kingdom of comparable stature in all Guinea. Based on a substantial core of Edo people living around the capital city, Benin expanded in all directions to assert its hegemony as far west as Lagos, as far east as the lower Niger, and both Yoruba and Ibo groups accepted the suzerainty of the *oba* (king of Benin). But from the seventeenth century onward Benin's hold on its remoter vassals weakened, though the kingdom's decline was not continuous. Indeed, so well constructed was the political structure of the kingdom that it endured with little change until the end of the nineteenth century.

Oyo was not drawn into the orbit of the Atlantic trade until the eighteenth century, when a route was established between the capital, Old Oyo, and Porto-Novo on the coast east of Ouidah. Benin, by contrast, had a long and intimate record of intercourse with Europeans. In the sixteenth century no kingdom in Guinea was on such cordial terms with the Portuguese, the *obas* sending an embassy to Lisbon, allowing Portuguese missionaries to build a church in their capital, and requesting Portuguese firearms for their army. By the eighteenth century, however, Benin's trade with Europe was at a low ebb. And so Benin, at one time seemingly wide open to outside influences, became the most isolated of all the major kingdoms of Guinea.

Benin's decline coincided with the rise of a number of powerful trading communities among the Ijaw of the eastern Niger delta and the Ibibio of the Cross River. Confusingly termed "city-states" by recent writers— there were no urban graces in the squalid villages that became their capitals—these owed their rapid growth entirely to the Atlantic trade. With the densely populated Ibo country as their hinterland the trading states of the Oil Rivers, as the network of creeks and estuaries came to be known in the nineteenth century, were exceptionally well sited to act as middlemen in the slave trade. Using the guns and cannon obtained from Europe to arm their massive war-canoes, each state carved out its own commercial sphere of influence, developing as it did so remarkable new forms of political organization.

Although the Ibo came in the eighteenth century to supply a greater number of slaves than any other ethnic group in Guinea, their own small village-states possessed an internal vitality which appears to have left them little disturbed by the effects of the trade. But as an expanding commerce multiplied contacts between communities, certain groups whose prestige was derived from the control of important religious centers gradually began to establish their commercial hegemony over extensive areas. The Aro of Aro Chuku became the best known of these local imperialists, and it may well be that the Aros' skillful blend of religious propaganda, military force, and commercial acumen reproduced the same set of qualities that had led to the predominance of Ife among the Yoruba many centuries earlier.

THE MUSLIM REVOLUTIONS

By the beginning of the eighteenth century the Muslim religion had been practiced in the Sudanic belt of West Africa for more than five hundred years. And yet there were still very few parts of the region which the traveler from North Africa or the Middle East could confidently describe as *Dar al-Islam,* "Abode of Islam." Only in the famous cities of the middle Niger and in the capital of Bornu would a Muslim visitor be able to find a substantial part of the population regularly observing the ritual obligations of the faith and being governed in accordance with the *Shari'a,* the Muslim code of law. In most of the principal towns of the Western and Central Sudan there were small communities of Muslims, usually engaged in trade and often differing in language from the people among whom they lived. As for the rulers of the Sudan some, particularly in the Hausa states, were Muslims at least in name, but the majority—notable among them the kings of the Bambara, the Mossi, and the Wolof—still supported the traditional religion of their peoples. On both sides religious intolerance was rare. Muslim rulers accepted many religious practices that stricter champions of the faith would have denounced as "heathen," while non-Muslim rulers were glad to make use of the services of Muslim secretaries and advisers.

Flexible and easygoing though these Sudanic societies may appear, they contained certain obvious sources of tension. A strict, well-educated Muslim, his knowledge of the world widened either by the experience of the pilgrimage to Mecca or by long trading journeys, could hardly avoid feeling a strong sense of cultural superiority over his parochial, illiterate, and pagan neighbors. The collapse of the Songhai empire, whose later rulers had been such staunch upholders of Islam, must have impoverished many of the *ulama,* but the tradition of Muslim learning was by this time too deeply rooted to be destroyed. Certain groups had come to acquire a special reputation for their devotion to the faith. Prominent among these "missionary clans" as they have been called were the Kunta, a tribe of Arab nomads whose main encampments lay north of Timbuktu, and the Torodbe, a Fulfulde-speaking group (akin to the Fulani) whose members were to be found in many countries between Futa Toro, their original home, and the Hausa kingdoms. Leading members of both the Kunta and the Torodbe belonged to the Qadiriyya *tariqa,* one of the major religious fraternities of North Africa. The gradual expansion of such a fraternity established a far-flung network of contacts which made it easier for serious practitioners of the faith to keep in touch with one another, while the regular meetings of local branches served to strengthen the devotion of ordinary Muslims.

The more conscious a Sudanic Muslim became of the obligations of his religion, the less easy it was for him to tolerate the abuses he saw around him. In circumstances such as these and especially when they found themselves being persecuted for their faith, devout Muslims were bound to pay special attention to those passages in the Prophet's teaching in which he laid stress on the duty of the Muslim community to take part in a jihad or holy war for the protection and expansion of the faith. In the eighteenth and nineteenth centuries no less than five jihads were proclaimed in various parts of Western and Central Sudan. Each of these jihads had a revolutionary effect on the politics, the social structure, and the culture of the people in whose areas it was waged.

The first in this series broke out in Futa Jallon (now part of the Republic of Guinea) about 1725. At this time the Futa Jallon plateau contained a mixed population of Fulani pastoralists and farmers of Susu or Jallonka stock. In the early eighteenth century a number of marabouts (Muslim divines) of Fulani or Malinke origin began to settle in the area and soon came into conflict with the local pagan rulers. Fifty years of confused fighting ended in the establishment of a Muslim state whose rulers' title, *almami,* derived from the Arabic *al-imam,* denoted that their authority was conceived primarily in religious terms, the imam being in origin the leader of a community in its ritual prayers.

The foundation of a Muslim state in Futa Jallon had a profound impact on the surrounding peoples. Dispossessed chiefs of the Susu ruling houses and Muslim adventurers from Futa Jallon began establishing themselves as alien rulers among the Temne and other peoples of Sierra Leone and the Windward coast. Muslim traders from the interior attracted by the success of their coreligionists began to do more business in the area, pioneering as they did so new routes to the coast. By the end of the eighteenth century the main towns of Futa Jallon, such as Timbo, with their more spacious houses and their flourishing and well-attended Koranic schools presented a striking contrast to the villages of their pagan neighbors.

In the 1770's a second jihad was proclaimed in Futa Toro in the Senegal Valley where the Torodbe took the lead in overthrowing the pagan Fulani dynasty. But neither in Futa Jallon nor in Futa Toro did the jihads lead to the erection of strong centralized states. In both countries effective power lay in the hands of provincial chiefs, the descendants of the original war leaders. These chiefs elected the *almami* who was rarely allowed to hold office for more than a few years and so had no opportunity to build up an effective governmental machinery at the center.

The caliphate of Sokoto, the state born of the third in the series of jihads, contrasted sharply in size and political organization with the two Futas. Destined to form for a time the most extensive imperial structure in tropical Africa, the caliphate was in a large measure the creation of three outstanding men, Usuman dan Fodio, his brother Abdullahi, and his son Muhammad Bello. This remarkable triumvirate came of a Torodbe family that had been settled for generations in the Hausa kingdom of Gobir. Usuman, born in 1754, was by profession a religious teacher whose piety and sweetness of character invested him with that quality of charismatic saintliness Muslims call *baraka*. "He filled the western country with learning and with seekers after learning," his son said of him. "He was a reformer at the head of his generation, an excellent orator, a fine classical poet." [20] Usuman was not a violent revolutionary of the same stamp as the Almoravid or Almohad leaders, but a gradualist who directed his call for a stricter adherence to the original principles of Islam to his fellow Muslims and who hoped by the use of peaceful admonition to persuade the rulers of the Hausa states to amend their ways. But since he found himself bound to denounce as "impious" the cruel and oppressive practices of the governments of his day, his message inevitably acquired a much wider appeal, and Hausa peasants and Fulani cattlemen, hitherto quite untouched by Islam but with many grievances against their rulers, flocked to hear him preach. The semipagan ruling elite of Gobir naturally began to see in the ever-growing number of Usuman's followers a serious threat to their authority. A number of violent incidents took place. Usuman and his disciples were clearly in danger of their lives. There was no alternative for them but to flee Gobir and proclaim a jihad against their sacrilegious oppressors.

From a serious disturbance in one corner of Gobir the war spread to engulf all of the Hausa states. Men enrolled themselves under the banner of the Shehu (the title, a Hausa form of the Arabic *shaikh,* by which Usuman was known to his followers) for many reasons: ideological zeal, eagerness to avenge old wrongs, love of adventure, or lust for booty, and later when it became clear which side was going to win, a shrewd calculation of self-interest. Though the Shehu's message was universalistic in intent, the majority of his supporters came from a single ethnic group, the Fulani, with which Usuman himself, as a Torodbe, was closely linked. Most of the Fulani had been living in Hausa country, either as settled farmers or as nomadic pastoralists, for many generations, but they still retained a strong sense of separate identity. Usuman's jihad should not, however, be thought of in such simple terms as a war between Muslim Fulani and pagan Hausa. Many of the Fulani pastoralists who fought for the jihad remained pagans, and Hausa, Tuareg, and members of other ethnic groups were to be found in Usuman's camp. On the other hand some Fulani and not a few Muslims supported the cause of the Hausa kings. But there can be no doubt that the involvement of such large numbers of Fulani gave to the jihad a strength and range it would not have possessed as a purely religious or social movement, for by this time the

Fulani had become an influential minority not only in the Hausa states but in many other parts of the Central Sudan.

The jihad began in 1804. By 1808 after a fierce and close-fought struggle the Shehu's followers were masters of Gobir. The next year Sokoto was founded as the capital of the new state. Usuman who had been invested with the Hausa title of *sarkin musulmi*, "Lord of the Muslims," concerned himself primarily with religious propaganda and exegesis, leaving in the capable hands of his brother and his son the practical problems of administration. Already before the final defeat of Gobir, Usuman's supporters had succeeded in seizing power in the Hausa states of Kano, Zaria, and Katsina. From the Hausa country the jihad was carried eastward against Bornu, southeastward into the Benue Valley, and southward to Nupe and Oyo in a movement which, despite some fluctuations, retained its momentum until well into the second half of the nineteenth century.

At an early stage in the jihad Fulani living in the western marchlands of Bornu threw off Kanuri rule and founded a number of minor emirates, including Hadeija and Katagum. From these bases they carried the war into the heart of Bornu, destroying the capital and forcing the *mai* and his effete courtiers to flee eastward. Bornu was saved from ruin and dismemberment by a marabout of mixed Kamembu and Fezzani ancestry, Muhammad al-Amin, usually known as al-Kanemi, "the man from Kanem." Al-Kanemi was fully the equal of the great leaders of the jihad, both as a religious scholar and as a soldier and practical administrator. Bringing with him a force of Kamembu spearmen and Shuwa Arab cavalry, on two occasions he drove the Fulani from the metropolitan provinces of Bornu. This powerful and popular hero thus made himself the de facto ruler of Bornu, but he was shrewd enough to allow the *mai,* the representative of the ancient Saifuwa dynasty, to remain as titular sovereign, while he himself took over the administration of the country and embarked on a policy of reform designed to rebuild the crumbling structure of the state and to enforce a proper observance of the obligations of the faith with a zeal no less ardent than that of the jihadists themselves. Muhammad al-Amin proved himself the founder of a new dynasty, though it was not until 1846, eleven years after his death, that the last Saifuwa *mai* was removed by Umar, Muhammad al-Amin's son and successor. Under its Kanemi rulers Bornu was a more tightly governed state than it had been under the Saifuwa, but the ancient kingdom had lost its old position of hegemony in the Central Sudan. The Fulani conquest turned the face of the former Hausa states, once vassals of the *mais,* westward to Sokoto; at the same time Bornu found itself faced with an increasingly formidable neighbor to its east through the rise of the kingdom of Wadai.

To the south and southwest of Bornu there lived a great variety of ethnic groups whose polities varied from minor kingdoms such as Mandara to a multitude of independent village communities. The Fulani had been moving into this area during the eighteenth century, attracted by the lush grazing of the Benue Valley. Already by 1800 some Fulani had achieved positions of local importance by marrying into the families of the chiefs of other groups. The jihad provided the scattered bands of nomads with a unique opportunity for concerted action, as the Fulani flocked to enroll themselves under the banners which enterprising warriors of the faith had brought from the Shehu himself. Thus formed, the Muslim war bands set about conquering neighboring pagan communities and so built up a string of new states—Bauchi, Gombe, Adamawa, and others—all tributary to Sokoto and larger than any polities the area had known before. Adamawa, which took its name from its founder, Mobiddo Adama, was the most extensive of these new emirates. Its capital was at Yola on the Benue, but it stretched deep into the grassy highlands of Cameroun, where ambitious provincial chiefs found it easy to carve out new fiefs for themselves.

Fulani expansion in the Benue country was facilitated by the natural divisions between diverse ethnic groups. But the Fulani proved no less successful in their drive to the south which brought them up against the substantial kingdoms of Nupe and Oyo. Suave, well-informed, determined, and unscrupulous, their morale strengthened not only by their recent successes but by an arrogant conviction of racial and cultural superiority, the Fulani proved themselves, here as in other parts of West Africa, masters of the arts of diplomacy and politics. In Nupe a dispute over the succession played into their hands; in Oyo they profited from a long drawn-out civil war between the Alafin and one of the great warlords based on the provincial town of Ilorin. By a shrewd blend of guile and force the Fulani made themselves masters both of Nupe and of Ilorin. From these bases the jihad was carried eastward to the peoples living about the Niger-Benue confluence and southward deep into Yoruba territory.

Oyo had begun to show signs of serious internal weakness toward the end of the eighteenth century. The establishment of a Fulani emirate at Ilorin in the heart of the kingdom was a disastrous blow. The capital, Old Oyo, was abandoned and thousands of refugees poured southward, shattering the relatively peaceful relationship that had existed in the past between the various Yoruba states. Thus, there began a period of civil war that convulsed Yoruba communities for the rest of the century and led to the emergence of a number of new centers of power. Of these new centers the most prominent was Ibadan, founded in 1829 as a war camp by a group of soldiers of fortune from Oyo. Ibadan took the lead in resisting the Fulani who suffered a decisive check in 1840.

While the jihad of Usuman dan Fodio was running its course, two new holy wars broke out in the area of the upper Niger. The first of these—and the fourth in the series of jihads—was proclaimed in 1818 by a Fulani marabout, Seku Ahmadu, against the pagan Fulani rulers of Macina, a little state in the neighborhood of Jenne on the upper Niger and a vassal of the Bambara kingdom of Segu. By the time of Seku Ahmadu's death in 1844, his empire embraced an area of about fifty thousand square miles from Jenne to Timbuktu. Eight years later the last great jihad leader, al-Hajj Umar Tal, a Torodbe from Futa Toro, launched his followers on a holy war that gave him mastery by 1864, the year of his death, over the two Bambara kingdoms of Segu and Kaarta, the recently established theocratic state of Macina, and many smaller principalities between the Niger and the Senegal.

Both Ahmadu and Umar had close contacts with the leaders of the jihad in the Hausa country. Ahmadu had been a disciple of Usuman dan Fodio in 1805 and had sent a flag to Sokoto to be blessed by the Shehu before launching his own jihad. Umar's relations with Sokoto were even closer, for he had spent several years at the court of Muhammad Bello, Shehu Usuman's son and successor, and married one of Bello's daughters. The success of the jihad in the Hausa states undoubtedly inspired both Ahmadu and Umar Tal to undertake similar wars in their own countries.

But although the three nineteenth-century jihads presented obvious similarities in the religious zeal of the leaders and the revolutionary nature of their message in regard to the old social order, there were also striking differences between them. These differences were most apparent in the case of al-Hajj Umar, for he, unlike Shehu Usuman and Seku Ahmadu, who belonged to the old, established Qadiriyya fraternity, was a member of the Tijaniyya, a new religious order founded in the Maghrib in the late eighteenth century. Much simpler in its ritual, the Tijaniyya made a wider and more egalitarian appeal than the sophisticated Qadiriyya. At the same time members of the new tariqa believed themselves to be superior to all other Muslims; compared to Qadiris they were, Tijanis claimed, as gold to iron. The introduction of this new religious order, whose tenets were ideally suited to a militant and revolutionary movement, represents al-Hajj Umar's most substantial contribution to West African Islam.

Umar's early life had been devoted to travel and scholarship, but once he had established a base for himself at Dinguiray to the east of Futa Jallon, he proved himself an outstanding military leader with a keen interest in weaponry. Unlike the other jihad leaders his position brought him into close contact with Europeans and especially with the French on the Senegal, and he developed a vigorous trade in firearms, weapons which had been little used in other jihads.

Unlike the Sokoto leaders, whose empire, though conquered by the British, preserved many of its characteristics during the period of colonial rule, neither Seku Ahmadu nor al-Hajj Umar were the founders of long-lasting states. Ahmadu was an administrator of genius who made Macina for a time one of the best governed polities in Africa, but in 1862 the kingdom was overwhelmed by al-Hajj Umar, who made use of highly specious arguments to justify his attack on so strictly Muslim a state. Umar himself was killed fighting in Macina two years later. In the course of the next thirty years the territory he had conquered was taken over by the French. But even without French intervention it seems unlikely that his empire would have held together as well as that of Sokoto. The natural base for Umar's state was Futa Toro, his own homeland and the country from which he drew his most ardent supporters. But when he started his jihad, Futa Toro was coming under French domination, and so he had to impose the structure of his rule over people of alien stock, Bambara, Fulani, and others, who soon had cause to regard their new Tukulor masters as a tyrannical minority.

Whatever the outcome of the individual jihads, there can be no doubt that taken as a whole they represent one of the great revolutions of African history. The jihad leaders introduced new forms of political organization which at their most successful provided certain parts of the Sudanic belt with a measure of political unity they had never known before. Even more significant was their impact on the general culture of the population of wide areas. If today a majority of the population of Senegal and Gambia, Mali and Guinea, Niger and Northern Nigeria can be classified as Muslims, this is due in large part to the impulses set in motion by the jihads of the eighteenth and nineteenth centuries. Acceptance of Islam brought with it not only new political allegiances and new religious formulas, but also new customs that affected the dress a man wore, the food he ate, the education he received, and the family relationships he maintained.

But like all violent revolutions, the West African jihads present savage paradoxes. Begun in part as movements of social protest against unjust practices, they led in most areas to the establishment of new aristocracies little less oppressive than those they had overthrown. These aristocracies derived a large part of their wealth from slaves obtained by attacking their pagan neighbors in raids hypocritically sanctified as continuations of the holy war. Indeed, though they undoubtedly brought about a new measure of internal security in some areas, these *empires combattants* [21] were always engaged in warfare. One knows too little about the state of the Western and Central Sudan before the jihads to make comparative generalizations with any great assurance. But it does not seem unreasonable to suppose that many parts of West Africa were experiencing a greater amount of violence in the 1850's than they had known a century earlier and that most of this violence was directly or indirectly a result of the jihads. Certainly, the prevailing violence and the divisions that it engendered would seem to provide one of the reasons for the ease with which a new race of conquerors succeeded in the latter half of the nineteenth century in taking over the entire region.

THE IMPACT OF EUROPE: THE ANTECEDENTS OF IMPERIALISM, 1750 TO 1850

By 1750 most of the maritime nations of Western Europe had a share in the Guinea trade. But as the volume of trade steadily increased, one nation began to outstrip its continental rivals. The British had taken a comparatively modest part in the West African trade in the seventeenth century; in the decades after 1750 they established themselves as by far the most successful slave traders in the world. An estimate made in 1787 reckoned that the British were then purchasing thirty-eight thousand slaves a year, the French between twenty and thirty thousand, and the Portuguese ten thousand.

This burgeoning trade meant that more Europeans than ever before, particularly in Britain and France, the two most powerful nations of contemporary Europe, had some reason to take an interest in Africa—or rather, other parts of the continent being of little concern at this time, in Guinea. Only a few Europeans—the slave dealers of Liverpool and Bordeaux, their agents on the West Coast, their customers, the plantation owners of Jamaica or Virginia—had direct contact with Africans. But there was a much wider circle of businessmen—gunsmiths in Birmingham, for example, or silk manufacturers in Lyon—who were partly dependent on some aspect of the African trade for their livelihood. This steadily mounting interest generated by commercial activities had a range of consequences that led to the gradual transformation of European ideas about the tropical regions of the continent.

Globally conscious statesmen in London and Paris began to appreciate the strategic importance of their countrymen's trading posts in West Africa with the result that the Anglo-French conflicts of the period produced a series of minor campaigns between British and French forces in the Senegambia area. Of little importance in their immediate consequences, these petty colonial skirmishes foreshadowed the intense rivalry between the two powers that was to become a major factor in shaping the political destinies of West Africa.

The proliferation of books about Africa meant that the continent was beginning to stir the imagination of a public far wider than the small group of merchants and politicians with a practical stake in the affairs of Guinea, a public whose members reacted to the new horizons opened up to them in many different ways. Men of scientific inclination looked at maps of the continent and wondered what that vast, uncharted interior might contain. Men of sensibility, many of them under the spell of such dynamic advocates of a more humane system of human relationships as John Wesley or Jean Jacques Rousseau, were horrified by the casual brutalities of the African slave system. Rationally minded men, proudly conscious of the remarkable achievements of their own culture and age, or men of religion, enthusiastically convinced that they were the privileged possessors of divine truth, read of the "barbarous customs," the "heathen practices" of contemporary African societies, and experienced emotions of distaste, pity, or contempt, sublimated in some cases by an urge to bring to these unfortunate black men the blessings of Christianity and civilization.

And so, as the eighteenth century drew to an end, there emerged among Europeans a strange assortment of attitudes to Africa—commercial interest, national competitiveness, scientific curiosity, simple compassion, and a generous, if patronizing, zeal to "civilize" and "convert." These attitudes were to serve as springboards for future European activities, first in West Africa and later in other parts of the continent. From such diverse antecedents the conquering colonialism of the latter half of the nineteenth century was formed.

These different strands of thought and action were closely intertwined, but for clarity's sake they must be examined separately, beginning with the impact of European curiosity. One can find no more striking illustration of the extent of Europe's ignorance of the geography of the interior of Africa than the opinion widely held until as late as the 1790's that the Niger flowed not eastward but westward, to enter the Atlantic through the Senegal and the Gambia. There was nothing surprising about European ignorance of the interior; most traders living on the coast of West Africa had had no incentive to travel inland. But as Europe's knowledge of more distant continents was dramatically enlarged by the exploits of such men as Captain James Cook, the wide blanks on contemporary maps of Africa began to seem a reproach to the spirit of the age. So it struck a select group of Englishmen who came together in 1788 to found the first learned society ever to be devoted to the study of Africa. This body, "the Association for Promoting the Discovery of the Interior Parts

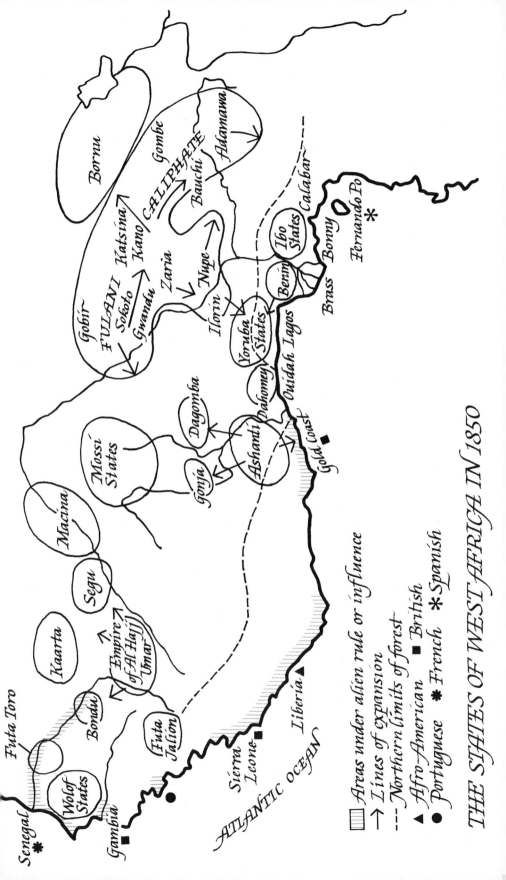

THE STATES OF WEST AFRICA IN 1850

Legend:
- ⬚ Areas under alien rule or influence
- → Lines of expansion
- --- Northern limits of forest
- ▲ Afro-American ■ British
- Portuguese * French * Spanish

Labels on map:

Senegal *
Futa Toro
Wolf States
Gambia ■
Kaarta
Bondu
Bonn
Empire of Al Hajj Umar
(Futa Jalon)
Segu
Macina
Mossi States
Gonja
Dagomba
Ashanti
Sierra Leone ■
Liberia ▲
ATLANTIC OCEAN
Gold Coast ■
Dahomey
Ouidah
Gobir
FULANI
Sokoto
Gwandu
Katsina
Kano
Zaria
Nupe
Ilorin
Yoruba States
Benin
Lagos
Brass
Bonny
Calabar
Ibo States
Fernando Po *
Bornu
Gombe
CALIPHATE
Bauchi
Adamawa

of Africa," was concerned, as its grandiloquent title clearly affirmed, with the task of exploration, but it may well be regarded as the forbear of many of those learned societies founded in various European countries and in the United States whose members have devoted themselves to the study of the land, the peoples, and the resources of Africa. The most substantial achievements of the first phase of the exploration of the interior took place in West Africa. Between 1788 and 1830 a succession of daring young men, drawn from several different parts of Europe and financed first by the African Association and later by the British government and other agencies, provided the outside world with accounts of many of the major states of West Africa and showed that the Niger was a great navigable waterway which appeared to provide easy access from the much frequented creeks and inlets of its confusing delta to the populous countries of the Central Sudan. This was a discovery which commercial interests, even though they had given no support at all to the initial work of exploration, were to exploit in time with increasing vigor.

Even more important in its consequences for the future than this relatively sudden enlargement of Europe's knowledge was the movement of conscience and compassion that found practical expression in the campaign to abolish the slave trade. The campaign was begun by a small group of Englishmen in the 1780's and rapidly developed into a national crusade with international ramifications, for ardent abolitionist lobbies emerged in most of the European and American countries with a stake in the trade. In 1807 the British Parliament made it unlawful for British subjects to take part in the trade. And from then on successive British governments used all the means at their disposal—from a naval squadron in West African waters to insistent diplomatic pressure on slave-trading nations, European, American, and African—to bring about the complete termination of the trade in slaves. But it was not until the 1860's—after a period of unprecedented activity by slave dealers from the Americas in the 1820's and 1830's—that the export of slaves from Guinea finally came to an end.

Among the problems of particular concern to the abolitionists was the fate of ex-slaves in England and North America. To return the "Black Poor" as they were termed in eighteenth-century England to their land of origin seemed an undertaking at once practical and humane. Two settlements for freed slaves were founded in Guinea, one on the Sierra Leone peninsula, the other, later to become the Republic of Liberia, farther east on the littoral sometimes termed the Grain Coast. The two settlements differed in origin and development: Sierra Leone, founded in 1787 as a result of largely private English philanthropy, was taken over by the British government in 1808 and became the first Crown Colony in tropical

Africa. Its population, a mere two thousand settlers, mostly ex-slaves from Jamaica or Nova Scotia, increased rapidly when British warships began landing "liberated Africans" rescued from the holds of captured slavers. Liberia, whose first settlements were founded in 1822 as a result of the work of the American Colonization Society, drew its immigrants almost entirely from the Negro population of the United States. The Afro-American community was never a political colony of the United States, and its anomalous status led to practical difficulties when it became necessary to raise revenue by imposing custom duties on foreign traders. The settlers, therefore, decided in 1847 to end the legal confusion by declaring their community a sovereign republic.

The English abolitionists were for the most part men of ardent faith who saw it as part of their duty to bring to Africa the blessings of their religion. Abolitionist zeal fusing with evangelical fervor led to the formation in the 1790's of a number of Protestant missionary societies, some of which devoted their attention to West Africa. With the help of workers drawn from most Protestant countries mission stations were founded first in those parts under British control, then in the 1840's in places such as Calabar and Abeokuta, beyond the pale of British jurisdiction. By 1850 it was clear that these Protestant evangelists were making a substantial impact on the peoples among whom they worked. For the first time Christianity was to be regarded as a force in the affairs of West Africa.

Slaves had for so long formed the major export of Guinea that the extraordinary volte-face of the nation most deeply involved in the trade was bound to produce changes profound enough to be described as revolutionary. This was particularly obvious in the field of commerce. Slaves were gradually replaced by palm oil as the principal export of the Guinea coast. Palm oil had hitherto been a substance of little importance in the Guinea trade, but once it was discovered early in the nineteenth century that the oil could be used both as a lubricant for machinery and as a constituent in soap manufacture, demand rose rapidly in a Britain caught up in the first, grimy stages of its industrial and urban revolution. The boon in palm oil preserved the prosperity of Bonny and Calabar as much as of Liverpool, for the trading states of the Niger delta were fortunate in having as their immediate hinterland the most favorable territory for the oil palm in all West Africa. Elsewhere, other vegetable products—peanuts in Senegal, timber in Sierra Leone—began to take the place of slaves as major exports, while in kingdoms such as Dahomey rulers started to employ the slaves they could not sell overseas to produce plantation crops. Ultimately, the transition from the Atlantic slave trade to "legitimate commerce" was made without causing economic disaster in any part of Guinea.

Politically, the abolition of the slave trade introduced a new element into the affairs of Guinea, for the British in their zeal to extirpate the slavers and to protect their own legitimate commerce, were driven to intervene in local politics on a scale which no European power had ever done before. The transformation of Sierra Leone into a Crown Colony was the first step. In 1816 Bathurst was founded to check the slave trade on the Gambia. In 1821 the government took over the British posts on the Gold Coast, previously administered by a company of merchants. Seven years later, after a distastefully expensive war with the Ashanti, the government returned the posts to the merchants. There followed a remarkable period in which the initiative of a single man transformed the situation on the coast. George Maclean, a Scottish army officer appointed governor by the merchants, established excellent relations with the Ashanti and persuaded the Fante rulers to submit their disputes to his arbitration. Maclean's system of jurisdiction became the foundation of the colony of the Gold Coast when the British Government resumed direct control of the area in 1844.

While the British were thus beginning to construct the colonial framework of the countries that are now the independent states of Gambia, Sierra Leone, and Ghana, they were also becoming more deeply involved in the area of the future Nigeria. In 1830 fifteen years of intensive exploration financed by the British government ended with the voyage of two young Cornishmen, Richard and John Lander, down the Niger to its mouth. Two years later a Liverpool merchant attempted to exploit the Landers' discovery by sending a commercial expedition up the river. In 1841 another, even larger expedition was sent to the Niger; organized by the British government at the behest of the abolitionist lobby, it was intended to establish centers for legitimate trade and missionary enterprise deep in the interior. So heavy was the mortality among the Europeans taking part in these two expeditions that both were regarded as dismal failures; but by making use of steamships—the most spectacular manifestation of the technological superiority of Europe West Africa had yet seen—they pioneered a method of penetration that enabled the next generation of Europeans, once they had found a prophylactic against malaria, to make themselves masters of the navigable stretches of the lower Niger and the Benue.

Along the coast in the 1840's the British government began to use the methods of gunboat diplomacy to persuade local rulers to sign treaties renouncing the slave trade. In 1849 a full-time consul was appointed to "the Bights of Biafra and Benin." Based on the Spanish-owned island of Fernando Po and with a formidable naval force within easy call, the holders of this post, the first European diplomatic agency ever to be established in West Africa, began to intervene ever more vigorously on behalf of British nationals and British protégés in what had hitherto been regarded as the purely domestic affairs of the coastal states. Certainly, there was no intention of establishing any political dominion in this area, and yet the contacts formed by the actions of consuls and naval officers, traders, missionaries, and explorers were to prepare the way for the creation of by far the most substantial of British colonies in tropical Africa.

Compared with this brisk expansion of British interests, the growth of French influence in this period appears very modest. The Senegal remained the main area of French activity, though by 1850 the French presence on the river was not much more powerful than it had been a century earlier. In the 1830's and 1840's French traders with a certain amount of official backing began to develop new commercial links with the Casamance country south of the Gambia, with the stretch of coast north of Sierra Leone, with the Ivory Coast, and with Dahomey. The small trading posts of this period were to become two generations later the growing points of the colonies that were to develop into the modern states of Guinea, Ivory Coast, and Dahomey.

Among the European powers with interests in West Africa the future clearly lay with the British and the French. On the Gold Coast the Danes, who had declared the slave trade illegal as early as 1804, sold their posts to the British in 1850, while the Dutch gave up their trading stations in 1872. Farther east on the stretch of coast between Ouidah and Lagos traders from Brazil had begun a flourishing trade in slaves in the early eighteenth century, a trade which reached its peak in the 1830's, when the Yoruba wars flooded the markets on the coast with captives and the Brazilian port of Bahia was importing close to twenty thousand slaves a year. Strong action by the British in ejecting the slave-trading ruler of Lagos in 1851 ended both the trade in slaves and the political influence of Brazil in West Africa.

It is easy to appreciate the political consequences of the complex of actions associated with the abolition of the slave trade. But historians of the future, when distance will reveal more sharply the ephemeral nature of European colonial rule in West Africa, may well lay greater stress on the cultural consequences of European activities in the age of abolitionist enthusiasm. This period marked the beginning of a real meeting of minds between Europe and tropical Africa. For the first time—if one leaves aside the handful of West Africans who managed to gain an education in Europe in the eighteenth century—substantial numbers of Africans began to be influenced not only by the techniques and the material innovations introduced by Europeans but by European ideas. These ideas, being concerned with man's place in the universe and with the right ordering of society, were no less forceful and no less far-reaching than those being propagated at this time by Muslim zealots in the Sudan. The first agents of this revolution were Protestant missionaries, evangelically minded administrators, and God-fearing British naval officers, all men with a confidence verging on arrogance in the superiority of their own social and religious concepts over anything Africa could offer. In Sierra Leone they had at their disposal an ideal laboratory for their ideas, a community that could produce a truly Afro-European culture.

The nucleus of original settlers, made up of men who, though of Negroid stock, had been brought up to accept European ways, acted as a leaven on the thousands of "liberated Africans" brought to the colony after 1807. These "recaptives," as they were sometimes termed, were drawn from almost every part of West Africa. All of them had undergone the shattering experience of capture and liberation. Brutally torn from their own well-established societies, they had found themselves transported to an entirely alien part of Africa, an extraordinary country in which many black men lived like white men, attended schools, flocked to churches, and succeeded, if they were industrious enough, in acquiring substantial houses and trading establishments. Little wonder that the most enterprising of the recaptives found compensation for the world they had lost in the new ideas, the new institutions, and the new techniques they saw around them.

From Sierra Leone these men, later to call themselves Creoles, eager to profit from new opportunities of trade or of employment or anxious to return to their homeland, spread out along the coast, to Bathurst and Accra, to Lagos and Abeokuta, and later to the Ibo country. Holding in their minds firm convictions about the blessings of Christianity, the value of European education, and the importance of modern technology, they served as gentle pioneers of change in the societies in which they settled. Through men such as these would come, so their European supporters believed, "the regeneration of Africa." As they prospered they would form, in the words of an English missionary, "an intelligent and influential class" who might become "the founders of a kingdom" which would "render incalculable benefits to Africa and hold a position among the states of Europe." [22] This was, indeed, a prophetic vision, for this generation of Europeanized Africans introduced a new element into the structure of many existing societies, a class of men who developed under European protection into a new elite, the vigorous advocates of a modern nationalism whose concepts were in time to sweep the entire continent.

❦ WEST AFRICAN TRADE

Linked by the caravan trails of the desert to Egypt and the Maghrib, connected by Atlantic sea-lanes with Western Europe and the Americas, and possessing an intricate network of internal trade routes, West Africa presented by the beginning of the nineteenth century the spectacle of a system of commerce more elaborate than any elsewhere in tropical Africa.

For a period of more than a thousand years from the eighth to the nineteenth centuries West African exports to the outside world were based on two major commodities, gold and slaves. Gold is found close enough to the surface to be mined by relatively simple methods in several parts of West Africa. In the past, four areas were of especial importance: Bambuk lying between the Senegal and its tributary the Faleme, Bure on the upper Niger, the Lobi country on the upper Volta, and the forest country of Ashanti. When gold-mining first took place in West Africa is not known; it may well have been undertaken as early as the first millennium B.C. But it is clear that from the eighth century onward external demand led to a steady increase in production, first Bambuk and Bure, then Lobi and the Ashanti country being drawn into the system of external trade. The total West African production of gold in the sixteenth century has been estimated at no more than nine metric tons, about two-thirds of which may have been exported. Minute though this figure must seem by modern standards, it represented at the time a substantial proportion of world production. From the seventeenth century on gold production seems to have suffered a serious decline. At any rate the Saharan trade shrank to a trickle, while the European trade on the Gold Coast, where most of the precious metal came from local mines, was estimated in 1700 at no more than one and three-fourths metric tons.[23]

The export of slaves was a regular feature of trans-Saharan trade from the time of its development by Muslim merchants from the Maghrib at the end of the first millennium A.D. The trans-Saharan slave trade thus lasted more than twice as long as the Atlantic trade. In the absence of any reliable statistics it is impossible to compare the total value of the two branches of the trade, but it seems clear that the annual export of slaves across the Sahara never approached the figures of the Atlantic slave trade at its height. In the 1780's Bonny, then the principal slave market on the Guinea Coast, was reported to be sending out twenty thousand slaves a year; in the 1850's the slave trade of Kano, the largest commercial center of the Sudanic belt, was reckoned not to exceed five thousand.[24]

If gold and slaves made up by far the greatest part of the export trade of West Africa, the region possessed a number of other products to offer the outside world. Ivory, though never in the quantities obtainable in other parts of tropical Africa, malaguetta pepper, though inferior to the pepper of the East Indies, hides and skins, the source of the famous "Morocco" leather, gum, obtainable in southern Mauritania and used for a wide variety of manufacturing processes: all these materials were handled both on the trans-Saharan routes and at some of the ports of Guinea. In addition there was some export trade in cloth of West African manufacture. Kano cloth was sent northward across the desert, while for a time Benin cloth was bought by European merchants for sale on the Gold Coast and in Angola.

At the beginning of the nineteenth century changes in the economy of Western Europe led to a demand for other raw materials of West African origin, a demand vigorously encouraged by those who sought to bring about the complete elimination of the slave trade. Peanuts from Senegal, timber from Sierra Leone and the Gold Coast, and above all palm oil from the Niger area began in the 1830's and 1840's to show that they were to become the new staples of West Africa's overseas trade.

In return for this comparatively wide range of commodities West Africa received an even greater variety of goods from other parts of the world. Something has already been said of these imports in general terms; two contemporary lists provide a detailed and vivid illustration of the same theme. The first describes Dutch imports to Benin in the seventeenth century as being made up of "cloth of gold and silver; red and scarlet cloth; drinking vessels with red stripes round the mouth; all kinds of fine cotton; linen; candied oranges, lemons, and other green fruit; red velvet; brass bracelets weighing 5½ ounces; lavender; violet embroidery silk; coarse flannel; fine coral; Harlem fabrics, starched and flowered; red glass earrings; gilded mirrors; iron bars; crystal beads; *boesjes* or Indian cowries which serve as local currency." [25] The second is Heinrich Barth's list of the imports of Kano, "the great emporium of Negroland" in the 1850's: "Bleached and unbleached calicoes, and cotton prints from Manchester; French silks and sugar; red cloth from Saxony and other parts of Europe; beads from Venice and Trieste; common paper with the sign of three moons, looking-glasses, needles and small ware from Nuremberg; sword blades from Solingen; razors from Styria," together with coarse embroidery silk from Tripoli, "articles of Arab dress" from Egypt and Tunis, frankincense and spices, a small quantity of firearms of American origin brought up from the Niger, and copper from the mines south of Darfur. [26]

From the main termini of the Saharan and the Atlantic trade these exotic articles of merchandise were distributed over a wide area and so helped to stimulate the internal trade of the region. This internal trade also had its staples: salt, kola nuts, and cloth. Salt came not only from the

Saharan deposits but also from salt pans on various parts of the coast. Kola nuts grown in the forest country between Futa Jallon and northern Ashanti were carried by caravans of Dyula or Hausa merchants to the countries of the Sudanic belt, where they were greatly appreciated as a stimulant. Cloth was woven at a number of local centers, of which Kano was the most famous. Salt, kola nuts, and cloth could easily be transported over long distances. But there was also a considerable traffic in more perishable commodities. Timbuktu, for example, was supplied with foodstuffs brought by canoe from far up the Niger, the trading states of the Niger delta obtained yams from their hinterland, while every large town maintained a flourishing market stocked with local produce.

So lively a system of production and distribution made possible the existence of substantial urban centers not only as was the case in other parts of Africa, on the coast or on the borders of the Sahara, but also in the very heart of the region. Dyula merchants, for example, developed the town of Kong in the northern Ivory Coast into a place with fifteen thousand inhabitants, a remarkable urban population for tropical Africa in the mid-nineteenth century. Kong possessed its own cloth industry and traded in gold, kola nuts, and salt. Nowhere indeed in the entire continent outside Egypt, parts of the Maghrib and of the Swahili coast, and a handful of cities of European foundation in southern Africa did there exist in the mid-nineteenth century an urban civilization comparable to that to be found in the most prosperous parts of West Africa.

WEST AFRICA IN THE 1850'S

Compared with other regions of Africa in the middle of the nineteenth century West Africa stands out for two reasons. In the first place, it was by far the most populous part of Africa—today West Africa contains more than a third of the population of the entire continent, and the proportionate differences between regions must have been much the same in the 1850's as they are today. At the same time West Africa presented a political pattern more complex than that of any other region. It was not merely that West Africa contained a very large number of independent political units—this was a characteristic common to all parts of tropical Africa at this time—but the pattern appeared confusing because there was to be found among these polities a quite extraordinary variety of forms of political organization, a variety unmatched, it might well be supposed, in any other part of the world of comparable size.

In Ashanti and the Fulani caliphate of Sokoto the region possessed the largest, in Benin and Bornu the oldest, in Dahomey possibly the most autocratic, in Macina the most truly theocratic of all the states of tropical Africa. Nor could one find anywhere else in the continent trading states of the same character as Bonny or Calabar nor such a galaxy of diverse polities created by a single ethnic group as the states of the Yoruba. And to these must be added the village states of the Ibo and the Ewe, the petty chiefdoms—repositories of the traditions of long past imperial greatness—of the Songhai and the Malinke, the kingdoms of the Mossi, the Bambara, the Wolof, and others, the Muslim principalities of the two Futas, and many other substantial polities—Kong, Idah, or Bussa, for example—which would have stood out more prominently in other parts of the continent but here admit only of a passing mention.

The area covered by these relatively elaborate political structures was a very considerable one, but there were still many parts of the region where people lived in communities on which the organization of a state with its hierarchy of officeholders had not been imposed. Indeed, one may think of most of the major polities of West Africa as being surrounded by zones of territory occupied by people in stateless societies. Though these peoples—the Tiv of the Benue Valley, for example, or the Senufo of the northern Ivory Coast—figure hardly at all in the conventional annals of West Africa, they represent a very substantial element in the population of the region as a whole, primitive perhaps in the eyes of their more sophisticated neighbors but maintaining a vigorous culture of their own.

In the political mosaic of West Africa the establishments created by Europeans stand out by virtue of the exotic culture of their rulers and the rather more formidable armaments at their disposal. But in 1850 these European possessions were still very modest in extent, their total area to be measured in hundreds rather than in thousands of square miles, and they can hardly be regarded as the dominant polities of the region. And yet there was something illusory about their modesty. The unimpressive colonial townships of Senegal, Sierra Leone, and the Gold Coast in fact represented the temporary terminals of the influence of two of the wealthiest and most vigorously expansionist powers in the world. Along the lines that connected Paris with St. Louis, London with Freetown and Cape Coast, there was beginning to flow a current that would come, as it increased in strength, to penetrate, galvanize, and partly transform the entire region.

CHAPTER VIII

Equatorial Africa

𝕴 GEOGRAPHY

The extremities of Africa can be divided into regions with fairly obvious
frontiers; the great central block, the heart of the continent, is more
amorphous. Much of this part of Africa is occupied by the basin of the
great river Congo, but one cannot define the region simply on the basis of
its hydrography. Nor are modern political boundaries, the product of the
historical accidents of a particular epoch, of much assistance. (It is a little
absurd that the group of territories known until recently as French Equatorial Africa should have included in northern Chad several hundred
thousand square miles of the Sahara.) To west and east, indeed, there are
certain obvious natural features to act as frontiers, the mountain ranges
of Cameroun and the Atlantic Ocean to the west, the chain of great lakes
from Albert to Nyasa in the east. But to north and south historians concerned with the precolonial period find themselves having to act in almost
as arbitrary a fashion as nineteenth-century diplomatists hovering over
the map of Africa are alleged to have done. Lines of latitude—fifteen
degrees north and twenty degrees south—must be used as rough and
ready frontiers. But the area that lies between these latitudes is too large
and too diverse to be studied as a single region. One may divide it—
roughly along the line of five degrees south—into two parts, "Equatorial Africa" to the north, "Central Africa" to the south.

Equatorial Africa thus defined is a block of territory, about a million
square miles in extent, that embraces the modern states of Cameroun,
Gabon, Central African Republic, and Congo (Brazzaville) together with
the northern half of Congo (Kinshasha) and all but the Saharan provinces
of the Republic of Chad.

Geographically, the region might be summed up as a land of plateaus,
rivers, and dense forest. Most of the region lies above two thousand feet,
and there are mountains on the Nigeria-Cameroun border which rise to

over eight thousand feet. These plateaus are cut into by many rivers. The greatest of these is the Congo. With its headwaters far to the south it describes a vast bend, its stream swollen by innumerable tributaries, of which the Ubangi flowing from the northeast and the Kasai from the southeast are the largest. To the north of the Congo basin the main river is the Chari that flows, fed by many tributaries, into Lake Chad, while the mountains of Cameroun are divided by the upper waters of the Benue. Farther west there is yet another complex of rivers, those that run directly into the Atlantic, among them the Ogowe of Gabon and the Sanaga of Cameroun. Most of these rivers are navigable at their mouths and for long stretches on their middle reaches, but those that reach the Atlantic have to pass through gorges and over rocky outcrops that effectively prevent them from being used as easy lines of penetration from the seacoast.

Even more than its plateaus or its rivers, however, the forest has given the region its especial character. The tropical rain forest extends some hundreds of miles on either side of the equator to form the densest mass of vegetation in the entire continent. But it does not completely dominate the whole region. To the north it thins out to woodland savanna, the vegetation becoming progressively sparser as one moves northward to the plains of Central Chad. And these broad lines of savanna and forest that extend across the region contain many areas with a distinctive character of their own: the grassy uplands of central Cameroun, the barren Teke plateaus north of Stanley Pool, the marshes of the Chari delta or of the Ubangi-Congo confluence, the rocky massifs that occur in much of eastern Chad. Taken as a whole Equatorial Africa is a region of considerable geographical diversity.

✻ THE PEOPLES OF EQUATORIAL AFRICA

Diversity is no less apparent in the pattern of the region's population. Today Equatorial Africa contains peoples of three racial types: Caucasoid, Negroid, and Pygmoid. The Caucasoids are represented by the latest comers to the region, the Arab pastoralists of Chad who began to move westward from the Eastern Sudan in the fourteenth century and the Fulani pastoralists of Cameroun who reached the valley of the Upper Benue before 1800. As in all the other regions of tropical Africa people of Negroid stock make up the vast majority of the population. But Equatorial Africa also contains a sizeable number, today put at about one hundred seventy thousand, of Pygmies, an element in the population not to be found elsewhere in the continent. The domain of those Pygmies, who still maintain themselves by hunting and gathering, is now confined to certain stretches of the Equatorial rain forest, but there is evidence to suggest that Pygmy hunters were once to be found dispersed over a much larger area that included the edges of the savanna.

If the Pygmy peoples originally possessed distinctive languages of their own, no trace of these appears to have survived; all the Pygmy groups now use the speech of their Negroid neighbors. In the languages spoken by the Negroids five stocks are represented: Chadic (a branch of Afro-Asiatic), Adamawa (a branch of Western Sudanic), Central Sudanic (a subbranch of Nilo-Saharan), Maban (another branch of Nilo-Saharan), and Bantu. Chadic languages are spoken by some of the peoples living to the south of Lake Chad, both in the plains of the Chari-Logone and in the mountains of Mandara. Adamawa languages are spoken not only in the geographical province of that name in central Cameroun but also much farther to the east where they have been carried by such people as the Zande, who now live astride the Sudan-Congo boundary. Central Sudanic languages are chiefly spoken in the northeast of the region, but they have been carried farther west by the Sara and farther south by the Mangbetu. Maban is confined to Wadai. Finally, the entire southern part of the region from Mount Cameroun to the Congo and the great lakes is occupied by the speakers of Bantu languages.

Different linguistic stocks mingle with one another in the country that lies immediately to the north of the equatorial forest to form an exceedingly confusing pattern. This confusion must be regarded as the reflection of a particular stage of historical evolution. Clearly, this area—southern Chad, northern Cameroun, the entire Central African Republic—has received in the course of the past two to three thousand years peoples coming from every point of the compass. Yet until very recent times the backwardness of the area, shown in the lack of large-scale political structures and in the equally striking absence of vigorously maintained trade routes, made it impossible for any one people to impose its language and culture on its neighbors.

Farther south the remarkable dispersal of Bantu languages indicates a historical phenomenon of a different kind—the movement of a rapidly multiplying group of peoples into an almost empty land. The problems raised by the Bantu migrations are discussed in the next chapter, Central Africa being the region of the continent most clearly dominated by these peoples. Here, however, it should be noted that linguistic evidence suggests that the ancestral homeland of the Bantu lay in the area of the Upper Benue. But one should not think in terms of a steady expansion from this area. On the contrary it seems more likely that large-scale expansion only took place after Bantu groups had established themselves south of the equatorial forest. Obscure though the early migrations that

Figures indicate percentage of general
roots in particular Bantu languages

▨ Rain forest

‑‑→ Conjectured route of pre-Bantu

CONJECTURED SPREAD OF
BANTU SPEAKERS (After Guthrie)

Labels on map:
- Ganda 37
- Kikuyu 32
- Sukuma 41
- Swahili 44
- Yao 35
- Rwandi 44
- Luba Katanga 50
- Bemba 54
- Luba Kasai 47
- Shona 37
- Zulu 29
- Sotho 28
- Xosa 26
- Kongo 44
- Teke 28
- Duala 14
- Mbundu 38
- Herero 33
- Pre-Bantu
- ATLANTIC OCEAN

led to the peopling of Equatorial Africa still remain, one point, at least, can be stressed. The historian is concerned here not with simple population movements, compared to the flood of immigrants from Europe to the United States in the nineteenth century, but rather with a pioneering process made up of many different currents. Thus, in Gabon, a country with an area of more than a hundred thousand square miles and a population of half a million, oral traditions indicate that forty named groups of Bantu-speakers entered the territory, some from the north, some from the east, some from the south, while yet others regard themselves as completely autochthonous.

At present archeology can add little—except in parts of central Chad, which have been the scene of more extensive research—to our knowledge of the distant past of Equatorial Africa. But the variety of stone implements that have been discovered makes it clear that at least in some parts of the region human occupation can be traced back to paleolithic times. It is clear, too, that although the forest might have appeared an oppressive environment to early man accustomed to the open plains of the savanna, some groups, notably the ancestors of the Pygmies, learned to adapt themselves to forest life with remarkable success. But the present low density of population—an average of no more than five people to the square mile for most parts of the region—suggests that Equatorial Africa must have always been a very thinly populated area in comparison to adjoining regions. This thinness of population clearly affects the quality of the region's history. Here there has never existed so spectacular a diversity of states and kingdoms, so vigorous a record of external influences as West Africa affords to the historian. Consequently, information about the past of the kind preserved in the detailed traditions of court chroniclers or in the written accounts of foreign visitors is much less extensive. Indeed, over much of the region outside the Sudanic belt in the north and the coastal area in the west, one has to wait until the nineteenth century to obtain any impression of the development of the great mass of the population. The picture that then emerged from the accounts of European travelers showed that most of the peoples of Equatorial Africa were living in small, independent communities bound together largely by ties of kinship and presenting few or none of the characteristics of an organized state. Only in certain limited areas situated for the most part on the periphery of the region were more elaborate forms of political organization to be found. Any attempt to sketch the broad outline of the region's history must then begin by considering the evolution of this galaxy of miniscule polities that covered so much of the region's territory.

✈ THE MINOR POLITIES OF EQUATORIAL AFRICA

At first sight these simple "stateless communities" seem to possess a quality of timelessness, as if they were suffering from a paralysis of immobility while other more elaborate societies were subject to the evolutionary processes of change. This notion of the changelessness of simple societies is an illusion. Each of these communities possesses a highly complex culture of its own, the product in part of local adaptation to a particular environment, in part of a long process of borrowings from neighboring peoples. Ideally, the historian should be able to trace this millenary development and to know when and how a particular food crop or type of weapon or building technique or religious ritual was introduced, to describe the varied movements that led to the establishment of a particular people in a particular locality. Unfortunately, in the present state of knowledge no studies of the necessary depth, using all the possible sources—archeology, oral tradition, linguistic research, comparative ethnology—have yet been undertaken to enable one to speak with any assurance of the past of any of these Equatorial societies. One can, however, say something of the diversity to be found among them, a diversity well illustrated by three highly distinctive groups of people, the *montagnards* of Mandara in northern Cameroun, the Bangala or *Gens d'Eau* of the Ubangi-Congo confluence, and the Pahouin (Fang) of south Cameroun and Gabon.

In their stone-walled villages, sited fortress-like among the rocky massifs of Mandara, the *montagnards*—Matakam, Mofu, and other groups distinguished from one another mainly on grounds of language— appeared to their neighbors, the sophisticated Muslim communities of the plain, as turbulent and anarchic savages. Each village was largely independent of its neighbors. "Their political ideas," an early European administrator, Gordon Lethem, wrote of the *montagnards*, "can scarcely rise beyond harrying the neighbour and the stranger and vicious resistance to the invader." [1] In their resistance to the slave raids of their formidable neighbors, the Muslims of Bornu or Adamawa, the pagan tribesmen proved remarkably successful. Their warriors, equipped with bows or with swords, spears, and shields and fighting often behind walls built across their upland valleys, were often more than a match for the heavy cavalry of the plains.

Within their villages the *montagnards* developed an impressive material culture. "In visiting the hills," Lethem noted, "I was astonished at the comfort and cleanliness of their homes and the order and neatness of their farms and the remarkable development of the rotation of crops." Clearly, the point is well worth stressing for it applies to many other African communities; small-scale political organization should not be thought of as implying backwardness in the field of economic development.

The marshy country at the confluence of the Ubangi and the Congo was occupied by a cluster of peoples whom the earliest European travelers, mistakenly believing them to form a single ethnic group, named the Bangala. Later research has shown that these marsh dwellers, whose environment distinguishes them from their neighbors, represent a collection of many different groups, some Sudanic, others Bantu in origin, and Belgian ethnologists now prefer to apply to them the generic name of *Gens d'Eau*. These people lived in compact villages sited along the banks of rivers, some villages being completely independent of their neighbors, others grouped together under the authority of a local leader. They adapted themselves most successfully to their difficult environment. Skillful fishermen and enterprising dealers in slaves, ivory, and other local products, they dominated a long stretch of the Congo with their barge canoes. Their regular long-distance fishing and trading expeditions brought them into contact with many other peoples. Thus, the *Gens d'Eau* came to act as the major agents of change over a wide area as they passed on new materials, techniques, and ideas from one people to another.

Pahouin is the name applied to a group of people, now numbering close to one million and occupying most of southern Cameroun and northern Gabon, who speak basically the same language and possess common traditions of origin. These traditions tell how the Pahouins were forced by the pressure of invaders of uncertain origin to leave their homeland on the edge of the savanna in central Cameroun and move into the forest following a southwesterly direction that was to lead them to the sea. This movement appears not to have begun until the end of the eighteenth century, but it developed a rapid momentum as the Pahouin clans, their numbers swollen by the peoples they conquered and absorbed, constantly jostled one another, forcing individual village settlements to break away and move onward. Their success gave them the élan of a people very conscious of their superiority over their neighbors. "The Prussians of Africa," an English trader called them in the 1870's,[2] while a generation later Mary Kingsley summed up the Fang, that section of the Pahouin who had occupied northern Gabon, as being "full of fire, temper, intelligence and go; very teachable, rather difficult to manage, quick to take offence and utterly indifferent to human life." [3]

The *montagnards* of Mandara, the *Gens d'Eau* of the Congo, the Pahouin of Gabon and Cameroun—these are only three among a dozen ethnic groups of equal importance in the development of Equatorial

Africa. Banda and Baya, Sara and Mongo—fully to explore the history of the region it would be necessary to study all these peoples and to take into consideration a hundred smaller groups, many similar to the village communities of the Amba described in Chapter XVII, in order to present the historical pattern in its true complexity.

𝌆 THE KINGDOMS AND CHIEFDOMS OF EQUATORIAL AFRICA

Compared with the states of West Africa, those of the Equatorial region were fewer, smaller, and later in their development. This last point was true even of the Sudanic belt between Lake Chad and Darfur. By 1500 the only substantial polities in this area were the Bulala kingdom—an offshoot of ancient Kanem—around Lake Fitri and the cluster of So/Kotoko city-states in the valley of the lower Chari. Wadai and Baguirmi, which were to develop into the most powerful kingdoms in the region, were only founded in the sixteenth century.

Both states came into existence when small immigrant groups—in Wadai the Tundjur, a branch of the ruling dynasty of Darfur, in Baguirmi the Kinga coming from a mountainous district east of the Chari—imposed their hegemony on the scattered and culturally diverse communities occupying what was to become the central area of the new kingdoms. In Baguirmi the founding dynasty, whose rulers were converted to Islam in the seventeenth century, survived unchanged. In Wadai the pagan Tundjur were overthrown about 1630 by a revolt of their Maba subjects led by an Arab, Abd al-Karim, who persuaded his followers to become Muslims and who established a dynasty that lasted until the French occupation. Both kingdoms were advantageously placed for raiding their hitherto unmolested southern neighbors, the Sara, Banda, and other peoples. The wealth thus obtained from slaves enabled them in the eighteenth century to throw off the overlordship of their powerful neighbors, Bornu and Darfur. But in the early nineteenth century the fortunes of the two kingdoms diverged sharply: Wadai steadily increased in wealth, its economy greatly stimulated by the opening of a new trans-Saharan route which provided direct access to the Mediterranean, whereas Baguirmi found itself caught between a revived Bornu and a more militant Wadai, its territory ravaged by the armies of both sides.

On the cool and fertile highlands of central Cameroun, some three hundred miles south of Baguirmi, there developed a cluster of kingdoms and chiefdoms associated with the Mbum, the Tikar, and the Bamileke, remarkable not for their size—Bamum, the largest of them, was no more than three thousand square miles in extent—but for their complex political organization and their elaborate material culture.

The early history of these peoples is completely unknown, for they were not described by any outsiders until the late nineteenth century and their oral traditions reach back no more than two or three centuries. These traditions indicate that the settlement of most of the highlands by the present inhabitants took place fairly recently, that many groups came from farther north, though records of migrations refer to no area more distant than the northern edge of the highlands, and that two peoples, the Mbum and the Tikar, played the major role in state formation. Among the Mbum whose four kingdoms, largely destroyed by the Fulani in the nineteenth century, appear to have been the most ancient, the ruler (*bel-laka*) was attended with elaborate ritual—his regalia included finely wrought bronze trumpets—and surrounded by a court made up of titled dignitaries. The Tikar, who may have been an emigrant offshoot of the Mbum, were responsible for creating many of the other states of the area, including Bamum, states which came to exhibit a high degree of centralization.

At the same time some of the highland peoples achieved great skill as craftsmen. The Bamileke, in particular, were renowned for their wood carving, while Fumban, the capital of Bamum, with its wide range of local crafts, including bronze-casting, could be regarded at the end of the nineteenth century as one of the major artistic centers of tropical Africa.

Population densities in the highlands were among the highest in Equatorial Africa—today they stand at over fifty to the square mile in many districts, while in parts of Bamileke country they reach the astonishing figure of more than eight hundred. These figures provide one clue to help explain the area's historical development, for they imply an efficient system of agriculture capable of producing the surplus needed to support a substantial number of craft-specialists and administrative officials. Such an agriculture must have been made possible by the fertility of local soils and the regularity of local rainfall. But the highlands must originally have derived certain elements in their culture from neighboring peoples. On this point the traditions are not helpful, but it would seem that the most likely source of external stimulus was to be found among the people of the middle Benue, notably the Jukun, the masters of a very powerful kingdom in the seventeenth century.

Along the coast from Cameroun Mountain to the mouth of the Congo only a handful of polities larger than village chiefdoms were to be found. At the head of the estuary known to the Portuguese as Rio dos Camaroes, "river of prawns," the Duala people, enriched by their control of the trade of the hinterland, established a single chiefdom that broke up into four parts in the early nineteenth century. North of the mouth of the Congo there came into existence at least as early as the sixteenth century three states—Loango, Kakongo, and Ngoy—founded by peoples of the same stock as the Kongo, who established the great kingdom of that name south of the river. Their development was profoundly influenced by the consequences of a vigorous trade with Europeans.

The dominant people on the right bank of the lower Congo were the Teke, who began, possibly as early as the fifteenth century, to construct a kingdom that in time stretched over a wide expanse of plateau country north of Stanley Pool. The Teke kingdom was remarkable for its extraordinary degree of decentralization, the king being little more than a religious leader elected by the territory's more powerful chiefs.

Most of the peoples of the cluster known collectively as Mongo, occupying the country lying within the great bend of the Congo, lived in independent village communities, but among their southwestern section a number of small kingdoms were created in the area around Lake Leopold II. The history of these states is still obscure. With the Kuba, by contrast, a people of different stock living on the southern edge of the forest, it has been possible to trace in some detail the growth of a remarkable kingdom.

Kuba is the name applied by their neighbors to a cluster of eighteen closely connected groups most of whom came from farther west and reached their present homeland on the middle Kasai in the sixteenth century. Here they established a number of chiefdoms one of which, that founded by the Bushongo, achieved a position of paramountcy. At this time the Kuba were primarily hunters and fishermen, but in the middle of the seventeenth century the initiative of a new line of powerful rulers, possessing close connections with the more highly developed peoples to the west, brought about an economic revolution. New crops of American origin were introduced, and new techniques in a wide range of handicrafts were adopted from neighboring peoples. As a result population grew rapidly, craftsmen became increasingly specialized, and trade connections multiplied. The Kuba kingdom did not expand beyond its late seventeenth-century limits; its population was less than a hundred thousand; but it remained until the twentieth century a state outstanding for the material prosperity and the high standard of living of its people. "Charmingly decorated houses each of them a work of art," "every cup, every pipe, every spoon a piece of artistry," so the German ethnologist Leo Frobenius noted in Kuba country in 1906, describing at the same time how "there was not a man who did not carry sumptuous weapons of iron or copper, with inlaid hilts and damascened blades." [4]

Six hundred miles northeast of the Kuba kingdom and divided from it by the great rain forest another group of states was being created in the eighteenth and nineteenth centuries by warriors of Zande stock. The

Zande, whose language is in the Adamawa branch of Western Sudanic, expanded eastward in the woodland-savanna country lying north of the forest. In the process they imposed not merely their political domination but also their language on the heterogenous peoples inhabiting the area. But Zande polities were subject to a constant process of fission, as the adventurous sons or disappointed rivals of an established chief broke away to found new chiefdoms for themselves. Consequently, by the mid-nineteenth century the country between the Bomu and the Uele rivers contained more than a score of Zande polities, some of which were substantial enough to be described as kingdoms.

The eastern point of their advance brought the Zande into contact with another conquering people, the Mangbetu. The history of this people, who speak a Central Sudanic language, is still extremely obscure, but it is clear from the account of the German traveler, Georg Schweinfurth, who visited their country south of the Uele in 1873, that they had reached a stage of development far in advance of their neighbors. Schweinfurth called Mangbetu country "an Eden upon earth"; he regarded their handicrafts—and especially the work of their smiths—as being superior even to those of the Muslims of North Africa; and though he did not disguise their relish for human flesh—indeed he considered their cannibalism to be "unsurpassed by another nation in the world"—he summed them up as "a noble race of men" and praised "the order and stability of their national life." Some years earlier the Mangbetu kingdom had split into two parts. But the Mangbetu king with whom Schweinfurth stayed possessed a territory far greater than that of any Zande chief, and his opulent court with its swarm of retainers, its lavish treasure chambers, and its splendid hall of audience indicate a high degree of centralization comparable to that achieved in the greatest of the interlacustrine kingdoms of East Africa. The history of Equatorial Africa abounds in unsolved problems; that of the genesis of the Mangbetu kingdom is one of the most intriguing.[5]

✳ EXTERNAL INFLUENCES AND THE DEVELOPMENT OF TRADE

At the beginning of the nineteenth century Equatorial Africa could be regarded as the most isolated of the continent's regions, the least affected by external influences. In part, of course, this isolation was merely a reflection of the geographical remoteness of most of the region from the major centers of cultural innovation. But there is another point that helps to explain the indifference of outsiders: Equatorial Africa was not merely remote, it offered little to attract the interest of foreign merchants. Gold, so potent in stimulating long-distance trade in other parts of Africa, was completely lacking. Copper, second in importance to gold as a trade metal, though found between Loango and the Teke country, was only of significance in local trade. As for slaves and ivory, the region's major products, it was not until the seventeenth century that they could be exported in any quantity, for the trade was dependent partly on regular visits by Europeans to the coast, partly on the establishment of Baguirmi and Wadai as polities powerful enough to attract slave dealers from adjoining areas.

But though the country between Chad and Darfur was drawn into the wide-ranging system of Muslim trade considerably later than other parts of the Sudanic belt, it had been exposed to the movements of peoples from adjoining regions for a very long time. Over a period extending back perhaps as far as three thousand years there had been a slow seepage of cattle-owning peoples from Borku and Ennedi. It is possible that small groups of refugees or adventurers from ancient Kush and Christian Nubia reached the country west of Darfur. In the fourteenth century Arab pastoralists began moving in from the east. By 1600 Arab nomads had reached the country south of Lake Chad and were in contact with Fulani cattle-herders coming from the west. By this time, too, Muslim holy men had begun to settle in the area and Muslim pilgrims from the Western Sudan to pass along the route that led to Darfur, Kordofan, and the Nile. For trade purposes, however, the pilgrims' road to the east was of little importance. Before 1800 merchants from North Africa wishing to visit Baguirmi or Wadai found it necessary to travel by way of the Fezzan to Bornu or from Egypt to Darfur. Massenia and Wara, the capitals of the two kingdoms, must have been regarded at least until 1750 as termini on the Muslim traders' frontier.

The Equatorial coast was explored by the Portuguese at the end of the fifteenth century. A hundred and fifty years later the firstcomers were being pushed out by the English, the French, and the Dutch. Loango and Cabinda became the main centers of European commerce—in 1788 thirteen thousand five hundred slaves were exported from these places. Duala, too, attracted a considerable number of ships, and there was some intercourse with the Mpongwe on the Gabon River. Outside these centers very little trading appears to have been done.

The interior of Equatorial Africa contained no long-distance trade routes comparable to those of other regions. Indeed, some of the inland peoples had no commercial dealings of any kind with their neighbors. Between Yaounde and Brazzaville, for example, there was not a single market of any importance at the time of the European occupation. Elsewhere, however, local trading systems developed, some of which interlocked one with another. In this way certain commodities passed from middleman to middleman and so came to be diffused over a very wide area. By the 1870's some European trade goods could be found a thousand miles up the Congo.

The major polities of the region provided the natural centers for such local systems of trade. In Loango, for example, the Vili organized caravans that traveled as far as Stanley Pool in search of slaves and ivory. The commercial activity thus generated induced people living farther inland to carry on the trade, and riverain groups, the Teke, the Bobangi, the *Gens d'Eau,* established their control over the commerce of long stretches of the Congo. Loango was also in touch with its neighbors to north and south and carried on a flourishing coastal trade with the Portuguese, who bought elephant hair and raphia cloth to sell in the markets of Angola.

The trade of Loango owed its rapid development to the European demand for slaves and ivory. With polities more remote from the coast an external stimulus of this nature was hardly apparent. In the Kuba kingdom, for example, the vigorous internal trade was based on the exchange of special products of local manufacture, while in their trade with neighboring peoples the Kuba dealt almost entirely in articles drawn from different parts of the Congo basin—slaves, ivory, iron, copper, salt, and so on. Indeed, so content were the Kuba with their own manufactures that they refused to buy the European cloth brought from Angola in the nineteenth century.

EQUATORIAL AFRICA IN THE 1850'S

A ring of substantial polities on the periphery, a multitude of independent village communities in the center: thus briefly might one describe the political pattern that had emerged in Equatorial Africa between 1500 and 1800. Like all such patterns it was never static. About 1850 the first stage in a new process of transformation brought about by the increasing pressure of outsiders became apparent.

In the northeast a cosmopolitan assortment of traders, most of them Arabic-speakers from the Nile Valley, began to search for ivory among peoples hitherto untouched by the commercial currents of a wider world. By the 1860's the traders reached Zande country. In contrast to their northern neighbors who suffered terribly from the traders' depredations, the Zande were well enough organized to hold their own, the wealthiest chiefs acting as middlemen and acquiring substantial supplies of firearms in exchange for slaves and ivory.

Wadai, too, was more open to external influences than ever before. About 1810 the ruler succeeded in developing a new trans-Saharan route that gave his kingdom direct access to the Mediterranean coast by way of the lonely oasis of Kufra. This route rapidly increased in importance and provided Wadai with firearms and other European commodities in exchange for slaves and ivory. The rapidly growing strength and wealth of Wadai attracted traders and adventurers from other parts of the Sudan, some of whom obtained permission to establish tributary fiefs for themselves among the peoples living beyond Wadai's southern borders.

Meanwhile, from the west bands of Fulani, inflamed by jihadist zeal, were fanning out from the valley of the Upper Benue. Nominally owing allegiance to the *lamido* of Adamawa, himself a tributary of Sokoto, these turbulent and arrogant frontiersmen disrupted the life of many communities of northern and central Cameroun. In this area they wrought a profound transformation, creating a cluster of new states—Ngaundere, Tibati, and others-opening the area to new commercial currents. Hausa traders were quick to take advantage of the new sources of slaves and ivory, and to set against the old traditions and customs the new immensely attractive culture of Islam.

Far to the east yet another Muslim invasion was starting, as Arab and Swahili traders from the East Coast extended their activities west of Lake Tanganyika. Before long the lure of untapped stocks of ivory was to lead these enterprising and adventurous men into the heart of Equatorial Africa.

On the coast changes were more difficult to detect. In the 1850's the slave trade was still flourishing, though confined to merchants possessing contacts with Cuba and Brazil. But one significant innovation had taken place. In the 1840's the French established an administrative post on the north bank of the Gabon estuary, a site that later developed into the freed slave settlement of Libreville. At the same time a handful of American Protestant missionaries began work in the area. Only the villages of the estuary were affected by these alien influences. To have seen in this modest establishment one of the major European bases for the penetration of the interior would have required in the 1850's almost superhuman powers of foresight. No part of the map of Africa was still so blank as that which covered the Equatorial region. Even the course of the Congo was still completely unknown. All this was to be astonishingly transformed before the end of the century.

CHAPTER IX

Central Africa

🌿 GEOGRAPHY

The term Central Africa is used here to denote that great bloc of territory whose bounds are the tropical forest to the north, the line of great lakes to the east, the northern frontier of South Africa and Botswana to the south and the Atlantic Ocean to the west. Thus, it embraces modern Angola, Zambia, Rhodesia, and Malawi and the southern half of Congo-Kinshasha and has an area of about a million and a half square miles.

The geography of Central Africa is less varied than that of any other region of the continent. Here are no mountain ranges, though most of the land lies three thousand feet above sea level and there are highlands in southern Angola and eastern Rhodesia; no deserts except a small coastal strip in southern Angola; only the rolling stretches of "bush"—vegetation of varying density, part savanna grasslands, part woodland—broken by the lines of great rivers or by occasional swamp-fringed lakes. No part of Africa is so rich in waterways—the Congo and the Zambezi with their tributaries and the numerous rivers of Angola, most of them broken by falls or rapids, but some easily navigable for long stretches.

Rainfall is sufficient for agriculture over most of the region, but much of the soil is poor and the bush infested with tsetse fly. Basically, then, one may think of Central Africa as reproducing many of the environmental features found over large parts of West Africa. And indeed, one can trace a certain similarity in the historical development of the two savanna belts north and south of the equator, for the history of both regions over the last thousand years is concerned with the rise and fall of substantial kingdoms in a pattern that contrasts sharply with the record of smaller polities that makes up the greater part of the history of East and South Africa.

But the comparison must not be pushed too far. West Africa has been more exposed to external influences, and its cultures are exceedingly varied. Central Africa, by contrast, although certainly not unaffected by the impact of outsiders, presents a greater degree of cultural homogeneity than any other region in the continent.

🎏 BANTU MIGRATIONS

All the indigenous peoples of Central Africa are of Negroid stock and speak Bantu languages. Yet two thousand years ago the region was probably populated only by small groups of Pygmoid and Bushmanoid hunters. Thus, the major theme of Central African history is the migration and dispersal of Bantu peoples. This is a movement not confined to Central Africa, for Bantu peoples have had a powerful impact on both East and South Africa as well. Today the Bantu occupy about a third of the entire continent, and their dispersal represents one of the greatest movements of population in the history of the world during the last two thousand years.

But despite their vast scale, the Bantu migrations present possibly the most challenging problem in the field of African history, for they are illuminated by no written sources and by no oral traditions except in their last stages. Fortunately, the historian now has other sources at his disposal. Within very recent years the work of linguistic scholars and of archeologists has led to the formulation of the most persuasive hypotheses yet advanced to account for the Bantu migrations.[1]

The linguistic evidence provides three important clues. In the first place, though there are some three hundred Bantu languages, they are all closely related to one another. This close relationship, comparable to that of English and German, contrasts with the great divergences that exist between most other African languages, even when they belong to the same branch of the same stock. From this it may be deduced that while the speakers of other languages—such as Yoruba and Ibo, both members of the Kwa branch of Western Sudanic—must have diverged from their parent branch at a very remote date, the speakers of Bantu languages must have separated much more recently and they must have moved comparatively rapidly to account for their present dispersal from the Atlantic to the Indian Ocean.

The second linguistic clue was provided by Greenberg when he pointed to the connection between the Bantu languages and the languages of the Benue-Congo branch of Western Sudanic. Making the reasonable assumption that the speakers of these languages moved from the savanna southward to the forest, this classification suggests that the home of the earliest Bantu speakers or "pre-Bantu" as Guthrie calls them, was in the area of the Upper Benue. The third clue comes from Guthrie's immensely detailed analysis of the Bantu languages themselves. Guthrie discovered that five hundred word roots were distributed throughout the Bantu area. He then counted the word roots to be found in each Bantu language and expressed these numbers as a percentage of the whole. His figures indicate that the center of the Bantu world—the area whose languages contain the greatest percentage of word roots—lay in northern Katanga and that expansion took place first to the east and to the west, then to the north and south of these two wings.

Now the significant feature of northern Katanga is that its light woodlands reproduce the environment of the Upper Benue. In between lie the vast, forbidding stretches of equatorial rain forest, but certain easily navigable rivers—the Chari, the Ubangi, the Congo, and the Kasai—provide obvious routes through this otherwise almost impenetrable barrier. Guthrie has therefore suggested that the first Bantu migrations may be represented by small bands of canoemen making their way down these waterways. But what provoked this migration and when did it occur? Many scholars have suggested that it must have been connected with the coming of iron to the Sudanic belt. Iron clearly enabled men to acquire better weapons for hunting and fishing and better tools for boat-building. Radio carbon dating reveals that iron was being used in the Nigerian plateau in the third century B.C., while the earliest Iron Age site yet discovered in Central Africa lies in eastern Barotseland and has been dated to the first century A.D. Tentatively, then, it would seem that the original migration took place about the beginning of the Christian era.

But how is one to account for the extraordinary expansion of the Bantu? Earlier scholars have visualized the Bantu as a conquering minority, not unlike the Nguni hordes of the nineteenth century. But there can only have been a sparse population for them to absorb or conquer. It is far more reasonable, as the historian Roland Oliver has pointed out, to connect their expansion with a rapid growth of population. And this growth can be accounted for initially by the fact that the Bantu brought with them not only ironworking but also food-producing techniques.

Guthrie's linguistic evidence suggests that from the central area the first stage of expansion in an easterly direction led to the East Coast. Ptolemy's *Geography,* which is probably a fourth-century compilation, refers to "man-eating Ethiopians" living in the southernmost part of the East Coast known to the Mediterranean world. "This," Oliver suggests, "may well be the first documentary record of the Bantu." [2] At any rate it is clear from Arabic sources that by the tenth century Negroid peoples were established as far north as the Juba in southern Somalia.

The Bantu reached the coast of East Africa at a time when it was being regularly visited by Indonesian seafarers. Among the goods these Mongoloid migrants brought with them were three plants domesticated in

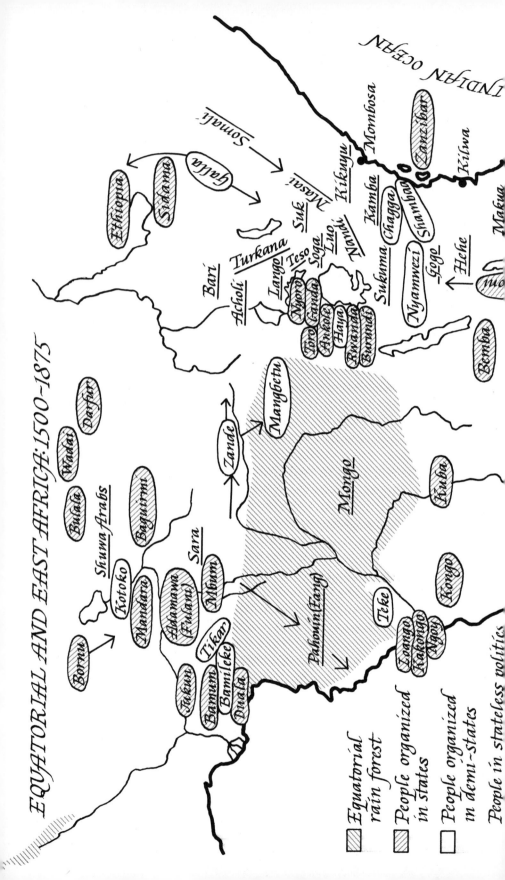

EQUATORIAL AND EAST AFRICA: 1500–1875

INDIAN OCEAN

Somali

Galla

Ethiopia

Sidama

Masai

Somali

Suk

Nandi

Kikuyu

Mombosa

Zanzibar

Kilwa

Makua

Kamba

Chagga

Shambaa

Turkana

Bari

Lango

Teso

Soga

Luo

Sukuma

Nyamwezi

Gogo

Hehe

Achoü

Nyoro

Toro

Ganda

Ankole

Haya

Rwanda

Burundi

Bemba

Mangbetu

Darfur

Wadai

Zande

Bulala

Baguirmi

Kuba

Mongo

Shuwa Arabs

Sara

Kotoko

Mandara

Adamawa
(Fulani)

Mbum

Kongo

Pahouin (Fang)

Tke

Jakun

Tikar

Bamum

Bamileke

Duala

Loango

Kakongo

Ngoy

Bornu

Equatorial
rain forest

People organized
in states

People organized
in demi-states

People in stateless polities

Southeast Asia but hitherto completely unknown in Africa—the banana, the Asian yam (a species far superior to the indigenous African yams), and the coco yam or taro. The introduction of these three plants must have had a revolutionary effect on the economy of the humid parts of the continent, for the millets and sorghum of the savanna could not be grown in a damp, hot climate; and indigenous food plants, such as the oil palm or the various local species of yam, could not form the basis of a diet. With yams and bananas as their staple food African farmers could move into lands they would otherwise have been forced to avoid.

How these plants spread across the continent is a matter of speculation and controversy. Probably, a number of routes were used. But it is reasonable to assume that the Bantu must have played a considerable part in the dispersal of the new crops. With new sources of food at their disposal, the Bantu population steadily expanded. And constantly, on the perimeter of favored areas, small groups broke away to seek new lands for themselves. Gradually, then, not in the spectacular manner of an entire people on the march, but rather by a process of steady seepage spreading in all directions, small groups of Bantu colonists moved out until in the course of fifteen hundred years most of the southern half of Africa was covered by their communities.

‌ LUBA EXPANSION; MONOMOTAPA; KONGO

Linguistic research throws some light on the broad pattern of Bantu expansion; detailed evidence can only come from archeology. At present, though large parts of the region remain completely unexplored by archeologists, far more work has been done on Early Iron Age sites in Central Africa, particularly in Zambia and Rhodesia, than in any other part of the continent, and it has recently become possible for scholars to describe at least in outline the early history of some parts of the region.

The existing evidence shows that men with a knowledge of iron were living in eastern Barotseland as early as the first century A.D. Three hundred years later Iron Age settlements existed in Rhodesia. By the eighth century there was a considerable number of communities using iron, extending from southern Zambia across western and central Rhodesia into northern Transvaal. These people were mixed farmers, cultivating millet, herding cattle, and acquiring additional food by gathering and by hunting. Not all the peoples living in these settlements were Negroid Bantu; in some sites skeletal remains of Bushmanoid types have been found, suggesting that some of the original inhabitants of the region had taken over the culture of the invaders. Besides Bantu and Bushmen there is some archeological evidence to suggest a third element in the population—small groups of people, neolithic in culture, and possessing cattle, who had moved down from the highlands of East Africa. It is likely that these were the first people to introduce cattle into the region.

Meanwhile, remarkable developments were taking place in the Luba country at the center of the Bantu world. Excavations at a cemetery site on the shore of Lake Kisale in northern Katanga have revealed that by the eighth century the area contained a dense population. Fine pottery and elaborate copper jewelry indicate, as Oliver has pointed out, that these people had achieved an "astonishing level of wealth and technical skill." [3] They were already exploiting the copper mines of Katanga and importing glass beads from the East Coast. Luba traditions speak of the Kisale area as being the original home of the Luba people, but these traditions reach back no further than the sixteenth century in their narrative of events. Much of Luba traditional history is concerned with the movement of small emigrant groups who established chieftaincies in the areas that surround the Luba heartland. It seems reasonable to assume that this was a process that had been going on for many centuries before the period covered by Luba tradition.

One group who may have come from the Luba area is represented by the people who constructed the first stone walls at Zimbabwe, the most famous and the most spectacular complex of ruins in the southern half of Africa. In the eleventh century immigrants from the northwest established their domination over the first Iron Age settlers living between the Zambezi and the Limpopo and merged with them to become the ancestors of the Karanga (Shona) people of modern Rhodesia.

Already, before the arrival of these immigrants, the Early Iron Age settlers had begun to exploit the area's deposits of gold and copper and to carry on trade with the Swahili-Arab communities of the East Coast. The wider political groupings established by the eleventh-century immigrants provided even better conditions for trade and encouraged coastal merchants to make their way into the interior in their search for gold, ivory, and slaves.

By the fifteenth century one of the Karanga clans, the Rozwi, had established domination over a "loose confederacy of vassal chieftains," [4] who paid them tribute in ivory and gold dust. The Rozwi probably owed their importance to their skill as ritual experts, mediators between their subjects and the spiritual world. A variety of reasons induced them to become great territorial rulers. Pressure from people living to the west forced them to build up a more effective military system. Muslim traders in the country, an influential community numbering several thousands, encouraged them to extend their rule, knowing that political stability would aid their commercial activities. Finally, the growth in population led to a shortage of salt, a vital commodity for any people living in the tropics.

In the mid-fifteenth century a Rozwi king, Mutota, embarked on a series of campaigns with such ardor that his people gave him the praise name of *mwene mutapa,* "master pillager." This title was used by all his successors and in the form Monomotapa was applied by the Portuguese to the kingdom as a whole. Mutota's son was no less successful, and by 1480 the new empire extended over most of modern Rhodesia and reached down the Zambezi Valley in a broad belt of territory to the Indian Ocean. But so wide-flung an empire could not be held together for long. By 1500, when the Portuguese arrived on the coast, the southern part of the empire had broken away to form the kingdom of Changamire.

Monomotapa was not the only substantial kingdom in Central Africa at this time. Far to the west a group of states had been established at the mouth of the Congo River. Their early history, at present unillumined by archeological research, is extremely obscure. But it is clear from Portuguese sources that by 1500 the largest of the states, the kingdom of Kongo, occupying the plateau country of north Angola, a state created by immigrants who imposed their domination on many of the small chiefdoms of the area, had already achieved a considerable measure of centralization, with the king appointing officials chosen by himself to the posts of provincial governor and district head.

✻ LUBA AND LUNDA STATES

Four themes dominate the history of Central Africa from the beginning of the sixteenth to the middle of the nineteenth century: the expansion of Luba-Lunda political institutions, the activities of the Portuguese, the disturbances caused by indigenous military powers such as the Jaga or the Ngoni, and the spread of the slave trade together with the emergence of long-distance trade routes. These themes are, of course, interconnected, but the pattern of Central African history may emerge more clearly if they are examined separately.

The early history of that part of Central Africa which now forms the southern part of Congo-Kinshasa is extremely obscure. There is a complete gap between the eighth century—when, as archeologists have revealed, a remarkable culture flourished in northern Katanga—and the sixteenth century, which is the earliest point in time reached by local traditions. According to these traditions the first major kingdom of the Luba was created about 1500. This main Luba kingdom lay to the north of Lake Kisale. It was formed by an invading clan, the Balopwe who came from somewhere farther north and established their supremacy over some of the petty chiefdoms which existed in the area.

Toward the end of the sixteenth century some members of the Luba royal house traveled westward to establish a new kingdom among the Lunda, a people closely related to the Luba, who lived between the Lualaba and the Kasai. Among the Lunda a form of political organization was evolved which led to the rapid proliferation of Lunda-type polities over an immense area stretching from eastern Angola to northeastern Zambia. Groups of adventurers, some of them members of the Lunda royal clan, left the original Lunda kingdom and set out to seek their fortunes among the surrounding peoples. These peoples were living in miniscule polities, small chiefdoms or independent lineages. When a Lunda chief and his followers settled in an area, the newcomers made no attempt to remove the local chiefs who were accepted as "owners of the land." Local communities were required to pay tribute to the Lunda overlord or his representative. At the same time the Lunda settlement became a center for arbitration, where disputes between local communities could be peacefully settled.

During the seventeenth and eighteenth centuries there was a double movement of Lunda expansion. The original Lunda kingdom, the kingdom of the Mwata Yamvo, "Lord of the Vipers," as the ruler was titled, was gradually extending its domains. At the same time break-away Lunda groups were founding new kingdoms much farther afield. One such state was Kasanje in Central Angola, another the Bemba kingdom in northeastern Zambia, a kingdom whose rulers appear to be descended from some of the original Luba founders of the Lunda kingdom.

By far the largest and most important of the new Lunda states was the kingdom of the Kazembe—again the name is a title applied to the ruler of a specific territory—which occupied the Luapula Valley south of Lake Mweru. This territory was conquered by the armies of the Mwata Yamvo in the early eighteenth century, a conquest probably inspired in part by a desire to acquire the rich salt pans and the copper mines of the area. By the end of the eighteenth century the new colony was almost as substantial a state as the original Lunda homeland. Its rulers, the Kazembes, acted as independent monarchs, though they maintained good relations with the Mwata Yamvo kings and sent them occasional tribute.

At the beginning of the nineteenth century the two great Lunda kingdoms were at the height of their power. But both suffered from their inability to weld their widely scattered provinces into a fully integrated state. When a ruler behaved oppressively, the outlying provinces naturally revolted. In the second half of the nineteenth century both kingdoms had to face the threat posed by groups of well-armed foreign traders, settled in their midst—the Cokwe in Mwata Yamvo's, the Nyamwezi (Yeke) in Kazembe's. Unable to resist the encroachments of these enterprising newcomers, who played skillfully on the discontents of their subjects, both kingdoms were on the verge of complete disintegration when the area came under European control.

✻ THE PORTUGUESE

Up to 1850 the Portuguese were almost the only Europeans to maintain contact with Central Africa. Their activities were concentrated in three main areas: the kingdom of Kongo, the valley of the Cuanza in central Angola and the valley of the lower Zambezi. They reached Kongo in 1482, established a fort at Sofala near the mouth of the Zambezi in 1505, and founded Luanda, the capital of Angola, in 1576.

Portuguese relations with Kongo opened in an atmosphere of remarkable cordiality. Kongolese ambassadors were sent to Lisbon, Portuguese missionaries and craftsmen to Kongo, and in 1506 one of the first members of the Kongolese royal family to be baptized became king as Affonso I. Affonso accepted the Christian teaching with passionate conviction and wanted his people to adopt the new religion and to acquire with it something of the technical skills possessed by the Portuguese. But the rulers of Portugal could not afford to meet his insistent appeals for aid, nor could they restrain the lawless group of Europeans of various nationalities recently settled on the island of São Tomé, who looked to the well-populated kingdom of Kongo for slaves to work their sugar plantations.

The kingdom of Kongo possessed certain innate weaknesses: the death of the reigning monarch was usually followed by a bitter struggle between rivals for the throne, and the ensuing disorder made it easy for powerful provincial chiefs to assert their independence. These weaknesses were disastrously compounded by the activities of the slave traders who intrigued with rival factions, encouraged local wars, and removed many thousands of the population.

In the mid-sixteenth century individual Portuguese traders came into contact with the kingdom of Ndongo which lay to the south of Kongo. The dynastic title *ngola* borne by the kings of Ndongo provided the name which, in the form Angola, the Portuguese applied to all the territory south of Kongo. In the 1570's an enterprising soldier of fortune, Paolo Dias, was given a grant by the Portuguese Crown to found a colony on the coast of Ndongo. Dias hoped to find land suitable for European settlement and rich mines of silver in the Cuanza Valley. The silver mines proved an illusion, and the land never attracted settlers. Instead, Luanda, the town founded by Dias, became the most important base for the slave trade in the whole of western Africa.

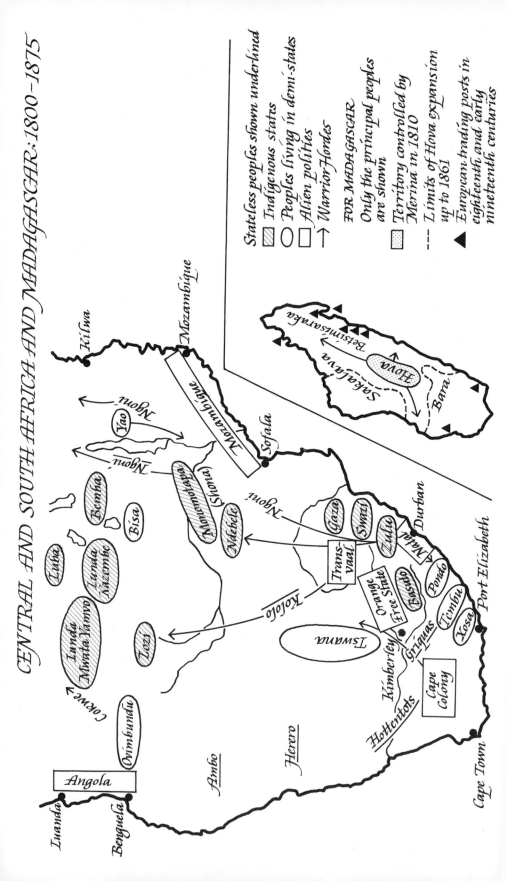

CENTRAL AND SOUTH AFRICA AND MADAGASCAR: 1800–1875

Stateless peoples shown underlined
- ▨ Indigenous states
- ◯ Peoples living in demi-states
- ▭ Alien polities
- ↑ Warrior Hordes

FOR MADAGASCAR
Only the principal peoples are shown
- ▦ Territory controlled by Merina in 1810
- --- Limits of Hova expansion up to 1861
- ▲ European trading posts in eighteenth and early nineteenth centuries

Kilwa

Mozambique

Sofala

Mozambique

Ngoni

Yao

Ngoni

Bemba

Bisa

Monomotapa (Shona)

Luba

Lunda Kazembe

Ndebele

Ngoni

Gaza

Swazi

Durban

Zulu

Luba

Lunda Mwata-Yamvo

Lozi

Kololo

Transvaal

Basuto

Orange Free State

Pondo

Natal

Tembu

Xosa

Port Elizabeth

Corwe

Ovimbundu

Kimberley

Griquas

Tswana

Herero

Hottentots

Cape Colony

Ambo

Angola

Luanda

Benguela

Cape Town

Sakalava

Betsimisaraka

Hova

Bara

Inevitably, the Portuguese were drawn into conflict with Ndongo. Intermittent fighting went on for no less than a hundred years until the struggle came to an end with the complete destruction of the kingdom. At the same time there was a steady deterioration in Portuguese relations with Kongo. Existing tensions between Portuguese traders and Kongolese kings were rendered more acute by the sudden appearance of the Dutch. The Dutch began trading to the north of the Congo River in the early seventeenth century; in the 1640's they captured Luanda and held the town for some years before being driven out by a Portuguese expeditionary force sent from Brazil. In spite of this victory the Portuguese never found a way of preventing the Dutch and other European interlopers from carrying on a vigorous trade along the coast north of Luanda. The Kongolese, who had naturally welcomed the Dutch intervention, could be dealt with more effectively. In 1665 a Portuguese army invaded the country and killed the king together with many of his nobility in a battle that was catastrophically decisive, for in the disorders that followed Kongo fell apart into a multitude of petty chiefdoms. The process of fragmentation was a continuous one, and by the end of the nineteenth century almost every village was an independent unit.

By 1700, then, the Portuguese had shattered Kongo and Ndongo. But they lacked the means to dominate the states which lay deeper in the interior. With the kingdoms of Kasanje and Matamba and with the Ovimbundu states of the Benguela highlands a modus vivendi was established. Basically, the situation resembled that prevailing on the Guinea coast. Both sides were equally interested in a flourishing trade in slaves. The Portuguese needed to maintain a regular flow of slaves to Brazil, while the native states reaped fat profits by sending slaving caravans deep into the interior to Lunda country and beyond. Without the assistance of these African middlemen the Portuguese could never have met the demands of Brazil.

The Angolan slave trade provided such easy remuneration for those who were engaged in it that it removed every incentive to seek other forms of economic development. Slaves supplied up to 90 percent of Angola's exports. Consequently, when in the 1840's the slave trade was finally abolished, the colony seemed threatened with economic collapse. Luanda had had a population of more than three thousand Europeans in the late seventeenth century and Angola had been the most extensive European colony in Africa. In 1850 the city contained less than a thousand white men, and the colony struck visitors as being little better than a penal settlement.

Both in Kongo and in Angola the Portuguese had picked up reports of rich mineral deposits, yet found nothing in sufficient quantities to meet the expense of exploitation. In their East African colony of Mozambique, on the other hand, they were within reach of one of the richest gold-bearing areas in Africa, and the Zambezi provided them with an obvious avenue into the interior. By 1540 they had established two posts, Sena and Tete, high up the river, the latter nearly three hundred miles from the sea.

From these posts free-lance traders set out for the kingdom of Mono-motapa. They were followed in the 1570's by a Portuguese expeditionary force, sent out from Lisbon ostensibly to avenge the murder of a Jesuit missionary at the court of Monomotapa. The expedition ended in complete disaster, but Portuguese influence in Monomotapa continued to increase, until in 1629 the ruler was constrained to acknowledge himself a vassal of the Portuguese Crown.

The Portuguese traders in Monomotapa behaved in as harsh and arrogant a manner as did their compatriots in Kongo, but their power was based on less secure foundations. Consequently, they were unable to withstand a general revolt, encouraged by the ruler of Changamire, which swept them from the country in the 1690's. Throughout the eighteenth century trade with Monomotapa and Changamire was carried on by means of African middlemen who brought their caravans to the Portuguese posts on the Zambezi.

By the nineteenth century the Portuguese presence in Mozambique consisted of no more than a few settlements on the coast and two posts on the Zambezi, together with the great estates (*prazos*) of a number of half-caste adventurers whose political status was not unlike that of independent African chiefs.

WARRIOR HORDES: THE JAGA, THE NGONI, AND OTHERS

Much of the history of Central Africa from 1500 onward is concerned with the wars that accompanied the expansion of Portuguese power. But there are two periods in the region's history—one beginning in the 1560's, the other in the 1830's—when wide areas were devastated by warrior hordes whose incursions were the result of purely indigenous causes.

In the 1560's the country to the west of the Kwango River was invaded by the war bands of the Jaga. In 1568 the Jaga sacked San Salvador, the capital of Kongo, but the kingdom was saved by a Portuguese force of six hundred musketeers sent from São Tomé. Most of the Jaga then turned south to raid central Angola and the Benguela highlands, until at length they settled down in the kingdoms they had conquered or created from Yaka on the Kwango to some of the Ovimbundu states in the highlands.

It seems likely that the Jaga began as a small group living in the Lunda-

Luba country to the east. Forced by unknown causes to organize themselves in disciplined warrior bands they developed extremely effective tactics, being highly mobile, masters of all the stratagems of war, and brutally conscious of the advantages of a policy of "frightfulness"—stories of their hideous cannibal feasts were current in Kongo three centuries after their passing—prepared to kill their own children if they impeded their march, but always willing to accept new recruits from the villages they overwhelmed.

The invasions that afflicted most of the southern part of Central Africa in the 1830's and 1840's were a direct result of the *mfecane,* the "time of troubles" of the Sotho and Nguni peoples of South Africa. Three main hordes made their way into Central Africa at this time: the Ngoni, the Ndebele, and the Kololo. The nucleus of the Ngoni was a small Nguni group led by Chief Zwangendaba, who began moving northward in the 1820's to escape Zulu domination. In the early 1830's the Ngoni stormed Zimbabwe and shattered the ancient kingdoms of Changamire and Monomotapa. In 1835 they crossed the Zambezi, settled at various points west of Lake Nyasa, ravaged the surrounding countryside, and passed on into southern Tanzania.

The Ndebele under their chief Mzilikazi had been part of the Zulu army until Mzilikazi revolted against Shaka and was forced to flee northward to escape vengeance. In the early 1830's the Ndebele made themselves masters of the Transvaal. But they were not able to hold their own against those other immigrants from the south, the Boer trekkers. After suffering two serious defeats in 1837, they resumed their northward march until they reached the Rhodesian plateau, where they settled, dominating as they did so the local Shona, once the subjects of Monomotapa.

The Kololo were a mixed group of Sotho peoples led by Chief Sebitwane. After years of wandering which took the horde as far west as Lake Ngami in the northern Kalahari, the Kololo settled in the floodplain of the upper Zambezi and conquered the kingdom of the Lozi.

These three groups have much in common with the Jaga. The Ngoni and the Ndebele were trained in Zulu tactics and had no difficulty in absorbing the men of other tribes into their regiments. To many of the small communities which lay in their path the passage of these ferocious bands brought utter disaster; yet from another point of view the wanderings of these peoples are to be counted among the epics of African history and their chiefs stand out as leaders on a heroic scale. They plundered to survive, and when at last they found a land where they could live in peace and plenty they settled down and made their homes there.

The Ngoni split up after Zwangendaba's death and founded a number of small kingdoms north and west of Lake Nyasa. The Ndebele remained united; their kingdom dominated western Rhodesia. The Kololo were less fortunate. In the 1860's they were annihilated in a counterrevolution led by survivors of the original Lozi dynasty.

⚑ THE CREATION OF LONG-DISTANCE TRADE ROUTES

In the fifteenth century there was only one long-distance trade route in Central Africa: the ancient route, along the valley of the Zambezi, by which gold and ivory passed from the Rhodesian plateau to the Muslim cities of the East African coast. Over the rest of Central Africa such trade as existed appears to have been on a more modest scale, being confined to the exchange of commodities such as raffia cloth and salt.

The arrival of the Portuguese in Kongo soon led to the development of wider trading contacts. The Portuguese needed slaves and ivory. To satisfy their demands native traders went from Kongo to the Stanley Pool area and later to the lands east of the Kwango.

By the middle of the seventeenth century the Imbangala of Kasanje had become the chief suppliers of slaves for the Portuguese of Angola. From them the Mwato Yamvo, the great Lunda king, obtained a steady supply of European trade goods, including firearms. The Imbangala maintained their monopoly over the trade with the interior until the late eighteenth century, when their southern neighbors, the Ovimbundu, began to break into their preserves. The Ovimbundu, occupying a score of little states on the Benguela highlands, appear to have been encouraged to participate in the trade by Portuguese adventurers who began to settle in their country in the mid-eighteenth century. The Ovimbundu showed commercial enterprise, pioneering many new routes which drew the lands of the upper Zambezi within the orbit of long-distance trade.

The insatiable demands of the Portuguese colony of Brazil for slave labor provided the motivating force that stimulated the enterprise of Angolan, Imbangala, and Ovimbundu slave traders. On the eastern side the slave trade remained on a very much smaller scale until the establishment of plantations in the French Indian Ocean colonies of Île de France (Mauritius) and Bourbon (Réunion) in the mid-eighteenth century. By the end of the same century it had become commercially profitable to send slaves on the long voyage round the Cape; and as increasingly efficient restrictions began to be imposed on the West African trade the export of slaves from Mozambique to Brazil became more and more important, reaching its peak in the 1830's and 1840's, only a few years before its final suppression.

The slave trade was of minor importance in the first three centuries of Mozambique as a Portuguese colony. Gold and ivory were the major exports. But the gold trade never met Portuguese expectations and gradually disappeared. For the decline in this lucrative commerce the Portuguese were themselves largely responsible. Their ruthless methods alienated the Swahili middlemen who had done so much to develop the trade of the interior, and the increasing disorder consequent on the decline of Monomotapa discouraged the local miners.

During the eighteenth century Bisa traders living north of the Zambezi established trading connections between the kingdom of the Kazembe in the Luapula Valley and the Portuguese posts at Sena and Tete. Two expeditions sent out by the Portuguese, one in 1798, the other in 1830, succeeded in reaching the Kazembe's capital, but the Portuguese were never able to develop a substantial trade with the new Lunda kingdom.

Other traders were more successful. At the beginning of the nineteenth century Nyamwezi traders whose homeland lay east of Lake Tanganyika reached the Kazembe's country, attracted probably by the copper and salt to be found there. Nyamwezi influence was becoming a factor of major political significance in the Luapula Valley by the 1850's.

The Nyamwezi were not the only African people to emerge as traders between the east coast and the interior. The Yao, who lived in the country east of Lake Nyasa, stimulated by the increasing demand for slaves, made themselves the principal slave merchants of the Nyasa area. The Bemba, after ousting the Bisa, came to occupy a similar position farther west in northeastern Zambia. Finally, in the 1820's and 1830's Swahili and Arab adventurers began to appear in the country west of the Lakes Nyasa and Tanganyika. In the 1850's their caravans were reaching ever deeper into the basin of the Congo.

Thus, by the 1850's a network of long-distance trade routes had been laid across the breadth of Central Africa. The Portuguese had dreamed of the *traversia,* a transcontinental route, since the early sixteenth century; and it was the new impulse that they imparted to the economic life of Central Africa that ultimately called such a route into existence. By 1850 men from the Atlantic and Indian Ocean coasts were meeting at the courts of the Lunda kings. But though the impulse came largely from Europe, the agents were African. And the routes which Europeans "explored" in the second half of the nineteenth century had been created years earlier by African pioneers.

CENTRAL AFRICA IN THE 1850'S

The political consequences of the developing trade were basically the same in Central Africa as they were in other tropical regions of the continent. Those who participated in the trade, whether as middlemen or as ultimate suppliers of slaves or ivory, increased in power, for the trade with all its tempting luxuries—brandy, tobacco, cloth, beads—provided ambitious chiefs with an incentive to extend their power and with an instrument to assist them in doing so. Firearms had reached the heart of Central Africa by the early eighteenth century, and the Kazembes had made use of them in their conquest of the Luapula Valley. But trade and firearms were not the only foundations of political power: a closely knit social organization and an army well disciplined in the use of traditional weapons could prove, as the Ndebele and Ngoni had shown, equally effective.

In 1500 there appear to have been only two major kingdoms in Central Africa, Kongo and Monomotapa. By 1850 these two great states had disappeared, their internal weaknesses having been aggravated by the encroachment of the Portuguese. But many other new states had emerged, some undoubtedly the equal of the old kingdoms in their size and power: the kingdoms of the Luba and the Lunda and their offshoots, which included the Bemba kingdom, Kasanje, the states of the Ovimbundu and the Ngoni, the Barotse (Lozi/Kololo) kingdom, and the kingdom of the Ndebele. The Portuguese colonies of Angola and Mozambique were certainly no more powerful than these substantial African states. Indeed, in southern Mozambique the Portuguese were at one time almost overwhelmed by the Nguni hordes.

The territory occupied by the major states comprised perhaps half the total area of Central Africa. Between most of the major states there lay broad belts of country whose inhabitants were organized in smaller polities, petty chiefdoms, or independent village communities. The existence of these buffer zones meant that the major states rarely came into conflict one with another. But it was the people of these minor polities who suffered most from the depredations of their more powerful neighbors, and some of them were to find the burden of their tribulations increased still further in the course of the next half century.

CHAPTER X

East Africa

ꙮ GEOGRAPHY

Today the term East Africa is usually understood to refer only to the three countries of Kenya, Tanzania (Tanganyika and Zanzibar), and Uganda. For historical purposes it is worth giving the region a somewhat larger extent to include Burundi, Rwanda, and northern Mozambique. Thus defined, East Africa possesses certain obvious geographical boundaries: the Somali deserts and the mountains of Ethiopia to the north, the chain of great lakes—Albert, Kivu, Tanganyika, Nyasa—to the west, the lower Zambezi to the south, the Indian ocean to the east. But these boundaries should not be thought of as natural frontiers limiting movement. The history of East Africa has been profoundly influenced by people coming from adjoining regions of Africa and from across the Indian Ocean.

Geographically, East Africa—a little less than one million square miles in area—is a region of striking contrasts: a coast of easy access and inviting aspect, backed by an arid and desolate hinterland that rises gradually to a plateau, parts of which—the highlands of Kenya, southern Tanzania, Ruanda, Burundi, and the borders of Lake Victoria—contain some of the richest and most delectable landscapes of the whole continent. It is in these favored areas that the present population is densest. One of the best ways of visualizing East Africa is to think of the region as made up of islands of fertility, with good soil and regular rainfall, separated or bounded by harsher lands of desert scrub as in northern Kenya or tsetse-infested bush as in central Tanzania.

ꙮ BUSHMEN AND ANCIENT AZANIANS

By the end of the Old Stone Age, after many millennia of evolution, East Africa had acquired a population whose type is regarded as ancestral to the modern Bushmen. Today the greatest concentration of Bushmen is to be found in the western half of South Africa. But there are still a few small Bushmen groups surviving in East Africa, some of whom speak a Khoisan language.

For the early Bushmen, as for their modern descendants, the most attractive parts of East Africa were not those well-watered districts where the modern population is densest, but the dry grasslands of central Kenya and Tanzania. It was here that the game animals which provided much of the food of these hunting peoples were most abundant.

This broad wedge of highland steppe that stretches deep into East Africa continues northward along the Rift Valley through Ethiopia to the Red Sea. Southward along this "ecological bridge" that connects East Africa with regions to the north there appear to have come, beginning perhaps about ten thousand years ago, a stream of people of Caucasoid stock whom some archeologists describe as "proto-Hamites." This movement of Caucasoid peoples from Northeast Africa has continued until modern times, its latest phase being the migration of Somali pastoralists into northern Kenya in the early years of the present century.

The earliest Caucasoid immigrants settled beside the lakes in the Kenya Rift Valley. They possessed finer stone implements than any previously known in East Africa. Fishing supplied them with much of their food, and they were able, like the mesolithic Negroids of Khartoum, to live a settled life with leisure to produce other artifacts, such as pottery.

Many centuries later other Caucasoid groups, arriving in East Africa about 1000 B.C., introduced domestic cattle and possibly also cereal cultivation. By the first millennium A.D. these "ancient Azanians," as some historians have termed them (Azania was the name given by Greek writers to the coast of East Africa), had come to populate most of the Kenya highlands and adjoining areas in northern Tanzania. They have left many traces of their occupation: stone burial chambers, hut circles, terraced fields, even the traces of roads and irrigation works. They are recalled in the earliest tradition of the present inhabitants as a race of tall, bearded, red-skinned people. And they have their living descendants in the Iraqw of northern Tanzania, whose language has been identified as Cushitic. But it was the lot of the great majority of these Caucasoid Azanians to succumb to the pressure and to be absorbed in the mass of later waves of immigrants, the Nilo-Hamites and the Bantu.

✺ BANTU MIGRATIONS AND SWAHILI CIVILIZATION

Today Bantu-speaking peoples of basically Negroid stock form so large a part of the total population of East Africa that it is difficult to imagine that there was once a time when people of Negroid stock were not to be found in the region. Yet at the beginning of the first millennium A.D. the population of East Africa consisted of Bushmen hunters and of Caucasoid communities dependent on agriculture and cattle raising, with possibly a few Negroid groups speaking Central Sudanic languages in the extreme northwest.

According to the tentative reconstruction of Bantu migrations by Guthrie and Oliver, Bantu settlers began to move into East Africa from the southern Congo in the first centuries of the Christian era. By 1000 A.D. Negroid groups were to be found along the coast from the Zambezi to the Juba. They had reached an area particularly well sited for intercourse between peoples of different cultures.

The east coast of Africa is also the western shore of the Indian Ocean; many threads link African history with that of the maritime lands of southern Asia. The regime of the winds—the northeast monsoon blowing from December, the southwest monsoon from March—makes it easy for sailors from the lands around the Arabian Sea to make trading voyages to the East African coast. No archeological evidence has yet been uncovered to reveal when this trade began, but it is clear from a Greek commercial handbook, the famous *Periplus of the Erythrean Sea,* that a flourishing commerce was being carried on in the first century A.D.

Sailors from South Arabia were probably the pioneers of the East African trade; they established a connection that has continued to this day. Between the first and the fifth centuries A.D. Greek merchants from Egypt had some stake in the trade. About the middle of the first millennium A.D., if not earlier, traders from the Persian Gulf, southern India, and Indonesia made contact with East Africa. From an early date some foreign traders probably established commercial posts at convenient sites along the coast. By the tenth century some of these posts were growing into flourishing city-states under rulers who had accepted Islam.

Muslim traders from Kilwa, Sofala, and other towns between the Rufiji and the Zambezi made their way into the interior in order to have direct access to the gold mines of Rhodesia. The part they played in the history of the kingdom of Monomotapa has already been noticed. North of the Rufiji there is no evidence of a Muslim penetration of the interior until the late eighteenth century. It would seem that there was no incentive for coastal traders to venture inland. The goods they sought—ivory, slaves, tortoiseshell, rhinoceros horn—could be more conveniently collected by the local people who attended the seasonal markets at the coast.

But one should not suppose that there existed a complete barrier between the coast and the interior. If there were no trade routes, there were certainly trade contacts, and it was through such contacts that new materials and new techniques gradually percolated into the interior. The *Periplus* makes pointed reference to the sale of iron implements to the natives of Rhapta, a site probably on the northern Tanzanian coast. It was through such contacts that iron, which may also have reached the Kenya area from southern Ethiopia, came to be more widely used by the Caucasoid Azanians. The introduction of the Asian yam and the banana by Indonesian seafarers has already been noted. Among the other novelties brought by the Indonesians and of especial value to the people of the coast were the coconut palm and the outrigger canoe.

The majority of Indonesian migrants passed on to colonize the vast, uninhabited island of Madagascar. No archeological evidence of their presence has yet been discovered in East Africa. The impact of Muslim immigrants from Persia and Arabia, on the other hand, is clearly manifest in many ways. There are the ruins at many sites along the coast of mosques and palaces built in medieval Muslim styles of architecture. There are references to the Persian and Arab origin in the chronicles of the dynasties of the coast. There are the many Arabic loanwords in Swahili (the word itself is derived from the Arabic *sahil*, "coast"). And there is the unmistakable impact of Muslim culture on many of the peoples of the coast.

One should not think of the Islamization of the coast as being the work of a large number of foreign settlers. It was the product of a movement similar to that taking place at the same time on the southern "shore" of the Sahara. A small minority of Muslim traders, with perhaps a few political refugees, introduced the political structure of an Islamic state to a population in which the Bantu Negroid element predominated. In many of the medieval states, as in nineteenth-century Zanzibar, the "White Moors"—to use a Portuguese term—formed a ruling aristocracy; but it was a natural process for the descendants of these Arab and Persian rulers gradually to become indistinguishable in appearance or language from many of their subjects. Thus, there developed a civilization that has been called by one of its most recent historians "something unique, neither wholly Arab nor exclusively African, eclectic but not cosmopolitan." [1]

〰️ THE EARLY HISTORY OF THE NORTHEASTERN INTERIOR

The impact of other peoples of the Indian Ocean on the coastal Bantu was a spectacular development; and the accounts of Arab and Portuguese travelers present a vivid picture of the wealthy city-states that existed in the fourteenth and fifteenth centuries on the East African coast. Far more obscure but historically no less important is the story of what was happening in the northeastern interior at the same time—the impact of the Negroid Bantu on the Caucasoid Azanians, combined with the arrival in the same area of new groups from the north, the Nilo-Hamites and people speaking Cushitic languages such as Galla.

The problem of Nilo-Hamitic origins is highly complicated. Recent linguistic research suggests that the Nilo-Hamitic languages represent a blending of three linguistic stocks, Nilotic as spoken by the Negroid peoples of the Upper Nile, Cushitic as spoken by the mainly Caucasoid Sidama of southern Ethiopia, and a third language spoken by a people not yet identified. As for their tradition of origin it would seem that the basin of Lake Rudolf on the Kenya-Ethiopia border was their earliest known dispersal point. From here groups went either westward toward the Nile or southward into the lands already occupied by the Azanians.

It is clear that there were various waves of Nilo-Hamitic migration. The Masai, the best known of the Kenya Nilo-Hamites, were the latest to reach the highlands. The Nandi and other smaller tribes, such as the Kipsigis or the Suk, were already established to the west of the Rift Valley when the Masai arrived. And the Nandi had been preceded by yet another Nilo-Hamitic group, the Tatoga, who were dispersed over country to the south of the Kenya-Tanzania border.

The Masai appear to have reached the Kenya highlands about the sixteenth century. At the same time the ancestors of the Kikuyu, affected possibly by the pressure of Galla coming down from the north, were moving up the Tana River to the fertile country around Mount Kenya. Other Bantu-speaking peoples such as the Kamba and the Chagga also appear to have moved inland from the coast.

The thinness of our present knowledge of the history of the northeastern interior until the middle of the nineteenth century, when it began to be illuminated by the accounts of European travelers, makes the picture look very confusing. But three facts stand out. The civilization of the ancient Azanians was largely destroyed. (It is tempting to ascribe its destruction to the depredations of pastoral nomads, such as the Masai, on sedentary agriculturalists.) The eastern Bantu were profoundly influenced by their contact with the Azanians and the Nilo-Hamites. They accepted certain social institutions, such as the division of society into age-sets, from their new neighbors; they copied their weapons, their adornments, and their hair styles; and their lighter skin suggests there must have been a considerable amount of intermarriage with people of Caucasoid stock. Finally, it is clear that no major kingdom ever arose in this area, which comprises most of modern Kenya and northeastern Tanzania; and it is only in the eighteenth century that one can begin to trace the emergence of chieftainship among the Chagga of Kilimanjaro and the Shambaa of Usambara. The acephalous societies of the Nilo-Hamites and the eastern

Bantu contrast sharply with the hierarchical states that were established in the area of the great lakes.

⚜ THE EARLY HISTORY OF THE INTERLACUSTRINE AREA AND THE SOUTHERN INTERIOR

In time archeological research should be able to dispel much of the obscurity that envelops the history of the interlacustrine area of East Africa before 1500 A.D. At present historians can do no more than put forward an almost entirely hypothetical reconstruction.

For much of the first millennium A.D. the population may well have been confined to a few Pygmy groups living in the forests to the west, a few Bushmen hunters to the northeast, and possibly a number of Negroid agriculturists speaking Eastern or Central Sudanic languages moving in from the northwest. Before the end of the first millennium the first Bantu-speakers must have arrived, moving into the area from the west and southwest. It is reasonable to associate the intensive colonization of much of the area with the introduction of the banana, the staple crop of the Ganda and other peoples living to the north and west of Lake Victoria. How the banana reached the area is uncertain. It may have been transmitted by the Azanians, or it may have passed along a chain of Bantu peoples in southern Tanzania.

There is no evidence to show when Caucasoid groups first reached the interlacustrine area, but it is clear that some centuries before 1500 a wave of light-skinned pastoralists, usually referred to as Hamites and probably associated with the Cushitic peoples of southwest Ethiopia, reached the country north of Lake Victoria and came to dominate the scattered and stateless groups of Bantu farmers. In the territory between Lakes Victoria and Kyoga later to be occupied by the kingdoms of Buganda and Bunyoro they established a centralized kingdom of considerable extent, known as Kitara.

Kitara was overwhelmed by Nilotic invaders from the north in the sixteenth century. But some of the pastoral aristocracy of Kitara moved westward to found new kingdoms for themselves. Rwanda and Ankole were the most prominent of these new states. In Rwanda the immigrants were known as Tutsi, in Ankole as Hima. From these two bases Hima/Tutsi groups carried their form of political organization, with its elaborate form of chieftainship and its social division between pastoral aristocrats and Bantu serfs, into the area between Lakes Victoria and Tanganyika.

The Nilotic groups who began to enter East Africa about the sixteenth century were entirely different from the Hima pastoralists, the Nilo-Hamites, or the early Caucasoid settlers in the Kenya highlands. The

Nilotes were a Negroid people whose homeland lay between the Bahr-al-Ghazal and the White Nile. Consequently, they can have had little or no contact with the elaborate culture developed in Ethiopia, a culture that had some influence on the other three groups which had entered East Africa from the north. The Nilotes appear to have had no form of technological superiority over the people among whom they settled. They did not have a great reputation as warriors. But they brought with them more elaborate notions of political organization, and their prowess as arbitrators and rainmakers led many Bantu and Sudanic peoples to accept their domination.

In northwest Uganda the Nilotes merged with Sudanic groups to form the Alur and Acholi, among whom there developed a multiplicity of tiny chiefdoms. Very different was the political situation farther south, where a Nilotic clan, the Bito, overthrew the Hima kingdom of Kitara and established the powerful state of Bunyoro. From Bunyoro Bito groups founded chiefdoms among the Ganda and Soga to the south and southwest. The Soga chiefdoms never achieved any great territorial extent, but Buganda, originally a vassal of Bunyoro, grew so powerful that by the nineteenth century it was in a position to eclipse its former overlord.

It would seem that the already considerable Bantu population of Bunyoro, Buganda, and Busoga made it impossible for these areas to absorb more than a conquering minority of Nilotes. And so the main body of Nilotic immigrants avoided these lands, passing north of Lake Kyoga and finally settling around the Kavirondo Gulf on the northeastern corner of Lake Victoria. Surrounded by Bantu and Nilo-Hamitic groups, the Luo, as this last group of Nilotes came to be called, were numerous enough to preserve their language, but they never merged their loosely organized clans to form a substantial state.

The interlacustrine area enjoyed a more regular rainfall than almost any other part of East Africa. At the same time it was little affected by the tsetse fly. With the advantage of a better food supply the population must have increased more rapidly than elsewhere in the region. Consequently, men must have begun breaking away from the settled areas in search of new pastures for their cattle and new areas of untouched soil to cultivate. As they moved away they took with them the forms of political organization with which they were familiar.

By the early nineteenth century most of western Tanzania was occupied by a considerable number of petty chieftaincies. The ruling dynasties to the southeast of Lake Tanganyika traced their origins back to the Luba country west of Lake Tanganyika; those at the northern end of the lake had links with Burundi and Rwanda. Farther east, among the Sukuma and Nyamwezi, the chieftainship appears to be derived from the interlacustrine area and to represent a form of political organization that existed before the coming of the Hima. There is clear evidence of a movement of Sukuma and Nyamwezi groups eastward into the dry central belt of Tanzania in the eighteenth century. But local traditions suggest that several centuries earlier cattle-owning migrants had brought the Sukuma form of chieftainship to people living north of Lake Nyasa, whence it spread northeastward to the Hehe, to the Gogo, and possibly even to the Chagga. This movement in the dispersal of chieftainship appears not to have affected people, such as the Yao and the Makua, living in southeastern Tanzania or northern Mozambique.

There is a marked contrast in the historical pattern of the northern and southern interiors of East Africa. In the northern half people of four main stocks met and mingled; in the south the population is almost exclusively Bantu. In the interlacustrine area of the north and in the Kenya highlands natural conditions make possible the development of an agriculture that can provide the surplus to support elaborate states. Over most of the south the fertile areas are separated from one another by miles of dry or tsetse-infested bush. In the favored districts of the north major movements of migration had come to an end by the nineteenth century; the south, by contrast, could be regarded as still in its pioneering phase, and the spread of chieftainships may be seen as part of the steady process of populating an almost empty land.

PORTUGUESE, OMANI ARABS, AND THE DEVELOPMENT OF TRADE ROUTES

In 1498 European intercourse with East Africa was resumed after an interval of about a thousand years when a Portuguese squadron under Vasco da Gama sailed up the coast on its way to India. The cities of the coast were then at the height of their prosperity. In the previous century there had been a great expansion of Islam on the farther side of the Indian Ocean; new markets were revealed for African products and more reliable contact established with old trading partners. This great movement of peaceful development was shattered by the Portuguese. Within twenty years the newcomers were masters of the coast. It was a sterile conquest. The Portuguese rendered one great service to the people of East Africa by introducing certain food crops, particularly maize and manioc, from the New World. They contributed little else to Swahili civilization.

At the end of the seventeenth century the Portuguese were driven from all their posts north of Cape Delgado by the Omani Arabs. The suzerainty claimed by the Omani over the coast was not made effective until the second quarter of the nineteenth century, when a highly enterprising ruler of Oman, Sayyid Said, made Zanzibar first his base, then from 1840 his capital. He forced the coastal states to accept him as their overlord and set about transforming his new domain into a profitable commercial venture.

The tradition of Arab-Swahili enterprise in the interior of East Africa was a very old one. The gold and ivory of the Rhodesian plateau had attracted coastal traders from Kilwa and Sofala for many centuries before the coming of the Portuguese. But there was no incentive to make direct contact with the lands lying to the north of Lake Nyasa until the end of the eighteenth century. A combination of factors led to the sudden expansion of the East African trade. The demand for slaves to be sent to Brazil or to work the newly established plantations in the French Indian Ocean islands has already been noted in connection with the history of Central Africa. Zanzibar, too, needed slaves after the introduction of cloves to the island in 1818 and the establishment of more and more plantations. At the same time the growing prosperity of the middle classes of Western Europe and America greatly enlarged the market for ivory. Slaves and ivory were the traditional exports of the East Coast, but in the early nineteenth century they provided an opportunity for greater profits than ever before.

Nevertheless, it was not the coastal people who took the first step in initiating long-distance trade routes. These routes were created by people of the interior—notably the Yao, the Bisa, the Nyamwezi, and the Kamba—who began to organize regular caravans to the coast. It was not until the middle years of the nineteenth century that Arab traders were to be found in any numbers in the interior. Firearms had never been known in the interior of East Africa before. Now they began to pass into the hands of local men. By 1850 the inexorable consequences, so familiar from other parts of the continent, that flowed from the export of slaves and the import of guns were also to be observed in East Africa. But the turmoil which afflicted the region was made worse by the depredations of the warrior bands of the Masai and the Ngoni.

The Masai were at the height of their power in 1850. They were interested in acquiring cattle not slaves, and their weapon was the spear, not the gun. But they terrorized the plains of central Kenya and northern Tanzania, and their ferocious reputation discouraged traders from attempting to penetrate their country. For some of the peoples of southern Tanzania the Ngoni invasions brought utter destruction. Others, such as the Hehe, responded by forming themselves into larger political units and by adopting Ngoni military techniques. Thus, they were better equipped to meet the growing tide of violence that affected so much of Tanzania in the second half of the nineteenth century.

🜉 EAST AFRICA IN THE 1850'S

There were three major areas of political power in East Africa in the 1850's: the fertile interlacustrine lands, the Zanzibar-dominated coast, and the Masai plains. The interlacustrine area contained by far the most powerful states of the interior—Buganda, Bunyoro, Rwanda, Ankole, and others. The cities of the coast, the only substantial urban centers in the region, were caught up in the loosely organized commercial empire of Zanzibar. The Masai were true pastoralists who never attempted to create an organized state. These major centers of power occupied only a small part of the total area of East Africa. Most East Africans still lived in small societies, petty chiefdoms, or acephalous communities such as those of the Kikuyu, and their contacts with a wider world were far more limited than was the case in West or Central Africa where long-distance trade routes had developed at a much earlier date.

In 1850 not a single European could be found in the interior of East Africa and only a handful on the coast—a few merchants and consuls at Zanzibar and a tiny group of Protestant missionaries near Mombasa. Even the broad outline of the geography of the interior was unknown to Europeans. It could, indeed, be said at this time that there was no region of the continent in which Europeans had so little interest, no region on which they had made so little impact as East Africa. This situation was to be dramatically transformed in the course of the next generation.

CHAPTER XI

South Africa

𝕏 GEOGRAPHY

South Africa—a region which comprises the present republic of that name, together with the territories of Botswana, Lesoto, Swaziland, and southern Mozambique—has an area of about a million square miles. The massive plateau that occupies so much of East and Central Africa dominates South Africa even more clearly. The plateau is tilted up on its eastern side, where the high veld of the Transvaal lies at over six thousand feet. Its edge is marked by the almost unbroken line of an escarpment that falls steeply, in parts precipitously, to the low-lying lands of the coast. This coastal belt is never less than fifty miles across and has a width of two hundred miles and more in southern Mozambique.

South Africa is usually thought of as a land of wide open spaces, of grassy plains stretching away to the flat lines of remote horizons. This is, indeed, the characteristic landscape of the veld of the eastern and central interior; but the periphery is more varied. There is the favored corner of the Cape, where a Mediterranean climate in southern latitudes produces a unique ecology; the great range of the Drakensberg, ringing Lesoto (Basutoland), with peaks rising to eleven thousand feet; the lovely green hill and valley country of Natal; the swamps of the Okovango in northern Botswana; the Namib desert that forms the "skeleton coast" of South-West Africa.

Variations in rainfall explain many of South Africa's contrasts in landscape. The eastern coastal lands may expect thirty inches or more of rain every year. But the volume and the regularity of the rainfall declines steadily as one moves over the interior. Much of the western half is termed "desert"—the Kalahari and the Karroo. But there is not complete aridity (the rainfall averages eight to sixteen inches a year), and these "deserts" should be thought of as lands of dry steppe, comparable not with the Sahara but with the Sahel that fringes the great desert.

The pattern of rainfall, favoring the eastern coastal lands, has naturally had a profound influence on the distribution of population. But the environment has influenced human activity in a number of other, quite different ways. There is the simple and obvious fact of South Africa's remoteness. Lying at an extremity of the continent, bounded on all its coasts by vast expanses of ocean, no part of Africa has been so far removed from the main centers of human activity—at least for most of the last twenty to thirty thousand years (in paleolithic times the situation was different). Moreover, as if to discourage still further approach from the sea, the coasts are storm-girt, limited in their number of natural harbors, and backed, on the western side, by an almost waterless hinterland. Nor does the region possess any navigable rivers to facilitate penetration by seafarers; even the Orange, the greatest of South Africa's rivers, dries up in certain places.

In compensation South Africa has an advantage over other regions of the continent. Its cooler climate protects it from many of the disease-bearing pests of the tropics, and especially from the tsetse fly and the anopheles mosquito. The absence of the tsetse fly means that almost every part of the region can serve as reasonable cattle country. Over most of tropical Africa one of the major themes in the history of the past two thousand years is the work of peasant farmers, clearing the woodland or the forest. In South Africa, by contrast, where agriculture alone could not always be counted on to supply a livelihood, the lives of men have been profoundly influenced by the ways of cattle. As for the region's immense mineral wealth, this did not become a factor in its development until late in the nineteenth century.

✢ BUSHMEN AND BANTU

Today South Africa possesses a greater assortment of races than any other region of the continent; three thousand years ago its population was made up exclusively of people of Bushmanoid stock. About the beginning of the Christian era these hunting folk probably came into contact with small groups of Caucasoid pastoralists who had made their way southward from the highlands of East Africa. Stone bowls of a type associated with the neolithic culture of Kenya have been found in South-West Africa, a Caucasoid strain has been noted in the physical characteristics of the pastoral Herero of that territory, and skeletal remains from Later Stone Age sites in other parts of South Africa possess Caucasoid features. From these Caucasoids some Bushmen probably acquired cattle and so evolved the distinctive culture of the Hottentots.

In the latter half of the first millennium A.D. Negroid Bantu began to filter into the region. By the sixteenth century the Southern Bantu contained four main linguistic groups: Nguni, Sotho, Venda, and Southwestern. The Nguni, all of whose peoples—Xosa, Tembu, Pondo, Zulu, and others—speak dialects of the same language, moved into the fertile lands of the east coast. This favored area probably already contained a considerable Bushmanoid population. That a good deal of intermarriage took place between the two races is suggested by the presence of a large number of words with Khoisan click sounds in the Nguni language. But relations were not always peaceful: many of the pastoral Hottentots retreated westward to the Cape; many Bushman groups sought refuge in lonelier and less hospitable districts. By the end of the seventeenth century Nguni settlements had spread over most of modern Natal, and their occupation of the northern parts of the country could be traced back for at least four hundred years.

Traditions suggest that the Sotho once occupied the area lying to the northeast of the Kalahari. From there, about the fifteenth century, they began fanning out over the high plateau to the east and south. In the Limpopo Valley they came into contact with the Venda, a people closely related to the Shona of Monomotapa. Among the gentle hills of Swaziland Sotho and Nguni groups met and overlapped. Farther south the Drakensberg divided the two peoples, while to the east the desolate stretches of the Kalahari separated the Sotho from the southwestern Bantu. This distinct group of Bantu peoples, comprising the Herero, the Ambo, and others, had moved south from the highlands of Angola.

Not until their time of troubles at the beginning of the nineteenth century did any of the Southern Bantu establish a territorial state comparable to the large and powerful kingdoms of Central Africa. There was nothing surprising about this apparent backwardness. The Southern Bantu—like the Anglo-Saxon invaders of Britain in the Dark Ages—were colonists in a half-empty land, and their political institutions were of a kind natural to pioneers. Originally, no doubt the Bantu were only organized in small kin groups. But as population increased, groups came together to form tribes under the rule of a chief. Succession to chieftainship was on a hereditary basis; the chief's family or clan formed the core of the tribe; and the tribe usually took its name from one of its rulers.

By the eighteenth century the number of such tribal chieftaincies among the Southern Bantu ran into several hundreds. They varied greatly in size, some chiefs having only a few hundred followers, others many thousands. Settlement patterns were not the same in all areas: in Natal homesteads were usually isolated from one another, whereas on the fringes of the Kalahari substantial towns grew up around the few good water holes. There were differences, too, in social organization between Sotho and Nguni. But all the tribal chieftaincies of the Southern Bantu were subject to the process of "fissiparous multiplication." As the population, both of men and of cattle, increased competition for pasture land and water holes grew more intense. The still unoccupied lands provided a safety valve. And so disputes between tribes or within tribes could be resolved by the departure of the weaker party in search of vacant lands. There was conflict, too, with Hottentots and Bushmen—Bushmen hunters naturally regarded the cattle of the strangers as fair game—but it was conflict on a minor scale, not of a kind that made necessary the creation of elaborate military organizations. Ineluctable forces were to transform this pattern of comparatively peaceful development.

🕮 THE DUTCH AT THE CAPE

South Africa was the last region in the continent to attract the attention of Europeans. A temperate climate and an absence of tropical fevers were no compensation for the region's remoteness, its apparent lack of mineral resources, and the backwardness of its population. And so it was not until 1652, more than a century and a half after the first Portuguese landfall in South Africa, that the first European settlement was established by the Dutch at the Cape. It was intended only as a victualing station, a convenient halfway house on the sea route to the Indies, not as a gateway to the interior. Yet this is what it became. For the settlement needed colonists, soldiers to guard it against attack by European rivals, farmers to provide food for visiting ships. And some of the colonists needed land and a life free from the restrictions of the East India Company's rule.

Men could make a living beyond the borders of the colony as hunters in search of ivory, or as traders bartering with the Hottentots for their cattle, or even as cattle farmers themselves. Gradually, on the frontiers a new type of European evolved, the Trek Boer, the "migrant farmer." The Boers represented only a minority of the European community, but more than any other group, European or African, they were to dominate the future development of South Africa. With their numbers increased by natural reproduction, the frontiersmen from the Cape advanced northward and eastward. The Bushmen they hunted down; the Hottentots provided them with cheap labor; but the Bantu whom they encountered on the Great Fish River in the 1770's presented a block of population too massive for them to penetrate. Between Boer and Bantu, then, an uneasy march land—the Eastern Frontier of the Cape—came into existence where black men and white were to raid and counterraid each other for the next hundred years.

𝕏 THE MFECANE

Meanwhile, an even more explosive situation was developing among the Nguni living in the rich lands of Natal. The safety valves that had prevented major conflict in the past were being removed, for the population continued to increase and less and less land became available. In self-defense tribes began to unite with their neighbors to form tribal confederations and to experiment with new forms of military organization. It was the beginning of the *Mfecane*, the term applied by the Nguni to the wars and disturbances that occupied most of the first half of the nineteenth century.

The central event of the *Mfecane* was the emergence of the military state of the Zulu. The Zulu kingdom was created by Shaka, a leader of genius who developed into a ruthless despot. Shaka hit on a way of bringing separate tribes together by recruiting all their young men into his regiments. Thus, provided with a permanent army, highly disciplined and trained in new fighting methods, Shaka was able to defeat all his neighbors and devastate their lands. But Shaka had established a model which his neighbors hastened to adopt. Other remarkable Nguni leaders emerged, men who, having either quarreled with Shaka or been defeated by him, found it necessary to escape his wrath. Training their followers in Zulu methods of warfare, adapting Zulu forms of political organization to their needs, they set out on their wanderings.

These powerful warrior hordes left in their wake a trail of devastation, of rotting corpses and burning villages and plundered herds. But not all those who lay in their path were killed; survivors from defeated tribes were taken along as captives and gradually absorbed into the community of their conquerors. And when at last a horde ceased its wanderings and established itself permanently in some favored land, it possessed sufficient discipline to achieve the transformation into a territorial state. Thus, Sobhuza and his followers laid the foundation of the Swazi kingdom, Soshangane created the Gaza kingdom in southern Mozambique, and the Nguni of Zwangendaba and the Ndebele of Mzilikazi left a deep mark on the history of East and Central Africa.

In the past there had been comparatively little contact between Nguni and Sotho. But as Nguni hordes began to pour onto the plateau, the Sotho found themselves caught up in the convulsions of the *Mfecane*. Tribes fled the plains to seek sanctuary in the mountains or along the fringes of the Kalahari. In the Drakensberg another remarkable leader, Moshesh, welded a great number of minor groups together to form the Basuto nation. Other Sotho leaders created warrior bands of their own—the most successful being Sebitwane, who led his people, the Kololo, northward to the Zambezi.

Thus, within half a century the *Mfecane* had transformed the political pattern of much of South Africa. In place of the multitude of small tribes there were now a number of substantial kingdoms. At the same time a vast expanse of territory—most of the modern Transvaal, Orange Free State, and Natal—was denuded of its population. Had the *Mfecane* occurred a century earlier, these lands would have been reoccupied by Nguni and Sotho when settled times returned and population began to increase. It was one of the ironies of history that just at this time Boer cattle farmers should have been impelled to seek new lands far beyond the frontiers of the Cape.

✠ BRITISH AND BOERS

The British occupied the Dutch colony at the Cape in 1795, after Britain's mortal enemy, France, had overrun Holland in the first years of the French Revolution wars. The Cape was a colony of no economic value; nor was it needed, with the empty lands of Canada and Australia lying open, for white settlement. But its strategic importance to the masters of India was immense; it seemed, in the words of the first British governor, "the master link of connection between the western and eastern world." [1] And so the British made sure that the colony remained in their hands when peace was made in Europe in 1815.

In 1798 the Cape had a European population of twenty-one thousand. By 1832 the number of Europeans had increased to sixty-six thousand, among whom were the survivors and offspring of the five thousand British settlers sent out in 1820 to occupy the Eastern Frontier of the colony. For the Boer cattle farmers figures such as these spelled overpopulation. Boer families were large, younger sons needed land, and a respectable farm required no less than six thousand acres. The Boers had acquired an unshakable conviction of their natural superiority over all "coloured" peoples. The new administration at the Cape, on the other hand, under the influence of humanitarian sentiments, appeared more interested in safeguarding the basic rights of the native population. Political resentment sharpened the force of the economic necessity that drove the Boers to look beyond the bounds of the colony.

By the 1820's Europeans at the Cape were becoming increasingly well informed about the lands that lay beyond the frontiers. Traders were doing regular business with the Nguni tribes: in 1824 a trading post was established at Port Natal, a site whose name was later changed to Durban. By the 1820's Protestant mission stations had been established far to the north of the Orange River and beyond the Eastern Frontier of the

Cape in territory belonging either to Sotho or Nguni peoples. From sources such as these and from the accounts of hunters and other adventurers who had pushed even farther into the interior came back reports of the empty grasslands of the High Veld and—even more attractive— the recently depopulated country of Natal, a land described by one contemporary as "inexhaustible in natural resources." [2]

The natural line of European advance was eastward along the fertile coastal belt. But it was here that African population was densest. The story of the Eastern Frontier was one of almost constant disorder. In the early 1830's Xosa war bands devastated European farms in the frontier district. The Colonial government retaliated with a formidable punitive expedition, but it lacked the military resources to control the land it had overrun. Finally, the metropolitan government decided that the conquered territory should be returned to the local chiefs. To the Boer farmers this act of an apparently "Kaffir-loving," missionary-influenced British government was utterly exasperating. In 1835 the Great Trek— one of the most dramatic migrations in history—began.

In the course of the next decade about fourteen thousand people— men, women, and children—joined in the exodus to the interior. They did not travel in a single mighty host but in smaller parties, groups of neighbors setting out under an elected leader. They traveled in lumbering wagons drawn by up to twenty oxen. The first wheeled form of transport ever to be seen in sub-Saharan Africa, these vehicles proved highly effective on the firm open stretches of the veld. They enabled the trekkers to carry with them much more baggage than any African migrant band dependent solely on head porterage; they provided Boer families with mobile homes, and they could be swiftly transformed, when drawn up in laager, into easily defensible strongpoints.

The trekkers were entering territories where violence had been endemic for a generation. Conflict between these land-hungry white farmers and local Bantu chiefs was inevitable. In some areas, such as the mountainous districts of Lesoto, there was a reasonable chance of successful African resistance to this European invasion. In Natal the Zulus under Shaka's successor, Dingane, massacred the first party of settlers. But the combination of guns, wagons, and horses gave the Boers in the long run a decisive tactical advantage over foot soldiers equipped only with shields and spears. By the end of 1838 the Boers had inflicted crushing defeats on the two major military powers of the area, Dingane's Zulus in Natal and Mzilikazi's Ndebele in the Transvaal. Mzilikazi led his people northward out of range of Boer attacks: Dingane was overthrown in a civil war and his successor, Mpande, made peace with the Boers.

By the early 1840's there were half a dozen petty Boer republics established beyond the frontier of Cape Colony, the most important being the Republic of Natal with its capital at Pietermaritzburg and its territory reaching to the sea to include Port Natal. Unwilling though the British government was to assume new commitments, it could not ignore these developments. Port Natal was a site of potential importance on the imperial highway to India: it could not be left in hostile hands. There were reports of Boer actions which suggested the revival of a form of slavery on their new farms. Above all, the Boers were coming into conflict with Bantu chiefs, some of whom looked to the government at the Cape for protection. Far from stabilizing the situation on the frontiers of the Cape, the Boer exodus exposed it to the shock of new waves of unrest. And so reluctantly the British found themselves having to take action over an extent of territory whose bounds were forever widening.

In 1842 British troops were sent to drive the Boers from Port Natal. The next year saw the annexation of Natal as a British colony followed by the gradual disintegration of the Boer republic. In 1847 yet another war on the Eastern Frontier of the Cape led to the permanent occupation of all the territory up to the Kei River. Known as British Kaffraria, the conquered areas were placed under military control and administered separately from the Cape until 1866. Finally, in 1848 British sovereignty was proclaimed over all the country occupied by Boers between the Orange and the Vaal. Only those trekkers who had moved beyond the Vaal River lay outside the sphere of British influence, and even they were still regarded as being legally subject to British justice.

Thus, within little more than a decade European power, manifested in the well-armed Boer farmers or the British magistrates and redcoats, had penetrated deep into the interior. Nowhere else in Africa in recent times, save only in Algeria and, more fleetingly, in Egypt, had European might been displayed on a comparable scale.

✥ THE BEGINNINGS OF THE "NATIVE PROBLEM"

Rivalry and tension between the two groups of Europeans provided the most publicized crises in nineteenth-century South Africa. Less dramatic was the development of the really major theme in the region's modern history, the interaction of peoples of African and of European descent.

As early as the 1650's, the first decade of the Cape as a European settlement, many of the main elements in what was later to be known to Europeans as the "native problem" could be discerned. There was the constant undertone of violence—Hottentot marauding countered by Dutch punitive expeditions. There was the bitter dispute over land, as the Hottentots found themselves steadily dispossessed of pastures that had been theirs since time immemorial. There was among many of the white colonists the emergence of an attitude of harsh racial superiority, strengthened by a narrow-minded religious faith and expressed in crude stereotypes that described the "natives" as "dull," "stupid," "incredibly idle," or—in the savage phrase of Van Riebeck, the first governor of the Cape—as "black, stinking dogs."

Aware of the problems likely to arise from the evolution of a society containing such disparate elements, some of the early administrators sought a solution by means of racial segregation. There was talk, in the early years, of constructing a canal across the Cape peninsula, and serious consideration was given in the early nineteenth century to plans for creating an empty neutral zone on the turbulent Eastern Frontier. It was, of course, utterly impossible to keep the races apart. From the start there had been intercourse between Dutch settlers and Hottentot women. As the Hottentots gradually collapsed as a distinct ethnic group—their lands occupied by European settlers, their numbers decimated by epidemics of smallpox, a disease hitherto unknown to them—a new ethnic group known as the "Coloureds" began to emerge in the population of the Colony.

Though the majority of the Cape Coloureds were of Hottentot origin with some infusion of European blood, their numbers also came to include the descendants of the Indian, Malay, Malagasy, and African slaves brought to the Cape by the Dutch East India Company. Many of the Cape Coloureds lived the wretched life of landless laborers or squatters on European farms, but some, especially those of Asian origin, set themselves up as skilled craftsmen in Cape Town, and a few enterprising individuals, having acquired horses and guns, copied the methods of Boer frontiersmen and carved out independent domains for themselves beyond the Orange River. The largest of these new groups, the Griquas or Bastards, played an important part in the politics of the frontier for more than half a century.

The Dutch settlers at the Cape were insulated by their remoteness from the currents of liberal thought circulating in late eighteenth-century Europe. The arrival of British administrators, missionaries, and settlers exposed Dutch society to the uncomfortable draft of contemporary "winds of change." Under the Dutch company's rule the Hottentots had possessed no legal status; one of the earliest enactments of the new government at the Cape was to publish a code which brought the resident native population within the bounds of the law. Soon the Protestant missionaries, whose newly established stations served as focal points for the "civilization" of the Hottentots, began to take note of the injustices suffered by their charges at the hands of local farmers and officials. Missionary agitation, carried on with the support of the powerful humanitarian pressure group in London, led in 1828 to the famous Fiftieth Ordinance, which guaranteed to the Coloured population of the Cape "the same freedom and protection as are enjoyed by other free persons of the Colony, whether English or Dutch." [3] Six years later there followed the emancipation of the Cape's thirty thousand slaves. Later still, when in 1853 the Cape received its first constitution, Coloured men possessing the requisite qualifications were not excluded from the vote. In social and economic terms the Cape Coloureds formed a rural and urban proletariat, but there were no political or legal restrictions on their advancement. Had the Cape not been so powerfully influenced by the tide of events beyond its frontiers, the colony might well have evolved into a truly multiracial society.

To the Boers of the frontier, with their absolute conviction that racial equality was "contrary to the laws of God," with their resolute determination to maintain "proper relations" between masters and servants, the legislation introduced by the British was utterly abhorrent. It was natural, therefore, that they should strive to reestablish the old order in their new homes. Moreover, they acquired their new lands by right of conquest. Bantus living in the territory of the new republics were tolerated as squatters on Boer farms or driven into the less accessible and less fertile areas where they were subject to occasional visitations by Boer officials. "The better disposed emigrants," wrote David Livingstone in 1847, when he was living at a mission station on the edge of Boer territory, "lament the evils they witness. But the absence or laxity of law leaves the natives open to the infliction of inexpressible wrongs." [4]

In the British colony of Natal a different policy was followed. Here lands denuded of their population during the Zulu wars began to fill up with returning refugees once law and order had been reestablished. By this time much of the best land had been taken over by European settlers, and so it was decided to set aside special areas as "native locations" or "reserves," where the Bantus could still remain largely subject to their own chiefs in accordance with their own customs, while at the same time being brought into contact with the "civilizing" influence of European missionaries and magistrates. Given the temper of the local white settlers, who deeply resented the creation of the reserves, and the practical weakness of a colonial government continually short of money, it was impossible to achieve a more liberal settlement. But to cram eighty thousand Bantus into one-tenth of the area occupied by less than eight thousand white farmers was to establish from the start a situation that no peaceful process of change could ameliorate.

✻ THE DEVELOPMENT OF TRADE

It is one of the paradoxes of African history that South Africa, until 1800 economically by far the least developed region of the continent, should have been transformed within the past hundred years into the richest and most advanced. Remoteness from the major centers of vigorous commercial activity and the apparent lack of obviously attractive resources provide an explanation for the region's long backwardness. The immensely rich gold deposits of the Transvaal lay too deep to be reached by simple African mining techniques, and no attempt was made to draw the expanding Bantu population into the slave-trading systems of the Atlantic or of the Indian Ocean. Even when a European settlement was made at the Cape, it could offer nothing in the way of exports but wine and wheat, commodities little in demand in contemporary Europe or Asia.

Before the establishment of the Dutch at the Cape most African communities engaged in some local trade, and there is archeological evidence to show that the Bantus of the Transvaal acquired some trade goods from the East Coast. But neither the South African Bantus nor the Hottentots developed a more elaborate commercial system based on regular markets and a class of professional traders. Thus, Cape Town, the earliest and until 1850 the only European settlement with more than five thousand inhabitants, represents the first important commercial center in the history of the region. Gradually, as European frontiersmen pressed further eastward along the coast or deeper into the interior, more and more of the local peoples, Hottentot and Bantu alike, were introduced to new forms of commerce, bartering cattle, ivory, ostrich feathers, animal skins, and agricultural produce for European trade goods.

The transfer of the Cape from the Dutch to the British helped to stimulate the colony's economy. The old monopolistic restrictions imposed by the Dutch East India Company were abolished, the new colonial government spent more freely than the impoverished Company, new markets opened overseas, and new immigrants brought with them new commercial interests. Government revenue rose from £50,000 a year in the 1790's to £150,000 in the 1820's and £300,000 in the 1850's, while exports, worth a mere £15,000 a year in the last years of Dutch rule, brought in £250,000 in the 1820's and more than £750,000 in the 1830's. Until 1842 wine—given preferential treatment for a time in the British market, where it was used largely to adulterate more expensive foreign vintages—was the colony's major export; but in that year it was replaced by wool. Wool exports, presented with an insatiable market by the rapidly expanding British textile industry, soared from 20,000 pounds in 1832 to 25,000,000 pounds in 1862 and provided in the latter year more than 80 percent of the colony's total exports.

By the 1850's Cape Colony had acquired the rudimentary infrastructure of a modern economy. Cape Town was a flourishing town of 25,000 people, with five banks and some industrial establishments. Port Elizabeth, founded in 1826, was playing an important part in opening up the Eastern Cape. Graaff-Reinet and Graham's Town, the capitals of the Western and the Eastern provinces, were developing into pleasant, well-ordered towns. Increasing attention was being paid to road construction, and there were plans for a railway at the Cape. But taking the region as a whole, the vast majority of its inhabitants, black and white alike, were still tied to a subsistence economy. No one could have predicted the extraordinary transformation the future had in store.

✳ SOUTH AFRICA IN THE 1850's

By the 1850's the political geography of South Africa presented a pattern as complex as that of any of the regions of the tropical part of the continent. Moreover, in one important respect the pattern was even more varied, for by this time the region contained four European polities, more substantial than those to be found anywhere else in the continent, except in Algeria.

Of these four the Cape was by far the most important. In 1856 its population was 267,000, of whom 119,000 were Europeans, the majority being of Dutch descent. Natal had a mere 6500 settlers, with the English just outnumbering the Boers. Of the Boer polities the Orange Free State had some 12,000 Europeans, the Transvaal 18,000. By the mid-1850's both of these Boer states were completely independent of British control. In 1852 the British government abandoned its claim that all "the emigrant farmers" were still subject to British jurisdiction, turned its back on the humanitarian policy of attempting to protect the more distant tribes against Boer injustices, and recognized the independence of all the Boers living beyond the Vaal. Two years later the government, anxious to disentangle itself from expensive new commitments, abandoned its sovereignty over the Orange River territory. But the European communities in South Africa were bound together by so many ties that the political divisions accepted in the early 1850's could not provide the basis of an enduring political settlement.

Although the territory under European domination had expanded very rapidly in the past twenty years—the total area of Natal, the Orange Free State, and the Transvaal was put at about 150,000 square miles in 1858—most of the African peoples of the region were still independent of European rule. Between British Kaffraria and Natal lay a number of minor chiefdoms, founded by the Tembu, the Pondo, and other Nguni groups. North of Natal were the far more substantial polities of the Zulu and the Swazi, while most of southern Mozambique was dominated by the kingdom of Gaza, created at the time of the *Mfecane* by a Nguni leader using Zulu military techniques. Between Natal and the Orange Free State many different groups mainly of Sotho origin were being molded into a single kingdom by the Basuto chief, Moshesh, a political leader of outstanding ability. Between the Orange Free State and Cape Colony lay a narrow stretch of territory controlled by Griqua chiefs. North of Griqualand, between Boer territory and the Kalahari, stretched a chain of Tswana chiefdoms, while the vast expanse of territory later called South-West Africa was occupied by the smaller polities of the Ambo, the Herero, and others.

Though all these African polities were still completely independent, there were few, if any, of them which had not had by the 1850's some contact with white men. The missionary travels of David Livingstone which took him in the early 1850's first as far north as the Zambezi, then west to Luanda and back across the continent to Mozambique, represented not an isolated feat of exploration but the most remarkable of many strenuous journeys undertaken at this time by European traders, hunters, missionaries, and explorers. The activities of these frontiersmen served not only to stimulate a more vigorous interest in the "far interior," they also placed over the African polities of the region the first thin mesh of the net of European influence, a net whose thickening, tightening strands were to draw the indigenous communities of South Africa into a closer and more lasting contact with an alien people and culture than any other African people have experienced since the Arab conquest of North Africa more than a thousand years earlier.

CHAPTER XII

The Islands

🌿 ATLANTIC ISLANDS

Like miniscule satellites a variety of islands lie off the great landmass of Africa. Historically, they have been bound more closely to Africa than to any other continent, and so it is fitting to consider them here.

The islands of the southern half of the eastern Atlantic include two archipelagos, the Canaries and the Cape Verde islands, and a number of isolated islands or island groups, of which the most important are Madeira, Fernando Po, São Tomé, and St. Helena. Almost all the islands are of volcanic origin, and their violent geological past has endowed them with spectacular natural beauty and with patches of very fertile soil.

The most easterly of the Canaries lies only sixty miles from the coast of Africa, and Fernando Po is even nearer to the mainland. As both places were within the range of the simple canoes of coastal peoples, the Canaries came to be colonized by a people of Berber stock, the Guanche, and Fernando Po by a Bantu-speaking group, the Bubi. But the other islands, separated from the mainland by three hundred miles and more of stormy ocean, were beyond the reach of African craft and remained uninhabited until the end of the Middle Ages.

The people of the ancient Mediterranean world were dimly aware of the existence of islands off the western coast of Africa and surrounded them with many legends. But it was not until the fourteenth and fifteenth centuries that the more northerly islands, the Canaries, Madeira, and the Cape Verde group, were explored by adventurous European seafarers—Genoese and Portuguese, Spaniards and Norman French. To the Portuguese alone belongs the credit for the discovery of the southern islands. They sighted "Formoso," "the beautiful" (it was renamed Fernando Po, after its discoverer, three centuries later) and São Tomé in 1471 and St. Helena in 1502.

Fernando Po was too unhealthy to attract settlement and St. Helena too remote—at least until the middle of the seventeenth century, when the English East India Company took it over as a victualing station on the long sea route to the Indies. But the other islands soon acquired a motley collection of European colonists. The Canaries came under Spanish sovereignty, and their Guanche inhabitants, like the Caribs of the West Indies, were exterminated or absorbed. All the other islands were claimed by the Portuguese, though their European population contained settlers from other parts of the western Mediterranean.

Many of the islands were ideally suited to become producers of lucrative tropical crops such as sugar, that luxury of sixteenth-century Europe. Plantations required slave labor, and the islands became the first communities in the world to evolve a social pattern—white aristocracy, freed men of mixed origin, black slaves—that was later to become widely diffused in the New World.

None of the islands had to face so many vicissitudes as São Tomé. A prosperous start with wealth coming from sugar plantations and a flourishing slave trade with the Congo was followed in the seventeenth century by a disastrous decline. Competition from Brazilian sugar and the ravages of gangs of ex-slaves ruined the plantations and forced the planters to move away. The introduction of coffee and cocoa in the early nineteenth century revived interest in São Tomé and brought a fresh generation of planters to the island, but the new arrivals soon found themselves engaged in fierce competition for land with the old-established and racially mixed Creole community. Indeed, they too would have been ruined when their slaves were emancipated in 1869 if a new means of obtaining plantation workers had not been evolved—the recruitment of contract labor in Angola.

Fernando Po, which was transferred from Portugal to Spain in 1778, had a less eventful history. Indeed, the Bubi can hardly have been aware of European activities until the late 1820's when the British received Spanish permission to establish a settlement on the island as a base in their campaign against the slave trade. The British connection brought freed slaves and a group of Baptist missionaries to Fernando Po, but the Spanish government rejected British offers to buy the island and began to administer it effectively in the 1840's. Little, however, was done to develop its economic resources until Spain found herself deprived of her other tropical colonies in the Far East and the Caribbean after the war of 1898 with the United States.

In their historical development the more northerly islands presented sharp contrasts both among themselves and with the remoter islands farther south. The Cape Verde archipelago was clearly a colonial territory, though lawless and ill-administered like the other Portuguese possessions on the African mainland. The majority of the islands' population was descended from Negro slaves, though many of them had a trace of white blood. Madeira and the Canaries were clearly provinces of their metropolitan powers, Portugal and Spain. Their population was almost entirely European; indeed, in the 1830's when the Canaries had two hundred thousand inhabitants and Madeira over one hundred thousand, there were about three times as many Europeans living in these small islands as were to be found on the entire African mainland.

In their economy the Cape Verde islands presented a depressing picture: early settlers had destroyed much of the original vegetation, soil erosion had set in, and the population suffered on occasion from famine and drought. Madeira and the Canaries, on the other hand, had experienced periods of considerable prosperity. Sugar came to be replaced by wine as the islands' main export—the wine trade, greatly stimulated by British demand, reaching its peak in the early nineteenth century. In the 1830's the Canaries began to export cochineal (a dyestuff produced from the bodies of insects that infest a certain species of cactus); thirty years later cochineal accounted for 90 percent of the islands' exports. There were dangers in excessive dependence on a single product: the vineyards of Madeira were ravaged by disease in the 1850's, the advent of chemical dyes ruined the cochineal market in the 1870's. But in general it was clear that the islands with their favorable position—they served as regular ports of call for ships bound for West Africa, the Cape, and South America—their excellent climate, and their area of fertile soil, could indeed be described as "fortunate" when compared with most parts of the mainland.

ISLANDS OF THE WESTERN INDIAN OCEAN

The islands of the western Indian Ocean have a geographical pattern not altogether dissimilar from that of the eastern Atlantic islands. Here, too, are a couple of archipelagos, the Comoros and the Seychelles, and a number of other islands, some—notably Zanzibar and Pemba—within easy reach of the mainland, others—Réunion, Mauritius, and its Dependencies—set, like St. Helena, many hundreds of miles from land. Moreover, in their physical features several of these islands resemble their counterparts off western Africa, for they are also of volcanic origin. But overshadowing the minor islands—at least on the map—lies the massive shape of Madagascar, the fifth largest island in the world.

Madagascar has an area two and a half times that of Great Britain or more than twice that of New England, and its landscapes are more varied than those of many African countries of considerably larger size. A highland mass, running from north to south, dominates the island.

Made up of lofty plateaus cleft by deep valleys and rising to occasional massifs, it slopes down gradually to the dry savanna plains of the western coast and falls by sudden escarpments to the narrower and more humid plains of the eastern side. Today Madagascar lies stripped of the primeval forests that covered the island two thousand years ago. Poor laterite soils abound, and the island has been harshly described as having "the shape, the colour and the fertility of a brick."

Mauritius and Réunion received their first inhabitants only in the seventeenth century, while most of the remote Dependencies of Mauritius, including the Seychelles, were not settled until the latter half of the eighteenth century. The date of the first settlement on Zanzibar and the Comoros is uncertain. As for Madagascar, it seems highly probable that the island remained unknown to man until the end of the first millennium B.C. and that it was first drawn into the realm of history by Indonesian seafarers.

✸ THE COLONIZATION OF MADAGASCAR

By virtue of the length and daring of their voyages the Indonesians might well be called the Norsemen of the Indian Ocean. For more than a thousand years their ships—outrigger canoes later reinforced by sails— made the passage from Southeast Asia to East Africa. At first they seem to have come by way of the convenient landfalls spaced around the northern perimeter of the Indian Ocean. Later, they may have struck straight across several thousand miles of open sea, using the westward-flowing equatorial current to help them on their passage. It seems likely that some of them settled for a time on the east coast of Africa, although none of the present inhabitants of that area can claim to be their descendants. But their colonization of Madagascar is indisputable.

Even today many of the Malagasy—the collective name applied to the native inhabitants of Madagascar—possess physical features of an obviously Mongoloid character; they speak a language closely related to other Indonesian languages; and their culture is dominated by Indonesian characteristics. Nevertheless, the Malagasy are not a uniform but a mixed people. The ancestors of many of them were of Negroid origin, while in some coastal areas the people were influenced by Muslim culture and may have received some Arab blood.

There is no direct historical evidence to show how Negroid people first came to Madagascar. The most likely hypothesis suggests that they were brought over as the concubines or slaves of Indonesian colonists who had already resided for some time on the East African coast. Later, there was probably some direct immigration across the Mozambique channel, where the Comoros, whose population is of mixed African, Malagasy, and Arab origin, served as convenient stepping-stones. It has been suggested that these Negroid immigrants possessed greater immunity to malaria than the Indonesians and that therefore their numbers increased at a much greater rate. Certainly, in many areas Negroid features predominate: among the Betsileo, for example, living in the southern part of the island, 51 percent of the population are of Negroid type, only 3 percent Mongoloid, and the remainder mixed. But despite their numerical superiority the Bantu-speaking immigrants, like Africans in the New World, abandoned both their language and many of their customs and adopted those of their Indonesian masters and Malagasy neighbors.

The establishment of Muslim trading posts on the northern and eastern coasts of the island about the beginning of the second millennium A.D. only represented the continuation in a new guise of a movement that had already been under way for a thousand years: most of these Muslims were not pure Arabs but Swahili or Indonesian converts, but they introduced a distinctive new strand into Malagasy culture. Meanwhile, the original settlers, their numbers reinforced by new arrivals from Indonesia or from Africa, were spreading round the coasts and moving into the more favored districts of the interior. Gradually, local groups based on kinship began to coalesce to form a large number of chiefdoms and petty kingdoms. These polities were often isolated from their neighbors in the vast, thinly populated island; their peoples were of varying racial mixture and had behind them different historical experiences; and they were subjected to the pressure of many different kinds of environment and so came to evolve many distinct forms of economy, from cattle herding on the dry plains of the southwest to the farming of rice in irrigated fields in the high interior. Thus, despite the basis of a common language and a common culture, in the political field there was an intense feeling of ethnic diversity and no consciousness of national unity.

⚜ THE EUROPEAN IMPACT

When the Portuguese burst into the Indian Ocean at the beginning of the sixteenth century they were naturally drawn to the rich mainland bases of commerce in East Africa and South Asia. The islands of the western Indian Ocean held little to attract them. But their impact on Madagascar, though indirect, was nevertheless profound, for the havoc that they caused on the oceanic trade routes put an end to the passage of ships between Indonesia and Madagascar. Asia and Africa had come together to form the Malagasy people. Henceforward the inhabitants of the great island were to become increasingly subject to the influence of Europe.

In the mid-seventeenth century both the French and the English tried to establish colonies on the coast of Madagascar. The attempts of neither power succeeded, but the French effort, more elaborately planned and sustained over a much longer period than that of the English, had two important consequences. It produced an abiding French interest in Madagascar, and it led to the annexation of the beautiful uninhabited island that was first called Bourbon but whose name was changed during the revolution to Réunion.

Meanwhile, the Dutch were attempting to transform the equally alluring island they had named Mauritius into a profitable colony. They found the task too difficult for them and abandoned the island early in the eighteenth century. Unlike Bourbon, whose development had proved equally arduous, Mauritius possessed an excellent natural harbor, and the French were moved to take over the again uninhabited island. Within a generation they had found the key to commercial prosperity. The provision of highly efficient harbor services—invaluable to ships making the long passage to the Indies—and the establishment of plantations, some growing crops introduced from the East Indies, induced a steady stream of Frenchmen to settle in the Île de France, as the French renamed the island, or in neighboring Bourbon.

The transformation of the Mascarenes—the name applied to the two islands and their dependencies—had many profound consequences. It greatly stimulated the slave trade in East Africa, for slaves were required to work the plantations. It led to the establishment of a few French trading posts on the east coast of Madagascar, and it affected the balance of naval power in the Indian Ocean ultimately, as it turned out, to France's disadvantage. During the Napoleonic wars the success achieved by French privateers based on Mauritius in their attacks on British shipping led the British to invade and capture the Mascarenes and to retain Mauritius when peace was made in 1815. Finally, the wealth acquired by the Mascarenes from plantations attracted the attention of the Arabs of Zanzibar. Cloves were introduced into Zanzibar in 1818 and within a few years became the basis of the island's economy. The clove plantations of Zanzibar and Pemba served to maintain the demand for slaves at a time when the new masters of Mauritius had forbidden the import of slaves into the island and were striving to curtail the trade in other parts of the Indian Ocean.

Meanwhile, the traditional state system of Madagascar with its multitude of petty principalities was being transformed by the efforts of the rulers of the little inland kingdom of Merina to enlarge their domains and later to attempt the conquest of the whole island. In the first third of the nineteenth century Merina had two remarkable monarchs who possessed, like Muhamad Ali of Egypt, a shrewd appreciation of the value of European techniques, especially in the military field, and who welcomed the British and French agents, missionaries, traders, and adventurers who came to their kingdom. By organizing a standing army on European lines the Merina kings were able to dominate two-thirds of the island.

By the 1860's it could be said that Merina, despite a period of sharp reaction in the 1840's and 1850's against European ways, was more open to European influence than any other indigenous state in Africa. As for Mauritius and Réunion, they had overcome the difficulties caused by the emancipation of the slaves, in Mauritius by encouraging Indian emigration, in Réunion by developing other forms of contract labor. Sugar now dominated their economies and provided the livelihood of European plantocracies, nearly all of whose members, even in British Mauritius, were of French origin. These island aristocracies were in general far more sophisticated but clearly no less vigorous than any of the European communities to be found on the mainland of Africa.

CHAPTER XIII

Variety and Classification

✣ THE VARIETY OF AFRICA

To trace, however briefly, the historical development of each of the regions of Africa is to provide some indication of the continent's variety.
Clearly, the differences between regions are very substantial; hardly less
striking are the internal contrasts each region affords. This protean diversity needs further emphasis, for it serves as the most effective antidote
to those facile generalizations which superficial observers have been
applying to Africa, more than to any other continent, for many hundreds
of years. To convey as vividly as possible an impression of multiformity
must then be one of the major preoccupations of a historian who takes the
whole continent as his subject. Vividness comes not from the general but
from the particular, and so it seems appropriate to turn away for a section
from the broad impressionistic treatment of massive regions and long
stretches of time and concentrate on the more precise delineation of certain societies at a specific moment in time—the middle of the nineteenth
century.

One cannot, of course, hope to convey in so short a space a truly
rounded impression of the complex individuality of each of these societies. For such a purpose it would be necessary to examine every one of
their facets—social structure, economic organization, material culture,
system of ideas, and so on. But if of necessity one must isolate a single
aspect of a people's culture, it seems best to concentrate on their form of
political organization. This has the advantage of being a well-
documented subject and one that has received increasing attention within
recent years. At the same time the study of the diverse forms of polity to
be found in Africa provides more effectively than an examination of any
other aspect of African culture an indication of the extraordinarily wide
range of societies to be found in the continent.

✣ THE CLASSIFICATION OF AFRICAN POLITIES: SOME INITIAL DIFFICULTIES

In the middle of the nineteenth century the number of autonomous political units to be found in Africa ran into thousands. In part a figure such as this was the product of the multiplication of miniscule forms of political organization among certain peoples; the Berbers of Morocco, for example, were reckoned to be divided into no less than six hundred tribes, most of which could be subdivided into several completely autonomous fractions. Even if one counts a group such as this as a single type of polity, the total number and variety of types still remains remarkable. In seeking to convey some impression of this variety one must select, basing one's choice of polities to be described on a reasoned system of classification. Certain criteria come immediately to mind when thinking of the polities of nineteenth-century Africa. One can make a division between territories dominated by aliens—the colonies of European and Asian powers—and indigenous polities. One can lay special stress on the state religion and distinguish between Muslim, Christian, and "Pagan" polities. One can follow the conventional European practice and speak of "great" powers and "lesser" powers, using extent of territory, size of population, and degree of wealth at the ruler's disposal as the obvious measuring rods. Such systems of classification help to indicate some of the striking differences that existed between polities in mid-nineteenth-century Africa. But they make no allowance for the great contrast between polities that fell within the same category. Thus, the list of Muslim states in nineteenth-century Africa includes the Ottoman pashalik of Egypt, the Omani sultanate of Zanzibar, and the Fulani caliphate of Sokoto, but though Islam served as a common denominator, there existed between these three states far-reaching differences in political and social structure.

Over the last thirty years African political systems have become the subject of a steadily expanding body of research by social anthropologists, political scientists, and historians. The analyses which these scholars are making should lead to the construction of a system of classification elaborate enough to embrace a range of polities very diverse and complex in their structure. No universally accepted system of classification has yet been established. Indeed, the data required for such a system are far from complete, for there are still many African peoples whose political systems remain to be studied. Nevertheless, enough material is now available to allow a tentative and provisional classification to be suggested. European political scientists tend to assume that systems of classification based only on European samples possess universal validity.

African experience shows that while many European and African polities possess certain common characteristics, they cannot be exactly equated. Moreover, there are many other African forms of government for which it is quite impossible to find an approximate European equivalent.

There is another difficulty to be faced in attempting to classify African polities as they existed at any one moment in time. The nineteenth century was a period of steadily accelerating change, such as could drastically transform within the space of a few years the structure of an old, established polity. In these circumstances it is hardly sufficient to provide—in the manner of a constitutional handbook—a static description of the organization of a particular polity. One must also attempt to give some indication of the forces both internal and external to which it was exposed, to see it, in other words, in its historical context. But if individual polities change, types remain constant. These types one must now seek to define.

All the polities of nineteenth-century Europe could be described as states. A state may be defined as consisting of a number of communities over which there has been imposed a centralized superstructure of authority. This centralized authority, represented either by a single individual or by an association of individuals, has at its disposal some form of administrative machinery, manifested by the existence of a body of officeholders whose function is to carry out its orders. Many nineteenth-century African polities come within this definition of a state. A much larger number of African polities, however, did not possess these characteristics. Some of them may be described as "stateless polities," for they possessed none of the essential characteristics of a state; to others the term "demi-state" may be applied, for these polities displayed some but not all of a state's characteristics. Here then are three broad categories— stateless polity, demi-state, and state—into which all African polities can be fitted.

𝕊 STATELESS POLITIES

Stateless polities varied greatly according to the environment and the historical forces to which their people had been exposed, but they possessed by their very nature certain common characteristics. Above the local community there existed no formally constituted political superstructure. Circumstances might make it advisable for a number of communities to come together for military action or for other purposes, but such groupings—like alliances between sovereign states—were temporary phenomena and did not alter the fact that local communities were basically independent political units. Within these stateless polities society was egalitarian rather than hierarchical: most men had the opportunity to participate at some period in their lives in the decision-making processes of their community. In most stateless polities the community was bound together by ties of kinship. Kinship ties also influenced relations between neighboring polities; the people of communities linked by an assumed common ancestor could thus see themselves as forming part of associations, sometimes described as clans or tribes, much wider than the local community in which most of their lives were spent. To external observers stateless societies seemed often to present a spectacle of complete anarchy; in fact the obligations of kinship within and between polities created a subtle web binding the peoples of stateless areas together and giving a certain stability to their social and political structures. Inevitably, there was a good deal of local violence but it was always violence on a minor scale.

Stateless polities were to be found in many parts of nineteenth-century Africa, usually in areas where little contact had yet been made with a wider world. Consequently, trade played little or no part in their economies. In other respects the nature of their economies varied greatly, some being dependent on agriculture, others on pastoralism, yet others on hunting and gathering to provide their livelihood. At one time there must have been many independent bands of hunters and gatherers in Africa, but their numbers had steadily declined. By the nineteenth century only a very few groups—the Bushmen of the Kalahari, some of the Pygmies of the Congo forest, and a few bands in East Africa—were still able to retain their political independence. Other hunting peoples had been exterminated, absorbed, or reduced to a servile status by more powerful neighbors. Among the Bushmen and the Pygmies the local community consisted of a small nomadic band of hunters operating within a well-defined territory.

Among agriculturists living in stateless polities the pattern of the local community varied. With the Amba and many other Bantu-speaking peoples of Central and Equatorial Africa the political unit was the compact village settlement governed by an informal council in which all adult males could participate. With the Kikuyu of the Kenya highlands the basic unit was a cluster of homesteads, linked to other clusters within a limited area by an age-grade system. With the Ibo of West Africa groups of villages formed substantial units that might almost be regarded as demi-states.

Stateless pastoralists, of whom the Nuer, the Masai, and the Somali provide the most prominent examples, differed greatly in the organization of their communities. The Nuer of the southern Sudan alternated between isolated wet-season agricultural villages and dry-season cattle camps, where people from several different villages came together. The

Masai, living in the excellent cattle country of the East African Rift Valley, had no need to follow the same pattern of migration; their communities were divided into age-grades of warriors and elders, the men of each grade of a particular area living together in substantial kraals. The Somali, occupying a much harsher environment in the semidesert scrub country of the Horn of Africa, divided into small units which moved over extensive areas, the men of these movable hamlets being linked by kinship ties to wider communities.

✿ DEMI-STATES

The term "demi-state" is applied here to those polities that occupy an intermediate position between stateless polities and fully organized states. Within the demi-state the local community is no longer completely autonomous; above it there exists some form of political superstructure. At the apex of this superstructure there stands, as in the state, a dominant individual or group of individuals. But whereas in the state the ruling authority has at its disposal the means of enforcing its decisions over a wide range of activities, in the demi-state such competence is severely restricted. Compared with stateless societies demi-states present a less egalitarian social structure; some form of social stratification is usually to be noted with royals or nobles being distinguished from commoners. But in terms of material wealth this distinction is much less apparent. Indeed, even the dominant individual of the polity is hardly to be distinguished in this respect: his dwelling is no palace, his entourage not to be described as a court. This modesty of means at the center is a reflection of the weakness of the whole political structure; a ruler cannot amass wealth or command labor service unless he has some form of bureaucracy at his disposal. Lacking the framework of an effective administration to hold their structures together, demi-states tend to form highly unstable political units, easily fragmented and possessing strong fissiparous tendencies.

Demi-states were to be found in every region of nineteenth-century Africa, in environments ranging from the lonely valleys of the Moroccan Atlas to the vast expanses of the South African veld and from the deserts and massifs of the Sahara to the swamps of the Niger delta. Despite the basic structural characteristics that served to distinguish them from other types of polity, demi-states varied greatly in their constitution: the village republics of the Berber *montagnards,* the tribal confederations of the Tuareg, the "kingdoms" of the Shilluk of the southern Sudan and of the Teke of the lower Congo, the trading communities of the Niger delta, the petty chiefdoms formed by so many Bantu-speaking peoples of the southern half of Africa—all these polities may be regarded as falling into the category of demi-state. In the Berber village republics the dominant individual was an elected president, in the "kingdoms" of the Shilluk and of the Teke a "divine king" or supreme ritual expert, in the chiefdoms of the Zande or of the Tswana often the enterprising son of an established chief who had broken away from his father's chiefdom to found a new polity for himself. Some demi-states, such as the tribal confederations of the Tuareg, represented a loose hegemony extending over thousands of square miles; in general, however, demi-states were confined to a handful of villages or a group of hamlets. Though larger in area and population than the polities of stateless peoples, they were far inferior to those of organized states.

The nature of any polity may be transformed by revolution or conquest, by internal stresses or external pressures; demi-states may emerge from stateless polities, states from demi-states. Thus, the stateless polities of the Yao of the Lake Nyasa area were profoundly affected in the first half of the nineteenth century by the demand of coastal merchants for slaves and ivory and began to throw up adventurous men whose success in trade enabled them to become the founders of petty chiefdoms. An even longer and more intensive experience of external trade led the modest communities of the Niger delta to develop new institutions and gradually to take on the character of a new state. In the sedentary Berber communities of the Atlas ambitious men occasionally overthrew the representative institution of the village republic, made themselves masters of the local territory, conquered neighboring polities, and so transformed themselves into the rulers of petty principalities. Even more dramatic were the revolutionary changes that took place in the nineteenth century among the Southern Bantu, a people who had hitherto known no polity more elaborate than the petty chiefdom, changes that led to the emergence of several substantial kingdoms.

✻ STATES

The first African polities to develop the characteristics of a state were in the valley of the Lower Nile as early as the fourth millennium B.C. By the end of the first millennium B.C. states had come to be established in other parts of North Africa (Carthage, the Berber kingdoms, the Greek and Roman colonies), in the eastern Sudan (Kush), and in Ethiopia (Axum). By 1500 A.D. states had evolved in many parts of West Africa (Ghana, Mali, Songhai, the Hausa kingdoms, Kanem-Bornu, the Yoruba states, Benin), in limited areas of Central Africa (Kongo, Monomotapa), on the Ethiopian plateau (Ethiopia, the Sidama kingdoms), and on the East African coast (the Swahili city-states). By the nineteenth century many areas which in 1500 contained no polities larger than petty chiefdoms had seen the development of considerable states. This movement occurred in West Africa among the Wolof, the Mossi, the Akan, the Adja, and others; in Equatorial Africa among some of the peoples of the central Sudan (Baguirmi, Wadai) and of the Cameroun highlands (Tikar, Mbum, Bamum); in Central Africa among the Luba, the Lunda, the Lozi, the Ovimbundu, and others; in East Africa among many of the interlacustrine peoples (kingdoms of Buganda, Bunyoro, Ruanda, Ankole, and others); in South Africa among the Zulu, the Swazi, and the Basuto; and among several of the peoples of Madagascar (notably the Hova of Merina). Between 1500 and 1850 a number of alien peoples that possessed a state organization established colonies in Africa: the Turks in Egypt, the Sudan, Tripoli, Tunis, and Algiers, the Omani Arabs in Zanzibar, the Portuguese in Angola and Mozambique, the French in Algeria, Senegal, and Réunion, the English in Sierra Leone, on the Gold Coast, in parts of South Africa, and in Mauritius, the Dutch Boers in the interior of South Africa and freed slaves of American origin in Liberia. Before 1500 the majority of Africans almost certainly lived in stateless polities or in demi-states; by 1850 probably more than half the people of the continent were within the territories of organized states.

States were to be found in every region of Africa and in almost every natural area—in the tropical rain forest, on the savannas, on the lofty plateaus, and by the seacoasts. Even in the desolate Sahara, states, such as the oasis kingdom of the Fezzan, were not unknown. Vastly different though the environments in which states had developed must appear, all of them had one point in common—the capacity to produce an economic surplus, to provide resources above the needs of mere subsistence. African states varied in their degree of dependence on the three means—agriculture, trade, and industry—of producing such a surplus. Buganda with its banana groves and Merina with its rice fields possessed a particularly productive agriculture; both kingdoms were noted, too, for the craftsmanship of their peoples, but their commercial contacts with the outside world were very modest. Ashanti derived much of its strength from its trade in slaves, gold, and kola nuts carried on with the Muslim states to the north and the Europeans on the coast. The Hausa kingdom of Kano, by 1850 a part of the Fulani empire of Sokoto, was as renowned for its agriculture as for its trade and industry: so well balanced a development of the country's resources was a feature of all the more prosperous states in African history. In wealth there were great contrasts in African polities. No measuring rods comparable to those used by modern economists have yet been devised for the past, but if the degree of urbanization be taken as a rough and ready gauge of development, then obviously the North African states were more advanced than any of the kingdoms of tropical Africa. It would be rash to affirm that those who lived in states necessarily enjoyed a higher standard of living than the people of demi-states or stateless polities, but it does seem evident that the population of states had a wider range of economic activities open to them and hence greater opportunities of accumulating wealth.

Superficially, most indigenous nineteenth-century African states could be described as monarchies with supreme power—executive, legislative and judicial—appearing to lie in the hands of a ruler descended from a well-established line of kings. "Despotism," "absolutism," and "autocracy" have been the terms most frequently applied by European observers to these African kingdoms. Among these states, however, there were profound differences beneath the surface similarities, differences that become apparent as soon as one begins to study specific aspects of their constitutions. Six aspects require special comment: the composition of the ruling class, the system of provincial administration, the organization of military force, the sources of revenue, the means used to regulate succession to the throne, and the nature of the ideological basis of the state. In one or more of these aspects African monarchies might vary greatly one from another.

The essential characteristic of a state is the existence of a body of administrators who assist the ruler in the work of government, their activities serving to bind the scattered communities of a particular territory into a permanent association. Those administrators who play some part in the making of decisions on major matters of state form the polity's ruling class or political elite. Broadly speaking, political elites may be regarded as falling into one or the other of two distinct categories, which may be described as "open" or as "closed." If open, almost any member of the community may aspire to membership in the elite; if closed, membership is limited to certain clearly defined social groups.

Most nineteenth-century African states possessed closed elites. There were a number of different ways in which such elites could be recruited. In ethnically homogeneous societies the major offices might be entrusted only to members of the royal lineage or clan: such was the case in the old kingdom of Kongo and in the Bemba paramountcy. Alternatively, in polities possessing a heterogeneous population, only those who belonged to the dominant ethnic group might aspire to reach the inner councils of the state. All the European and Asian colonies fell into this class; so too do such indigenous polities as Ankole with its dominant Hima pastoralists and the caliphate and empire of Sokoto, where the Fulani conquerors monopolized all the important posts. A third class of closed elite could be seen in states where the ruler entrusted most of the major offices to individuals, usually of slave origin, drawn from outside his territory and so entirely dependent on his goodwill: the regency of Tunis provides the most striking nineteenth-century example of such a slave elite. At earlier periods slave officials played an important part in the administration of many of the Muslim states of North Africa and the Sudan.

Open elites can be recruited either through representation or through association. Assemblies in which the representatives of a community came together to discuss major political issues were to be found in almost all stateless polities and demi-states. There is little evidence of the existence of institutions of this kind in nineteenth-century African states. This must not be interpreted as meaning that African rulers were indifferent to the opinions of their subjects. There were a number of channels by means of which rulers could make themselves aware of what was happening in their countries. Every monarch was assisted by an advisory council which was bound to include among its members some senior administrators. The views of such a council even the most absolute of monarchs could not afford entirely to disregard. Most monarchs also possessed their own private means of obtaining information, court messengers and other royal servants being given the task of reporting on the behavior of provincial magnates and other high officials. In their judicial capacity as a final court of appeal many monarchs were brought directly in touch with the affairs of their subjects. In some states mass assemblies were regularly held at the capital. On such occasions the monarch might publicly perform certain religious rites, receive tribute and pledges of allegiance from his most prominent subjects, and address the people on matters of national importance. Such ceremonies—vividly exemplified by the Annual Customs of the kings of Dahomey—provided intelligent rulers with an excellent opportunity for assessing the mood of their people. But the practical difficulties imposed by poor communications and the absence of powerful "estates" possessing their own sources of wealth, comparable to the clergy and the burgesses of medieval Europe, appear to have made the evolution of truly representative institutions impossible in any indigenous African state. Only among the closed elites of the British and the Boers in South Africa were parliaments to be found in the 1850's—and these two colonial societies were profoundly influenced by metropolitan examples.

In some African states rulers had at their disposal a large number of offices to which they were prepared to appoint any subject possessing the right qualifications. Such states, of which Buganda provides a particularly striking example, exhibited open elites recruited by association. In Buganda a man entering the Kabaka's service as a page might rise in time to the highest posts in the land. But though recruitment to state offices might in theory be open, there was an inevitable tendency for certain families with a long tradition of public service to monopolize important posts and so to transform the character of the elite. This, indeed, is what happened in Buganda toward the end of the nineteenth century.

Systems of provincial administration in African states presented varying degrees of centralization. In the most highly centralized states the ruler was free to appoint officials of his own choice to all major posts in the provincial administration. Such was the position in Egypt, in Tunis, in Buganda, and in Dahomey. At the other extreme a high degree of decentralization was to be found in those states in which provincial governors had established local dynasties and enjoyed complete autonomy within their own spheres, while rendering certain services to their suzerain. The empire of Sokoto was organized in this fashion; so too were certain parts of sixteenth-century Ethiopia and nineteenth-century Ashanti. Between these two extremes there existed various intermediate forms of administration. Provincial governorship might be entrusted only to members of the ruling lineage or clan (as in the Bemba paramountcy); alternatively, under a system that came to be described as "indirect rule" by European administrators, the members of a local elite might be allowed to continue in office subject to the supervision of an official sent from the metropolis. This form of administration was used by many expanding states—by the Turks in certain parts of the Sudan, by the Merina kings in Madagascar, and by the rulers of Ashanti. The power of these local "residents" could be strengthened by providing them with a garrison of troops; an even more effective form of insurance against rebellion was to establish colonies of settlers drawn from the metropolitan provinces in the newly conquered districts.

For a variety of reasons every African ruler needed a substantial military force: to protect himself against internal threats to his authority, to defend his kingdom against external attack, and to provide the means for raiding or conquering neighboring polities and for garrisoning subject provinces. Armed forces might be recruited either on a temporary or on a permanent basis. A large standing army was too heavy a burden for the economy of most indigenous states. A state possessing a simple technology could be kept permanently prepared for war only by introducing revolutionary changes in the structure of its society; nowhere in Africa was such a development more strikingly illustrated than in the kingdoms of the Zulu and of peoples related to them such as the Ngoni. In training and in discipline the Zulu army might well be considered the most formidable fighting force in Africa, but it lacked firearms. The only substantial standing armies to be found in the continent in 1850 were those supported by alien powers—the French forces in Algeria, the British troops in South Africa, and the Turkish-officered Egyptian army. In Madagascar the rulers of Merina had also built up a powerful standing army.

The armies both of Egypt and of Merina were trained by Europeans and largely equipped with European weapons.

In place of a standing army many African rulers maintained a substantial bodyguard, taking care to provide these household troops with the best equipment—horses, firearms, and armor—available. In war the royal bodyguard could be used as a *corps d'élite* to stiffen the fighting quality of the militia. To ensure the loyalty of such a force some rulers considered it advisable to employ not free-born male subjects but slaves, mercenaries, or even—in the extraordinary case of the Amazons of Dahomey—women. But there was always the danger that a really powerful body of household troops might turn into an unruly Praetorian Guard; the anarchy that afflicted Morocco in the eighteenth century was greatly aggravated by the indiscipline of the army of Negro slaves formed by Mulay Ismail but too turbulent a force for that ferocious sultan's milder successors to control.

In most African kingdoms free men of military age were under the obligation to turn out for service in the militia when summoned by their superiors. A militia so composed made up in numbers what it lacked in equipment, discipline, and training. It served effectively enough on brief military expeditions when the objective was the agreeable one of securing slaves or other loot from less powerful neighboring polities—a form of military activity common to most African states. It could be used, too, to swell the sovereign's retinue on a tour of his own dominions; the more energetic rulers of Ethiopia, Morocco, and Tunis knew well that tours of this kind, regularly conducted, provided the most effective means of keeping their kingdoms in order. In war against neighboring states of equal strength the value of the militia was more questionable; much depended on its morale, but even the most enthusiastic volunteers were no match for small bodies of well-equipped professionals.

The ruler of even the smallest of states had to maintain a household very much larger than that of an ordinary extended family. As a state expanded in territory and population, the ruler's household developed into a court, which in turn became transformed into an increasingly elaborate bureaucracy. To find the means of maintaining such a household, court, or bureaucracy was a major preoccupation for any conscientious ruler. In all states the revenue at the ruler's disposal depended partly on the economy of the territory, partly on the efficiency of its system of administration. But given substantial variations from state to state, there were certain basic requirements that every African ruler had to bear in mind. It was essential to provide sufficient food to support the royal household and to entertain the constant stream of visitors. Even in African states such as Tunis or Morocco which made use of a local currency it was customary for the peasantry to pay their taxes in kind. After local officials had deducted their share of the tax, which served them in lieu of a salary, the remainder of the produce was passed on to the royal establishments. A ruler could supplement this supply of food by the produce of his own estates, farms worked by palace servants, or more extensive plantations cultivated by slaves. In some polities food could also be obtained by war—by raids on the granaries or on the cattle herds of neighboring peoples.

Besides feeding many hundreds of guests and retainers, rulers had to make lavish presents to their more substantial subjects and in some cases to pay tribute to distant overlords. Slaves and cloth were the most widely acceptable presents. Slaves could be obtained through trade or as tribute from subject provinces or could be captured in raids launched by the ruler himself, in which he could retain for his own use a major part of the booty. Cloth might be manufactured locally, but in many parts of the continent the best quality cloth came from the outside world. There were other exotic products, notably firearms and gunpowder, which African rulers came to regard as increasingly important and which they could only acquire through long-distance trade. To meet their needs rulers were obliged to assert a measure of control over imports and exports. Foreign traders were required to pay customs duties or tolls of passage, and certain items, such as ivory or firearms, were often made into royal monopolies. A ruler might also seek to engage in trade on his own account: the career of Sayyid Said of Zanzibar provides a notable example of a successful merchant prince. An expanding revenue could only be achieved by introducing changes in the character of the administration. A ruler who sought to increase his resources inevitably found himself faced with new administrative, fiscal, and political problems, a situation vividly illustrated by the late-nineteenth-century history of Egypt, Tunis, and Morocco. Difficulties over revenue were not confined to indigenous African polities. European colonies found it hard to raise enough money from customs duties—the main form of revenue at their disposal—and were compelled to look to their metropolitan governments for financial assistance.

Succession to the highest office was a matter of major importance for every African kingdom; for states not laced together by a highly developed bureaucracy a disputed succession almost invariably involved a period of grave internal weakness, of civil war, and of increased risk of foreign invasion. There are three ways in which succession may be arranged: by hereditary right, by election, or, as in the case of colonial governorships, by appointment. Election to the highest office—the method followed by modern democratic states—was almost unknown in nineteenth-century Africa. Only in Turkish Algiers was this office filled by election, candidates being confined in this case to members of the closed military elite. Nevertheless, in African monarchies the hereditary principle did not preclude an element of selection. Nowhere, indeed, in the continent could one find a system of succession by primogeniture comparable to that so firmly established in most nineteenth-century European monarchies. In African kingdoms the choice of heir was normally, though not universally, confined to a single dynasty; in a few cases two or more royal houses in turn provided the ruler.

Succession was, of course, profoundly affected by the rule of descent locally accepted. In patrilineal societies the king's immediate heirs were his sons, in matrilineal societies his brothers born of the same mother and his sister's sons. Since all African societies were polygynous, a ruler was likely to have a considerable number of sons. The range of possible successors was increased still further in those states where all the descendants of certain famous kings were allowed to put themselves forward as candidates for the throne; the history of the kingdom of Kongo graphically illustrates the instability that could result from such a system of succession. Other states found it advisable to reduce the number of candidates by limiting eligibility to the sons of the king's most important wife or by laying special stress on seniority or competence.

Nevertheless, however small the number of candidates, the need for a choice remained. Selection could be made either by the reigning sovereign during his lifetime or by some formally constituted electoral council after his death. In Dahomey the king nominated his successor and granted the chosen son important privileges. In Buganda, Ashanti, and Sokoto an electoral council, varying in composition but always including the highest officials, came together to choose a new ruler. Ankole resorted to the drastic and unusual device of allowing the king's sons to fight it out between them in the most literal manner until one contender was left victorious.

Even after a smoothly conducted succession a new ruler might find himself faced with the danger of revolt from disappointed claimants to the throne. There were a number of ways in which this danger could be minimized: royal contenders could be liquidated, imprisoned, deprived of all political power, debarred by custom from putting themselves forward once again, or given the hope of success at a later selection. African states varied considerably in their practice. The nineteenth-century kings of Buganda found that immediately after their accession it was advisable to kill off all their brothers. In seventeenth-century Ethiopia all possible claimants to the throne were incarcerated for life on an inaccessible mountaintop. In Dahomey the king's brothers were regarded as ineligible to succeed him and debarred from all political offices. In Sokoto seniority of descent from the founder of the dynasty was a major factor in favor of a candidate; thus, both the brothers and the sons of a new caliph could nurture hopes of eventually becoming caliphs themselves.

Kingship was an exacting occupation. Inevitably, cases occurred when a ruler lost the confidence of his people. Some states developed constitutional means by which a monarch could be removed. Among the Ashanti and other Akan peoples it was accepted that a ruler who offended greatly against the customs of the land could suffer "destoolment." Yoruba sovereigns were required to commit suicide when their powers were obviously failing. States which lacked such constitutional devices were forced to fall back on the classic methods of assassination—the fate suffered by Shaka, the first Zulu king—or revolt. Alternatively, an effete ruler might find himself gradually deprived of power by an able and ambitious "mayor of the palace"—a process well illustrated by the history of Bornu in the first decades of the nineteenth century.

In every indigenous African state ideology supplemented force in helping to cement the political structure. If historical experience showed that force was the more important element in the formation of most states, ideology tended to become increasingly significant in the maintenance and preservation of their political structure. An effective ideology provided the people of a given community with an explanation that justified and so strengthened the ordering of the society in which they lived. In practice ideology supported the established order of indigenous monarchies in three ways: by ascribing to the ruler a personality that raised him above the level of ordinary men, by endowing the kingly office with extraordinary powers over natural forces, and by making the monarchy a symbol of the unity of an entire people and a focus for their sentiments of loyalty.

African monarchs vividly exemplified the rule that in all monarchical societies before the age of rationalism the king appears in the eyes of his subjects as a person "hedged" with divinity, an individual utterly different from ordinary mortals. Some African rulers provided evidence of their special character by tracing their line of descent back to gods or supermen: in Ankole, for example, the Hima kings claimed to be the descendants of the fabulous Chwezi. Myths of this kind were not confined to pagan societies. In Christian Ethiopia the emperors laid great stress on an ancestry reaching back to King Solomon, while many Muslim rulers, including the later sultans of Morocco, made themselves out to be descendants of the Prophet Muhammad.

Whatever their origins, most rulers were credited with the magical power of being able to influence the natural order so as to ensure prosperity for their people. This power did not come to them spontaneously: it was imparted through the initiation rituals that took place at a ruler's accession, was often regarded as being dependent on the observance of certain rules affecting the sovereign's food, dress, and other aspects of his daily life, and needed to be replenished at certain annual ceremonies. The practical duties associated with the royal office meant that the rulers of African states—in contrast to the "divine kings" of certain demi-states—could not devote more than a limited part of their time to religious duties, but they were usually required to play the leading role in certain major religious ceremonies. Vast though the difference in religious concepts might be, the Muslim sultan leading his people in prayer was fulfilling a function not so far removed from that of the pagan king making sacrifices to his ancestors on behalf of his people.

Many rulers served to personify the unity of their people. Sometimes they acted as the guardians of sacred objects—a golden stool in Ashanti, a drum in Ankole—that symbolized the collective soul of the people or the spirit of the land. Usually, a ruler's titles conveyed some impression of his position in the eyes of his subjects. Thus, the Southern Bantu spoke of their chiefs as their "fathers" or their "herdsmen"; the Ganda gave to their Kabaka titles indicating that they regarded him as embodying the power of the nation; and many Muslim peoples honored their sovereigns with the title *Amir al-Mu'minin,* "leader of the faithful."

However exalted a ruler's position might be, his people expected him to use his powers in a responsible manner. Monarchical forms of government carry with them an ideal of kingship. However tyrannical or effete individual rulers might prove, this ideal concept—made explicit in some African states in the ruler's coronation oath to cherish and defend his people—gave a powerful measure of stability to the institution of monarchy.

No less than more easily visible political institutions, ideologies are susceptible to the processes of change. Sacred objects gradually gain or lose their significance; rituals are devised, elaborated, discredited; ceremonies arranged or prohibited; systems of belief handed down from one generation to another until some rival system modifies them or takes their place. All these changes are the product of human actions. Thus, some African monarchs made a point of destroying or transferring to the shrines of their capital the regalia of conquered chiefs and peoples; others took care to associate with their rule the ritual experts of the polities they had overrun, sometimes, as happened in the Kongo kingdom, by marrying into priestly lineages. Orthodox Muslim or Christian rulers condemned the beliefs and rituals of older religions and sought to bring their pagan subjects to a proper realization of the true faith.

Any all-embracing system of beliefs, once it has become deeply rooted in the minds of a particular people, acquires great resilience and is likely to prove exceedingly difficult to eradicate. In the history of most African states one can find evidence of the capacity of old ideas to survive for very long periods of time. Ethiopia provides a particularly striking example of the strength of ideology. In the eighteenth century the kingdom collapsed completely, yet this collapse did not discredit the traditional concept of monarchy and the kingdom was revived under the old inspiration in the latter half of the nineteenth century.

The Ethiopian example points toward a generalization that would seem to be true of all African societies before the twentieth century. These societies were certainly not immune to the processes of change, but one cannot instance a single example of an African people deliberately rejecting through a profoundly revolutionary movement their traditional ideology and institutions. Such a movement occurred in France in the eighteenth century and, to a more limited extent, in England and the American colonies; in the twentieth century movements aiming to re-shape a country's ideology and institutions were to take place in many different parts of the world. Initially, it would seem that revolutions of this profundity can occur only in countries whose economies are suffi-ciently evolved to allow the emergence of a greater diversity of social groups; later, countries with simpler economies may well choose to copy the revolutionary doctrines and methods of their more highly developed neighbors. This was to be the experience of Africa in the twentieth cen-tury.

When one turns from indigenous kingdoms to those African territories dominated by alien minorities, one immediately becomes aware of a sharp difference in the ideological basis of the polity. A dominant alien minority inevitably stresses its cultural superiority over its subjects. Some of the subject people are likely to accept this claim and to attempt to assimilate themselves to the culture of their foreign masters. Others are likely to reject the claim entirely and to do all that they can to resist the intruders, but the great mass of the population, overawed by the force at the aliens' disposal and seeing perhaps some material benefits—increased security, new opportunities for trade, and so on—in the aliens' rule, may well accept the situation passively for a long time. Among themselves the aliens tend to develop a set of ideas designed to bolster up their self-assurance: the Arab pride of race, French and British talk of a civilizing mission, and Boer theories of racial superiority pro-vide examples of this process. But for a group of alien conquerors to develop an ideology that is entirely acceptable to their subjects is an exceedingly difficult undertaking. To gain acceptance such an ideology

needs to challenge and modify ancestral systems of belief at every level
—to put forward new ideas not only about man's ordering of society but
also about man's place in the universe. Here an alien group which regards
itself as the advocate of a new religion has a massive advantage over
aliens who come merely as temporal conquerors. Thus it was that of all
the alien groups to settle in Africa before 1850 the Arabs, as bearers of
Islam, achieved the greatest measure of acceptance. Indeed, in certain
parts of Africa they came in time to lose the character of aliens. But even
with the backing of an immensely powerful ideology the full process of
acceptance required the passage of many centuries and the pressure of
many thousands of alien immigrants. The manifestations of a profound
European impact on North Africa in the centuries on either side of the
start of the Christian era had been erased by the Arab conquest. Since
then Europeans had had neither the time nor the numbers to make a
really profound impression on indigenous institutions and ideologies. By
1850, however, it was clear that Europeans were developing a passionate
conviction of cultural superiority, a conviction based partly on pride in a
rapidly developing technology, partly on a new-sprung missionary ardor
to propagate their own forms of Christianity. This conviction was to provide the driving force behind their assumption of new political responsibilities in every part of Africa. Time would show whether the European
conquerors could devise an ideology really acceptable to their subjects.

In the chapters that follow an account is given of more than a dozen
African kingdoms ranging from Ethiopia and Morocco to the kingdoms
of the Zulu and the Bemba and including most of the really substantial
indigenous states together with a few lesser kingdoms such as Kaffa and
Ankole. Though chosen partly to illustrate the many differences to be
found in the structure of indigenous states, it would be a mistake to
regard this list as presenting anything in the nature of a representative
sample. It is, indeed, an illusion to think in terms of samples when dealing with such subtle and complex organisms as large-scale political societies. Every substantial state possesses its own distinct character—a fact
of which European and American observers are vividly aware when they
consider their own continents but which they often forget when general-
izing about other parts of the world.

Given the extraordinary number and variety of polities to be found in
Africa, any account by a general historian must be highly selective. But to
consider a dozen or so African kingdoms and all the main alien-
dominated territories together with a number of demi-states and stateless
polities should stimulate an awareness of the variety of Africa. It should
also serve to convey an impression of the nature and strength of local
forces. To think of Africa only in terms of broad movements—the ad-

vance of Islam, the impact of Europe, and so on—is to fall far short of a proper comprehension of events. The warp of these broad movements needs to be woven into the woof of the local scene. A study of a considerable range of African polities in the middle of the nineteenth century provides one of the surest foundations for a proper understanding of the massive changes that were to affect the continent in the years after 1850.

POLITICAL DIVISIONS

There is one important aspect of the political structure of mid-nineteenth century Africa that cannot be adequately illuminated through the presentation of individual polities—the nature of the continent's political divisions. By the nineteenth century most Europeans had come to acquire a very clear conception of the form political divisions between sovereign states should take. They saw such divisions as boundary lines visibly defined on maps, delimited by treaties, and demarcated on the ground by specially appointed officials. All political divisions must be seen as the product of particular forms of political organization at specific stages of technological development. Different political structures and different technologies produce different concepts of political divisions. Inevitably, therefore, the divisions between African polities took a form quite unlike the standard boundaries with which Europeans were familiar.

Perhaps the most helpful way to reach some understanding of different concepts of political division is to think in terms of the rights that the people of a polity regard as important and which they are prepared to defend by means of force. Every African polity, whatever its nature, sought to define its rights in some material sphere. Thus, bands of Pygmy hunters asserted exclusive hunting rights over well-defined territories, pastoral nomads laid claim to grazing grounds or watering places, and communities of agriculturalists found it necessary, whenever land came into short supply, to establish divisions between neighboring communities. Given this emphasis on the right to use land for a particular purpose, it was quite possible for two communities, differing in their economies and possessing distinct and independent forms of political organization, to coexist harmoniously in the same area. The relationship established in some areas between Fulani pastoralists and Hausa or Malinke farmers or between Pygmy hunters and Bantu villagers illustrates this type of situation.

To the rulers of states it was important to assert the right to levy tribute from particular communities. Yet most African rulers would have found it impossible to define the exact extent of their territories. The core of closely administered central provinces merged imperceptibly into borderlands whose communities paid tribute with a frequency that depended partly on their distance from the capital, partly on the force at their over-lord's disposal. It was not uncommon for minor polities situated uncomfortably in zones between two major states to find it necessary to pay tribute to both their powerful neighbors.

States faced three possible types of neighbors: minor polities with a population made up mainly of peasant cultivators, groups of nomads, or states possessing an organization similar to their own. The first type presented the easiest problem: minor polities could be intimidated, conquered, and eventually absorbed. Nomads provided much more troublesome neighbors: such was the experience of the ancient Egyptians with the Libyans, of the states of the medieval Maghrib with the Bedouin Arabs, of Songhai and Bornu with the Tuareg, and of Ethiopia and the Sidama kingdoms with the Galla and the Somali. Protection against raids by unruly pastoralists could only be achieved by constant vigilance. Some highly organized states created specially defended frontier districts: the ancient Egyptians at certain periods built massive fortresses on their southern border, the Romans in North Africa created a system of defense in depth known as the *limes*, many of the Sidama kingdoms such as Kaffa surrounded themselves with long stretches of palisaded ditches. Alternatively, nomads could be intimidated by well-planned punitive expeditions, a policy followed by all the states with nomadic neighbors at certain periods in their history. But once a state relaxed its guard it was likely to suffer grievously from the depredations of infiltrating nomads.

When highly organized states, claiming a wide range of rights and anxious to control the passage of men and of goods into their territories, come directly into contact with one another, it becomes necessary, so European experience had shown, to define with great care the territorial division between them. In mid-nineteenth-century Africa there were very few areas where such a situation existed. In the seventeenth century the states of the Maghrib—Morocco and the two Turkish regencies of Tunis and Algiers—had discussed and defined their respective boundaries. In the 1840's Morocco and France reached agreement over the western boundary of Algeria, and an imperial firman from the Porte defined the boundary between Egypt and the Ottoman domains in Palestine. In the 1850's the English and the Boers in South Africa agreed on some of the boundaries between their territories. Elsewhere in Africa, as a glance at any contemporary map will indicate, well-defined boundaries in the European sense did not exist. The rivalry of alien powers rather than, as in Europe, the clash of indigenous states was the force that eventually imposed on Africa the political divisions it now bears.

CHAPTER XIV

Northeast African Polities about 1850

❧ THE PASHALIK OF EGYPT: "ORIENTAL DESPOTISM"

No polity in Africa, no polity, indeed, anywhere in the world surpassed Egypt in the length of its record as an organized state. For more than five thousand years the peoples of Egypt had been subject to the pressures of a highly elaborate system of government. Inevitably, there had been changes in the character of the ruling elite, inevitably, too, there had been periods marked by the breakdown of the machinery of the state; but the territorial bounds of the country—the union of Upper and Lower Egypt —had been firmly established, and it had become the accepted practice for a successful ruler to impose over his domain a type of government to be found nowhere else in Africa, a system that involved a high degree of centralization with the ruler having at his disposal an administrative machinery that enabled him to intervene forcefully in the affairs of all his subjects. Egypt provides then the only African example of a type of polity that has been termed "Oriental despotism."

Three factors made the construction of such a polity possible—the relatively small size of the country, the fertility of its soil, and the density of its population. Although Egypt might claim to exercise a hegemony over a very much larger territory, the core of the country—the settled areas of the Nile Valley, the delta and the adjoining oases—comprised less than fifteen thousand square miles. The extraordinary richness of the soil, annually renewed by the Nile floods, made it easy to provide the surplus needed to support an elaborate political superstructure. Finally, the density of the population—estimated at two and a half million in 1821 and at five million fifty years later—increased the need for an elaborate form of government. But once the machinery of centralized administration had fallen into disrepair, as happened under the Mamluk beys of the eighteenth century, it needed a man of exceptional ability to re-create the structure of despotism. Early nineteenth-century Egypt was presented with such a ruler in the person of Muhammad Ali.

Muhammad Ali never became the ruler of a sovereign state. He recognized the suzerainty of the Ottoman sultan, paid tribute to Constantinople, and never assumed for himself a title more exalted than that of pasha or viceroy. (His grandson, Ismail, was granted the title of khedive or king after agreeing to increase his tribute from £375,000 to £675,000 a year.) Yet no ruler in Africa possessed such a wide range of powers as the pasha of Egypt. It was not merely that he could order an execution with a casual gesture: other African rulers, such as Mutesa of Buganda or Shaka Zulu, did the same. The essence of his power lay in the fact that he succeeded in transforming the whole land of Egypt into a vast private estate. "All the nobles were humbled and nothing remained in the country," wrote Muhammad Abdu, a famous late nineteenth-century Egyptian nationalist, "save instruments of his will which he used to collect soldiers and wealth by any and every means. Thereby was wiped out any element of good life, such as opinion, will and personal independence in order to make the entire Egyptian realm one big feudal domain for himself and his children where it had been many domains under many princes." [1]

The son of an Albanian tobacco merchant, Muhammad Ali had come to Egypt as a soldier and an alien, and men of the same background as himself, soldiers and aliens rather than native-born Egyptians, occupied the most important positions in his political system. In the early 1830's, when he was at the height of his power, the pasha had at his disposal an army of about a hundred thousand men and a navy with eighteen thousand sailors, and he was spending 60 percent of his total revenue, then estimated at three million pounds, on his armed forces. All the most important offices in the military and court administration were occupied by aliens. Of these expatriates in Egypt Turks, whose numbers were put at thirty-two thousand in 1835, formed the largest and most important group. They staffed the officer corps of the army and the senior posts of the civilian administration. But since Muhammad Ali was also anxious to modernize the country he made it his policy to employ Europeans possessing special technical qualifications in a great variety of posts. Thus, during his reign the director of public works, the head of the medical services, the manager of his private estates, and many of the specialists in his army and navy were European. These aliens naturally possessed a vested interest in the regime which helped to ensure their loyalty.

A hierarchy of officials linked the inhabitants of the remotest village with the center. At village level authority lay with the local headman, the *shaykh al-bilad,* who was responsible for the collection of taxes and the recruitment of forced labor for the corvée. The headman was always a native Egyptian; the office of *mamur* (district head) was occasionally held by Egyptians; the post of *mudir* or provincial governor was reserved for the Turks. Finally, at the center were the various departments of state and their respective councils. By the side of all these officials from village headmen to the grandees of the capital there stood that modest but quite indispensable individual, the Coptic clerk or accountant, secretary or scribe. Without the support of this native-born minority of Egyptian Christians—the Coptic population was put at one hundred and fifty thousand in the 1830's—a reasonably efficient system of administration could never have been achieved.

This elaborate superstructure of government rested on the backs of the fellahin, the peasant farmers of the villages, who made up nine-tenths of Egypt's population. To the fellahin—"the most patient, the most pacific, the most home-loving and withal the merriest race in the world" as one European described them [2]—Muhammad Ali's regime had little to commend it. Taxes were collected more vigorously than ever before, and men were liable to be press-ganged into the army to serve for quite indefinite periods or ordered to perform corvée service under gruelling conditions. "It would be scarcely possible for them to suffer more and live," wrote E. W. Lane of the fellahin in the 1830's.[3] And a generation later another equally sensitive European observer, Lucy Duff-Gordon, quoted a peasant as saying after he had described how a village accused of "insurrection" had been destroyed by soldiers, "truly, in all the world none are miserable like us Arabs. The Turks beat us, and the Europeans hate us and say 'quite right.' By God, we had better lay our heads in the dust [die] and let the strangers take our land." [4]

⚜ TURCO-EGYPTIAN RULE IN THE SUDAN

In the 1850's the Sudan could be regarded as a colony of a province of the Ottoman Empire. Muhammad Ali had undertaken the conquest of the country on his own initiative, and he and his successors had no intention of allowing their suzerain at Constantinople to interfere in the administration of the conquered territory.

By 1850 the Turco-Egyptians controlled an area of about four hundred thousand square miles, rather more than two-fifths of the size of the modern republic. This territory which embraced most of the country between Kordofan and the Red Sea was divided up into seven provinces. Khartoum, the administrative capital and seat of the governor-general, was also the largest town in the country; it had developed within little more than twenty years from an insignificant fishing village at the confluence of the two Niles to an urban center with a population of more than thirty thousand.

Muhammad Ali visited the Sudan only once, but he kept a close watch on the administration of the territory. The government at Cairo had the final word in the appointment, promotion, or discharge of all but the most junior officials, and the pasha himself frequently intervened in these matters. Up to 1835 each provincial governor communicated directly with Cairo; after 1835 a more centralized system was established with the appointment of a governor-general to superintend the administration of all the provinces. When it appeared in the mid-1840's that the holders of this office might accumulate a dangerous amount of power, the practice developed of changing governors-general at very frequent intervals. The four governors-general in Muhammad Ali's reign were all senior army officers who had given proof of their ability either in the Sudan itself or in the Arabian, Greek, and Syrian campaigns. The officials in charge of provinces and districts were also drawn from the army. As in Egypt these senior posts were invariably given to Turks. At the same time Coptic clerks, many of whom came to settle permanently in the country, were brought in to fill the subordinate posts in the administration.

Turco-Egyptian rule in the Sudan was based on the presence of a very substantial military force. In 1850 the army numbered thirty thousand, but soon afterward it was reduced to half that figure. Most of the regular infantry were recruited from slaves obtained in raids on the Dinka, Nuba, and other neighboring peoples. At first all the officers were Turks, but as early as the 1840's it was decided to allow Sudanese to enter the officer corps. The cavalry, organized not as disciplined troops but as irregular levies, came increasingly to be provided by the Shaiqiya, a Bedouin tribe from the Dongola area with a formidable military reputation behind it. Every provincial governor had a substantial garrison barracked at provincial headquarters and every *kashif* (district official) was given a small detachment of irregulars to serve as a local constabulary and to assist in the collection of taxes.

As in Egypt, so in the Sudan Muhammad Ali's regime brought a far greater measure of internal security than the area had known before and so greatly improved the opportunities for economic development. Some Sudanese collaborated advantageously with the conquerors, but to the mass of the population Turkish military rule must have appeared harsh and oppressive. Dissident movements were savagely suppressed: thus, in 1844 forty Beja notables, suspected of disloyalty to the government, were hanged in a Khartoum marketplace, after a punitive expedition had ravaged their tribal area. For most Sudanese the greatest abuse sprang from the ruthless methods used to collect taxes, a task frequently entrusted to the barbarous irregulars. There is no doubt that some senior Turkish officials deplored these excesses, but in attempting to control them they were faced with two almost insuperable difficulties—the chronic shortage of money, which meant that many officials were themselves months overdue with their pay, and the remoteness of the areas in which many subordinate officers operated.

If there were abuses, there were also safety valves. Many of the peoples of the conquered territory were pastoral nomads. Unable to subject them to direct administration, the Turkish officials adopted a system of indirect rule, using the tribal chiefs as their intermediaries but leaving the old political structure virtually intact. The development of a pioneering trading frontier up the White Nile and the Bahr al-Ghazal provided many Sudanese from the settled districts of the middle Nile Valley with the opportunity of following a profitable career as traders or soldiers of fortune in areas where the writ of the government hardly ran. Finally, there existed between the limits of effective Turco-Egyptian occupation on the Blue Nile and the highlands of Ethiopia a broad belt of wild, mountainous country where Sudanese in trouble with the Turkish authorities could seek refuge and even succeed in setting up petty polities of their own.

The faults and weaknesses of the Turco-Egyptian regime are easily apparent; they were to contribute to its downfall in the 1880's. But the extent of the Turco-Egyptian achievement should not be underestimated: the tough and resolute Turkish army officers in Muhamad Ali's service succeeded in establishing a more substantial political superstructure than the Sudan had known since the days of ancient Kush. This superstructure was to be used by their successors, first the Mahdists, then the British, as the foundation for still more substantial polities. The modern Republic of the Sudan occupies a land area (967,000 square miles) larger than that of any other state in contemporary Africa: it owes its size in no small degree to the initiative of the Turkish imperialists of the early nineteenth century.

ETHIOPIA: WARLORDS AND THE IMPERIAL TRADITION

No African monarch possessed so imposing a title or laid claim to so illustrious a lineage as did the ruler designated by Europeans as emperor of Ethiopia. This potentate, to whose Amharic title, *negus nagasti,* "king of kings," were added the grandiloquent honorifics "Conquering Lion of the Tribe of Judah, Elect of God," was regarded by many of his people as the descendant of King Solomon and the Queen of Sheba. Yet in the first half of the nineteenth century the numerous occupants of this exalted position were the most wretched of political puppets; the old imperial structure was nothing but a memory, though one which might provide farsighted men with inspiration for the future. Real power lay with the Galla and Amhara warlords whose armies engaged in the endless struggles of constantly shifting alliances on the high Ethiopian plateau.

Modern Ethiopia has an area of 395,000 square miles; historical Ethiopia was a country of about a third this extent. Before the conquest of Menelik II at the end of the nineteenth century the term "Ethiopia" could properly be applied only to the central provinces of the modern kingdom, Tigre, Amhara, Gojam, Shoa, and others. These provinces served as the foundations on which the medieval kingdom had been constructed. Beyond them lay an outer ring of tributary kingdoms brought under Ethiopian hegemony in the fourteenth and fifteenth centuries. Both provincial governors and vassal kings rendered tribute to the emperor, each province being required to send to the imperial court its own distinctive produce—horses from Tigre, silk and brocades from the ports of the Red Sea coast, gold, cattle, and slaves from the provinces of the interior —but the degree of imperial control naturally varied from area to area. In many of the remoter territories the dynasties of the original rulers were left in place, their links with the imperial house strengthened in some cases by diplomatic marriages. The governors of the inner provinces, on the other hand, could be appointed and dismissed at the emperor's pleasure. Indeed, it became the practice to put these lucrative posts up to auction, the highest bidder recouping his expenses by "fleecing the people" of his province and by putting all subordinate posts for sale.[5]

The Ethiopian plateau did not possess a natural unity. Deep gorges separated district from district, rendering communications extremely difficult and emphasizing the isolationism of peoples already distinguished one from another by custom and language. To establish any form of political superstructure over such a country was a herculean undertaking; its successful accomplishment required a skillful blending of ideology and force. The visible display of imperial might presented by the great tented camp with which the emperors toured the country served to overawe potential rebels. But it needed the teachings of the Church, for whom the emperors were the most munificent of patrons, to stress the divine character of the Solomonid dynasty and to render acceptable to the greatest of their subjects the absolutist claims of the emperors.

Cracked by the hammer blows of the Somali invasions, undermined by the Galla penetration of the central plateau, seriously weakened by the substitution of a fixed capital at Gondar for the mobile court of earlier centuries, the imperial superstructure collapsed. But the imperial tradition survived. Even the most impious of Galla warlords paid lip service to the mystique of the ancient dynasty. And yet under the conditions that prevailed in Ethiopia during the first decades of the nineteenth century it was difficult to see how this tradition could have had much meaning for the future.

The country was given up not merely to interregional conflicts but to an even more widespread factionalism. The great warlords were, after all, no more than "the most powerful of a number of competitors." In the society of the time every man seemed to regard himself, so Walter Plowden, a perceptive British consul, noted, as "born to great destinies," "the smallest spark" sufficing to "set fire to his ambitions." With no body of landed proprietors possessing a practical stake in the maintenance of order, almost every man appeared to think he had "something to gain by anarchy." In such circumstances no chief could be absolutely sure of his followers; he could attempt to bind them to him only by the lavishness of his generosity, "slaughtering many oxen daily" and "pouring out mead in torrents" to satisfy his meaner retainers, rewarding his more noble supporters with the grant of villages and districts.

Compared with contemporary Egypt, which Europeans regarded as the most "civilized" country in Africa, Ethiopia presented a spectacle of utter barbarity. Superficial impressions were deceptive. Behind Egypt's development lay a deep malaise; behind Ethiopia's barbarity a rude vigor. "In some respects," wrote Plowden with great discernment, the Ethiopians "are a happy people. They possess in their own land all the necessaries and many of the luxuries of life in abundance; they have great freedom of speech and action and are always gay, systematically, as by constitution. It is hard to convince them that they will benefit either by our science or our wealth." "In Europe," an Ethiopian who had visited Rome told Plowden, "the rich can live more luxuriously but there is no country like Ethiopia for the poor." [6]

To many observers, Europeans and Ethiopians alike, the country's anarchy must have presented a vicious circle from which there was no escape. In fact, already by 1850, powerful forces of change were at work. Firearms in increasing supply were beginning to revolutionize warfare, while the presence of acquisitive foreigners, the Turks in the Sudan, the Europeans on the Red Sea coast, could be regarded as an external threat of a kind Ethiopia had not known since the sixteenth century. Both these forces served in different ways to revive the possibility of national unity. Impossible though it would have been to predict in 1850, the second half of the nineteenth century was to produce, through the achievements of three highly remarkable emperors, Theodore, John, and Menelik, a revival of the glories of the ancient imperial house.

⁂ THE SIDAMA AND GALLA POLITIES OF SOUTHWESTERN ETHIOPIA

In 1850 northeastern Ethiopia was a land of priests and *rases,* of monasteries and of half-ruined monuments of ancient empires. Very different was the social and political pattern of the southwestern section of the Ethiopian plateau. Here there had come into existence, at least as early as the fifteenth century, a number of kingdoms founded by the Cushitic Sidama, a people differing both in language and in religion from the Semitized Christian Amhara. The Sidama had suffered even more grievously than the Amhara from the devastating migrations of the pastoral Galla. But two Sidama kingdoms, Kaffa and Janjiro, had survived. Their highly elaborate monarchical institutions presented a striking contrast to the egalitarian age-grade system of the Galla. In those areas where they still followed a pastoral way of life the Galla preserved their traditional polities, but in the fertile Sidama country they turned to agriculture, abandoned their nomadic life, and came at the beginning of the nineteenth century to create substantial kingdoms of their own. Thus, by 1850 there were three major elements in the political pattern of southwestern Ethiopia: the still surviving Sidama kingdoms, the cluster of newly created Galla states, and the traditional polities of the remaining Galla tribes.

Kaffa, about four thousand square miles in extent, was the more substantial of the two Sidama kingdoms. It occupied an area of remarkable fertility, producing a wide range of crops, and its wealth was further enhanced by a flourishing trade based on the export of coffee, civet, ivory, and slaves. A variety of institutions testified to the complexity of the superstructure that a line of kings reaching back in 1890 more than nineteen generations had created. There was an imposing court, a well-developed system of provincial administration to supervise the collection of revenues from a variety of sources, including custom duties and—perhaps most remarkable of all—an efficient system of frontier defense. The kingdom was surrounded with a deep, wide ditch defended by a tall palisade, except in those stretches where rivers afforded natural obstacles. Strangers coming to the kingdom had to pass through certain well-guarded gates. Points most likely to be attacked by the neighboring Galla were defended by still more elaborate fortifications. But the policy of Kaffa was not purely defensive; indeed, during the early nineteenth century it conquered a substantial amount of new territory.

The Galla hordes who swept over so much of the Ethiopian plateau in the sixteenth and seventeenth centuries might be compared to the Teutonic invaders of the Roman Empire in the Dark Ages of European history. The Galla, a bellicose, mobile, and highly adaptable people, were divided into a large number of tribes or clans linked loosely together by ties of genealogy. Each tribe was bound together by an elaborate system of age grades known as *gada*. All the male members of a tribe participated in the system, moving from grade to grade at eight-year intervals, but a boy was usually not allowed to enter the first grade until his father had completed the fifth and final grade. At each grade men and boys were required to observe certain well-defined forms of behavior and perform specific duties. The members of the fourth grade were responsible for the government of the tribe, taking over all administrative, judicial, and priestly offices relinquished by their predecessors who, on entering the fifth grade, had to content themselves with a purely advisory role in tribal affairs. The fourth grade elected its own leaders, though these were usually chosen from certain prominent families. Most tribes possessed a number of titled offices, the most important being that of the *abba boku,* "the father of the sceptre," who presided over the tribal assembly, acted as chief judge, and led the tribe in time of war.

The Galla who settled down in Sidama country gradually abandoned this system of election and allowed the main offices to become hereditary in certain families. This change, which may well have owed something to Sidama influence, prepared the way for the emergence of a group of five Galla monarchies. The history of one of these states, Limu-Enarea, illustrates clearly the revolutionary processes that transformed the democratic polities of the Galla into an absolute monarchy.

The ancient Sidama kingdom of Enarea was overrun by the Limu Galla at the beginning of the eighteenth century. The Galla then split up into a multitude of groups smaller than their old tribes and fought unceasingly among themselves and with the Galla of neighboring territories. At the beginning of the nineteenth century all the groups of the Limu Galla agreed to accept as their chief a certain Bofo, a notable warrior who had led Limu resistance against the invasion of another Galla tribe.

Enarea lay on an important trade route running from Massawa and Gondar to Kaffa. Bofo's rise to power coincided with a notable revival in trade between the Red Sea and southwestern Ethiopia. The Muslim merchants who passed through Enarea helped Bofo consolidate his power, not only by providing him with new sources of wealth but also by introducing him to new political techniques and novel religious concepts of a kind highly relevant to a ruler with absolutist ambitions. The Galla possessed a religion of their own, but Bofo and many of the leading men of the kingdom became converts to Islam. By 1825 when Bofo was succeeded by his son, Abba Begibo, Limu-Enarea had developed within a generation into a wealthy and stable state.

In Abba Begibo's reign (1825–61) Limu-Enarea had an area of more than three thousand square miles and a population of about one hundred thousand. The kingdom possessed a system of frontier defense as elaborate as Kaffa's, detachments of cavalry being stationed on all the main roads leading into the country. The mass of the Galla population lived in scattered homesteads grouped into hamlets, but around the *masseras,* the residences of the king and of the provincial governors, villages and even small towns began to develop with a fluctuating population of officials, traders, slaves, and other retainers. The most important royal residence was the site of the country's largest market, which had a population of ten thousand.

Abba Begibo ruled with the assistance of an advisory council made up of some of his relations—a few of whom had posts as provincial governors—and of important court officials. But the king's powers were regarded as absolute, and he could dismiss whom he pleased. His court was large and imposing. He had twelve official wives; his concubines were numbered in hundreds, his slaves in thousands. His bodyguard, the nucleus of the kingdom's armed forces, contained a detachment of musketeers, all Amhara mercenaries. To supervise trade he employed a special group of "passport men" or customs officials. In order to conduct a vigorous diplomacy—he was particularly adept at arranging political marriages—the king maintained a large staff of messengers and interpreters. And he regularly led his army in slave raids against neighboring tribes.

Kaffa, Limu-Enarea, and the neighboring Galla kingdoms must be reckoned as being among the most prosperous states in all Africa in the middle of the nineteenth century. But their prosperity and their internal organization could not protect them in the last decade of the nineteenth century from being overrun by a revived Ethiopia whose armies were equipped with an overwhelming preponderance of modern firearms.

THE "DIVINE KINGSHIP" OF THE SHILLUK

In 1850 most of the peoples of the territory now known as the southern Sudan—it lay then beyond the bounds of Turco-Egyptian administration—lived in stateless polities. But there were some groups which had evolved polities of the kind classified here as "demi-states." Of these the Shilluk—a Nilotic people who today number about one hundred ten thousand—provide the most notable example.

The Shilluk occupied a narrow strip of territory along the White Nile extending about one hundred miles downstream from Lake No. Originally, they had formed part of a large group of Nilotic peoples known collectively as the Lwo. The Lwo lived to the south of the other main group of Nilotes represented by the Dinka and the Nuer. Sometime before 1500, as a result possibly of overpopulation, possibly of pressure from Nilo-Hamitic peoples coming in from the east, Lwo groups began to move into other areas. Many of the Lwo went south into modern Uganda, but one large group led by a certain Nyikang moved northward and occupied the area that now forms the Shilluk homeland. Here they settled as farmers in isolated hamlets that came in time to form an almost continuous line along the river frontage. Their agricultural way of life contrasted sharply with the pastoral pursuits of their neighbors, the Dinka and the Nuer.

Shilluk hamlets were grouped together to form settlements. Each settlement managed most of its own affairs under its own chief. But all the Shilluk recognized a supreme head in the person of the *reth* or king.

In most monarchical societies an attempt has been made to give to the kingly office a certain sacred aura. The Shilluk invested their king with a very precise form of divinity. They believed that when a *reth* had been properly installed through a highly elaborate ceremony in which representatives of every section of the Shilluk people took part, he became possessed by the spirit of Nyikang, who was more to them than a great historical figure, the founder of the Shilluk nation; he was a semidivine being in direct communication with Juok (God), the controller of all the forces of nature. Thus, it was possible for the *reth,* who was in a sense Nyikang reincarnate, to provide for the well-being of his people. By the performance of sacrifices and other rites he could influence Juok and so ensure that the crops would grow, disease be averted, enemies defeated, and so on. The primary function of the *reth* was to perform those ritual ceremonies on which the livelihood of the whole people depended.

The extent of the *reth's* administrative and judicial powers are not easy to determine. It appears that he did not have the right to nominate settlement chiefs, for these chiefs were elected by the lineage heads of the settlement. In the event of a serious quarrel between settlements the *reth* might act as a peacemaker, but he had no means of enforcing his decisions except by sending his retainers to support one side or another. The *reth* did not have a standing army at his disposal nor a body of regular officials posted around the country. But one early European traveler noted that settlement heads regularly sent their deputies to report to the *reth;* and it is possible that this practice represents the first stage in the establishment of a system of centralized administration.

The cult of Nyikang, to whom there were shrines in every village, helped to give the Shilluk a remarkable degree of unity, but it could not protect the *reth* against rebellion. Only members of the royal clan—the descendants of Nyikang—whose fathers had been *reths* were eligible for the kingship. At any one time there must always have been a number of possible candidates, all of whom were required to live away from the capital. Most *reths* appear to have met with violent deaths and to have lived in constant fear of assassination. According to tradition a *reth* never let it be known where he was going to sleep and spent his nights prowling around the capital watching for intruders.

To justify rebellion the Shilluk evolved an ingenious theory. When the *reth* was growing too weak or too old he could be ritually killed, and at any time in his reign he could be challenged to single combat by one of his rivals. European observers at one time accepted this theory as literal fact, but there is no historical evidence to indicate that any *reth* was put to death by ritual murder or killed in a duel with a rival. It would seem, however, that by legitimizing rebellion the Shilluk were able to preserve the divine character of their monarchy. For the spirit of Nyikang was immortal; Nyikang always reigned, passing from the body of an old and feeble *reth* into that of a more vigorous successor.

Remarkable though the Shilluk kingship was, it could not provide an organization strong enough to hold at bay the Turkish and Arab merchants with their bands of armed retainers. In 1860 there were a considerable number of Arabs recently settled in the northernmost Shilluk villages. By 1870 the whole country had come under Turkish administration.

THE "ORDERED ANARCHY" OF THE NUER

There are a number of African peoples whose history before the twentieth century has not yet been properly studied but whose social and political institutions have been made the subject of detailed investigation by social anthropologists. Their accounts are mainly in terms of the present, and it is obviously misleading to assume that a people's institutions functioned in the 1930's or 1940's, when the pressure of the colonial superstructure was beginning to weigh upon them, just as they had done in the middle of the nineteenth century. But with certain peoples—particularly those living in stateless polities in areas where the influence of a colonial government was still slight—it is not unreasonable to assume that the main features of their society had changed comparatively little and that an account written in the colonial era may be taken as providing a fairly accurate picture of the state of that people two generations earlier. The Nuer fall into this category. They were not brought under effective colonial administration until 1930. A few years later they were studied by the distinguished social anthropologist E. E. Evans-Pritchard, whose account of their social structure soon established itself as one of the classic works of modern social anthropology.[7] In the absence of other sources a historian can do no more than follow this account.

Evans-Pritchard summed up the political system of the Nuer in the phrase "ordered anarchy"; alternatively, Nuer politics might be regarded as an extreme form of what other social anthropologists have termed "minimal government," for the Nuer had no chiefs, no councils, no courts of law, and the influence exerted by their ritual experts, known as "leopard-skin chiefs," was exceedingly modest. Nevertheless, these people evolved a form of society that possessed a remarkable stability. The Nuer, whose numbers were put at three hundred thousand in the 1930's, occupied an area of about forty thousand square miles on either side of the White Nile, mainly to the south of the point where the river is joined by its tributaries, the Bahr al-Ghazal and the Sobat. To outsiders Nuer land, with its flat clay plains and intersecting swamps, is monotonous to the point of repulsion, but the Nuer adapted themselves completely to their harsh environment. Unlike desert nomads who succumb to the lure of more fertile lands, they appear never to have wished for any other home.

Great herds of cattle provided the Nuer with their livelihood, supplemented by the produce of modest garden plots. As with all pastoral peoples, the needs of their cattle dictated the pattern of their lives. They spent the wet season in villages built on sandy ridges above the flooded plains, but the droughts of the long dry season compelled them to move with their herds to cattle camps on the banks of rivers or near pools of permanent water. Cattle were their obsession, cattle their pride and joy, and they heartily despised those peoples, whatever other material advantages they possessed, who had few cattle of their own.

A common language and other common cultural features enabled the Nuer to think of themselves as a distinct people, but they possessed no political unity, being divided into a number of tribes, each with its own territory. Tribes were of unequal size: in the 1930's tribal populations ranged from five to fifty thousand. Every tribe could be divided into two or more segments, every segment subdivided into sections; every section consisted of a number of villages. Within a village—the basic political unit of Nuer society—most men regarded themselves as kinsmen, with an obligation to help one another. In most respects Nuer villages were autonomous units, but they were not completely self-contained. People from neighboring villages came together at dry-season cattle camps or joined forces to form raiding parties in attacks on other tribes.

There were no courts of law, no official leaders at any stage in Nuer society. Every Nuer had to be ready to stand up for himself and fight for his rights. There were frequent feuds between local communities. If a man was killed in one of these quarrels, his kinsmen were bound to avenge his death. A blood feud thus started could be ended by the killer and his kin paying compensation; in such affairs the local ritual expert, the "leopard-skin chief," was expected to act as mediator. Blood feuds caused such inconvenience to local communities that the pressure of public opinion often served to bring the contending parties to a settlement.

Tensions within Nuer society would undoubtedly have been greater in the nineteenth century, if the tribes had not found room for expansion. The Nuer regarded the neighboring Dinka—Nilotic pastoralists like themselves—as their hereditary enemies. Both peoples coveted each other's cattle, but the Nuer were the more successful warriors. Throughout the nineteenth century they expanded eastward, conquering Dinka territory and absorbing the defeated groups into their own tribes. They were strong enough, too, to prevent the Arab traders who caused so much suffering to other peoples of the Southern Sudan from establishing *zeribas* in their country.

It was easy for outsiders to think of the Nuer as a race of surly and turbulent savages. As Evans-Pritchard's study reveals, they were and still remain a very remarkable people, tough, resilient, "deeply democratic," "easily roused to violence," and immensely proud. "They strut about," Evans-Pritchard has written, "as lords of the earth, which indeed they consider themselves to be." [8]

CHAPTER XV

Northwest African Polities about 1850

✣ THE VILLAGE REPUBLICS OF BERBER MONTAGNARDS

Superficially, the tapering belt of territory lying between the Sahara and the Mediterranean appeared in the middle of the nineteenth century to be controlled by four powerful regimes—the Alawite sultans in Morocco, the French military governors in Algeria, the Husainid beys in Tunis, and the Ottoman pashas in Tripoli—in whose organization the native Berber population of the Maghrib had no part. But there were many areas where the Berbers enjoyed complete independence, for the terrain of much of the Maghrib was peculiarly well adapted for resistance to foreign invaders. In the lonely upland valleys of the Atlas and in the outlying massifs of the Rif and of Kabylia a sedentary Berber population living in scattered hamlets or compact villages presented a form of polity that appears to have changed little in the course of two thousand years.

The basic political unit of these Berber *montagnards* was—to use the terms employed by French scholars—the "canton" or the "village republic." A canton was made up of a group of villages or hamlets, its population rarely exceeding three or four thousand, its territory usually confined to a single valley. Every village possessed a council in which all grown men could participate, but the council of the canton was much less democratic in its character, only the heads of the most important lineages taking part in its deliberations. The canton council elected a president (*moqaddem*) who held office for a year at a time and who served as the council's chief executive.

With no formal staff of officials at its disposal and with much depending on the personality of the *moqaddem* the cantonal government could impose on its constituent villages only the most modest of superstructures. A strong council could punish wrongdoers by the infliction of fines. Two-thirds of the sums thus raised were set aside for the remuneration of the president and members of the council; the remainder was kept in a cantonal treasury to meet certain communal expenses. In southern Morocco the sense of cantonal solidarity found expression in the construction of communal granaries—massive buildings of stone that could easily be transformed into fortresses. Regular festivals and common participation in certain communal labors connected with irrigation helped to foster the spirit of community.

The Berber *montagnards* were a passionately independent and egalitarian people. Should any individual show signs of developing too avid a taste for power, he ran the risk of meeting a violent death at the hands of one of his compatriots. Many cantons, particularly in the Rif and in Kabylia, were permanently divided into family leagues (*soffs*) constantly feuding one with another. Factionalism made it difficult for these village republics to develop more elaborate political institutions. This basic conservatism was reinforced by the existence of an elaborate system of alliances (*leffs*) that helped to preserve a balance of power between the cantons of a particular area. Within such an area every canton belonged to one or other of two rival *leffs*. Should any canton be attacked by a neighbor belonging to a rival *leff*, it could count on receiving immediate assistance from its own allies. Cantons were also grouped together to form tribes, but tribes rarely possessed specific institutions and tribal membership implied little more than a vague sense of fraternity.

For most of their history the Berber *montagnards* appear not to have lifted their eyes above the narrow horizon of their miniscule republics. But there were a few exceptional occasions—under Masinissa, under the Fatimids, and under the Almohads—when they succeeded in creating much more substantial polities. The process by which this revolutionary transformation of traditional Berber institutions could take place has been described by Robert Montagne in his classic study of the Berber of southern Morocco,[1] a work in which he traced the emergence of the great late nineteenth-century Berber kaids who came to be known as the lords of the Atlas and suggested that the methods they employed may well have been used by earlier state builders in Berber history.

Although the constitution of every Berber canton was designed to ward against the concentration of power in the hands of a single individual, an able and ambitious man, supported by a powerful lineage, could sometimes find a way of dominating his neighbors. Elected *moqaddem,* he would proceed to reduce the power of his fellow notables, using bribery to gain supporters and violence to eliminate opponents. Then, having taken over all the funds of the canton, he would assume the title of *amghar* (despot). A formidable fortress (*kasba*), erected by forced labor in his home village, would serve at once to symbolize and to consolidate the tyrant's power; here he could both entertain his supporters and incarcerate his opponents. To meet his rising expenses and to divert the energies of his kinsmen, he would then proceed to attack neighboring cantons, using his allies of the *leff* to assist him and placing his kinsmen in charge of the conquered territories. Thus, within the space of a few years a vigorous village chief might find himself the ruler of a substantial little state, but such a state could be held together only by force and so might collapse as rapidly as it had been formed.

Only by inspiring his followers with an ideology at once binding and dynamic could a successful leader hope to achieve still wider conquests. No system of ideas, as Berber history showed, was more potent than religious enthusiasm directed against the infidel or the heretic, the spiritual rewards of the warriors of the true faith being supplemented by more mundane benefits in the form of ample booty. But even as the rulers of empires, the Berbers could not succeed in overcoming a factionalism too deeply engrained by centuries of feuding between rival *soffs* and *leffs*. The threat of revolt was constant and as soon as the caliber of the ruling dynasty declined, the great state fell apart and the tribes returned to their immemorial form of political organization. In the history of the Maghrib only outsiders—Phoenicians and Romans, Turks and Arabs—have succeeded in creating large states capable of enduring for a span of several centuries.

✥ THE SULTANATE OF MOROCCO: THE POLITIES OF THE MAKHZEN

In Morocco the Arabic word *makhzen* developed from its original meaning of "storehouse" to be applied first to the treasury and then to the entire governmental structure controlled by the sultan. There had been sultans and a *makhzen* in Morocco ever since the end of the eighth century, and despite revolutionary changes of dynasty it is possible to trace over the centuries a gradual development in the structure of this form of government. But no sultan however powerful was ever able to control more than half the area of modern Morocco (171,000 square miles). One of the abiding themes of Moroccan history is the conflict between the government-controlled territory (*bilad al-makhzen*) and the "land of dissidence" (*bilad as-siba*).

The nature of Morocco's terrain dictated that the great range of the Atlas and the massif of the Rif should lie almost invariably within the *bilad as-siba*, leaving to the *makhzen* the fertile Atlantic plains with their flourishing urban centers, Fez and Marrakesh, the regional capitals of the north and the south, and the string of ports from Tangier to Mogador. The personnel of the *makhzen*, both civilian and military, was drawn in the nineteenth century from a number of Arab tribes who were granted certain privileges in return for their services. Islam provided the sultanate with its ideological basis, for the reigning monarch had always been regarded as the religious leader of his people, and the ruler's religious prestige was enhanced still further when the latest Moroccan dynasties, the sixteenth-century Saadians and their successors, the Alawites, were able to claim direct descent from the Prophet. As *sharif* (descendant of Muhammad), as *imam* (religious leader), as *amir al-Muminin* (commander of the Faithful), the sultan was regarded, even by the most independent of Berber *montagnards,* as standing apart from ordinary men and as being powerfully endowed with the mystic force of *baraka,* a force that enabled him to induce well-being among his subjects.

Superficially, the ruler of Morocco appeared to be an absolute Muslim potentate whose least caprice had to be obeyed. To see the sultan in the oriental splendor of one of his palaces or on one of his regular tours of his dominions, accompanied by an army of horsemen—"the great migration," in the words of one observer,[2] "stretching from horizon to horizon, a rainbow of colour upon the green plains"—was to have this impression of absolutism seemingly confirmed. In reality, however, every Moroccan sultan, of whatever period, was poised uneasily on a pinnacle of power. His empire was not a solidly centralized state but "a vague federation" of tribes and clans, each anxious to assert its own independence.[3] To maintain his position the sultan had to devise a subtle blend of diplomacy and force, holding the Berbers of the *bilad as-siba* in check by bribery, intrigue, or punitive expeditions, at the same time keeping a constant watch on the tribes of the *bilad al-makhzen,* who might at any time launch a revolt in favor of one of his kinsmen.

The personnel of the *makhzen* represented "the only disciplined body" in the midst of what most European observers described as "Moroccan anarchy." [4] Over the course of centuries the *makhzen* officials had developed the self-confidence, the *esprit de corps* of a class of mandarins, their characteristic manner of thinking marking them off no less distinctly than their uniform from the mass of Moroccans both in the cities and in the countryside. The *makhzen* was divided into two sections, one concerned with the administration of the court, the other with affairs of state. The "Court Service" consisted of a large number of retainers, some drawn from the privileged tribes, others black slaves, each with a title—"man of the bath," "man of the tea," "man of the stable," and so on—indicating his special responsibilities. The "Court Service" also included two cavalry corps, one providing mounted couriers, the other the sultan's bodyguard. The "Service of State" was a very much smaller section; it was headed by the grand vizier who was supported by a number of secretaries. All members of the *makhzen* from the sultan down had to be prepared to lead a nomadic life, for only through continual tours could the sultan impress on the country the reality of his power and ensure a steady stream of the revenue needed to support his magnificent establishment.

Nominated kaids and pashas, usually chosen from the ranks of local chiefs or prominent landowners, were responsible for the administration of the tribes and cities of the *bilad al-makhzen*. Though possessing virtually autocratic powers within their own districts, they could be removed at any time by the sultan. Their main obligation to the central government was to keep it supplied with the revenue and the troops that it needed. So long as the *makhzen* refrained from importing expensive foreign luxuries, local sources of revenue were sufficient for its needs. During the latter half of the nineteenth century this economic balance was to be disrupted by increasing foreign pressure, with consequences that were ultimately to prove disastrous for the old regime. In 1850, however, the country was experiencing one of the more stable periods in its history.

It was easy for contemporary Europeans, infected by the brash self-confidence of their age, to write Morocco off as a barbarous land, its society stagnant, its empire decaying. The absence of all those institutions—well-kept roads, hospitals, schools, factories—regarded as essential in a modern state, seemed to confirm this view. And yet, as an acute and sympathetic European observer pointed out, there was to be found "in the great cities and in the kasbas of the plain an orderly and civilized society" which had developed a "special form of Arab civilization." [5] The emergence of so refined, gracious, and alluring a culture was rendered possible by the relative degree of political stability that the *makhzen* had succeeded in impressing on a land whose natural features presented such daunting obstacles to the development of a strong form of government.

✻ MILITARY RULE IN ALGERIA: TURKISH DEYS AND FRENCH GENERALS—AND THE AMIRATE OF ABD AL-KADIR

When the French occupied Algiers in 1830, they brought to an end three centuries of Turkish sovereignty in the central Maghrib. Nominally a province of the Ottoman Empire, the regency of Algiers—as the polity was usually termed by Europeans—had long been a completely autonomous state, a military republic controlled by a small class of Turkish janissaries. These capable and disciplined fighting men were drawn from the lower classes of Turkish society. Most of them married into local families and settled permanently in Algiers, but they never established a hereditary aristocracy. It was a strict rule that only men of pure Turkish origin could be members of the *ojaq*, the ruling military caste, and so the numbers of the janissaries were kept up by a steady stream of recruits from Constantinople, Smyrna, and the villages of Anatolia.

The head of state of the regency of Algiers, who bore the title of dey, was an elected despot, chosen by a council (*diwan*) made up of the senior officers of the *ojaq,* invested for life with autocratic powers, but needing always to tread warily in dealings with his compatriots: of the twenty-eight deys who reigned between 1671 and 1830, no less than half were removed by assassination and their successors imposed on the *diwan* by a mutinous soldiery.

Outside Algiers the country was administered along lines similar to those adopted by the *makhzen* in Morocco. The towns—Constantine and Oran were the major provincial centers—were occupied by Turkish garrisons. Certain Arab tribes collaborated with the Turks and were given exemption from certain taxes in return for their help in collecting revenue from their unprivileged neighbors. But the Berber *montagnards* of Kabylia and Arab nomads living on the edge of the desert remained well beyond the range of the Turkish beys and aghas. In their territorial policy the Turks were realists. Their own numbers never exceeded fifteen thousand; in the heyday of the regency most of their wealth came not from the land but—through the exploits of their privateers—from the sea; to confine effective administration to strictly limited areas was an eminently sensible line of action.

At first the French attempted to follow the same pragmatic policy of limited occupation. But in their ignorance of the internal polities of the regency they made a serious initial mistake. Wishing to pose as liberators come to free the native population from Turkish tyranny, they rounded up the janissaries and shipped them back to Anatolia. Every colonial power needs native collaborators. In Algiers the French found their most ardent supporters among the hitherto despised Jewish minority. In the interior they sought to establish treaty relations with local chiefs. But to the Arab and Berber population the French were not merely alien conquerors to be charged with all those abuses inevitably associated with any army of occupation but also infidels, many of whose actions were deeply offensive to Muslim susceptibilities. This widespread and passionate loathing for a brutal and sacrilegious invader served to provide the ideological basis for a new Muslim state, the most substantial indigenous policy the central Maghrib had known for centuries.

Abd al-Kadir, the founder of this state, is one of the great figures of nineteenth-century African history, to be remembered not only as the leader of Algerian resistance against the French but also as a reforming Muslim statesman, inspired, like his contemporaries, the great Muslim leaders of the Western Sudan, with the vision of establishing a truly theocratic state, a polity governed strictly in accordance with the laws laid down by the Prophet for the first community of Muslims. Born into a distinguished marabout family that claimed a sharifian origin, Abd al-Kadir was in his mid-twenties at the time of the French invasion, but he had already made the pilgrimage to Mecca and gained considerable experience of a wider world. In 1832 this remarkable young man, already revered for his piety, esteemed for his learning, and admired for his energy, was chosen by a group of Arab tribes in his home area in western Algeria to lead them in a jihad against the French. Taking the title of amir, Abd al-Kadir set about the task of creating something more substantial than a temporary coalition; his aim was to mold the petty Arab and Berber polities into a fully organized state.

By 1840 Abd al-Kadir had established an administrative superstructure over a large part of the interior. He used his own kinsmen and the members of other marabout families to act as his agents among local groups, giving them the title of *khalifa* (deputy) and instructing them to maintain a steady flow of tribute to the central treasury. This revenue he used to meet the cost of maintaining and equipping with firearms a regular army of ten thousand men and of constructing a chain of strategically placed fortresses. At the same time he encouraged the development of Muslim institutions, especially schools and courts of law, and took a sternly puritanical line in attempting to suppress prostitution, the drinking of alcohol, and other practices proscribed by the Koran.

At first the French were prepared to recognize Abd al-Kadir as ruler of most of the interior. But conflict between the two sides was inevitable, a series of local clashes gradually escalating into a full-scale war. The ruthlessness of French methods of total conquest and the sheer weight of French numbers—their army was increased from 18,000 men in 1831 to 108,000 in 1846—proved decisive. In 1847 Abd al-Kadir surrendered, to end his days in exile.

In the administration of a colony the first twenty years of whose existence were marked by almost continuous fighting the army inevitably played the dominant part. By a decree of 1834 "the French Possessions in North Africa"—the new name "Algeria" was not officially adopted until 1839—were placed under the supreme control of the Ministry of War at Paris. The senior army officers who were appointed governors-general acted as heads both of the military and of the civilian establishments. Within the colony the governor-general possessed virtually dictatorial powers; but only one governor-general, Bugeaud (1840–47), held the office long enough to make a really decisive mark on the country.

In their conquest of the interior the French could always find local chiefs willing to collaborate with them. But bitter experience showed that most collaborators needed to be closely supervised. Since most of Algeria was regarded as military territory, the task of acting as intermediaries between the Muslim population and the French authorities was given to army officers, seconded by the specially established *bureaux arabes*. "For most of these officers," an eminent French historian has recently pointed out, "the Arabs represented a mass of primitive humanity made up of lying, hypocritical, and cruel individuals who had to be kept in place by force, until social and economic changes made it possible for them to emerge slowly from their original barbarism. It was the duty of the *bureau arabe* to promote their well-being without either seeking their cooperation or taking their advice." [6]

To consolidate its conquests the French government began in 1840 to encourage the European colonization of Algeria. Twenty-five thousand Europeans had already settled in the occupied areas; by 1846 their numbers had risen to one hundred nine thousand. The early settlers came from every part of the western Mediterranean from Spain to Malta. Most of them were *petits blancs,* laborers or craftsmen, who settled in the towns. But some French capitalists bought up rural estates and many of the colonists brought over under official schemes were placed in agricultural settlements on land from which the native proprietors had been ejected.

By 1850, after only twenty years of French rule, Algeria had developed into a highly complex political community, with its cosmopolitan coastal cities, its new French settlements in the coastal plains, and its Arab and Berber tribes kept in check only by the application of massive military force. Its development was rendered the more complex by its proximity to the metropolis, for this meant that the colony was powerfully affected by any major political change that might take place in France itself. Thus, under the constitution of the Second Republic, born of the Revolution of 1848, Algeria was declared an integral part of France and its *colons* given representation in the National Assembly, only to revert to the earlier system of military rule with the establishment of the Second Empire in 1852.

THE REGENCY OF TUNIS

The regency of Tunis controlled an area of about fifty thousand square miles, with a population estimated in the mid-nineteenth century to number rather more than a million. Its terrain was for the most part open and easily governable. Indeed, no other country of the Maghrib had been so profoundly molded by external forces or possessed so long a record— reaching back to Carthaginian times—of organization as a substantial state. The rulers of Tunis were more fortunate than other Maghribi sovereigns. The inhabitants of certain areas, Berber *montagnards* toward the Algerian frontier, Arab camel-nomads on the Saharan fringes, successfully resisted their domination, but these dissidents never presented a serious threat to their authority. Unlike the sultans of Morocco, the beys of Tunis were not harassed by the need to keep constant watch on the uneasy frontiers of the *bilad as-siba;* unlike their immediate neighbors, the pashas of Tripoli, they were not obliged to mount frequent expeditions against threatening desert tribes. With more than half their subjects submissive city dwellers or sedentary cultivators the rulers of Tunis could pride themselves on having at their disposal one of the most peaceful and prosperous countries in Africa.

Like contemporary Egypt, like Algiers before 1830, Tunis formed part of the Ottoman Empire, yet possessed all the attributes of a fully sovereign state. Since the seventeenth century the country had been ruled by dynasties of beys of mamluk origin, first the Muradids, then after 1705 the Husainids. After a turbulent period in the middle of the eighteenth century, the Husainids had established the rule that succession should be by primogeniture in the male line and thus freed the country from the civil wars begotten of a disputed succession that were the bane of so many other African kingdoms.

The government of Tunis could be described as despotism pure and simple, for the bey was subject to no formal restraint and could appoint whomever he pleased to official posts not only in the capital but also in the provinces. A small group of mamluks, one-time slaves of Greek or Circassian origin, brought up from boyhood in the royal palace, together with occasional Italian adventurers provided the beys with their principal servants and advisers and formed the country's political elite. Such an elite was entirely dependent on the sovereign's favor: its members were granted many opportunities of acquiring substantial riches, but many a proud and prosperous mamluk found himself reduced to penury, thrown into prison, even condemned to death, as his master's favor suddenly shifted. Kaids, nominated by the bey and usually of mamluk origin, acted as provincial governors and supervised the collection of taxes, squeezing as much as they could from the defenseless peasantry, treating the nomadic pastoralists who made up about a third of the country's population with greater circumspection. Regularly, twice a year, the bey dispatched his army, made up mostly of irregular troops and commanded by his heir, the "bey of the Camp," on a tax-collecting *tournée* directed against the more turbulent tribes of the south and west.

Inevitably, as with almost every mid-nineteenth-century system of government in any part of the world, the beylical regime was riddled with corruption. Many of the mamluk ministers were more concerned to amass fortunes for themselves than to render their sovereign faithful service. Indeed, there were a number of cases when royal treasurers absconded overseas, taking with them vast sums of money. Important offices were put up for sale, and no tax could be collected without a sizable part of the produce—most taxes were paid in kind—remaining in the hands of the tax collector. Nevertheless, until the 1830's Tunis could be reckoned a reasonably prosperous country, with a balanced budget, moderate taxation, and a favorable balance of trade. This sensible, if unprogressive, equilibrium was first disrupted by the ambitions of Bey Ahmad (1837–55). He envied his great contemporary, Muhammad Ali, idolized that dangerous model Napoleon, and determined to modernize his country. With the aid of a French military mission he built up a regular army; other Europeans were invited to develop a wide range of new industries; and the bey indulged his own grandiose tastes by constructing a vast palace, a kind of Tunisian Versailles. Financial difficulties soon led to the ruin of all these projects. But Ahmad's principal minister, Mustapha Khaznadar, remained in office after his master's death and made himself, under Ahmad's effete successors, virtual ruler of the country; his unscrupulous and shortsighted policies prepared the way for the collapse of a form of government that had lasted for more than two hundred years.

𝕏 TUAREG CONFEDERATIONS

"A mighty people" the Tuareg were called by the first European traveler to write an account of them; and the same observer, the early nineteenth-century explorer Frederick Hornemann, went on to suggest that had the Tuareg lived in a more civilized environment, their "natural abilities" might well have led them to become "one of the greatest nations upon earth." These remarkable people dominated a vast block of central Saharan territory several hundred thousand square miles in extent: to the north their influence was felt in Ghadames and Murzuk, to the south their power troubled the rulers of all the northern Sudanic states from Bornu to Timbuktu, to east and to west their raiding parties clashed with their desert neighbors, the Tebu of Tibesti and the Moors of the western Sahara. Few other African peoples could claim so extensive a territory.

In the middle of the nineteenth century the Tuareg formed five groups or confederations of tribes: the Kel Ahaggar, the Kel Ajjer, and the Kel Air took their names from the massifs that made up the core of their respective territories, the Aulimmiden occupied a wide stretch of country on either side of the Niger at the northern point of the river's long drawn-out bend, while a fifth group, known by several different names, lived between the Aulimmiden and the Kel Air. These confederations varied greatly in size: in 1938 the smallest of them, the Kel Ajjer, contained no more than two thousand people, while the largest, the Aulimmiden, its numbers swollen by a high proportion of Negro serfs or slaves, had a population of one hundred sixty thousand. Even among the Kel Ahaggar, regarded as the purest of Tuareg groups and the least affected by external influences, nearly a quarter of the population (4250 in 1938) was made up of Negro slaves.

The nature of their environment forced upon the Tuareg the life of pastoral nomads, raising herds of camels, goats, and, on the southern fringes of the Sahara, cattle. But there were also a few places in the central Sahara, particularly in the massifs or in the Sahel, where a supply of permanent water made possible the cultivation of dates, millet, and other crops in garden plots worked by slaves. The most striking feature of Tuareg society was its class structure, with three well-defined classes— nobles, vassals, and slaves—and certain minor castes of blacksmiths and craftsmen. At the same time every confederation consisted of a number of tribes and clans, each with its own chief. Thus, among the Kel Ahaggar there were three tribes, each consisting of a noble clan from which the name of the tribe was derived and a number of vassal clans. A man's status was dependent on his clan; a member of a vassal clan could not hope to achieve nobility. Between nobles and vassals and the slaves there was a sharp racial distinction; the former showed by their lighter complexion that they were of proper Tuareg stock, the latter were invariably Negroid in origin.

The Tuareg nobles formed an aristocracy of warriors. Utterly contemptuous of any kind of manual labor, happy to sponge off their vassals for all the necessities of life, these lords of the desert never degenerated into effeteness. *Imouhar,* the Tamaheq word for nobles, is derived from a root meaning "pillage": in Tuareg society rapine was regarded as the proper occupation of a nobleman. Their raids, boldly and cunningly executed, were directed either against the encampments of a neighboring Tuareg group or against the villages of the settled cultivators of the Sudan. Booty ranged from slaves and camels to the ornaments stripped from an enemy's womanfolk. Whenever possible bloodshed was avoided, for killing brought with it the discomforting complications of the blood feud. Raids involved grueling rides, often across hundreds of miles of desert. Part sport, part product of economic necessity, such martial exercises made the arrogant and mysterious men of the desert among the most formidable fighting men in all Africa, their mounts swift, graceful riding camels, their arms sword, lance, and dagger, their defense great oryx-skin bucklers, their eyes piercing and imperious above the dark folds of their mouth veils.

Most confederations possessed a paramount chief who bore the title *amenokal* and came from a lineage of one of the noble clans. Succession was usually matrilineal, but there was always an element of choice among possible heirs and no *amenokal* could be confirmed in office without the approval of a council made up of all the clan heads of the confederation, vassal as well as noble. The *amenokal* acted as leader in time of war, served as arbitrator in intertribal disputes over grazing rights or stolen animals, and represented a confederation in negotiations with neighboring peoples. Every year he received a wide range of tribute in kind, young camels, butter, dates, millet, and other produce from the vassal clans, trade goods paid by caravan merchants as the tolls of passage, and a share of the booty of successful raids. But his office was surrounded with no great mystique; his tent might be more luxurious than tents of other men, but he maintained no court and could be approached without formality; even for the collection of tribute he was dependent on the chiefs of tribes and clans in whose internal government he had no say. Lacking the means to build up a machinery of administration, no *amenokal* could ever transform himself into the ruler of a proper state. His position, though nominally held for life, was a precarious one, and he could be deposed if his actions proved unpopular.

The Tuareg were of Berber stock. Their political system represented an adaptation of traditional Berber institutions to the harsh and competitive environment of the desert, an environment that offered opportunities for certain enterprising groups to dominate their neighbors and so establish themselves as nobles. Yet the politics of the desert were never static: vassal clans transferred their allegiance from one group of nobles to another, noble clans declined in power and were reduced to vassal status, factions broke away from one confederation and moved into the area of another. Even the confederations themselves appear to have taken the form they presented in the mid-nineteenth century only some hundred or two hundred years earlier. Beneath an apparently conservative surface one can detect the kaleidoscopic processes of change.

CHAPTER XVI

West African Polities about 1850

✣ THE ANCIENT SUDANIC EMPIRE OF BORNU

Of all the great kingdoms that had flourished in the Western and Central Sudan in medieval times Bornu alone survived in the nineteenth century as a substantial, independent state. Memories of the ancient imperial splendor were still preserved among local groups of the Malinke and Songhai people, but the heartland of the old empires of Mali and Songhai had been for many generations either under alien domination or fragmented into scores of miniscule polities. Bornu, with an area of about twenty-five thousand square miles and a population of perhaps half a million, could still be regarded as one of the major states of all Africa. Moreover, if some of its smaller neighbors among the Hausa states be excepted, it was unique in the sub-Saharan regions of the continent in possessing a history that reached back over a thousand years, a history in which the country's elite felt—and still feels—an immense pride.

During this long period the political structure of the state had naturally undergone profound changes. At first, when the center of power was based on Kanem, the country north of Lake Chad, the state was organized round a confederation of clans with one clan, the Magumi, and its senior lineage, the Saifuwa, being of superior status. At this time the ruler who bore the title of *mai* appears to have occupied a position not unlike that of a Tuareg *amenokal,* being advised by a council of nobles made up of leading members of the various clans in the area. The looseness of this structure was probably one of the reasons for the long period of civil war that ended in the mid-fifteenth century when the Saifuwa decided to shift their power from Kanem to Bornu, west of Lake Chad. In their new territory the Saifuwa were soon able to achieve a much greater degree of centralization. They appear to have left behind them the dissident nomadic clans and to have been accompanied only by their own clansmen, the Magumi. They established their power over the local people not by peaceful penetration but by the sword. In this way they acquired a territory considerably wealthier in natural resources than the arid wastes of Kanem.

About 1470 the *mais* founded their capital, Birni N'Gazargamo, at a site fifty miles west of Lake Chad. This great city, with its brick-built palaces, remained the capital of Bornu until it was abandoned after being sacked by the Fulani in 1812. Here the *mais* lived surrounded by their nobles, their great officials, and their spiritual advisers, the Muslim *mallams*. The members of this elite were rewarded by the gift of fiefs in outlying villages; from the peasantry of their fiefs they obtained tribute, part of which was passed on to the *mai*. With one exception, the Galadima, the warden of the western marches, the fief-holders were required to reside in the capital, their fiefs being dispersed around the country and seldom held on a hereditary basis. At the same time the *mais* developed the practice of entrusting some of the greatest offices of state to slaves or eunuchs of the royal household. A large part of the *mai*'s revenue came from the spoils of war—substantial neighboring states, such as the Hausa kingdoms and Baguirmi, were intimidated into paying regular tribute, while the smaller communities on the southern borders were raided for slaves. Some of these slaves were sold to North African merchants in exchange for horses and later for muskets; by this means the *mais* were able to build up a permanent cavalry force and a small corps of musketeers. Thus constituted, with a system of administration well devised to link people in the provinces to the capital and to prevent separatist movements among members of the nobility, and with a military force powerful enough to overawe all its neighbors, Bornu remained the most powerful state of the Central Sudan for some three hundred years (1500–1800).

The Fulani wars shattered the prestige of the Saifuwa and provided the opportunity for the emergence of a new dynasty founded by Muhammad al-Kanemi. Bornu under the Kanemi dynasty differed in some respects from the old Saifuwa kingdom. There was a change in the royal title from *mai* to *shehu* (sheikh); great stress was laid on the proper observance of the Sharia, the Muslim code of law; many members of the Magumi clan, the old aristocracy, lost their privileged position, their place being taken by the principal supporters of the new dynasty. Many of these newcomers were Shuwa Arabs; these pastoral nomads from the country east of Lake Chad were given land in Bornu and provided the *shehus* with a formidable force of cavalry. But the basic structure of the state remained much the same as it had been for the last three centuries, and many of the weaknesses which had been apparent in the last days of Saifuwa rule were reproduced in the latter half of the nineteenth century.

Much depended on the personal quality of the ruler; yet the development of a highly elaborate court etiquette had an enervating effect on the royal princes. At the same time it was essential to keep the kingdom in a state of constant military readiness in order to check the depredations of the turbulent Tuareg and Tebu nomads of the southern Sahara. Finally, although the dominant Magumi had merged with the indigenous So to produce the Kanuri people, the population of the kingdom as a whole was far from homogeneous. Most of the sedentary peoples of the western marches of Bornu remained untouched by Kanuri culture, and there were groups of pastoral nomads, both Fulani and Shuwa Arabs, to be found in the metropolitan provinces of the kingdom. In periods of crisis the presence of these alien groups proved a source of grave weakness: just as at the time of the jihad the Fulani struck viciously against the *mai,* so in the 1890's the Shuwa Arabs abandoned the *shehu* to join the invading forces of the Sudanese adventurer Rabih.

THE EMPIRE AND CALIPHATE OF SOKOTO

The empire of Sokoto was established as the result of the Fulani jihad launched in the first years of the nineteenth century. By 1850 it had developed into the most extensive political structure in tropical Africa, covering an area of one hundred fifty thousand square miles and stretching from the Sahara to the forest belt and from beyond the northwestern borders of modern Nigeria deep into the Adamawa plateau in the present Republic of Cameroun. To travel from one end of the empire to another required a journey to be measured not in days but in weeks and months. The empire consisted of about twenty provinces which varied greatly in size and in the number, wealth, and ethnic composition of their populations. Kano, for example, an old-established Hausa kingdom with an elaborate system of government before its conquest by the Fulani, had a population of about a million; some of the smaller provinces in the valleys of the Niger and of the Benue, formed through the conquest and amalgamation of many minor pagan polities, contained a population of less than fifty thousand. In organization the empire might almost be termed a confederation, for the provincial governors, the emirs, enjoyed virtually complete autonomy within their own territories, but they accepted the hegemony of the caliph, the ruler at Sokoto.

Born of the conflict between the semipagan rulers of the Hausa kingdom of Gobir and the Muslim community gathered around the Sheikh Usuman dan Fodio, the caliphate in its earliest form represented an attempt to establish a truly Muslim state. The constitution of the original Muslim community as it had existed in Mecca after the death of the Prophet provided Usuman dan Fodio and his followers with a model. The title of caliph with which the sheikh and later his successors were invested harked back to the purity of early Islam and stressed the essentially religious nature of the leadership. (The more familiar title sultan was originally applied to the ruler of Sokoto only by Europeans and other outsiders.) Usuman dan Fodio was primarily a teacher and a scholar; even as caliph he devoted most of his time to teaching and writing, acting as the spiritual adviser to his followers. Practical problems of war and administration were left to his principal supporters, the most prominent of whom were his own kinsmen, especially his brother Abdullahi and his son Muhammad Bello. Vizier, the title held both by Abdullahi and Bello, originally meant no more than "helper"; "an upright vizier," in the words of Usuman dan Fodio, was "the first pillar of the kingdom," being one "who is consulted by the caliph in all matters of his concern." [1] As the new state rapidly expanded, the sheikh's two principal advisers agreed on a practical division of the work of administration, Abdullahi making himself responsible for the supervision of the western provinces, which later included Nupe and Ilorin, while Bello took charge of the eastern provinces formed after the conquest of the Hausa kingdoms. This division continued after Bello had succeeded his father as caliph in 1817. Abdullahi moved to Gwandu, a town about fifty miles southwest of Sokoto. While recognizing the seniority of the caliph at Sokoto his successors, the emirs of Gwandu, continued to receive the tribute of the provinces that had been placed in Abdullahi's sphere of authority. Thus, the whole imperial structure could be described as a "Dual Empire," although the disparity between Sokoto and Gwandu became increasingly marked after Abdullahi's death in 1828.

Usuman dan Fodio's closest supporters had been responsible for the overthrow of the Hausa kingdoms of Gobir and Zamfara; the territories of these two states were incorporated in the metropolitan province of the empire. Outlying provinces were conquered by enterprising Fulani leaders most of whom had studied under the sheikh. Usuman dan Fodio presented them with a flag and invested them with the title of emir. They were then left free to raise their own band of followers and to fight their own battles, with little or no assistance from Sokoto, in the sphere of influence allocated to them. In most areas successful flag bearers were able to establish themselves as founders of dynasties in the territory they had acquired. As governors of provinces of the empire the emirs were under the obligation to send regular tribute to Sokoto, or in the case of the western provinces to Gwandu. The nature of the tribute paid depended on the economy of the province; some, notably Kano and Katsina which contained flourishing commercial centers, sent large quantities of cowries, the local currency, supplemented by horses and cloth; others, such as Bauchi and Adamawa, lying off the main trade routes, paid most of their tribute in slaves. On the death of an emir a local electoral council made up of the principal officials of the emirate chose a successor from among a number of candidates belonging to the ruling dynasty. The successful candidate was then presented to the caliph for his approval. Normally, the authorities in Sokoto were prepared to accept the local nominee, but after 1850 a number of cases occurred in which a provincial emir was deposed by his suzerain. To assert Sokoto's control over its dependent provinces the caliph's principal councilor, the vizier, made regular visits to the provincial capitals and maintained a correspondence—the letters being written in Arabic, the language of state—with the emirs.

In their administration the larger provinces reproduced the structure of the empire as a whole. Thus, the territory under the authority of the emir of Zaria comprised the old Hausa kingdom of the same name, six small vassal states which had also been vassals to Hausa Zaria, and four larger vassals made up of lands newly conquered by Fulani adventurers. Like England after the Norman conquest, the old Hausa kingdom was divided into fiefs given to the principal warriors of the jihad. The majority of fiefs were attached to certain offices of state whose incumbents owed their appointments to the emir, but a few important families succeeded in acquiring fiefs on a hereditary basis. All fief-holders were responsible for the administration of their own areas, for the collection of tribute due to the emir (one-fifth of which they were allowed to keep to themselves), and for the provision of contingents of fighting men in time of war. Every fief-holder gathered around himself "a set of henchmen" capable of being employed as messengers or tax gatherers, constables, or men-at-arms.[2] The larger vassal states possessed a system of administration comparable to that of the emirate itself, with an established dynasty and a hierarchy of officials; their relationship with Zaria was similar to Zaria's relationship with Sokoto. The smaller vassals enjoyed less freedom: unlike the larger vassals whose rulers could make raids on their pagan neighbors whenever they chose to do so, the lesser vassals had to seek the emir's permission before embarking on any military operation.

In theory both the caliph at Sokoto and the provincial emirs could be described as autocrats, for their powers were not limited by the need to consult any form of representative council. But as the rulers of truly Muslim states, they were required to observe the principles of Muslim law. Within every emirate there existed an influential pressure group made up of local Muslim scholars, many of whom were quick to criticize action that could be regarded as uncanonical. Equally influential were the great Fulani families who formed the local aristocracies and filled most of the great offices of state.

Inevitably, the Sokoto empire was subject to those weaknesses characteristic of all imperial structures rapidly established by people of one ethnic group imposing their rule on populations of different stock. On the borders of the empire Hausa groups maintained a successful and, indeed, an aggressive resistance to Fulani imperialism. Ambitious emirs occasionally revolted against the authority of Sokoto. And there were frequent cases of oppression by the Fulani nobility: at an early stage of the jihad the sheikh's brother, Abdullahi, bitterly condemned those members of the community who neglected the obligations of the faith and thought only of collecting "concubines and fine cloth and horses that gallop in the towns, not on the battlefields." [3] The practice of slave-raiding sanctioned by the concept of jihad and supported by the demands of a society and an economy partly dependent on slave labor led to the devastation of many pagan polities. But within the empire itself there existed a greater area of peace and security than was to be found in any other part of mid-nineteenth-century tropical Africa. Above all, Islam, as the religion of state, provided the empire through its stress on justice and brotherhood with a set of principles and a universalistic culture that could serve powerfully to break down or at least to ameliorate the tensions between different classes and peoples. The system of government established by Usuman dan Fodio and his followers survived the revolutionary strains of the colonial period; that it should have succeeded in doing so, that the emirates of modern northern Nigeria should still retain so many aspects of the past is evidence not so much of conservatism as of the strength and vitality of the system.

THE ASHANTI UNION AND EMPIRE

Few African courts were capable of making so striking an impression on outsiders as that of the *asantehene,* the ruler of Ashanti, in his capital Kumasi. To nineteenth-century Europeans Ashanti, both in the crude magnificence of its public displays and in the hideous cruelty of its rituals, seemed to epitomize what they conceived of as "barbarism." The first detailed accounts of Ashanti, both written by Englishmen who visited Kumasi on diplomatic missions in the second decade of the nineteenth century,[4] described the brilliant spectacle presented on certain royal occasions; the king surrounded by his chiefs and warriors, the great state umbrellas of crimson and yellow, the hammocks lined with scarlet taffeta, the sumptuous finely woven cloth worn in a style resembling a Roman toga and, above all, the abundance of ornaments of solid gold borne by all the great men. But they also described the desolate scenes on certain other festivals, besmirched by the ritual sacrifice of criminals and prisoners of war: the widespread sense of horror, the "doleful cries" of women, the stupefying clamor of the "death drums and horns," the clothes of the great officials stained with blood indicating that they had participated in the executions.[5] Such was the extraordinary impression conveyed by one of the most remarkable, as it was also among the richest and the most powerful, of all the states of Africa.

In the middle of the nineteenth century Ashanti was capable of making its ascendency felt over an area of more than one hundred twenty-five thousand square miles in extent, an area that embraced most of modern Ghana and that was reckoned to contain three to five million people. At the heart of this rambling empire lay the group of little Akan states that had come together toward the end of the seventeenth century under the leadership of the chief of Kumasi to form the Ashanti Union. Beyond this nucleus lay other Akan states conquered in the eighteenth century and reduced to the status of provinces within the Ashanti empire. More remote still from the capital were a number of non-Akan states, such as Dagomba, that had been forced after defeat in war to pay regular tribute to the *asantehene*.

At first the *asantehene* was regarded as no more than *primus inter pares* among the chiefs of the Union. In the nineteenth century some of these chiefs who bore the title *abrempon,* usually translated as "duke," particularly those of Juaben, Bekwai, and Mampong, still retained very great power. Within their own territories they were virtually supreme, but they owed allegiance to the *asantehene* and were bound to provide him with tribute and fighting men.

Three factors served to hold the Union together in its early days: the common interest of all the states in united military action, the political ability of the early *asantehenes,* and the steadily growing prestige that surrounded them as guardians of the Golden Stool, the sacred object that was held to contain the soul of the Ashanti people. The steady run of victories achieved throughout the eighteenth century served to strengthen the *asantehenes'* position and led them toward the end of that century to embark on a series of reforms designed to strengthen their own personal power and to provide the expanding empire with an efficient administrative superstructure.

As rulers of Kumasi the *asantehenes* were assisted by a number of hereditary local chiefs known as captains. Newly conquered provinces were placed under the supervision of these chiefs and not added to the territories of the *abrempon.* In order to keep a check on these captains, the *asantehenes* began the practice of appointing their own nominees, chosen on account of their ability and drawn from no single section of society, to the great offices of state. These appointed chiefs owed their office entirely to the *asantehene* and so could be "destooled"—each chief had a stool as symbol of his office—at will. Certain offices tended to remain in the hands of the same families, whose members came to acquire a tradition of public service. Thus, by the middle of the nineteenth century Ashanti possessed the rudiments of a bureaucracy with an exchequer staffed by Muslims scribes, a substantial diplomatic service, and a corps of administrators appointed to act as resident commissioners in the conquered provinces.

To maintain his officials the *asantehene* had at his disposal a considerable range of revenues: tribute from the subject states, poll tax and death duties paid by the people of Kumasi, tolls levied on merchants, and the profits derived from royal industries—the king had his own gold mines worked by slaves—and from trading operations. Whenever possible taxes were required to be paid in gold. Lacking gold, some of the tributary states offered other produce—livestock, foodstuffs, European trade goods, or slaves. In some years the northern tributary, Dagomba, was expected to supply two thousand slaves and had to employ mercenary horsemen, Zaberma from the borders of the Sahara, to mount the raids needed to acquire this amount.

Ashanti never built up a regular army, but since all able-bodied men were liable to military service, it could always put into the field very substantial forces equipped to a considerable extent with firearms. To strengthen and protect their own position the *asantehenes* established a personal bodyguard or security force commanded by members of the royal family.

One of the most striking features of the Ashanti system of government was the comparative absence of serious disputes over the succession. A new *asantehene* was chosen by the queen mother assisted by senior chiefs from a number of possible royal candidates. Despite the awe with which he was surrounded no *asantehene* could be regarded as a remote "divine king." His position compelled him to act as a hardworking head of state, but he was never an absolute despot. It was one of the firm principles of the Akan system of government that a chief who offended against the customs of his people should be subject to destoolment. Even the *asantehene* had to bear this in mind; indeed, two nineteenth-century rulers of Ashanti were removed for this reason. But most *asantehenes* appear to have been remarkably able men. "The King's manners," an Englishman wrote in 1817 of the *asantehene* Osei Bonsu, "are a happy mixture of dignity and affability. He excels in courtesy, is wisely inquisitive and candid in his comparisons: war, legislature, and mechanisms were his favorite topics in our private conversations." [6]

It was Ashanti's misfortune to become involved during the course of the nineteenth century in a long series of wars with an outside power that could, when pressed, dispose of forces far more formidable than all the war bands of the great forest kingdom. By Englishmen of the time the Ashanti wars were regarded as a struggle between civilization and barbarism, humanitarianism and savagery. Certainly, there was a sharp conflict of cultures, but beneath the ideological overtones one can detect a more familiar pattern—the political difficulties that invariably arise when rival imperialisms find themselves in uneasy juxtaposition.

✡ THE AUTOCRATIC KINGDOM OF DAHOMEY

In area, in population, and in natural resources the nineteenth-century kingdom of Dahomey was far inferior to its great neighbor Ashanti. It extended over not much more than twenty thousand square miles—a much smaller area than that of its successor-state, the modern Republic of Dahomey. Its population did not exceed a quarter of a million, and its territory, lying within that part of Guinea where a savanna-type vegetation reaches to the sea, was entirely lacking in such products as gold and kola nuts, which contributed so much to Ashanti's prosperity. Nevertheless, this modestly endowed kingdom developed a quite remarkable set of institutions that marked it out as one of the outstanding African states of the nineteenth century.

Two features of Dahomey's political system—the royal corps of women warriors, the notorious Amazones, and the "Annual Customs" at which numbers of slaves were sacrificed—made a particularly deep impression on contemporary Europeans. Seen in isolation the Amazones appear grotesque, the Annual Customs horrifying. They can be properly understood only when taken as parts of a highly elaborate polity.

The kingdom of Dahomey had grown rapidly from a small chiefdom founded by a single lineage, the Agasuvi, in the mid-seventeenth century on the Abomey plateau lying about fifty miles inland. The Agasuvi expanded first by defeating all the petty chiefdoms in their neighborhood, then by conquering the more substantial polities of the coast. Until the 1820's the kingdom was forced to accept the hegemony of the great Yoruba state of Oyo; indeed, the widespread fear of Oyo was one of the forces that helped to bind the heterogeneous ethnic groups of the new kingdom together under the leadership of the kings of Dahomey. These kings presented a remarkable line of rulers, famed not only for their martial prowess but also for their shrewdness as political innovators. They dispensed with the form of succession practiced in neighboring chiefdoms whereby brother succeeded brother—a form that involved the constant risk of fratricidal strife—and established the rule that a king should choose as his heir the son he deemed most fit to fill the kingly office. At the same time they developed the practice of excluding from posts of political importance all other members of the royal clan. These princes and princesses whose numbers rose in time to several thousand were well provided for and lived a life of luxurious and innocuous leisure. In this way the dynasty was able to secure a measure of internal stability that contrasted sharply with the disturbances experienced by neighboring polities. Between 1650 and 1889 the average length of reign for the kings of Dahomey was no less than twenty-four years; in neighboring states the average reign rarely lasted longer than a decade.

Royal authority was strengthened still further by the development of an unusual form of court service. The palace of the kings of Dahomey at their capital Abomey contained as many as eight thousand people, all of them, with the exception of a few eunuchs, women. These women, most of whom were figuratively known as the "king's wives," fulfilled a variety of functions. One important group made up the corps of Amazones who formed the royal bodyguard and provided a substantial part of the national army. Masculine in their physique—one sardonic European visitor who saw the Amazones on the march described them as "old, ugly and square-built frows trudging grumpily along" [7]—these formidable females put at the disposal of the kings of Dahomey a force on whose loyalty they could rely completely. Other women in the palace were given the task of supervising all the officials of any importance in the kingdom, keeping a close check on their behavior and acting as intermediaries between them and the king. These "outside" officials were all drawn from the clans of commoners. In theory each of them owed his appointment to the king; in practice many of the great offices of state tended to be hereditary in certain families. At their head was a small group of ministers who served the king as his principal advisers.

The Atlantic slave trade provided the rulers of Dahomey, at least until the middle of the nineteenth century, with the opportunity of acquiring the surplus wealth needed to maintain the royal clan, the palace women, and the great officials. Unlike Ashanti, Dahomey was in direct contact with European traders whose activities were closely supervised by one of the three great ministers of state. To the north and west of the kingdom lay a multitude of petty polities whose peoples became the victims of the "man-hunting" expeditions mounted by the army of Dahomey every dry season. Apart from the Amazones, the army was made up of local levies. Numbering about seven thousand men and five thousand women, the army was regarded by some observers as the best organized fighting force in West Africa.

The unity of the kingdom was given visual expression in the ceremonies that accompanied the long drawn-out festivities known to Europeans as the "Customs." The Customs which were attended by people from all parts of Dahomey involved every aspect of the state—political, judicial, economic, and religious. The festivities gave the king an opportunity to impress his subjects and foreign visitors by his wealth (though great by West African standards, this was less, in the opinion of the famous traveler Richard Burton, than that of "any petty hill rajah in India" [8]), to receive tribute and pledges of allegiance from local officials, to decide major law cases, to congratulate, promote, and reward his most faithful subjects, and to perform those rites needed to ensure the good will of his ancestors, the great kings of Dahomey. These rites involved the sacrifice of several score of human victims, usually condemned criminals and war captives. "You have seen me kill many men at my Customs," an eighteenth-century ruler is reported as saying to a European visitor. "This gives a grandeur to my Customs, far beyond the display of fine things which I buy. This makes my enemies fear me and gives me such a name in the bush. Besides, if I should neglect this indispensable duty, would my ancestors suffer me to live? Would they not trouble me day and night and say that I sent nobody to serve them?" [9]

Dahomey has often been described as the most highly centralized state of its size in West Africa and its ruler regarded as possessing absolute powers. To see the great ministers of state "wallowing in the mud" in the royal presence was to have the impression of absolute power seemingly confirmed. But though the king could dismiss individual officials, "collectively," as Burton pointed out, the ministers and the war captains were "too strong for him"; "without their cordial cooperation he would soon cease to reign." Great though the king's powers might be, he lacked the means to intervene in many of the affairs of his subjects. "Except in the case of serfs, slaves and captives, there is throughout Dahomey, and I may say Africa, more of real liberty and equality—I will not add fraternity—than in any other quarter of the globe, and the presence of the servile renders the free men only freer and more equal." [10]

❧ IBO VILLAGE-GROUPS AND THE "TRADING EMPIRE" OF ARO CHUKU

In the nineteenth century the Ibo people had no sense of national unity. Culturally, they were divided into a number of groups, differing from one another in dialect and in certain aspects of their social organization. Politically, they presented the spectacle of a mass of petty polities each independent of its neighbors but preserving the same basic form throughout Ibo country.

Each of these polities consisted of what has been termed a "village-group" made up of a number of villages whose member-families were linked together by descent from a common ancestor, by worship of a particular guardian deity, and by use of a central market. These village-groups, with populations varying from a few hundred to several thousand, were the largest political units in Ibo country. In contrast to the hierarchical structure of the societies of the neighboring Yoruba and the Edo of Benin, Ibo polities were remarkably democratic and egalitarian. Each village possessed its own council of elders, but matters of importance to the whole group were brought before a wider assembly, where every man had a right to contribute to the debate, special attention being paid to the words of men of wealth, valor, and ability. In some Ibo communities local affairs were dominated by associations of titleholders, in practice village plutocracies, for only those rich enough to pay the fees required for the purchase of a title could join them. Among certain Ibo groups age-sets made up of men or boys of the same age were highly developed, particular sets being made responsible for certain public duties —clearing paths, policing markets, or collecting fines. But even more important in preserving the orderly life of the community than institutions such as these was the intricate system of rules and customs backed up by strong religious sanctions that led people to regard criminal acts as offences against the earth spirit or against the ancestors of the village.

Relations between neighboring villages usually took the form of a state of armed neutrality, interspersed by periods of open warfare. But though villages might frequently attack one another, neighboring polities were usually so evenly matched in arms and equipment that it was virtually impossible for one village to overwhelm another. There were, moreover, a number of other factors that served to ameliorate this seemingly anarchic situation. Marriage customs encouraged intercourse between village-groups, for men were required to marry outside their own community. Markets, too, brought people of different groups together and served not only as places of business but also as social centers. The intricate mesh of personal relationships thus created—of business contracts and family ties—served to soften the acerbity of local conflicts.

There were, too, among the Ibo a few great religious centers whose influence was felt over a wide area. The most famous of these was Aro Chuku, lying on the eastern edge of Ibo country, the home of an oracle whom Europeans came to term "the Long Juju." To Aro Chuku, as to Delphi among the ancient Greeks, men came from far afield to seek the oracle's decisions in settling intervillage disputes. The local clan, the Aro, acted as agents of the oracle, traveling widely to advertise its powers, serving as guides to pilgrims and suppliants, setting up their own small colonies in important villages, and taking a keen interest in trade. To assist them the Aro began recruiting bands of professional warriors from other Ibo groups; villages that dared to question the oracle's decisions were attacked by these mercenaries and given a savage demonstration of the oracle's power. With such a force at their disposal, with their "colonies" established in a large number of Ibo communities and with their prestige as servants of the oracle giving them freedom to pass unmolested along routes barred to other travelers by intervillage feuds, the Aro were able to build up a highly profitable "trading empire." They became the great middlemen of the eastern half of Ibo country, dealing in slaves, palm oil, and European manufactures, and doing business with that other enterprising group of middlemen, the traders of the coastal states. But though they acquired great influence in the affairs of many Ibo communities, they made no attempt to build up a formal political kingdom. To construct an administrative superstructure over the mass of vigorous, self-willed Ibo polities was a task that called for the possession of a more formidable power than the priests, traders, and warriors of the Long Juju could ever hope to muster.

THE TRADING POLITIES OF THE EASTERN NIGER DELTA

Wealthy and powerful, enriched by the "comey" (customs duties) paid by European traders and rendered formidable by their fleets of war canoes, the trading polities of the eastern Niger delta—Brass, Kalabari, Bonny, and later Opobo—presented a striking contrast to the modest, egalitarian village-groups of their immediate hinterland. At one time the political system of these delta peoples had been very similar to that of neighboring Ibo communities. Their mid-nineteenth-century constitution was the product of three centuries of intensive commercial experience.

The "canoe-house"—to use the term suggested by a modern social anthropologist [11]—formed the basic unit of these polities. Such a unit was made up of freemen and slaves—many of the former being members of the original local lineages, most of the latter being aliens brought to the coast from the interior—knit together under the strict authority of the head of the house and so organized that they formed both an effective trading corporation and a fighting force capable of manning one or more war canoes. Each polity contained a number of such "houses" under the supreme authority of a chief to whom European traders applied the title of king. This ruler was drawn from a single royal lineage and derived his power partly from his headship of a major "house," partly from the prestige he acquired through his skill in dealing with European traders, partly from the ritual with which his office was invested. But unlike other African monarchs, the rulers of the delta polities had no hierarchy of officials at their disposal. The peculiar political conditions prevailing in the delta obviated the need for a corps of administrators.

The central territory of each polity was a compact area containing the capital—a contemporary description of Bonny as "an assemblage of mean houses with winding foot tracks for streets" [12] might serve for all the delta towns—together with its adjoining "river" (an estuary capable of taking ocean-going ships) and its outlying villages, fishing grounds, and plantations. Every polity also extended its influence over the neighboring creeks and waterways stretching northward to reach the firm land beyond the swamps. No attempt was made to administer the communities that lived within this sphere of influence; it was sufficient to ensure that they did not trade directly either with the Europeans on the coast or with merchants from rival delta polities. The delta peoples were middlemen rather than producers. A complete monopoly of trade within its own sphere of influence was the objective of every substantial polity.

Within the polity "houses" were responsible for their own internal administration. Matters of concern to the whole community were discussed openly in a general council in which the "house" chiefs naturally played a leading part or more intimately in the sessions of "secret societies" which brought together all the leading men of the polity and provided them with a body of younger men who could act as their agents.

Few societies in mid-nineteenth-century Africa were so forcefully exposed to the processes of change as the trading communities of the Niger delta. Among these tough, resourceful businessmen the atmosphere was one of vigorous competition, of violence between polity and polity, of intense rivalry between "house" and "house." In the eighteenth century "house" chiefs owed their positions largely to their birth; in the nineteenth century it became increasingly common for enterprising men, even of slave origin, to attract followers by their prowess in war and their skill in trade and so to rise to chiefly rank. Indeed, in the 1860's one "slave chief," Jaja of Bonny, was able to establish his own kingdom at Opobo.

Dangerous exposure to alien pressures was the price paid by the delta middlemen for their lucrative contacts with the outside world. The delta monarchies had been called into existence to meet the demands of European commerce; in the second half of the nineteenth century their independence was undermined by pressures of a different kind—the imperatives of British naval officers of the antislavery squadron and the interventions of British consuls in support of the interests of British traders.

ALIEN SETTLEMENTS: SENEGAL, SIERRA LEONE, LIBERIA, AND THE GOLD COAST

The history of West Africa in the latter half of the nineteenth century showed that the alien settlements established at various points on the coast had a greater capacity for expansion than did any other class of polity in the region. As late as 1850, however, it would have required remarkable prescience to have foretold such a development. Both in population and in area all the European coastal settlements were extremely modest and the metropolitan governments that controlled them did not appear to have any desire to take up expensive new commitments in an area of little value to their economies. Nevertheless, these small colonial polities became the nuclei around which some of the modern states of West Africa were formed; the political structures of Senegal, Sierra Leone, Liberia, and Ghana owe much to the patterns of government and society whose lineaments were clearly visible by 1850.

In that year the French colony of Senegal consisted of the town of St. Louis, the island of Gorée, and a number of trading posts (*escales*) on the Senegal River. The total population was no more than eighteen thousand, of whom only three hundred were Europeans. Before the emancipation of slaves in 1848 the African population was divided into three groups: mulattoes and freed slaves, "free" Africans (traders, artisans, and boatmen, drawn from neighboring territories), and slaves. A census held in St. Louis and Gorée in 1826 gave the number of these three groups as thirteen hundred and fifty, two thousand, and twelve thousand, respectively. The mulattos, freed slaves, and "free" Africans were known as *habitants*. Some of them, particularly the mulattos, had become completely assimilated to the French way of life; assimilation was carried further by frequent marriages between Frenchmen and mulatto women.

St. Louis and Gorée had been in French hands since the seventeenth century; they were among the most substantial European bases in tropical Africa. But the colony as a whole suffered from two fundamental weaknesses, one economic the other military. With the abolition of the slave trade gum became Senegal's main export; but the price of gum was falling on the world market and the trade, carried on at *escales* on the Senegal River, was subject to many local difficulties. The people on either side of the river—the Moors to the north, the Wolofs and others to the south—were sufficiently highly organized not only to interrupt the trade when they chose but also to contain other French activities. Thus, they completely disrupted the attempt made by the French after 1817 to establish plantation settlements outside St. Louis. Indeed they were strong enough to be regarded as a threat to the entire French presence. The parliamentary government of Louis Philippe was unwilling to meet the cost of reinforcing the modest colonial garrison. It required a change of regime in Paris—the establishment of the Second Empire of Napoleon III—before Senegal received the troops needed to permit a policy of vigorous expansion.

The British colony of Sierra Leone occupied a territory of about four hundred square miles, comprising the peninsula of Sierra Leone with a number of islands and coastal districts to the north and south. Founded in 1787 as a settlement for freed slaves and financed and administered by a group of English philanthropists, Sierra Leone was taken over by the government as a Crown Colony in 1808. At that time it had a population of two thousand black settlers drawn from Britain, Canada, and Jamaica. By 1850 the population had risen to forty thousand as a result of the influx of "liberated Africans," men, women, and children rescued by the British navy from foreign slave ships in West African waters.

In the middle of the nineteenth century Sierra Leone presented a clearly stratified society. A small group of Englishmen, numbering little more than a hundred, occupied the most important positions in government, commerce, and the church. Descendants of the original settlers formed a local aristocracy anxious to adopt all the manifestations of the culture of Victorian England and contemptuous of the "liberated Africans" whom they regarded as barbarous social inferiors. These "liberated Africans" formed by far the largest element of the population; among them were to be found representatives of almost every ethnic group in western Africa, with people of Yoruba and Ibo stock predominating. Settled for the most part in newly founded villages—villages to which the local authorities gave such sterling British names as Wellington, Hastings, and York—under the paternal supervision of Anglican missionaries, the more enterprising of the "liberated Africans" responded eagerly to the opportunities of their new environment, accepted the religion and the education offered by their benefactors, turned to trade, acquired property in Freetown, and in the case of the most successful achieved a substance and a status sufficient to put them in the same class as the old-established settlers. Finally, occupying the lowest place in Sierra Leone society came a steadily increasing number of local immigrants, drawn from the people of the interior and attracted to the colony by the opportunities of trade and employment to be found there. Over the flourishing urban community of Freetown, the villages of the peninsula, and the outlying districts was laid the modest superstructure of British colonial administration. A governor, usually an army officer, was assisted by a council of officials and nominated members—the division of the council into two parts, executive and legislative, did not occur until 1863 —and a military force was provided by a few companies of the West Indian Regiment, attempts to raise a local militia never having proved successful. The annual revenue brought in about £25,000 in the early 1850's and always needed to be supplemented by a grant from the home government.

The contrast between Sierra Leone and Liberia went deeper than the obvious fact that one was a British colony, the other an independent republic strongly influenced by American culture and with a constitution closely modeled on that of the United States. In 1850 Liberia consisted of a number of settlements strung along three hundred miles of coast. Nowhere did its authority, asserted through treaties with local chiefs, penetrate more than forty-five miles into the interior. Between 1822 and 1867 it received just under twenty thousand immigrants, less than a third of whom were Africans rescued from slave ships. Thus, though Liberia's territory was larger than Sierra Leone's, the total number of settlers, put at three thousand in 1847, was very much smaller, and the proportion of immigrants who had been born outside Africa very much higher. Except for the color of their skins the settlers had absolutely nothing in common with the local people. They had come to Liberia not out of any sentimental desire to return to a long-lost homeland but in the hope of being able to build up on African soil a society that would allow them to enjoy the rights denied to them in the country of their birth. In every aspect of their culture—religion, language, education, dress—they emphasized the difference between themselves and the "tribal Africans" who surrounded them; indeed, the more successful Liberians deliberately thought to model their way of life on that of their former masters, the slave-owning planters of the southern United States. Hardly less alien to Africa than the colonies established by European powers, Liberia inevitably developed a form of government that had more in common with European colonial administration than with indigenous African polities.

The British "forts and settlements" on the Gold Coast had a checkered administrative history behind them. Founded as trading posts in the seventeenth century, they had been administered by the monopolistic Royal African Company until 1750, by an association of independent British traders, the Company of Merchants Trading to West Africa, from 1750 to 1821, by the governor of Sierra Leone from 1821 to 1828, and by a Committee of Merchants, supported by a modest subsidy from the British government, from 1828 to 1843. Finally, in 1843 the Colonial Office assumed direct responsibility for the Gold Coast; after a period of remote control from Sierra Leone the settlements were made into a separate colony under its own governor in 1850. British responsibilities were not confined merely to the maintenance of a number of antiquated and unprofitable trade castles disposed along two hundred miles of coast; during the 1820's and 1830's many of the petty chiefdoms in the vicinity of the forts had come to look to the British first for protection against invasion from Ashanti, then for assistance in settling local disputes. In 1844 a number of Fante chiefs put their signatures to a document known as "the Bond," in which they acknowledged British "power and jurisdiction" and agreed that criminal cases should be tried before British "judicial officers" acting in concert with the local chiefs and "moulding the Customs of the Country to the general Principles of British Law." [13] The area regarded by the British as "Protected Territory" lacked well-defined limits, but it stretched at least fifty miles inland, included a large number of hitherto independent chiefdoms, and had a population reckoned to number four hundred thousand. Not only was British suzerainty ill-defined, but the British presence on the Coast was extremely modest, and the local administration depended on a number of Western-educated Africans, mostly of mulatto origin, to fill important posts in the service.

Unimposing though all these West African settlements must have appeared to any contemporary observer conscious of the massive establishments built up by Europeans in other continents, their political significance could be properly assessed only when they were regarded as places subject to the dynamic influence of powerful pressure groups in their metropolitan countries. Pressure groups of two different types—one concerned with humanitarian ends, the other with commercial objectives —were of particular importance. In Britain a variety of agencies expressed the Victorian public's passionate loathing of the slave trade and made it possible for the British government to maintain—at considerable expense for the British taxpayer—a squadron of a dozen warships in West African waters, a force that represented one of the most substantial instruments of power in contemporary Africa. At the same time the practical concerns of individual French and British merchants led the two metropolitan governments to interest themselves in the affairs of parts of the region well beyond the bounds of their formal administration. Moreover, as Britain and France grew steadily richer, so the resources their governments were prepared to set aside for use in West Africa gradually increased. No indigenous polity could hope to rival the military force, the financial reserves, and the far-flung commercial interests that Britain and France, technologically the two most advanced countries in the mid-nineteenth-century world, were beginning to display in West Africa.

CHAPTER XVII

Equatorial African Polities about 1850

✬ THE TEKE KINGDOM: EXTREME DECENTRALIZATION

The Teke inhabit the bare and sandy plateau country to the north of Stanley Pool on the lower Congo. Here at least as early as 1500 they established a kingdom that later stretched over a thinly populated area about seventy-five thousand square miles in extent, a kingdom quite unlike the elaborately organized states of West Africa, for it exhibited so extreme a degree of decentralization that the term kingdom is hardly appropriate and it seems more satisfactory to place it in the category of demi-states rather than of states.

The majority of the Teke have no traditions of migration and appear to have been settled in their present area for a very long time. Certain small groups, however, are known to have moved into Teke country from the south and east in the course of recent centuries. How the Teke kingdom came to be founded is not known, but local traditions give the Teke and the Kongo peoples a common ancestry, and it seems likely that the Teke were involved in the same process of political change that led to the emergence of the neighboring kingdoms of Kongo, Loango, and Kakongo.

In the nineteenth century the basic unit of the kingdom was the village chiefdom, each petty chief having within his domain his own village and a number of scattered hamlets. These were administered by headmen who possessed family ties with the inhabitants. New hamlets were constantly being founded by independent-minded heads of families.

Chieftainship was confined to certain noble families, the office usually passing from father to son. The local chief held a court in his village and collected tribute for the king, but his most important duties were of a ritual nature. The Teke believed that within each domain there dwelt an earth spirit; by attending to this spirit the chief ensured prosperity for his people.

The village chief occupied the lowest rank in a hierarchy of chiefs. His superiors were distinguished by the possession of a sacred basket (*nkobi*), which was regarded as the dwelling place of a more powerful spirit. The *nkobi* was kept in a shrine and attended by families of priests. A *nkobi* carried with it a special title for its possessor, each title having its own rank in the chiefly hierarchy. At the top stood two great chiefs, one for the south of the kingdom, the other for the north. These two chiefs passed on to the king the tribute collected in their areas. Each of them held a court beyond which there could be no further appeal to the king.

The king has been described as the "pope" of the Teke. He was the nation's supreme ritual expert, acting as the guardian of a hoard of sacred objects and holding communication with a spirit dwelling in the waterfalls of the Lefini River and regarded as the most powerful of all the spirits in the land. But the king's political powers were extremely modest. He appears to have possessed no special judicial authority, he had no strong bodyguard and no staff of officials at his disposal, his village was no larger than those of his greater chiefs, and he could only count on receiving tribute at irregular intervals. Moreover—and this was a source of fundamental weakness—among the Teke, kingship unlike chieftainship was not hereditary. Members of certain noble families were eligible to put themselves forward as candidates, the election being decided by a council which included many of the greatest chiefs. Obliged to some of his most powerful subjects for his election, dependent on their support if he wished to repel an enemy or curb a rebellion, the position of the Teke king was weaker than that of almost any other African ruler to whom a royal title could be applied.

ZANDE POLITIES: CONQUEST AND FISSION

The Zande, today numbering about half a million, were one of the most dynamic peoples of tropical Africa in the nineteenth century. The creators of a string of polities in the country that forms the watershed between the basins of the Congo and the Nile, they represented a constantly expanding agglomeration of many ethnic groups originally differing from one another in language and customs but molded into a common pattern by one dominant group, the Ambonu, under their ruling clan, the Avungara.

The Avungara myth of origin tells how a certain Kuramgbwa, a great hunter, attracted men to him by his prowess in the chase and by his skill as an arbitrator of disputes, came to be recognized as a chief, and was thus able to unite many different clans into a single people. His son, who is said to have invented the name Avungara, began to expand the kingdom by attacking neighboring peoples and appointing his own sons chiefs of conquered provinces. The subject peoples began rapidly to adopt the language and the customs of the conquerors who had settled in their midst. But Zande history does not present the steady consolidation of a large centralized state. Among the Zande the center never held. While a chief lived, his sons often went off with their followers to found new chiefdoms for themselves. At the death of a chief a fierce battle for succession often ended with the defeated party leaving the territory to create some new independent polity elsewhere. In a kingdom containing a number of dependent provinces local chiefs were constantly seeking occasions to revolt against their suzerain. Thus, the history of the Zande is in part a record of the constant spinning off of warrior bands to found new polities and of the emergence of a great number of independent kingdoms and chiefdoms. The German traveler Schweinfurth, who became in the 1870's one of the first Europeans to enter Zande country, counted no less than thirty-five "independent Chieftaincies" in the parts he visited.[1]

Each of these polities was ruled by a member of the Avungara clan; this gave to the Zande galaxy a measure of uniformity. The Avungara also provided the aristocracy of every chiefdom—an aristocracy which possessed many traits in common with the aristocracies of more complex societies, an intense interest in genealogy, a contempt for manual labor, a love of finery, and a passionate predilection for the gossip and intrigue of the court. In these petty courts the political life of the community centered: the rulers dispensed justice, kept their faithful bodyguard—the nucleus of their armed force—received the foreign traders, and asserted their monopoly over the trade in guns and ivory. In Zande society the bonds that held polities together were based on loyalty to persons rather than to institutions. There were no sacred regalia, no fixed capitals, no well-defined territorial boundaries. In such circumstances stability depended largely on the personality of the king or chief. Here the Avungara were remarkable for the quality of the rulers that sprang from their line. "The defiant, imperious bearing of the chiefs," wrote Schweinfurth, "alone constitutes their outward display. . . . The dread which they inspire is incredible." [2] But it was respect as well as fear that the Zande felt for their rulers. To their natural imperiousness the Avungara added, as a modern observer has noted, "courteous manners, cordiality, self-assurance, composure, reserve, reflectiveness and generosity," together with "intelligence and calm, sound judgment, firmness, astuteness and prudence." [3]

⁂ THE HUNTING BANDS OF THE MBUTI PYGMIES

"Imagine," wrote H. M. Stanley, the first outsider ever to describe the equatorial rain forest of the eastern Congo, "the whole of France and the Iberian peninsula closely packed with trees varying from 20 to 180 feet high, whose crests of foliage interlace and prevent any view of sky and sun." And he went on to evoke vividly the sensations produced by this primeval wilderness: "an awe of the forest rushed upon the soul and filled the mind . . . one became aware of its eerie strangeness, the absence of sunshine, its subdued light, and marvelled at the queer feeling of loneliness . . . it was as if one stood amid the inhabitants of another world." [4] For a period of time that may well stretch back for thousands of years this extraordinary environment, so oppressive, so repulsive to most outsiders, has been the cherished home of certain groups of Pygmy hunters.

Of these groups the Mbuti of the Ituri forest are the best known. First described by Stanley in 1890, they have been the subject of detailed study by modern social anthropologists, one of whom, Colin Turnbull, has presented a remarkably intimate account of the Mbuti way of life.[5] In the nineteenth century their hunting bands formed an important element in the pattern of polities of the eastern Congo, but the historian has a much more general reason for studying the political organization of these nomadic hunters, for it seems reasonable to assume that the present structure of these hunting bands provides some impression of a type of polity that must once, before the development of agricultural communities, have been common in many parts of Africa.

Today the Mbuti, who number about thirty-two thousand, form not only "the largest single group of Pygmy hunters and gatherers in Africa" but also "probably the purest in both the biological and cultural senses." [6] Unlike other Pygmies who intermarried with their Negro neighbors, the Mbuti remain sharply distinct from the groups of cultivators who have penetrated the Ituri forest both in their physical appearance and in their means of livelihood. Their food supply, though supplemented by the plantation crops obtained from the villagers, is still derived from the animals they hunt and the wide range of foodstuffs they collect in the fastnesses of the forest. Such an economy forces the Mbuti to lead a nomadic life, shifting their forest camps from one point to another of their hunting territory every few weeks.

Although the Mbuti possess a certain sense of common identity, today they are divided into three distinct linguistic groups, each group having derived its language from its Negroid neighbors, the Central Sudanic Mangbetu and Lese and the Bantu Bira. The Mbuti have also been divided into three cultural groups, one using the bow, a second the spear, and the third the net as the main implement for hunting. But in all the groups of the Mbuti the only form of political organization is the hunting band. These bands vary greatly in size, some containing as many as thirty nuclear families, others as few as three, the average band numbering about fifty men, women, and children. Most bands are made up of families derived from a variety of lineages; all of them are subject to the processes of fission or amalgamation with other bands. Within the band there is no chief or leader, no ritual specialist, no council of elders. But the band possesses a strong sense of solidarity, each of its members knowing that survival in the forest depends on constant cooperation among all the individuals in the band. Thus, decisions are reached in the most democratic manner possible as the result of discussions around the campfire. Each band has its own hunting territory whose boundaries, defined by obvious natural features such as rivers, are recognized by neighboring bands. Even today these territories are regarded as providing ample grounds for the needs of any one band, and thus there appears to have been little cause for interband conflict.

Negroid cultivators, organized in village communities, probably began to move into the Ituri forest three or four hundred years ago. In time a symbiotic relationship was established with the Mbuti. Bands of hunters found it convenient to attach themselves to village-groups that had settled themselves in their territories, assisting the villagers by acting as spies or scouts in war and providing them with game and other forest products in return for plantation crops or metal implements such as arrowheads. Though the villagers liked to regard the Mbuti as their dependents, it was the Pygmies who gained most from the relationship. "The tribes of the Central African forest have much to bear," Stanley noted, "from these little, fierce people who glue themselves to their clearings, flatter them when well-fed, but oppress them with their extortions and robberies." [7] In their social structure and their technology the villagers were clearly far more advanced than the hunters; but to the villagers the forest has always been an alien environment regarded with dread and as peopled with malevolent spirits. The Mbuti consider the forest, so bountiful to them in all its gifts, the manifestation of a benevolent deity: they refer to it as "father" or "mother" and talk of the affection that it feels for them. Confident that the forest will always provide their basic needs, their lives are marked by what Turnbull has called "a general lack of crisis." [8] The absence of external stresses and of political and economic pressures would seem to explain why both the economy and the political structure of many Mbuti communities have changed so little over the centuries.

✸ THE INDEPENDENT VILLAGES OF THE AMBA

Many of the peoples of Equatorial Africa were members of societies in which the village community represented the only form of political unit. One such society was that of the Amba whose territory, Bwamba, is today bisected by the Uganda-Congo border. The Amba live in a spectacular setting on the floor of the western Rift Valley with the snowcapped peaks of the Ruwenzori to the east, a high escarpment to the west, the grasslands that lead to Lake Albert to the north, and the great Ituri forest to the south.

Today the Amba are strongly influenced by their neighbors, the people of Toro. But in physique and general culture they are much closer to the other Bantu groups of the Congo basin than to the interlacustrine Bantu living farther east. Four languages—three Bantu, one Sudanic, the latter being spoken today only by a few hundred people—are found in Bwamba, all of them being mutually unintelligible. The inhabitants of any one village all speak the same language, but their neighbors may speak another language, for Bwamba is not divided into blocks of territory possessing linguistic unity.

The floor of the Rift Valley is cut by transversal valleys formed by streams flowing down from the Ruwenzori. The Amba sited their compact villages on the ridges between these minor valleys on land that had first to be cleared of forest. Each village was an independent political unit. Its members were grouped around a single lineage and most of the men could trace their descent from a common ancestor five or six generations back. But no village was completely self-contained. Men were required to seek wives in other villages, and sometimes a wife's male relatives were invited to settle in the husband's village. It was, indeed, an asset for a village to attract outsiders in such a way; by so doing it increased its own population and added to its fighting strength.

Within the village polities there was no chief and no regular council of elders. Disputes between villagers were settled at informal meetings in which every man might express his opinion. Should a man from one village be killed by a man from another village, there was no higher body to whom the relatives could appeal. As such a death had to be avenged by the killing of someone from the murderer's village, a blood feud was started, a petty war in which the two rival bodies often sought the support of other villages. Further deaths in these intervillage fights only served to prolong the feud, which might drag on for years.

Intervillage warfare was a constant feature of Amba life. But no village ever attempted to conquer its neighbors. There existed, indeed, no incentive for conquest: land was abundant, captives—if held as slaves

—could not be prevented from escaping, and there was little in the way of booty—for the Amba possessed no cattle—to excite the victors. With their neighbors the Konjo, who lived on the slopes of the Ruwenzori, there was little contact, except for the purposes of trade. The most powerful external pressure came from the kingdom of Toro lying to the east of the Ruwenzori. The sophisticated inhabitants of Toro regarded the Amba as savages who filed their teeth and ate revolting foods; in the late nineteenth century they began raiding Bwamba, and their influence steadily increased after the British occupation, when Toro officials were given posts in Amba country.

CHAPTER XVIII

Central African Polities about 1850

✻ THE PORTUGUESE COLONIES IN ANGOLA AND MOZAMBIQUE

For the Portuguese, as for the Arabs, the age of their greatest activity in Africa lay, by the middle of the nineteenth century, far in the past. "Lord of the conquest, navigation and commerce of Ethiopia, India, Arabia and Persia," Manuel I of Portugal had called himself in 1501, and the exploits of his countrymen in the succeeding century had gone far to justify that splendidly grandiloquent title. The Portuguese had ringed the Moroccan coast with their military posts, colonized Madeira, the Cape Verde islands, and São Tomé, engrossed a large part of the trade of both West and East Africa, made themselves a major force in the affairs of three of the greatest African states of their day, Ethiopia, Kongo, and Monomotapa, captured much of the spice trade of the East Indies, and laid the foundations of a great new country, Brazil, with their settlements on the coast of South America. Yet by 1850 Portuguese possessions in Africa amounted to no more than the two bankrupt and decaying colonies of Angola and Mozambique together with a few small posts in West Africa and some of the principal islands of the eastern Atlantic.

It became fashionable for the more vigorous colonial powers of the late nineteenth-century world to take a censorious view of Portuguese activities in Africa. A greater awareness of the particular pressures to which the Portuguese were subject might have induced a more sympathetic attitude. Portugal was a small country—its population was three and a half million in 1850—and a poor one. In 1861 the government's total revenue was no more than three million pounds, an amount which had hardly changed in the past thirty years. Its politics had been extremely unstable: foreign invasion, military rule, revolution, civil war— Portugal had experienced all of these in the first half of the nineteenth century. The political and economic weaknesses of Portuguese governments made them vulnerable to foreign pressure from great powers such as France and England; it also meant that they lacked both the money to develop their African colonies and the force to control their colonists.

There is another factor that has to be considered when judging the Portuguese. Their activities in Africa between 1550 and 1850 can be properly understood only when they are seen in conjunction with the development of Brazil. For European colonists Brazil offered much greater attractions than any Portuguese territory in Africa. There were more favorable lands for settlement, the native population made up of Amerindians was more primitive than almost any African people and it was also comparatively sparse, and the interior of Brazil contained—so the Portuguese discovered to their astonishment and delight in the 1690's— large quantities of alluvial gold. No wonder that Angola found it impossible to attract settlers, no wonder that most of the population of the Portuguese African territories consisted of social castaways, political exiles, criminals, ne'er-do-wells, when such an alternative existed for men of enterprise and talent. In the 1850's Brazil had a population of eight million, of whom five million were free men, the majority of Portuguese origin. In 1845 the total white population of Angola was put at just over eighteen hundred, while the number of whites in Mozambique must have been even smaller.

But if Brazil, until its independence in 1825, was the "milch-cow" of the Portuguese crown, Africa, especially Angola, was the "black mother" of Brazil. The whole economy of Brazil was dependent on African slaves to provide labor for the sugar plantations and the mines. "Our African colonies," João de Andrade Corvo, a Portuguese colonial minister, wrote in the 1870's, "were little more than parks for the production and creation of slaves." [1] The poverty of the Portuguese government and the insatiable demands of Brazil for slave labor were the factors that shaped the administration and social structure of Portugal's African colonies until the 1850's, when the slave trade reached its last decade.

It was a long-established tradition that the Portuguese Crown should exercise a tight control over its colonies. The Crown's representative in Angola and Mozambique was the governor. Some governors were able and honorable men who tried to develop their territories in an enlightened manner. But they faced insuperable difficulties. Their term of office lasted only a few years, and they were subject to fierce local pressure. In 1839 a governor of Angola who attempted to enforce the home government's legislation against the slave trade was thrown out of the country by the whites of Luanda. In these circumstances most governors regarded their service in the colonies as an opportunity for personal enrichment. Some proved extremely successful at feathering their own nests: one, a governor of Mozambique, was reported to have made £800,000 from the slave trade.

Local officials, army officers, and traders took their cue from the men at the top. "What do I care for this country?" a merchant in Tete on the Zambezi remarked to Livingstone. "All I want is to make money as soon as possible and then go to Bombay to enjoy it." [2] The meager salaries received by the servants of government made corruption inevitable; the power at their disposal made exploitation easy. Up-country the territories were divided into captaincies (*presidios*), each with a military post as its headquarters and a small garrison to keep order. To these posts local chiefs brought tribute, usually in the form of slaves.

In the valley of the Zambezi Portuguese and Goan traders, some of whom had come to the country as soldiers, acquired great estates known as *prazos*. Until late in the nineteenth century the *prazeros* were the lords of Zambezia. Many of them lived in great luxury, protected by private armies of well-armed retainers. Although they acknowledged the over-all authority of the Portuguese Crown, their wealth and power made it easy for them to disregard the Crown's local representatives.

In Angola there were no *prazeros*. Instead, traders settled beyond the bounds of the colony at the capitals of local rulers. At Kasanje, for example, forty Portuguese traders had their homes in the 1850's. From these bases they sent native agents, known as *pombeiros,* to carry European trade goods deep into the interior and to bring back slaves and ivory.

Very few European women chose to come to Angola and Mozambique. (Benguela, the second town of Angola, contained only one white woman in 1845.) Inevitably, therefore, Portuguese traders and officials took African wives and mistresses. Miscegenation eased race relations. "Nowhere else in Africa," so Livingstone, one of the harshest critics of Portuguese rule, noted in Angola in 1854, "is there so much good will between Europeans and Africans as here." [3]

The Cross and the Sword were the symbols of Portuguese authority in the great days of the empire. The Cross was sadly lacking in the mid-nineteenth-century African colonies. There had been a time in the seventeenth century when a hundred missionaries were at work in Angola and Mozambique. By 1850 there were only a dozen priests in the two territories. Their reputation was shocking—"greedy, lustful, rebellious, and libertine" were the epithets applied by an Angolan bishop to his subordinate clergy in 1773—their influence negligible.

Oxen stalled within the stately walls of Luanda's cathedral, the once great fortress of Sofala garrisoned by convicts, the town a huddle of miserable shanties—sights such as these seemed to Livingstone and other

English travelers clear evidence of the Portuguese colonies' "miserable state of decay." Yet individual Portuguese—in particular the lawless *prazeros* of Zambezia and the bush traders of Angola—showed themselves men of courage, resource, and tenacity. Indeed, it might be said that no other Europeans had succeeded in adapting themselves to the rigors of tropical Africa more effectively than had the Portuguese.

🦋 KONGO: THE POLITICS OF FRAGMENTATION

In the sixteenth century the kingdom of Kongo was one of the most substantial states in tropical Africa; by the nineteenth it had fallen apart into a multitude of independent chiefdoms. Other great African states—the Western Sudanic empires of Mali and Songhai and both Egypt and Ethiopia at certain periods in their history—had experienced a similar process of fragmentation, but nowhere is this process so well documented as in the history of Kongo.

The kingdom of Kongo came into existence in the fourteenth century when a conquering group moved south from the Congo River onto the plateau that now forms part of northern Angola. The invaders allied themselves by marriage with the main lineages of the region, their leader taking to wife a woman of the priestly clan and thus securing the blessing of the supreme earth-priest of the old society.

By the end of the fifteenth century when the Portuguese first made contact with the kingdom Kongo covered an area of about forty thousand square miles. Its ruler, the *mani-Kongo*—*mani* was the title applied to all those holding positions of authority in the kingdom—had his court and capital at the town which later came to be known as San Salvador. The kingdom was divided into six provinces; these in turn were subdivided into districts, each district being made up of a number of villages. Villages were governed by headmen who were the leaders of local lineages; all higher posts were filled by appointment. The king nominated all but one or two of the provincial governors—the exceptions being in provinces where the governorship remained in the hands of local families—and some district chiefs. To these posts it was normal practice to nominate his closest relatives, which meant that he had to remove the nominees of his predecessor. Subordinate authorities paid taxes to their superiors, the higher officials bringing the products of their provinces and districts to the royal court at an annual ceremony, where they also renewed their oaths of allegiance. The king received a substantial revenue to maintain his court with its large company of officials, pages, craftsmen, soldiers, and musicians. During the sixteenth century Portuguese cultural influence gave the Kongolese court an exotic veneer: great men who were also Christian converts, were baptized with European names, took to

European dress, and even adopted European titles of nobility. But spectacular though the consequences of cultural intercourse with Europe might seem, they could not fundamentally transform the structure of the kingdom.

The great weakness of this structure lay in the regulations for succession to the throne. In the sixteenth century it was accepted that any male descendant of the great King Affonso I (1506–c.45) was eligible for consideration as a candidate. The new ruler was chosen by an electoral college made up of a dozen great officials, including after 1558 the king's Portuguese confessor. Candidates began canvassing for support long before the death of a reigning sovereign, with the result that the court and the provincial aristocracy were continually finding themselves divided into rival factions.

These internal weaknesses were aggravated by external pressures. The Portuguese merchants residing in the country were a small but turbulent group whose power was strengthened by the establishment of a permanent Portuguese base in Luanda in 1575. The developing slave trade provided local magnates, especially those living near the coast, with an opportunity of acquiring new sources of wealth and of gathering round them bands of armed retainers whom they could use to assert their independence. The catastrophic defeat suffered by Kongo at the hands of the Portuguese in 1665 certainly accelerated the process of disintegration, but even before this date there was ample evidence of the breakdown of authority, a breakdown occurring not only between the royal court and the provinces but also within the provinces themselves.

By the middle of the nineteenth century, after a hundred and fifty years of continuous fragmentation, the area formerly occupied by the unified kingdom was divided up among a multitude of petty chiefdoms, most of them no larger than a single village. These chiefdoms were ruled either by *infantes*, descendants of the old royal lineage, or *fidalgos*, free men who had established their own domain; most of their subjects were regarded as slaves. Among the ruins of San Salvador a *mani-Kongo* still reigned, lord now of little more than a few huts and a small company of slaves, but inheritor, like some latter-day Holy Roman emperor, of the memories of a great past and still invested with a certain prestige. Thus it was that independent *infantes* continued to come to San Salvador to receive from the *mani-Kongo*, after payment of a suitable fee, some more exalted title.

 It is natural to think of this process of fragmentation as "decay" with the population, ravaged by the endemic wars produced by the slave trade, steadily declining. But it also needs to be seen, as Jan Vansina has pointed out,[4] as the emergence of a new kind of society called into being by the demands of the slave trade. Within this society a man's power could be assessed in practical terms by the number of slaves he had at his disposal. In such an intensely competitive society many individuals found it possible to carve out independent polities for themselves, but no single polity was able to accumulate sufficient resources to enable it to dominate its neighbors and so create a new political superstructure.

THE BEMBA PARAMOUNTCY

The area, some fifty to sixty thousand square miles in extent, which now forms the northeastern part of Zambia, might be described as a Central African interlacustrine region, for it lies between the four great lakes of Tanganyika, Nyasa, Mweru, and Bangweulu. In the course of the eighteenth and nineteenth centuries this area came to be dominated by the Bemba people, who succeeded in constructing one of the major polities of Central Africa. Lubemba, "land of the Bemba," is a high plateau, the country open and well-watered but tsetse-infested and with poor soil. Even today population density is little more than five to the square mile.

Into this interlacustrine area there had come over a period of many hundreds of years small groups of agriculturalists moving in an easterly or southeasterly direction from the basin of the Upper Congo. Toward the end of the seventeenth century a new group that was to play a leading role in the political development of the area arrived. This group was led by members of a clan which used a crocodile as its totem and claimed to have broken away from one of the Luba kingdoms to the west. Gradually, the Luba immigrants established their hegemony over many of the small polities already existing in the area. In time Luba immigrants and earlier inhabitants, divided from the start by no great cultural differences, fused to form a single people, a new ethnic group, the Bemba.

By the middle of the eighteenth century lineages of the Crocodile clan had founded five substantial chiefdoms in the interlacustrine area. The ruler of one of these chiefdoms, who bore the title *chitimukulu,* was accepted as paramount of the Bemba confederacy. But at this time the chitimukuluship was not confined to a single lineage and chiefs of other lineages competed fiercely for the post when occasion arose. Early in the nineteenth century, however, one lineage succeeded in consolidating its hold over the chitimukuluship. As new chiefdoms came to be created through the conquest of neighboring peoples, they were placed in the charge of close relatives of the reigning *chitimukulu.* By 1850 Arab and Swahili traders were doing business in Lubemba, opening the country for the first time to trade with the outside world and offering Bemba chiefs guns, cloth, and other trade goods in return for ivory and slaves. The Bemba were thus enabled to enhance their superiority over their neighbors and at the same time provided with an incentive to engage in further conquest.

Within Lubemba the basic political unit was the compact village settlement. The villages, often as much as twenty miles apart, were governed by headmen, elderly men for the most part who gathered relatives around them to form a distinct community. Since there was no shortage of land, villages often moved their sites in response to the needs of shifting cultivation. They were also liable to break up on the death of a headman.

Chiefdoms were formed by grouping a number of villages together, the chief's own village, always very much larger than those of his subjects, serving as the local capital. To Bemba commoners their chiefs, who could be drawn only from lineages of the royal Crocodile clan, appeared at once oppressive and almost divine—oppressive, because they were, in popular opinion, indeed "like crocodiles that seize hold of the common people and tear them to bits with their teeth," semidivine since their supernatural powers enabled them "to spit blessings over the land."

A chief's power was manifest in the size of his following. Messengers carried his commands to outlying villages, war captains called up men to serve in his army, other officials superintended the payment of tribute or the performance of the labor duties he had the right to demand of his subjects. But neither the *chitimukulu* nor the other major chiefs were complete autocrats, for they were assisted by a group of hereditary councilors. These discussed matters of major importance to the chiefdom, but their primary duty was to carry out certain ritual ceremonies. By refusing to carry out these duties this secretive and aristocratic body—its members conducted their business in an archaic language not understood by commoners—could put subtle pressure on the chief.

The Bemba were a matrilineal people, tracing descent on the mother's, not the father's side; thus, a man's direct heirs were not his sons but his brothers or his elder sisters' sons. This system had an important bearing on the structure of the paramountcy. Once the chitimukuluship had come to be confined to a single lineage, the younger brothers and nephews of a ruling *chitimukulu* knew that in time they would probably succeed to the title and thus they had little incentive to plot rebellion. Nineteenth-century *chitimukulus* were particularly anxious to place their closest relations in major chieftainships. Thus, when in time a member of the royal family succeeded to the chitimukuluship, he brought with him a wealth of experience gained during his tenure of other great offices.

To assert their powers still further these nineteenth-century rulers attempted to impose a monopoly over external trade. In this they were never completely successful. Chiefs ruling newly conquered border provinces found it more profitable to trade on their own account, even if this insubordinate attitude deprived them of the chances of promotion to a more exalted but less lucrative post. Indeed, by the end of the nineteenth century one newly created chiefdom, Mwamba, was powerful enough to rival the *chitimukulu*. Thus, the Bemba paramountcy never achieved a degree of centralization comparable to that reached in some other major tropical African polities. But the extensive political superstructure constructed by the ruling Crocodile clan was in sharp contrast to the miniscule polities of other peoples in the area and gave to the Bemba people a cohesiveness and an esprit de corps that persists strongly to this day.

THE POLITIES OF THE LAKE NYASA AREA

The country around Lake Nyasa presented a striking contrast to those parts of Central Africa where a single people—the Lunda or the Luba, the Bemba or the Lozi—had succeeded in elaborating their own characteristic form of political organization, thus giving to wide areas a substantial measure of cultural uniformity. The Nyasa area was occupied by five substantial clusters of peoples: Maravi, Yao, Tumbaka, Nyakyusa, and Ngoni. The Maravi cluster, from whom Malawi, the modern name of the country, is derived, included the Cewa and Nyanja peoples living around the southern end of the lake in a country rough and broken for the most part but well wooded and well watered. The dry plateau above the western littoral was the domain of the Tumbaka cluster, while the Nyakyusa cluster occupied the intensely fertile section of the Rift Valley at the northern end of the lake, together with the high mountains of the Livingstone Range to the north. On the eastern side of the lake the Yao formed the dominant group; in the first half of the nineteenth century small bands of Yao adventurers began to penetrate Maravi territory lying to the southwest of the Yao homeland. Finally, the disciplined horde of the Ngoni, an offshoot of the Nguni-speaking peoples of distant Natal, moved into the area in the late 1830's, devastating as they passed many Maravi and Tumbaka communities.

Culturally, the Maravi, the Tumbaka, and the Yao peoples possessed certain affinities; indeed, it seems likely that all three groups once formed part of a movement of matrilineal Bantu-speaking peoples coming from the Congo basin. None of these peoples had ever created a really substantial state of its own. Among the Yao and the Maravi the characteristic form of polity was the petty chiefdom in which a number of villages were somewhat loosely bound together. For several generations before 1850 the Yao had been in touch with Arab and Swahili traders on the east coast. These traders visited Yao villages in the country between the lake and the Indian Ocean, offering guns, cloth, and other goods in return for slaves and ivory. To meet the traders' demands Yao adventurers began moving steadily farther afield. Men who had made a name for themselves as warriors and traders naturally attracted followers whom they could equip with firearms. Thus, they acquired sufficient strength first to raid, then to dominate completely many of the Maravi chiefdoms south of the lake. But it was never possible for even the most successful Yao leader to establish a really substantial state. His closest advisers, the most powerful headmen of the villages lying within his chiefdom, were bound to him largely by ties of self-interest; the more ambitious were naturally anxious to assert their independence and so retain for themselves the ivory and other produce they were required to offer as tribute to their chief. Nineteenth-century Yao history contains many examples of village headmen who succeeded in establishing their own chiefdoms.

Most of the peoples that formed the Tumbaka cluster lived in small village units controlled by informal councils of elders. One part of Tumbaka country, however, had seen the introduction of more elaborate political institutions, when about 1780 a group of ivory traders, said to have come from the east, though their ethnic origin is uncertain, settled at Karanga on the Nyika plateau. The newcomers carried on a peaceful trade, bartering cloth and beads for ivory and skins, and their leader, Mlowoka, soon came to be held in high esteem by the local people on account of his generosity. After a time Mlowoka began to give public recognition to the elected headmen of Tumbaka villages by investing them with a turban and to appoint his own companions as heads of districts made up of groups of villages. In this way a little kingdom was established which lasted under Mlowoka's successors until the 1850's, when it was shattered by the Ngoni.

The Nyakyusa peoples living at the northern end of the lake differed sharply from the other Nyasa groups. They appear to have come from the north rather than from the west. They reckoned descent on the male, not —as with the peoples coming from the Congo—on the female, side. Cattle played a particularly important part in their economy, and their political institutions were quite unlike those of their southern neighbors. The Nyakyusa proper had developed the practice of forming new villages every generation, when the young men who had already spent many years together herding their fathers' cattle, split off from the parental village to form a new village of their own, the most vigorous among them serving as village headmen. A number of these "age-villages" as they have been termed formed a chiefdom. Every Nyakyusa chief was required to hand over power toward the end of his life not to one but to two of his sons, each of whom established his own chiefdom. Thus, there was a constant multiplication of Nyakyusa polities, keeping pace with the steady expansion of population made possible by the occupation of an area of exceptional fertility. By the end of the nineteenth century there were nearly a hundred Nyakyusa chiefdoms, their populations ranging from a few hundred to several thousand people.

Among the Ngonde, one group in the Nyakyusa cluster, political evolution had proceeded a stage further with the establishment of a paramount who bore the title *kyungu*. The first *kyungu* appears to have been the leader of an emigrant band whose members settled on the northwestern littoral of Lake Nyasa, an area then occupied by Tumbaka-type peoples, about the end of the sixteenth century. By the nineteenth century the *kyungu* had come to be regarded as a "divine king" who was kept in ritual seclusion and suffocated when his physical powers showed signs of failing. His establishment was enriched by the profits drawn from controlling a large part of the ivory trade, but he was not in a position to exercise much authority over the territorial nobility of Ngonde country. These local chiefs accepted the *kyungu's* religious paramountcy, but spent much of their time fighting among themselves.

The political systems of the Nyakyusa peoples were, then, hardly less fragmented than those of the Yao or the Maravi. In striking contrast to all these peoples the Ngoni invaders who burst into the area in the late 1830's had evolved a highly disciplined form of political organization. The core of the Ngoni horde was formed by a Nguni-speaking tribe, the Jere, whose original numbers appear not to have exceeded a thousand. In the early 1820's the Jere, under their formidable chief, Zwangendaba, were forced to flee from Natal to escape the violence of the *Mfecane*. However they had already come to adopt the new military tactics developed by the Zulu, and they were able to overwhelm all the peoples who lay in their path as they advanced northward. As they moved on, leaving a swath of desolation behind them, their numbers snowballed. Able-bodied men and women, the survivors of the ravaged villages of many different ethnic groups, were taken into the horde and affiliated to Jere lineages, the women providing additional wives for the victorious warriors, the men, despite their semiservile status, being given the opportunity to serve in the Ngoni regiments. After Zwangendaba's death about 1848 the horde broke up into a number of segments, but each segment was still a very substantial body retaining the basic characteristics that had given the horde its original cohesion. At the top of a well-defined pyramidal structure stood the chief, supported by his relatives and other members of the original Jere nucleus, an aristocracy intensely proud of its distinctive Nguni culture. Regiments were formed of all the men of a particular age group. Thus, military service brought together men belonging to different lineages, living in different villages, and so served powerfully to develop a sense of unity. And this sense of unity was further strengthened by the fact that even when they began to settle down in the latter half of the nineteenth century, the Ngoni were still an alien people operating in a hostile environment.

With Ngoni raiding parties ravaging wide stretches of country, with Tumbaka villagers fleeing for refuge to inaccessible mountains or to new settlements built on piles in the lake, with Yao adventurers carving out new principalities for themselves at the expense of the Maravi, and with Nyakyusa chiefdoms constantly proliferating, the Nyasa area presented in the 1850's a picture of turbulent complexity, a pattern that was to become still more complex in the course of the next decades as new groups, Kololo, Swahili-Arab, and European, came to settle in the area. Yet the pattern is far from meaningless, for here, on a comparatively small stage, one can see vividly presented the dynamics of political development, the influence of war and trade, the impact of new technologies and new institutions.

CHAPTER XIX

East African Polities about 1850

🌿 THE OMANI ARAB SULTANATE OF ZANZIBAR

In 1800 the town of Zanzibar had little to distinguish it from other Arab-Swahili urban communities on the coast of East Africa; by 1850 it had developed, through the political genius of Sayyid Said, sultan of the Persian Gulf state of Oman, into the center of one of the most influential polities in tropical Africa. "When one pipes in Zanzibar, men dance on the Lakes"—this Swahili proverb of the latter half of the nineteenth century testified to the range of the place's influence. And yet the sultans of Zanzibar were never the rulers of a great territorial domain, and the content of their power was in many ways exceedingly modest.

In 1840 Sayyid Said, while remaining ruler of Oman, took up his residence in the town of Zanzibar. Three years earlier he had ended a long duel with Mombasa, the most powerful city-state of the coast, by forcing the inhabitants to accept his authority. By the time of his death in 1856 his claim to suzerainty was accepted by almost all the polities from Mogadishu in the north to Kilwa in the south.

Said's power was based on a small army, no more than three thousand strong, made up of mercenaries known as "Baluchis" and recruited from the borderlands between India and Persia, together with a navy of about a dozen vessels, frigates and sloops for the most part. But Said's armed forces were in turn dependent on his success in securing sufficient revenue to pay for them. Most of the sultan's revenue—in Said's reign it cannot have exceeded fifty thousand pounds in any one year—came from duties charged on all imports and some exports.

"I am nothing but a merchant," Sayyid Said once remarked in an appealing but disingenuous manner to a European visitor, for he was an astute politician with a complete grasp of the connections between commerce, revenue, government, and security. And he pursued every line of action that would serve to increase the wealth at his disposal. He quickly perceived the importance of cloves, introduced to Zanzibar in 1818, and himself established numerous plantations. He welcomed Indian traders for the capital they brought with them: it was, indeed, Indian credit that enabled Arab merchants to take thousands of pounds' worth of goods into the interior. He improved the local currency by importing small coins from India. He was glad to see Europeans and Americans show an increasing interest in the trade of East Africa, and he himself participated in this trade by sending his own trading expeditions into the interior.

Said's ambitions were sensible and moderate; he needed no elaborate machinery of government to achieve them. His government was almost entirely personal, patriarchal in its simplicity. His principal followers, the leading Arabs of Zanzibar, attended his daily durbars, but he appears to have had no regular council to advise him. The collection of taxes, principally customs duties, was farmed out to an Indian businessman who contracted an agreed sum that was subject to periodic increases. In time Said's successors were able to appoint governors, garrisons, and customs officials to most of the towns along the coast. Said could only afford a few such posts; elsewhere he had no alternative but to leave the traditional rulers in place. Even on Zanzibar island itself the local inhabitants, the Tumbatu and the Hadimu, did not come under the direct supervision of an official of the sultan until the 1890's.

The personality of the sultan was, of course, one of the major factors in the politics of Zanzibar. Sayyid Said was a model ruler. "He wishes to do good to all," one British consul wrote of him; [1] and even the poorest could count on receiving justice at his hands. His four sons who succeeded him were men of lesser ability, but they had to cope with problems that Said had never faced in Zanzibar, the rivalry of their own relatives and the growing pressure of European powers.

Although the sultans of Zanzibar might be constitutionally described as autocrats, their actions were subject to pressure from many different directions. There were the Arabs of Zanzibar, who became the landed gentry, the plantocracy of the island. Their numbers were put at four thousand in the 1860's. Many of them had come with Said from Oman, but some had been settled longer in the island and resented the influx of newcomers. There were the "northern Arabs," the crews of the dhows that visited the island regularly: "turbulent, plundering, filthy, squalid, ill-featured savages" in the words of one British consul, [2] they represented a serious threat to law and order. Then there were the Indians, about six thousand in East Africa in the 1860's, on whose business acumen the whole economy depended. Finally, there were the consuls of Britain, France, and the United States.

Of these representatives the British consuls were by far the most important. They were supported by the presence of a naval squadron in East African waters, and they had the advantage of a long association with Oman, reaching back to the early years of the century, when the British had helped Said to suppress the pirates of the Persian Gulf. The close connection with Britain protected Zanzibar against the threat of possible encroachment by the French. It also provided a reigning sultan with a measure of security in the event of internal disturbances. After Said's death his successor, Majid, relied on the British to suppress a revolt by one of his brothers, Bargash, in Zanzibar and to turn back an invading fleet launched by another brother, Thuwain, who had become ruler of Oman. But the price that had to be paid for British support was increasing compliance with the British aim to abolish the slave trade. Already by 1860 the informal empire created by Sayyid Said in East Africa lay clearly within the wider sphere of the informal empire maintained by the British around the shores of the Indian Ocean.

BUGANDA: A HIGHLY CENTRALIZED KINGDOM

Along the northwestern shore of Victoria Nyanza, greatest of the East African lakes, there stretched the crescent-shaped kingdom of Buganda. Modern Buganda, as a province of Uganda, has an area of twenty thousand square miles; the mid-nineteenth-century kingdom was considerably smaller, but its population was reckoned to be about a million, and another million people lived in the petty Soga and Haya states to the east and southwest, whose rulers regularly paid tribute to the kabaka, the king of Buganda.

The Ganda were fortunate in occupying one of the most naturally favored districts in tropical Africa. Rainfall was regular and abundant, the soil rich and the staple crop, bananas, so easy to produce that "one old woman," it was said with only slight exaggeration, "could produce enough to feed ten men." Cultivation among the Ganda was women's work, the men being left free to develop their skills as craftsmen—the huts, the dress, the implements, and the ornaments of the Ganda were among the finest in tropical Africa—and above all to take part in military expeditions.

Nineteenth-century Buganda was, as modern historians have pointed out, a highly acquisitive society. Wealth came from war. Raids against neighboring peoples—no less than sixty such expeditions took place in the reign of Mutesa I (1854–83)—produced slaves, cattle, and ivory. The women slaves served to swell the retinue of the kabaka and his chiefs, cattle could be used to reward and feast the rank and file, and men slaves and ivory were sold to the Zanzibari merchants, who had reached

Buganda in the 1840's, bringing with them cotton cloth and other luxuries and—most significant of imports—guns.

In Mutesa's reign Buganda's policy toward its neighbors was to raid or to extract the regular payment of tribute, but not to conquer or absorb. At an earlier period, however, in the seventeenth and eighteenth centuries, the kingdom had maintained a steady process of expansion. The ruling dynasty was a section of that Nilotic clan, the Bito, from which came also the rulers of Bunyoro, Buganda's powerful northern neighbor, and many of the small Soga states to the east. In the sixteenth century Buganda was a vassal of Bunyoro, and its territory extended no farther than twenty-five miles from the capital, Kampala. But Bunyoro overextended its power, suffered a serious defeat, and in the late seventeenth century allowed its small but compact neighbor an opportunity to expand.

The modesty of Buganda's beginnings was an advantage to the development of the kingdom. It gave time for the Nilotic dynasty to form links of marriage and of office with all the clans, most of them Bantu, in the kingdom. Local chieftainships were hereditary, but as the kingdom expanded, the rulers developed the practice of placing newly conquered territory under the charge of officers appointed by themselves; later nearly all the hereditary chieftainships of the country were taken over by appointed officials. These officers were not drawn from any one class or clan, as was the case in neighboring interlacustrine kingdoms. Thus, by the mid-nineteenth century Buganda had developed into probably the most homogenous and highly centralized state of its size in tropical Africa.

Few African rulers possessed such power as the kabaka of Buganda. In other kingdoms the ruler had to accept the fact that some of his subordinates were great territorial lords with their own sources of wealth, their own bands of armed retainers, too powerful to be removed. The kabaka suffered no such frustrations. He could appoint, transfer, or dismiss whom he pleased. This high degree of royal power made it possible for the Ganda to enjoy a far greater equality of opportunity than was the case in most other African kingdoms. A man of spirit could go far in the kabaka's service. The greatest opportunities came to those who started their careers as boy pages in his court. Men who proved their ability in the royal service were rewarded by the grants of authority over certain areas with the right to the tribute and labor services of the local peasantry. The ladder of promotion reached up to the posts of the great provincial chiefs, who enjoyed high prestige and received many perquisites of office. A great officeholder could find many ways of advancing the interests of his kinsmen and his clients, but he could never pass his post on to one of his sons.

The kabaka had another advantage over many African monarchs. He did not have to contend with the rivalry of ambitious kinsmen. There was no royal clan, for princes took the clan of their mother. Only the son of a kabaka could succeed to the throne. When the kabaka died, his successor was chosen from among his sons by the *katrikiro* (chief minister) and another official. Those royal brothers unsuccessful in the election were usually put to death. This cruel but effective method spared nineteenth-century Buganda the sort of civil conflicts that wrecked neighboring states and so contributed to the kingdom's predominance in the interlacustrine area.

To Speke, the first European traveler to describe Buganda, Kabaka Mutesa appeared as a bloodthirsty and capricious despot who inflicted hideous punishments for apparently trivial offences—a page, for example, had his ears cut off for repeating a message wrongly, and executions at the court were of almost daily occurrence.[3] But the Ganda viewed their monarch in a different light. To them he was, in the imagery of one of his titles, "the charcoal fire of the smith who can forge the kingdom as a smith forges iron." The kabaka personified the power of the Ganda nation. It was natural that he should behave in an arbitrary manner. And if some innocent people suffered from his acts, this was nothing when compared to the benefits he rendered his people. Moreover, his caprices affected comparatively few of his subjects. In countries with a modest technology and indifferent communications—though Buganda was one of the very few African kingdoms with a regular system of roads—a despotic ruler can never build up a machinery of government elaborate enough to enable him to impose his will on the lives of all his subjects.

Since war played so important a part in the life of Buganda—indeed one historian has described the nineteenth-century Ganda state as "essentially a military machine"[4]—any change in the character of the army was bound to have a profound effect on the structure of Ganda society. Such a change began to take place in the 1860's. The traditional army consisted of militia bands of peasant soldiers, armed with spears and led by local chiefs. (There was also a considerable navy, made up of large canoes and used for transport and for raiding on Lake Victoria.) The introduction of firearms by Arab traders enabled Kabaka Mutesa to establish a Praetorian Guard, a *corps d'élite* of musketeers, whose officers were recruited from the pages of the royal palace. In war this regiment of musketeers bore the brunt of the fighting, leaving the old-fashioned militia to act as auxiliaries.

The creation of a standing army increased the kabaka's power. At the same time it became possible for young men with the requisite skills to rise to prominent positions with a rapidity which their seniors, working their way up the traditional hierarchy of royal offices, must have envied. It was a profoundly significant coincidence that these changes should have taken place at a time when revolutionary ideas were being introduced into the religious life of the country.

In Buganda, as in all long-established kingdoms in tropical Africa, the ruler was surrounded by much religious ritual. But since his personal powers were so great and since he was continually engaged in the active process of ruling, a monarch like Kabaka Mutesa could not afford to allow himself to be seriously restricted by ritual observances. So Mutesa felt himself free to take a keen interest in the teachings of Islam as revealed by Arab traders and to invite Christian missionaries, both Anglican and Roman Catholic, to come to Buganda in the late 1870's. Mutesa himself was never formally converted, but some of the young men at court became the first Ganda to accept the new religions.

Thus, in the 1880's a revolutionary oligarchy was beginning to emerge in Buganda—a group of men deeply interested in the techniques and ideas of the outside world and holding positions of power. When, in the next decade, Buganda came under British protection, these men were able to turn this loss of sovereignty to their kingdom's advantage by collaborating with the protecting power and to obtain for themselves a dominant position in the newly created territory. This predominance was symbolized by that territory's name, for though Uganda contains a great variety of peoples, the term itself *U-ganda* is merely the Swahili equivalent of *Bu-ganda,* "land of the Ganda."

ANKOLE: THE DOMINATION OF A PASTORAL ARISTOCRACY

The kingdom of Ankole formed during the colonial period a district of the Western Province of Uganda, a district somewhat larger both in area (six thousand square miles) and population (five hundred thousand) than the nineteenth-century kingdom. Ankole is a country of rolling grasslands to the east and of grassy hills with some patches of dense forest and papyrus swamps in the valleys to the west—a country which possesses splendid grazing land and at the same time receives sufficient rainfall to allow a productive agriculture.

Ankole traditions tell of a time before the creation of the kingdom, when Negroid Bantu agriculturalists, a dark stocky people known as the Iru, and immigrant cattle herders, the tall, shapely, lighter-complexioned Hima, lived peacefully side by side. The Hima, however, possessed both the means and the incentive to dominate the Iru. The cattlemen lived in kraals, much larger social units than the scattered homesteads of the Iru. The prevalence of cattleraiding schooled the Hima in military pursuits and made it advantageous for a number of kraals to come together for raiding their neighbors or protecting themselves against the attacks of rival Hima groups. Finally, by forcing the Iru to accept an inferior status it was possible to extract tribute from them in the form of beer and millet and services such as those performed by specialists in crafts and in magic.

Ankole tradition ascribes the creation of the kingdom to the Chwezi, that mysterious people who before 1500 ruled the ancient kingdom of Kitara in the area of Bunyoro and Buganda. In Ankole legend the Chwezi are credited with superhuman qualities—so bright were their eyes that it hurt lesser mortals to look them in the face—but they were afflicted by a series of calamities and disappeared from the land, leaving only one of their number behind, a certain Ruhinda, an illegitimate son of the last Chwezi king. Ruhinda became the founder of the existing dynasty of Ankole, and from his clan came many of the dynasties of the other Hima states.

The political structure of Ankole was based on the need to maintain Hima domination. The Iru peasantry occupied a position of permanent inferiority: no Iru was allowed to own productive cattle, to marry a Hima woman, to occupy any major office, or even to start a blood feud with a Hima who had murdered one of his kinsmen. The Iru made payments of agricultural produce in tribute to local chiefs, part of which was passed on to the *mugabe* or king. The relationship of the Hima to the *mugabe* was much less onerous than that of the exploited Iru. Herdsmen offered the king cattle as a sign of homage and willingness to follow him in war and so established bonds of clientship with him. In return, as clients, they could count on the *mugabe's* protection and assistance should their cattle be raided by outsiders, and they could have access to his court in the event of a dispute with fellow herdsmen.

Supported by the tribute of Iru serfs and the gifts of Hima clients, the *mugabe* was able to maintain an extensive and elaborate court. The circumstances of his accession guaranteed his fitness to rule, for in Ankole the custom had developed of allowing the sons of a dead king to fight among themselves for the succession. For several months after the death of a *mugabe* the interior of the country was in a state of chaos, but the powerful chiefs who guarded the border provinces prevented foreign enemies from taking advantage of the confusion. Every stratagem— poison, ambush, assassination—was permissible between the competing bands, until one brother was left victorious, his rivals dead or in exile. Thus deprived of male relatives on his father's side, the new *mugabe* inevitably came to depend on his mother's kin. His mother and chief sister enjoyed positions of special prominence, while his mother's brothers and their sons were appointed to the most important offices.

The new ruler took over the guardianship of the royal drum, Bagyendanwa, which was believed to have come down from the Chwezi. Bagyendanwa was neither a mere piece of regalia nor the dwelling place of a spirit but rather a force in itself of tremendous power. To the shrine of the drum there came a constant stream of offerings, for Bagyendanwa needed food to remain strong. Warriors setting out on a raid, rich men afraid of the malevolence of their neighbors, barren women, and farmers anxious for their crops all believed that the drum could succor them. The cult of Bagyendanwa gave added prestige and sanctity to the *mugabe*. But it did more than that: the cult was open to all men, Hima and Iru alike. Deeply divided though Ankole society may appear to have been, the political power of the king and the cult of the drum acted as acceptable unifying agents. "We," all the people of Ankole could declare, "are the children of Bagyendanwa"—as such they regarded themselves as different from all their neighbors.

❧ THE WARRIOR COMPANIES OF THE MASAI

The Masai are the best known of all the Nilo-Hamitic peoples of East Africa. Their fame is understandable. They are among the most numerous of Nilo-Hamitic groups (there are today about a quarter of a million people of Masai stock in Kenya and Tanzania). Their imposing height and bearing and their adherence to their traditional way of life mark them off sharply from their neighbors. Their prowess as warriors once made them one of the most widely feared of African peoples. Indeed, at the height of their power in the mid-nineteenth century Masai influence extended far more widely than that of any of the other indigenous peoples of East Africa.

In 1850 the Masai dominated an area of about eighty thousand square miles, from the country south of Lake Rudolf, along the line of the Rift Valley across the Kenya Highlands, and on along the wide corridor of grassland, known today as the Masai steppe, deep into modern Tanzania. But Masai power was felt even beyond the bounds of this vast territory, and there were occasions when their raiding parties reached almost to the shores of the Indian Ocean to the east and of Lake Victoria to the west.

The Masai had two abiding passions—cattle and war—and the two were intimately connected. God, so the Masai believed, had created cattle for their exclusive benefit—a highly convenient notion, elevating the filching of the cattle of neighboring peoples into a moral duty. But there was also a strong economic motive behind Masai raids: unlike many pastoral peoples, the Masai had a taste for beef. Moreover, since they did not practice agriculture, they had regularly to sell animals—albeit the skinniest in their herds—to their agricultural neighbors in exchange for

grain. The easiest way to replenish their herds, always liable to be reduced still further by disease, was to take their neighbors' cattle. But cattle raiding and the bloody fights that accompanied it were far more than an
economic necessity. To the Masai they were sport and glory, the true test
of manhood.

The Masai were a single people in the sense that they spoke the same
language and observed the same customs, but politically they were divided up into at least a dozen tribes of varying size. Within Masai society
there was a sharp distinction between the age-grades—each grade being
composed of a number of age-sets—of the warriors and the elders. The
warriors and elders of a given district lived apart from one another, each
grade in its own kraal. Warriors living in the same kraal were attended by
their mothers and girl friends and formed a company with a war captain
at their head. This captain was responsible for maintaining discipline,
planning raids, and settling disputes. Within the elders' kraal disputes
came before a council of heads of families. There appears to have been no
political authority linking elders and warriors of the same district.

A number of warrior companies, accustomed to joining forces in large-
scale raids, formed a tribal section. A number of such sections loosely
confederated formed a tribe. Within a Masai tribe there was one person
whose influence was universally recognized, the superior *laibon,* who
provided, in G. W. B. Huntingford's phrase, "a mystical focus for tribal
activities." [5] He was the intermediary between his people and the spirit
world; he could make the rain fall and provide in other ways for the prosperity of his fellow tribesmen; he could make medicine that would protect the warriors and ensure the success of their raids. This last function
increased his political powers, for it meant that the war captains had to
seek his permission before embarking on any major raids. The office of
senior *laibon* was hereditary, and all the most important *laibons* throughout Masailand came from the same subclan and so had some connection
with one another. But great though the influence of certain *laibons* is
known to have been, none of them had at his disposal the machinery of
government of a territorial chief.

The Masai were formidable fighters: a company of these warriors in
panoply—ostrich-feather headdress, painted face, gleaming spear, oval
shield—presented a truly frightening sight. But they lacked both the
numbers and the techniques to dominate all their neighbors. Lords of the
open plains, they found it impossible to overrun the steep, fertile, densely
populated areas occupied by such people as the Kikuyu. Indeed, it has
been suggested that by the mid-nineteenth century a certain balance of
power had been established between the Masai and their neighbors.
After 1860 the Masai were rent by a series of civil wars, which may have

had their ultimate origin in the fact that it was becoming easier to carry off the cattle of a neighboring Masai tribe than to raid the heavily defended stockades of the Bantu peasant communities.

But even more damaging than civil war were the lethal epidemics—cholera in 1869, rinderpest and small-pox in the 1880's—that ravaged Masai territory. (The Masai, making contact with so many peoples in the course of their raids, were particularly exposed to infectious diseases, whether human or animal.) Thus weakened, the Masai themselves came under attack from their neighbors, particularly from other Nilo-Hamitic peoples, the Nandi and the Kipsigis. By the 1890's the great days of Masai military domination were over, which greatly facilitated the British occupation of the Kenya Highlands.

✿ THE STATELESS POLITIES OF THE KIKUYU

The Kikuyu are today the most prominent of all the peoples of Kenya. Numerically—their population exceeds a million—they are the most numerous people in East Africa and their energy, ability, and readiness to accept modern ways have made them one of the best known of all African peoples. A century ago they were almost completely unknown to the outside world. Their isolation was not surprising, for they occupied a small territory, not much more than one thousand square miles in extent, which was only just beginning to be visited by traders from other parts.

Kikuyu territory stretched as a belt some twenty to thirty miles in width southwestward from Mount Kenya. Though modest in size, their home had many advantages: the soil fertile, the water abundant, the climate—for it lay at an altitude of between six and seven thousand feet—exhilarating. Kikuyu traditions tell of a migration from the coast up the Tana River. The people appear to have reached the northeastern edge of their present homeland in the early sixteenth century. At this time the land was densely forested and inhabited only by a few Dorobo hunters. The Kikuyu purchased the land from the Dorobo and pressed forward —like the Anglo-Saxon settlers in the English Midlands a millennium earlier—cutting down the forest and bringing the land under intensive cultivation, so that it struck the first European travelers as having the appearance of "one vast garden." [6] Only on the edges of Kikuyu country was a belt of forest a mile or two wide left intact; it provided a most effective line of defense against the encircling and consistently bellicose Masai.

The Kikuyu were one people only in the sense that they spoke a common language, followed certain common rituals, and accepted a common tradition of origin. Politically, they were one of the most fragmented of African ethnic groups. The basic unit in Kikuyu society was the *mbari,* a term sometimes translated as "joint family." A *mbari* was made up of a number of homesteads, each of whose heads could claim descent from a common ancestor three or four generations back. The number of people living in a *mbari* varied greatly: some had as many as five thousand, others less than fifty, the average appearing to be about one hundred and fifty.

Kikuyu country is made up of wave upon wave of ridge-like hills. Each ridge usually formed the territory of a single *mbari*. No *mbari* was subject to the overriding power of any external authority, but for certain purposes members of different *mbari* living in a definite neighborhood found it necessary to come together. The link between *mbari* was provided by the Kikuyu age-grade system. Members of between five and thirty *mbari* came together for the initiation ceremonies which all youths and girls had to undergo. Those youths who attended the same initiation ceremony became age-mates and moved through the different age-grades from warrior to senior elder together. The warriors of the same age-sets were sometimes responsible for keeping order at markets.

There were certain matters that were of concern to all the *mbari* of a group or district: the settlement of disputes between members of different *mbari,* sacrifices and initiation ceremonies, diplomatic negotiations with external groups, and so on. These matters were the concern of the senior elders meeting in council. Age-sets were grouped together in generation-sets. A senior generation-set held power for a period of twenty to thirty years, before handing it over at a lengthy and elaborate ceremony to its successor.

In traditional Kikuyu society there existed no form of chieftainship. This did not mean that prominent men could not emerge in Kikuyu society: successful war leaders against the Masai are known to have attracted many followers and to have acquired considerable wealth in cattle. But in Kikuyu society as it existed in the nineteenth century there were no means by which an ambitious man could aspire to political overlordship.

The other striking feature of Kikuyu society was the power and privilege possessed by the older members of the community. Loosely, one might describe Kikuyu society as a gerontocracy, but one organized on an egalitarian basis, for all old men of the appropriate age-set could count on membership in the senior elders' council.

CHAPTER XX

South African Polities about 1850

✣ THE BRITISH COLONY OF THE CAPE OF GOOD HOPE

In the 1850's the British colony of the Cape of Good Hope represented by far the largest sub-Saharan territory under European control; it contained the most substantial number of European settlers, about 45 percent of its total population of a quarter of a million were classified as "white," and it had evolved the most elaborate institutions of any European territory in Africa.

When the British took over the Cape from the Dutch in the 1790's, they were content to impose above the Dutch system of local government with its landdrosts and its field cornets the superstructure of a colonial rule in which legislative and executive powers were concentrated in the hands of the governor. Thus, the early British governors of the Cape—most of them army officers who had first made a name for themselves in the Peninsular campaigns—could rule in an almost completely autocratic manner, subject only to the restraints imposed by a distant British government and by a parliament largely indifferent at this time to South African affairs. In 1825 an advisory council composed entirely of officials was appointed to assist the governor, and in 1833 this body was transformed into a legislative council by the addition of a handful of nominated unofficial members, drawn from the ranks of prominent local merchants or landowners.

The people of the Cape, especially the new English settlers, were not unaffected by the trend of political ideas in the England of the Great Reform Bill. Moreover, their own community was experiencing significant social changes: during the 1830's and 1840's the Cape saw the establishment of elected local government bodies, the development of vigorous church assemblies, the emergence of a politically conscious press, and the improvement of communications within the colony. Inevitably, many men became increasingly irritated with the spectacle of a legislative council on which officials, often openly contemptuous of public opinion, were in a permanent majority. (Indeed, one tactless governor went so far as to remark to members, "Do not waste your breath, gentlemen, important matters are decided elsewhere.") In 1849 popular feeling came to a head when the British government imprudently decided to transport convicts to the Cape. A colony-wide Anti-Convict Association was founded and forced the government to abandon the project by means of a campaign of passive resistance and public protest. The agitation thus aroused lent added urgency to the need already recognized by the British government for a more liberal political settlement. In 1853, after protracted discussions, the Cape received its first constitution.

The Cape constitution of 1853 remained in force, with some amendments, until the Act of Union in 1910. It established a bicameral legislature—a Legislative Council with fifteen members, a House of Assembly with forty-five—but the executive still remained in official hands, and it was not until 1872 that the Cape was granted full internal self-government with its own prime minister and Cabinet. The new constitution gave the vote to about 80 percent of the male population of the colony. But though many of the colony's colored people possessed the modest property qualifications that made them eligible to vote, they took little advantage of this opportunity. The Cape "coloured vote" was of little importance in the political development of the colony.

The path of constitutional advance followed by the Cape helped to create a pattern that was to be reproduced in the British territories of tropical Africa a century later. But the most significant features of Cape Colony when compared with other African polities of the mid-nineteenth century lie not in its constitutional development but in its administrative efficiency, its internal cohesion, and its military power. It was almost unique in contemporary Africa to find law and order maintained over an area as large as the two hundred thousand square miles controlled by the Cape government. This government had at its disposal a wide range of officials, judges, and magistrates, tax collectors and auditors, policemen and school teachers, road engineers and harbor masters. Divisions existed within the colony between Dutch and English and between the Eastern Province and the Western; nevertheless the two dominant European groups were coming steadily closer together. Thus, the colony was not confronted with the threat that hung over most other contemporary African polities of being torn apart by civil war. Above all, the colony had at its disposal by virtue of its imperial connections, very substantial military power. Its own military resources were limited, but in the early 1850's there were more than eight thousand British regulars stationed in the colony or in adjoining British Kaffraria. The cost of these troops was borne, albeit with much reluctance, entirely by the metropolitan power. In 1849, when the Cape's own revenue stood at £238,000, the British government spent no less than £370,000—10 percent of the country's total military budget—on maintaining troops in South Africa.[1] Nowhere outside Egypt or Algeria was military power on such a scale to be seen in contemporary Africa.

🌿 THE BOER REPUBLICS

With their capitals mere villages and with their European population spread so thinly over the ground that only one white man could be counted to every four or five square miles of territory, the Boer polities of the Orange Free State and the Transvaal—the latter adopted the grandiose title of the South African Republic in 1853—presented in the mid-1850's a political organization of extreme simplicity.

"We are resolved, wherever we go," the Trekkers had declared in one of their manifestos, "that we will uphold the just principles of liberty; . . . we will establish such regulations as may suppress crime and preserve proper relations between master and servant." [2] Two clauses in the South African Republic's constitution of 1858 gave forthright expressions to these resolutions. "The people demand," stated the eighth clause, "as much social freedom as possible." "The people desire," so ran the very next clause, "to permit no equality between coloured people and the white inhabitants, either in Church or State." [3] The contradiction, though glaring, is no more extraordinary than that presented by the slave-owning democracies of ancient Greece.

Both republics had similar institutions: a volksraad or parliament elected by all the male burghers, an executive council, and an elected president. Since there was no standing army and no civil service, all burghers between the ages of sixteen and seventy were liable to burgher service. Field cornets were responsible for the maintenance of law and order in their localities; field commandants led the commandos in which all burghers were liable for service in time of emergency; both these officials were elected to their offices by the people of their districts.

Though broadly similar in their institutions and their social structure, the two republics developed along different lines. The Orange Free State had the advantage of occupying a more compact territory; its position placed it more closely in contact with the outside world; and it was able to develop an economy based largely on the export of wool that provided the government with an adequate revenue. The South African Republic, by contrast, covered a very much larger area and was more isolated and much poorer in natural resources until the discovery of gold on the Witwatersrand transformed its situation. At the same time the republic represented an amalgamation of four earlier republics, many of whose citizens were drawn from the most turbulent and lawless elements of Trekker society. Thus, while the Orange Free State preserved a remarkable measure of political stability and accepted without difficulty a minority of English settlers, the South African Republic suffered from growing internal tensions that brought it in the 1870's to the verge of complete collapse.

✺ THE TRIBAL CHIEFDOMS OF THE TSWANA

At the beginning of the nineteenth century there appears to have existed among most of the Bantu peoples of South Africa a marked degree of uniformity in the character of their political institutions. This uniformity was in sharp contrast to the intense local diversity to be found in areas of comparable size in other parts of the continent, but it becomes perfectly understandable when seen against the background of the peoples' historical development. Most of the Southern Bantu had inherited certain common cultural traditions; the form of the economy, based on a combination of cattle raising, hunting, and agriculture, varied little from group to group; external influences had hitherto played virtually no part in the development of the area; indeed, all the Bantu groups, whether living on the high veld, on the arid fringes of the Kalahari, or among the fertile valleys of Natal, had behind them the same sort of experience— that of pioneers moving into an almost empty land.

The revolutionary stress produced by the *Mfecane,* the time of troubles in the 1820's and 1830's, disrupted this broadly uniform pattern. From the era of violence there emerged a number of polities—most notable among them the kingdoms of the Zulu and of the Basuto—more substantial than any that the Southern Bantu had ever known before. In some of these larger polities novel features of a revolutionary nature were grafted onto the traditional forms of political organization. But there were many peoples living on the periphery of the area thrown into turmoil by the *Mfecane* with whom the older political pattern with its multitude of tribal chiefdoms still persisted. Such was the situation among the Tswana, the collective name applied to the western group of Sotho-speaking peoples.

Today the Tswana number about a million, a third living within the borders of Botswana (formerly the Bechuanaland Protectorate), most of the remainder in the Republic of South Africa. In the past the Tswana were divided up into a large number of tribes—at least fifty of which survive to this day—the term "tribe" being defined as a politically independent unit under the authority of a single chief. Tribes—their names derived either from former chiefs or from animals revered as totems—

varied greatly in size. The largest of Tswana tribes, the Ngwato, today has a population of more than one hundred thousand and occupies an area of forty-two thousand square miles. But this is exceptional: in the past most tribes were very much smaller, many with a population of no more than one to two thousand, living in an area not exceeding a hundred square miles.

The history of the Tswana presents a kaleidoscopic impression of movement, fission, and absorption. Migrating from the north into areas sparsely populated by bands of wandering Bushmen hunters, they were not subject to the pressures that could lead to the establishment of con-solidated territorial states. Disputes within the ruling lineage of a chief-dom could easily be resolved by the disappointed party breaking away to form a new chiefdom for himself and his followers. At the same time, as chiefdoms declined in power, they were liable to be taken over by their more substantial neighbors. The size and power of individual chiefdoms were subject to constant fluctuations, a chief with a reputation for gen-erosity or for prowess in war being able to attract individuals from other chiefdoms or to enlarge by conquest the bounds of his own domain. Thus, in the larger Tswana chiefdoms a number of distinct classes could be ob-served—"nobles," the members of the ruling lineage; "commoners," the descendants of alien groups incorporated into tribal society several gen-erations back; and "immigrants," people more recently taken into the tribe.

Within his own tribe the prestige of a chief was as high as his duties were onerous. He was the focus for the unity of his people, their "father," their "herdsman." To him they paid tribute: from the hunters one tusk of every elephant they killed, the skin of every lion, the brisket of every antelope; from women at time of harvest a basketful of corn; from cattle owners an ox on certain major occasions. To the chief they brought their problems, their petitions, their complaints, for though regarded with great reverence, the Tswana chief was no remote "divine king," but the active leader of his people. "The chiefs," wrote a nineteenth-century ob-server, "are the great providers of the community. With the produce of their flocks they must feed the poor, furnish the warrior with arms, supply the troops in the field, and promote and strengthen the alliances which are to be contracted with neighboring nations." [4]

Chiefs, the same observer noted, were usually very dignified in their gestures and movements. Being descended from ruling lineages whose members had taken care to obtain the most beautiful women of the tribe as their wives, they usually possessed "great physical advantages over their subjects." But in dress and other forms of adornment they were hardly to be distinguished from the common people, and they could "be approached, addressed, contradicted even without ceremony." [5] For regular advice they turned to a small, intimate council of their own choosing, whose members usually included their paternal uncles and their brothers. But it was the practice to submit matters of public concern to a general assembly attended by all the men of the tribe. All men attending had the right to express their opinions freely; warriors often concluded a vigorous speech by hurling their spears into the ground to emphasize their point. No vote was ever taken and the chief invariably had the final word, but in summing up he always had to take into consideration the opinions that had been expressed.

Apart from the services of a few messengers maintained in their household, Tswana chiefs had at their disposal nothing that can be described as a bureaucracy. Every local group—family compound, village, or ward—had its own hereditary headman who was responsible for the maintenance of law and order, the adjudication of local disputes, and the collection of tribute, each headman being subordinate to his immediate political superior. Such a system worked effectively enough among the Tswana who lived in an arid land where people were compelled to gather together to form compact settlements in places containing permanent supplies of water. In every Tswana chiefdom the chief's own village was always the largest settlement—and sometimes the only substantial one—in the territory. Indeed, the capitals of the larger tribes sometimes contained as many as ten thousand people, an urban population which would be regarded as remarkable in any part of sub-Saharan Africa.

Compared with other Bantu polities—sixteenth-century Kongo, for example, or Buganda and the Bemba paramountcy in the nineteenth century—Tswana chiefdoms appear as less elaborate political structures. Not until the end of the nineteenth century in some of the largest Tswana chiefdoms did chiefs begin to adopt the practice of appointing governors over remote districts. Moreover, the small size and compactness of their domains enabled Tswana chiefs to establish an intimate accord with their subjects of a kind that was hardly possible in larger polities. And although Tswana society had its divisions, there was no class of slaves such as had appeared in so many other African polities. But there was nothing immutable about this social and political structure: while the Tswana retained their traditional form of chiefdomship, developments taking place among the Nguni-speaking peoples showed how revolutionary innovations could transform completely the whole pattern of Southern Bantu society.

🏹 THE ZULU KINGDOM: MILITARY DESPOTISM

Military power was an essential element in the development of all the major kingdoms of nineteenth-century Africa, but no kingdom was so systematically and efficiently organized for war as that erected by the Zulu chief Shaka in the first quarter of the nineteenth century.

In 1800 the Zulu clan was organized in a small chieftaincy, occupying an area of about a hundred square miles, with nothing to distinguish it from the scores of similar petty chieftaincies established by Nguni-speaking Bantu and extending over most of modern Natal. But the times were troubled; pressure of population had led to increasing conflict among the Nguni, and a number of wider political groupings, confederations of clans, began to emerge. The Zulus formed part of one such confederation under the paramountcy of Dingiswayo.

Among Dingiswayo's most notable warriors was a man named Shaka, born in 1787, the illegitimate and unwanted son of the chief of the Zulus. As a boy Shaka had endured many humiliations—even his name, meaning "beetle" in Zulu, was an insult—and the course of his later career must in part have been inspired by a ferocious determination to obtain compensation for the sufferings of his youth. Joining Dingiswayo's army as a young man, he soon proved himself an outstanding warrior. He was as popular as he was brave, excelling both on the battlefield and as a dancer and composer of songs. But he possessed another, rarer quality—a remarkable originality of mind. This led him to devise an entirely new form of tactics. He substituted for the traditional light throwing spear of the Nguni a much heavier weapon that was to be used for stabbing. A well-disciplined body of spearmen, thus armed, had only to ward off with their massive shields the missiles of their adversaries to have them at their mercy.

About 1817 Shaka became chief of the Zulus and so acquired his own following. He now carried his revolutionary ideas a stage further. Nguni chiefs had recently developed the practice of forming all the young men of the same age-set into a regiment. But these regiments were only called upon in the event of war. Shaka saw that it was essential for the success of his new tactics to subject his warriors to continuous training and strict discipline. Once the warriors of an age-grade had been called up, they were required to live in barrack-like settlements in the center of Shaka's territory, and they were not demobilized until they had completed many years of service.

This military revolution had profound political consequences. After

Dingiswayo's defeat and death at the hands of the chief of a rival confederation, Shaka was left as the most powerful chief in northern Natal. His military successes served to extend his domain. Young men flocked to join his famous army; neighboring chiefs hastened to recognize his hegemony. By recruiting all their followers of military age Shaka ensured that subordinate chiefs had no means of effectively rejecting his rule. At the same time he was able to develop an intense spirit of national consciousness among his soldiers. In the Zulu army men learned that they were completely dependent on the king: from him came their weapons, their food—the cattle captured on raids against neighboring peoples—their honors and promotion. *Isihlango senkosi* a man was called in Zulu: the words mean "war shield of the king."

Shaka's power was as near to being absolute as any ruler's could be in an age of simple technology. Indeed, few rulers have ever treated their subjects with such ruthlessness and ferocity. He expelled all the rainmakers on the grounds that only the king could make rain. He made his soldiers dance on thorns to harden their feet and had them clubbed to death if they showed any sign of weakness. He refused to take a legal wife for fear that an heir would plot against him, and he executed any of his concubines who became pregnant. When his mother died he mourned her death by massacring several thousand of his subjects. To one of his women who protested at his brutality, he justified himself thus: "Force is the only thing they understand, and you can only rule the Zulu by killing them. Who are the Zulu? They are parts of two hundred unruly clans which I had to break up and reshape and only the fear of death will hold them together. The time will come when they will be as one nation. In the meantime my very nature must inspire them with terror." [6]

For all his precautions Shaka died violently, assassinated in 1828 by his brothers. But within a mere ten years the Zulu kingdom, which extended over an area of eighty thousand square miles, had become too well integrated to break up on its founder's death. It withstood the shock of defeat at the hands of the Boers in the reign of Dingane, Shaka's successor, and enjoyed a generation of peace under its third king, Mpande. In Mpande's reign Zululand was estimated to have a population of between a quarter and half a million. By this time the Zulus had as their neighbors not the weak Nguni chieftaincies, but Boer and British settlers in the Transvaal and Natal. Cetewayo, Mpande's successor, found himself caught up in the toils of European conflict. In 1880 the British invaded Zululand, deposed Cetewayo, and eventually established their rule over the entire kingdom.

✻ MOSHESH'S PARAMOUNTCY: THE NATION-COMMUNITY OF THE BASUTO

The polity of the Basuto resembled the Zulu kingdom in two ways—as a product of the same violent era, the *Mfecane,* and as the creation of a single outstanding leader. But the personality of its founder, Moshesh, was almost diametrically opposed to that of the sullen and bloodthirsty Shaka, and the institutions of the Basuto state were characterized by no innovations as revolutionary as those established by the Zulu despot. Indeed, the polity constructed by Moshesh may well be regarded as representing the most successful example of the application of traditional methods of state-building in the history of the Southern Bantu.

Moshesh was born in 1784, the son of a minor Sotho chief. As a young man he made a name for himself as a bold warrior and successful cattle raider, his prowess attracting followers in the conventional manner. But from the start he appears to have dreamed of greater things, an ambition which led him to consult the most remarkable Sotho political leader of his day, the venerable chief Mohlomi, a visionary who claimed that in his youth he had been told by heavenly agents to "rule by love." Putting this strange doctrine into practice, he had come to acquire great prestige as a healer, a rainmaker, and an arbitrator of disputes. Mohlomi gave the young Moshesh much practical advice, warning him to distrust witch doctors as they were usually charlatans, recommending him to marry a large number of wives in order to create harmonious links with other chiefs, and urging him to relieve the afflicted, who would repay his generosity with devotion and so be drawn "within his shadow."

This advice accorded well with Moshesh's remarkably attractive personality. Immensely affable, endlessly patient in listening to others, and with a happy knack for remembering the names, faces, and life histories of his followers, Moshesh clearly possessed the charismatic quality of a successful leader. But the warm heart was combined with a mind of great shrewdness—penetrating, judicious, and far-sighted. His long career was to win him an undisputed place among the great African statesmen of his age.

In 1822, when the war bands of the Nguni first began devastating Sotho territory, Moshesh was no more than the chief of about two thousand people living in the exposed lowlands of northeastern Lesotho. To avoid annihilation in a period so dreadful that some Sotho groups were reduced to cannibalism in order to survive Moshesh led his people on a long and heroic march to a natural fortress far to the south, the flat-topped, precipice-flanked hill of Thaba Bosiu. Round this impregnable core the "nation-community" of the Basuto came to be formed.

Rather than expose his people to attack by the formidable warrior hordes in the vicinity, Moshesh paid the tribute that was demanded of him. At the same time he attracted smaller groups to whom he could offer a measure of protection. It was a custom for Sotho chiefs to loan cattle to their subjects; by following this practice Moshesh established material links between himself and those who accepted him as their chief. But these bonds were strengthened by the real devotion his courage and generosity inspired. As the troubles subsided, groups which had sought refuge in Cape Colony began returning to their old homes and tribes recently dispersed were reformed under his paramountcy. As a result the number of his followers increased from twenty-five thousand in 1836 to eighty thousand in 1848.

The structure of Moshesh's polity was closer to that of a confederation than of a unitary state. Moshesh's own personality and the threat presented by common enemies helped to hold the component parts together, and Moshesh as paramount was in a position to settle his brothers and sons in villages remote from the capital to act as his "eyes and ears." But every subordinate chief enjoyed complete local autonomy, and it was in practice impossible to restrain the more impulsive from engaging in cattle raids on their own accord or even from breaking away completely and moving to another area. To ensure the cooperation of his subordinates in his policies Moshesh made a point of holding regular assemblies at which matters of state were vigorously debated, and the paramount's suggestions sometimes overruled. Such assemblies bore witness to the significance of the Sesotho saying that "a chief is a chief by grace of the people."

In the 1840's the Basuto were threatened by a new invasion, the movement of Boer farmers into the country west of Thaba Bosiu, a movement which was followed in 1848 by the temporary British annexation of all the country between the Vaal and the Drakensberg. In his dealings with the European newcomers Moshesh was fortunate in having as his advisers a group of shrewd and devoted French Protestant missionaries whom he allowed to settle in his country in 1833. Moshesh himself was glad to welcome the superior techniques associated with European civilization, and he sincerely desired to live at peace with his neighbors. But the situation on his western frontiers was so explosive, with Boer farmers settling on land to which the Basuto laid claim, that conflict was unavoidable. Initially, the Basuto achieved considerable success in resisting Boer encroachments, but the war of 1865 finally demonstrated their weakness and brought Moshesh's polity to the verge of almost total breakdown. But Moshesh had long realized that the only way of preserving his people from Boer domination was to place them under British protection. In

1868 he surrendered Basutoland to the British. Two years later he died at the age of eighty-four.

Without the protective scaffolding of British rule to hold the polity together, there is no doubt that Moshesh's construction, weakened by the shocks of Boer attacks and cracked by bitter divisions among the old paramount's relatives and subordinates, would have collapsed completely. But by preserving the independence of his people for so long Moshesh enabled them to secure a special position in the evolving political pattern in Southern Africa and so to escape the fate of total subjection to alien rule that befell almost all their Bantu neighbors.

CHAPTER XXI

Island Polities about 1850

✳ THE MALAGASY KINGDOM OF MERINA

In the last quarter of the eighteenth century a French trader from Mauritius, Nicholas Mayeur, became the first European to visit parts of the high interior of Madagascar. "Europeans who know Madagascar," he wrote on his return, "will find it difficult to believe that in the interior of the island one finds a greater degree of civilization and a more efficient system of police than on the coasts where the people have maintained a constant intercourse with Europeans for centuries." And he went on to claim that the remarkable inhabitants of the interior, the Hova of Merina, possessed a greater "natural intelligence" and more "aptitude for work" than any of the other peoples of the great island.[1] Events were to prove this a prescient judgment.

The population of Merina presented one immediately striking characteristic: a large number of people possessed the long hair and olive complexion that denoted pure Indonesian descent. Even today no less than 45 percent of the Hova are classified as being of Mongoloid type, a very much higher proportion than is to be found elsewhere on the island, where the majority of the people are Negroid or mixed Negroid-Mongoloid in physical features. Of the early history of the Hova nothing certain is known. It is possible that they represent the last stream of Indonesian immigration into Madagascar and that they arrived a thousand years after the first Indonesian settlers. It seems probable that they were established on the high plateaus of the northern interior by the fifteenth century. In the sixteenth century the political organization of the Hova consisted of nothing more elaborate than a number of petty chiefdoms. But one of these gradually succeeded in dominating its neighbors and took to itself in the mid-seventeenth century the name Merina.

To strengthen their position the early rulers of Merina began to surround their office with an elaborate ritual: the ceremonial bathing of the king, for example, at the opening of every year was designed to suggest a deep religious significance. But the kingdom was also acquiring a sound economic foundation. The Hova had occupied a large marshy area which they transformed into skillfully irrigated rice fields. By so doing they were able to produce sufficient food for a steadily increasing population. At a later stage Merina's numerical superiority over its neighbors was to be one of the main causes of its success. As craftsmen, too, the Hova surpassed most other Malagasy peoples: Mayeur was deeply impressed by their work as blacksmiths and weavers. Nor were they completely isolated from the rest of the world: a modest trade was maintained with the east coast, sufficient to provide the Hova with European firearms in exchange for slaves.

There was nothing inevitable about the rise of Merina. Among the Malagasy there were other people as numerous and no less enterprising —the Sakalava, for example, who dominated much of the west coast. And in the mid-eighteenth century the political development of Merina gave no evidence of future greatness. Quite the reverse, indeed, for on the death of one of its rulers the little kingdom—its territory extended no farther than a twenty-mile radius around the capital, Tananarive—was divided into three parts, each with its own monarch. For a generation these petty principalities fought each other, leaving the country open through their disunity to the attacks of all its neighbors, until at last one of the three divisions acquired a ruler who was to prove himself the greatest figure in Malagasy history. His name was Andrianampoinimerina, usually abbreviated to Nampoina, "The Desired One."

Nampoina became king of one of the substates of Merina about 1770 and died in 1810. In the first twenty years of his reign he restored the old unity of the kingdom and developed an administrative structure that made it possible for him to pursue in the latter half of his reign a steady policy of expansion. Merina society possessed sharp social divisions, with an aristocracy made up of the clans which could claim royal descent. Nampoina had grown up in a time when the anarchical behavior of a multitude of independently minded chiefs had brought the country to the verge of ruin. To prevent this from happening again it was essential to build up a strong monarchy. New rituals and ceremonials were introduced to enhance royal prestige. The great men of the kingdom were made to realize that they held their land from the king and that he had the right to take it from them. A corps of officials was formed to act as the king's advisers, agents, and messengers. A *levée en masse* of Hova free men put at the king's disposal an army, seventy thousand strong, while local communities were required to provide corvée labor on works of public utility such as the construction of irrigation canals. Finally,

Nampoina instituted the practice of holding regular mass assemblies (*kabary*) at which he told the people his plans and sought their approval. It was an effective means of giving a popular gloss to an absolutist regime.

To extend the bounds of Merina, Nampoina used a combination of force and diplomacy, and he devised effective methods for keeping the new territories under his control. Hova colonists were sent out to develop hitherto unpopulated areas or to provide garrisons to overawe the more recalcitrant of the recently conquered peoples; independent chiefs who peacefully accepted Merina hegemony were left in office, but were required to send a modest tribute to Tananarive and to accept the advice of the local Hova governor or resident. Nampoina had seen his kingdom grow to about ten times its original size. He left to his successor an even vaster ambition. "The sea marks the limits of my rice-fields": this was the aphoristic advice that Nampoina, whose domains had at no point yet reached the sea, gave on his deathbed to his chosen son and heir, Radama. It was the first time a Malagasy ruler had dreamed of uniting all Madagascar, an island larger in area than most of the countries of Europe.

Radama was a gay, lively, dashing young man, as shrewd and intelligent as his father, "exceedingly proud" and "jealous of absolute authority" in the opinion of his courtiers [2] and with a mind avid for information about the outside world. His attitude toward Europeans was the reverse of his father's. Nampoina viewed European traders with distrust and discouraged them from visiting Merina. But a few Frenchmen reached the Hova capital. From them Radama heard of the exploits of their emperor and learned of the wonders of European technology. Napoleon became his model, the possession of an army—trained and equipped on European lines—his dream: with such an instrument he would be able to fulfill the charge his father had laid upon him. A curious concatenation of circumstances made Radama's dream come true.

In 1810 the British captured Mauritius from the French. The first British governor of Mauritius, Robert Farquahar, was a passionate opponent of the slave trade. It seemed to Farquahar that the best means of suppressing the trade on the coasts of Madagascar was to assist one of the many Malagasy states in dominating the entire island and so put an end to intertribal war. Having found that Merina was ideally suited for this role, Farquahar sent envoys to Radama and negotiated a treaty whereby Radama agreed to renounce the slave trade in return for an annual subsidy, part of which would take the form of military supplies. Radama also managed to obtain the services of three European instructors. These remarkable men, a Frenchman, an Englishman, and a Jamaican mulatto,

sergeants in their own armies but generals in Merina, succeeded in substituting for the unwieldy amateur levies a standing army fifteen thousand strong, organized, disciplined, uniformed, and equipped with some
of the latest weapons. Such a force was practically invincible. Taking advantage of Merina's central position, Radama sent out expeditions in
every direction and proved himself an even greater conqueror than his
father. On many a stretch of coast the rice fields of Merina reached, figuratively at least, to the sea.

Radama's innovations were not confined to the military sphere. He
welcomed Protestant missionaries and lay workers to his capital and allowed them to establish schools and workshops; he abolished certain
barbarous practices, such as trial by ordeal; and—like another Peter the
Great—he forced some of his subjects to wear their hair short in the
European manner. But he did not have time to infect enough of his people with his ideas, and his death in 1828 was followed by a long period of
reaction. A small group of conservative army officers and aristocrats ele-
vated Radama's chief wife, Ranavalona, to the throne, encouraged her to
believe herself sacred, hunted down and killed Radama's closest associates, expelled the missionaries, and persecuted their converts. In the
past there had been no great difference in wealth among the social classes
of Merina. In Ranavalona's reign the new men in power established what
has been called "an authoritarian form of plutocracy." [3] They asserted a
monopoly over foreign trade and limited it to the import of munitions and
luxury goods for themselves; they kept in their own hands the slaves and
cattle that formed the booty of war; and they oppressed and exploited the
people.

So intent were these traditionalists on preserving Madagascar from
possible European encroachments that they even thought of building a
wall round the island. But it was impossible to follow a policy of complete
isolation: indeed, a handful of Frenchmen who rendered essential service
in the field of trade and technology were allowed to reside in the country.
It was from these men that the queen's son, Radama II, acquired a com-
pulsive conviction of the blessing of European civilization. When in 1861
he succeeded his mother, he immediately opened the country to Europeans, allowed the missionaries to return, gave concessions to traders,
and signed treaties of friendship with Britain and France. Radama was
an impractical idealist; the oligarchy of traditionalists saw to his speedy
removal. But the floodgates, once opened, could never again be closed
completely. Shortly after Radama's murder power came into the hands of
a court official, Rainilaiarivony, who as chief minister was able to make
himself virtual ruler of Merina—for the queens who were his sovereigns were only figureheads—during the last thirty years of its existence

as an independent kingdom. Rainilaiarivony stood for a policy of moderate reform.

ISLAND PLANTOCRACIES: MAURITIUS AND RÉUNION

Mauritius has an area of seven hundred twenty square miles, Réunion of nine hundred seventy. On the map, set beside the vast bulk of the African continent, the two island colonies seem insignificantly small, but in the middle of the nineteenth century they possessed a dense and rapidly expanding population. Indeed, in 1850 there were rather more people in the two islands—Mauritius had a population of one hundred fifty-eight thousand in 1846, Réunion one hundred eight in 1847—than in the whole of Cape Colony. Even more significant, the two islands possessed an elite of landowners, merchants, and professional men which in wealth and culture surpassed every other European community in Africa. "The extraordinary richness and prosperity of Mauritius, and its long settled law and civilization," wrote an English governor in the 1880's, "have nourished an island aristocracy, which is, perhaps, without example in any country of similar extent, for its numbers, its social refinement, and its intelligence and activity of mind." [4] Much the same could be said of Réunion, which later claimed to have provided the *Académie Française* with more members during the nineteenth century than any department of metropolitan France.

There were obvious similarities between the two islands, for both had developed as plantation colonies under French rule in the eighteenth century. In character they were far closer to the European colonies in the Caribbean than to any of the settlements on the mainland of Africa. In 1807—three years before its capture by the British—Mauritius had a population of sixty-five hundred whites, fifty-nine hundred freed slaves, and sixty-three thousand slaves. Moreover, both colonies, though administered by metropolitan powers with very different political traditions, presented systems of government in 1850 that had many features in common—notably the substantial powers allowed to the local bureaucracy headed by the governor and the existence of an advisory council with nominated members drawn largely from the class of prosperous merchants and planters.

Before 1815 the differences in social structure between the two islands had been relatively slight; after 1815 a number of new developments began to make their mark on the societies of the two colonies, developments that in the long run were to have a profound effect on their political evolution. On becoming a British colony, Mauritius was naturally placed under the superstructure of British colonial administration. British officials were brought out to fill most of the senior posts in the local civil service, a British garrison—seventeen hundred strong in 1850—was stationed on the island, and a number of Anglican missionaries began work among the African population. But the British did not come to the island as settlers, and so the leading families of the old French-settler population retained their position as the island's aristocracy, vigorously preserving their culture, their religion, and their code of law. There was one substantial difference between the French population of the two islands. In 1818 the white population of Réunion was fifteen thousand, more than double that of the white population of Mauritius. Immigration from France led to further increases in the European population of Réunion, stressing still further the disparity between the two islands. While Réunion, like Mauritius, possessed its class of wealthy plantation owners living in conditions of luxury and elegance, it also contained a large number of *petits blancs,* most of them smallholders, whose standard of living was no higher than that of the slaves on the wealthier plantations.

Emancipation came to the slaves of Mauritius in 1834, to those of Réunion fourteen years later. In both islands the ex-slaves gradually withdrew from the great plantations, forcing the planters to look elsewhere for laborers. India provided Mauritius with the labor force it required for the sugar fields. In the early 1830's the first Indian contract-laborers reached the island, many of them later deciding to settle there and not to return to their homeland. Already by 1846 Indians made up more than a third of the island's population, and their numbers increased rapidly in the next few decades. In Réunion the settlers looked first to Africa for contract-labor, but the system of recruitment employed by French agents on the African coast in the 1850's was so little different from the slave trade that it had to be abandoned. Not until the 1860's did Réunion begin to receive contract-labor from India in any numbers and then only for a limited period.

After 1815 both islands had come to concentrate on the production of sugar. In the 1850's, when the market for cane sugar enjoyed boom conditions, both islands experienced a period of hitherto unrivaled prosperity. Wealthy, cultured, and cosmopolitan, Mauritius and Réunion occupied in 1850 a place of some distinction among the territories of their respective metropolitan powers.

CHAPTER XXII

Africa from 1850 to 1875

✂ EXTERNAL PRESSURES AND INTERNAL DYNAMICS

Impressionistic titles for any but the shortest periods of history are inevitably imprecise and misleading. Nevertheless, if one is to attempt to sum up in a phrase the character of African history in the third quarter of the nineteenth century, the title given to this section—"the last years of the old order"—may perhaps suffice. It is true that the indigenous political order in many parts of Africa was far less ancient than the term "traditional," which Europeans later applied to it, would seem to suggest. Many of Africa's most substantial polities represented in their mid-nineteenth-century forms comparatively recent creations. The revivified pashalik of Egypt with its dominions in the Sudan, the caliphate of Sokoto, the kingdoms of the Zulus, the Ndebele and the Ngoni, the Malagasy kingdom of Merina—all these powerful states were the products of political changes that had taken place only a generation or two earlier. The history of many other African states—Ashanti, Dahomey, Wadai, Darfur, Buganda, the Lunda kingdoms—reached back no more than two to three hundred years. Yet all these indigenous polities had their roots in a more distant past; in this they were in a sharp contrast to the novel regimes to be established by the European conquerors of the continent.

By 1900 the old order was clearly in ruins. Many of the great African states had been shattered or reduced to the humiliating status of protectorates, and those kingdoms which still retained their independence were to lose it within the space of a few years. In 1875, on the other hand, the old political order was still flourishing vigorously. None of the major states of the continent had yet come under European domination. Indeed, except in Algeria, Senegal, and South Africa, the areas under immediate European control were not much more extensive than they had been at the beginning of the century.

Nevertheless, though the indigenous system still stood secure, between 1850 and 1875 it became increasingly subject to alien pressures. Not all the outsiders were Europeans. On the frontiers of the Egyptian Sudan individuals drawn from many provinces of the Ottoman Empire sought profitable employment. In parts of East Africa and even in the eastern Congo basin Arab merchants acquired considerable political power. And there was a steady growth in the Indian business community in Zanzibar. Asian enterprise had for centuries been a major factor in the development of Africa, but by the middle of the nineteenth century the contemporary achievements of Arabs, Turks, and Indians were far outclassed by the extraordinary expansion of European activities. The third quarter of the nineteenth century saw a very substantial increase in the interest of European businessmen and politicians in the affairs of Egypt and Tunis, the consolidation of French rule in Algeria, the opening of Morocco to European commerce, the conquest by the French of a deep wedge of territory along the Senegal River, the expansion of British interests on the coasts of Guinea and East Africa, the exploration of many previously uncharted regions, the steady expansion of European power in South Africa, and a notable advance of Christian missionary pioneers in many parts of the continent.

To concentrate, as so many European historians have done, on these external pressures is to lose sight of the true complexity of events, and to ignore the indigenous forces of which some were still completely unaffected in their operation by external pressures. Every African ruler operated in a highly involved political situation. For some rulers—particularly in North and South Africa and in the coastal districts of Guinea and of East Africa—relations with Europeans presented problems of almost daily occurrence. For many others European activities were still matters of marginal significance and of only occasional interest. The Shehus of Bornu, for example, were inevitably far more concerned with the policies of their neighbors in Wadai, Baguirmi, and Sokoto than they were with the actions of the British on the Niger or of the French on the Senegal. Inevitably, too, every ruler was preoccupied with the need to maintain and consolidate his own authority and so was constantly immersed in the tangled politics of his own domain.

When due allowance has been made for these internal dynamics, the most significant developments of this quarter century are to be associated with the activities of outsiders. Clearly, one can begin to detect signs of that acceleration in the process of change that was to represent the profoundest theme in the history of modern Africa.

❧ FORCES OF CHANGE

For any period of African history before the nineteenth century twenty-five years would seem too short a span of time in which to detect significant change. By 1850, however, certain parts of the continent had begun to be caught up in that process of accelerating change that distinguishes the history of modern times so sharply from that of any other period. In Chapter IV a distinction was drawn between the forces and the manifestations of change. Six distinct forces making for change were identified: alterations in the natural environment, population growth and pressure, the peaceful pursuit of well-being, the violent pursuit of well-being, the impact of ideas, and the stimulus of intercourse. To gain some understanding of the transformation undergone by Africa in the years that preceded the age of avowed European imperialism something must be said about each of the forces mentioned.

Already by 1875 men in certain parts of Africa and its adjoining islands were commenting on the change that had taken place, largely as a result of recent alien enterprise, in the natural environment. In the valley and delta of the Egyptian Nile and on the coastal plains of Algeria the landscape was changing as effective measures of irrigation or of drainage brought waste or marshy tracts under cultivation. In Mauritius the expansion of sugar plantations reduced the island's forest cover from two-thirds of its total surface in 1825 to one-sixth in 1875. In other parts of the continent the most striking change in the environment came from the annihilation of most of the larger fauna, a process particularly marked in South Africa. Lion, elephant, and rhinoceros, once common even in the western Cape, were no longer to be found in any part of Cape Colony by 1860 and disappeared shortly afterward from Natal and the Orange Free State. One South African animal, the quagga, a species akin to the zebra, became completely extinct by the 1870's; the great herds that once roamed the plains of the Orange Free State were massacred by Boer hunters who sold the hides for export or kept them to be made into grain sacks. The same process of destruction, brought about by the combination of an increased demand for hides and ivory with the introduction of more effective firearms, could be observed in many other parts of Africa.

Another aspect of the changing environment was presented by the emergence of different patterns of disease. Certain diseases—among them tuberculosis and measles—appear to have been introduced, at least into sub-Saharan Africa, by aliens from Asia and Europe. The spread of disease was encouraged by the growing mobility of peoples associated with increasing trade. One particularly well-documented example is provided by the cholera epidemic of the late 1860's.[1] Cholera reached Arabia from India in 1865. Pilgrims returning from Mecca carried the disease across the Red Sea, and in the course of the next three years the infection spread along the trade routes of Ethiopia and the Horn of Africa to reach Zanzibar in 1869. From Zanzibar it was carried by trading caravans as far west as the upper Congo, while slave dhows brought the disease to Madagascar from where it was taken to the Mascarenes. The outbreak of cholera in Algeria at this period was probably part of the same epidemic, with Maghribi pilgrims acting as the carriers. The number of deaths caused by this wide-ranging epidemic cannot be assessed, but it certainly ran into hundreds of thousands. A natural calamity on such a scale was more destructive of human life than any of the wars of the period.

The middle of the nineteenth century saw a number of significant changes in the pattern of population movement in Africa. The collapse of the Atlantic slave trade put an end to the forced migration of Africans to the New World. But in other parts of the continent, notably in the southern Sudan and in the Congo-Tanganyika-Nyasa area, the trade developed afresh and sent a steady stream of men, women, and children, drawn from regions never touched by the Atlantic system, northward to Egypt, eastward to Zanzibar, and across the seas to Arabia and to parts of the Middle East. The trade in slaves also made for many local shifts in population, as the rulers of most of the major polities of sub-Saharan Africa continued to seek to increase their wealth and strength by raiding their weaker neighbors and enslaving their able-bodied captives. A large proportion of the population of almost all the major towns of tropical Africa was of slave origin; besides being used as domestic servants, slaves were employed in many African states to do agricultural work in newly founded villages or plantations.

Since the ending of the large-scale movements of population from Arabia that occurred during the early centuries of the Muslim era, Africa received comparatively few foreign immigrants. By 1850, however, a notable change had taken place with the development of a steady flow of immigrants from most of the countries of southern Europe across the Mediterranean to Algeria and Egypt and with a much more modest movement of population from Britain and other parts of Europe to South Africa. In 1800 there cannot have been more than twenty-five thousand Europeans resident in the entire continent (excluding the neighboring islands), the majority of them settled at the Cape. By 1875, with more than a quarter of a million European settlers in Algeria, eighty thousand Europeans in Egypt, and about three hundred thousand in South Africa, the total European population for the whole continent was approaching three quarters of a million.

Egypt and Cape Colony are the only major mainland territories possessing census figures relating to this period. In both territories there was a substantial increase in population: in Egypt from an estimated three million in 1836 to five and a quarter million in 1871, in Cape Colony from one hundred twenty-nine thousand in 1832 to four hundred ninety-six thousand in 1865. There are other parts of the continent where the evidence suggests a substantial increase in the population for this period. In the northern interlacustrine area of East Africa, for example, the expansion of the Teso, today the third largest ethnic group in Uganda, appears to have taken place about the middle of the nineteenth century. Originally a pastoral people of Nilo-Hamitic origin, the Teso migrated in a southwesterly direction to settle in a more fertile country than any they had known before, and lying to the east of Lake Kyoga. They took enthusiastically to agriculture, established permanent homesteads, and experienced a notable increase in population. Many other parts of the continent were less fortunate, with disastrous epidemics such as cholera or recurrent famines restraining population growth. And there were certain districts, particularly in the Nigerian "Middle Belt" and in the southern province of Tanzania, where the devastation caused by mid-nineteenth-century slave raiding left a scar that persists to this day; in these areas, after a village had been completely destroyed, bush encroached on the deserted lands and with the bush came the tsetse fly, whose presence proved a powerful deterrent to resettlement at a later date.

Population changes within indigenous African societies inevitably had some effect on the political and economic structure of the areas in which they occurred. But of all the population changes of the period the most significant for the future of Africa were those taking place outside the continent, especially in Great Britain, the country which by 1850 had come to develop a wider range of contacts with Africa than had any other alien power. In 1811 the population of Britain stood at eighteen million; by 1871 it had risen to thirty-one million. An increase of this magnitude, unparalleled in any earlier period of history, was one of the factors involved in that highly complex historical phenomenon, the Industrial Revolution. Of all the forces making for change in nineteenth-century Africa none was so far-reaching in its consequences as the great expansion of trade made possible by a rising demand for African products in the newly industrialized countries of Western Europe and North America.

The Industrial Revolution brought with it entirely new concepts of well-being for those most closely involved in its processes. The factory worker living in one of the grimy towns of Victorian England may hardly have been aware of Africa, but through his increased consumption of soap (much of it manufactured from Nigerian palm oil), through his growing expenditure on clothing (shirts made from Egyptian cotton), and through his ambition to acquire those symbols of contemporary respectability, a sideboard of mahogany and a piano with a keyboard of ivory, he was contributing directly to the economic development of certain parts of Africa. Between 1854 and 1874 in a Britain that was then clearly the greatest trading nation in the world, expenditure on imports rose, at a time when the country's population was still increasing rapidly, from £5. 10s to £11.8s per head. Admittedly, British trade with Africa represented only a very small proportion of the country's total overseas commerce. But modest increases in external trade could have profound consequences for the African country concerned: more European merchants taking up residence in its ports, consuls appointed to protect the merchants' interests and almost invariably intervening in local affairs, politicians and civil servants in the metropolitan country forced by the representations of the merchants to take an interest in a part of the world that had previously lain beyond the horizon of their knowledge, local people brought closely into contact with Europeans as their servants, their customers, or their trading partners and gaining through this experience some knowledge of new techniques, some concept of different worlds, a still wider range of consumers acquiring a taste for the seductive novelties—cotton goods or muskets, trade gin or tea—introduced by the newcomers and so finding themselves forced to think of new methods of developing their own economy in order to produce the commodities sought by foreign merchants. A process such as this could be observed in all its complexity in centers such as Lagos or Zanzibar, Alexandria or Tangier, and in simpler form on those trading frontiers pushed forward along the lower Niger or the upper Congo, the White Nile or the Zambezi, where alien entrepreneurs sought to interest peoples hitherto untouched by the commerce of a wider world in the products of American cloth manufacturers, English gunsmiths, or German distillers.

The opponents of the slave trade advanced the argument that the development of "legitimate commerce" would put an end to the violence associated with the traffic in human beings. In fact "legitimate commerce" could also lead to violence. The course of events in the Niger delta after 1850 showed that African middlemen were prepared to use force to prevent their European rivals from breaking into their trading preserves; at the same time alien intruders in the southern Sudan were finding that the trade in ivory could be rendered profitable only when accompanied by the capture and sale of slaves. Indeed, in this period the pursuit of commercial gain and the practice of violence went closely together in many parts of the continent.

The acquisition of improved instruments of destruction greatly increased the possibilities of profitable violence. Flintlock, muzzle-loading muskets were in great demand, and their use spread with expanding trade to areas where they had not been known before. Used in sufficient quantities, especially against an enemy unfamiliar with the sound of gunfire, these muskets could produce a decisive military advantage, but as firearms they were inaccurate, dangerous to handle, and achieved only a very slow rate of fire. Thus, they were completely outclassed by the new breech-loading rifles that began to make their appearance in Africa in the 1860's. Farsighted African rulers were quick to appreciate the value of the newer firearms.

These changes in military technology clearly increased the advantages which the richer and larger indigenous polities possessed over their smaller neighbors. But at the same time the greater African states found that they themselves were no longer in a position to overcome determined European opponents. It was not simply a matter of guns; European armies, with experience in many different campaigns to assist them, were better disciplined, better trained, and better equipped than any military force to be found in Africa. Bonaparte's defeat of the Egyptian Mamluks at the Battle of the Pyramids in 1798 had provided a foretaste of what was to come. The British-Ashanti War of 1875, which ended with General Wolseley's successful march on Kumasi, showed how effectively European troops could now operate in tropical conditions. The Ashanti, like the Egyptian Mamluks, were famed for their prowess as warriors. If they could no longer resist an European invasion, what chance had other African states of averting defeat?

The advance in the technology of the newly industrialized nations powerfully affected European attitudes toward the people of Asia and Africa, strengthening already existing notions of superiority and thus rendering still more difficult the growth of a proper understanding between the peoples of the Old World. Terms such as "civilized" and "barbarous" or "savage," which had long formed part of the intellectual stock-in-trade of literate Europeans, stressed the differences between European and African societies while ignoring their similarities. At the same time these epithets, crude simplifications of a complex reality, helped to bolster the Europeans' sense of superiority. Other factors worked toward the same end. Most contemporary interpretations of Christianity contained a dogmatic insistence on the "falsity" of all other religions and in particular of Islam. But then it must be remembered that centuries of conflict between Muslims and Christians had created a dense ideological fog which prevented men of religion on either side from understanding each other's point of view. Nor was there any comprehension at this time, at least among European Christians, of the nature of indigenous African religions. Moreover, Africans of Negroid stock were not merely to be regarded pejoratively as pagans; for centuries both Christians and Muslims had been accustomed to think of black men as slaves. And though by 1850 slavery as a social institution found hardly any supporters in Europe, at least one group of Europeans in Africa—the farmers of the Boer Republics—believed that there could be found in the Bible irrefutable evidence that colored men were predestined to occupy a position of servile inferiority in white society.

During the late eighteenth and early nineteenth centuries Europeans were provided with a new justification for their notions of superiority through the development of the concept of "race." Humanity could be divided, as the proponents of the new science of ethnology pointed out, into a number of "races," each of which possessed its own distinctive set of physical characteristics and mental attributes. From this point some ethnologists went on to devise systems in which races were set in positions of superiority or inferiority and individuals described in terms of racial stereotypes. Theories of race seemed to accord with the revolutionary new scientific ideas put forward by Darwin and other evolutionists. The "white race"—and especially its "Anglo-Saxon" branch—was spreading over the entire earth. Clearly, this process provided an illustration of the Darwinian theory of the survival of the fittest. To become popular ideas must be simple; to become powerful they must gratify the self-esteem of those who hold them. For nineteenth-century Europeans the ideology of race was simple and flattering. There was no talk now, as there had been in the eighteenth century, of the "noble savage": who would be so absurd as to prefer "barbarism" to "civilization"? Commanding such a wide measure of assent, contemporary ideas about "race" gave Europeans a new élan, a new self-confidence in dealing with other peoples, and provided the basis for seemingly moral arguments in justification of imperial rule.

Notions of ethnic superiority were not confined to Europeans; cultural arrogance was a trait displayed by many people in the more powerful African states in their attitudes toward their neighbors. But European attitudes toward Africa were given a peculiar twist when small but influential groups of men and women in the metropolitan countries began to argue that it was Europe's duty to raise Africa from "barbarism." Religious conversion to Christianity, education, the development of agriculture and other useful crafts—these were the ways in which Africans would learn to acquire the virtues of civilization, exchanging indolence for industry, deceitfulness for honesty, drunkenness for sobriety, and superstition for the eternal truths of the Gospel. In Europe Africans would find the ideal they should follow. Assimilation should be the object of European enterprise.

Ideas such as these were most vigorously expressed in missionary circles and by those laymen influenced by missionary ideals. In an African context the missionaries were clearly revolutionaries who attacked long-accepted beliefs and attempted to transform many of the basic institutions of society. Contemporary ideas of progress blended with evangelical fervor to give these pioneers the confidence needed for such a task. "The earth shall be filled with the knowledge of the glory of the Lord. The obstacles to the coming of the Kingdom are mighty, but come it will for all that. . . . The world is rolling down to the golden age. The inmates of our workhouses have more comforts than rich chieftains in Africa . . . and travelers are conveyed on the ocean and on the land with a celerity which our forefathers could not comprehend and which Africans now consider fabulous." [2] The words are those of David Livingstone; they would have found an echo in the minds of many other missionaries and mission-supporters of the time.

The missionaries and other humanitarians were not indifferent to the problems of economic development; most of them shared Livingstone's conviction that "no permanent elevation of a people can be effected without commerce." [3] But to the missionaries African advancement was naturally of more concern than European profits. Other Europeans with an interest in the economic possibilities of Africa regarded the continent in a different light: to them it appeared as an undeveloped estate capable of yielding substantial profits, once the labor of its inhabitants had been subjected to European direction and supervision. The idea was not a new one. As early as the fifteenth century European plantations had been established in many of the Atlantic islands off the western coast of Africa; in 1798 the French, recently deprived of their richest colonies in the West Indies, sought compensation in Egypt, which was to be transformed into a colony capable of providing both the products and the markets needed by France; and there had been a number of abortive attempts to establish plantation colonies in Madagascar and on the West African coast. Practical experience of the difficulties of colonial rule in Africa, together with the infinitely greater attraction of other parts of the world as fields for profitable investment, led politicians and businessmen in England and France to take a skeptical view of the possibilities of African economic development. But during the 1860's the reports brought back by European explorers began to suggest that Africa did indeed contain great riches. "It is not long since Central Africa was regarded as nothing better than a region of torrid deserts or pestiferous swamps," declared the London *Times* in 1873 in a leading article written to commemorate the return of the explorer Samuel Baker from an expedition to the southern Sudan. "There now seems reason to believe that one of the finest parts of the world's surface is lying waste . . . under the barbarous anarchy with which it is cursed." [4]

The notion of racial superiority, the concept of a civilizing mission, the belief that Africa contained rich lands waiting to be exploited—here were three of the intellectual strands that came together in the aggressive European imperialism of the late nineteenth century. In the 1850's and 1860's, however, Africa was an area of concern only to small groups of public men in Western Europe. No politician could have relied on obtaining popular support for a policy of territorial aggrandizement in what was still for most Europeans the least inviting of the continents. But as the wealth, the power, and the self-confidence of the peoples of Western Europe steadily increased, so the ground was prepared for an assault on Africa, ranging wider in its impact, reaching further in its consequences than any other alien intrusion experienced by the continent in all the millennia of its history.

Mid-nineteenth-century European ideas about Africa were, then, of immense significance for its future development. But it would be a mistake to assume that the ideas only of Europeans are of interest to the historian of this period. Islam also possessed its missionaries, and in the work of the Sanusiyya and other religious fraternities one can see manifested the concept of a civilizing mission, possibly even more potent as an instrument of change than the activities of contemporary Christian missionaries. There existed, too, among many African peoples—the Amhara, the Fulani, the Ganda, the Ndebele, for example—an intense ethnic consciousness, a pride of race that certainly possesses some affinities with early forms of European nationalism and is worth considering as one of the major ideological forces of the period.

Few processes are so productive of change as is prolonged intercourse between peoples of alien culture. Yet this was an experience many African communities, prevented by the nature of their environment from establishing contact with a wider world, had never known. Gradually, however, with the expansion of long-distance trade, the emergence of larger political units and the intrusion of alien travelers, missionaries, traders, and administrators, the old isolation began to break down. One must not think of this process exclusively in terms of European initiative; fruitful intercourse was constantly taking place between different African peoples. The boy from a hill village in Adamawa (Cameroun/northern Nigeria) taken captive by the neighboring Fulani and given employment in the household of a local emir found himself seeing things (new styles of dress, new methods of building, new types of weapons and so on), meeting people (couriers from Sokoto, traders from Kano, pilgrims returned from Mecca), and hearing conversations (talk of a wider world, of more elaborate polities, of the religion of Islam), of a kind he would never have known had he remained in his ancestral village.

The consequences of intercourse were naturally most clearly visible in those places where Africans, Asians, and Europeans, each with their strikingly different cultures, came most closely into contact. In Algeria, South Africa, and the slave-trading districts of East and Central Africa and southern Sudan this intercourse involved much suffering for the local people. Elsewhere, however, contact between peoples of different continents proved more fruitful. A small but significant number of young men from Egypt, Morocco, Sierra Leone, and Senegal were sent to Europe for their education; some of them returned as dedicated innovators. The career of the first African bishop of the Anglican Church, Samuel Ajayi Crowther, provides one striking example of this personal evolution; another, equally noteworthy, may be seen in the experience of the Egyptian Muslim scholar al-Tahtawi (1801–73), who spent five years in Paris in the late 1820's, became familiar with the political writings of the eighteenth-century philosophers of the Enlightenment, and learned of the recent discoveries made by European Egyptologists. These intensely exciting intellectual experiences aroused in al-Tahtawi a passionate pride in Egypt's glorious past, made him aware of contemporary ideas of nationalism, and led him to become the first Egyptian in modern times to think of the people of his country as forming a distinct national community. Returning to Egypt, he devoted himself to writing, translating, and teaching, touching in his books on every aspect of Egyptian life, putting forward for the first time many of the themes to be accepted and developed by later generations of Egyptian nationalists, and building up for himself a reputation as "the greatest single influence in the thought of Egypt in the nineteenth century." [5]

MANIFESTATIONS OF CHANGE

Manifestations of change, it has been suggested, can be observed in many different fields, in material objects, techniques, settlement patterns, lines of communication, institutions, and modes of thought. By the middle of the nineteenth century evidence of change in all these fields was becoming increasingly apparent in many parts of Africa.

The gradual dispersal of cultivated plants, one of the most significant manifestations of change in the history of Africa, appears to have aroused little comment among contemporary observers of the African scene. There can be no doubt that the process begun in the sixteenth century with the introduction of American food crops—maize, manioc (cassava), peanuts, and others—continued through the nineteenth century, serving gradually to enrich the economies of local peoples. But one can make no easy generalizations about this internal dispersal, for its rate varied from area to area and from crop to crop. The most important stages in the development of the major cash crops of modern Africa occurred after 1875, but a beginning had been made before that date with the expansion of cotton-growing in Egypt, the introduction of cloves to Zanzibar, and the establishment of sugar plantations, worked by indentured Indian labor, in Natal in the 1860's.

Nineteenth-century European travelers in the interior of Africa sometimes came across unexpected material innovations such as manufactured objects of European origin. Clapperton, for example, was surprised to find on his visit to Kano in 1824 that he could buy in the market "an English green cotton umbrella." Away from the coast such exotic innovations remained unusual throughout this period; indeed, in most parts of the continent goods of alien manufacture still retained the character of luxury items. Gradually, however, as the volume of trade increased, more and more Africans began to acquire a taste for alien imports. Except in areas of European settlement, the range of foreign commodities was still almost as limited as it had been a hundred years earlier, with cotton goods, firearms, and alcohol or, in certain Muslim countries such as Morocco, tea and sugar, the imports most in demand. Only in some of the major ports and urban centers of North and South Africa and to a lesser extent in colonial capitals such as Freetown (Sierra Leone) and St. Louis (Senegal) could the contemporary traveler expect to find any trace of these modern amenities—large public buildings, schools, hospitals, libraries, newspapers, well-stocked shops—that served as the material hallmarks of "civilization."

Of the new techniques introduced into Africa in the nineteenth century the reading and writing of Roman script was almost certainly the most important. Before 1820 a small number of Africans—Egyptian and Maghribi Muslims who had visited Europe, mulattos in Senegal, Creoles in Sierra Leone, and Niger delta traders taught by their European acquaintances—had acquired this form of literacy. (Many more Africans were, of course, able to read Arabic script.) But it was not until Christian missionaries began to embark on sustained programs of education that really significant advances took place. Particularly striking were the results achieved in the Malagasy kingdom of Merina which received its first missionaries, Englishmen in the service of the London Missionary Society, in 1818. Working in collaboration with a Frenchman already settled at the court of the king, Radama I, the missionaries devised a method of writing down the Malagasy language, using French vowels and

English consonants. In 1827 more than four thousand local people were literate in their own language. At the same time the missionaries introduced new techniques of carpentry, metalworking, tanning, and other industrial skills. This was a pattern followed at most of the larger mission stations established on the African mainland: an intense study of the local language, the teaching of literacy, the translation and printing of parts of the Bible and other works, and the training of converts in practical skills previously unknown to them.

Missionary societies were not the only bodies anxious to introduce new techniques. In Egypt Muhammad Ali had established a number of educational institutions whose primary purpose was to train the specialists needed by the pasha to staff the modern military machine on which his power was based. Muhammad Ali's schemes were expanded by his grandson, Ismail, to provide Egypt with the foundations of a modern educational system. By 1875 more than a hundred thousand Egyptians were attending government schools. Innovations ranged from the new methods of arithmetic taught at the primary level to the training at specialized institutions designed to turn out surveyors, veterinary surgeons, and agriculturalists. By comparison with this vigorous Egyptian effort, the support given by the newly established British and French colonial governments to the development of native education appears extremely modest. In the Gold Coast, for example, five thousand children were attending school in 1880; 90 percent of them were being educated in missionary establishments. In the same year expenditure by the colonial government on education, including a grant to the missions, was less than a thousand pounds, barely more than 1 percent of the colony's total revenue.

Formal schooling has never been the only way to acquire new techniques. The Wolof soldier who took service in a regiment of Senegalese *tirailleurs,* the Algerian Muslim who became the servant of a French army officer, the Bantu farmer who made his way to the diamond fields at Kimberley—men such as these were likely to become familiar with many things they could never have known before, learning how to use new tools, enriching their spoken language with new words, and acquiring— even at the cost of hardship and humiliation—a vision of the world different from that of their fathers. But the really striking technicians of a new age were to be found among those who had experienced a long period of formal education based on European models. These were the men who qualified as clerks or skilled mechanics, priests or teachers, doctors, army officers, or civil servants. Their numbers were still very small; they were to be found only in a few parts of the continent, most notably in Egypt, in the British West African settlements, and among the "Coloured" community in Cape Colony. But the appearance of these new professionals was a social portent of immense significance for the future.

The pattern of major settlements was less firmly established in sub-Saharan Africa than in the Mediterranean lands to the north. Revolutionary political movements could lead to the complete destruction of old urban centers and to the rapid development of new foundations. Thus, in the fighting that accompanied the Fulani jihad in the Nigerian area the capitals of the states of Gobir, Bornu, and Oyo were razed to the ground, never to be reoccupied. The victorious Fulani built an entirely new town, Sokoto, as capital of their empire, together with a considerable number of new provincial centers of which Bauchi and Yola were the most important. At the same time the people of Bornu created a new metropolis in Kukawa, while Yoruba refugees from old Oyo founded a new Oyo and several other large towns, including Ibadan and Abeokuta.

From the time of the Phoenicians there had been a close connection between colonial enterprise and urban development. The process was well illustrated in the nineteenth century. In the Sudan the Turco-Egyptians transformed Khartoum from a small fishing village into the commercial and administrative center of a vast area. Zanzibar underwent a similar development as a result of Omani enterprise. In Senegal the French founded the new town of Dakar; in Algeria they created a number of new urban centers, among them Orléansville, which began as an army camp, and Philippeville, a new port built on a deserted Roman site. In the same way the expansion of European rule in South Africa led to the foundation of urban settlements of a kind the region had never known before. Most of these new towns were no more than modest market centers for agricultural districts, but some, particularly the new ports, Durban, Port Elizabeth, and East London, underwent a steady expansion; and there was no town anywhere in the continent that could compare with Kimberley's phenomenal growth after the discovery of diamonds in 1867.

Rapid expansion was not confined to new foundations. The growth in overseas trade revitalized many old cities. Before 1875 this process could most clearly be seen in the ports of North Africa. In Morocco, for example, the population of the country's eight main ports was put at sixty-seven thousand in 1836; thirty years later it had increased to one hundred one thousand. Even more striking was the transformation of Alexandria from a semiderelict town with a population of fifteen thousand in 1821 to a booming modern city with close to two hundred thousand inhabitants by 1875.

Another consequence of the expansion of overseas trade was to be found in the development of new trade routes in the interior. From the middle of the nineteenth century the southern Sudan and parts of East, Equatorial, and Central Africa, all areas previously neglected by long-distance traders, were drawn, largely as a result of the growing demand for ivory, into the orbit of a wider economy. Meanwhile, most of the old established routes, though subject as always to the disruptions caused by local political disturbances, retained their importance. Along the trans-Saharan caravan route that linked Morocco with the Western Sudan there was, as trade returns collected by European consuls at the Moroccan port of Mogador clearly proved, a substantial increase in the volume of trade. In the 1860's Timbuktu acquired, possibly for the first time in its history, a small colony of Moroccan Jews; their arrival in the main entrepôt of the Western Sudan was a sure indication that trade was flourishing.

Methods of land transport changed little in the course of the century: human or animal power continued to provide the only means of transportation in most parts of the continent. By 1875 Egypt, with more than a thousand miles of track, was the only African country to possess a network of railroads. In Algeria and South Africa railroad construction had only just begun. Properly maintained roads were to be found only in a few indigenous states, most notably in Buganda, and in parts of Egypt, Algeria, and South Africa. Nowhere in tropical Africa was it yet practicable to use wheeled vehicles. In the field of marine and river transport, on the other hand, a notable revolution was already well under way. Steamships had first appeared in African waters as early as the 1820's. By 1860 regular steamship services had been established between Western Europe and many of the major ports of North, West, and South Africa. The new services shortened the length of the voyage, reduced the cost of freight, and made commercial relations between Europe and Africa easier and safer than ever before. Steamships were also employed by European pioneers for river transport first on the Niger and later on the Zambezi and the White Nile. Indeed, by 1875 steamships had come to be regarded as an invaluable aid for explorers, and they were soon to make their appearance on most of the great lakes of the interior.

Some African communities probably experienced no significant change in the structure of their institutions during the course of the nineteenth century. But in many parts of the continent local peoples found themselves caught up in events of a violence such as they had never known before, events which caused the very framework of their society to be transformed. Usually, such changes were associated with conquest by an alien invader. Most of the military powers of nineteenth-century Africa, whatever their ethnic origin, French or Turk, British or Fulani, Ngoni or Arab, created new political superstructures, forcing many previously independent peoples to acknowledge political superiors of a kind they had never known before. The conquerors themselves also experienced institutional change, as the obligations of formal empire or informal hegemony led them to devise new methods through which to maintain their power. The French army officer in the Algerian *bureaux arabes,* the British consul on the Nigerian coast, the Arab merchant prince in the southern Sudan, the Nyamwezi warlord in Western Tanzania were men performing functions of a kind entirely novel for the areas in which they operated.

Even more unusual than these new political structures were the religious and social institutions—especially the European type of church and school—introduced as a result of Christian missionary enterprise. For some Africans, torn from their own kindred by the slave trade and later rescued by European liberators, the Christian mission station provided the nucleus for a new community. Taking the culture of their European pastors as a model, African converts in centers such as Freetown and Lagos began to establish within their own society many of the institutions of Victorian England. Men whose fathers had been rescued from slave ships became the founders of modern businesses, successful lawyers, respected clergymen or civil servants, active members of chambers of commerce, vigorous participants in voluntary associations formed to secure some local improvement. Experience of so wide a range of modern institutions led logically to the foundation of local political parties. Indeed, as early as 1871, one can see in the plans to form a Fante Confederation on the Gold Coast evidence of political activity of a kind that represented a remarkable blending of European and African ideas.

Colonial territories such as Cape Colony or the British settlements in West Africa provided an ideal environment for the missionary seeking to establish new institutions. Much more arduous was the task of the Christian evangelist working beyond the colonial frontier, for he usually found himself operating in a society which sanctioned many practices, ranging from polygamy and domestic slavery to witchcraft, slave raiding, and human sacrifice, that he was bound to regard as utterly abhorrent. The missionary's primary task was to preach the Gospel, but sermons were of little avail in persuading a people to abandon long-established customs. Only a colonial government with the power to prohibit and to punish could bring about most of the changes the missionaries desired. Inevitably, therefore, as the implications of their position became clearer, many missionaries developed into ardent advocates of an extension of European rule.

Islam, with its power to create new institutions or to transform old ones, was a social force no less revolutionary than Christianity. It was also, especially in those parts of West Africa affected by the jihads of the first half of the nineteenth century, an expansionist religion. A society newly subjected to Muslim influence might display many manifestations of change: the building of a mosque, the establishment of a Koranic school, the presence of a new social grouping made up of Muslim clerics, the introduction of the *Sharia* (the Muslim code of law), the adoption of new forms of dress. As a community became more accustomed to the new culture, profounder changes were likely to occur. Ancestor worship, for example, a cult observed in many pagan societies, might disappear in the face of Muslim disapproval. Its passing was likely to weaken the ties that held very large extended families together, thus making possible the emergence of smaller family groupings. The consequences of the initial impact of Islam must not be exaggerated. A small group of Muslim traders or a garrison of Muslim soldiers stationed in a pagan village could exercise only a very limited influence on their neighbors; first-generation converts inevitably continued to observe many uncanonical practices; and there were certain peoples in the Sudanic belt whose hostility to neighboring Muslim states made them particularly unresponsive to the appeal of Islam.

Most nineteenth-century Christian observers regarded Islam with contempt. In fact the dedicated Muslim and the evangelical Christian— each with a clear vision of the pattern of an ideal society, each fortified by a sense of absolute superiority over the beliefs of other religions—had many mental attributes in common. Moreover, in many parts of the continent Islam possessed a clear advantage over missionary Christianity: it was an old established religion and its adherents were deeply involved in the life of local societies. In the shaping of nineteenth-century Africa Islam was a force no less significant than the Christianity of the mission stations.

For men and women brought up in communities hitherto little affected by the outside world conversion to Christianity or to Islam added a new and sometimes disturbing strand to the complex web of accepted ideas. But there were many other ways in which men's modes of thought might be changed. A people caught up in the violence that accompanied the slave trade found their ancestral sense of values suddenly shattered. When famine, caused by the destruction of crops, became a yearly hazard, when men could not walk abroad without fear of being kidnapped, when every stranger was a potential enemy, then "the free hospitality, the ready transit, the giving and receiving of news in turn"—the characteristics of "the good old days" as described to an English missionary in the Nyasa area by an elderly Yao informant in the 1880's [6]—disappeared, to be replaced by meanness, obstruction, suspicion, and the habit of violence.

No less traumatic was the experience of alien conquest, especially when it was accompanied—as happened in parts of Algeria and South Africa—with the loss of an agricultural people's most cherished possession, their land. The historian usually has to content himself with the complacent annals of the conquerors. Occasionally, however he may come across a source that throws some light on the attitude of mind of the conquered. Some of the mournful songs composed by the Berbers of Kabylia after the defeat of their revolt against the French in 1871 have been recorded. One tells of the landowner who was forced to sell his best land, his fruit trees, even his clothes. "Now he does not possess even a single sheep of his own. He is destitute and suffers from hunger. It is the will of God. Let us resign ourselves." [7] But one may well imagine that resignation was laced in many vigorous minds with a bitterness, a deep-rooted hatred of the invader, emotions of a kind the Kabyles—and other societies that suffered similar experiences—may never have known before.

Experiences of this terrifying intensity were confined to comparatively limited areas. In most parts of Africa the course of men's lives followed an old established pattern. Yet occasional incidents might bring to hitherto isolated peoples the disturbing realization that strange worlds existed beyond the narrow bounds of their horizons. During the middle years of the nineteenth century many communities in tropical Africa made their first acquaintance with that astonishing phenomenon—a *white* man. At first sight a European traveler, carrying with him all the gadgetry of contemporary technology, was a very strange apparition; it is not in the least surprising that he should have been greeted—as explorers' narratives so often testify—with intense curiosity, awe, or even terror. The profound differences in culture continued, even after the initial shock had worn off, to invest Europeans with an aura of mystery in African eyes; for exactly the same reason Africans—especially those of Negroid stock—remained a profoundly mysterious people to many Europeans. But whatever the initial misunderstandings, these contacts with solitary white men were events of historical significance for many African peoples, for they represented the first stage in the growth of direct contact with a wider world.

Intercourse with Europeans introduced Africans to a new expression and a new concept: *Africa*. The division of the world into continents—a concept derived from the work of ancient Greek geographers—was meaningful only to people living in societies brought by the demands of their economy or for other reasons into constant contact with distant lands. During the nineteenth century Europeans themselves became more aware of Africa than they had ever been before. Through many different channels—missionary meetings, explorers' narratives, newspaper reports of colonial wars, scholarly publications on geography or ethnography—information about Africa reached the educated public. Paradoxically, however, as the volume of information increased, so stereotyped images became more common. Africa was "dark" or "mysterious," its people "savage" or "child-like," "naturally indolent" or "grossly sensual," and so on.

Already by 1875 a few Africans, familiar with European culture, were beginning to attack these crude simplifications. Undoubtedly, the most powerful Negro African writer of his day was E. W. Blyden. Born in 1832 in the West Indies of parents probably of Ibo origin, Blyden spent most of his working life in Liberia. A prolific writer and one of the most learned and widely traveled men of his day, Blyden worked out "a complete and consistent philosophy of Africanism." [8] Accepting the concept of racial differences, he argued that races were not, as Europeans so often declared, either superior or inferior but equal and complementary, each making its own distinctive contribution to the totality of human civilization. African culture was characterized by an intense sense of community and a deep responsiveness to religion. Historically, Africa had made notable contributions to human development. As for the future, "Africa," Blyden wrote in 1874, "may yet prove to be the spiritual conservatory of mankind. . . . When the civilized nations, in consequence of their wonderful material development, shall have had their spiritual perceptions darkened . . . through the agency of a captivating and absorbing materialism, it may be that they may have to resort to Africa to recover the simple elements of faith." [9]

Blyden's thought was clearly a product of his age, a reaction against the offensive doctrines of European racism, a passionate attempt to bolster up African self-respect at a time when the material power of Europe was growing ever more formidable. But he spoke also for the future, and so his ideas, first put forward in the 1870's and vigorously expounded until his death in 1912, came to serve as one of the shaping forces in the intellectual development of twentieth-century African nationalism.

🎏 NORTHEAST AFRICA

"My country," declared Ismail, khedive of Egypt, in 1878, "is no longer in Africa; we now form part of Europe." [10] It was an astonishing claim, one which might well seem not unjustified to a European visitor to Egypt in the 1870's who confined his attention to the country's two greatest cities: Alexandria, where nearly half the population was by that time of European origin, and Cairo, recently adorned with modern boulevards, hotels, an opera house, and a club described as possessing "billiard and reading rooms not unworthy of Pall Mall." [11] The khedive himself was one of the most striking personalities of his age, a new sort of man who personified the changes that were beginning to transform the "unchanging" East. A grandson of Muhamad Ali, Ismail had been educated at the French military academy of St. Cyr, had learned to speak French like a Parisian, and had acquired the seductive manners of a *grand seigneur.* Succeeding his uncle, Muhammad Said, as pasha of Egypt in 1863, he proved himself an intelligent, hard-working autocrat. But he was also a man of vaulting ambition, who dreamed of modernizing his country, founding a great African empire, and winning for himself a place as an equal among the sovereigns of the world.

The expansion in Egypt's economy—particularly marked during the cotton boom caused by the temporary collapse of American production in the early 1860's—provided Ismail with solid foundations on which to build. New irrigation works brought a steady increase in the amount of land under cultivation and a rapid rise in the output of cotton, the country's major export crop. Moreover, in his scheme for Egyptian advancement Ismail was able to count on the support of a wide range of collaborators. For centuries Egyptian society had been divided between a Turkish-speaking governing class and the Arabic-speaking masses. These ethnic distinctions now began to disappear, as the Turkish minority—their numbers no longer replenished as in Mamluk days by a constant stream of new recruits—were gradually absorbed into the mass of the population, while native-born Egyptians came to be appointed to some of the highest posts in the land. Promising young men were sent to Europe for their education, and in increasing numbers Europeans were introduced to fill the many new posts for which trained Egyptians could not yet be found.

Even Ismail's bitterest critics could not deny that his reign (1863–79) was full of remarkable achievements. Work on the Suez Canal, begun in Muhammad Said's reign as a result of the initiative and perseverance of a French ex-consul, Ferdinand de Lesseps, was completed in 1869. The country was equipped with the infrastructure of a modern communications system, large sums being spent on the construction of modern port facilities, roads, railroads, and postal services. At the beginning of the nineteenth century Egypt was a notoriously dangerous country for travelers; in Ismail's time an English observer could remark that it was "much safer than many parts of Ireland." [12] While these internal developments were taking place, Egyptian influence was making itself felt on an ever-widening frontier. In the 1860's and 1870's the peoples of the southern Sudan and of Darfur, of Ethiopia and the Somali coast, and even of distant Uganda felt the impact of Egyptian power. Never in all the millennia of the country's history had Egypt made so deep a penetration into the interior of Africa. Yet, irksomely for its ruler, the country's subordinate status still persisted. Ismail might play host to the royalty of Europe at the opening of the Suez Canal; his legal status remained that of a vassal of the Ottoman sultan. His grandfather's experience had shown that the Great Powers would not allow Egypt to assert its claims to independence; in such circumstances Ismail could do no more than obtain a few minor concessions—the substitution of the title khedive for that of pasha, the cession of the Red Sea ports of Suakin and Massawa, the right to negotiate loans with foreign governments—all of which had to be paid for by lavish bribes in court circles and an increase in the amount of annual tribute sent to the Porte.

So vigorous a policy of internal development and external aggrandizement would probably have been beyond Egypt's means, even if the country's revenues had been as carefully husbanded as they were in the days of Muhamad Ali. Ismail, for all his shrewdness, was the very reverse of economical; he soon showed himself to possess, in the nice phrase of a modern historian, "an appalling talent for spending money." [13] His extravagance spread to his entourage. An Egyptian princess was found to have run up a bill for one hundred fifty thousand pounds with a French dressmaker; hearing that a new cannon had been invented in Europe, the head of the Ordnance Department ordered not one as an experiment but a couple of dozen on the grounds that "Egypt could not remain behind other nations in military matters"; [14] and there were many, even grosser examples of squandermania. Spending on such a scale could, of course, be met only by borrowing, and for a time there were plenty of Europeans willing to lend money to the khedive and his associates on highly usurious terms. Between 1863 and 1876 Ismail borrowed an average of seven million pounds a year, an amount sometimes exceeding his annual revenue. By 1875 the khedive had brought his country to the brink of bankruptcy.

Expansion on many of the colonial frontiers of the nineteenth-century world was due more to private enterprise than to official initiative. This was certainly the case on Egypt's colonial frontier in the southern Sudan, where from the 1840's a motley collection of traders of many nationalities, stimulated by the increasingly high prices paid for ivory, had been extending their activities over a great arc of territory. At first the traders moved along the lines of the rivers, the White Nile and its tributaries; later, accompanied by bands of well-armed Arab servants, they began to move into the interior. They found themselves operating among peoples living in stateless polities, possessing no previous experience of long-distance commerce, and showing no great interest in the conventional trade goods of the outside world. It soon became apparent that the easiest way of paying one local group for its ivory was to present it with the cattle stolen from its neighbor; the same raid might also provide slaves who could be used to reward a trader's servants or sold in northern markets to help defray the heavy expenses involved in operating under such arduous conditions. Thus brutally, the Dinka, the Nuer, the Bari, the Bongo, and a score of other peoples were drawn into the economy of a wider world.

The career of Zubair Pasha shows how the possibilities inherent in this situation could be exploited by an intelligent and adventurous man. Born in 1831 of a Sudanese Arab family that claimed descent from the Abbasids, Zubair began modestly enough by attaching himself in 1856 to a trader from Lower Egypt. Within two years he had made enough money to set up on his own and return to the Bahr al-Ghazal, determined to explore areas not yet visited by any trader. His travels brought him as far as Zande country, at that time particularly rich in ivory. To provide himself with a secure base he followed the usual practice and built himself a zariba or fortified encampment. By 1870 Zubair's zariba had grown into a regular town, Zubair himself giving employment to a thousand armed men, selling as many as eighteen hundred slaves a year, and maintaining a court described by one European traveler as "little less than princely." [15] Zubair was certainly conscious of the regal nature of his position. "I ruled over the land," he wrote in his autobiography, "in accordance with the Book and the Law of Muhammad. I undertook the civilization of the country, . . . causing it to progress along the lines of commerce and peace." [16]

Humanitarians in Britain could not possibly accept such an interpretation of this merchant prince's activities. To them it became increasingly obvious, as a succession of travelers brought back first-hand reports of the Sudan, that yet another part of Africa had been given up to the horrors of the slave trade. Ismail, who claimed to stand "at the head of civilization on the African continent," [17] was particularly susceptible to their criticisms. Moreover, he needed British diplomatic support in his international relations, and he was anxious to assert his authority on the frontiers of his empire. In 1869 he decided to appoint an Englishman, the explorer Samuel Baker who already possessed considerable first-hand experience of the Sudan, to lead a lavishly equipped expedition up the Nile. Baker's task, defined in grandiose terms, was "to annex the countries that constitute the Nile Basin with the object of opening those savage regions to legitimate commerce and establishing a permanent government." [18] In practical terms the expedition was largely a failure; it achieved little beyond reestablishing government control of the post of Gondokoro. But Baker's appointment served as a precedent. In 1874 he was succeeded as governor of "Equatoria" by another Englishman, an army officer named Gordon, who had made a name for himself in China and who was destined to do more than any other European of his day to involve his country in the affairs of the Sudan.

While Ismail was attempting to assert his control over Equatoria, Zubair's power was steadily increasing in the area of the Bahr al-Ghazal. In 1873 Ismail decided to accept the situation and appointed Zubair as governor of the province, supplying him with a garrison of regular troops in return for tribute paid in ivory. The next year Zubair, in the most astonishing coup of his career, attacked Darfur, for three centuries one of the most powerful states of the Sudanic belt, defeated the sultan in pitched battle, and overran the country. Ismail himself had long looked covetously at Darfur and was determined to appoint his own nominee as governor of the newly conquered territory. Imprudently, Zubair traveled to Cairo to protest the khedive's decision; by imposing restrictions on his movements Ismail made sure that his ambitious subordinate did not return to the Sudan.

Darfur was not the only ancient kingdom to arouse Egyptian interest. Beyond the rugged borderlands of the southeastern Sudan lay Ethiopia. During the century of anarchy known to Ethiopian chroniclers as "the time of the princes," the country could hardly be described as a kingdom, but the coronation of the warlord Kassa as the Emperor Theodore (Tewodoros) in 1855 marked the opening of a new era in Ethiopia's long history. Theodore was one of the most extraordinary figures of his age. Born in 1818 the son of a minor chief on the Ethiopia-Sudan border, he made a name for himself as the leader of a band of freebooters and gradually fought his way to supreme power. As emperor he was made vividly aware of his country's many weaknesses—the endemic warlordism, the ravages caused by Galla inroads, and the revived threat of foreign intervention posed by Egyptian expansion in the Sudan and European activities on the Red Sea coast. Dreaming of re-creating the ancient glories of the Solomonid kingdom, he saw clearly that the country needed a strong central government with the turbulent local chiefs reduced to the position of salaried officials, a powerful standing army equipped with modern weapons, and a reformed Church stripped of much of its wealth and power. Only a man of herculean energy would have attempted to embark on such a program. In the conditions of the time it could never be successfully completed. "If I go to the south," Theodore once told a British visitor, "my people rebel in the north; when I go to the west, they rebel in the east. I have pardoned the rebels over and over again; meanwhile they persist in their disobedience and defy me. I am now determined to follow them into every corner and shall send their bodies to the grave and their souls to hell." [19]

Frustration blended with megalomania—"are you not aware," he once remarked, "that India and half the world belongs to me" [20]—transformed this shrewd, courageous man into a terrible figure, a brutal and bloodthirsty tyrant. A train of relatively trivial events led to his downfall. The British Foreign Office forgot to answer a letter from Theodore to Queen Victoria; the British consul recently accredited to Ethiopia was imprisoned, so too was a second British representative and a group of other Europeans residing in the country. British prestige required that they should be rescued and so, in 1868, a large British expeditionary force was sent from India under the command of an engineer officer, General Napier. The British advance from the Red Sea into the heart of Ethiopia was one of the most remarkable feats of military organization of its day. There was not much need for fighting: by this time most of the provincial leaders were in revolt against the emperor and his army had dwindled from one hundred thousand to ten thousand men. Theodore killed himself as the British stormed his mountain fortress of Magdala.

The British had no territorial ambitions in Ethiopia, but to Ismail the revived anarchy that followed Theodore's death offered yet another opportunity for Egyptian aggrandizement. Massawa, acquired from the Ottoman sultan in 1865, was an ideal base from which to launch an attack. But by the time the Egyptian army was ready to embark on the only major campaign of Ismail's reign, the Ethiopians had found a new leader in the ras of Tigre who was crowned as the Emperor John (Yohannes) in 1872. Three years later two Egyptian expeditions suffered crushing defeats at the hands of the new emperor. Mutilated Egyptian prisoners were sent back to Ismail with the savage message, "If you want any more eunuchs for your harem, drive me up the rest of your army." [21] The brandnew rifles and artillery captured by the Ethiopians were kept for use against later invaders.

Egyptian activities were not confined to the Eritrean coast. In 1870 an Egyptian force occupied the Somali ports of Zeila and Berbera, both of which had long been under nominal Turkish suzerainty. From the coast the Egyptians advanced inland to establish a garrison in the independent sultanate of Harar. Other intruders, too, had begun to stake their claims on unoccupied stretches of the western littoral of the Red Sea. In 1862 the French purchased the little port of Obock from a local Danakil chief, while in 1869 an Italian shipping company obtained the port of Assab in the same way. The British already possessed a secure base in the port of Aden. They had no desire to increase their responsibilities in the area, but they were acutely sensitive to moves by foreign powers in the neighborhood of any of the main arteries of their empire.

Ever since the French invasion of Egypt in 1798 British statesmen had been aware of the significance of Northeast Africa in general and of Egypt in particular in the strategy of empire. "We do not want to have Egypt," Palmerston wrote in 1857, "what we wish about Egypt is that it should continue to be attached to the Turkish Empire, which is a security against its belonging to any European Power. We want to trade with Egypt, and to travel through Egypt, but we do not want the burthen of governing Egypt." [22] Disraeli's masterly coup of 1875—his purchase for Britain of Ismail's shares in the Suez Canal Company—did not present any departure from the policy so clearly defined by Palmerston. "The question for us," wrote Foreign Secretary Lord Derby in explanation of the purchase, "is not one of establishing an exclusive interest but of preventing an exclusive interest from being established as against us." [23] But for all the negatives surrounding British policy the events of the last quarter of the nineteenth century were to reveal it as a force capable of transforming the political structure of the entire continent.

NORTHWEST AFRICA

Nowhere in Africa, during the third quarter of the nineteenth century, were Europeans to be seen in such numbers as in Algeria. In 1856 the *colon* population stood at one hundred sixty thousand; by the late 1870's it had risen to over three hundred thousand. Only about half of the settlers were of French origin, drawn mostly from the Midi and Corsica; the remainder came from other parts of the western Mediterranean and included Spaniards, Italians, and Maltese. From the early days of the French conquest most of the *colons* had made their homes in the towns, earning their living as administrators, shopkeepers, or artisans; only a minority were pioneering farmers settled in the countryside. In addition Algeria supported a powerful army of occupation whose numbers, put at sixty thousand in 1875, could easily be increased to meet any emergency. The settler and the soldier—not as in so many other parts of Africa at this time the trader and the missionary—represented the European presence; their impact on Algeria was harsh.

In the 1850's the occupation of the oases of the northern Sahara and the penetration of the highland fastness of Kabylia marked the final stages of the French conquest. As a defeated people, the Arab and Berber masses were at the mercy of their conquerors. For many of them the price of defeat was the loss of much of their land, confiscated to satisfy the needs of French settlers. "There is not an Arab, with a tent and a family of his own," wrote a sensitive French army officer in 1850, "who does not feel a sense of desolation when he thinks about the past nor a sense of anxiety when he tries to make out the future." [24] Revolt, itself often no more than a violent reaction at the prospect of growing impoverishment, was punished by the confiscation of a tribal group's best lands. Forced into cultivating tracts where the soil was poorer and therefore exposed all the more cruelly to the disastrous effects of frequent droughts, many Algerian peasants found themselves being plunged deeper into pauperism. By encouraging the introduction of individual landholding, the French brought about the ruin of the traditional system of collective land tenure and made it easy for European speculators to purchase land cheaply, thus reducing the once-free occupants to the status of tenants or landless laborers.

The ruthlessness that characterized *colon* attitudes toward the natives was in part a reflection of their own insecurity. For European settlers, too, Algeria was a harsh and cruel land. It was an extremely difficult country to develop: dependent almost entirely on its agricultural resources, yet incapable of producing lucrative crops such as cotton or sugar, the colony began to yield reasonable returns only when in the late 1870's French viticulturists brought their skills to the country. Its marshy coastal plains, the main areas of European settlement, proved to be very unhealthy until they had been effectively drained. Above all, compared with the colonies of Anglo-Saxon settlement in the New World or Australasia, Algeria contained a massive native population, outnumbering the settlers in the proportion of ten to one, surly and farouche, if not belligerently hostile, in its attitude toward European intruders. Army officers in the *bureaux arabes* saw at close quarters the consequences of the settlers' policy of *refoulement* (pushing back the natives) and became increasingly critical of the behavior of the *colons,* who, for their part, loathed the arrogant autocracy of military administrators. During the reign of Napoleon III the *colons* could not obtain the free hand they so passionately desired. Indeed, the emperor was anxious to protect the natives whom he admired from exploitation by the settlers whom he despised. But given the strength of local pressure groups and the vacillations of Napoleon's own policy, his talk of establishing an "Arab kingdom" in Algeria was empty rhetoric. The alienation of land continued, and the afflictions of the Algerian people were increased still further in the late 1860's by a dreadful series of natural disasters—locusts, drought, and cholera—reckoned to have cost no less than three hundred thousand lives.

Few Frenchmen welcomed the collapse of the Second Empire on the battlefields of the Franco-Prussian War in 1870 so vociferously as the *colons* of Algeria. To them the Third Republic brought the end of military autocracy, representation in Paris, and a measure of control over their own affairs. But to the mass of Algerians the prospect of unfettered settler rule was utterly abhorrent. The revolt that broke out in Kabylia in 1871 developed into one of the most serious insurrections ever faced by a colonial power. Inevitably, after its suppression, the rebels were stripped of their most precious possession, their land. For the triumphant *colons* there opened a golden age of settler domination and for the Algerian masses long years of bitter, silent resignation.

With their power so firmly established in Algeria, the French were bound to interest themselves in the affairs of their North African neighbors, Tunis and Morocco. To French expansionists Tunis seemed a country ripe for the picking. In the 1860's Mustapha Khaznadar, the cunning, avaricious, and entirely self-interested mayor of the palace, who possessed virtually dictatorial powers until his fall in 1873, became entangled, like his contemporary the Khedive Ismail, in the toils of shady European financiers, and with the same disastrous chain of consequences: ambitious schemes for modernization, loans raised at exorbitant rates of interest in the money markets of London and Paris, the country overrun by European speculators whom the local Arabs compared to "flies swarming over a wounded ass," taxes raised to meet the cost of interest or debt-repayment, revolts by a peasantry oppressed beyond endurance, savage repression, and growing pressure from foreign interests culminating in the establishment in 1869 of an international commission to control the country's finances.

France was not the only great power with an interest in Tunis. The regency was still nominally a vassal state of the Ottoman Empire—a status which the British were particularly anxious to see maintained, for to the rulers of India, who still regarded the French as the most dangerous of potential enemies, Tunis occupied a position of some significance in the strategy of empire. Should the French take over the regency and transform the port of Bizerta into another Toulon they would be in a position to cut one of the main British routes to the East. The newly established government of a united Italy also had a stake in Tunis. Italian nationals, ranging from wealthy Genoese merchants to impoverished Sicilian fishermen, made up about half the country's fifteen thousand Europeans. In these circumstances Tunis presented the most obvious field for future Italian expansion. Rivalry between the great powers provided the only effective guarantee of Tunisian independence.

Much the same could be said of Morocco. At first glance the country seemed far better placed than Tunis to defend itself, and until the middle of the nineteenth century its rulers had succeeded in keeping Europeans at a distance. But two major military defeats, the first inflicted by the French in 1844, the second by the Spaniards in 1860, revealed the grave weakness of the once-formidable empire. At the same time a commercial treaty negotiated with the British in 1856 removed many of the vexatious restrictions hitherto imposed on European businessmen. From the late

1850's there was a rapid expansion of European influence in Morocco. The European population rose from four hundred in 1854 to fifteen hundred in 1867. Steamship services, offering regular connections with French and British ports, came into operation. Most significant of all, there was a notable increase in consular representation and in consular power, for the consuls were authorized to extend the privilege of "protection" to Moroccans in the service of their own nationals. Protection brought with it exemption from local taxation and the right to be tried in consular courts. From a reasonable provision designed to protect a handful of Europeans the practice developed into a serious abuse, as increasing numbers of Moroccans found ways of acquiring the privilege and so removed themselves from the jurisdiction of their rightful sovereign.

Sidi Muhammad, sultan of Morocco from 1859 to 1873, was an intelligent ruler who appreciated the need for development and reform. Taking up some of the ideas suggested by the more congenial European consuls and making use of the services of a variety of Europeans—Spanish exiles, French deserters and British engineers—he sought to modernize his army, start new industries, improve certain roads and harbors, and render the administration less corrupt and more efficient. Such a policy could never be popular, for the mass of Moroccans were acutely distrustful of all Europeans, and their intellectual leaders among the ulama were deeply committed to a highly conservative form of Islam. Moreover, any increase in the power of the *makhzen* (central government) threatened to reduce the prestige of powerful provincial governors. The local Europeans put further obstacles in the path of the reforming sultan. They resisted any attempt to curb the abuses of the system of protection; at the same time any scheme for improvement put forward by the consul of one nation was likely to arouse the jealous opposition of his diplomatic colleagues. Spain, France, and Britain were the European powers most deeply involved in Moroccan affairs. The Spaniards, some of whom were still animated by the passions of the *reconquista,* claimed it as their "historic right" to intervene in Morocco, while the French argued that their stake in Algeria gave them a predominant interest in the country. The British, ever mindful of the need to safeguard their base at Gibraltar, wished to see Morocco's independence preserved; they also saw in the country a valuable market for an expanding trade. British diplomatic support certainly afforded Morocco some protection against the grosser forms of French and Spanish pressure, yet it was largely due to British influence that the sultan had agreed to reverse a well-established policy of isolation and open the country to foreign traders. There was little comfort for Moroccan patriots in the realization that the independence of their country depended on the patronage or the rivalry of foreign powers.

The evident weakness of Muslim states when faced with the more aggressive or expansionist powers of Europe led many Europeans to assume that Islam was a decadent religion. European attitudes toward Islam were vitiated, no less than Muslim attitudes to Christianity, by ignorance and prejudice. The history of Northwest Africa in the latter half of the nineteenth century affords in the rise and expansion of the Sanusiya order a striking indication of the inherent vitality of the religion of the Prophet. The Sanusiya was a missionary fraternity comparable to those other Muslim orders, the Qadiriyya and the Tijaniyya, whose impact on the Western Sudan has already been noted. Its founder, Sayyid Muhammad al-Sanusi, known to his followers as the Grand Sanusi, was born in Algeria in 1787 and devoted himself to a peripatetic life of learning and teaching. His ambition, like that of most of the great Muslim reformers of the early nineteenth century, was to create a society based on the ideals of primitive Islam. To this end he founded his own religious order in 1837. At this time he was at Mecca. A few years later local opposition forced him to leave Arabia; finding himself prevented by the French occupation from returning to his homeland, he took up his residence in the remote Cyrenaican oasis of Jaghbub.

Rapidly, Jaghbub developed into one of the major intellectual centers of the Muslim world. Like all great religious teachers, the Grand Sanusi attracted men of pious and scholarly temperament to become his disciples. The newcomers made a profound impression on the Bedouin tribesmen and were invited by one tribe after another to found lodges (*zawiya*) in tribal territory. Like European monasteries in the Dark Ages, these lodges soon came to serve a variety of purposes, "schools, caravanserais, commercial centers, social centers, forts, courts of law, banks, storehouses, poor houses, sanctuary and burial grounds, besides being channels through which ran a generous stream of God's blessing." [25] Founded for purely religious purposes "these centers of culture and security," whose sheikhs were under the direction of the Grand Sanusi, soon acquired political significance, for they introduced a new element of justice and order to a country hitherto divided between a score of warlike and fiercely independent Bedouin tribes. The Grand Sanusi died in 1859, but under his son and successor, Muhammad al-Mahdi, the movement maintained its momentum as a missionary order, its members moving along the caravan routes of the central Sahara to found new lodges as far afield as the Fezzan, Tibesti, and Wadai. The Ottoman authorities wisely treated the Sanusiya with great circumspection: indeed, the government of Cyrenaica toward the end of the nineteenth century has been described as a "Turco-Sanusi condominium." [26] Thus, gradually and by purely peaceful means the order laid the foundations of a novel theocratic state.

To the turbulent Bedouin of the eastern Sahara the Sanusi divines brought a more refined culture and a wider sense of political community; in so doing they proved themselves among the most successful innovators in the history of nineteenth-century North Africa.

✻ WEST AFRICA

In the complex pattern of West African polities three groups stand out as the major initiators of political change in the third quarter of the nineteenth century: the Tukolors under the leadership first of al-Haji Umar Tall then of his son Ahmadu, the French, and the British. Of the rise of the Tukolor empire and the career of its founder something has already been said; Umar's polity had grown rapidly in the 1840's and 1850's to become the major state in the area of the upper Niger. As it expanded it came directly into contact with the French on the Senegal.

The French posts on the Senegal were in an area possessing only modest natural resources, but if French influence could somehow be spread over the country that lay between the upper reaches of the Senegal and the Niger, then, so colonial policymakers rather too glibly assumed, it should be possible to attract to French trading posts the allegedly lucrative trade of the interior. To secure a proper hold on the line of the Senegal, thus putting an end to the vexations suffered by French traders at the hands of local riverain rulers, was an essential preliminary to such a policy. It was the achievement of a young engineer officer, Captain Faidherbe, whose service in Algeria had given him some understanding of Muslim peoples, to establish for the first time a firm French control of the river, thus ensuring an ideal springboard for future expansion. In his career as governor of Senegal Faidherbe enjoyed three advantages: he could count on the support of an autocratic imperial government in Paris far less averse to a vigorous colonial policy than its parliamentary predecessor, he was provided with more troops than any earlier governor had ever been allowed, and he held office for the unusually long period of nine years (1854–61, 1863–65). Combining force with diplomacy, Faidherbe got the better of the Moor and Wolof rulers who posed the most immediate threat to the French position, inaugurated the policy of recruiting local Africans to increase the number of troops at his disposal, and set about the task of winning men's minds to the French cause by establishing a school for the sons of chiefs and by developing St. Louis into a dignified colonial capital.

Of all the rulers with whom Faidherbe came into contact, al-Haji Umar was by far the most powerful. Many Frenchmen, recalling the savage struggle waged against Muslims in Algeria, thought of the Tukolor leader as a fanatical enemy of all Christians. Undoubtedly, some of Umar's followers, especially those from Futa Toro, would have welcomed a jihad aimed at expelling the French, but Umar himself was more interested in conquering the country of the pagan Bambara. In 1857 after his troops had failed to capture the French fort at Medina, recently established by Faidherbe at the furthest limit of French influence, Umar turned eastward to consolidate his dominion on the Niger. There could be no thought of challenging Umar's supremacy in this area, but Faidherbe hoped it might be possible to secure permission for French traders to do business within Tukolor territory. To this end he sent a diplomatic mission to Umar in 1863. Nothing came of this advance, for Umar was killed in 1864 and his son Ahmadu was preoccupied with internal political difficulties. Faidherbe left Senegal for good in 1865 and his successors were men of less vigorous imagination. The catastrophic French defeat in Europe in 1870 put an end to all talk of colonial expansion, but Faidherbe's ideas were not forgotten.

French activities were not confined to the Senegal Valley. In the late 1850's and in the 1860's military posts were established both to the north and south of the Gambia, while French merchants from Gorée island moved across to the mainland to lay the foundations of Dakar. Elsewhere in West Africa, on the Ivory Coast and on the Slave Coast west of Lagos, French initiative was due to the enterprise of individual traders. To Faidherbe, preoccupied with the interior, French establishments lying to the east of Sierra Leone seemed of little value, but the Gambia, where the British maintained a modest colony, was an area of vital interest to the French. Faidherbe suggested a territorial exchange; his ideas were taken up in the early 1870's and led to prolonged but fruitless Anglo-French negotiations. Had agreement been reached, the final partition of West Africa might have been made on "strikingly different" lines, with French power concentrated in Senegambia and the British masters of all the coast between Lagos and Accra.[27]

"To encourage and extend British Commerce and thereby to displace the Slave Trade": this neat blending of "self-interest and the general good" was Lord Palmerston's definition of British policy in West Africa [28]—and Palmerston personified the exuberant confidence of mid-Victorian Britain. "If we wish Commerce to prosper," Palmerston declared in 1860, "we must employ Force or the threat of Force to keep these Enemies of Legitimate Commerce [the slavers] quiet." [29] On these dynamic concepts the circumstances of the age imposed certain restraints. West African settlements, especially when their governments became involved in local wars, were expensive to maintain; the West Coast was notoriously unhealthy for Europeans; and once the Atlantic slave trade had been effectively suppressed, the need for vigorous British intervention seemed less pressing. In 1865 a Select Committee of the House of Commons showed itself strongly opposed to a further extension of British territory and contemplated eventual withdrawal, following the gradual transfer of administrative responsibility to the "natives," from the Gold Coast, Gambia, and Lagos, leaving Sierra Leone as the only British colony in the area. Whatever the contradictions of British policymakers in Westminster, the men on the spot—the administrators, the traders, the missionaries and their protégés, the Creoles of Sierra Leone—expected support and protection. Through the activities of this relatively small group of individuals the sphere of British influence was gradually expanded.

The most striking advances took place within the area of modern Nigeria, an approach being made from the north as well as from the south. In 1849 James Richardson, an ardent opponent of the slave trade, which he had observed at first hand while traveling in the central Sahara, persuaded the British government to send him on a mission of exploration across the desert. Richardson died at an early stage of the expedition, but one of his companions, a Prussian university lecturer, Heinrich Barth, succeeded in spending five years traveling between Bornu and Timbuktu and produced on his return one of the most thorough and scholarly narratives in the annals of exploration. The information sent back by Barth prompted the British government to dispatch a second expedition under Dr. W. B. Baikie to explore the Niger's great tributary, the Benue. Previous British expeditions up the Niger had lost many men from malaria. The regular use of quinine enabled Baikie and all his men to return safely.

Now at last it was possible to fulfill the dreams of the explorers and geographers and develop the Niger as a highway for commerce into the interior. By establishing posts along the line of the river British merchants, it was thought, would be able to purchase forest produce more cheaply than on the coast and at the same time attract much of the long-distance trade that passed northward across the Sahara. A Liverpool shipowner, Macgregor Laird, was the pioneer of the Niger trade. Supported by a government subsidy, Laird began sending steamers regularly up the river. To the merchant princes of the delta states and to their trading partners from Liverpool this move was a serious threat to their livelihood. But by attacking the ships and trading posts of the intruders they provoked the British into sending gunboats up the Niger. Despite the violence the Niger trade expanded. By the late 1870's there were fourteen British steamers operating on the river, amicable contacts had been established with Nupe, one of the southern provinces of the Sokoto caliphate, and, significant omen for the future, other Europeans were beginning to look with interest at what had previously been an undisputedly British preserve.

Meanwhile, along the Nigerian coast a steady increase in British influence was taking place. The official British presence was vigorously represented by a permanent consul supported by a substantial naval force, while the "palm-oil ruffians"—their numbers swollen by newcomers taking advantage of the establishment in 1852 of regular steamship services with West Africa—served as the frontiersmen of an expanding commerce. In circumstances such as these interference in the domestic affairs of the coastal polities—to settle disputes or remove offensive rulers—developed into a regular practice. The petty state of Lagos was the scene of the most far-reaching British action. Its ruler, Kosoko, fell foul of the British by continuing to engage in the slave trade; in 1851 a British naval squadron attacked Lagos, expelled Kosoko, and replaced him by a more pliant successor with a British consular representative at his side.

With British missionaries stationed at Abeokuta and other Yoruba towns to the north and Lagos developing as a major center of legitimate commerce the British government found itself drawn even more deeply into the violent politics of the Yoruba states. In 1861 the "anomalous quasi Protectorate" of Lagos [30] was transformed into a British Crown Colony. If the new colony were to prosper and provide sufficient revenue to meet the cost of its administration, there must be peace on the trade routes to the interior. But these routes, along which an increasing number of firearms were beginning to pass in exchange for local palm oil, were of vital importance to the warring Yoruba states. Intervention in Yoruba politics, the policy favored by J. H. Glover, the colony's energetic administrator in the 1860's, led to what the men in Whitehall regarded as "dangerous complications"; nonintervention, the policy forced on Glover's successors by the home government, led to commercial stagnation. The dilemma—commonplace enough for an imperial power—existed for three decades. As late as 1881 the British colonial secretary could set his face firmly against "direct interference with the inland tribes." [31]

Already, however, far beyond the colonial frontiers such interference was taking place. For the 1850's and 1860's saw a vigorous expansion of the missionary work begun in the Nigerian area in the 1840's. Europeans, Americans, and Africans, drawn from different denominations, were the pioneers of a movement that can reasonably be described as revolutionary, for it aimed at a radical transformation of local societies. Particularly striking were the results achieved through "native agency," through the work of men of African origin such as Samuel Ajayi Crowther. Crowther, a Yoruba by birth, had been caught as a slave in his youth, rescued by a British warship, and taken to Sierra Leone. There his remarkable intellectual gifts and his ardent faith led him on a career that culminated in his consecration as the first African bishop of the Anglican Church, his diocese being defined as "the countries of western Africa beyond the limits of our dominion," his activities concentrated on the mission stations established along the Niger.

The work of the missionaries was reinforced by the influence of the "emigrants," the returned captives and ex-slaves from Sierra Leone and Brazil, returning in sufficient numbers—there were three thousand of them in Lagos in the 1870's—to constitute a powerful leaven in the societies among which they settled. Gradually, a new type of West African began to emerge, the man or woman who without the experience of being forcibly removed from his native society, as the Creoles had been, had nevertheless been brought in touch with the techniques and ideals of Europe and America through education at the mission school and close contact with missionaries and emigrants.

Similar in character and no less striking in its consequences was the cultural revolution taking place at the same time along the Gold Coast. Here the European presence was far more firmly established than in the Nigerian coastal areas to the east. But the situation with which the British found themselves faced in the 1850's and 1860's was a tiresome and embarrassing one. The loosely defined protectorate established in the 1840's had led them to intervene ever more frequently in the internal affairs of the protected states. Yet commercially the protectorate was an area of comparatively little value; moreover, the continuing presence of a string of Dutch forts along the coast made it impossible to establish an effective system of customs administration, a serious weakness since customs duties provided the chief means of building up local revenue. In 1872 the Dutch handed over their forts to the British and revenue jumped from a mere nine thousand pounds a year in the early 1860's to more than sixty thousand pounds a year in the mid-1870's. But the vacillations of British policy and the complications caused by the negotiations with the Dutch led to serious difficulties both with the protected chiefs and with the great military power of Ashanti.

Resentful of British interference and encouraged by British talk of withdrawal, some of the Fante chiefs, assisted and advised by the growing class of Western-educated men on the coast, came together in 1871 to form a confederation. Weakened by internal rivalry the movement was brought to an end by British opposition, but the elaborate constitution drawn up by the supporters of the confederation deserves to be remembered as the first attempt made by a West African people to establish through the blending of European and African institutions a new form of polity. It was a polity, too, with avowedly progressive aims: "We contemplate," declared the signatories of the constitution, "means for the social improvement of our subjects and people, the growth of education and industrial pursuits, and, in short, every good which British philanthropy may have designed for the good of the Gold Coast." [32]

In the 1860's Ashanti armies invaded the protectorate and the British seemed incapable of resisting them. In 1873 a more formidable invasion was launched, provoked by Ashanti resentment at the cession to the British of the Dutch fort at Elmina, which was regarded as subject to Ashanti sovereignty. This time the British launched a massive counteroffensive. Sir Garnet Wolseley, "the very model of a modern major-general," was despatched to the Gold Coast with a picked force of twenty-five hundred men. Within a few weeks he had shattered the Ashanti armies, burned Kumasi, and forced the Asantehene to sue for peace. This brilliant feat of arms, by far the most successful yet recorded in the limited annals of European campaigning in tropical Africa, was a portent for the future. There was no talk now of withdrawal from the Gold Coast. Instead, a few months after Wolseley's triumph the protected areas of the Gold Coast were transformed by unilateral declaration into a British Crown Colony.

EQUATORIAL AND CENTRAL AFRICA

Hitherto Equatorial and Central Africa have been considered as two distinct regions. In this chapter it is worth abandoning this purely arbitrary division, for during the third quarter of the nineteenth century a common theme—the pressure and penetration of outsiders—dominates the history of this great territory, hitherto the most isolated of all the parts of the continent. At the same time one can see in what is perhaps the most spectacular episode in the area's history for this period, the voyage down the Congo of the explorer H. M. Stanley, the first indication that the basin of the Congo might possess a certain natural unity, a novel geographical concept that was to have a profound influence on the European approach to this part of Africa in the last decades of the century.

Something has already been said of the variety of intruders who began pressing in on Equatorial and Central Africa in the middle of the nineteenth century: Fulani horsemen in the northwest, traders from the Nile Valley in the northeast, yet other traders, Portuguese mulattoes, Ovimbundu, and Cokwe in the west, Arab, Swahili, and Nyamwezi in the east, and in the south the warrior bands of the Nguni diaspora followed by the first Europeans—missionaries, hunters, and traders—to move across the Limpopo into the "far interior." All these movements retained—and in the case of the Arabs and the Europeans increased—their momentum. Some light on certain aspects of these movements is thrown by a brief study of three of the outstanding figures of this period: the Nyamwezi adventurer, Msiri, the Scottish missionary-explorer, David Livingstone, and the Welsh-American journalist and traveler, H. M. Stanley.

By the later 1870's most of the country between the Luapula and the Lualaba, once largely part of the territory of the Lunda Kazembe, later known from the name of a local chief as Katanga, had been brought under the domination of a Nyamwezi adventurer, nicknamed Msiri, "the mosquito." Nyamwezi traders from east of Lake Tanganyika first visited Katanga, a country famous for its copper, early in the nineteenth century. Some of them took up permanent residence in the territory, where they became known as the Yeke. Msiri, whose father was a minor chief in Unyamwezi and a famous and widely traveled trader, reached Katanga about 1856. As a trader, dealing in copper, slaves, and ivory, he was able to acquire a plentiful supply of firearms with which to arm his Yeke followers. Inevitably, this rich and energetic man was drawn into Katangan politics. Local chiefs solicited his aid to deal with rebellious vassals. Before long he had established himself as a chief in his own right. To retain the goodwill of his followers he found it necessary to reward them with lavish gifts of women and cattle, commodities only to be obtained by launching constant raids on neighboring polities. Msiri was immensely successful; his capital, Bunkeya, became one of the largest towns in Central Africa, attracting traders from as far afield as Angola and Zanzibar; his harem contained five hundred wives, chief among whom was a "white woman," a Portuguese mulatto from Angola. But Msiri had created a kingdom that could be ruled only by terror. The grounds of the fortress-palace at Bunkeya were littered with the skulls of the men and women he had executed, often after they had been subjected to revolting tortures. In his cruelty Msiri reminds one of Shaka, but he was a less profound political innovator than the great Zulu despot. His empire was not to endure many years after the close of the 1870's.

A far more potent political and cultural revolutionary was the lonely Scottish traveler who spent thirty years tramping the bush paths of Central Africa. The career of David Livingstone provides a splendid illustration of the power of human personality. Born in 1813, the son of "poor and pious parents," Livingstone went to South Africa in 1841 as a medical missionary in the service of the London Missionary Society. From the first he was marked out as a pioneer. Kuruman, to which he was posted, was at that time the most northerly mission station in South Africa. To the north there stretched, so Robert Moffat, Livingstone's immediate superior, told him, "a vast plain, where I had sometimes seen, in the morning sun, the smoke of a thousand villages, where no missionary had ever been." [33] The lure of the unknown, the unevangelized village on the horizon, was to be with Livingstone for the rest of his life. And so, after a few years' apprenticeship based on fixed mission stations, Livingstone devoted himself to a life of constant movement. Between 1852 and 1856 he accomplished the journey that took him across the breadth of Africa from Angola to Mozambique. In 1858 he was appointed by the British government to lead an expedition up the Zambezi and spent the next five years in exploring the Lake Nyasa area. His last expedition, launched from Zanzibar in 1866, developed into an almost mystical quest for the sources of the Nile. Death came to him in 1873 after seven years spent wandering over much of the territory of modern Zambia and the southeastern Congo.

Behind this movement there was always purpose. An "intense love of nature," refined by scientific training, made him one of the most scholarly and observant travelers of his day, with an interest in every aspect of the new life he saw around him and a capacity to describe it in straightforward, yet often poetic prose. No less profound was his passionate resolve, formed in his youth, to devote his life to "the alleviation of human misery." This remarkable combination of qualities, nourished by an unshakable religious faith, made of Livingstone a man at once practical and idealistic, a realist and a visionary. Constantly, he was turning over in his mind plans for African advancement, for he possessed a vigorous belief in the inevitability of "progress," a generous appreciation of African capacity, and a vivid awareness of the down-drag of a savage environment. "The promotion of commerce," he wrote in *Missionary Travels,* "ought to be specially attended to." [34] Colonization, the settlement of Christian families from Britain in the healthier areas of the interior, would also stimulate economic development and at the same time make possible "the wide diffusion of better principles." In Christian trade, Christian colonists, and Christian civilization lay the deliverance of Africa, not only from the degradation of barbarism but—and it was this that gave such urgency to Livingstone's action—from the appalling miseries associated with the developing Arab slave trade in East and Central Africa. "I beg to direct your attention to Africa," Livingstone declared in the peroration of his famous Cambridge lecture in 1857. But it was only after his death that the British public really heeded his call. Before the 1870's were over, however, two substantial mission stations, Livingstonia and Blantyre, founded by the enterprise of Scotsmen in the Lake Nyasa area, gave the British a substantial stake in a part of Africa with which they had never been concerned before the days of the great explorer.

It was to be the achievement of Henry Morton Stanley, the other great Victorian explorer, to direct the attention of Europe no less forcefully to another part of Africa that had previously lain completely beyond the range of European interest and knowledge. Between 1874 and 1877 Stanley accomplished the greatest and also the most violent of all the expeditions of African exploration. Starting from Zanzibar, he made a circuit of the great lakes, Victoria and Tanganyika, struck across to the upper reaches of the Congo, and followed the great stream to its mouth. The Congo basin, the very heart of Africa, was thus exposed to the outside world.

Stanley—a journalist by profession, whose motive for going to Africa was to win "kudos" for himself by performing incredible feats—stands apart from all the other Africanists of his day. Most nineteenth-century explorers were financed by scholarly societies or by their own governments; Stanley's great expedition was paid for by two popular newspapers. Compared to Livingstone, Stanley was crude, coarse, and insensitive; yet there was an elemental force about the man that made him a historical figure on a grand scale. Fittingly, it was his destiny to become one of the architects of the Congo Free State, the most curious polity to be founded in nineteenth-century Africa. In 1879 Stanley returned to the Congo in the service of the *Comité d'Études du Haut-Congo,* an ostensibly international body with commercial interests cunningly constructed as a cover for the imperialist ambitions of Leopold II, king of the Belgians.

The careers of Msiri, Livingstone, and Stanley illustrate the activities of some of the intruders into the region during this period. There are many others of whom one could speak—Tippu Tib, a trader of mixed Arab and Swahili parentage, who in the 1870's began building up a territorial state for himself in the Manyema country of the eastern Congo; or the young French naval officer of Italian origin, Savorgnan de Brazza, who in the same period embarked on his career as an explorer-administrator with an expedition up the Ogowe; or Silva Porto, the hero of the Portuguese frontier in Angola in this period. Of these three men who stand as representatives of Arab, French, and Portuguese initiative in the area, there will be cause to speak later; all three reached the climax of their careers in the last decades of the century.

To think of the history of Central and Equatorial Africa between 1850 and 1875 simply in terms of powerful intruders battering on an impotent native population is to adopt too crude and simple a view of a complex period, for these years saw many developments in which outsiders were not involved. There was the growth of certain indigenous polities: Wadai, for example, lying far to the north, appears to have increased steadily in strength in the 1860's and 1870's. There were some dramatic reversals of political fortune: in the Barotse kingdom the Lozi princes who had been driven from the country in the 1840's by the invading Kololo took advantage in 1865 of a struggle for the throne among their overlords, staged a successful revolution, and massacred almost all the male Kololo. There was the rise to prominence of certain new ethnic groups; particularly striking as an example of this process was the emergence of the Cokwe.

The Cokwe were a seminomadic people of Lunda origin living between the headwaters of the Kwango and the Kasai and gaining their livelihood from hunting. As hunters, they were well placed to profit from the growing demand for ivory which could be exchanged for the firearms and other trade goods brought into the interior by their western neighbors, the Ovimbundu. At the same time their mode of living enabled the Cokwe to fill what has been termed an unoccupied "ecological niche" [35] in neighboring agricultural communities. Working in small bands, they infiltrated thinly populated country, used their firearms to dominate local villages, and added to their own modest numbers by taking many of the local women as slaves. Rapidly, the Cokwe spread eastward, their bands steadily increasing in size. By the 1870's there were many Cokwe groups settled within the territory of the Mwata Yamvo. Soon these fierce, well-armed elephant hunters were in a position to play as destructive a role in the lands of the western Lunda as their contemporaries, the Yeke, among the eastern Lunda peoples.

EAST AFRICA

Few parts of the continent had been so effectively shielded against external influences as the interior of East Africa. Suddenly, in the years after 1850 the old isolation ended, as a motley collection of alien intruders, some Asians, some Africans, a few Europeans, entered the region from the north, the east, and the south, harassing its borderlands or penetrating deep into its heart, transforming the lives of those with whom they came directly into contact.

One group of African intruders was made up of Somali pastoralists who moved into the valley of the river Tana in northeastern Kenya and routed a section of the Galla that had for long dominated the area; another, far to the south, was formed by the war bands of the Ngoni, who continued to practice the successful military tactics that had preserved them on their long march from distant Zululand. By the 1860's one Ngoni splinter group was established as a powerful political force among the Nyamwezi in the Tabora district of Tanzania, while another Ngoni band carved out a kingdom between the Rufiji and the Rovuma. Other Africans—the wandering Swahili traders who made their way to so many parts of the region and the Sudanese soldiers and porters who moved up the Nile into northern Uganda—were also looked on as aliens by the local populations with whom they came into contact, but their movements could not be described as exclusively African, for they were closely associated with the sudden Asian impact on the East African interior.

Khartoum and Zanzibar were the centers from which Asian influence spread southward and westward. The movement into the region from the north along the line of the White Nile formed part of that remarkable outburst of commercial activity among the peoples of the Nile Valley following the Turco-Egyptian conquest of the Sudan. In the late 1850's Khartoumers began operating among the Acholi of northern Uganda. This drive from the north was powerfully reinforced by the imperialist ambitions of the Khedive Ismail: in 1870 Ismail launched a grandiose expedition under the command of the British explorer Sir Samuel Baker "to annex the countries constituting the Nile Basin." In 1875 the khedive, in his anxiety to secure a new line of access to the interlacustrine districts, sent a force to annex Brava and other East African ports. Egyptian involvement in East African politics proved abortive. British pressure led to the evacuation of Brava, while growing financial weakness made it impossible to support further expeditions in equatorial regions. But the depredations of the Khartoumers caused much suffering to the Acholi and the machinations of the khedive's agents introduced a new factor into the politics of Buganda and Bunyoro, the two most powerful interlacustrine states. To counterbalance Egyptian pressure Mutesa of Buganda sought to attract the support of Britain by professing an interest in Christianity to the explorer H. M. Stanley, who visited him in 1875. The flurry of missionary activity set in motion by the newspaper letter in which Stanley reported his conversation with the kabaka led to a series of events that were to prove of crucial importance for the future of the interlacustrine area.

The Khartoumers and the Egyptians affected only the fringes of East Africa; the influence of the "coast men"—a few of them purebred Arabs from Muscat or South Arabia, the majority Swahili, many touched only lightly by Muslim Arab culture—was far more pervasive. From the coast there were three main lines of advance to the interior; one cut across central Tanzania to Lake Tanganyika, another ran from Kilwa to the northern tip of Lake Nyasa, the third struck across the Kenya highlands to Lake Victoria. By the 1870's there cannot have been more than two or three thousand "coast men" in the interior; they represented not a powerful current of pioneering frontiersmen but a steady trickle of merchant adventurers or enterprising caravan leaders who branched off the main routes to seek their fortunes in areas where ivory was plentiful and the local people cooperative. Their status and the nature of their settlement varied from place to place. To the rulers of the more powerful states of the interior they were little more than valuable commercial agents who might, through their knowledge of a wider world, achieve in time a certain degree of influence. In minor polities, on the other hand, an able and ambitious "coast man" might settle down, marry into the local chiefly family, and in time acquire substantial political power. Nowhere, however, within East Africa did any coastal adventurer succeed in building up so impressive a hegemony as that established by Tippu Tib in the eastern Congo. Only in Ujiji and Tabora were substantial communities of Arab and Swahili traders to be found; elsewhere small groups or even individuals operating on their own were easily integrated into the local population.

The reports of great lakes in the far interior brought back by Arab traders to the coast stimulated the curiosity of scientific circles in Europe about a hitherto neglected part of the continent. The trading nexus built up by the "coast men" greatly facilitated the process of European exploration. More swiftly than in any of the other parts of the continent regarded by Europeans as unknown the broad lines of the region's geography were uncovered through the activities of a handful of British explorers, Burton, Speke, Grant, Baker, Livingstone, and Stanley. The missionary advance proceeded more slowly, and it was not until the late 1870's that plans devised in response to the current of emotion sweeping through British missionary circles after Livingstone's death and reinforced by Stanley's dramatic call from Buganda led directly to the founding of the first mission stations in the interior.

The rapid development of European interest in the East African interior was accompanied by a marked increase in European activity on the coast. Zanzibar's trade with Europe and America expanded rapidly after the opening of the Suez Canal. In 1879, when rubber replaced ivory as the principal export, sixty-nine British ships visited the harbor compared with seventeen in 1871. Zanzibar might be of interest as a center for legitimate commerce; far more significant, however, in the eyes of many British observers was its notorious connection with the slave trade. Livingstone's dramatic revelations of the brutality of the trade in the interior came at a time when the Atlantic trade had at last been checked; they served to direct the attention of powerful humanitarian pressure groups in Britain to the exploits of Arab slavers in East African waters. In the 1860's the Zanzibar market was reckoned to be handling twenty thousand slaves a year. But Zanzibar was singularly vulnerable to pressure from the greatest naval power in the Indian Ocean. In 1873 Sultan Barghash reluctantly accepted British demands and agreed to abolish the slave trade throughout his dominions.

The impact of alien activity on the settled communities of the interior varied greatly from district to district. The peoples of the Kenya highlands—the Masai, the Kikuyu, the Nandi, and others—were powerful enough to force the coastal traders who passed through their country to act with great circumspection. By contrast, for many of the peoples of southern Tanzania afflicted by Ngoni raids and slavers' forays the latter half of the nineteenth century was a disastrous period. But this turbulent era which brought sudden death, famine, or enslavement to so many, provided some individuals with new opportunities for advancement. Bands of mercenary warriors, "somewhat reminiscent," a recent historian has suggested, "of the predatory companies of the European Hundred Years' War," [36] began to make their appearance; known as *ruga-ruga*, they copied the tactics of the Ngoni warriors and recruited their members from "all the most restless elements of a fluid society." Bands such as these provided ideal instruments for resolute men who sought to create a new political order.

The most prominent of these innovators was a young Nyamwezi chief, Mirambo. In the 1870's Mirambo succeeded in imposing his hegemony over most of the country between Tabora and Lake Victoria. He had learned much about war from the Ngoni and about trade from the Arabs and had gained a reputation as an exceptionally courageous and intelligent warrior. Thus, he was able to attract a stream of adventurous young men to his cause; arming as many as he could with firearms he put himself in a position to dominate all his neighbors. There were other warlords in central and southern Tanzania who adopted similar tactics, offering protection to their heterogeneous followers by erecting massive palisaded enclosures known as *bomas* at the center of their domains. Developments such as these served to indicate that East Africa's "time of troubles," like South Africa's *Mfecane,* was not, for all its suffering, entirely barren of political innovation and advance.

𝌤 SOUTH AFRICA

The impact of alien intruders on the peoples of East and Central Africa in the latter half of the nineteenth century seems modest in its effect when set against the cataclysmic disintegration of local communities that was taking place among most of the Bantu peoples of South Africa at this time. On every frontier of the European polities a motley concourse of white men—missionaries and elephant hunters, bush traders and land-hungry farmers, administrators and soldiers—pushed forward. A few dated events—the Caledon Valley annexed by the Orange Free State in 1866, Griqualand West by the Cape Colony in 1871—mark the major cessions of territory, but the process of advance was at once piecemeal and continuous. By the end of the 1870's there was hardly an indigenous community in South Africa that had not been affected by the coming of the white man, although there were still pockets of territory that had not yet been brought under direct European administration.

Many Bantu societies had suffered revolutionary changes during the violent years of the *Mfecane* in the early decades of the century. The arrival of Europeans allowed them no respite. Traders moving among local African communities found that guns and hard liquor—a cheap brandy known as Cape Smoke was now being manufactured by local winegrowers no longer able to sell their produce in European markets—were the most saleable commodities. The import of arms set in motion a vicious spiral of profitable violence. Thus, in the wastes of Southwest Africa the Namaqua Hottentots, who were closely in touch with European traders, raided the pastoral Herero, their northern neighbors, and drove off their cattle to sell for yet more guns.

Gun-peddling traders were not unwelcome visitors in African kraals. Missionaries, too, were not unacceptable. Their ideas about the world might seem incredible or ridiculous to African ears, but their settlements often developed into oases of order and decency in an anarchic land, centers where men, even if unimpressed by the religious teaching of the missionaries, might acquire certain useful skills and pick up interesting information about the outside world. Land-grabbing white farmers could not be regarded so tolerantly. It was so easy, especially in the Boer republics, for a white man to acquire land: he had only to ride out, see a tract that appeared unoccupied, note down the main natural features, obtain a certificate from the local landdrost, and so make himself lord of several thousand acres with the right to eject any Africans he might find living there or to compel them to labor for him. Many white men, not only the missionaries and liberal-minded officials of the Cape Colony but also, as Livingstone noted in 1847, "the better disposed emigrants," deplored what was happening. But, as Livingstone went on to point out, "the same absence or laxity of law" left "the natives open to the infliction of inexpressible wrongs." [37]

Even the partial expropriation of their land was a disaster for any people to whom land with the cattle and the crops that went with it was the only source of wealth. Many of the economic problems of modern Lesotho stem directly from the fact that in the 1860's after a decade of warfare, the Basuto lost to the farmers of the Orange Free State the fertile lands of the Caledon Valley. Deprived of half their arable land, the

Basuto were forced to content themselves with a territory of barren mountains and eroded valleys. At least the Basuto, who accepted British protection in 1868, remained to a considerable extent their own masters. Many other Bantu peoples suffered a harsher fate. Forced into limited reserves or reduced to the status of squatters on European-held land, they experienced a cruel impoverishment. The lands left to them were barely sufficient to meet their simple needs, especially in those seasons of drought that occur all too frequently in many parts of South Africa. A monotonous protein-deficient diet of maize porridge replaced the varied foodstuffs, supplemented by the proceeds of food-gathering and hunting, of the older more spacious days. The European trade goods that now came their way—tea, soap, shirts, buckets—offered poor compensation for what they had lost; moreover, these goods could only be obtained if a man was prepared to work for Europeans at meager wages.

The poverty of the Bantu in the South Africa of the 1860's could not be set against the opulence of the Europeans. The four European polities— Cape Colony, Natal, the Orange Free State, and the Transvaal—were all struggling communities. They differed greatly from the other colonies of European settlement in the Americas and Australia. Being poor, they failed to attract immigrants and so were deprived of the stimulus imparted by a steady stream of newcomers bringing with them new ideas, new techniques, and sometimes even new wealth. Suddenly, in 1867 an event occurred that no prophet could have foretold, an event of seminal importance in the history of South Africa and of profound significance for the later development of almost the entire continent: diamonds were discovered in the wedge of territory then occupied by the Griquas between Cape Colony and the Orange Free State. Of all the natural resources known to nineteenth-century technology none was better adapted to stimulate a laggard economy: diamonds could, in the initial stages, be effectively mined by primitive methods, they were easily transportable, and they were, of course, the most lucrative of all the gem stones known to man. Within a few years the foreign trade of the Cape Colony and of Natal doubled, the colonial governments' revenue doubled, money could be more easily borrowed and at lower interest rates on the London market, and ambitious public works, such as the extension of the country's hitherto diminutive railroads, could be undertaken in a spirit of confidence. At the same time Kimberley, the center of diamond mining, mushroomed into an ugly, brawling town of fifty thousand people, a town that could be regarded as the first truly industrial community in the entire continent, a town which saw the emergence of a class Africa had never known before, a shifting black proletariat.

In the 1850's the two Boer republics had been given their independence; the pattern of four distinct European polities continued through to the 1870's, Cape Colony being granted responsible government in 1872, while Natal remained under Colonial Office control. To British statesmen forced by their imperial responsibilities to view the South African situation in a broader context, this political pattern was aggravating and potentially dangerous. Even after the opening of the Suez Canal in 1869, the Cape Colony was still regarded as a major bastion in the grand strategy of the Empire. Imperial interests dictated that South Africa should remain an area of British paramountcy. But South African colonies had the serious disadvantage of involving the mother country in fighting costly native wars. The "native problem" was aggravated by the increasing number of firearms passing into Bantu hands; indeed, during the 1870's there was a widespread fear of a general native uprising.

In such a situation the establishment of a federation of the four white territories seemed to cool and logical minds in distant Whitehall to offer an ideal solution. If all four territories could be induced to harmonize their native policy, the tensions on the frontiers might be eased. Federation would also make possible substantial economies in the cost of administration and defense and so lessen the burden of the British taxpayer. At the same time the two Boer republics, which had already begun to look to other European countries for aid, would be brought firmly within the sphere of British influence. In 1875 Cape Colony and Natal, with a quarter of a million settlers, had four times the European population of the Boer republics and more than four times their revenue. To contemporaries, figures such as these must have suggested that for many generations to come the British were likely to remain the dominant group in South Africa.

🎝 THE ISLANDS

In 1850 the island colonies of Réunion and Mauritius possessed European communities more prosperous than any to be found on the mainland of Africa. The same could not be said of them in 1875. Not only had they been overtaken by other centers of European enterprise, notably Algiers, Alexandria, and Cape Town, but both islands had experienced in the late 1860's a cruel run of disasters. The price of cane sugar on which their economies depended began falling in the mid-1860's as a result of increased competition from the West Indies and from the newly developed beet-sugar industry in Western Europe. The opening of the Suez Canal in 1869 diverted to the shorter route much of the Indies-bound shipping that had formerly called at the Mascarenes. Most grievous of all, a series of epidemics scourged the islands. Between 1840 and 1870 both islands experienced a number of outbreaks of cholera and in the mid-1860's malaria was introduced to the Mascarenes. In the year 1868, when the malaria epidemic was at its height, one in every four of the eighty thousand inhabitants of Port Louis, the capital of Mauritius, died of the fever.

Compared with other lands around the Indian Ocean the great island of Madagascar appeared to be of relatively minor concern to Europeans. Traders from the Mascarenes—and especially from Réunion—carried on a regular trade with Tamatave and other ports of the east coast, where they could obtain supplies of cattle and rice. In 1841 the French government annexed two islands, Mayotte in the archipelago of the Comoros and Nossi-Be off the northwest coast of Madagascar, but the hope that Mayotte might develop into a major naval base in the Indian Ocean was never fulfilled and Nossi-Be attracted only a handful of settlers. European enterprise around the coasts of Madagascar remained on a very modest scale.

More significant were the developments that took place in the great inland kingdom of Merina. In the reign of Radama I (1810–28) a wide range of new ideas and techniques was introduced by the small group of European missionaries, military advisers, and technicians who had come to Merina on the king's invitation. Radama's successor, Queen Ranavalona, expelled the missionaries and broke off the amicable relations Radama had established with the British. But the queen and her entourage did not completely reject European ways, for they had acquired a taste for many European products and were glad to make use of the services of a handful of French technicians, the most remarkable of whom, Jean Laborde, proved to be a mechanical genius. Using a cheap encyclopedia as his guide, Laborde developed the manufacture of a wonderful variety of products, including guns, gunpowder, glass, bricks, and soap; turning his attention from industry to agriculture, he introduced new breeds of cattle and new species of plants, besides making the first ox carts ever seen in Merina; and he provided the queen with a magnificent palace, a pleasure garden, and a zoo. On Ranavalona's death in 1862 the missionaries were allowed to return. English Protestants of the London Missionary Society took up the work they had begun in Radama's reign and achieved an outstanding success. In 1868 the reigning queen and her immensely powerful chief minister, Ranilairivony, were baptized, together with many members of the Merina aristocracy. By the late 1870's Protestant converts numbered forty thousand. In no indigenous polity of mainland Africa could one find in 1875 a governing class so enamored of European ways as the aristocracy of Merina.

The success of British Protestants among Merina nobles aroused the jealousy of the French Catholics who found themselves forced to proselytize among the humbler classes and in districts remote from the capital.

Catholic missionaries were not the only Frenchmen with a passionate interest in Madagascar. The planters of Réunion, feeling that their small,
crowded island needed *lebensraum,* were vigorously expansionist in their
ideas: as early as 1845 the island's Council sent a memorandum to Paris
expressing its members' hope of founding "a great and important colony"
in Madagascar.[38] On the other hand British and British Indian traders
had acquired the largest stake in Madagascar's export trade, and British missionaries possessed great influence at the court of Merina. In such
a situation no contemporary observer of the Malagasy scene in the 1870's
could possibly have made an accurate prediction of the actual course of
events. Set securely on an inland plateau of a remote island, Merina
might well have been regarded as occupying as good a position as any
kingdom in the Afro-Asian world for resisting the encroachments of foreign powers.

Epilogue

Hindsight is a dubious advantage for the student of the past. Knowing what is going to happen next, the historian can never really put himself in the position of the men and women whose words he reads and whose actions he studies. The future to which they looked with confidence or foreboding has become the past. Events, once they have occurred, seem set in a pattern of inevitability; yet in any human situation there must always be, through the play of chance or the vagaries of individual initiative, a number of possible outcomes. Nevertheless, events in themselves can rarely be more than ripples in the great sea of history. They may deflect but cannot decisively alter the broad currents that determine the character of an age. And so, though men can never hope accurately to predict the complex pattern of forthcoming events, they may well identify the shaping currents of their time and point with visionary power to the perspectives of the future. Certainly, in 1875 there were men living in or concerned with Africa who thought they could discern the shape of things to come.

For more than a generation before 1875 some Africans appear to have been aware of the danger that a large part of the continent might be overrun by Europeans. As early as 1824 the English traveler Denham recorded a conversation with the Sheikh al-Kanemi, the ruler of the Central Sudanic state of Bornu, in which he was questioned closely about recent British moves in India. When Denham diplomatically explained that the British were always friends to Muslims, a Moroccan who was present exclaimed bitterly, "By God! they eat the whole country—they are no friends: these are the words of truth." [1] In the same way French operations in Egypt in 1798 and in Algeria after 1830 sent currents of alarm along all the trade and pilgrimage routes of the Muslim world. Nor was it only from fellow Muslims that unsettling rumors reached the rulers of the interior. In 1858 an Englishman who visited Nupe, one of the southern provinces of the Sokoto caliphate, found there was a widespread belief that the British intended to seize "a part of the country"; local men who had visited Lagos had learned from Spaniards and Portuguese that the British were "a very dangerous and encroaching nation." [2]

Some African rulers with greater experience of Europeans had developed a clear view of the tactics they employed. "First they send out missionaries," Theodore, emperor of Ethiopia, explained to a French visitor, "then consuls to support the missionaries, then battalions to support the consuls." [3] This was a shrewd and, in Theodore's case, a prophetic analysis of imperialist methods. Yet at the same time it would be true to say that there was probably not a single major political figure in the Europe of the 1860's and 1870's who thought of Africa in terms of conquest. To European statesmen burdened by their own local problems Africa was remote, barbarous, and relatively unimportant, though a few areas were regarded as possessing some strategic value. Only a few small groups of individuals thought differently.

In the first place there were the missionaries. Men like J. L. Krapf, a German Protestant who established the first mission station in East Africa, were moved by a sense of "the spiritual darkness of the tribes and nations of Inner Africa" and dreamed of founding a chain of mission stations that would stretch across the continent from east to west.[4] David Livingstone, who saw himself as "trying to make a path for commerce and Christianity," [5] became obsessed by the horrors of the slave trade and in the "solitude" of his last journey invoked "Heaven's rich blessing on every one—American, English, Turk—who will help to heal this open sore of the world." [6] The fiery Catholic priest Charles Lavigerie is said to have remarked to a friend when in 1867 he accepted an appointment as bishop of Algiers, "Algeria is but an open door to an untamed continent of two hundred million souls." [7]

Then there were the traders, men from many different parts of Europe, attracted to Africa by the prospect of new economic opportunities. "Where there is money to be made," wrote a discerning British civil servant in 1876, with special reference to the Niger trade, "our merchants will be certain to intrude themselves, and if they establish a lucrative trade public opinion in this country practically compels us to protect them." [8] And so, as European contacts with Africa steadily increased, new pressure groups of a kind unknown before began to emerge: French businessmen with a stake in Egypt or Morocco, Englishmen concerned about the future of the new South African mining industry, Italian shipping magnates interested in the trade of the Red Sea, and others, all of whom were likely to lobby their governments to gain metropolitan support for their own local ends.

Finally, there were the public men, politicians, journalists, and others. In the 1850's and early 1860's there had been little talk of the desirability of overseas expansion; on the contrary public men, both in Britain and in France, the two major colonial powers, tended to regard their country's colonies as tiresome and expensive liabilities. But in the late 1860's and early 1870's a perceptible change in the public mood became apparent. In Britain a young radical politician, Charles Dilke, secured an immense success in 1868 with his book, *Greater Britain,* in which he spoke "of the grandeur of our race, already girding the earth, which it is destined, perhaps, eventually to overspread." [9] In France a young political economist, Paul Leroy-Beaulieu, produced in 1874 a massive thesis on modern colonization; having proved to his own satisfaction that colonies were likely to be a source of immense profit to the mother country, Leroy-Beaulieu came to the resounding conclusion that "a people which colonizes is a people which projects into the future the foundations of its grandeur and eventual supremacy." [10] In Germany Friedrich List had argued as early as 1841 that colonies provided "the best means of developing manufactures, export and import trade, and finally a respectable army" and had urged the "German seaports to buy land in foreign countries and settle them with German colonies." His ideas, little heeded when they first appeared, were taken up in 1867—by which time German trade contacts with Africa had greatly increased—and vigorously endorsed in an important series of newspaper articles written by a Prussian diplomat closely associated with Bismarck. [11]

Even in Portugal, a country little affected by the economic forces so powerfully felt elsewhere in Western Europe, the new mood became apparent. "We can no longer continue to live isolated, as we could when our African colonies were no more than parks for the production and creation of slaves," wrote João de Andrade Corvo, a former professor of history who held a number of ministerial posts in the 1870's, "Today the world is one of work and not indolence; the earth is for men, and no one can keep civilization from it." [12] The concept of a Portuguese imperial mission was an old one and could easily be revived. Extremely surprising, on the other hand, was the dedication to the cause of imperial expansion of the ruler of one of the smaller states of Europe, Leopold II, king of the Belgians. Belgium, a kingdom formed as recently as 1830, possessed virtually no overseas contacts, yet it was from the Belgian king that there came in the mid-1860's a declaration that provided a striking foretaste of the new imperialism: "We shall point out the domains that the State will acquire, where there are people to be civilized and led towards every kind of progress, and which will guarantee for us new revenues, for our middle classes the new occupations they are looking for, for our Army a little action, and for all Belgians a chance to show the world that they also are an imperial people capable of dominating and teaching others." [13]

By 1875, then, an observer of the European scene might note that there were a number of public men being listened to with increasing attention as they exuberantly pointed out the lineaments of the future. These confident exponents of the new imperialism gave little thought to the reaction of those "lesser breeds" whom they intended to dominate and civilize. Yet by 1875 in some parts of Africa most exposed to European pressure there had appeared the first indications of that new spirit which was to develop into the mighty force of African nationalism. In Cairo in the 1870's there gathered round the strange figure of Jamal al-Din al-Afghani—"wild man of genius" to some observers, cynical adventurer to others—a small group of university students. From their widely traveled master these young men learned of "the danger of European intervention, the need for national unity to resist it, the need for a broader unity of the Islamic peoples, the need for a constitution to limit the ruler's power"; by him they were urged "to write, to publish newspapers, to form a public opinion." [14] In West Africa, too, there were to be found among the small group of Western-educated Africans in the European colonies on the coast men such as E. W. Blyden or Africanus Horton, who looked prophetically forward beyond the period of colonial tutelage to the emergence of modern African states.

Imperialism and nationalism were to provide the dominant themes of the century that lay ahead. But for the historian to think of the development of Africa only in terms such as these is to accept far too narrow a view of historically significant activities. The pioneering of the bush, the slow peopling of plains and forests, the gradual growth of centers of settlement, the diffusion of useful plants and animals, the proliferation and refinement of crafts, the development of commerce, the emergence of institutions, the evolution of philosophies are all great movements that lie within the compass of the historian's vision. To reflect on movements such as these in an African context is to realize the shallowness of ethnocentricity as an attitude toward the past. The history of a continent is a compound of the actions of an immense variety of men and women. The skill of the Bushman hunter or of the Moroccan craftsman, the perseverance of the Kikuyu farmer in the highlands of Kenya or of the Egyptian fellah in the valley of the Nile, the business acumen of the merchant from Ghadames, of the Jellaba trader, of the "palm-oil ruffian" in the creeks of the Niger delta, the martial pride of the Zulu warrior or of the Fulani horseman, the courage of the Boer voortrekker, of the Maghribi pilgrim, of the Cokwe elephant hunter, the faith of the Christian missionary or of the Muslim divine have all contributed to the making of Africa. Africa is the product of all its peoples.

Notes

❧ NOTES TO INTRODUCTION

1. Hassan ibn Muhammad al-Fasi was captured by Italian pirates off the Tunisian coast in 1518, taken to Rome and presented to Pope Leo X, who persuaded him to be baptized and stood as his godfather. Leo Africanus, "the African," as he was thenceforward known, wrote a *History and Description of Africa* which was first published in an Italian version in Venice in 1550 and later translated into Latin, French, and English. Leo's work, based on his own extensive experiences, provided European readers with an account of North Africa, the Sahara, and the Sudan that remained a standard work of geography until it was finally supplanted by the accounts of European travelers of the early nineteenth century.
2. A. J. Toynbee, *A Study of History* (London, 1948), III, 322.
3. J. Vansina, "Recording the Oral History of the Bakuba—I. Methods," *Journal of African History*, I/1 (1960), 45.
4. W. E. F. Ward, *A History of Ghana* (London, 1959), p. 6.
5. *An Arab Philosophy of History, Selections from the Prolegomena of Ibn Khaldun . . .* , tr. and arr. by C. Issawi (London, 1963), pp. 26–27.

❧ NOTES TO CHAPTER II

1. See for example the map provided in the end pocket of G. P. Murdock, *Africa, Its Peoples and Their Culture History* (New York, 1959).
2. W. Macgaffy, "Concepts of Race in the Historiography of North East Africa," *Journal of African History*, VII/1 (1966).
3. J. H. Greenberg, *Languages of Africa*, 2d revised ed. (Bloomington, Ind., 1966), pp. 149–60.
4. Murdock, *op. cit.*, p. 12.

❧ NOTES TO CHAPTER III

1. L. S. B. Leakey, "The Evolution of Man in the African Continent," *Tarikh*, I/3 (1966) and "The Earliest Toolmakers," in M. Posnansky

(ed.), *Prelude to East African History* (London, 1966). Leakey's earlier ideas are presented in *The Progress and Evolution of Man in Africa* (London, 1961).

2. R. G. Armstrong, "The Use of Linguistic and Ethnographic Data in the Study of Yoruba and Idoma History," *The Historian in Tropical Africa*, ed. by J. Vansina, R. Mauny, and L. V. Thomas (London, 1964), p. 135.

🕮 NOTES TO CHAPTER IV

1. R. N. Cust, *A Sketch of the Modern Languages of Africa* (London, 1883), pp. 23–24.
2. A. Moorehead, *The White Nile* (London, 1964), p. 44.
3. H. Vedder, *South West Africa in Early Times* (London, 1932), p. 145.
4. The notorious phrase used in 1963 by H. R. Trevor-Roper, regius professor of modern history in the University of Oxford, with reference to African history, *The Rise of Christian Europe* (London, 1966), p. 6.
5. J. D. Omer-Cooper, *The Zulu Aftermath* (Ibadan History Series, 1966), p. 37.
6. A. Billiard, *Voyage aux colonies orientaux* (Paris, 1829), p. 46.
7. A. M. Jones, "Indonesia and Africa: the Xylophone as a Culture Indicator," *Journal of the Royal Anthropological Institute*, 89/II (1959).
8. S. F. Nadel, *A Black Byzantium* (Oxford, 1942), p. 267.
9. *Ibid.*, pp. 299–300.
10. Abd ar-Rahman as-Sadi, *Tarikh es-Soudan*, tr. and ed. by O. Houdas (Paris, 1964), pp. 35–37.
11. W. K. R. Hallam, "The Bayajidda Legend in Hausa Folklore," *Journal of African History*, VII/1 (1966).

🕮 NOTES TO CHAPTER V

1. B. G. Trigger, "The Languages of the Northern Sudan: an Historical Perspective," *Journal of African History*, VII/1 (1966).
2. W. S. Smith, *The Art and Architecture of Ancient Egypt* (Baltimore, 1958), p. 20.
3. Quoted in H. Frankfurt, *Ancient Egyptian Religion* (New York, 1948), p. 43.
4. *Ibid.*, pp. 44–45.
5. Murdock, *op. cit.*, pp. 64–68.
6. J. D. Clark, "The Spread of Food Production in Sub-Saharan Africa," *Journal of African History*, II/2 (1962).
7. Murdock, *op. cit.*, p. 182.
8. Quoted in J. Boardman, *The Greeks Overseas* (Harmondsworth, 1964), p. 42.
9. M. Rostovtzeff, *The Social and Economic History of the Roman Empire* (Oxford, 1957), p. 278.
10. N. H. Baynes, *The Byzantine Empire* (London, 1949), p. 78.
11. E. Ullendorf, *The Ethiopians* (London, 1960), p. 97.
12. Quoted in J. M. Ahmed, *The Intellectual Origins of Egyptian Nationalism* (London, 1960), pp. 5–6.

13. H. H. Dodwell, *The Founder of Modern Egypt* (Cambridge, 1931), p. 195.
14. H. S. Lewis, "The Origins of the Galla and Somali," *Journal of African History*, VII/1 (1966).
15. I. M. Lewis, "The Northern Pastoral Somali of the Horn," *Peoples of Africa*, ed. by J. L. Gibbs (New York, 1965), p. 348.
16. I. M. Lewis, *A Modern History of Somaliland* (London, 1965), p. 32.
17. This phrase was used by George Sandys, an English traveler who visited Egypt in the seventeenth century.
18. D. S. Landes, *Bankers and Pashas* (London, 1958), p. 86.

✣ NOTES TO CHAPTER VI

1. Some confusion arises from the double meaning of the term "Sudan." Today it is usually understood in a political sense to apply to the republic of that name. Originally, the term, an abbreviation of the Arabic *Bilad as-Sudan*, "land of the blacks," was applied in a geographical sense to all the countries lying south of the Sahara. In any history of Africa before modern times the term "Sudan" must be understood in this older and wider sense.
2. S. Gsell, *Histoire ancienne de l'Afrique du nord* (Paris, 1913–28), III, 301; V, 189.
3. Plutarch *Praecepta Gerendae Rei Publicae* III, 6.
4. E. Gibbon, *The Decline and Fall of the Roman Empire*, abridged ed. (Harmondsworth, 1963), p. 474 (chap. xxxiii of original edition).
5. C. A. Julien, *Histoire de l'Afrique du nord*, rev. ed. (Paris, 1961), I, 188.
6. B. Lewis, "The Invading Crescent," *The Dawn of African History*, ed. by R. Oliver (London, 1961), p. 34.
7. Ibn Said quoted in N. Barbour, *Morocco* (London, 1865), p. 52.
8. Julien, *op. cit.*, II, 134.
9. Barbour, *op. cit.*, p. 46.

✣ NOTES TO CHAPTER VII

1. The term "Guinea," today applied only to the republic of that name and to the adjacent Portuguese territory, is derived from a Berber word *aguinaou* meaning "black" and thus identical with the Arabic word *sudan*. The term was first used in the fifteenth century by the Portuguese, who applied it to the entire coast of West Africa. It remained in active use among Europeans until the eighteenth century. Recently, geographers and historians have found it convenient to revive the term.
2. There is a brief report on the Akure excavations by T. Shaw, "Excavations at Iwo Eleru," *West African Archaeological Newsletter*, No. 3 (1965).
3. The excavations conducted by G. Connah at Daima are described in an anonymous article, " 'Classic' Excavation in North-East Nigeria,"

Illustrated London News, October 14, 1967, Archaeological Section, No. 2276.

4. Some historians divide the Sudanic belt into two parts, Eastern and Western, with Lake Chad serving as the point of division. But it seems more satisfactory to divide the Sudan into three parts, with the western border of Nigeria acting as the dividing line between the Western and Central parts and the western border of the Sudan Republic providing the line between the Central and Eastern parts. The eastern half of the Central Sudan falls into the region of Equatorial Africa, but up to 1500 A.D. the history of this stretch of country is so closely linked with that of the country west of Lake Chad that it is better to consider it in this chapter.

5. A translation of this extract from al-Muhallabi (d. 963), preserved in the geography of Yaqut (d. 1229), is given by H. R. Palmer, *The Bornu Sahara and Sudan* (London, 1936), p. 196.

6. Abd ar-Rahman as-Sadi, *Tarikh es-Soudan,* tr. and ed. by O. Houdas (Paris, 1964), pp. 6–7. It seems likely that the references to Yemen, Mecca, or Arabia in the legends of the Central and Western Sudan represent later interpolations by local Muslim scholars.

7. The most recent advocates of this theory are G. P. Murdock in *Africa: Its Peoples and Their Culture History* (New York, 1959), pp. 36–39, and R. Oliver and J. D. Fage in *A Short History of Africa* (Harmondsworth, 1962), pp. 44–53.

8. This passage from ibn Battuta's *Travels* is given in B. Davidson, *The African Past* (Harmondsworth, 1964), pp. 90–91.

9. Leo Africanus, *History and Description of Africa,* tr. by J. Pory and ed. by R. Brown (London, 1896), III, 825.

10. J. S. Trimingham, *A History of Islam in West Africa* (London, 1962), p. 101.

11. Quoted in *ibid.,* p. 145.

12. D. Zahn, "The Mossi Kingdoms," *West African Kingdoms in the Nineteenth Century,* ed. by D. Forde and P. M. Kaberry (London, 1967), pp. 152–78.

13. H. R. Palmer, *Sudanese Memoirs* (Lagos, 1928), III, 97.

14. Ibn Khaldun, *Histoire des Berbères,* quoted in T. Hodgkin, *Nigerian Perspectives* (London, 1960), p. 74.

15. Palmer, *op. cit.,* III, 112; see also M. G. Smith, "The Beginnings of Hausa Society," *The Historian in Tropical Africa,* ed. by J. Vansina, R. Mauny, and L. V. Thomas (London, 1964), pp. 346–47.

16. P.R.O. C.O. 267/6, Board of Trade to William Pitt, 23.11.1758.

17. J. Barbot, *A Description of the Coasts of North and South Guinea* (London, 1732), quoted in F. Wolfson, *Pageant of Ghana* (London, 1958), p. 68.

18. The phrase is used by the Dutch trader W. Bosman in *A New and Accurate Description of Guinea* (London, 1705), p. 185.

19. *Ibid.,* quoted by A. A. Boahen, "The Rise of the Akan," *The Middle Age of African History,* ed. by R. Oliver (London, 1967), p. 23.

20. Muhammad Bello, *Infaq al-Maysur,* in Hodgkin, *op. cit.,* p. 196.

21. This phrase is applied by A. Gouilly in *L'Islam dans l'Afrique occidentale française* (Paris, 1952), p. 77, to the states created by Samory

and Rabeh in the late nineteenth century, but it is no less applicable to the states formed as a result of the jihads.

22. H. Venn, general secretary to the Anglican Church Missionary Society, in a letter written in 1857, quoted by J. F. A. Ajayi, "Nineteenth Century Origins of Nigerian Nationalism," *Journal of the Historical Society of Nigeria,* II/2 (1961), 199.

23. Estimates of West African gold production have been worked out by R. Mauny, *Tableau géographique de l'ouest africain au moyen âge* (Dakar, 1961), pp. 375–77.

24. The figure for Bonny is given by Captain John Adams, that for Kano by Heinrich Barth; both passages in which these estimates occur are given in Hodgkin, op. cit., pp. 178 and 261.

25. O. Dapper, *Description de l'Afrique* (Amsterdam, 1686), tr. in Hodgkin, *op. cit.,* p. 128.

26. H. Barth, *Travels and Discoveries in North and Central Africa* (London, 1857), II, 135.

NOTES TO CHAPTER VIII

1. Rhodes House, Oxford: British Empire MSS 276/4. G. J. Lethem, "Report on the Dikwa Emirate" (c. 1921), p. 19.

2. Trader Horn, quoted in P. Alexandre and J. Binet, *Le Groupe dit Pahouin* (Paris, 1958), p. 88.

3. M. Kingsley, *Travels in East Africa* (London, 1897), p. 329.

4. L. Frobenius, *Histoire de la civilisation africaine* (Paris, 1936), p. 16, quoted in R. Slade, *King Leopold's Congo* (London, 1962), p. 52.

5. G. Schweinfurth, *The Heart of Africa* (London, 1878), II, 33–64.

NOTES TO CHAPTER IX

1. M. Guthrie, "Some Developments in the Prehistory of the Bantu Languages," *Journal of African History,* III/2 (1962); R. Oliver, "The Problem of the Bantu Expansion," *Journal of African History,* VII/3 (1966).

2. Oliver, *op. cit.,* p. 368.

3. *Ibid.,* p. 374; see also J. Nemquin, "Notes on Some Early Pottery Cultures in North Katanga," *Journal of African History,* IV/1 (1963).

4. B. Fagan, *Southern Africa* (1965), p. 120; see also D. P. Abraham, "Maramuca: An Exercise in the Combined Use of Portuguese Records and Oral Tradition," *Journal of African History,* II/2 (1961).

NOTES TO CHAPTER X

1. G. S. P. Freeman-Grenville, "The Coast, 1498–1840," in R. Oliver and G. Mathew (eds.), *History of East Africa* (Oxford, 1963), I, 168.

NOTES TO CHAPTER XI

1. Earl Macartney to Dundas, July 10, 1797, quoted in V. T. Harlow, "The British Occupations, 1795–1806," *Cambridge History of the British Empire, South Africa* (Cambridge, 1963), VIII, 168.

2. The chairman of a meeting held in Cape Town in 1833 to consider establishing a settlement in Natal; P. R. Kirby, *Andrew Smith and Natal* (Cape Town, 1955), p. 147, quoted in J. D. Omer-Cooper, *The Zulu Aftermath* (London, 1966), p. 178.

3. This sentence occurs in a motion proposed by Thomas Fowell Buxton in the British House of Commons and accepted by the House on July 15, 1828, shortly before the publication of the Fiftieth Ordinance at Cape Town: H. Gailey, "John Philip's Role in Hottentot Emancipation," *Journal of African History*, III/3 (1962), 431.

4. Quoted in J. A. I. Agar-Hamilton, *The Native Policy of the Voortrekkers* (Cape Town, 1928), p. 167.

NOTES TO CHAPTER XIV

1. Muhammad Abdu quoted in N. Safran, *Egypt in Search of Political Community* (Cambridge, Mass., 1961), p. 33.

2. J. C. McCoan, *Egypt as It Is* (London, 1878), p. 25.

3. E. W. Lane, *The Manners and Customs of the Modern Egyptians* (Everyman ed., n.d.), p. 131.

4. L. Duff-Gordon, *Letters from Egypt 1863–65* (London, 1865), p. 363.

5. C. F. Beckingham and G. W. B. Huntingford (eds.), *Some Records of Ethiopia 1593–1646*, extracts from *The History of High Ethiopia* by M. de Almeida (Hakluyt Society, 1954), p. 72.

6. W. Plowden to Lord Clarendon, 9.7.1854, *Correspondence Relating to Abyssinia 1846–1868* (London, 1869), pp. 99, 101, 107, 115.

7. E. E. Evans-Pritchard, *The Nuer* (Oxford, 1940).

8. *Ibid.*, pp. 181–82.

NOTES TO CHAPTER XV

1. R. Montagne, *Les Berbères et le Makhzen dans le sud du Maroc* (Paris, 1930).

2. W. B. Harris quoted in G. Maxwell, *Lords of the Atlas* (London, 1966), p. 36.

3. E. Aubin, *Morocco of Today* (London, c. 1906), p. 191.

4. *Ibid.*, pp. 182–83.

5. *Ibid.*, p. 37.

6. C. A. Julien, *Histoire de l'Algérie contemporaine, la conquête et les débuts de la colonisation 1827–1871* (Paris, 1964), p. 336.

NOTES TO CHAPTER XVI

1. Quoted in M. Last, *The Sokoto Caliphate* (London, 1967), p. 147.

2. H. A. S. Johnston, *The Fulani Empire of Sokoto* (London, 1967), p. 167.

3. Abdullah ibn Muhammad, *Tazyin al-Waraqat*, tr. and ed. by M. Hiskett (Ibadan, 1963), p. 22.

4. T. E. Bowdich, *Mission from Cape Coast Castle to Ashantee* (London,

1819); J. Dupuis, *Journal of Residence in Ashantee* (London, 1824).
5. *Ibid.*, p. 164.
6. Bowdich, *op. cit.*, pp. 247–48.
7. Sir Richard Burton, *A Mission to Gelele, King of Dahome*, ed. by C. W. Newbury (London, 1966), p. 262.
8. *Ibid.*, p. 214.
9. A. Dalzel, *The History of Dahomey* (London, 1793), p. 221.
10. Burton, *op. cit.*, p. 159.
11. G. I. Jones, *The Trading States of the Oil Rivers* (London, 1963), p. 55.
12. Rev. Hope Waddell quoted in an anonymous article, "Bonny," *Nigeria Magazine*, No. 58 (Lagos, 1958).
13. The text of the "Bond" is given in C. W. Newbury, *British Policy Towards West Africa* (London, 1966), p. 298.

✷ NOTES TO CHAPTER XVII

1. G. Schweinfurth, *The Heart of Africa* (London, 1878), I, 274.
2. *Ibid.*, I, 285.
3. E. E. Evans-Pritchard, "Zande Kings and Princes," in *Essays in Social Anthropology* (London, 1957), p. 116.
4. H. M. Stanley, *In Darkest Africa* (London, 1896), II, 70–75.
5. C. M. Turnbull, *Wayward Servants* (London, 1967).
6. *Ibid.*, p. 17.
7. Stanley, *op. cit.*, II, 95.
8. Turnbull, *op. cit.*, p. 254.

✷ NOTES TO CHAPTER XVIII

1. Quoted in J. Duffy, *Portuguese Africa* (London, 1959), pp. 195–96.
2. Quoted in H. A. C. Cairns, *The Clash of Cultures* (New York, 1965), pp. 127–28.
3. D. Livingstone, *Missionary Travels and Researches in South Africa* (London, 1857), p. 372.
4. J. Vansina, *Kingdoms of the Savanna* (Madison, Wis., 1966), p. 194.

✷ NOTES TO CHAPTER XIX

1. A. Hamerton, "Report on the Affairs of the Imam of Muscat, 1844," *Bombay Records*, 238, p. 5, quoted in J. M. Gray, "Zanzibar and the Coast," *History of East Africa*, ed. by R. Oliver and G. Mathew (Oxford, 1963), I, 220.
2. C. P. Rigby, *Report on the Zanzibar Dominions* (Bombay, 1861), p. 4.
3. J. H. Speke, *Journal of the Discovery of the Sources of the Nile* (London, 1863).
4. C. C. Wrigley, "The Changing Economic Structure of Buganda," *The King's Men*, ed. by L. A. Fallers (London, 1964), p. 19.
5. G. W. B. Huntingford, *The Southern Nilo-Hamites, Ethnographic Survey of Africa* (London, 1953), p. 122.

6. L. von Höhnel, *The Discovery of Lakes Rudolf and Stefanie* (London, 1894), I, 302, 352.

❧ NOTES TO CHAPTER XX

1. Details of British military expenditure in South Africa: *Parliamentary Papers*, 1852/3, LIX, Troops (South Africa).
2. P. Retief's declaration, Grahamstown, 2.1.1837, quoted in J. P. Fitzpatrick, *The Transvaal from Within* (London, 1895), p. 5.
3. The constitution of the South African Republic is printed in full in G. W. Eybers, *Select Constitutional Documents Illustrating South African History 1795–1910* (London, 1918).
4. E. Cassalis, *The Basutos* (London, 1860), p. 216.
5. *Ibid.*, p. 218.
6. E. A. Ritter, *Shaka Zulu* (London, 1955), p. 319.

❧ NOTES TO CHAPTER XXI

1. N. Mayeur, "Voyage dans le sud et dans l'intérieur des terres," *Bulletin de l'Académie Malgache* (Tananarive, 1913), XIII, 167–68.
2. W. Ellis, *History of Madagascar* (London, 1838), II, 400.
3. H. Deschamps, *Histoire de Madagascar* (Paris, 1960), p. 165.
4. Quoted in J. Pope Henessey, *Verandah* (London, 1964), p. 240.

❧ NOTES TO CHAPTER XXII

1. J. Christie, *Cholera Epidemics in East Africa* (London, 1876).
2. I. Schapera (ed.), *Livingstone's Private Journals, 1851–53* (London, 1960), pp. 167–68.
3. D. Livingstone, *Missionary Travels and Researches in South Africa* (London, 1857), p. 199.
4. *The Times*, 9.12.1873, quoted in R. Gray, *A History of the Southern Sudan, 1839–1889* (Oxford, 1961), p. 173.
5. J. M. Ahmed, *The Intellectual Origins of Egyptian Nationalism* (Oxford, 1960), p. 115.
6. W. P. Johnson, quoted in A. Smith, "The Southern Interior, 1840–1884," *History of East Africa* (Oxford, 1963), I, 255.
7. Quoted in C. A. Julien, *Histoire de l'Algérie contemporaine, 1827–1871* (Paris, 1964), p. 590.
8. R. W. July, *The Origins of Modern African Thought* (London, 1968) p. 232.
9. E. W. Blyden, *The Prospects of the African* (London, 1874), quoted in July, *op. cit.*, p. 219.
10. Quoted in the Earl of Cromer, *Modern Egypt* (London, 1911), p. 48.
11. J. C. McCoan, *Egypt as It Is* (London, 1877), p. 53.
12. Quoted in A. E. Crouchley, *The Economic Development of Modern Egypt* (London, 1938), p. 78.
13. D. S. Landes, *Bankers and Pashas* (London, 1958), p. 134.
14. Cromer, *op. cit.*, p. 39.

15. G. Schweinfurth, *The Heart of Africa* (London, 1878), II, 216.
16. H. C. Jackson, *Black Ivory and White, or the Story of El Zubeir Pasha, Slaver and Sultan, as Told by Himself* (Oxford, 1912), p. 31.
17. Ismail used this phrase in an interview with Sir Bartle Frere in 1873, quoted in R. Gray, *op. cit.*, p. 176.
18. S. Baker, *Ismailia* (2d ed.; London, 1879), p. xi.
19. H. Rassam, *Narrative of the British Mission to Theodore* (London, 1871), I, 251.
20. *Ibid.*, II, 153.
21. Quoted in R. Greenfield, *Ethiopia* (London, 1965), p. 89.
22. Quoted in Cromer, *op. cit.*, p. 71.
23. Quoted in R. E. Robinson, J. Gallagher, and A. Denny, *Africa and the Victorians* (London, 1961), p. 83.
24. Pélissier de Reynaud quoted in Julien, *op. cit.*, p. 341.
25. E. E. Evans-Pritchard, *The Sanusi of Cyrenaica* (Oxford, 1949), p. 79.
26. *Ibid.*, p. 98.
27. J. D. Hargreaves, *Prelude to the Partition of West Africa* (London, 1965), p. 195.
28. Robinson, Gallagher, and Denny, *op. cit.*, p. 35.
29. Minute by Lord Palmerston, 20.4.1860: C. W. Newbury, *British Policy Towards West Africa, Selected Documents, 1786–1874* (Oxford, 1965), p. 120.
30. The phrase used by Lord John Russell in a letter to the Duke of Newcastle, 7.2.1861: C. W. Newbury, *op. cit.*, p. 426.
31. Lord Kimberley to the governor of Lagos, 26.8.1881, quoted in Robinson, Gallagher, and Denny, *op. cit.*, p. 40.
32. Quasie Edoo to Sir A. E. Kennedy, 24.11.1871: G. E. Metcalfe, *Great Britain and Ghana, Documents of Ghana History, 1807–1957* (University of Ghana, 1964), p. 335.
33. W. G. Blaikie, *Personal Life of David Livingstone* (London, 1917), p. 28.
34. Livingstone, *op. cit.*, p. 24.
35. J. Vansina, *Kingdoms of the Savanna* (Madison, Wis., 1966), p. 219.
36. A. Smith, *op. cit.*, I, 280.
37. Quoted in J. A. H. Agar-Hamilton, *The Native Policy of the Voortrekkers* (Cape Town, n.d.), p. 167.
38. H. Deschamps, *Histoire de Madagascar* (Paris, 1960), p. 167.

✠ NOTES TO EPILOGUE

1. E. W. Bovill (ed.), *Missions to the Niger* (Cambridge, 1966), III, 479.
2. W. B. Baikie in a despatch to the Foreign Office, 5.7.1858, quoted in K. O. Dike, *Trade and Politics in the Niger Delta, 1830–1885* (Oxford, 1956), p. 177.
3. G. Lejean, *Voyage en Abyssinie* (Paris, 1872), p. 185.
4. J. L. Krapf quoted in C. P. Groves, *The Planting of Christianity in Africa* (London, 1964), II, 99.
5. D. Livingstone, *Cambridge Lectures* (London, 1858).
6. These famous words, which were inscribed on Livingstone's tomb in Westminster Abbey, occur in a letter written by the explorer to the

New York Herald: R. Coupland, *Livingstone's Last Journey* (London, 1945), p. 222.

7. Quoted in Groves, *op. cit.,* II, 210.

8. Minute by W. H. Wylde of the Foreign Office, 6.8.1876, quoted in Dike, *op. cit.,* p. 205.

9. Quoted in C. A. Bodelsen, *Studies in Mid-Victorian Imperialism* (Copenhagen, 1924), p. 69.

10. Quoted in A. Murphy, *The Ideology of French Imperialism, 1871–1881* (Washington, D.C., 1948), p. 137.

11. C. J. H. Haynes, *A Generation of Imperialism, 1871–1900* (New York, 1941), p. 221.

12. Quoted in J. Duffy, *Portugal in Africa* (Harmondsworth, 1962), p. 106.

13. Quoted in N. Ascherson, *The King Incorporated* (London, 1963), p. 58.

14. A. Hourani, *Arabic Thought in the Liberal Age, 1798–1939* (London, 1962), p. 109.

Suggested Readings

The primary aim of the Suggested Readings is to provide a guide for those who wish to explore certain aspects of the African past in greater detail. For this reason Part I, which is concerned mainly with general works, contains a good deal of information of a kind not easily accessible elsewhere about bibliographies and periodicals. Part II gives details of the main sources drawn on for individual chapters.

Anyone who attempts to range over the whole field of African history soon finds himself faced with two formidable difficulties: the multiplicity of languages in which important works about the African past have been written and the ever-increasing mass of material at the historian's disposal. Something should be said about both of these problems. Works relating to Africa have been written in Arabic and Turkish and in most of the major languages of Europe including Latin, Greek, Portuguese, Spanish, Italian, French, English, German, Dutch, Flemish, and Russian. In addition, there is a considerable literature of historical importance in certain African languages, including Afrikaans, Amharic, and Ge'ez, Hausa, Luganda, Malagasy, and Swahili. The student whose knowledge is confined to English has a wide range of general works at his disposal and many detailed studies of areas formerly under British rule, but he will find himself debarred from wide reading about those parts of Africa—the Maghrib, much of West and Equatorial Africa and Madagascar—that once formed part of the French empire. Moreover, French scholars have written penetratingly about many other parts of Africa. Any serious student of general African history must be prepared to read as much in French as he does in English.

Other languages are somewhat more limited in their range, but clearly it is impossible to make a detailed study of the history of the Portuguese territories in Africa without a knowledge of Portuguese or of South African history without knowing Afrikaans. In the same way a knowledge of Arabic is essential for any one concerned with the detailed history of much of Muslim Africa. German and Italian scholars have written much about the territories that once formed part of the German and Italian colonial empires, and there are a number of works by nineteenth-century German and Italian travelers that have never been translated. There are also numerous early works in Dutch relating to West Africa that have not been translated, while some of the literature on the former Belgian Congo is in Flemish. A number of scholars in the Soviet Union and in other Eastern European countries, including Poland and Czechoslovakia, have produced works on Africa. In Turkey a considerable amount is now being written about the Ottoman Empire, which included in its territories a large part of North Africa. Works in African languages other than Arabic and Afrikaans are confined mainly to chronicles, memoirs, legends, and poetry. Social anthropologists have long accepted the necessity of learning the language of the people whose institutions they study. Historians are now finding the same linguistic fluency equally necessary when studying the historical traditions of any particular people.

Ideally, then, a gift for languages is one of the most valuable qualities for the African historian to possess. Some of the most eminent Africanists of the past, men such as Heinrich Barth, Richard Burton, and Harry Johnston, were remarkable for their ability as linguists. But the learning of languages is not dependent entirely on natural ability or inclination; perseverance and opportunity are also important. With the development of new techniques for teaching languages and the lengthening of periods of postgraduate study it is becoming easier for a new generation of Africanists to acquire a knowledge of languages. In the meantime students of African history who, like the present author, find their ability to read fluently confined to English, French, and German have at their disposal a formidable amount of material.

Some idea of the mass of material already available may be obtained from the most detailed of the bibliographies mentioned below. But it needs to be emphasized that the amount of this material increases year by year. New sources of archival material are constantly being brought to light. At the same time there is a steady proliferation of new publications. Twenty years ago only a small group of scholars were actively engaged in the study of the African past; "there must today," so Roland Oliver, one of the most prominent of English Africanists, has recently pointed out, "be getting on for a thousand people around the world who are actively engaged in extending the frontiers of knowledge in one part or another of this subject." There can be few fields of historical research that have ever witnessed so explosive an expansion of knowledge. In such a situation it is particularly important for the serious student of African history to keep up with the latest developments in research.

Finally, it is worth reemphasizing the point made in the last paragraph of the Introduction about the limitations of any general history. By the time this book is published a number of important studies of different aspects of the African past at present in press will have appeared. There are also a number of very recent publications to which I have not been able to devote sufficient attention. Such deficiencies are aggravating but unavoidable. The critical reader must be prepared to demolish those parts of this historical framework that he finds unsatisfactory and erect new scaffolding in their place.

PART I

𝄞 BIBLIOGRAPHIES

Recent developments in African studies have been accompanied by a steady improvement in the quality of bibliographical material. The *Bibliography of African Bibliographies* compiled by A. Garling of the African Studies Centre, Cambridge (1968), is a valuable guide but not altogether a complete one, for it does not mention the important bibliographies contained in some recent studies in African history, geography, and anthropology. Special mention should be made of the bibliographies contained in each of the volumes of the Ethnographic Survey of Africa. These are never less than adequate and the best are exceedingly well done. Here one can mention only those bibliographies of special value to the student of African history before 1875.

Africa, General: *Africa South of the Sahara: a Selected Annotated List of Writings,* compiled by H. Condover of the Library of Congress (Washington, 1963).

Africa, Prehistory: The *Surveys and Bibliographies* published by the Council for Old World Archaeology (C.O.W.A.) at Boston University provides the most useful guide to recent research. The "Old World" is divided into twenty-two areas, six of which—nos. 9–14—are in Africa.

Africa, History: R. Mauny, "Contribution à la bibliographie de l'histoire de l'Afrique noire des origines à 1850," *Bulletin de l'Institut d'Afrique Noire,* Série B, XXVIII/3–4 (1966) lists works relating to Tropical Africa published before 1850; R. I. Rotberg's *Political History of Tropical Africa* (New York, 1965) contains a bibliography valuable for the prominence given to recent articles in periodicals.

Muslim Africa: J. Sauvaget, *Introduction to the History of the Muslim East. A Bibliographical Guide,* 2d edition recast by C. Cahen (Berkeley, 1965), is invaluable for students of Islam but devotes relatively little space to sub-Saharan Africa. The *Encyclopedia of Islam* gives useful bibliographical notes for all the main articles. J. D. Pearson, *Index Islamicus, 1906–1955. A Catalogue of Articles on Islamic Subjects in Periodicals and Other Collective Publications* (Cambridge, 1958), is arranged to permit easy reference to works on particular countries. A supplement covering the years 1956–60 was published in 1962.

Northeast Africa: R. Jones, *North-east Africa* (London, 1959), is one of the volumes of the Africa Bibliography Series published by the International African Institute and defined as covering "Ethnology, Sociology and Linguistics": this volume does not include Egypt.

Egypt: There is no compact bibliographical guide to the whole span of Egyptian history. For a bibliography of ancient Egypt see the work by

Drioton and Vandier cited on p. 456; for the classical period, see the relevant chapter bibliographies in the *Cambridge Ancient History;* for the Muslim period see the works cited above for Muslim Africa; for the modern period there is no up-to-date bibliography, but a great deal of bibliographical information is contained in the collective work edited by P. M. Holt, *Political and Social Change in Modern Egypt* (London, 1968).

Sudan: R. L. Hill, *A Bibliography of the Anglo-Egyptian Sudan from the Earliest Times to 1937* (London, 1939); A. R. El Nasri, *A Bibliography of the Sudan 1938–1958* (London, 1962); A. Ibrahim and A. R. El Nasri, "Sudan Bibliography, 1959–1963," *Sudan Notes and Records,* XLVI (1965).

Ethiopia: There is no adequate bibliography covering the whole of Ethiopian history; for select bibliographies see the works by Ullendorf and Pankhurst cited on p. 457.

Somalia: There is no complete bibliography; for a select bibliography see I. M. Lewis, *Peoples of the Horn of Africa* (London, 1955), a volume in the Ethnographic Survey of Africa.

Libya: R. W. Hill, *A Bibliography of Libya* (Durham, 1959).

Algeria, Morocco, Tunisia: C. A. Julien, *Histoire de l'Afrique du Nord,* revised edition, 2 vols. (Paris, 1961), contains two excellent bibliographies prepared for the first volume by C. Courtois and for the second volume by R. Le Tourneau. An English translation of this work with revised and extended bibliographies is to be published in 1970.

Sahara: B. M. S. Blaudin de Thé, *Essai de bibliographie du Sahara français et des regions avoisantes* (Alger, 1959).

West Africa: R. Jones, *West Africa* (London, 1958), a volume in the Africa Bibliography series. For the early history of West Africa there is a valuable bibliography in the work by Mauny, *Tableau géographique* cited on p. 463. See also H. A. Rydings, *The Bibliographies of West Africa* (Ibadan, 1961).

French West Africa: E. Joucla, *Bibliographie de l'Afrique Occidentale Française* (Paris, 1937).

Sierra Leone: H. C. Luke, *A Bibliography of Sierra Leone,* 2d edition (London, 1925); P. E. H. Hair, "A Bibliographical Guide to Sierra Leone, 1460–1650," *Sierra Leone Studies,* no. 10 (1958), continued from 1650–1800 in no. 13 (1960).

Liberia: M. D. Solomon and L. d'A. Warren, *A General Bibliography of the Republic of Liberia* (Evanston, Ill., 1962).

Ghana (Gold Coast): A. W. Cardinall, *A Bibliography of the Gold Coast* (Accra, 1932).

Nigeria: J. Harris, *Books about Nigeria.* 3d edition (Ibadan, 1962).

French Equatorial Africa: G. Bruel, *Bibliographie de l'Afrique Equatoriale Française* (Paris, 1914).

Belgian Congo: For a brief guide to the complex bibliographical material relating to the ex-Belgian Congo see H. P. Condover, *Africa South of the Sahara,* pp. 281–82. For a select bibliography, see R. Cornevin, *Histoire du Congo-Léo* (Paris, 1963).

Angola: See the select bibliographies in the works by Vansina, Boxer, and Birmingham cited on p. 468.

Mozambique: See the select bibliographies in the works by Axelson cited on p. 468.

East Africa: R. Jones, *East Africa* (London, 1960), a volume in the Africa Bibliography series; the first two volumes of the *History of East Africa* (Oxford, 1963 and 1965) contain valuable select bibliographies.

Southern Africa (including South Africa and the former British Central Africa, now Zambia, Rhodesia, and Malawi): R. Jones, *South-East Central Africa and Madagascar* (London, 1961), a volume in the African Bibliography series; there are extensive bibliographies covering both South Africa and the territories to the north in E. Walker, *A History of Southern Africa* (London, 1957) and in the *Cambridge History of the British Empire*, VIII: *South Africa*, revised edition (Cambridge, 1963).

South Africa: In addition to the works cited above see S. Mendelssohn, *Mendelssohn's South African Bibliography*, 2 vols. (London, 1910), and I. Schapera, *Select Bibliography of South African Native Life and Problems* (London, 1941).

Madagascar: G. Grandidier, *Bibliographie de Madagascar*, 3 vols. (Paris, 1906, 1935, 1957).

Mauritius: A. Toussaint, *Bibliographie de Maurice, 1502–1954* (Port Louis, 1956).

Réunion: For a select bibliography see the work by Scherer cited on p. 473.

The journal *Africa* published quarterly by the International African Institute (London) regularly includes a "Bibliography of Current Publications," one section of which is now devoted to history and archeology. Summaries of many of the articles cited in this bibliographical section may be found, though usually after an interval of two years, in *African Abstracts*. Useful bibliographical essays have recently appeared in *Africana Newsletter* (Stanford) and *African Studies Bulletin* (New York, later Boston).

Some important work in the field of African history is to be found in unpublished theses. The Library of Congress published a guide to theses produced up to 1962, *American Doctoral Dissertations on Africa* (Washington, D.C., 1962). From 1961 the Hoover Institute has published an annual bibliography, *U.S. and Canadian Publications on Africa*. Beginning with the issue covering the year 1965 this publication also includes details of theses. In Britain the Standing Conference on Library Materials on Africa (Scolma) published *Theses on Africa* (Cambridge, 1964) and *U.K. Publications and Theses on Africa for 1963* (1966) with issues for 1964 (1966) and 1965 (1967).

✥ HISTORIOGRAPHIES

Particularly valuable, especially for those making their first acquaintance with the history of a particular area, are the historiographical

essays that provide critical surveys of a wide range of historical literature.

Sauvaget's *Introduction to the History of the Muslim East* is in part a
historiography. It should be consulted for guidance in all aspects of the
history of Islam up to the nineteenth century. It should be supplemented
by B. Lewis and P. M. Holt (eds.), *Historians of the Middle East* (London, 1962), which considers both contemporary Muslim historians and
later European historians of Islam. The opening chapters of P. M. Holt
(ed.), *Political and Social Change in Modern Egypt* (London, 1968),
consists of a series of historiographical essays on Turkish, Arabic, and
English sources for the history of Ottoman Egypt.

The historiography of Algeria is well covered by two collections of
essays: *Histoire et historiens de l'Algérie, 1830–1930*, published as a
supplement to the *Revue historique* (Paris, 1931), and *Vingt-cinq ans
d'histoire algérienne, 1931–1956* (Alger, 1956). For recent developments in Algerian historiography see J. Wansborough, "The Decoloni-
zation of North African History," *Journal of African History* (J.A.H.),
IX/4 (1968).

The collection of historiographical essays edited by R. W. Winks, *The
Historiography of the British Empire-Commonwealth* (Durham, N.C.,
1966), contains two excellent chapters on "South Africa" by L. M.
Thompson and "British West Africa" by H. M. Wright; chapters dealing
with other parts of Africa refer to the period after 1875. On the literature
of French activities in Africa there is a useful study by R. Lebel, *Histoire
de la littérature coloniale en France* (Paris, 1931); this work has sections
on all the territories later incorporated in the French empire.

※ GUIDES TO ARCHIVES AND LIBRARIES

Some material of interest to the historian of Africa is probably to be
found in the archives of almost every country in the world, but the most
important collections are concentrated in Western Europe, North America, and in various parts of Africa. Useful guides to archives and libraries have now been published. For Great Britain see A. R. Hewitt,
*Guide to Resources for Commonwealth History in London, Oxford and
Cambridge* (London, 1957). For other Western European countries see
the series *Guides to Materials for West African History* (London). This
includes reports on material in the archives of Belgium and Holland
(1962) and on French archives (1968) by P. Carson, on Italian archives
(including the Vatican) by R. Gray and D. Chambers (1965), and on
Portuguese archives by A. F. C. Ryder (1965).

On the nature of Muslim archives see J. Sauvaget, *Introduction to the
History of the Muslim East*, pp. 16–21. A. Garling's *Bibliography of
African Bibliographies* contains a considerable number of references to
reports of manuscript collections relating to Ethiopian, Egyptian, and
North African history.

E. W. Dadzie and J. T. Strickland's *Directory of Archives, Libraries
and Schools of Librarianship in Africa* (Unesco, 1965) provides brief
notes on the archives of tropical Africa. On Southern Africa see the first

section of the bibliography in *Cambridge History of the British Empire:* VIII, *South Africa.*

P. Duignan, *Handbook of American Resources for African Studies* (Stanford, 1967), covers the American field with great thoroughness.

Reports on individual collections in Europe, America, and Africa are published regularly in *Africana Newsletter* (Stanford).

✣ ENCYCLOPEDIAS AND OTHER REFERENCE WORKS

Current editions of the *Encyclopaedia Britannica* and *Chambers Encyclopedia* contain a number of articles of interest to the African historian, but it must be remembered that there is always a considerable time-lag before the product of recent research reaches the pages of an encyclopedia. Historical articles dealing with tropical Africa are usually less adequate than those devoted to countries such as Egypt, Ethiopia, or Morocco, broad outlines of whose histories have long been clearly established. Early editions of encyclopedias contain material of great interest to the historian of European ideas about Africa.

The Encyclopedia of Islam (Leiden) is an indispensable reference for any one concerned with the study of the Muslim parts of Africa. Its articles cover the whole range of Muslim culture; it contains long studies of the historical development of individual countries, briefer accounts of the history of major urban centers, and many biographical entries. The first edition was published in four volumes between 1913 and 1934; the second edition, to which reference should be made whenever possible, began publication in 1954 and as of 1969 was about half way to completion.

Students of the Greek and Roman period in North African history should refer to the various classical encyclopedias, details of which are given in the bibliography to the first volume of Julien's *Histoire de l'Afrique du Nord.*

There is a great need for a large-scale reference work, edited with the same scholarly thoroughness as the *Encyclopedia of Islam,* to cover sub-Saharan Africa. The two encyclopedias produced by the French and Belgian governments during the colonial period, *Encyclopédie coloniale et maritime,* 7 vols. (Paris, 1944–51), and *Encyclopédie du Congo Belge,* 3 vols. (Bruxelles, 1950–52), are of interest to the historian of the colonial period, but their ethnographic and historical sections have been superseded by later research. The same may be said of the handbooks published by the British colonial governments of Nigeria, Uganda, and Tanganyika. For Southern Africa there is a compact reference work compiled by E. Rosenthal, *Encyclopaedia of Southern Africa* (London, 1961).

There are two biographical dictionaries devoted to limited parts of Africa: R. L. Hill, *A Biographical Dictionary of the Anglo-Egyptian Sudan* (Oxford, 1951), and E. Rosenthal, *Southern African Dictionary of National Biography* (London, 1966). Some of the Europeans who left their mark on Africa from the fifteenth century on find a place in their country's dictionary of national biography.

𝕏 ATLASES

African history introduces the student to so many unfamiliar places that good maps are an essential standby. The most useful historical atlas is that compiled by J. D. Fage, *An Atlas of African History* (London, 1958). For the location and dispersion of particular ethnic groups the maps contained in each of the volumes of the Ethnographic Survey of Africa should be consulted; they have been drawn with beautiful clarity and precision. The best general atlas of Africa is *The Times Atlas of the World*, Vol. 4: *Southern Europe and Africa* (London, 1956).

Northern Africa in Muslim times is included in the *Historical Atlas of the Muslim Peoples*, edited by R. Roolvink and others (Amsterdam, 1957; Harvard, 1958). For Southern Africa see E. A. Walker, *Historical Atlas of South Africa* (Cape Town, 1922).

Single-country atlases, some of which contain an historical section, have been prepared for the following territories:

Algeria—*Atlas historique, géographique, économique: L'Algérie* (Paris, 1934).

Morocco—*Atlas historique, géographique, économique: Le Maroc* (Paris, 1935).

Tunisia—*Atlas historique, géographique, économique: La Tunisie* (Paris, 1936).

West Africa—Y. Urvoy, *Petit atlas ethno-démographique du Soudan entre Sénégal et Tchad* (Paris, 1942).

Sierra Leone—J. I. Clarke, *Sierra Leone in Maps* (London, 1966).

Ghana—T. E. Hilton, *Ghana Population Atlas* (University of Ghana, 1960).

Congo-Kinshasa—R. de Rouck, *Atlas géographique et historique du Congo Belge et des territoires sous mandat du Ruanda-Urundi.*

Rhodesia—*Rhodesia: Its Natural Resources and Economic Development* (Salisbury, 1965).

Mozambique—*Atlas de Moçambique* (Lourenço Marques, 1962).

Kenya—*Atlas of Kenya* (Nairobi, 1962).

Tanganyika—*Atlas of Tanganyika,* 3d edition (Dar-es-Salaam, 1956).

Uganda—*Atlas of Uganda* (Department of Lands and Surveys, 1962).

South Africa—A. M. and W. J. Talbot, *Atlas of the Union of South Africa* (Pretoria, 1960).

𝕏 PERIODICALS

A list of periodicals "regularly containing material on Africa" recently prepared by the African Studies Centre at Cambridge runs to more than seven hundred publications, while the invaluable *Serials for African Studies* compiled by H. F. Condover of the Library of Congress (Washington, 1961) lists "two thousand-odd titles." Figures such as these give some indication of the mass of periodical material now being produced in the field of African studies. A large number of these periodicals are concerned only with contemporary affairs and may be disregarded by the student of African history before 1875; on the other hand the historian may find it necessary to consult a number of periodicals not listed in Condover's *Serials*, for they have now ceased publication. Thus, it would be possible to produce a list of several hundred periodicals of concern to the historian in Africa. A brief historical sketch of the development of periodicals may serve to provide a few guidelines for those who wish to explore this type of material.

Possibly the first scholarly article on an African subject was the study of the rivers of the interior of Africa written by the famous French cartographer D'Anville; it was published in 1759 in the *Mémoires* of the Académie Royale des Inscriptions et Belles Lettres (Paris). A generation later the growing interest in geography led to the publication of the *Allgemeine geographische Ephemeriden* (Weimar) and the *Annales de voyages* (Paris), both of which drew much of their material from travelers' accounts of parts of the world, including Africa, little known to Western Europeans. The first decades of the nineteenth century saw the foundation of new learned societies in the fields of geography, history, archeology, ethnology, and Oriental studies, most of these societies producing their own regular publications. Of particular value to the historian of Africa are the geographical journals of the nineteenth century. In the closing decades of the nineteenth century there was a steady proliferation in the number of learned societies both in Europe and in America. (See the article "Societies, Learned" in the eleventh edition of the *Encyclopaedia Britannica* for an extensive list of nineteenth-century societies.)

The nineteenth century also saw the appearance of other kinds of periodical publications of interest to the historian in Africa. The missionary societies and other humanitarian associations such as the English Anti-Slavery Society began to produce regular publications which devoted much of their space to accounts from missionaries or other supporters working overseas. These accounts often provide much information useful in helping the historian to reconstruct a picture of the political, social, or economic situation of a particular area of Africa.

The last decades of the nineteenth century saw the emergence of a new range of societies with a special interest in the problems of colonial expansion. These societies—the *Comité de l'Afrique Français*, the African Society (London), the *Deutscher Kolonialverein*, and others—produced their own journals, which often contained articles of interest to the student of precolonial history.

The growth of communities of European settlers or administrators in many parts of Africa led in time to the establishment of periodicals and learned societies based on metropolitan models. The earliest of these colonial journals was the *Revue africaine* founded in 1856 by the *Société historique algérienne*. Other journals that come into this category are *Sudan Notes and Records* issued by the Sudan Philosophical Society and the *Uganda Journal* issued by the Uganda Society. Scholarly minded administrators and missionaries contributed to journals of this type.

Between the two World Wars a number of research institutes were founded, among them the International African Institute, the Institut

Français d'Afrique Noire, and the Institut des Hautes Études Marocaines. The journals and other publications of bodies such as these are of direct interest to the historian. Historical research received a further impetus after World War II with the establishment of new universities with vigorous departments of history. In Nigeria, for example, the Historical Society was founded as a result of the initiative of members of the University of Ibadan. The growing interest in the African past in the older universities of Europe and North America led in the 1960's to a new range of periodicals including the *Journal of African History* (*J.A.H.*) (Cambridge) and *African Historical Studies* (Boston). The proliferation of periodicals of interest to the historian in Africa continues: new issues are regularly noted in *Africa* (London), in the *Africana Newsletter* (Stanford), and in the *Bulletin* of the African Studies Association of the United Kingdom. The list of periodicals that follows is confined to journals entirely devoted to subjects of interest to the historian in Africa; historical, geographical, and anthropological journals that occasionally contain articles of interest to Africanists have, for reasons of space, been omitted. Nor has any mention been made of the missionary periodicals that appeared during the nineteenth century.

1. EUROPE AND ASIA

GREAT BRITAIN:

Africa (International African Institute, London), from 1928.

Bulletin of the African Studies Association of the U.K., from 1964.

Bulletin of the School of Oriental and African Studies (London), from 1917.

Journal of African History (Cambridge), from 1960.

Journal of the Royal African Society (London), from 1901; title changed to *African Affairs* in 1944.

FRANCE:

Arabica, from 1954.

Bulletin du Comité de l'Afrique Française (Paris), from 1891: title changed to *L'Afrique française* in 1908; supplements published under the title *Renseignements coloniaux;* ceased publication in 1960.

Cahiers d'études africaines (Paris), from 1960.

Cahiers d'outre-mer (Bordeaux), from 1948.

Journal de la Société des Africanistes (Paris), from 1931.

Revue du monde musulman (Paris), from 1906; title changed to *Revue des études islamiques* in 1926.

Revue d'histoire des colonies (Paris), from 1913; title changed to *Revue française d'histoire d'outre-mer* in 1959.

GERMANY:

Der Islam (Berlin), from 1910.

For a list of German colonial periodicals, many of which contain material of value for the precolonial history of the areas under German rule, see the bibliography compiled by J. Bridgman and D. E. Clarke, *German Africa* (Stanford, 1965).

HOLLAND:
Journal of the Economic and Social History of the Orient (Leiden), from 1957.
SPAIN:
Al-Andalus (Madrid), from 1933.
PORTUGAL:
Estudos ultramarinos (Lisbon), from 1948.
Studia, published by the Centro de Estudos Historicos Ultramarinos (Lisbon), from 1958.
ITALY:
Africa italiana (Bergamo), from 1927 to 1941.
POLAND:
Africana Bulletin (Warsaw), from 1964.
ISRAEL:
Asian and African Studies, from 1965.

2. NORTH AMERICA
UNITED STATES:
Africana Newsletter (Stanford), from 1962.
African Historical Studies (Boston), from 1968.
African Studies Bulletin (New York), from 1958.
Journal of Near Eastern Studies (Chicago), from 1942.
Journal of Negro History (Washington, D.C.), from 1916.
Middle East Journal (Washington, D.C.), from 1947.
Muslim World (Hartford, Conn.), from 1911.
CANADA:
Canadian Journal of African Studies (Montreal), from 1967.

3. AFRICA (including periodicals relating to individual African countries published outside Africa).
EGYPT:
Annales du Service des Antiquités de L'Égypte (Cairo), from 1897.
Bulletin de l'Institut d'Égypte (Cairo), from 1857.
Bulletin de la Société Royale de Géographie d'Égypte (Cairo), from 1879.
Bulletin of the Faculty of Arts (Alexandria), from 1943.
Bulletin of the Faculty of Arts (Cairo), from 1915.
Bulletin de l'Institut Français d'Archéologie Orientale (Cairo), from 1901.
Chronique d'Égypte (Brussels), from 1926.
Journal of Egyptian Archaeology (London), from 1914.
SUDAN:
Sudan Notes and Records (Khartoum), from 1918.
Kush: Journal of the Sudan Antiquities Service (Khartoum), from 1953.
Bilad as-Sudan (Khartoum), from 1967.
ETHIOPIA:
Annales d'Éthiopie (Paris), from 1955.
Journal of Ethiopian Studies (Addis Ababa), from 1963.

LIBYA:
Libya Antiqua (Tripoli), from 1964.
Quaderni di archeologica della Libia (Rome), from 1950.

TUNISIA:
Revue tunisienne (Tunis), 1894–1952; succeeded by *Les Cahiers de Tunisie* (Tunis), from 1953.
Karthago: Revue d'archéologie africaine (Tunis), from 1950.
Les Cahiers de Byrsa (Paris), 1951–61.

ALGERIA:
Revue africaine (Alger), from 1856.
Bulletin de la Société de Géographie d'Alger et de l'Afrique du Nord (Alger), from 1880.
Libyca: Série anthropologie et archéologie préhistoriques (Alger), from 1953.
Libyca: Série archéologie et épigraphie (Alger), from 1953.
Bulletin d'archéologie algérienne (Alger), from 1967.

MOROCCO:
Revue de géographie marocaine (Rabat), from 1916.
Hespéris: Archives berbères et Bulletin de l'Institut des Hautes-Études Marocaines (Rabat), 1921–59.
Tamuda: Revista de investigaciones maroquies (Tetuan), 1953–59; merged with *Hespéris* in 1959 to become *Hespéris-Tamuda* (Rabat), from 1960.
Bulletin d'archéologie marocaine (Rabat), from 1956.

SAHARA:
Travaux de L'Institut des Recherches Sahariennes (Alger), from 1942.

WEST AFRICA: FRANCOPHONE
Institut Français d'Afrique Noire. Annuaire et mémoires, 1916–17; superseded by *Bulletin du Comité d'Études Historiques Scientifiques de l'A.O.F.,* from 1918 to 1938; superseded by *Bulletin de l'Institut Français d'Afrique Noire* (Dakar), from 1938 to 1953. From 1954 the *Bulletin de l'I.F.A.N.* has appeared in two parts: *Série A. Sciences naturelles; Série B: Sciences humaines.* In 1966 I.F.A.N.'s title was changed to Institut Fondamental d'Afrique Noire.
Notes africaines (I.F.A.N., Dakar), from 1959.

MAURITANIA:
Études mauritaniennes (St. Louis), from 1948.

SENEGAL:
Études sénégalaises (Dakar), from 1949.

GUINEA:
Études guinéennes (Conakry), from 1947 to 1955; superseded by *Recherches africaines* (Conakry), from 1959.

IVORY COAST:
Études éburnéennes (Abidjan), from 1950.

MALI:
Études soudanaises (Bamako), from 1953.

UPPER VOLTA:
Études voltaiques (Ouagadougou), from 1950.

DAHOMEY:
Études dahoméennes (Porto-Novo), from 1948.

NIGER:
Études nigériennes (Niamey), from 1953.
(All *Études* published at irregular intervals by the local I.F.A.N.)

SIERRA LEONE:
Sierra Leone Studies (Freetown), 1918 to 1939 and from 1953.
Sierra Leone Geographical Association (Freetown). *The Bulletin,* from 1957; title changed to *The Journal* in 1967.

GHANA:
Historical Society of Ghana (title changed from Gold Coast and Togoland Historical Society). *Transactions* (Achimota), from 1952.
Ghana Geographical Association. *Bulletin,* from 1955.
Ghana Notes and Queries (Kumasi), from 1961.

NIGERIA:
The Nigerian Field (London), from 1931.
The Nigerian Teacher (Lagos), 1934–36; title changed to *Nigeria,* 1939–59; title changed to *Nigeria Magazine,* from 1960.
Historical Society of Nigeria (Ibadan). *Journal,* from 1956; *Bulletin of News,* from 1956.
Nigerian Geographical Journal (Ibadan), from 1957.
Tarikh: a New Journal of African History for Schools (Ibadan), from 1965.
Bulletin of the Centre of Arabic Documentation (Ibadan), from 1964.
Kano Studies (Kano), from 1965.

PORTUGUESE GUINEA:
Boletim cultural da Guiné portuguesa (Bissau), from 1946.

CAMEROUN:
Bulletin de la Société des Études Camerounaises, 1935–47.
Études camerounaises (I.F.A.N., Douala), 1948–57.
Institut des Recherches Scientifiques du Cameroun (Yaoundé). *Recherches et études camerounaises,* from 1960.

CONGO-BRAZZAVILLE:
Bulletin de la Société des Recherches Congolaises, 1922–39.
Bulletin de l'Institut d'Études Centrafricaines, 1945–60.
Bulletin de l'Institut de Recherches Scientifiques au Congo, from 1962.

CONGO-KINSHASA:
Congo: Revue générale de la colonie belge (Brussels), 1920–47.
Zaire: Revue congolaise (Brussels), 1947–60.
For details of other periodicals relating to Congo-Kinshasa, see J. Vansina, *Introduction à l'ethnographie du Congo* (Kinshasa, 1965), pp. 21–22.

ANGOLA:
Arquivos de Angola (Luanda), 1933–39 and from 1943.
RHODESIA:
Nada: Southern Rhodesian Native Affairs Department Annual (Salisbury), from 1923.
Rhodesian Scientific Association. *Proceedings* (Salisbury), from 1899.
ZAMBIA:
Rhodes-Livingstone Institute, now incorporated in the University of Zambia (Lusaka). *Communications*, from 1943. *Journal*, from 1944; title changed to *African Social Research* in 1967; *Papers*, from 1938; title changed to *Zambian Papers* in 1967.
Northern Rhodesia Journal (Livingstone), from 1950; title changed to *Zambian Journal* in 1965.
The Nyasaland Journal (Blantyre), from 1948; title changed to *Society of Malawi Journal* in 1965.
EAST AFRICA:
East African Swahili Committee (Kampala). *Bulletin*, 1930–52; *Swahili*, from 1952.
East African Geographical Review (Kampala), from 1963.
Azania: Journal of the British Institute of History and Archaeology in East Africa (Nairobi), from 1966.
KENYA:
Kenya History Society (Nairobi). *Transactions*, from 1957; *News Bulletin*, from 1955.
TANZANIA:
Tanganyika Notes and Records (Dar es-Salaam), from 1936.
UGANDA:
The Uganda Journal (London), from 1934.
SOUTH AFRICA:
Bantu Studies (Johannesburg), 1921–41; superseded by *African Studies*, from 1942.
South African Geographical Journal (Johannesburg), from 1917.
South African Archaeological Bulletin (Claremont, Cape Province), from 1946.
South African Archives Yearbook.
MALAGASY REPUBLIC:
Bulletin de l'Académie Malgache (Tananarive), from 1902.
MAURITIUS:
Société de l'Histoire de l'Île Maurice. Bulletin (Port Louis), from 1938.

𝕫⊫ GENERAL HISTORIES OF AFRICA

The student of African history now has a number of general works at his disposal, some of which range over the entire continent while others are confined to sub-Saharan or Tropical Africa. One may draw a distinction between the relatively short works which stimulate and provoke by their generalizations and longer works more useful for purposes of reference. Recent studies that fall into the first category include R. Oliver and J. D. Fage, *A Short History of Africa* (Harmondsworth, 1962), R. Oliver and A. Atmore, *Africa since 1800* (Cambridge, 1967), and B. Davidson, with photographs by W. Forman, *Africa: History of a Continent* (London, 1966). The text of the last-named work, whose magnificent illustrations make it the most lavish work so far produced in the general field of African history, has been published in handier format and with some additional material under the title *Africa in History: Themes and Outlines* (London, 1968). More detailed general studies of African history include R. Cornevin, *Histoire des peuples d'Afrique noire* (Paris, 1960) and *Histoire de l'Afrique*, 2 vols. (Paris, 1962–66); G. P. Murdock, *Africa: Its Peoples and Their Culture History* (New York, 1959); and R. I. Rotberg, *A Political History of Tropical Africa* (New York, 1965). All these works contain useful reading lists or bibliographies.

Also to be noted in the category of general works are the two short collections of broadcast talks on different aspects of African history edited by R. Oliver, *The Dawn of African History* (London, 1961) and *The Middle Ages of African History* (London, 1967), and the exciting work by B. Davidson, *Old Africa Rediscovered* (London, 1959), published in the United States under the title *The Lost Cities of Africa*.

✹ HISTORICAL ANTHOLOGIES

Many of the basic sources for African history are to be found in works that are exceedingly difficult to obtain for those who do not have access to a really good library. Those who find themselves in this situation will gain some assistance from historical anthologies. Three such anthologies range over much of sub-Saharan Africa: B. Davidson, *The African Past* (London, 1964); C. Coquery, *La Découverte de l'Afrique* (Paris, 1965); and J. Simmons and M. Perham, *African Discovery* (London, 1942).

For West Africa see C. Howard, *West African Explorers* (London, 1951), and the anthologies edited by Hodgkin, Fyfe, and Wolfson cited on p. 465. For East Africa see C. Richards and J. Place, *East African Explorers* (London, 1960) and the collection of documents on the Coast edited by Freeman-Grenville and cited on p. 470. For South Africa see E. Axelson, *South African Explorers* (London, 1954).

Two volumes of *Readings in African History* edited by P. J. M. McEwan, *Africa from Early Times to 1800* and *Nineteenth Century Africa* (London, 1968), contain a wide range of extracts from the work of modern historians.

✹ SINGLE-COUNTRY HISTORIES

Concise histories have now been written for most of the countries of modern Africa. Many of these works are referred to in the suggestions for further reading related to the chapters on regional history. But for ease of reference a brief list of these works is provided here.

Egypt: G. Hanotaux (ed.), *Histoire de la nation égyptienne*, 7 vols. (Paris, 1931–37). In English there is a useful summary of Egyptian history in the *Encyclopaedia Britannica*.

Sudan: A. J. Arkell, *A History of the Sudan to 1821*, 2d revised edition (London, 1961); P. M. Holt, *A Modern History of the Sudan* (London, 1961).

Ethiopia: A. H. M. Jones and E. Monroe, *A History of Abyssinia* (London, 1935); E. Ullendorf, *The Ethiopians* (London, 1960).

Somalia: I. M. Lewis, *The Modern History of Somaliland* (London, 1965).

North Africa (the Maghrib): C. A. Julien, *Histoire de l'Afrique du Nord*, revised edition (Paris, 1961); N. Barbour (ed.), *A Survey of North West Africa* (London, 1959).

Morocco: H. Terrasse, *Histoire du Maroc*, 2 vols. (Casablanca, 1949–50); N. Barbour, *Morocco* (London, 1965).

Algeria: S. Gsell, G. Marçais, and G. Yver, *Histoire de l'Algérie* (Paris, 1927); J. Alazard and others, *Initiation à l'Algérie* (Paris, 1957).

Tunisia: R. Brunschwig and others, *Initiation à la Tunise* (Paris, 1950).

West Africa: J. D. Fage, *An Introduction to the History of West Africa*, 3d edition (Cambridge, 1962); J. F. A. Ajayi and I. Espoe (eds.), *A Thousand Years of West African History* (Ibadan, 1965).

Senegal: H. Deschamps, *Le Sénégal et la Gambie* (Paris, 1964), a volume in the *Que sais-je?* series.

Gambia: J. M. Gray, *A History of the Gambia* (Cambridge, 1940); Lady Southorn, *The Gambia* (London, 1952); H. A. Gailey, *A History of the Gambia* (London, 1964).

Mauritania: A. Gerteiny, *Mauritania* (London, 1967).

Sierra Leone: A. P. Kup, *A History of Sierra Leone, 1400–1787* (Cambridge, 1961); C. Fyfe, *A History of Sierra Leone* (London, 1962).

Liberia: G. W. Brown, *The Economic History of Liberia* (Washington, D.C., 1941); E. J. Yancy, *The Republic of Liberia* (London, 1959).

Ivory Coast: G. Rougerie, *La Côte d'Ivoire* (Paris, 1964), a volume in the *Que sais-je?* series.

Ghana: W. E. F. Ward, *A History of Ghana*, 2d edition (London, 1958); J. D. Fage, *Ghana, A Historical Interpretation* (Madison, 1959).

Togo: R. Cornevin, *Histoire du Togo* (Paris, 1959) and *Le Togo* (Paris, 1967), a volume in the *Que sais-je?* series.

Dahomey: R. Cornevin, *Histoire du Dahomey* (Paris, 1962) and *Le Dahomey* (Paris, 1965), a volume in the *Que sais-je?* series.

Nigeria: A. C. Burns, *History of Nigeria*, 6th edition (London, 1963); M. Crowder, *The Story of Nigeria* (London, 1962).

Niger: E. Sérié des Rivières, *Histoire du Niger* (Paris, 1965).

Cameroun: E. Mveng, *Histoire du Cameroun* (Paris, 1963); B. Lembezat, *Le Cameroun* (Paris, 1964).

Chad: P. Hugot, *Le Tchad* (Paris, 1965).

Central African Republic: P. Kalck, *Réalités oubanguiennes* (Paris, 1959).

Congo-Kinshasa: R. Slade, *King Leopold's Congo* (London, 1962); R. Cornevin, *Histoire du Congo-Léo* (Paris, 1963).

Angola and Mozambique: J. Duffy, *Portuguese Africa* (Cambridge, 1959) and *Portugal in Africa* (Harmondsworth, 1962).

British Central Africa: A. J. Hanna, *The Story of the Rhodesias and Nyasaland*, 2d edition (London, 1965); A. J. Wills, *An Introduction to the History of Central Africa*, 2d edition (London, 1967).

Rhodesia: L. H. Gann, *A History of Southern Rhodesia* (London, 1965).

Zambia: L. H. Gann, *A History of Northern Rhodesia* (London, 1964); B. M. Fagan (ed.), *A Short History of Zambia* (Nairobi, 1966).

East Africa: R. Oliver and G. Mathew (eds.), *History of East Africa*, Vol. I (Oxford, 1963); K. Ingham, *A History of East Africa* (London, 1963).

South Africa: E. A. Walker, *A History of Southern Africa* (London, 1957); C. W. de Kiewiet, *A History of South Africa, Social and Economic* (Oxford, 1941); *The Cambridge History of the British Empire*, Vol. VIII: *South Africa*, revised edition (Cambridge, 1963).

Madagascar: H. Deschamps, *Histoire du Madagascar* (Paris, 1960).

Mauritius: P. J. Barnwell and A. Toussaint, *A Short History of Mauritius* (London, 1949).

Réunion: A. Scherer, *Histoire de la Réunion* (Paris, 1965), a volume in the *Que sais-je?* series.

An excellent series of brief introductory histories, *The Modern Nations in Historical Perspective* (Englewood Cliffs, N.J.), considers groups of African countries. The series includes volumes on Central Africa by P. Gifford, the Congo by H. R. Rudin, Egypt and the Sudan by R. Tignor and R. Collins, Ethiopia, Eritrea, and the Somalilands by W. H. Lewis, former French West Africa by J. D. Hargreaves, Morocco, Algeria, Tunisia by R. M. Bruce, Portuguese Africa by R. Chilcote, and Sierra Leone and Liberia by C. Fyfe.

👁 ALIENS IN AFRICA TO 1875

The activities of aliens, whether of Asian or of European origin, provide one of the recurrent themes of African history. A number of works on alien enterprise are mentioned under the chapter headings in Part II of the Suggested Readings: for the Phoenicians see Chapter VI, Section 3; for the South Arabians, Chapter V, Section 7; for the Arabs, Chapter V, Sections 8, 9, and 11, and Chapter VI, Sections 5 and 7; for the Ottoman Turks, Chapter V, Section 13, and Chapter VI, Section 8; for the Indonesians, Chapter XII, Section 3.

European activities in Northern Africa in classical times need to be seen in the context of the entire Mediterranean world. In addition to the works on Greek and Roman rule in Egypt (Chapter V, Section 6) and on Roman rule in North Africa (Chapter VI, Section 4) one should consult the appropriate volumes of the *Cambridge Ancient History* or the more concise studies contained in the French general histories in the series *Peuples et civilisations, Clio: Introduction aux études historiques; Histoire générale* (Collection G. Glotz) or the recent *Histoire générale des civilisations*. The two great works by M. Rostovtzeff, *The Social and Economic History of the Hellenistic World* (Oxford, 1941) and *The So-*

cial and Economic History of the Roman Empire (Oxford, 1957), contain sections relating to Egypt and other parts of North Africa.

The Arab conquest of North Africa shattered the unity of the Mediterranean world. The economic consequences for Europe of the rise of Islam formed the subject of the famous and controversial work by H. Pirenne, *Mohammed and Charlemagne,* English translation (London, 1939). On the issues raised by Pirenne see *The Pirenne Thesis,* edited by A. Havighurst in the "Problems in European Civilization" series (Boston, 1958). Works on European knowledge of Africa in classical and medieval times are listed on p. 451. On European commercial contacts during the medieval period with North Africa and Egypt the works by Mas Latrie (p. 462) and Heyd (p. 458) should be consulted.

The fifteenth century saw the opening of a new phase in which European contacts with Africa became at once more intense and more extensive. There are two excellent general studies which between them cover the period of European expansion in Asia and in America as well as in Africa up to the end of the nineteenth century: J. Parry, *The Age of Reconnaissance* (London, 1963), and D. Fieldhouse, *The Colonial Empires* (London, 1966). The appropriate volumes and chapters of the *New Cambridge Modern History* and of the various series of French general histories cited above may also be consulted. One aspect of European activities in Africa, the growing interest in the interior of northern and western Africa in the late eighteenth and early nineteenth centuries, is considered in R. Hallett, *The Penetration of Africa* (London, 1965). The growth of Europe's interest in Africa may be traced through a number of notable general works dating from the sixteenth century onward. These include F. da Montalboddo, *Paesi novamente retrovati* (Venice, 1507); S. Munster, *La Cosmographie universelle* (Basle, 1552); G. B. Ramusio, *Navigationi e viaggi,* 3 vols. (Venice, 1560); F. de Belleforest, *La Cosmographie universelle de tout le monde* (Paris, 1575); J. Ogilby, *Africa* (London, 1670); T. Astley, *A New General Collection of Voyages and Travels,* 4 vols. (London, 1743–47); J. Pinkerton, *A General Collection of the Best and Most Interesting Voyages and Travels in All Parts of the World,* 17 vols. (London, 1808–14), Africa is covered in volumes 15 and 16.

Most of the nations of Western Europe developed a stake in Africa, the Portuguese and the Spaniards being followed by the French, the English, the Dutch, and other people of northwestern Europe. The most important general works are noted here, together with some of the best known contemporary works produced by the nationals of individual countries.

PORTUGAL. For a general history of Portugal see H. V. Livermore, *A New History of Portugal* (Cambridge, 1966). On the Portuguese expansion see E. Prestage, *The Portuguese Pioneers* (London, 1933), and C. R. Boxer, *Four Centuries of Portuguese Expansion* (Johannesburg, 1961). Brief accounts of the papers, some of which are given in English or in French, delivered at the Congresso Internacional de Historia dos Descobrimentos held in Lisbon in 1960 to commemorate the quincentenary of the death of Henry the Navigator have been published in *Resumio das comunicacoes* (Lisbon, 1966). For general accounts of Portuguese activities in Africa see J. Duffy, *Portuguese Africa* (London, 1959), and R. J. Hammond, *Portugal in Africa, 1815–1910* (Stanford, 1966). For Portuguese activities in West Africa see the works cited for Chapter VII, Section 9, and in Central Africa, Chapter IX, Section 5. The most notable contemporary account of the first stage of the movement of Portuguese expansion, the *Chronicle of the Discovery of Guinea*, was written by G. E. de Zurara c. 1452 but not published until 1831: the English edition is cited on p. 464. Zurara's account was continued by João de Barros, *Decadas da Asia*, first published in Lisbon between 1552 and 1615, a new Portuguese edition being in 4 vols. (Lisbon, 1945–46). This great work, the major Portuguese chronicle of the sixteenth century, has never been completely translated into another European language, but an English translation of the most important passages relating to West Africa has been made by G. R. Crone (see his edition of Cadamosto cited on p. 464) and of passages relating to Mozambique and East Africa by G. M. Theal in *Records of South East Africa*, Vol. VI, pp. 1–306. In the same collection of *Records* Theal also gives extensive translated extracts from the seventeenth-century Portuguese chroniclers, D. de Couto (Vol. VI, pp. 307–410), A. Bocarro (Vol. III, pp. 254–435), and M. Faria e Sousa (Vol. I, pp. 1–46). The most important accounts of parts of Africa written by Portuguese or by men of other nationalities in Portuguese service include for West Africa the works by Cadamosto and Pereira (p. 464), for Angola and Kongo those of Lopez and Cadornega (p. 468), for East Africa dos Santos (p. 468), and for Ethiopia Alvarez, Castanhoso, and Almeida (p. 458).

SPAIN. Spanish activities were confined to parts of the Maghrib and West Africa. For sixteenth-century Spanish activities in North Africa see the great work by F. Braudel, *La Méditerranée et le monde méditerranéen à l'époque de Philippe II*, new edition, 2 vols. (Paris, 1966). For early Spanish activities in West Africa see the two works by J. W. Blake cited on p. 464. Major contemporary works by Spanish writers on Africa include Marmol Caravajal, *Descripción general de Africa*, 3 vols. (Granada and Málaga, 1573–99), and Ali Bey, *Travels in Morocco, Tripoli, Cyprus, Egypt, Arabia, Syria and Turkey* (London, 1816). (On the extraordinary character and adventures of Domingo Badía y Leblich *alias* Ali Bey see Hallett, *Penetration of Africa*, pp. 310–20.)

FRANCE. Between the sixteenth and the nineteenth centuries the French developed interests in the Maghrib, Egypt, Senegal, a number of coastal districts in West and Equatorial Africa, Madagascar, and the Mascarenes. There are a number of general works that cover the history of French expansion: H. Blet, *Histoire de la colonisation française*, 3 vols. (Paris, 1946–50); J. Saintoyant, *La Colonisation française sous l'ancien régime*, 2 vols. (Paris, 1929), *La Colonisation française pendant la Révolution, 1789–1799*, 2 vols. (Paris, 1930), *La Colonisation française pendant la période napoléonienne, 1789–1815* (Paris, 1931); H. J. Deschamps, *Les Méthodes et les doctrines coloniales de la France du XVIe siècle à nos jours* (Paris, 1953). The 6-volume work edited by G. Hanotaux and A. Martineau, *Histoire des colonies fran-*

çaises et de l'expansion française dans la monde (Paris, 1930–34), contains separate sections devoted to the colonial history of individual territories. See also for the mid-nineteenth century the opening chapters of J. Ganiage, *L'Expansion coloniale de la France sous la Troisième République, 1871–1914* (Paris, 1968), and H. Brunschwig, *Mythes et réalités de l'impérialisme colonial français, 1871–1914* (Paris, 1960). Brunschwig's work is one of the very few works that have been translated into English—*French Colonisation, 1870–1914* (London, 1966). For more detailed studies of French activities in North Africa see P. Masson, *Histoire des établissements et du commerce français dans l'Afrique barbaresque, 1560–1793* (Paris, 1903), and the works cited for Chapter VI, Section 10; for Egypt see the works cited for Chapter V, Section 13, for West Africa Chapter VII, Sections 9 and 12, for Equatorial Africa Chapter VIII, Section 6, and for Madagascar and the Mascarenes Chapter XII, Sections 2 and 3. Among the most prominent works by contemporary Frenchmen with experience of Africa are those by Volney and the scholars who accompanied Bonaparte in 1798 on Egypt (p. 459), Cailliaud on the Sudan (p. 459), Guillain on the East African coast (p. 471), Flacourt and Guillain on Madagascar (p. 473), and J. H. B. de Saint Pierre and others on the Mascarenes. Among the most important French works on West Africa published before 1875 are J. B. Labat, *Nouvelle relation de l'Afrique occidentale*, 5 vols. (Paris, 1728), J. Barbot, *A Description of the Coasts of North and South Guinea* (London, 1732), and R. Caillié, *Travels Through Central Africa to Timbuctoo*, 2 vols. (London, 1830). For further information on French travelers in Africa see the work by Lebel (p. 432).

HOLLAND. The Dutch stake in Africa was largely confined to the Gold Coast, the Cape, and for a limited period Mauritius. C. R. Boxer's *The Dutch Seaborne Empire, 1600–1800* (London, 1965) is the best general work in English; the principal works in Dutch are listed in its bibliography. For the Dutch at the Cape see the works cited for Chapter XI, Section 3. The massive work compiled by the Dutch geographer O. Dapper from a wide range of sources, *Description de l'Afrique* (Amsterdam, 1684), is the most important Dutch work on Africa. Among other Dutch works relating to Africa that achieved a wide circulation through translation are those by I. H. van Linschoten, *His Discours of Voyages unto ye East and West Indies* (London, 1598), Hakluyt Society edition (London, 1885), and W. Bosman, *A New and Accurate Description of the Coast of Guinea* (London, 1705), facsimile edition with introduction by J. R. Willis and notes by J. D. Fage and R. E. Bradbury (London, 1967).

GREAT BRITAIN (ENGLAND). A direct English interest in Africa dates back to the first trading voyages to the West Coast made in the middle of the sixteenth century. By the end of the eighteenth century the British were becoming increasingly aware of the importance of guarding the sea routes to their empire in the East. During the Napoleonic wars they intervened in Egypt and occupied the Dutch settlement at the Cape and the French base in Mauritius. In the decades after 1815 the activities of British traders, missionaries, and explorers combined with vigorous naval action to suppress the slave trade gave the British an interest in almost every part of Africa. There is no compact introduction to the whole range of British activities in Africa from the sixteenth century on, but much information can be extracted from the *Cambridge History of the British Empire*, the most elaborate and richly documented of all the European imperial histories: Vol. I, *The Old Empire to 1783* (Cambridge, 1929); Vol. II, *The New Empire, 1783–1870* (Cambridge, 1940); Vol. III, *The Empire-Commonwealth, 1870–1919* (Cambridge, 1959). R. Robinson, J. Gallagher, and A. Denny's *Africa and the Victorians: the Official Mind of Imperialism* (London, 1961) is the most important of recent studies on nineteenth-century British expansionism in Africa. On Britain's interest in Egypt see J. Marlowe, *Anglo-Egyptian Relations, 1800–1953* (London, 1954). For British interests in West Africa in addition to the works cited for Chapter VII, Sections 9 and 12, and Chapter XXI, Section 6, see E. C. Martin, *The British West African Settlements, 1750–1821* (London, 1927); on British contacts with East Africa see R. Coupland, *East Africa and Its Invaders* (Oxford, 1938) and *The Exploitation of East Africa, 1856–1890* (London, 1939); on British actions in South Africa see the works cited for Chapter XI, Section 5, and Chapter XXI, Section 9; on the British and Mauritius, Chapter XII, Section 4.

Two important collections of travels—R. Hakluyt, *The Principall Navigations, Voiages and Discoveries of the English Nation*, 2d greatly expanded edition, 3 vols. (London, 1598–1600), new edition, 12 vols. (Glasgow, 1903–5), and S. Purchas, *Hakluytus Posthumus or Purchas His Pilgrimes*, 4 vols. (London, 1625), new edition, 20 vols. (Glasgow, 1905–7)—contain the accounts of the earliest English voyages to different parts of Africa. James Bruce, who traveled in North Africa, Egypt, Ethiopia, and the Sudan, is the most notable British explorer of the eighteenth century (p. 458). The roll of late eighteenth- or nineteenth-century British explorers and travelers in Africa includes Park (p. 465), Bowdich and Dupuis (p. 422), Denham and Clapperton (p. 476) and the Landeers (p. 465) in West Africa, Livingstone (p. 482) in Central Africa, Burton, Speke, Grant, and Baker in East Africa (p. 482), and Barrow, Burchell, and Campbell in South Africa (p. 472).

GERMANY. German interests in Africa date back to the sixteenth century, although it was not until the 1880's that the Germans acquired a firm political stake in Africa. For a study of German expansion see H. Brunschwig, *L'Expansion allemande outre-mer du XVe siècle à nos jours* (Paris, 1957). Notable German Africanists include the Ethiopian scholar Ludolphus (p. 458) and the travelers Barth in West Africa (p. 465), Nachtigal in the Central Sudan (p. 467), and Krapf in Ethiopia and East Africa (p. 482).

UNITED STATES. The United States developed a considerable commerce with many parts of Africa in the nineteenth century, besides having a special interest in Liberia. C. Clendenen, R. Collins, and P. Duignan, *Americans in Africa, 1865–1900* (Stanford, 1966) contains an introduction on "The United States and Africa up to 1865," together with an extensive bibliography. Among nineteenth-century travelers with American connections were Du Chaillu in Equatorial Africa (p. 467) and the Welsh-born H. M. Stanley (p. 482).

BRAZIL. For an introduction to Brazilian contacts with Africa, see J. H. Rodriguez, *Brazil and Africa* (Berkeley, 1965).

CHINA. For Chinese contacts with East Africa up to 1500 see J. J. L. Duyvendak, *China's Discovery of Africa* (London, 1949).

THE SLAVE-TRADE AND THE ABOLITIONISTS. The Arabs, the Turks, and most of the European powers with a stake in Africa participated in the export trade in slaves. Three recent works each provide a broad survey of the Atlantic trade: B. Davidson, *Black Mother* (London, 1961), D. Mannix and M. Cowley, *Black Cargoes: a History of the Atlantic Slave Trade, 1518–1865* (London, 1963), and J. Pope-Hennessy, *Sins of the Fathers: a Study of the Atlantic Slave Traders, 1441–1807* (London, 1967). A mass of previously unpublished material is contained in E. Donnan (ed.), *Documents Illustrative of the History of the Slave Trade to America*, 4 vols. (Washington, 1935). For detailed studies of the European organization of the trade see K. G. Davies, *The Royal African Company* (London, 1957), and Gaston-Martin, *Nantes au XVIIIe siècle: l'ère des négriers, 1714–1744* (Paris, 1931). First-hand accounts by men who engaged in the trade include H. Crow, *Memoirs* (London, 1830), and J. Newton, *The Journal of a Slave Trader*, edited by B. Martin and M. Spurnell (London, 1962). *Efik Traders of Old Calabar*, edited by D. Forde (London 1962), contains the remarkable diary of a late eighteenth-century African slave trader from Calabar. A number of African slaves wrote accounts of the experiences that accompanied their enslavement; some of these accounts have been edited by P. D. Curtin and others, *Africa Remembered* (Madison, 1967). Increasing attention is now being paid to the nature of the trade in slaves within Africa; see, for example, P. D. Curtin and J. Vansina, "Sources for the Nineteenth-Century Atlantic Slave Trade," *J.A.H.*, V/2 (1964). For the Atlantic trade see also the works cited for Chapter VII, Sections 9 and 12, and Chapter IX, Section 5. On aspects of the trade in slaves in North Africa see N. R. Bennett, "Christian and Negro Slavery in Eighteenth-Century North Africa," *J.A.H.*, I/1 (1960). Aspects of the Saharan slave trade are touched on in works by Mauny (p. 463), Miège (p. 462), and Boahen (p. 481). On the development of the slave trade in the southern Sudan after 1850 see the work by Gray (p. 481). The two works on East Africa by Coupland cited above contain much information on the East African slave trade.

R. Coupland's *The British Anti-Slavery Movement* (London, 1933) provides the best introduction to the history of the abolition of the slave trade. E. E. Williams' *Capitalism and Slavery* (Chapel Hill, N. C., 1944) is a passionate examination of the economic, as opposed to the humanitarian, motives of the antislavery movement. C. Lloyd's *The Navy and the Slave Trade* (London, 1949) examines the key role played by the British Navy in suppressing the slave trade. T. Clarkson, *History of the Rise, Progress and Accomplishment of the Abolition of the African Slave Trade by the British Parliament*, 2 vols. (London, 1808), and T. F. Buxton, *The African Slave Trade and Its Remedy* (London, 1841), are the two most important works by English abolitionists. See also R. Coupland's fine biography, *Wilberforce* (Oxford, 1923), and C. Buxton, *Memoirs of Sir T. F. Buxton* (Everyman ed., London, n.d.).

AFRICANS IN OTHER CONTINENTS

The activities of Africans in Europe, Asia, and the Americas is an aspect of the continent's history that has not been considered in this work, but a few basic studies may be given here for those who wish to pursue this subject further. On the part played by men of Berber stock in the development of Muslim Spain see the work by Lévi-Provençal cited on p. 461. On the African element in American Negro culture see M. Herskovits, *The Myth of the Negro Past*, new edition (Boston, 1958), and *The New World Negro* (Bloomington, Ind., 1966). On the African contribution to Brazil see G. Freyre, *The Masters and the Slaves*, translated from the fourth edition by S. Putnam (New York, 1946).

RELIGION AND IDEOLOGY

Ideally, the historian of a particular African society should make himself familiar with the whole range of its peoples' ideas concerning the supernatural, the natural environment, and the nature of human relationships. Ideally, too, the historian who takes all Africa as his theme should be able to indicate the wide range of intellectual systems to be found in the continent and the changes that have taken place within them. This is an aspect of African history that has been treated, at least insofar as indigenous systems are concerned, quite inadequately in the present work. But those who wish to pursue the subject further will find a wide range of studies at their disposal. Two recent symposia—D. Forde (ed.), *African Worlds* (London, 1954), and M. Fortes and G. Dieterlin (eds.), *African Systems of Thought* (London, 1965)—provide an introduction to the variety of African ideologies. For a brief introduction see E. G. Parrinder, *African Traditional Religion*, revised edition (London, 1962). Notable studies of the beliefs of individual peoples include P. Tempels, *Bantu Philosophy*, translated from the French (Paris, 1959); E. E. Evans-Pritchard, *Nuer Religion* (Oxford, 1956); G. Lienhardt, *Divinity and Experience: the Religion of the Dinka* (London, 1961); J. Middleton, *Lugbara Religion: Ritual and Authority Among an East African People* (London, 1960). See also the stimulating article by R. Horton, "African Traditional Thought and Western Science," *Africa*, XXXVII/1 and 2 (1967).

ISLAM. On the rise of Islam see the works cited for Chapter V, Section 8. On the developed form of Muslim culture and society see G. E. von Grunebaum, *Medieval Islam* (1953), and R. Levy, *The Social Structure of Islam* (Cambridge, 1957). For an introduction to the role of Islam in Africa see J. S. Trimingham, *The Influence of Islam upon Africa* (London, 1968), and I. M. Lewis (ed.), *Islam in Tropical Africa* (London, 1966). J. S. Trimingham has also written detailed studies of Islam in the

Sudan (London, 1949), in Ethiopia (London, 1952), in West Africa (Oxford, 1959), and in East Africa (Oxford, 1964). See also A. Gouilly, *L'Islam dans l'Afrique occidentale française* (Paris, 1952), and V. Monteil, *L'Islam noir* (Paris, 1964). On European attitudes to Islam see the two recent studies by N. Daniel, *Islam and the West: the Making of an Image* (Edinburgh, 1966) and *Islam, Europe and Empire* (Edinburgh, 1968).

CHRISTIANITY. On the spread of Christianity in Africa there are two broad factual surveys: K. S. Latourette, *A History of the Expansion of Christianity,* 7 vols. (New York, 1937–45), and C. P. Groves, *The Planting of Christianity in Africa,* 4 vols. (London, 1948–58). For further works on early Christianity in Egypt and North Africa see the bibliographies in N. H. Baynes, *The Byzantine Empire,* and C. A. Julien, *Histoire de l'Afrique du Nord,* Vol. I. The renewed movement of Christian missionary activity in the nineteenth century produced in time a mass of printed works including the histories of missionary societies and the biographies of individual missionaries. The works by Latourette and Groves contain a considerable amount of bibliographical information. Missionary ideas about Africa are discussed in the works by Curtin and Cairns cited for the Introduction, Section 1. Other notable recent studies of nineteenth-century missionary enterprise include J. F. A. Ajayi, *Christian Missions in Nigeria, 1841–1891* (London, 1965), and R. Oliver, *The Missionary Factor in East Africa* (London, 1952). See also the symposium edited by C. G. Baëta, *Christianity in Tropical Africa* (London, 1968).

⚜ ART IN AFRICA

A study of the African past can be greatly enhanced if it is broadened to include some consideration of the variety of forms of art developed by particular African peoples. This is yet another aspect of the past that has been mentioned only obliquely in the present study. A considerable number of splendidly illustrated art books are now available for those who wish to pursue this aspect of the past. The photographs by W. Forman taken to illustrate B. Davidson's *Africa: History of a Continent* provide an excellent introduction to the whole range of artistic achievement in Africa.

The Sahara and parts of southern Africa are particularly rich in rock paintings, some of which are of great antiquity. Lavishly illustrated volumes on rock paintings include J. D. Lajoux, *The Rock Paintings of Tassili* (London, 1963); E. Goodall and others, *Prehistoric Rock Art of the Federation of Rhodesia and Nyasaland* (Salisbury, 1959); and H. Breuil, *The Rock Paintings of Southern Africa,* 3 vols. (London, 1955–59).

I. Woldering, *The Art of Egypt* (London, 1965), and C. F. Nims and W. Swan, *Thebes of the Pharoahs* (London, 1965), illustrate different aspects of the art of ancient Egypt. On the most spectacular of ancient Egyptian monuments see I. E. S. Edwards, *The Pyramids of Egypt* (Harmondsworth, 1961). For pre-Muslim North Africa see A. Lézine, *Architecture punique* (Paris, 1959) and *Architecture romaine d'Afrique*

(Paris, 1960), and the volume of photographs by H. Wimmer and M. Vilinkova, *Roman Art in Africa* (London, 1962).

On Muslim architecture in North Africa there are two basic works: K. A. C. Cresswell, *The Muslim Architecture of Egypt*, 2 vols. (London, 1952 and 1959), and G. Marçais, *L'Architecture musulmane d'occident* (Paris, 1954).

The collection of essays by various scholars edited by A. Diop, *L'Art nègre* (Paris, 1951) and the collection of photographs by E. Elisofon with text by W. Fagg, *The Sculpture of Africa* (London, 1958), provide an introduction to the art of Tropical Africa. For more detailed studies see L. J. P. Gaskin and G. Atkins, *A Bibliography of African Art* (London, 1965).

PART II

✿ INTRODUCTION

1. *Images of Africa*. Almost everything written about Africa affords material for the student of imagery, but it is worth drawing special attention to the importance of those most widely distributed forms of printed matter, school text books, encyclopedias, and novels. Recent studies which touch on certain aspects of European ideas about Africa include H. N. Fairchild, *The Noble Savage* (New York, 1928); P. D. Curtin, *The Image of Africa* (London, 1965), a study of British ideas about West Africa between 1780 and 1850; and H. A. C. Cairns, *The Clash of Cultures* (New York, 1965), a study of British attitudes toward East and Central Africa before the establishment of colonial rule. I was first introduced to the concept of the "morality of amorality" by M. G. Smith.

2. *The Tradition of African Studies*. There is no single work that traces the development of African studies from Herodotus to the present day, but various aspects of the tradition have been studied in detail by modern scholars. On the classical world's knowledge of Africa: E. H. Bunbury, *History of Ancient Geography*, 2 vols. (London, 1879), and J. O. Thomson, *History of Ancient Geography* (Cambridge, 1948). On Muslim geography see the article "Djughrafiya" in the *Encyclopedia of Islam*. The development of African cartography from ancient to modern times is illustrated in the superb set of volumes produced by Yusuf Kamal, *Monumenta Cartographica Africae et Aegypti*, 5 vols. (Cairo, 1928–51). On European knowledge of Africa in the Middle Ages see C. R. Beazley, *The Dawn of Modern Geography*, 3 vols. (Oxford, 1897–

1900), and C. de la Roncière, *La Découverte de l'Afrique au moyen âge,* 3 vols. (Cairo, 1924–27). On the development of European knowledge of Africa in the fifteenth and sixteenth centuries see B. Penrose, *Travel and Travellers in the Renaissance, 1480–1620* (Cambridge, Mass., 1952), and W. G. L. Randles, *L'Image du sud-est africain dans la littérature européenne au XVIe siècle* (Lisbon, 1959). On the history of European exploration see J. N. L. Baker, *A History of Geographical Exploration and Discovery* (London, 1948), E. Heawood, *A History of Geographical Discovery in the Seventeenth and Eighteenth Century* (London, 1912), and H. Schiffers, *The Quest for Africa* (London, 1957). On Egyptology: S. R. K. Glanville, *The Growth and Nature of Egyptology* (Cambridge, 1947). On Ethiopian studies: E. Ullendorf, *The Ethiopians* (London, 1960). On the history of anthropology: A. C. Haddon, *History of Anthropology,* 2d edition (London, 1934). On recent developments in the study of African history see the inaugural lecture delivered by R. Oliver, *African History for the Outside World* (London, 1964). For developments in the study of particular areas see the section Historiographies (p. 431).

3. *The Sources of African History.* For an introduction to the problems involved in the study of African history see the opening section of *The Historian in Tropical Africa,* edited by J. Vansina, R. Mauny, and L. V. Thomas (London, 1964). See also the inaugural lecture delivered by J. D. Fage, *On the Nature of African History* (Birmingham, 1965). D. McCall, *Africa in Time-Perspective* (Boston, 1964), provides an excellent introduction to the wide range of unwritten sources available to the historian in Africa. On the study of oral tradition see J. Vansina, *Oral Tradition* (London, 1964).

4. *The Scope and Purpose of a History of Africa.* Ibn Khaldun's *Muqaddima* or *Prolegomena* has been translated into English by F. Rosenthal, 3 vols. (London, 1958). Selections have been translated by C. Issawi, *An Arab Philosophy of History* (London, 1950).

✻ I. AFRICA AND OTHER CONTINENTS: SOME HISTORICAL COMPARISONS

The time has yet to come when a knowledge of the broad outlines of African history forms part of the common stock of historical knowledge. In making comparisons with other continents a historian of Africa has no reliable predecessor to guide him. There is one general work, Gordon Childe, *What Happened in History* (first published in 1942, latest edition: Harmondsworth, 1964), that I have found particularly stimulating. In tracing the course of human progress to the middle of the first millennium A.D. Childe draws his material from many different parts of the world. His profound sense of the importance of technological developments in the history of the ancient world illuminates many aspects of the past likely to have been ignored by anyone brought up in the classical tradition of literary history.

🏵 II. LAND AND PEOPLE

1. *Geography*. Platitudinous though the point may seem, it is worth stressing that by far the most effective way of grasping the geography of a country very different from one's own is to live in it for a considerable length of time and so to experience the nature of its peculiar environmental pressures, the rhythm of its seasons, their monotony or exhilaration, their pleasures and their discomforts. The right sort of travel—not hasty flights from capital to capital but observant wanderings off the beaten track—provides a powerful stimulant for the historical imagination. Unfortunately, only a minority of those who now study Africa in the Western world have a chance of visiting the continent. In these circumstances photographs, whether presented in documentary films, in color slides, or in lavishly produced books, offer an invaluable aid. Their impact can do much to rouse that sense of curiosity and excitement which transforms the process of learning from a laborious chore into an invigorating intellectual adventure. For descriptions of landscape the best accounts are to be found in the narratives of the great eighteenth- and nineteenth-century explorers. The realization that they were often the first Europeans to look on a particular scene seems to have sharpened their powers of observation, and many of them were capable of describing their experiences in a style that contains an admirable combination of sobriety and vividness.

Overall geographies of the continent fulfill a useful function in helping the student of Africa to grasp the broad lines of his subject. Recent general works on African geography include W. A. Hance, *The Geography of Modern Africa* (New York, 1964); A. B. Mountjoy and C. Embleton, *Africa, a Geographical Study* (London, 1965); R. J. Harrison Church and others, *Africa and the Islands* (London, 1964); and B. W. Hodder and D. R. Harris (eds.), *Africa in Transition* (London, 1967). The last-named work is made up of a series of "geographical essays" whose authors pay special attention to the historical background of the region they describe.

2. *Peoples and Tribes*. G. P. Murdock's *Africa: Its Peoples and Their Culture History* (New York, 1959) provides the most comprehensive single-volume introduction to the human variety of the continent. C. G. Seligman, *Races of Africa*, 3d edition revised (London, 1957), provides a more concise introduction. Unaccountably, in spite of its revision by distinguished anthropologists, this work still contains a number of generalizations about the so-called "Hamites" that are no longer accepted by historians and social anthropologists. In J. L. Gibbs (ed.), *Peoples of Africa* (New York, 1965) there are a number of well-balanced studies of individual African peoples.

3. *Physical Features: "Race."* C. Coon's *The Origin of Races* (New York, 1963) is the most recent general work on the subject; it contains a number of chapters on Africa. For the development of racist theories in regard to the Negro see P. D. Curtin, *The Image of Africa* (London,

1965), and T. E. Gosset, *Race: the History of an Idea in America* (Dallas, 1963).

4. *Languages.* Until the widespread diffusion of the technique of writing throughout Africa in the nineteenth and twentieth centuries only a limited number of languages possessed a written literature. These languages—ancient Egyptian, Punic, Coptic, Arabic, Amharic, and Ge'ez—have been the subject of much specialist research. The articles on Egyptian language, Coptic, Arabic, and Semitic languages in the 1962 edition of the *Encyclopaedia Britannica* provide useful brief introductions for the nonlinguist.

The development of the study and classification of the great variety of sub-Saharan African languages can be traced through the publication of a number of major works of linguistic scholarship: S. W. Koelle, *Polyglotta Africana* (London, 1854); R. N. Cust, *A Sketch of the Modern Languages of Africa* (London, 1883); C. Meinhof, *An Introduction to the Study of African Languages,* translated from the German (London, 1915); H. H. Johnston, *A Comparative Study of the Bantu and Semi-Bantu Languages,* 2 vols. (London, 1919–22); D. Westermann, *Die westlichen Sudan Sprachen* (Berlin, 1927); M. Guthrie, *The Classification of Bantu Languages* (London, 1948). In a series of articles first published in the *Southwestern Journal of Anthropology* in 1949–50, J. H. Greenberg put forward a system of classification to cover the whole continent. Since then Greenberg has made a number of revisions of his system; it is important, therefore, to consult his latest work, *The Languages of Africa* (Bloomington, Ind., 1966). Greenberg also contributed the article on African languages to the 1962 edition of the *Encyclopaedia Britannica.* Historians have made much use of Greenberg's classification, but it should be noted that some of his hypotheses have been criticized by other African linguists—see, for example, the review by M. Guthrie in *J.A.H.,* V/1 (1964).

For information on individual African languages see the *Handbook of African Languages* published in a number of separate parts by the International African Institute. For recent work on sub-Saharan African languages see *African Language Studies* (London), from 1960.

III. PERIODS OF AFRICAN HISTORY

The suggested readings for this chapter are confined to works on African prehistory. For general histories of Africa see p. 440. Two articles by J. D. Clark, "The Prehistoric Origins of African Culture," *J.A.H.,* V/2 (1964), and "The Spread of Food-Production in Sub-Saharan Africa," *J.A.H.,* III/2 (1962), provide an invaluable introduction to the recent work in African prehistory. See also L. S. B. Leakey, *The Progress and Evolution of Man in Africa* (London, 1961). H. Alimen's *The Prehistory of Africa* (London, 1957) is concerned with Stone Age Africa. For detailed regional studies see L. Balout, *Préhistoire de l'Afrique du Nord* (Paris, 1955); C. B. M. McBurney, *The Stone Age of Northern Africa* (Harmondsworth, 1960); S. Cole, *The Prehistory of East Africa* (London, 1963); M. Posnansky (ed.), *Prelude to East African History* (London,

1966); J. D. Clark, *The Prehistory of Southern Africa* (Harmondsworth, 1955); O. Davies, *West Africa Before the Europeans: Archaeology and Prehistory* (London, 1967).

🎋 IV. CHANGE IN AFRICA

I have developed the analysis of change contained in this chapter from my own knowledge of African history; it seemed necessary to try to work out a theoretical framework capacious enough to embrace all the phenomena of concern to the historian.

Information on alterations to the natural environment is to be found in the general works of geographers and prehistorians already cited. On population growth and pressure there appears to be no satisfactory general work that examines the African situation in the precolonial period. A study of "the peaceful pursuit of well-being" involves an examination of many aspects of a people's culture: one needs to acquire a sense of the dynamism, the creativity inherent in all human societies. The best of the works of modern social anthropologists are particularly helpful in this regard. A study of "the violent pursuit of well-being" involves examination of the various forms of armed conflict to be found in Africa. There is a mass of relevant material in the detailed studies by historians or social anthropologists of individual African peoples, but there appears to be no satisfactory general work on the subject. A study of "the impact of ideas" leads on to a detailed consideration of African systems of thought and to the development and expansion of religions; a number of works on this subject are cited on p. 449. Material on the "stimulus of intercourse" or the consequences of culture-contact will be found in many of the detailed historical or anthropological studies cited for the chapters that follow.

One aspect of the "appearance of material innovations" is to be found in the diffusion of plants and livestock. G. P. Murdock lays special emphasis on this aspect of African history in his general study, *Africa, Its Peoples and Their Culture History,* but not all his hypotheses have been accepted by ethnobotanists. Several of the papers delivered at the Third Conference on African History and Archaeology deal with aspects of ethnobotany; they are reprinted in *J.A.H.,* III/2 (1962). For a recent study of the distribution of maize see J. M. P. Miracle, "The Introduction and Spread of Maize in Africa," *J.A.H.,* VI/1 (1965).

One aspect of "the acquisition of new techniques" is discussed by M. Posnansky in his chapter on "The Origins of Agriculture and Iron Working in Southern Africa," in *Prelude to East African History* (London, 1966). For other studies of the diffusion of ironworking, see R. Mauny, "Essai sur l'histoire des métaux en Afrique occidentale," *Bulletin de l'I.F.A.N.* (1955), and P. Huard, "Introduction et diffusion du fer au Tchad," *J.A.H.,* VII/3 (1966).

On "the development of new patterns of settlement and new lines of communication," an aspect of change that involves the study of the foundation and growth of towns and the emergence of trade routes, there is a mass of material to be obtained from a reading of general historical works. Particularly useful for the history of urban centers in Muslim Africa are the articles devoted to individual towns and cities in the *Encyclopedia of Islam.*

Changes in institutions are discussed in many of the works dealing with political organization in Africa cited in the suggested readings for Chapter XIII.

On "the emergence of new modes of thought" see the works cited under the heading Religion and Ideology on p. 449.

V. NORTHEAST AFRICA

1. *Geography.* The chapter by A. M. S. Graham on "Northeast Africa" in B. W. Hodder and D. R. Harris (eds.), *Africa in Transition* (London, 1967) provides an introduction to the geography of this region. Two other geographical studies should also be consulted: H. E. Hurst, *The Nile* (London, 1952), and K. M. Barbour, *The Republic of the Sudan: a Regional Geography* (London, 1961).

2. *Caucasoids, Negroids, and Others.* W. Macgaffy, "Concepts of Race in the Historiography of North East Africa," *J.A.H.,* VII/1 (1966), contains a stimulating discussion on some of the problems involved in the physical anthropology of this region. For an introduction to the prehistory of the Sudan: A. J. Arkell, *A History of the Sudan to 1821,* 2d revised edition (London, 1961), pp. 24–45. Extracts from Agatharchides were preserved in the *Historical Library* of the first century B.C. Greek historian Diodorus Siculus.

3. *The Growth of Egyptian Civilization.* No aspect of the African past has been studied so intensively as the history of ancient Egypt. A valuable bibliographical guide to the mass of material now available is contained in E. Drioton and J. Vandier, *Les Peuples de l'orient méditerranéen: II. L'Egypte,* 4th revised edition (Paris, 1962). Here one can only mention a few valuable introductory works: W. A. Fairservis, *The Ancient Kingdoms of the Nile* (New York, 1962); C. Aldred, *The Egyptians* (London, 1961), a volume in the *Ancient Peoples and Places* series; P. Montet, *Eternal Egypt* (London, 1964); W. B. Emery, *Archaic Egypt* (Harmondsworth, 1961); H. Frankfort, *Ancient Egyptian Religion* (New York, 1948); J. A. Wilson, *The Culture of Ancient Egypt* (Chicago, 1956). Two important primary sources: J. H. Breasted, *Ancient Records of Egypt,* 5 vols. (Chicago, 1906–7), and Herodotus, *The Histories,* Book II (the account of a highly intelligent fifth-century Greek tourist).

4. *The Impact of Egypt: the Spread of Pastoralism and Agriculture.* For Egyptian influence on Nubia: W. B. Emery, *Egypt in Nubia* (London, 1965), and A. J. Arkell, *A History of the Sudan to 1821.* Egyptian contacts with the Sahara are discussed in H. Lhote, *Les Touaregs du Hoggar* (Paris, 1955). For the diffusion of agricultural techniques I have followed the hypothesis put forward by J. D. Clark in the article cited in note 6 of Chapter V.

5. *Kush.* In addition to the works by Emery and Arkell cited above, see P. L. Shinnie, *Meroe* (London, 1967), a volume in the *Ancient Peoples and Places* series. B. Davidson provides a vivid evocation of Kush in *Old Africa Rediscovered*, pp. 40–60. A comprehensive bibliography has been produced by F. Gadallah in *Kush*, XI (1963), pp. 207–16.

6. *Greek and Roman Rule in Egypt.* For early Greek contacts with Egypt as revealed by archeology: J. Boardman, *The Greeks Overseas* (Harmondsworth, 1964). H. I. Bell, *Egypt from Alexander the Great to the Arab Invasion* (London, 1948) is an excellent short survey of this period of Egyptian history. On Egypt under the Ptolemies: E. Bevan, *A History of Egypt under the Ptolemaic Dynasty* (London, 1927). The two works by M. Rostovtzeff cited on p. 443 provide the best introduction to the social and economic history of Egypt in Hellenistic and Roman times. On the Roman exploitation of Egypt: J. G. Milne, "The Ruin of Egypt by Roman Mismanagement," *Journal of Roman Studies*, XVII (1927). Four volumes of *Papyri* relating to this period have been published in the Loeb Classical Library. For an introduction to the Byzantine period: N. H. Baynes, *The Byzantine Empire* (London, 1935). For early Christianity see the works by Groves and Latourette cited on p. 450.

7. *Axum.* There are three general works on Ethiopia each of which provide brief summaries of the Axumite period: A. H. M. Jones and E. Monroe, *A History of Abyssinia* (Oxford, 1935); J. Doresse, *Ethiopia* (London, 1960); E. Ullendorf, *The Ethiopians* (London, 1960). See also R. Pankhurst, *An Introduction to the Economic History of Ethiopia* (London, 1961). For a detailed account of the Axumite period: A. Kammerer, *Essai sur l'histoire antique d'Abyssinie* (Paris, 1926). The two main literary sources for the period are *The Periplus of the Erythraean Sea*, translated by W. H. Schoff (New York, 1912) and *The Christian Topography of Cosmas Indicopleustes*, translated by J. W. McCrindle (Hakluyt Society, London, 1897). Extracts from both these works have been reproduced in R. Pankhurst's anthology, *Travellers in Ethiopia* (London, 1965).

8. *The Rise of Islam.* H. A. R. Gibb, *Mohammedanism* (London, 1949), provides an excellent introduction to the religion of Islam. On the history of the Arabs: B. Lewis, *The Arabs in History* (London, 1949); a short introductory work: P. K. Hitti, *History of the Arabs*, 6th edition (New York, 1958). On the life and role of Muhammad: W. Montgomery Watt, *Muhammad at Mecca* (London, 1953) and *Muhammad at Medina* (London, 1956). Various translations of the Koran are available; I have found the one by N. J. Dawood in the Penguin Classics (Harmondsworth, 1956) vigorous and stirring.

9. *The Arabs in Egypt.* For brief accounts, see the works by Lewis and Hitti cited above. For a narrative of the conquest, A. Butler, *The Arab Conquest of Egypt and the Last Thirty Years of the Roman Domination* (London, 1902). For the period of Arab rule in Egypt: G. Wiet, *L'Égypte*

arabe . . . *642–1517* (Paris, 1937), and S. Lane-Poole, *A History of Egypt in the Middle Ages,* 5th edition (London, 1936).

10. *Medieval Egypt.* The works by Lewis, Hitti, Wiet, and Lane-Poole should all be consulted. On Egypt during the period of the Crusades see the chapters by H. A. R. Gibb, in K. M. Setton (ed.), *A History of the Crusades,* of which the first two volumes covering the period up to 1311 have been published (Philadelphia, 1955, 1962). On European commercial contacts with Egypt the basic work remains J. Heyd, *Histoire du commerce du Levant au moyen âge,* 2 vols. (Paris, 1885). For a guide to primary sources, mostly Arabic works some of which have now been translated, see Sauvaget's bibliography cited on p. 429. For medieval Muslim society see the works by von Grunebaum and Levy cited on p. 449.

11. *Christian Nubia and the Arabs in the Eastern Sudan.* Arkell's *History* and P. M. Holt's *A Modern History of the Sudan* (London, 1961) provide brief accounts of this period of Sudanese history. For more detailed accounts see J. S. Trimingham, *Islam in the Sudan* (London, 1949), and Y. Fadl Hassan, *The Arabs and the Sudan* (Edinburgh, 1967). For an introduction to the recent archeology of Christian Nubia: P. L. Shinnie, "New Light on Medieval Nubia," *J.A.H.,* VI/3 (1965). On the Funj: O. G. S. Crawford, *The Funj Kingdom of Sennar* (Gloucester, 1951), and P. M. Holt, "Funj Origins: a Critique and New Evidence," *J.A.H.,* IV/1 (1963). On the Beja: A. Paul, *A History of the Beja Tribes of the Sudan* (Cambridge, 1954).

12. *Christians and Muslims in Ethiopia and the Horn.* In addition to the general histories by Doresse, Jones and Monroe, Pankhurst, and Ullendorf cited in section 7, see J. S. Trimingham, *Islam in Ethiopia* (Oxford, 1952), and I. M. Lewis, *The Modern History of Somaliland* (London, 1965). D. Mathew's *Ethiopia: the Study of a Polity 1540–1935* (London, 1947) is a vivid narrative based largely on the accounts of European travelers. Translations of Ethiopian chronicles are listed in the bibliography of Pankhurst's *Economic History.* The sixteenth-century Arabic chronicle describing Ahmad Gran's invasion of Ethiopia has been translated by R. Basset, *Histoire de la conquête de l'Abyssinie par Chihab El-Din Ahmed Ben Abd el-Quader surnommé Arab-Faqi* (Paris, 1897–1909). Several of the accounts of early European travelers have now been published by the Hakluyt Society: O. G. S. Crawford (ed.), *Ethiopian Itineraries circa 1400–1524* (1958), C. F. Beckingham and G. W. B. Huntingford (eds.), *The Prester John of the Indies* by F. Alvarez (1961), and *Some Records of Ethiopia,* including Manoel de Almeida's *The History of High Ethiopia* (1954); R. S. Whiteway (ed.), *The Portuguese Expedition to Abyssinia in 1541–53, as Narrated by Castanhoso* (1902); W. Foster (ed.), *The Red Sea and Adjacent Countries* (1949), contains C. J. Poncet's *A Voyage to Aethiopia* (1709). Job Ludolph's *A New History of Ethiopia* (London, 1682) is an outstanding work of seventeenth-century scholarship. James Bruce, *Travels to Discover the Source of the Nile,* 5 vols. (London, 1790), is one of the classics of African travel; the latest abridged edition, edited by C. F. Beckingham, was

published in Edinburgh in 1964. Travelers in Ethiopia in the first half of the nineteenth century include H. Salt, *A Voyage to Abyssinia* (London, 1814), W. Cornwallis Harris, *The Highlands of Ethiopia* (London, 1844), and T. Lefebvre, *Voyage en Abyssinie* (Paris, 1845–46). Brief extracts from many of these travelers are included in Pankhurst's anthology cited on p. 457.

13. *The Ottoman Turks in Egypt.* P. M. Holt, *Egypt and the Fertile Crescent, 1516–1922* (London, 1966), provides a good introduction not only to Egyptian history in this period but also to the history of the Ottoman Turks. For an invaluable bibliography of the Ottoman Empire see Sauvaget's *Introduction to the History of the Muslim East*, pp. 191–215. A volume in the *Modern Nations in Historical Perspective* series, R. O. Collins and R. L. Tignor, *Egypt and the Sudan* (Englewood Cliffs, N. J., 1967), provides a brief introduction to Egyptian history and contains a useful reading list for this period. More detailed studies of the Ottoman period will be found in P. M. Holt (ed.), *Political and Social Change in Modern Egypt* (London, 1968). See also H. A. R. Gibb and H. Bowen, *Islamic Society and the West*. Vol. I: *Islamic Society in the Eighteenth Century*, 2 parts (London, 1954, 1957). J. Carré, *Voyageurs et écrivains français en Égypte*. Vol. I: *1517–1850* (Cairo, 1932), is the best work on European travelers in Egypt, outstanding among whom was C. F. Volney, *Travels Through Syria and Egypt* (London, 1787). Few episodes in African history have inspired so copious a literature as Bonaparte's expedition to Egypt in 1798. A. Moorehead has produced a vivid brief account of "the French in Egypt" in *The Blue Nile* (London, 1962). See also F. Charles-Roux, *Bonaparte: Governor of Egypt* (London, 1937), and S. Ghorbal, *The Beginnings of the Egyptian Question and the Rise of Mehemet Ali* (London, 1928). The massive work produced by the scholars who accompanied Bonaparte, *Description de l'Égypte*, 9 vols. of text and 10 vols. of plates (Paris, 1809–28), is a major source for this period.

14. *Muhammad Ali.* In addition to the general works cited for section 13, see H. H. Dodwell, *The Founder of Modern Egypt* (Cambridge, 1931); H. A. B. Rivkin, *The Agricultural Policy of Mohammad Ali in Egypt* (Cambridge, Mass., 1961); A. E. Crouchley, *The Economic Development of Modern Egypt* (London, 1938); and J. Heyworth-Dunne, *An Introduction to the History of Education in Modern Egypt* (London, 1939). On the Sudan, see Holt's *Modern History* (cited on p. 458) and R. L. Hill's *Egypt in the Sudan, 1820–1881* (London, 1958). In *The Blue Nile* A. Moorehead provides a vivid account of the Turco-Egyptian conquest of the Sudan. Muhammad Ali's policy of modernization made first Egypt and later the Sudan relatively easy countries for European travelers to visit. Consequently, from the second decade of the nineteenth century a steady stream of narratives of travel in Egypt and the Sudan began to appear. Notable contemporary accounts include J. L. Burckhardt's *Travels in Nubia* (London, 1819); F. Cailliaud, *Voyage à Méroé* (Paris, 1826); and E. W. Lane, *Account of the Manners and Customs of the Modern Egyptians* (London, 1836, often reprinted).

15. *The Somali Expansion.* For an introduction: I. M. Lewis, *The Modern History of Somaliland* (London, 1965). Two volumes of the Ethnographic Survey of Africa are devoted to this area: I. M. Lewis, *Peoples of the Horn of Africa: Somali, Afar and Saho* (London, 1955), and G. W. B. Huntingford, *The Galla of Ethiopia: The Kingdoms of Kafa and Janjero* (London, 1955). I. M. Lewis, *A Pastoral Democracy* (London, 1961), provides a clear account of the political institutions of the northern pastoral Somali. R. F. Burton, *First Footsteps in East Africa* (London, 1856), new edition with introduction by G. Waterfield (London, 1966), describes an exciting expedition to Harar and provides a notable account of the Somali in the middle of the nineteenth century.

16. *Long-Distance Trade Routes.* I know of no single work on the development of trade throughout the region as a whole, but a great deal of information both on routes and on the goods that passed along them is to be found in the accounts of European travelers. Particularly valuable is the account by J. L. Burckhardt in *Travels in Nubia* of the trade of the Sudan just before the Turco-Egyptian conquest. On Ethiopian trade: Pankhurst, *Economic History,* pp. 307–88; on British interest in the Red Sea: H. L. Hoskins, *British Routes to India* (London, 1928); on the opening of the Southern Sudan: R. Gray, *A History of the Southern Sudan, 1839–1889* (London, 1961).

VI. NORTHWEST AFRICA

1. *Geography.* There are two outstandingly good geographical studies that between them cover the entire region with the exception of Libya: J. Despois, *L'Afrique du Nord,* 3d edition (Paris, 1964), and R. Capot-Rey, *Le Sahara français* (Paris, 1953). For an introduction to North African geography in English see the chapter by D. R. Harris in Hodder and Harris (eds.), *Africa in Transition.*

2. *Berbers and "Ethiopians."* G. H. Bousquet, *Les Berbères* (Paris, 1956), a volume in the *Que sais-je?* series, and C. A. Julien, *Histoire de l'Afrique du Nord,* Vol. I: from the origins to the Arab conquest, 2d edition revised by C. Courtois (Paris, 1961), pp. 49–63, provide brief introductions to a study of the Berber people. For a more detailed study S. Gsell, *Histoire ancienne de l'Afrique du Nord,* 8 vols. (Paris, 1913–28), one of the greatest works of European scholarship in the field of African studies, should be consulted. H. Lhote discusses the early populations of the Central Sahara in *Les Touaregs du Hoggar* (Paris, 1955) and gives details of the various classical writers who describe this area. L. Cabot Briggs, *Tribes of the Sahara* (Cambridge, Mass., 1960), provides a useful introduction to the peoples of the desert.

3. *The Phoenicians, Carthage.* In addition to the works by Gsell and Julien cited above there are a number of more recent studies. D. B. Harden, *The Phoenicians* (London, 1962), a volume in the *Ancient Peoples and Places* series, studies the Phoenicians both in their homeland and in their North African colonies; B. H. Warmington, *Carthage* (Har-

mondsworth, 1964), is based primarily on literary evidence; G. Picard, *Carthage* (London, 1964), is an account by an archeologist. The histories written by Polybius in the second century B.C. and by Livy in the first century B.C. are the main classical sources for the wars between Rome and Carthage.

4. *Roman Rule in North Africa.* Julien's history provides the most comprehensive introduction. On the *limes* see J. Baradez, *Fossatum Africae* (Paris, 1949), a study based on aerial photography in southern Algeria. On the Roman army in Africa: R. Cagnat, *L'Armée romaine d'Afrique* (Paris, 1912). The best introduction to the cultural life of Roman Africa is to be found in two works by P. Monceaux, *Les Africains: études sur la littérature latine en Afrique: les païens* (Paris, 1894) and *Histoire littéraire de l'Afrique chrétienne*, 7 vols. (Paris, 1901–23). For general surveys of Christianity in North Africa see the works by Groves and Latourette cited on p. 450. *Roman Africa in Colour* (London, 1966), a book of photographs by R. Ward with text by Mortimer Wheeler, provides an exciting introduction to the many Roman sites in North Africa.

5. *Vandals, Byzantines, and Arabs.* The last chapters of the first volume of Julien's *Histoire de l'Afrique du Nord* and the first chapters of the second volume which covers the period from the Arab conquest to 1830, second edition revised by R. Tourneau (Paris, 1961), provide the best introduction to this period. On the Vandals and the Byzantines in North Africa there are two outstanding works: C. Courtois, *Les Vandales et l'Afrique* (Paris, 1955), and C. Diehl, *L'Afrique byzantine* (Paris, 1896). The sixth-century Greek historian Procopius provides a vivid account of the Byzantine invasion of North Africa. E. F. Gautier, *Le Passé de l'Afrique du Nord: les siècles obscurs* (Paris, 1937), is a stimulating and controversial study of the early Muslim period. On Morocco which begins to emerge as a distinct country at this time there are two introductory histories: H. Terrasse, *Histoire du Maroc*, 2 vols. (Casablanca, 1949–50), and N. Barbour, *Morocco* (London, 1965). The first three centuries of Muslim rule in Spain are covered in the great work of E. Lévi-Provençal, *Histoire de l'Espagne musulmane*, 3 vols. (Paris, 1944–53).

6. *The Sahara in Classical and Early Muslim Times.* The first chapters of E. W. Bovill, *The Golden Trade of the Moors*, 2d edition revised by R. Hallett (London, 1968), provide an introduction to this period of Saharan history. Two aspects of the subject are discussed in more detail in Mortimer Wheeler, *Rome Beyond the Imperial Frontiers* (Harmondsworth, 1955) and R. C. C. Laws, "The Garamantes and Trans-Saharan Enterprise in Classical Times," *J.A.H.*, VII/2 (1967). R. Mauny, *Gravures, peintures et inscriptions rupestres de l'ouest africain* (Dakar, 1954), is a useful introduction to the rock art of the Sahara; the most spectacular of the recent discoveries are splendidly illustrated in a volume of photographs by J. D. Lajoux, *The Rock Paintings of Tassili* (London, 1963).

7. *The Medieval Maghrib.* Julien is again essential, but G. Marçais' *Berbérie musulmane et l'orient au moyen âge* (Paris, 1946) should also be read for a general account. On Morocco see the works by Terrasse and Barbour; Bovill's *Golden Trade* has a chapter on the Almoravids. One period of Tunisian history is covered in a notable work by R. Brunschvig, *La Berbérie orientale sous les Hafsides*, 2 vols. (Paris, 1940–47). Ibn Khaldun, *Histoire des berbères*, translated by M. de Slane, 2d edition, 4 vols. (Paris, 1925) is the outstanding work by a contemporary Muslim historian. A detailed account of North Africa was written by the eleventh-century Muslim geographer al-Bakri and translated by M. de Slane, *Description de l'Afrique septentrionale* (Paris, 1913).

8. *Christians, Turks, and Moors.* The works by Julien, Terrasse, and Barbour should all be consulted. The great series of edited documents from European archives, *Sources inédites de l'histoire du Maroc*, begun in 1905 by H. de Castries and still in progress, contains many valuable commentaries on aspects of Moroccan history in the sixteenth and seventeenth centuries. E. W. Bovill's *The Battle of Alcazar* (London, 1952) is a vivid and well-documented account of an important episode in Moroccan history. G. Fisher, *Barbary Legend: War, Trade and Piracy in North Africa* (London, 1957), studies the polities established by Turkish corsairs. The great work by F. Braudel cited on p. 445 places sixteenth-century North Africa in the context of the Mediterranean world. Among contemporary accounts of North Africa the most detailed is that provided by the sixteenth-century Moroccan traveler known to Europeans as Leo Africanus; the edition by A. Epaulard *et al.*, *Description de l'Afrique*, 2 vols. (Paris, 1956), should be consulted.

9. *Trade in Northwest Africa.* On European trade with North Africa in medieval times: Mas Latrie, *Relations et commerce de l'Afrique du Nord . . . avec les nations chrétiennes du moyen âge* (Paris, 1886). E. W. Bovill's *Golden Trade of the Moors* is primarily concerned with the development of the trans-Saharan trade. A. A. Boahen, *Britain, the Sahara and the Western Sudan, 1788–1861* (Oxford, 1964) contains a useful survey of the trans-Saharan trade in the mid-nineteenth century.

10. *Northwest Africa in the 1850's.* Three major works by French historians provide the best introduction to the history of Morocco, Algeria, and Tunisia at this period: J. L. Miège, *Le Maroc et l'Europe, 1830–1894*, 4 vols. (Paris, 1961); C. A. Julien, *Histoire de l'Algérie contemporaine:* Vol. I . . . *1827–1871* (Paris, 1964); J. Ganiage, *Les Origines du protectorat français en Tunisie* (Paris, 1959). Brief accounts of North Africa in the nineteenth century are given in C. F. Gallagher, *The United States and North Africa* (Cambridge, Mass., 1963), and N. Barbour (ed.), *A Survey of North West Africa* (*The Maghrib*) (London, 1962).

VII. WEST AFRICA

1. *Geography.* R. J. Harrison Church, *West Africa*, 3d edition (London, 1963), provides a comprehensive introduction to the geography of the

region. Of the single country studies, K. M. Buchanan and J. C. Pugh, *Land and People in Nigeria* (London, 1955), is particularly useful.

2. *The Peoples of West Africa.* D. Westermann and M. A. Bryan, *Languages of West Africa* (London, 1952), is the most comprehensive linguistic survey. On the earliest periods of West African history the most comprehensive studies are by R. Mauny, *Tableau géographique de l'ouest africain au moyen âge* (Dakar, 1961), and O. Davies, *West Africa Before the Europeans (Archaeology and Prehistory)* (London, 1967).

3. *The West African States of the First Millennium A.D.* Mauny's *Tableau géographique,* Bovill's *Golden Trade of the Moors,* and J. S. Trimingham's *A History of Islam in West Africa* (Oxford, 1962) all cover this period from somewhat different angles. Mauny provides a useful guide to the Arabic geographers whose works contain references to West Africa.

4. *The Empire of Mali and the Mande Expansion.* In addition to the works by Mauny, Bovill, and Trimingham cited above, see the important study by C. Monteil, "Les Empires du Mali," *Bulletin du Comité d'Études Historiques et Scientifiques de l'A.O.F.* (1929). D. T. Niane, *Soundiata ou l'épopée mandingue* (Paris, 1960), presents the traditional account of the founder of the Mali Empire. Ibn Batuta's *Travels in Asia and Africa* is available in an abridged translation by H. A. R. Gibb (London, 1929).

5. *The Songhai Empire.* In addition to the works by Mauny, Bovill, and Trimingham, see J. Rouch, *Contribution à l'histoire des Songhay* (Dakar, 1953) and *Les Songhay,* Ethnographic Survey of Africa (Paris, 1954). The works of the two most famous Sudanese historians relate principally to the Songhai period: Abd ar-Rahman as-Sadi, *Tarikh as-Sudan,* trans. O. Houdas (Paris, 1900), and Mahmud al-Kati, *Tarikh al-Fattash,* trans. O. Houdas and M. Delafoose (Paris, 1913). In his *Description of Africa* Leo Africanus (p. 462) provides an account of Timbuktu, Gao, and other Sudanese towns at a time when the Songhai Empire was at its height.

6. *The States of the Upper Volta.* For an introduction see the essays by J. D. Fage, "Reflections on the Early History of the Mossi-Dagomba Group of States," and J. Goody, "The Mande and the Akan Hinterland" in Vansina, Mauny, and Thomas (eds.), *The Historian in Tropical Africa,* and the accounts of Gonja by J. Goody and of the Mossi kingdoms by D. Zahan in D. Forde and P. M. Kaberry, *West African Kingdoms in the Nineteenth Century* (London, 1967). The first outsider to write an account of this part of West Africa was L. Binger, *Du Niger au Golfe de Guinée* (Paris, 1892).

7. *Kanem-Bornu and the Hausa States.* Bovill and Trimingham provide a brief introduction. For a more detailed study see the two works by Y. Urvoy, *Histoire des populations du Soudan central* (Paris, 1936) and *Histoire de l'empire de Bornou* (Dakar, 1949). The essay by M. G.

Smith, "The Beginnings of Hausa Society, A.D. 1000–1500," in *The Historian in Tropical Africa,* provides a valuable introduction to Hausa history. Many documents relating to the history of the Central Sudanic states have been translated by H. R. Palmer and published in *Sudanese Memoirs,* 3 vols. (Lagos, 1928), and *The Bornu Sahara and Sudan* (London, 1936). Extracts from some of these documents are reproduced in the anthology edited by T. Hodgkin, *Nigerian Perspectives* (London, 1960).

8. *The People of Guinea to 1450.* For a brief introduction see J. F. A. Ajayi and I. Espie, *A Thousand Years of West African History* (Ibadan, 1965). The relevant volumes in the Ethnographic Survey of Africa provide useful introductions to the history of particular peoples: M. Manoukian, *The Akan and Ga-Adangme Peoples* (1950) and *The Ewe-Speaking People of Togoland and the Gold Coast* (1952); M. Mc-Culloch, *The Peoples of Sierra Leone* (1950); D. Forde and G. I. Jones, *The Ibo and Ibibio-Speaking Peoples of South-Eastern Nigeria* (1950); D. Forde, *The Yoruba-Speaking Peoples of South-Western Nigeria* (1951); D. Forde, P. Brown, and R. G. Armstrong, *Peoples of the Niger-Benue Confluence* (1955); D. Gamble, *The Wolof of Senegambia* (1957); R. E. Bradbury and P. C. Lloyd, *The Benin Kingdom and the Edo-speaking Peoples of South-western Nigeria* (1957). On the Yoruba see also the classic work by a Nigerian historian, S. Johnson, *History of the Yorubas* (Lagos, 1921); on Benin, see J. Egharevba, *Short History of Benin* (Ibadan, 1960).

9. *The Impact of Europe: the Era of the Slave Trade.* On early European voyages the essential work is R. Mauny, *Les Navigations médié-vales sur les côtes sahariennes antérieures à la découverte portugaise (1434)* (Lisbon, 1960). For the earliest phase of European contact: J. W. Blake, *European Beginnings in West Africa, 1434–1587* (London, 1937). Several contemporary works relating to the earliest European contacts have been translated and edited for the Hakluyt Society: C. R. Beazley and E. Prestage (eds.), *Chronicle of the Discovery of Guinea* by Gomes Eannes de Zurara, 2 vols. (1896–99); G. R. Crone (ed.), *The Voyages of Cadamosto* (1937), also includes extracts from the chronicle of De Barros; G. H. T. Kimble (ed.). *Esmeraldu de Situ Orbis* by Duarte Pachecho Pereira (1937); J. W. Blake (ed.), *Europeans in West Africa, 1460–1560,* 2 vols. (1942). Accounts of the earliest English voyages to West Africa are given in Hakluyt's *Voyages* (p. 447). For general works on the slave trade, see p. 448, on the Portuguese, p. 444, and on the Dutch, p. 446. Brief studies of the European impact on West Africa in the sixteenth, seventeenth, and eighteenth centuries are contained in *A Thousand Years of West African History* and in J. D. Fage, *Ghana: an Historical Introduction* (University of Wisconsin, 1959). For detailed studies of certain of the European trading companies that functioned at this time, see K. G. Davies, *The Royal African Company* (London, 1957) and A. Delcourt, *La France et les établissements français au Sénégal, 1713–1763* (Dakar, 1952). From the sixteenth century on the number of published works relating to West Africa and written for the

most part by European traders steadily increased. Extracts from these works are given in three excellent historical anthologies: C. H. Fyfe, *Sierra Leone Inheritance* (London, 1964); F. Wolfson, *Pageant of Ghana* (London, 1958); and T. Hodgkin, *Nigerian Perspectives* (London, 1960). A. W. Lawrence, *Trade Castles and Forts of West Africa* (London, 1963) provides a detailed and well-illustrated study by an archeologist of some of the most remarkable of European monuments in tropical Africa.

10. *The States of Guinea: 1450–1750.* Most of the works cited for sections 8 and 9 are relevant. For works on Ashanti, Dahomey, and the Ibo polities, see p. 476.

11. *The Muslim Revolutions.* Introductory accounts are contained in Trimingham, Bovill, and *A Thousand Years of West African History.* See also H. F. C. Smith, "The Islamic Revolutions of the Nineteenth Century," *Journal of the Historical Society of Nigeria,* II/2 (1961). For works on the caliphate of Sokoyo and on Bornu see p. 476. For a general survey of some of the problems connected with the Fulani jihad in northern Nigeria, M. R. Waldman, "The Fulani *Jihad:* a Reassessment," *J.A.H.,* VII/3 (1965). On the jihad in Macina: A. H. Ba and J. Daget, *L'Empire Peul du Macina:* I. *1818–1853* (Bamako, 1955). On Umar Tall: J. Abun-Nasr, *The Tijaniyya* (Oxford, 1965). The principal European traveler in the Sudanic belt of West Africa at the time of the jihads was H. Barth, *Travels and Discoveries in North and Central Africa,* 5 vols. (London, 1857–58). This massive work has been partly abridged and edited by A. H. M. Kirk-Greene, *Barth's Travels in Nigeria* (London, 1962).

12. *The Impact of Europe: the Antecedents of Imperialism, 1750–1850.* On the growth of European interest in West Africa: P. D. Curtin, *The Image of Africa* (London, 1965), and R. Hallett, *The Penetration of Africa* (London, 1965). On the antislavery movement see the works cited on p. 448. The best introduction to the activities of Europeans in various parts of West Africa is to be found in a number of single country histories: P. Cultru, *Histoire du Sénégal;* J. M. Gray, *A History of the Gambia* (Cambridge, 1940); C. H. Fyfe, *A History of Sierra Leone* (Oxford, 1962); E. J. Yancy, *A History of Liberia* (London, 1959); W. E. F. Ward, *A History of Ghana,* 2d edition (London, 1958); M. Crowder, *The Story of Nigeria* (London, 1962). See also C. W. Newbury, *The Western Slave Coast and Its Rulers* (Oxford, 1961), and K. O. Dike, *Trade and Politics in the Niger Delta* (Oxford, 1956). Among the most vivid accounts produced by European travelers of this period are those by Mungo Park, *Travels in the Interior Districts of Africa* (London, 1799, often reprinted), and by R. and J. Lander, *Journal of an Expedition to Explore the Course and Termination of the Niger,* 3 vols. (London, 1832), abridged with introduction by R. Hallett, *The Niger Journals of Richard and John Lander* (London, 1965). Three important collections of official documents relating to this period have been published: C. Schefer, *Instructions générales données de 1783 à 1870 aux*

gouverneurs et ordinnateurs des établissements français en Afrique Occidentale, 2 vols. (Paris, 1921); G. E. Metcalfe, *Great Britain and Ghana, Documents of Ghana History, 1807–1957* (University of Ghana, 1964); C. W. Newbury, *British Policy Towards West Africa, Selected Documents, 1786–1874* (Oxford, 1965). On Christian missions in West Africa see, in addition to the relevant works cited on p. 450, J. F. A. Ajayi, *Christian Missions in Nigeria, 1841–1891* (London, 1965).

13. *West African Trade.* Mauny, *Tableau géographique*, provides the most comprehensive account of early trade in West Africa. For a brief general account of West African trade from the years 1000 to 1800 see the chapter by C. H. Fyfe in *A Thousand Years of West African History.* As in other parts of Africa most accounts by contemporary European travelers contain a good deal of information about the commerce of the countries through which they passed.

VIII. EQUATORIAL AFRICA

1. *Geography.* For a brief introduction to the geography of the region see the chapter by B. W. Hodder in Hodder and Harris (eds.), *Africa in Transition.* More detailed surveys are given in the encyclopedias produced during the colonial period, the French *Encyclopédie coloniale et maritime.* Vol. 5. *Afrique équatoriale française* (Paris, 1950), and Vol. 6, *Togo et Cameroun* (Paris, 1951), and the Belgian *Encyclopédie du Congo Belge,* 3 vols. (Brussels, 1950–52).

2. *The Peoples of Equatorial Africa.* The encyclopedias mentioned above contain general surveys of the ethnography of their particular territories. In addition to the works devoted to single peoples or groups of people given below, the following studies should be noted: A. Le Rouvreur, *Sahéliens et sahariens du Tchad* (Paris, 1962); P. Kalck, *Réalités oubanguiennes* (Paris, 1959), a study of the area that now forms the Central African Republic; H. J. Deschamps, *Traditions orales et archives au Gabon* (Paris, 1962). J. Vansina's *Introduction à l'ethnographie du Congo* (Kinshasa, 1965) is an excellent guide to the peoples of the former Belgian Congo, some of whom lie within the area of Equatorial Africa. The most detailed archeological research has been done in the area south of Lake Chad: J. P. Lebeuf, *Archéologie tchadienne, les Sao du Cameroun et du Tchad* (Paris, 1962).

3. *The Minor Polities of Equatorial Africa.* On the *montagnards* of Mandara: B. Lembezat, *Les Populations païennes du Nord-Cameroun et de l'Adamawa* (Paris, 1962). On the Bangala or *Gens d'Eau:* H. Burssens, *Les Peuplades de l'entre Congo-Ubangi* (Brussels, 1958). On the Pahouin or Fang: P. Alexandre, *Le Groupe dit Pahouin* (Paris, 1958). All these works are volumes in the Ethnographic Survey of Africa.

4. *The Kingdoms and Chiefdoms of Equatorial Africa.* J. S. Trimingham's *A History of Islam in West Africa* gives a brief account of the

development of Wadai and Baguirmi; on these states see also A. M. D. Lebeuf, *Les Populations du Tchad* (Paris, 1959). On the states of Central Cameroun: M. McCulloch, M. Littlewood, and I. Dugast, *Peoples of the Central Cameroons* (London, 1954), and C. Tardits, *Contribution à l'étude des populations bamiléké de l'ouest Cameroun* (Paris, 1960). On the coastal polities: E. W. Ardener, *Coastal Bantu of the Cameroons* (London, 1956). On Loango and neighboring states: M. Soret, *Les Kongo nord-occidentaux* (Paris, 1959). On the Kuba: J. Vansina, *Les Tribus Ba-Kuba et les peuplades apparentées* (Brussels, 1954). On the Teke and the Zande see p. 477. The works by Lebeuf, McCulloch, and others, Ardener, Soret, and Vansina are volumes in the Ethnographic Survey of Africa.

5. *External Influences and the Development of Trade.* On the introduction of Islam see Trimingham's *History.* J. Vansina, "Long Distance Trade Routes in Central Africa," *J.A.H.,* III/3 (1962), covers the southern part of the region. Several of the European writers who described the Guinea coast in the seventeenth and eighteenth centuries also refer to trading conditions on the coast of Equatorial Africa.

6. *Equatorial Africa in the 1850's.* M. as-Tunisi, *Voyage au Quaday* (Paris, 1851), is the first account of Wadai written by an outside observer. Barth (p. 465) visited Baguirmi and gathered some information about Wadai. G. Nachtigal, *Sahara und Sudan,* 3 vols. (Berlin, 1879–89), was the first European traveler to describe the country between Lake Chad and Darfur. P. B. du Chaillu, *Expeditions and Adventures in Equatorial Africa* (New York, 1862) is the first work to describe the interior of modern Gabon. For a detailed account of the first French settlements in Gabon: H. Deschamps, *Quinze ans de Gabon: les débuts de l'établissement français, 1839–1853* (Paris, 1965).

🌿 IX. CENTRAL AFRICA

1. *Geography.* For that part of the region which later formed part of the Belgian Congo, see *Encyclopédie du Congo Belge;* for the area covered by modern Zambia, Malawi, and Rhodesia, J. H. Wellington, *Southern Africa,* 2 vols. (Cambridge, 1955); on Angola, see Chapter 19 of R. J. Harrison Church's *Africa and the Islands.*

2. *Bantu Migrations.* This section is based mainly on the articles by Oliver and Guthrie cited in note 1, Chapter IX; Oliver's article contains references to earlier hypotheses relating to the Bantu. For a guide to Bantu languages, see M. A. Bryan, *The Bantu Languages of Africa* (London, 1959).

3. *Luba Expansion: Monomotapa: Kongo.* B. M. Fagan, *Southern Africa During the Iron Age* (London, 1965), a volume in the *Ancient Peoples and Places* series, is the best introduction to the archeology of the region. J. Vansina, *Kingdoms of the Savanna* (Madison, 1966), discusses the development of the major polities of the Angola-Congo area. On the rise of Monomotapa: D. P. Abraham, "The Early Political History of

the Kingdom of Mwene Mutapa, 850–1589," *Historians in Tropical Africa* (Salisbury, 1960) and "Maramuca, an Exercise in the Combined Use of Portuguese Records and Oral Tradition," *J.A.H.*, II/2 (1961). For an introduction to archeological research at Zimbabwe: R. Summers, *Zimbabwe, A Rhodesian Mystery* (Johannesburg, 1963). On the kingdom of Kongo see the works cited in section 5.

4. Luba and Lunda States. Vansina, *Kingdoms of the Savanna,* pp. 70–98, 156–79, provides the best introduction to Luba-Lunda history. See also the volumes in the Ethnographic Survey of Africa by M. Mc-Culloch, *The Southern Lunda and Related Peoples* (London, 1951), and by W. Whiteley and J. Slaski, *Bemba and Related Peoples of Northern Rhodesia . . . and Peoples of the Lower Luapula Valley* (London, 1951). R. F. Burton (ed.), *The Lands of Cazembe* (London, 1873), contains a translation of the account written by the Portuguese explorer Lacerda, who visited the kingdom of Kazembe at the end of the eighteenth century. The account of another Portuguese traveler, Gamitto, first published in Lisbon in 1854, has been translated by I. Cunnison, *King Kazembe, and the Marave, Chewa, Bisa, Bemba, Lunda and Other Peoples of Southern Africa,* 2 vols. (Lisbon, 1962). See also I. Cunnison, "Kazembe and the Portuguese, 1798–1832," *J.A.H.*, II/1 (1961).

5. The Portuguese. The general works on Portuguese activities in Africa cited on p. 444 should all be consulted. Vansina's *Kingdoms of the Savanna* provides a useful summary of Portuguese activities in Kongo and Angola. On the Portuguese in Angola see also C. R. Boxer, *Salvador de Sa and the Struggle for Brazil and Angola, 1602–1682* (London, 1952), and D. Birmingham, *Trade and Conflict in Angola: the Mbundu and Their Neighbours under the Influence of the Portuguese, 1483–1790* (Oxford, 1966). E. Axelson's *South-East Africa, 1488–1530* (London, 1940) and *Portuguese in South-East Africa, 1600–1700* (Johannesburg, 1960) provide the best introduction in English to Portuguese activities in Mozambique and on the Zambezi. These works by Axelson, Boxer, and Birmingham are richly documented from Portuguese archives. The earliest traveler's account of Central Africa was produced by a Portuguese, Duarte Lopez, who described the kingdom of Kongo in a work published in Rome by F. Pigafetta in 1591, English edition by M. Hutchinson, *A Report of the Kingdom of Congo* (London, 1881). In 1625 Purchas (p. 447) published "The Strange Adventures of Andrew Battell Sent by the Portugals Prisoner to Angola"; Battell's account was edited by E. G. Ravenstein for the Hakluyt Society in 1901. Purchas also published extracts from the *Ethiopia Oriental* of João dos Santos, a Dominican priest who traveled widely in Mozambique in the 1590's: extracts in E. Axelson (ed.), *South African Explorers* (London, 1954). A. de O. de Cadornega, *Historia general das guerras angolanas,* written in Luanada in 1681–83 and published in Lisbon in 3 vols. (1940–42), is the principal contemporary source for Angolan history in the seventeenth century; it has not yet been translated. The account of Kongo published in Naples in 1692 by the Italian Capuchin missionary J. Merolla was translated for Pinkerton's *Collection* (p. 444), Vol. XVI.

Some of the documents relating to Portuguese activities have been published in English or French translations: J. Cuvelier and L. Jadin (eds.), *L'Ancien Congo d'après les archives romaines, 1518–1640* (Brussels, 1954); *Documents on the Portuguese in Mozambique and Central Africa, 1497–1840* (Lisbon, 1962—), the four volumes already published covering the period from 1497–1516.

6. *Warrior-Hordes; the Jaga, the Ngoni, and Others.* On the Jaga see Vansina's *Kingdoms of the Savanna* and Ravenstein's edition, cited above, of Battell's adventures. For an introduction to the history of the Ndebele, the Kololo, and the Ngoni see J. D. Omer-Cooper, *The Zulu Aftermath* (London, 1966). For a contemporary account of the Matabele see J. P. R. Wallis (ed.), *The Matabele Journals of Robert Moffat, 1829–1860,* 2 vols. (London, 1945). The Kololo were described by D. Livingstone, *Missionary Travels and Researches in South Africa* (London, 1857); see also the volume in the Ethnographic Survey of Africa by V. W. Turner, *The Lozi People of North-western Rhodesia* (London, 1952). For the Ngoni see the works cited on p. 478.

7. *The Creation of Long-Distance Trade Routes.* J. Vansina, "Long Distance Trade Routes in Central Africa," *J.A.H.,* III/3 (1962), provides the best introduction to routes in the western part of the region; see also Birmingham, *Trade and Conflict in Angola.* On the Ovimbundu, see the volume in the Ethnographic Survey of Africa by M. McCulloch, *The Ovimbundu of Angola* (London, 1952). On trade in the eastern half of the region much information is available in the works by the Portuguese travelers Lacerda and Gamitto cited above.

X. EAST AFRICA

1. *Geography.* For an introduction see the chapters by S. J. K. Baker on "The East African Environment" in *History of East Africa,* Vol. I (Oxford, 1963), and by A. Warren in Hodder and Harris (eds.), *Africa in Transition.* There is a valuable collection of maps contained in the Report of the East African Royal Commission (London, 1955); see also the atlases for Kenya, Uganda, and Tanganyika (p. 434).

2. *Bushmen and Ancient Azanians.* For an introduction see the chapters by S. Cole, "The Stone Age of East Africa," and by G. W. B. Huntingford, "The Peopling of the Interior of East Africa by Its Modern Inhabitants," in *History of East Africa.* For a critical view of Azanian culture, see J. E. G. Sutton, "The Problem of 'Sirikwa Holes' and the So-called 'Azanian' Remains of the Western Highlands of Kenya," in M. Posnansky (ed.), *Prelude to East African History* (London, 1966), and "The Archaeology and Early Peoples of the Highlands of Kenya and Northern Tanzania," *Azania,* I (1966).

3. *Bantu Migrations and Swahili Civilization.* On the early history of the East African coast see the chapters by G. Mathew, "The East African Coast until the Coming of the Portuguese," in *History of East Africa,* and by J. Kirkman, "The History of the Coast of East Africa up

to 1700," in *Prelude to East African History*. G. S. P. Freeman-Grenville (ed.), *The East African Coast: Select Documents* (Oxford, 1962), is an invaluable collection with extracts from Greek, Arabic, Swahili, Chinese, and European accounts of the coast. Kilwa, the most important medieval site on the East African coast, has been excavated by N. Chittick; his chapter, "Kilwa," in *Prelude to East African History* provides an introduction to the history of the site. Other coastal sites are described by J. S. Kirkman, *Men and Monuments of the East African Coast* (London, 1964). Two volumes by A. H. J. Prins in the Ethnographic Survey of Africa, *The Coastal Tribes of the North-Eastern Bantu* (London, 1952) and *The Swahili-Speaking Peoples of Zanzibar and the East African Coast* (London, 1961), provide a detailed account of the ethnography of the coast.

4. *The Early History of the Northeastern Interior*. In addition to the works cited for Section 2 see the chapter by R. Oliver, "Discernible Developments in the Interior c. 1500–1840," in *History of East Africa*, Three volumes of the Ethnographic Survey of Africa are devoted to the Nilo-Hamites: G. W. B. Huntingford, *The Northern Nilo-Hamites* (London, 1953) and *The Southern Nilo-Hamites* (London, 1953); P. and P. H. Gulliver, *The Central Nilo-Hamites* (London, 1953). See also p. 479 for works on the Kikuyu and the Masai.

5. *The Early History of the Interlacustrine Area and the Southern Interior*. The chapter by R. Oliver in *History of East Africa* provides the most comprehensive introduction. On the Nilotes: A. Butt, *The Nilotes*, Ethnographic Survey of Africa (London, 1952); J. P. Crazzolara, *The Lwoo*, 3 vols. (Verona, 1950–54); B. E. Ogot, "Kingship and Statelessness among the Nilotes," in Vansina, Thomas, and Mauny (eds.), *The Historian in Tropical Africa*. Three volumes in the Ethnographic Survey of Africa provide an introduction to the interlacustrine Bantu peoples: M. C. Fallers, *The Eastern Lacustrine Bantu* (London, 1960); B. Taylor, *The Western Lacustrine Bantu* (London, 1962); A. A. Trouwborst, M. D'Hertefelt, and J. H. Scherer, *Les Anciens royaumes de la zone interlacustre méridionale* (Brussels, 1963). Many of the peoples of Tanzania have been studied in three recent volumes of the Ethnographic Survey: R. G. Willis, *The Fipa and Related Peoples of South-west Tanzania and North-west Zambia* (London, 1966); T. O. Beidelman, *The Matrilineal Peoples of Eastern Tanzania* (London, 1967); R. G. Abrahams, *The Peoples of Greater Unyamwezi* (London, 1967). See also M. Wilson, *The Peoples of the Nyasa-Tanganyika Corridor* (Cape Town, 1958). See p. 479 for works on Ankole and Buganda.

6. *Portuguese, Omani Arabs, and the Development of Trade Routes*. For an introduction to the Portuguese and Omani period see the chapter by G. S. P. Freeman-Grenville, "The Coast, 1498–1840," in *History of East Africa*. The most detailed study of the Portuguese period is the work by the German scholar J. Strandes first published in Berlin in 1899 and now available in an English translation by J. F. Wallwork and J. S. Kirkman, *The Portuguese in East Africa* (Nairobi, 1961). Portu-

guese accounts relating to East Africa have been published by Freeman-Grenville in the collection of documents cited for section 3. On the development of Omani interest in East Africa see R. Coupland, *East Africa and Its Invaders* (Oxford, 1938). Works on Zanzibar are cited on p. 479. M. Guillain, *Documents sur l'histoire, la géographie et le commerce de L'Afrique orientale*, 3 vols. (Paris, 1856), the work of a French naval officer, presents by far the most detailed of early accounts of the coast. On trade and trade routes there is much information, derived largely from the accounts of post-1850 European travelers in East Africa (p. 482), to be found in three chapters of the *History of East Africa* by Sir J. Gray, "Zanzibar and the Coastal Belt, 1840–84," A. Smith, "The Southern Section of the Interior, 1840–84," and D. A. Low, "The Northern Interior, 1840–84."

XI. SOUTH AFRICA

1. *Geography.* There are two detailed regional studies: J. H. Wellington, *Southern Africa*, 2 vols. (Cambridge, 1955), and M. Cole, *South Africa* (London, 1955). N. C. Pollock and S. Agnew, *A Historical Geography of South Africa* (London, 1963) should also be consulted.

2. *Bushmen and Bantu.* B. M. Fagan's *Southern Africa During the Iron Age* (London, 1965) provides a brief and up-to-date account of the archaeology of South Africa in the centuries that preceded the coming of the Europeans. Two works edited by I. Schapera, *The Khoisan Peoples of South Africa* (London, 1930) and *The Bantu-speaking Tribes of South Africa*, 4th edition (London, 1953), provide the most compact introduction to the ethnography of South Africa. The earliest accounts of the South African Bantu are contained in the narratives of Portuguese who suffered shipwreck on the coast of South Africa; these accounts have been edited for the Hakluyt Society by C. R. Boxer, *The Tragic History of the Sea, 1589–1622* (Cambridge, 1957). For contemporary accounts of life beyond the colonial frontier before the *Mfecane* see the narratives of A. Sparrman, *A Voyage to the Cape of Good Hope* (London, 1785); C. P. Thunberg, *Travels in Europe, Africa and Asia*, 4 vols. (London, 1795); and J. Barrow, *An Account of Travels in the Interior of Southern Africa* (London, 1801); none of these three travelers shared the preconceptions of the European settlers, Sparrman and Thunberg being Swedish naturalists, while Barrow was an English civil servant.

3. *The Dutch at the Cape.* The best introduction to this period of South African history is to be found in the first chapter of C. W. de Kiewiet, *A History of South Africa, Social and Economic* (Oxford, 1941). For a more detailed narrative with an emphasis on political events, see E. A. Walker's *A History of Southern Africa* (London, 1957) and the relevant chapters of the *Cambridge History of the British Empire: VIII. South Africa*, revised edition (Cambridge, 1963). The Van Riebeck Society has published many documents relating to this period, including the *Journal of Jan van Riebeck, 1652–1662*, 3 vols. (Cape Town, 1952–58). An entertaining account of the Cape was published in London in 1731 by P.

Kolben, *The Present State of the Cape of Good Hope;* see also the accounts by Sparrman, Thunberg, and Barrow. I. D. MacCrone's *Race Attitudes in South Africa: Historical, Experimental and Psychological Studies* (London, 1937) is a well-documented study of the development of ideas about race among the settlers at the Cape from 1652 to 1806.

4. *The Mfecane.* J. D. Omer-Cooper, *The Zulu Aftermath. A Nineteenth-Century Revolution in Bantu Africa* (London, 1966) provides the best introduction to the subject. For works on the Zulu, the Tswana, and the Basuto see p. 480. On the Swazi see H. Kuper, *An African Aristocracy* (London, 1947). Among the most important accounts of travel by Europeans beyond the colonial frontier in the first half of the nineteenth century are the works of an English naturalist, William Burchell, *Travels in the Interior of South Africa,* 2 vols. (London, 1822–24), of Dr. John Campbell of the London Missionary Society, *Travels in South Africa* (London, 1815) and *Travels in South Africa . . . a Second Journey,* 2 vols. (London, 1822), and of Dr. Andrew Smith, *The Diary of Dr. Andrew Smith,* edited by P. R. Kirby, Van Riebeck Society, 2 vols. (Cape Town, 1939).

5. *British and Boers.* The general works cited for section 3 deal at considerable length with relations between the two European groups in South Africa. Many of the official documents relating to this period have been edited by G. M. Theal, *Records of the Cape Colony from 1793 to 1828,* 36 vols. (London, 1897–1905). E. A. Walker's *The Great Trek* (London, 1938) is the best narrative by a non-Afrikaner of one of the major episodes in South African history. For studies of the relations between Boers and Britons after 1848 see p. 452. On the early history of Natal see A. F. Hattersley, *The British Settlement of Natal* (Cambridge, 1950), and J. Bird, *The Annals of Natal, 1495 to 1845,* 2 vols. (Cape Town, 1885).

6. *The Beginnings of the Native Problem.* In addition to the general works and the study by MacCrone already cited see J. S. Marais, *The Cape Coloured People, 1652–1937* (London, 1939); W. M. Mac-Millan, *The Cape Colour Question* (London, 1927) and *Bantu, Boer and Briton* (London, 1929); and J. A. I. Agar-Hamilton, *The Native Policy of the Voortrekkers* (Cape Town, 1928). The most influential contemporary work on the native problem was the study by the missionary Dr. John Philip, of the conditions of the Hottentots in Cape Colony, *Researches in South Africa* (London, 1828).

7. *The Development of Trade.* No adequate study has yet been made of the economy of the indigenous peoples of South Africa. On the economy of the European settlers see, in addition to de Kiewiet's *History,* M. H. de Kock, *Selected Subjects in the Economic History of South Africa* (Cape Town, 1924), and C. G. W. Schumann, *Structural Changes and Business Cycles in South Africa, 1806–1936* (London, 1938).

✠ XII. THE ISLANDS

1. *Atlantic Islands.* For a brief survey of early European voyages see C. Brochado, *The Discovery of the Atlantic* (Lisbon, 1966). Contemporary accounts of navigation on the Saharan coast before 1434 are given in Mauny's study cited on p. 464. For an introduction to the Guanche of the Canaries, see G. P. Murdock, *Africa: Its Peoples and Their Culture History*, pp. 114–16 and 123–24 (bibliography). Information about the historical development of the Atlantic islands is to be found in a great variety of sources from the narratives of seventeenth-century voyagers to nineteenth-century guide books (particularly useful for the Canaries) and encyclopedias, but with the exception of St. Helena serious historical studies are confined to works in Spanish or Portuguese. On the history of St. Helena see P. Gosse, *St. Helena, 1502–1938* (London, 1938).

2. *Islands of the Western Indian Ocean.* The division of the islands of the Western Indian Ocean into British and French possessions has prevented the appearance of an overall study. A. Toussaint's *History of the Indian Ocean* (London, 1966) devotes relatively little space to the islands. C. Robequain, *Madagascar et les bases dispersées de l'Union Française* (Paris, 1958) is an excellent geographical study which includes the Comoros and Réunion. For a brief study in English see R. J. Harrison Church, *Africa and the Islands*, pp. 447–68. H. Deschamps' *Histoire de Madagascar* (Paris, 1960) is a model study. On Réunion A. Scherer, *Histoire de la Réunion* (Paris, 1965), a volume in the *Que sais-je?* series, provides a useful introduction. On Mauritius the only comprehensive history is a textbook by P. J. Barnwell and A. Toussaint, *A Short History of Mauritius* (London, 1949). For the Lesser Dependencies see Sir R. Scott, *Limuria* (London, 1961).

3. *The Colonization of Madagascar.* Deschamps' *Histoire* provides the best general account. The most comprehensive study of the ethnography of Madagascar is the massive survey by A. and G. Grandidier, *Ethnographie de Madagascar*, 5 vols. (Paris, 1908–28). Malagasy society is described at various stages in its more recent history in a number of important works by European observers: E. Flacourt, *Histoire de la Grande Île de Madagascar* (Paris, 1658); *Madagascar or Robert Drury's Journal During Fifteen Years on That Island* (London, 1729); W. Ellis, *History of Madagascar*, 2 vols. (London, 1838); M. Guillain, *Documents sur l'histoire, la géographie et le commerce de la partie occidentale de Madagascar* (Paris, 1845).

4. *The European Impact.* In addition to the general works cited for section 2, see S. Howe, *The Drama of Madagascar* (London, 1938), a well-documented account of European relations with Madagascar from the sixteenth century; A. Toussaint, *Port Louis, deux siècles d'histoire, 1735–1935* (Port Louis, 1935); and G. Hanotaux (ed.), *Histoire des colonies françaises*, Vol. VI (Paris, 1933). A. and G. Grandidier (eds.), *Collections des ouvrages anciens concernant Madagascar*, 9 vols. (Paris,

1903–20), contains accounts by Europeans dating from 1500 to the eighteenth century relating not only to Madagascar but also to the Mascarenes. Contemporary accounts of the Mascarenes include J. H. B. de Saint Pierre, *A Voyage to the Isle of France* (London, 1791); C. Grant, *The History of Mauritius* (London, 1801); J. B. G. M. Bory de St. Vincent, *Voyage dans les quatres principales îles des mers d'Afrique* (Paris, 1804); and A. Billiard, *Voyages aux colonies orientales* (Paris, 1829).

XIII. VARIETY AND CLASSIFICATION

There are a number of works which discuss the problem of classifying African polities or which deal with certain general aspects of African political systems: M. Fortes and E. E. Evans-Pritchard (eds.), *African Political Systems* (London, 1940), Introduction; I. Schapera, *Government and Politics in Tribal Societies* (London, 1956); J. Middleton and D. Tait (eds.), *Tribes without Rulers* (London, 1958); G. P. Murdock, *Africa: Its Peoples and Their Culture History* (New York, 1959); L. Mair, *Primitive Government* (Harmondsworth, 1962); J. Vansina, "A Comparison of African Kingdoms," *Africa*, XXXII (1962); P. C. Lloyd, "The Political Structure of African Kingdoms: an Exploratory Model," in *Political Systems and the Distribution of Power*, Association of Social Anthropologists of the Commonwealth, Monograph 2 (London, 1965); J. Goody, "Introduction," in *Succession to High Office*, Cambridge Papers in Social Anthropology (Cambridge, 1966).

XIV. NORTHEAST AFRICAN POLITIES ABOUT 1850

1. *The Pashalik of Egypt: "Oriental Despotism."* In addition to the works on Muhammad Ali cited on p. 459, see the studies on social change in Egypt by G. Baer and on the social hierarchy in Egypt during Muhamad Ali's reign by N. Tomiche in P. M. Holt (ed.), *Political and Social Change in Modern Egypt* (London, 1968). One of the most vivid and penetrating contemporary accounts of Egypt by an outsider is in *Letters from Egypt* by Lady L. Duff-Gordon, 1st edition (London, 1865), enlarged edition with introduction by G. Waterfield (London, 1969).

2. *Turco-Egyptian Rule in the Sudan.* R. Hill, *Egypt in the Sudan, 1820–1881* (London, 1959), and P. M. Holt, *A Modern History of the Sudan* (London, 1961), provide good accounts of Turco-Egyptian administration. Hill in his essay on "Historical Writing of the Sudan since 1820," in B. Lewis and P. M. Holt (eds.), *Historians of the Middle East* (London, 1962), comments on the accounts of contemporary European travelers. A succinct account of administration in the Sudan is given in J. Petherick, *Egypt, the Soudan and Central Africa* (London, 1861).

3. *Ethiopia: Warlords and the Imperial Tradition.* M. Perham's *The Government of Ethiopia* (London, 1948) provides a good introduction. See also the works by contemporary travelers cited on p. 458.

4. *The Sidama and Galla Polities of Southwestern Ethiopia.* Two volumes in the Ethnographic Survey of Africa provide the most concise introduction: G. W. B. Huntingford, *The Galla of Ethiopia: Kingdoms of Kafa and Janjero* (London, 1955), and E. Cerulli, *Peoples of Southwest Ethiopia and Its Borderlands* (London, 1956). On the kingdom of Limu-Enarea: M. Abir, "The Emergence and Consolidation of Enarea and Jimma in the First Half of the Nineteenth Century," *J.A.H.*, VI/2 (1965), a study based in part on the unpublished papers of the French traveler A. d'Abadie.

5. *The "Divine Kingship" of the Shilluk.* A. Butt, *The Nilotes,* Ethnographic Survey of Africa (London, 1952), contains a brief account of Shilluk government. See also E. E. Evans-Pritchard, "The Divine Kingship of the Shilluk of the Nilotic Sudan," in *Essays in Social Anthropology* (London, 1962).

6. *The "Ordered Anarchy" of the Nuer.* E. E. Evans-Pritchard's *The Nuer* (London, 1940) is the basic work on these people. There is a shorter account of their system of government by the same author in Fortes and Evans-Pritchard (eds.), *African Political Systems.*

❧ XV. NORTHWEST AFRICAN POLITIES ABOUT 1850

1. *The Village Republics of the Berber Montagnards.* R. Montagne's *Les Berbères et le Makhzen dans le sud du Maroc* (Paris, 1930) is the basic work; it contains references to Berber communities in other parts of the Maghrib.

2. *The Sultanate of Morocco: the Politics of the Makhzen.* No detailed study based on research in Moroccan archives has yet been made. Among contemporary accounts of Morocco that written by a French journalist, E. Aubin, at the beginning of the twentieth century, *Morocco of Today* (London, 1906), stands out as being both sympathetic and extremely well informed. See also the general histories of Morocco by Barbour and Terrasse cited on p. 442.

3. *Military Rule in Algeria: Turkish Deys and French Generals—and the Amirate of Abd al-Kadir.* The most comprehensive of recent studies is the massive work by C. A. Julien, *Histoire de l'Algérie contemporaine* (Paris, 1964). The bibliography to this work provides the best guide to contemporary sources.

4. *The Regency of Tunis.* The first chapters of J. Ganiage's *Les Origines du protectorat français en Tunisie* (Paris, 1959) contain an excellent account based on a wide range of sources of the administration of the regency in the middle of the nineteenth century.

5. *Tuareg Confederations.* There are three basic works on the Tuareg: H. Duveyrier, *Les Touaregs du nord* (Paris, 1864), the work of a young Frenchman who was the first European to become deeply acquainted with Tuareg society: F. R. Rodd, *People of the Veil* (London, 1926), an

account of the Tuareg of Air; and H. Lhote, *Les Touaregs du Hoggar* (Paris, 1955).

✻ XVI. WEST AFRICAN POLITIES ABOUT 1850

1. *The Ancient Sudanic Sultanate of Bornu.* Detailed accounts of Bornu were written by the British explorer Denham in the 1820's, by Barth (p. 465) in the 1850's, and by Nachtigal (p. 467) in the 1870's. Denham's account published with the report of his fellow explorer Clapperton on the journey from Bornu to Sokoto in *Narrative of Travels and Discoveries in Northern and Central Africa in the Years 1822, 1823 and 1824* (London, 1826) has been edited by E. W. Bovill, *Missions to the Niger*, Vols. II–IV (Hakluyt Society, London, 1966). For recent studies of Bornu see the works by Palmer and Urvoy's *Histoire* cited on p. 463 and the short work by R. Cohen in the *Case Studies in Cultural Anthropology* series, *The Kanuri of Bornu* (New York, 1967).

2. *The Empire and Caliphate of Sokoto.* The works written in Arabic by the Fulani leaders Usuman dan Fodio, Abdullahi, and Muhammad Bello, some of which are now available in translation, are the main sources for the history of Sokoto. They have been extensively used in two recent studies: M. Last, *The Sokoto Caliphate* (London, 1967), and H. A. S. Johnston, *The Fulani Empire of Sokoto* (London, 1967). M. G. Smith's *Government in Zazzau* (London, 1960) provides a detailed account of administration in one of the major emirates. On the other emirates see S. J. Hogben and A. H. M. Kirk-Greene, *The Emirates of Northern Nigeria* (London, 1966). Clapperton in the *Narrative* cited above and in *Journal of a Second Expedition into the Interior of Africa* (London, 1829) and Barth provide accounts of the empire by outside observers.

3. *The Ashanti Union and Empire.* The narratives of two of the first Europeans, the Englishmen Bowdich and Dupuis, to visit Ashanti (cited in note 4, Chapter XVI) provide much information on the structure of the state in the early nineteenth century. For recent studies see the works by I. Wilks, "Ashanti Government," in Forde and Kaberry (eds.), *West African Kingdoms in the Nineteenth Century* (London, 1967), and "Aspects of Bureaucratization in Ashanti in the Nineteenth Century," *J.A.H.*, VII/2 (1966), and M. Arhin, "The Structure of Greater Ashanti," *J.A.H.*, VII/2 (1967).

4. *The Autocratic Kingdom of Dahomey.* Dahomey was the most accessible of the major polities of West Africa to European visitors; it was frequently described in works on West Africa from the eighteenth century onward. The most notable of these accounts were written by A. Dalzel, *The History of the Dahomey* (London, 1793) and by R. F. Burton, *A Mission to Gelele, King of Dahome* (London, 1864), new edition with introduction by C. W. Newbury (London, 1966). For a concise account of government in Dahomey see J. Lombard, "The Kingdom of Dahomey," in Forde and Kaberry (eds.), *West African Kingdoms in the Nineteenth Century.* For more detailed studies of the kingdom's institutions and history see M. J. Herskovits, *Dahomey, An Ancient West Af-*

rican Kingdom, 2 vols. (New York, 1938), and I. A. Akinjogbin, *Dahomey and Its Neighbours, 1708–1818* (Cambridge, 1967).

5. *Ibo Village Groups and the "Trading Empire" of Aro Chuku.* Contemporary accounts of certain aspects of Ibo society by O. Equiano (1789), R. Lander (1832), and W. B. Baikie (1856) are given in T. Hodgkin (ed.), *Nigerian Perspectives* (London, 1960). There is a useful brief account of Ibo government in J. B. Webster and A. A. Boahen, *The Revolutionary Years: West Africa since 1800* (London, 1967), pp. 177–89. See also M. M. Green, *Ibo Village Affairs,* new edition (London, 1954), and D. Forde and G. I. Jones, *The Ibo and Ibibio-Speaking Peoples of Southeastern Nigeria,* Ethnographic Survey of Africa (London, 1950).

6. *The Trading Polities of the Eastern Niger Delta.* Contemporary accounts by Barbot (1732), Adams (1823), Winwood Reade (1863) and others are given in Hodgkin, *Nigerian Perspectives.* The most detailed recent study is by G. I. Jones, *The Trading States of the Oil Rivers* (London, 1963). See also K. O. Dike, *Trade and Politics in the Niger Delta, 1830–1885* (Oxford, 1956).

7. *Alien Settlements: Senegal, Sierra Leone, Liberia, and the Gold Coast.* P. D. Boilat's *Esquisses sénégalaises* (Paris, 1853) is the most detailed contemporary account of Senegal. See also G. Hardy, *La Mise en valeur du Sénégal de 1817 à 1854* (Paris, 1921), and M. Crowder, *Senegal. A Study in French Assimilation Policy,* revised edition (London, 1967). On the British settlements in West Africa a mass of material is to be found in the *Report of the Select Committee on Africa (Western Coast), Parliamentary Papers* (1865), Vol. V. An impressionistic account of Sierra Leone is given in F. H. Rankin, *The White Man's Grave,* 2 vols. (London, 1836). On the Gold Coast the outstanding mid-nineteenth-century account was written by a British official, B. Cruickshank, *Eighteen Years on the Gold Coast of Africa,* 2 vols. (London, 1853). For more recent works on British West African settlements see p. 465. There is no adequate contemporary account of Liberia. For recent studies of the earliest period of Liberian history see the first chapter of M. Fraenkel, *Tribe and Class in Monrovia* (London, 1964); C. H. Huberich, *The Political and Legislative History of Liberia,* 2 vols. (New York, 1947); and P. J. Staudenraus, *The African Colonization Movement, 1816–1865* (New York, 1961).

XVII. EQUATORIAL AFRICAN POLITIES ABOUT 1850

1. *The Teke Kingdom: Extreme Decentralization.* The account of the Teke by J. Vansina, *Kingdoms of the Savanna,* pp. 102–10, is based on recently collected oral traditions.

2. *Zande Polities: Conquest and Fission.* G. Schweinfurth's *The Heart of Africa,* 2 vols. (London, 1878), contains the first detailed account by an outsider of Zande polities. For a general survey see the volume in the Ethnographic Survey of Africa by P. T. W. Baxter and A. Butt, *The*

Azande and Related Peoples of the Anglo-Egyptian Sudan and Belgian Congo (London, 1953). See also E. E. Evans-Pritchard, "Zande Kings and Princes" in *Essays in Social Anthropology* (London, 1962).

3. *The Hunting Bands of the Mbuti Pygmies*. C. M. Turnbull's *Wayward Servants* (London, 1967) is a detailed account by a modern social anthropologist.

4. *The Independent Villages of the Amba*. The Amba have been extensively studied by a modern social anthropologist, E. H. Winter: *Bwamba* (Cambridge, 1956); "The Aboriginal Political Structure of Bwamba," in Tait and Middleton (eds.), *Tribes Without Rulers* (London, 1959); *Beyond the Mountains of the Moon* (London, 1959).

✻ XVIII. CENTRAL AFRICAN POLITIES ABOUT 1850

1. *The Portuguese Colonies in Angola and Mozambique*. See the works on the Portuguese cited on p. 444 and p. 468.

2. *Kongo: the Politics of Fragmentation*. Early accounts of Kongo are cited on p. 469. A mid-nineteenth-century account was written by the German traveler A. Bastian, *San Salvador* (Berlin, 1859). For a recent study see Vansina, *Kingdoms of the Savanna*.

3. *The Bemba Paramountcy*. For a general survey see the volume in the Ethnological Survey of Africa by W. Whiteley and J. Slaski, *Bemba and Related Peoples of Northern Rhodesia* (London, 1951). On Bemba institutions: A. I. Richards, "The Political System of the Bemba Tribe," in Fortes and Evans-Pritchard (eds.), *African Political Systems*. For an introduction to Bemba history: A. Roberts, "The History of the Bemba," in R. Oliver (ed.), *The Middle Ages of African History* (London, 1967), and A. Tweedie, "Towards a History of the Bemba from Oral Tradition," in E. Stokes and R. Brown (eds.), *The Zambesian Past* (Manchester, 1966).

4. *The Polities of the Lake Nyasa Area*. For contemporary accounts of the area see D. and C. Livingstone, *Narrative of an Expedition to the Zambezi and Its Tributaries* (London, 1865); E. D. Young, *Nyasa* (London, 1877); J. Thomson, *To the Central African Lakes and Back* (London, 1881); W. A. Elmslie, *Among the Wild Angoni* (Edinburgh, 1899). A volume in the Ethnographic Survey of Africa provides a good general survey: M. Tew, *The Peoples of the Lake Nyasa Region* (London, 1950). On the Nkonde: M. Wilson, *The Peoples of the Nyasa-Tanganyika Corridor* (Cape Town, 1958). On the Ngoni: J. A. Barnes, *Politics in a Changing Society* (London, 1954). There is a chapter on the Yao by J. C. Mitchell in E. Colson and M. Gluckman (eds.), *Seven Tribes of British Central Africa* (London, 1954).

✻ XIX. EAST AFRICAN POLITIES ABOUT 1850

1. *The Omani Arab Sultanate of Zanzibar*. The most detailed mid-nineteenth-century account of Zanzibar was written by R. F. Burton,

Zanzibar, City, Island, Coast, 2 vols. (London, 1872). A great deal of contemporary material mainly drawn from consular correspondence was used by R. Coupland in his two studies, *East Africa and Its Invaders . . . to 1856* (London, 1938) and *The Exploitation of East Africa* (London, 1939). See also J. M. Gray's *A History of Zanzibar up to 1856* and the works on the East African coast cited on p. 470.

2. *Buganda: a Highly Centralized Kingdom.* For early accounts by European visitors see J. H. Speke, *Journal of the Discovery of the Nile* (London, 1863), and H. M. Stanley, *Through the Dark Continent,* 2 vols. (London, 1878). For later works based in part on a study of oral tradition see J. Roscoe, *The Buganda* (London, 1911); L. M. Fallers (ed.), *The King's Men* (London, 1964); and *History of East Africa,* Vol. I, pp. 187–91, 332–37, 345–50.

3. *Ankole: the Domination of a Pastoral Aristocracy.* K. Oberg, "The Kingdom of Ankole in Uganda," in Fortes and Evans-Pritchard (eds.), *African Political Systems,* is a valuable study by a social anthropologist. For other kingdoms and chiefdoms in Uganda and western Tanzania see A. I. Richards (ed.), *East African Chiefs* (London, 1960).

4. *The Warrior Companies of the Masai.* The Masai were first described by J. Thomson, *Through Masai Land* (London, 1885). For modern studies see the volume in the Ethnographic Survey of Africa by G. W. B. Huntingford, *The Southern Nilo-Hamites* (London, 1953), and *History of East Africa,* Vol. I, pp. 74–77, 301–13 and 414–19.

5. *The Stateless Polities of the Kikuyu.* L. von Höhnel, *The Discovery of Lakes Rudolf and Stephanie,* 2 vols. (London, 1894), contains the first account by a European traveler of a journey through Kikuyu country. For later studies see J. Kenyatta, *Facing Mount Kenya* (London, 1938); H. E. Lambert, *Kikuyu Social and Political Institutions* (London, 1956); J. Middleton, *The Kikuyu and Kamba of Kenya,* Ethnographic Survey of Africa (London, 1953); and *History of East Africa,* Vol. I, 202–3, 306–20.

✣ XX. SOUTH AFRICAN POLITIES ABOUT 1850

1. *The British Colony of the Cape of Good Hope.* Documents relating to the political development of the Cape are given in G. W. Eybers, *Select Constitutional Documents Illustrating South African History, 1795–1910* (London, 1918). In addition to the general works cited on p. 472, see S. Trapido, "The Origins of the Cape Franchise Qualification of 1853," *J.A.H.,* V / 1 (1964). There is a mass of material relevant to the political structure of the Cape to be found in the official publications of this period listed in the bibliography of Vol. VIII of the *Cambridge History of the British Empire.*

2. *The Boer Republics.* The constitutions of the republics are printed in the volume by Eybers cited above. Recent Afrikaner studies of the republics are listed by L. M. Thompson in his historiographical essay on

South Africa in R. W. Winks (ed.), *The Historiography of the British Empire-Commonwealth* (Durham, N. C., 1966), p. 225.

3. *The Tribal Chiefdoms of the Tswana.* For a general survey of all the Tswana tribes see the volume in the Ethnographic Survey of Africa by I. Schapera, *The Tswana* (London, 1953). For a historical study of the Tswana, see A. Sillery, *The Bechuanaland Protectorate* (London, 1952).

4. *The Zulu Kingdom: Military Despotism.* For an introduction to Zulu history see J. D. Omer-Cooper, *The Zulu Aftermath* (London, 1966), and M. Gluckman, "The Rise of a Zulu Empire," *Scientific American,* April 1960. E. A. Ritter's *Shaka Zulu* (London, 1955) is an excellent biography based on a study of oral tradition. On Zulu political organization see M. Gluckman, "The Kingdom of the Zulu of South Africa," in Fortes and Evans-Pritchard (eds.), *African Political Systems.*

5. *Moshesh's Paramountcy: the Nation-Community of the Basuto.* The best contemporary account of the Basuto is by a French missionary who lived with them for more than twenty years, E. Casalis, *The Basutos* (London, 1861). G. M. Theal, *Basutoland Records,* 3 vols. (Cape Town, 1883), contains much material from official archives relevant to Moshesh. For a history of the Basuto see J. D. Omer-Cooper, *The Zulu Aftermath,* and D. F. Ellenburger and J. C. Macgregor, *History of the Basuto, Ancient and Modern* (London, 1912). For modern studies of the Basuto see V. G. Sheddick, *The Southern Sotho,* Ethnographic Survey of Africa (London, 1953), and H. Ashton, *The Basuto* (London, 1952).

✲✲ XXI. ISLAND POLITIES ABOUT 1850

1. *The Malagasy Kingdom of Merina.* Of the works on Madagascar cited on p. 473 the most informative for mid-nineteenth-century Merina are the histories by Ellis (1838) and Deschamps (1960).

2. *Island Plantocracies: Mauritius and Réunion.* The general histories by Scherer and Barnwell and Toussaint cited on p. 473 contain much useful information. The *Mauritius Almanac,* published annually from the 1820's onward, contains much detailed information about the island's administration.

✲✲ XXII. AFRICA FROM 1850 TO 1875

1. *External Pressures and Internal Dynamics.* For general works on European activities in Africa see p. 446.

2. *The Forces of Change.* On changes in African fauna see F. Harper, *Extinct and Vanishing Mammals of the Old World* (New York, 1945). On the development of European ideas about Africa in the course of the nineteenth century see P. D. Curtin, *The Image of Africa* (London, 1965), and H. A. C. Cairns, *The Clash of Cultures. Early Race Relations in Central Africa* (New York, 1965). Information on most of the topics

discussed in this and the following section is derived from a great variety of sources: on such subjects as changes in population or the impact of improved firearms there is no obviously outstanding work to which the reader can be directed.

3. *The Manifestations of Change.* On the introduction of plants see the works cited on p. 455. The ideas of E. W. Blyden are discussed by R. W. July, *The Origins of Modern African Thought* (London, 1968).

4. *Northeast Africa.* For Egypt in the reign of Ismail see J. C. McCoan, *Egypt as It Is* (London, 1877); D. S. Landes, *Bankers and Pashas* (London, 1958); and M. Rifaat Bey, *The Awakening of Modern Egypt* (London, 1947). On the Suez Canal: J. Marlowe, *The Making of the Suez Canal* (London, 1964). On social changes during Ismail's reign: Ibrahim Abu-Lughod, "The Transformation of the Egyptian Elite," *Middle East Journal,* Summer 1967. On intellectual developments in nineteenth-century Egypt: A. Hourani, *Arabic Thought in the Liberal Age, 1798– 1939* (London, 1962); J. M. Ahmed, *The Intellectual Origins of Egyptian Nationalism* (London, 1960). On the financial difficulties of Ismail's reign see the opening chapters of the Earl of Cromer's *Modern Egypt* (London, 1911). On Ismail's activities in the Sudan and on the Red Sea coast: G. Douin, *Histoire du règne du Khédive Ismail,* 3 vols. (Cairo, 1936–41). For developments in the Southern Sudan: R. Gray, *A History of the Southern Sudan, 1839–1889* (Oxford, 1961). The major works of Sir Samuel Baker are *The Albert N'yanza* (London, 1866), *The Nile Tributaries of Abyssinia* (London, 1867) and *Ismailia* (London, 1874); for a recent biography see D. Middleton, *Baker of the Nile* (London, 1949). For a contemporary account of the British expedition to Ethiopia see C. R. Markham, *History of the Abyssinian Expedition* (London, 1869), and for a vivid account by a modern historian, A. Moorehead, *The Blue Nile* (London, 1962).

5. *Northwest Africa.* The works cited on p. 462 by Julien on Algeria, Ganiage on Tunisia, and Miège on Morocco should all be consulted. On Morocco see also F. R. Flourney, *British Policy Towards Morocco in the Age of Palmerston* (Baltimore, 1935), and E. F. Cruickshank, *Morocco at the Parting of the Ways. The Story of Native Protection to 1885* (Philadelphia, 1935). On the Sanusi: E. E. Evans-Pritchard, *The Sanusi of Cyrenaica* (Oxford, 1949).

6. *West Africa.* The works cited on p. 465 by Cultru on Senegal, Ward on the Gold Coast, Crowder on Nigeria, Newbury on the western slave coast, and Dike on the Niger delta should all be consulted. J. D. Hargreaves's *Prelude to the Partition of West Africa* (London, 1963) deals with both British and French activities in the region. For a detailed study of developments on the Gold Coast see D. Kimble, *A Political History of Ghana, 1850–1928* (Oxford, 1962). The British approach to West Africa from the north is traced by A. A. Boahen, *Britain, the Sahara and the Western Sudan, 1788–1861* (Oxford, 1964). For intellectual developments among West Africans in contact with Europeans: R. W. July, *The Origins of Modern African Thought* (London, 1968).

7. *Equatorial and Central Africa.* On Msiri: A. Verbeken, *Msiri, roi du Garenganze* (Brussels, 1956). Livingstone's principal published works are *Missionary Travels and Researches in South Africa* (London, 1857), *Narrative of an Expedition to the Zambezi and Its Tributaries* (London, 1865), and *The Last Journals,* edited by H. Waller, 2 vols. (London, 1874). I. Schapera has edited *David Livingstone: Family Letters, 1841–1856,* 2 vols. (London, 1959) and *Livingstone's Private Journals 1851–53* (London, 1960). For recent studies of Livingstone see R. Coupland, *Livingstone's Last Journey* (London, 1945), M. Gelfand, *Livingstone the Doctor* (Oxford, 1957), and O. Ransford, *Livingstone's Lake. The Drama of Nyasa* (London, 1966). H. M. Stanley's major works for this period are *How I Found Livingstone* (London, 1872) and *Through the Dark Continent,* 2 vols. (London, 1878). For recent studies of Stanley see I. Anstruther, *I Presume: Stanley's Triumph and Disaster* (London, 1956), and B. Farwell, *The Man Who Presumed* (London, 1958). On the Cokwe: J. Vansina, *Kingdoms of the Savanna,* pp. 216–27. Other works by European travelers of importance for this region and period: V. L. Cameron, *Across Africa* (London, 1877); H. Capello and R. Ivens, *From Benguella to the Territory of the Yacca,* 2 vols., translated from the Portuguese (London, 1882); A. De Serpa Pinto, *How I Crossed Africa,* 2 vols., translated from the Portuguese (London, 1881).

8. *East Africa.* The three chapters in the *History of East Africa,* Vol. I, covering the period 1840–84 and cited on p. 471 are invaluable for this section. See also the two works by Coupland, *East Africa and Its Invaders* and *The Exploitation of East Africa* cited on p. 479. After 1850 there is a steady increase in the number of accounts by European travelers of the interior of East Africa: J. L. Krapf, *Travels, Researches and Missionary Labours* (London, 1860), new edition with introduction by R. C. Bridges (London, 1968); R. F. Burton, *The Lake Regions of Central Africa,* 2 vols. (London, 1860); J. H. Speke, *Journal of the Discovery of the Source of the Nile* (London, 1863) and *What Led to the Discovery of the Source of the Nile* (London, 1864); J. A. Grant, *A Walk Across Africa* (Edinburgh, 1864), together with the works by Baker, Livingstone, and Stanley cited above. Extracts from these works are given in the anthology edited by C. G. Richards, *East African Explorers* (London, 1958). A. Moorehead's *The White Nile* (London, 1960) is a highly readable account of the search for the Nile sources. On Mirambo see the study by N. R. Bennett in *Studies in East African History* (Boston, 1963).

9. *South Africa.* In addition to the general works by De Kiewiet and Walker and the *Cambridge History of the British Empire* cited on p. 471 see C. W. de Kiewiet, *British Colonial Policy and the South African Republics, 1848–1872* (London, 1929) and *The Imperial Factor in South Africa* (Cambridge, 1937) for well-documented studies of British policy; W. B. Campbell, "The South African Frontier, 1865–1885: A Study in Expansion," *South African Archives Yearbook* (1960); J. A. I. Agar-Hamilton, *The Native Policy of the Voortrekkers* (Cape Town, 1928);

H. Vedder, *South West Africa in Early Times* (London, 1938). See also the works on the Zulu, the Basuto, and the Tswana cited on p. 480.

10. *The Islands.* The general works cited on p. 473 may be supplemented by a number of contemporary accounts for this period: W. Ellis, *Three Visits to Madagascar* (London, 1859) and *Madagascar Revisited* (London, 1867); Ida Pfeiffer, *Last Travels* (London, 1861), the remarkable adventures of a Viennese lady who visited Merina in the 1850's; N. Pike, *Sub-tropical Rambles in the Land of the Aphanapterix* (London, 1873), an account of Mauritius.

🏴 EPILOGUE

Africa's Future: the Perspectives in 1875. On British ideas about imperialism for this period see C. A. Bodelsen, *Studies in Mid-Victorian Imperialism* (Copenhagen, 1924). For French ideas, A. Murphy, *The Ideology of French Imperialism, 1871–1881* (Washington, D. C., 1948). For the early ideas of Leopold of the Belgians see A. Roeykens, *Leopold II et l'Afrique, 1855–80* (Brussels, 1952) and *Les Débuts de l'oeuvre africain de Leopold II* (Brussels, 1955), and N. Ascherson, *The King Incorporated* (London, 1963). On al-Afghani see A. Hourani, *Arabic Thought in the Liberal Age,* and on Africanus Horton, R. W. July, *The Origins of Modern African Thought.*

INDEX